SENDA MAN 1000

Book of circular play system
SENDA MAN 1000

First Printing, October 30, 2011
Bijutsu Shuppan-Sha Co., Ltd.
9F Jinbocho Place 3-2-3, Kanda jinbo-cho Chiyoda-ku, Tokyo 101-8417, Japan
Tel +81-3-3234-2153

Author	Mitsuru Senda + Environment Design Institute
Photograph	Mitsumasa Fujitsuka
Art direction	Kan Akita
Design	Yuji Hashimoto, Ryota Iwamatsu (Akita Design Kan Inc.)
Editing, Production	Mitsumasa Fujitsuka Hiroshi Mizukoshi, Shogo Kawasaki (Koryusha)
Talk manuscript	Chisai Fujita
Publishing	Kentaro Oshita
Printing direction	Katsumi Kumakura (Yamada Photo Process)
Printing	Yamada Photo Process Co., Ltd.
Binding	Shibuya Bunsenkaku Co., Ltd.

©2011 Man SENDA
Printed in Japan ISBN978-4-568-60040-7 C3052

遊環構造BOOK

SENDA MAN

Environment Design Institute
Book of circular play system

1000

著＝仙田 満＋環境デザイン研究所
撮影＝藤塚光政

目次 Contents

2011-2008

- 014　広島市民球場
  Hiroshima Municipal Baseball Stadium
  "Mazda Zoom-Zoom Stadium Hiroshima"
- 042　緑の詩保育園
  Green Note Day Nursery
- 046　中軽井沢山荘
  Villa Nakakaruizawa
- 052　一の台幼稚園
  Ichinodai Kindergarten
- 058　勝川幼稚園
  Kachigawa Kindergarten
- 064　慶應義塾日吉キャンパス 協生館
  Keio University Collaboration Complex
- 076　広島県立可部高等学校
  Hiroshima Prefectural Kabe High School
- 082　東大柏どんぐり保育園
  Tokyo University Kashiwa Donguri Day Nursery
- 086　岡崎げんき館
  Okazaki Genkikan
- 092　あづみの公園 サテライトハウス
  Alps Azumino National Government Park
- 100　上海STEP
  Shanghai STEP
- 108　国際教養大学図書館棟
  Akita International University, Library
- 124　国際教養大学講義棟
  Akita International University, Lecture Building
- 138　国際教養大学多目的ホール
  Akita International University, Multi Purpose Hall
- 144　東山動植物園探検温室
  Higashiyama Zoo and Botanical Gardens Adventure Glasshouse Project

2007-2005

- 172　河口湖ステラシアター
  Kawaguchiko Stellar Theatre
- 176　港区立飯倉保育園・学童クラブ
  Iigura Day Nursery, Iigura After School Club
- 182　四街道さつき幼稚園
  Yotsukaido Satsuki Kindergarten
- 190　多治見市立滝呂小学校
  Takiro Elmentary School, Tajimi
- 194　愛和病院ANNEX
  Aiwa Hospital ANNEX
- 200　猿島公園
  Sarushima Park
- 206　尼崎スポーツの森
  Amagasaki Sports Forest
- 212　佛山市岭南明珠体育館
  Foshan Pearl Gymnasium
- 228　上海旗忠森林体育城テニスセンター
  Shanghai Qizhong Forest Sports City Tennis Center
- 236　浪速スポーツセンター
  Naniwa Sports Center
- 242　よつば循環器科クリニック
  Yotsuba Circulation Clinic
- 246　こばと幼稚園絵本館
  Kobato Children's Library
- 250　ゆうゆうのもり幼保園
  Yuyu-no-Mori Nursery School and Day Nursery

2004-2000

- 268　福井まちなか文化施設［響のホール］
  Fukui Cultural Complex "Hibiki Hall"
- 274　健康パークあざい
  Wellness Park Azai
- 282　やすらぎの杜
  Yasuragi-no-Mori
- 288　ふじえだファミリークリニック
  Fujieda Family Clinic
- 292　わかくさ保育園
  Wakakusa Day Nursery
- 296　秋田市太平山自然学習センター
  Akita Taiheizan Nature Learning Center
- 304　関門海峡ミュージアム
  Kaikyo Dramaship
- 316　きききのつりはし＋御所野縄文博物館
  Bridge Kikiki + Goshono Jomon Museum

326	東京工業大学大学会館 ［すずかけホール］ Tokyo Institute of Technology "Suzukake Hall"	464	山梨県立科学館 Yamanashi Prefectural Science Center
330	弘法湯 Bath House "Kobo-Yu"	470	福井県児童科学館 Fukui Children's Science Center
334	ほうとく幼稚園 Houtoku Kindergarten	478	兵庫県立但馬ドーム Hyogo Prefectural Tajima Dome
340	京都アクアリーナ Kyoto Aquarena	496	川崎市向丘小学校 Mukaigaoka Elementary School, Kawasaki
352	アクアワールド大洗水族館 Oarai Aquarium "Aqua World"	500	愛知県児童総合センター Aichi Children's Center
366	佐久市子ども未来館 Saku Children's Science Dome for the Future	512	五藤光学研究所山梨工場 Goto Optical MFG. Yamanashi Factory
372	浜松こども館 Hamamatsu Children's Center	516	珠洲ビーチホテル Suzu Beach Hotel
378	国立成育医療センター National Center for Child Health and Deveropment	522	長崎市科学館 Nagasaki Science Museum
386	七尾希望の丘公園 ［ブリッジ遊具］ Nanao Bridge Play Structure	528	鈴廣かまぼこ博物館 Suzuhiro Kamaboko Museum
390	桜山の家 Sakurayama House	534	由比ヶ浜の家 Yuigahama House
398	海南市わんぱく公園 Kainan Wanpaku Park	538	藤野芸術の家 Fujino Workshop for Art
410	和歌山県動物愛護センター Wakayama Prefectural Animal Welfare Center		

1999-1995

1994-1990

426	世界淡水魚園オアシスパーク Oasis Park	562	旭川春光台 ［風の子館］ Asahikawa Shunkodai Park "Kaze no Ko Kan"
432	岐阜県先端科学技術体験センター Gifu Advanced Science and Technology Experience Center	570	兵庫県南但馬自然学校 Minami Tajima Nature School, Hyogo
440	富岩運河環水公園 Fugan Canal Park	576	ミュージアムパーク茨城県自然博物館 Ibaraki Nature Museum
450	やすらぎミラージュ Yasuragi Mirage	588	相模湖カルチャーパーク ［漕艇場］ Lake Sagami Culture Park, "Rowing space"
454	大森の家 Omori House	592	信州博アルピコ広場 ［円環遊具］ "Circular Play Structure" in the Shinshu Expo Alpico Plaza
460	春日部の家 Kasukabe House	598	姫路御立公園 ［たつまきロード］ Himeji Mitate Park "Tornado Road"
		602	国営ひたち海浜公園 ［たまごの森］ "Tamago no Mori" in Hitachi Seaside Park

606	相模原市星が丘こどもセンター Sagamihara Municipal Hoshigaoka Children's Center	722	渋谷区散策路整備計画［旧玉川上水ルート］ Shibuya Promenade Design "Hatsudai District"
612	多摩六都科学館 Tama Rokuto Science Museum	726	1万Mプロムナード三笠アプローチ Mikasa Park Approach Road in the ten thousand Meter Promenade
620	常滑市体育館 Tokoname Municipal Gymnasium	730	名古屋市宝くじモデル児童遊園［わいわい広場］ Nagoya Children's Play Park "Wai Wai Plaza"
628	東京辰巳国際水泳場 Tokyo Tatsumi International Swimming Center	734	山手ヨットクラブ Yamate Yacht Club
638	稲荷山公園わんぱく広場 Inari Park Wanpaku Plaza	740	相模川ふれあい科学館 Sagamigawa River Museum
642	スターズ・アート23 Stars Art 23	746	浜松科学館 Hamamatsu Science Museum
646	滋賀県立びわ湖こどもの国 Lake Biwa Children's Land	758	多摩動物園猛禽舎 Tama Zoo "Raptores House"
652	富山県こどもみらい館 Toyama Children's Center	762	筑波科学万国博覧会こども広場 Tsukuba Science Expo Children's Plaza
664	中国北京科普楽園 Beijing Children's Science Park	776	軽井沢640 Karuizawa 640
668	営団地下鉄南北線 Eidan Subway, Nanboku Line	782	静岡県吉原林間学校 Yoshiwara Camping School
672	弁天町ウォーターランド［プールズ］ Bentencho Waterland "Pools"	786	鳥居平やまびこ公園 ［ローラースケート場・風のとりで］ Toriidaira Yamabiko Park
678	鳥の家 Bird House	790	太刀の浦緑地 Tachinoura Port Park
682	鵠沼の家 Kugenuma House	794	脇田和邸 K. Wakita House
688	松庵の家 Shoan House	798	バナナハウス Banana House

1989-1980

704	白金台ガーデンハウス Shiroganedai Garden House	804	八日市市城砦公園 Yokaichi Rampart Park
708	軽井沢C山荘 Mountain Villa "C", Karuizawa	808	横浜市ほどがや地区センター Hodogaya Community Center, Yokohama
712	伊勢原市立図書館・こども科学館 Isehara Library and Science Museum	812	秋田県営御野庭団地 Akita Prefectural Onoba Housing
718	渋谷区散策路整備計画［美術館ルート］ Shibuya Promenade Design "Route to shoto Museum"	816	片瀬山の家 Kataseyama House
		822	秋田県立児童会館・こども博物館 Akita Prefectural Children's Center, Children's Museum

1979-1969

- 848 串木野児童館
  Kushikino Children's Center
- 852 横浜市赤城林間学園
  Akagi Camping School, Yokohama
- 856 沖縄県立石川少年自然の家
  Ishikawa Children's Nature School
- 866 愛知こどもの国［ドラゴン］
  Giant Play Structure "Dragon"
  Aichi Prefectural Children's Land
- 870 山梨県愛宕山少年自然の家
  Atagoyama House of Nature for Young People
- 874 野中保育園［野中丸］
  Nonaka Day Nursery "Nonaka-Maru"
- 884 野中保育園［野中ザウルス］
  Nonaka Day Nursery "Nonaka-Saurus"
- 904 神保医院
  Jinbo Clinic
- 908 鳥取砂丘こどもの国
  Children's Land at Tottori
- 912 愛宕山こどもの国［展望広場］
  Observation Square, Atagoyama Children's Land
- 918 新川シーサイド遊園
  Shinkawa Seaside Children's Park
- 922 ランニングサーキット
  "Running Circuit"
- 926 キシャコゾウ
  Kishakozo
- 930 道の巨大遊具
  "Giant Path Play Structure"
- 934 黒い家
  Black House
- 938 遊具
  Play Structure

- 008 はじめに
  Preface
- 010 遊環構造理論
  Circular play system theory

対談 Dialogue

- 148 斎藤公男
  Masao Saito
- 156 内田祥哉
  Yoshichika Uchida
- 544 植田 実
  Makoto Ueda
- 828 藤塚光政
  Mitsumasa Fujitsuka
- 944 塩川壽平
  Juhei Shiokawa
- 952 藤森照信
  Terunobu Fujimori

作品データ Data Index

- 164 2011-2008
- 260 2007-2005
- 414 2004-2000
- 552 1999-1995
- 692 1994-1990
- 836 1989-1980
- 960 1979-1969

- 968 年表
  Chronological table
- 992 SENDA・MANを撮影して40年
  藤塚光政
  Forty Years of shooting Senda Man
  Mitsumasa Fujitsuka
- 996 おわりに
  Acknowledgements
- 998 仙田 満 略歴
  MITSURU MAN SENDA Biography

はじめに

私は環境建築家と自称している。
建築設計者を越える新しいプロフェッショナルを追求している。
私の好みの空間、形はある。
しかしその優先度は低い。
私にとって重要なのはその土地、歴史であり、
私のつくる環境に住み、利用する人々の生き方なのである。
クライアントのためだけの建築をつくらない。
クライアントの満足は大事だが、その背後の利用する多くの人々を
元気にする建築、そして環境をつくりたい。
私にとって建築家としての個性的な空間や形はさほど重要ではない。
私がこだわっているのは、私の環境のつくり方である。
環境をデザインするつくり方である。
私のこだわりを一言でいえば
「遊環構造」というデザインの手法である。
「遊環構造」はこどものあそびやすい空間の構造原則であるが、
それは人の生きる意欲、学ぶ意欲、交流する意欲、
運動する意欲、あそぶ意欲、創造する意欲を
喚起する原則となっていると考えている。
私は遊環構造の環境建築家だ。
環境デザイン領域という新しい領域のデザイナーである。
多くの分野を通貫するデザインが環境デザインだ。
参加というキーワードは環境デザインにおいて
最も重要な言葉であり、行動だ。
私は多くの創造者と共同する。
多くの考えの異なる創造者といっしょに仕事をするのは楽しい。
又、一緒に多くの仕事を出来たことに感謝したい。

Preface

I call myself an environment architect,
and I pursue a new type of professionalism
that surpasses that of a conventional architect.
I have spaces and shapes that I prefer, but those are low priority.
The important factors to me are the location and its history,
as well as the way that the people that inhabit
and use the environments that I construct live.
I do not create buildings for the sole purpose of serving clients.
Customer satisfaction is important,
however I am more concerned in creating a building, or environment,
that delivers vitality to the many people that use it after them.
To me, spaces and shapes that boast individuality
as an architect are not very important.
I am pickier about how the environment is created
—that is to say, the way of making a design for an environment.
To put it short, I call my method of design "circular play system."
The structural principle behind circular play system is
that they are areas that are easy for children to play in.
However, I believe that is also the principle of
inciting people's urge to live, learn, socialize, exercise, and create.
I am an environment architect.
I am a designer in a new field called "environment a design."
Design that passes through ample different fields of design is
referred to as environmental design.
In environmental design the most important keyword is "participation."
Participation is action.
I work together with a large number of creators.
That is why I feel pleasure in creating these environments together.
It is enjoyable working together with creators
that offer a wide range of differing views.

遊環構造理論

私が環境デザイン研究所を設立したのは1968年のことである。現在まで40余年、私たちの事務所は巨大遊具、都市の木、環築、プレイストラクチャー、世界を望む家、意欲を喚起する環境等というデザインコンセプトを考え、それを具体的な形や空間や景観として設計し、デザインしてきた。

私たちの事務所は設立時より建築のみ設計するのではなく、物から広場、都市までを含む広範な領域をデザインしてきた。そしてその中心的なテーマが「こどものための環境デザイン」であった。これまでの歳月は私たちのデザイン分野を「こどものための環境」からその展開へと拡げつつある。しかし、私たちの中心的なテーマは今後も変わらずに、らせん状に拡大するデザイン活動の渦の核となっている。

この本には、40余年の作品を集めている。

そのテーマは「遊環構造」である。

この本のタイトルは『SENDA MAN 1000』としているが、1000頁の本である。SENDA MANのSENは1000に通じるが、1000に大きな意味はなく、たくさんという意味にかけたあそびで、サブタイトルの『遊環構造BOOK』がテーマである。

「多くの遊環構造の仕事」というような意味にとっていただければよい。「遊環構造」は30年におよぶ"こどものあそび"の調査から得た「あそび空間の構造」である。遊具の調査によってゲームが発生しやすい遊具は、あそび動線が必ず循環していることがわかった。（遊具におけるゲームは多くの場合、「追いかけっこ」が基本であるから、その動線がひとつのクローズした系を持つのは当然であるが）さらに、永年の"あそびの原風景"の調査から、こども達があそび場としていたのは街区がひとまわりでき、しかも抜け道、つまりショートカットがあり、また、それにいつもこども達が集まる小さな広場がとりついた構造であることを明らかにした。

循環とショートカット、そしてそれに取り付く小さな広場というこの構造を、さらに遊具、あそび場、建築、公園といろいろ調べていくと、その循環の中に"めまい"の体験要素が不可欠だということがわかってきた。またシンボル性の高い空間、場、あるいは物も必要であること、そ

して全体がやわらかな循環—いくつかの選択が許され、またさらに外に抜けることのできるような—穴だらけの空間であることが要求されていると考えている。すなわち回遊性と多様性である。

このように、遊具においても都市においても、共通したあそび空間の構造があり、このあそび構造が私達のデザインの基本となっている。

私はこれに「遊環構造」と名づけ、その特徴を次の7つの条件として整理した。

①循環機能があること
②その循環(道)が安全で変化に富んでいること
③その中にシンボル性の高い空間、場があること
④その循環に"めまい"を体験できる部分があること
⑤近道(ショートカット)ができること
⑥循環した広場、小さな広場等が取り付いていること
⑦全体がポーラス(多孔質)な空間で構成されていること

これらの条件、すなわち「遊環構造」の条件をここに発表する作品が全て満たしているわけではない。それは常に建築があそびを目的としているわけではないからである。しかしその場合でもイメージの「遊環構造」を私たちはデザインのコンセプトとしている。

本書に収録した作品を通して、どこまでこのコンセプトを表現できたかわからないが、本書によって環境における「遊環構造」の有効性を読みとっていただければ幸いである。

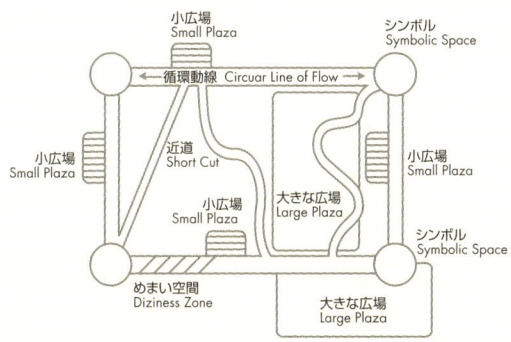

Circular play system theory

I established the Environment Design Institute in 1968. In the over 40 years since then our offices have fashioned numerous design concepts—including giant play facilities, city trees, environment architecture, play structures, the House with a View of the World, and Inspire Environments (environments that inspire)—and have designed those into concrete shapes, spaces, and landscapes.

Since the beginning our offices have not only designed buildings, but have provided design for a broad scope of fields, including objects, common areas, and even cities. A central theme across all of those, however, has been environment design for children. Our time until now has expanded our field of design from "environments for children" into that direction. However, our core theme will not change in the future, as it remains the core of our spiraling design activities that seem to expand like a corkscrew.

This book compiles more than 40 years of creations.

The theme is "circular play system."

This book is titled *Senda Man 1000*. However, the number "1000" carries little significance. It is merely a fun way of saying "a lot." The subtitle *Book of circular play system* is the main theme, which should be taken to mean "a large number of circular play system works."

"Circular play system" is play structures developed from over 30 years of surveying children's play. From the survey on play structures we discovered that the play flow line for play structures that tends to elicit game playing always circulates. (However, as in many cases these games are limited to "tag," it is obvious that this flow line is a single closed thread.)

Moreover, from the survey on play landscapes of childhood that was conducted over many years, we learned that the areas that children used to play allowed children to travel around the entire area, contained shortcuts, and always had a structure where there was a small communal space for children to gather.

After researching the structure circular shapes, shortcuts, and those with a small communal space attached, along with play structures, play areas, architecture, parks, and many other items, we found out that the experience element of "dizziness" was vital to the cycle. In addition, spaces, areas, and objectives with a strong symbolic value as well as an overall flexible cycle are necessary—there can be several options in a space covered with holes that lead to the outside. In other words mobility and diversity are important.

In this way both play equipment and cities alike have common play structures, and it is this play structure that lies at the foundation of our design.

We call these "circular play system" and have organized the inherent characteristics into the following seven conditions:

1) Possesses a circular function.
2) That cycle (path) is safe and rich with change.
3) Inside there is space and areas of high symbolic value.
4) The cycle contains a portion that allows one to experience the sensation of "dizziness."
5) There are shortcuts.
6) A cycled common area or small common space is attached.
7) The entire facility is constructed of porous material.

Nevertheless, all of the works presented in this book do not fulfill all of the conditions of a "circular play system." This is due to the fact that not all buildings are constructed for the purpose of playing. However, even in such instances we have utilized the design concept of circular play system as an overall theme. I am uncertain to what extent I have been able to express this concept through the works included in this book, but I hope that readers will be able to interpret the effectiveness of circular play system contained within environments.

2009
広島市民球場
Hiroshima Municipal Baseball Stadium "Mazda Zoom-Zoom Stadium Hiroshima"

夢の器

広島市民球場

広島県広島市南区南蟹屋／2009
Hiroshima Municipal Baseball Stadium
"Mazda Zoom-Zoom Stadium Hiroshima"
Minamikaniya, Minami-ku, Hiroshima-shi, Hiroshima

敷地は旧国鉄のヤード跡地であり、北側には在来線・山陽新幹線が走る。鯉の、優美で躍動するイメージをコンセプトとして掲げ、左右非対称のデザインとした。線路外の野外席を大きくとることで正面側に広場をゆったりと設けることができ、街に開かれた野球場が目指された。多様な観客席、開放的なコンコースは、来場するすべての人々を楽しませ、興奮と感動を街にもつなげる役割を担う。一周800mのメインコンコースを中心に遊環構造が形成され、27種類の多様なシートとショップがとりついている。

The site used to be a switchyard for the former National Railways, where the local line and Sanyo Shinkansen now run on the north side. The concept was based on the image of the graceful movement of a carp, and the design was made to be asymmetrical on the right and left sides. A great portion of the outside seating located around the tracks was taken out to create a large opening to the front, and also to make a baseball field that seems to open up to the city. Various types of seats and an open-style concourse provide enjoyment to everyone that visits, and also contributes to giving excitement and awe to the city.

2009

広島市民球場

Hiroshima Municipal Baseball Stadium "Mazda Zoom-Zoom Stadium Hiroshima"

駅からスロープの下まで600m、スロープは200m
駅から800mで夢の器に
600m from the station to the foot of the slope,
and the slope is 200m long—travel for about 800m
before arriving at the entrance to the dream vessel.

2009

広島市民球場

Hiroshima Municipal Baseball Stadium "Mazda Zoom-Zoom Stadium Hiroshima"

メインコンコースは一周600m、幅12m
The main concourse has a circumference of 600m and spans 12m in breadth.

2009

広島市民球場

Hiroshima Municipal Baseball Stadium "Mazda Zoom-Zoom Stadium Hiroshima"

メインコンコースは開放的で立体的な遊環構造
The main concourse is an open, stereoscopic circular play system.

2009

広島市民球場

Hiroshima Municipal Baseball Stadium "Mazda Zoom-Zoom Stadium Hiroshima"

サブコンコースから、コンコースを抜けて
グラウンドが望めるのが設計者の自慢だ

The Architect's pride—going through the concourse from the sub-concourse, one will be greeted with a view of the grounds.

2009

広島市民球場

Hiroshima Municipal Baseball Stadium "Mazda Zoom-Zoom Stadium Hiroshima"

グラウンドが近い
The grounds are near to visitor.

2009
広島市民球場
Hiroshima Municipal Baseball Stadium "Mazda Zoom-Zoom Stadium Hiroshima"

新幹線が見える、新幹線からも見える、
もちろん在来線からだって見える
It is possible to see the Shinkansen,
and to be seen from the Shinkansen.
Of course, it can also be seen from
the regular train lines.

2009

広島市民球場

Hiroshima Municipal Baseball Stadium "Mazda Zoom-Zoom Stadium Hiroshima"

2009

広島市民球場

Hiroshima Municipal Baseball Stadium "Mazda Zoom-Zoom Stadium Hiroshima"

下からも上からもあらゆる見方を追求
In pursuit of all perspectives, from below, and from the top.

2009

広島市民球場

Hiroshima Municipal Baseball Stadium "Mazda Zoom-Zoom Stadium Hiroshima"

頑張れカープ、嘆け!! Kuwahara!
Keep trying, Carp! Ke

2009

パフォーマンスシートは空中の応援席
The performance seats are rooters' seats suspended in mid-air.

広島市民球場
Hiroshima Municipal Baseball Stadium "Mazda Zoom-Zoom Stadium Hiroshima"

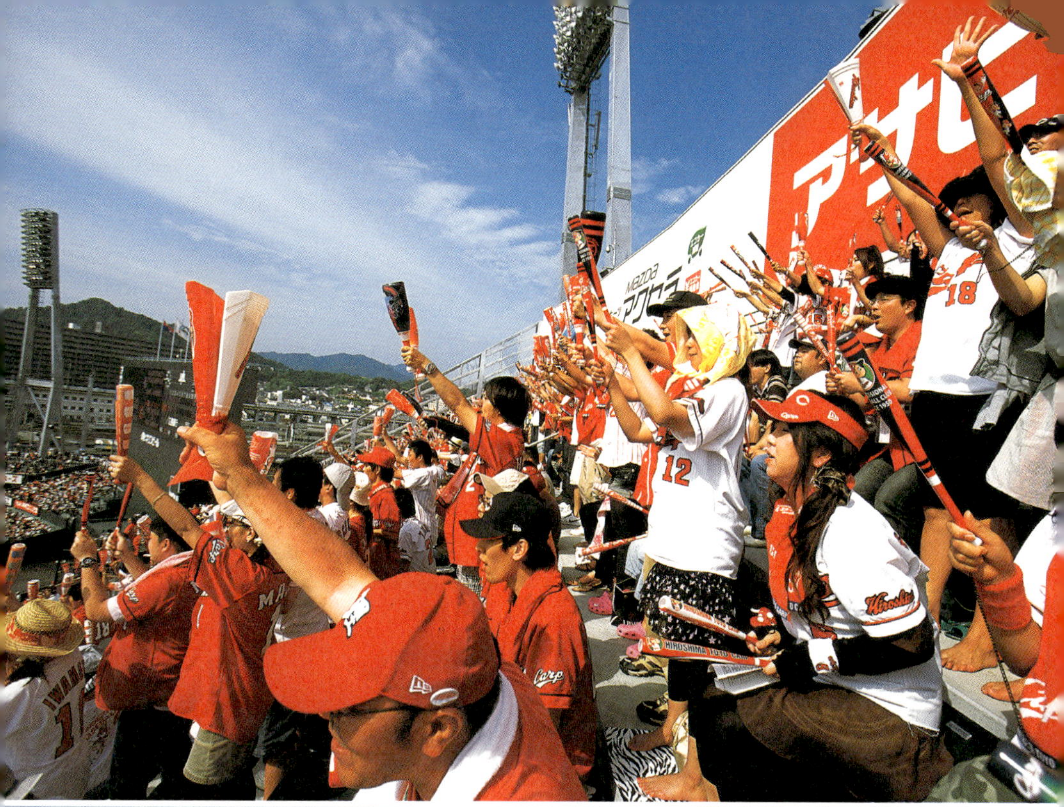
MAZDA
アクセラ
18
12

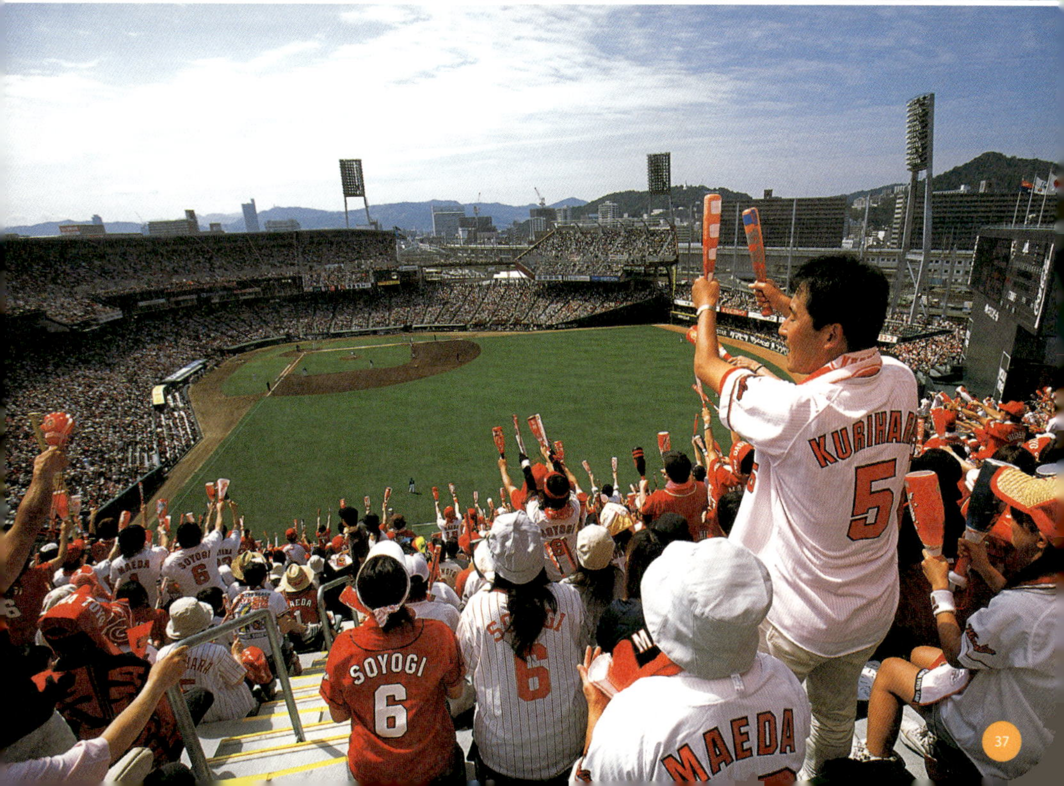
SOYOGI
6
MAEDA

2009

広島市民球場

Hiroshima Municipal Baseball Stadium "Mazda Zoom-Zoom Stadium Hiroshima"

フレー、フレー、かっ飛ばせー
Hurray! Hurray! Hit a ball! Hit it far!

2009

騒ぐ、叫ぶ、踊る、みんな一緒
Raise a racket, shout, dance! All together now!

広島市民球場
Hiroshima Municipal Baseball Stadium "Mazda Zoom-Zoom Stadium Hiroshima"

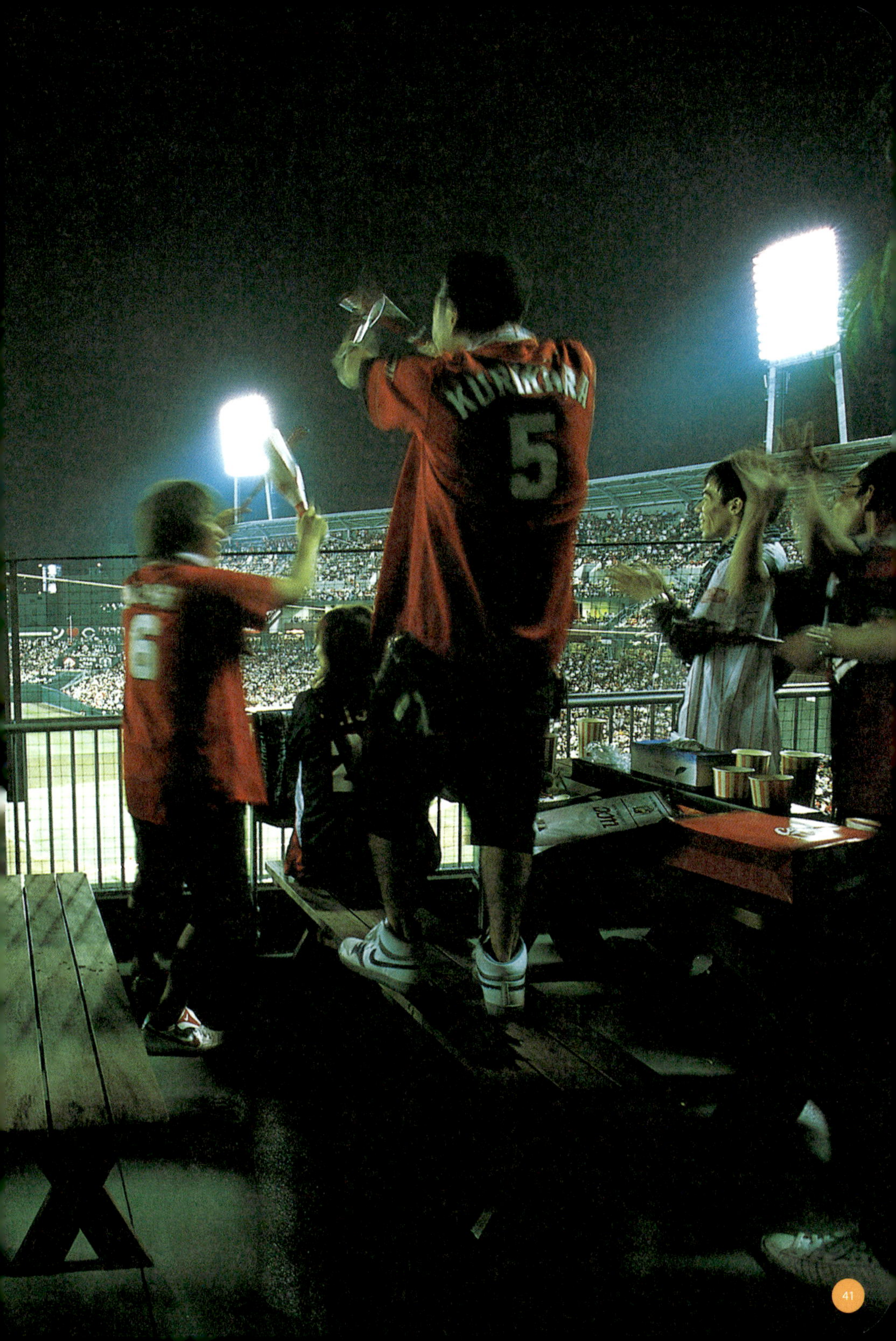

2011

緑の詩保育園

Green Note Day Nursery

木の円環

緑の詩保育園

埼玉県北本市深井／2011
Green Note Day Nursery
Fukai, Kitamoto-shi, Saitama

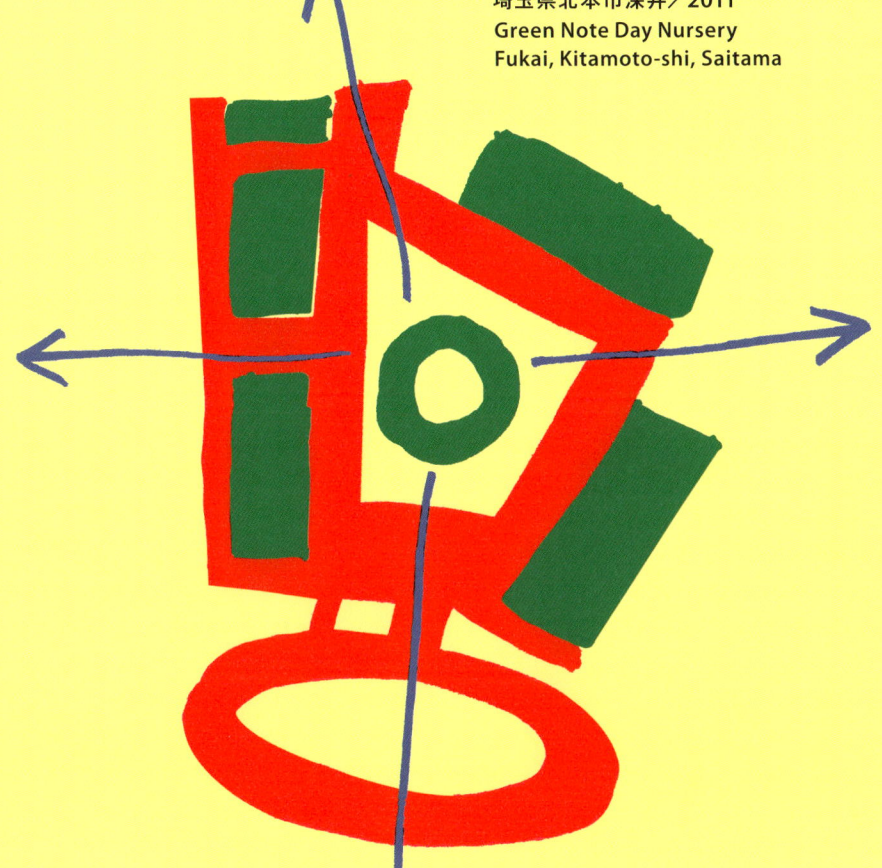

緑の詩保育園は、埼玉県の農地と住宅地が混在する郊外に立地している。敷地の広さは約3000㎡で、隣接する内井昭蔵氏が設計した同クライアントの幼稚園の1/3ほどである。この保育園の保育室は木造の平屋で、園長室、会議室のみが2階である。円環状のトップサイドライトを持つ大きな広場を囲んで、中央からカスケード状に室内の高さは低くなり、外周部はエントランスのあるテラスとなっている。全体が中央の遊戯室機能を持つ広場を中心とした遊環構造となっている。

Midori-no-uta Day Nursery is located at suburban area in Saitama Prefecture. The site has approx. 3000㎡ which is one third of the same client's kindergarten designed by Shozo Uchii. The school building is wooden structure and classrooms are on the first floor and rooms for headteacher and meeting are on the second floor. There is a large hall with toric top side light in the middle of the building and the height of the room becomes lower like cascade, and at the end of the circle, there is an outside terrace with entrance. The whole building has circular play system centering square with function of play hall.

2011

緑の詩保育園

Green Note Day Nursery

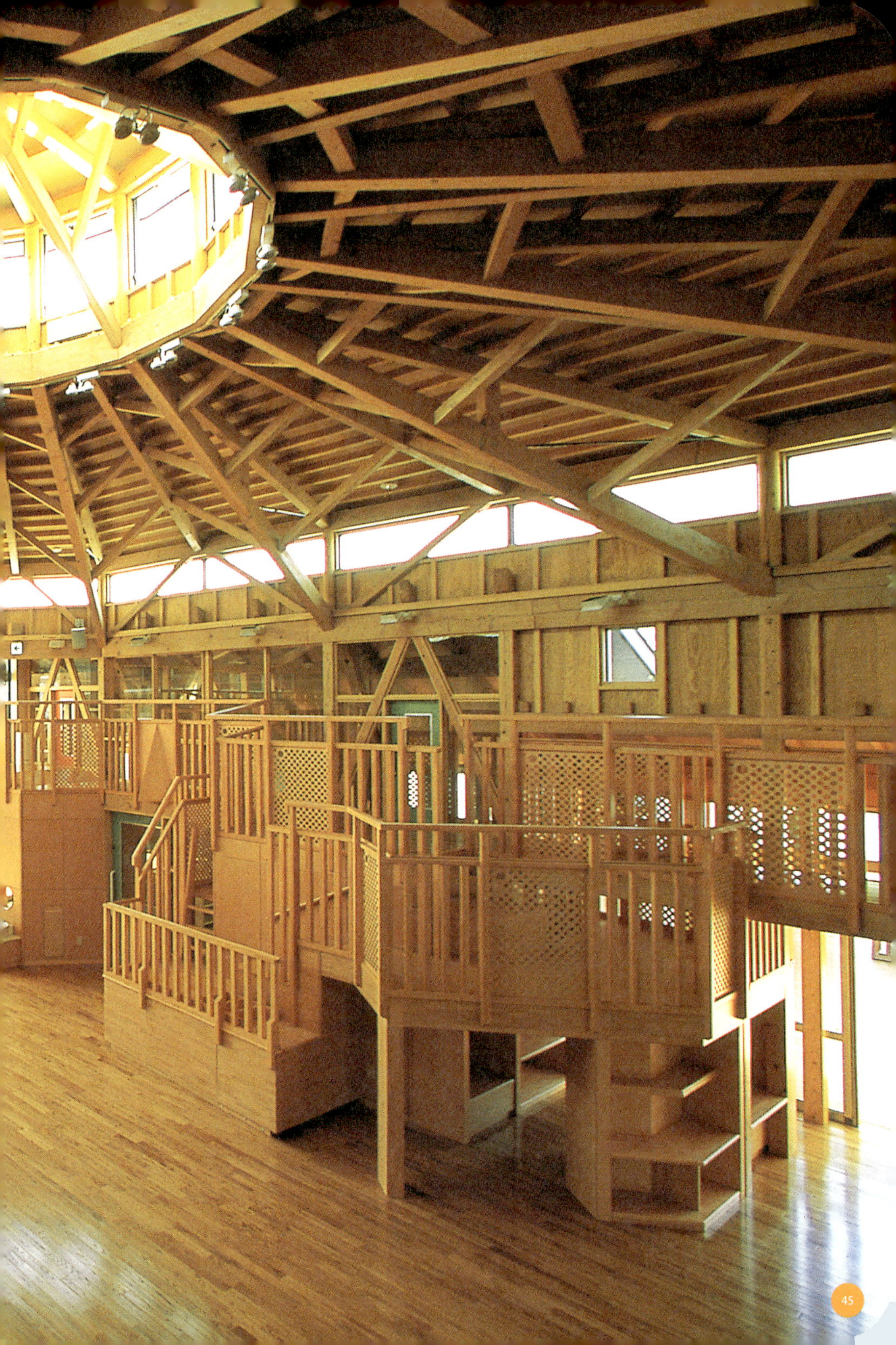

2009

中軽井沢山荘
Villa Nakakaruizawa

浅間山を望む家

中軽井沢山荘

長野県北佐久郡軽井沢町／2009
Villa Nakakaruizawa
Karuizawa-machi, Kitasaku-gun, Nagano

敷地は中軽井沢の野鳥の森、星野温泉の南に位置した山頂にある。山荘は母屋と客屋の分棟とし、間に中庭を設け渡廊下でつなぐ構成としている。既存樹林を残す配置計画とし、母屋・客屋ともに自然を満喫できるよう開口部・バルコニーを充分な形で設けている。母屋居間と客屋食堂からは正面に浅間山が望める。敷地の高低差を生かし様々な視界・シーンが展開するような空間構成としている。

This location is set at the peak of a mountain located at Naka-Karuizawa. The mountain lodge has a main building that stands separately from the guest rooms with a hallway that passes through a garden set in the middle. The plot's layout makes use of the existing trees and the main and guest buildings all have extensive openings and balconies that allow for enjoying the surrounding nature. There is also a view of Mt. Asama from the entrance of the main building and the guest building restaurant. The difference in levels of height around the vicinity offers a wide variety of views and scenes for visitors to enjoy.

2009

中軽井沢山荘
Villa Nakakaruizawa

2階の居間は真っ正面に浅間山と対峙する
The living room on the second floor stares Mt. Asama in the face.

2009

中軽井沢山荘　Villa Nakakaruizawa

家族そして働く仲間と
美しい一時を共有する
Share a beautiful moment
with family and colleagues.

2009

大きな門

一の台幼稚園
Ichinodai Kindergarten

一の台幼稚園

千葉県流山市東深井／2009
Ichinodai Kindergarten
Higashifukai, Nagareyama-shi, Chiba

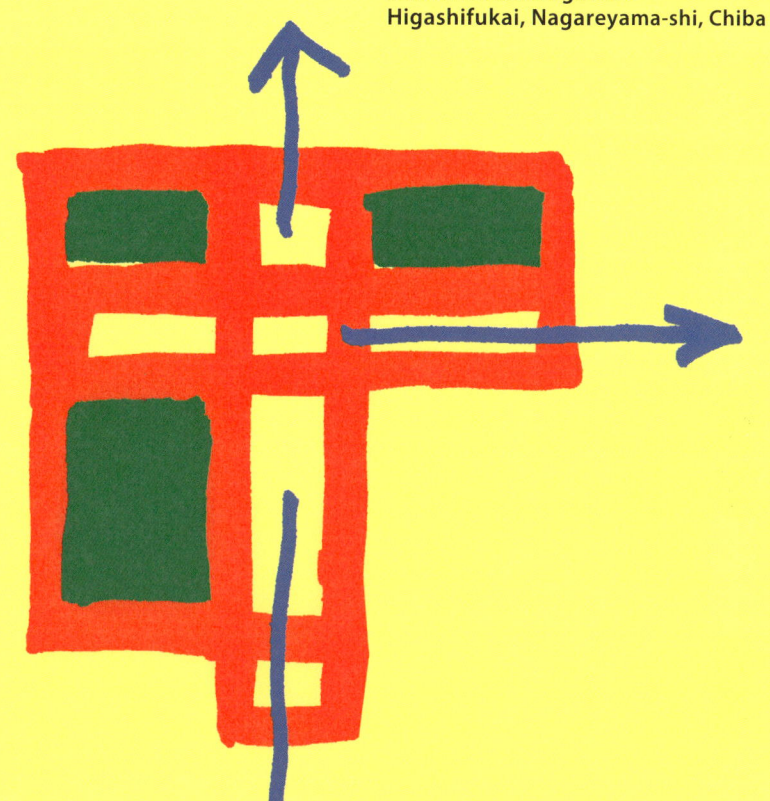

郊外の住宅街に立地する緑豊かな木造平屋建ての幼稚園。幅員5m超の廊下の両側に面して保育室を配している。間仕切りの開放により保育室と廊下全体が一室空間として利用でき、可動家具のレイアウトにより多様な活動空間を提供している。かつての旧園舎跡が新しくアプローチグラウンドとして整備され、旧グラウンドにつくられた園舎は大きな門としてこどもを迎えている。

This kindergarten is a single-story wooden structure located in a richly green residential area in the suburbs. The nursery rooms are on both sides of a spacious corridor with a width of over 5 meters. The room partitions can be removed to make one large space comprising the rooms and overall corridor, and the use of movable furniture allows the layout to be changed to create various types of space. The old remnants of a kindergarten have been revamped as a new approach ground, and the large gate built on the old grounds remains standing to greet children when they come.

2009

一の台幼稚園

Ichinodai Kindergarten

幼稚園は小さな学校、大きな家、そして中くらいの遊園地

The kindergarten is a small school, a large house, and a medium-sized amusement park.

2009

一の台幼稚園　Ichinodai Kindergarten

57

2009

勝川幼稚園
Kachigawa Kindergarten

楠の木を囲む

勝川幼稚園

愛知県春日井市旭町／2009
Kachigawa Kindergarten
Asahi-machi, Kasugai-shi, Aichi

名古屋近郊の商店街に近接した幼稚園の全面改築である。既存の園舎を残しながらグラウンドに新園舎を建て、旧園舎の位置にグラウンドを整備した。既存のクスノキを中心として、放射状に保育室を配置した。保育室と保育室の間は中庭形式とし、どの保育室にも3面の開口部を設け、光と風を取り入れることができる。中央のクスノキの周りには、大きなネット遊具をすり鉢状に取り付け、遊環構造を形成することによってこども達のあそびの中心としている。

This building is a total reconstruction of a kindergarten located near a shopping area in the outskirts of Nagoya. A new building was built on the grounds with the older one left standing, and the grounds surrounding the older building was thereafter developed. A group of nursery rooms is set in a radial form surrounding an old camphor tree. With small gardens set between each nursery room, each room is equipped with three entrances that allow for light and air to breeze into the building. A large net shaped like a bowl is set around the camphor tree, forming circular play system that provides a place for children to play in the middle.

2009

勝川幼稚園

Kachigawa Kindergarten

クスノキは残った
こども達の一日はクスノキからはじまりクスノキで終わる
The camphor tree has remained.
The children's days begin and end with the camphor tree.

2009

勝川幼稚園

Kachigawa Kindergarten

63

2008

跳躍台

慶應義塾日吉キャンパス 協生館

Keio University Collaboration Complex

慶應義塾
日吉キャンパス 協生館

神奈川県横浜市港北区日吉／2008
Keio University Collaboration Complex
Hiyoshi, Kohoku-ku, Yokohama-shi, Kanagawa

協生館は、慶應義塾の「開かれた学塾」というコンセプトで計画、設計された。そのデザインコンセプトは「世界に発信する学び舎」である。東側に広がる慶應の森とグラウンドを望みながら健康で活力に満ちた学習・研究活動に塾生が参加し展開される環境建築は、世界へ羽ばたく跳躍台としてイメージされた。大きな段状の建築構成が特徴的だが、50ｍプールなどの運動施設を地下に備え、イベントホール・講堂・学生生活支援施設と地域利用にも配慮され、従来の学校建築には見られない高度に複合化された遊環構造建築である。

Kyosei-kan was created based on Keio University's concept of an "open school." The design concept is "a place of learning that communicates to the world." The forest and sports grounds of Keio that spread out on the east side form an environmental architecture where students can partake in learning and research activities in a space that is healthy and rich with vitality. The structure's image is of a springboard for dissemination around the world. Student activity facilities made in consideration of local use, making this a highly multi-purpose, structure with circular play system that cannot be seen at conventional schools.

2008

慶應義塾日吉キャンパス 協生館

Keio University Collaboration Complex

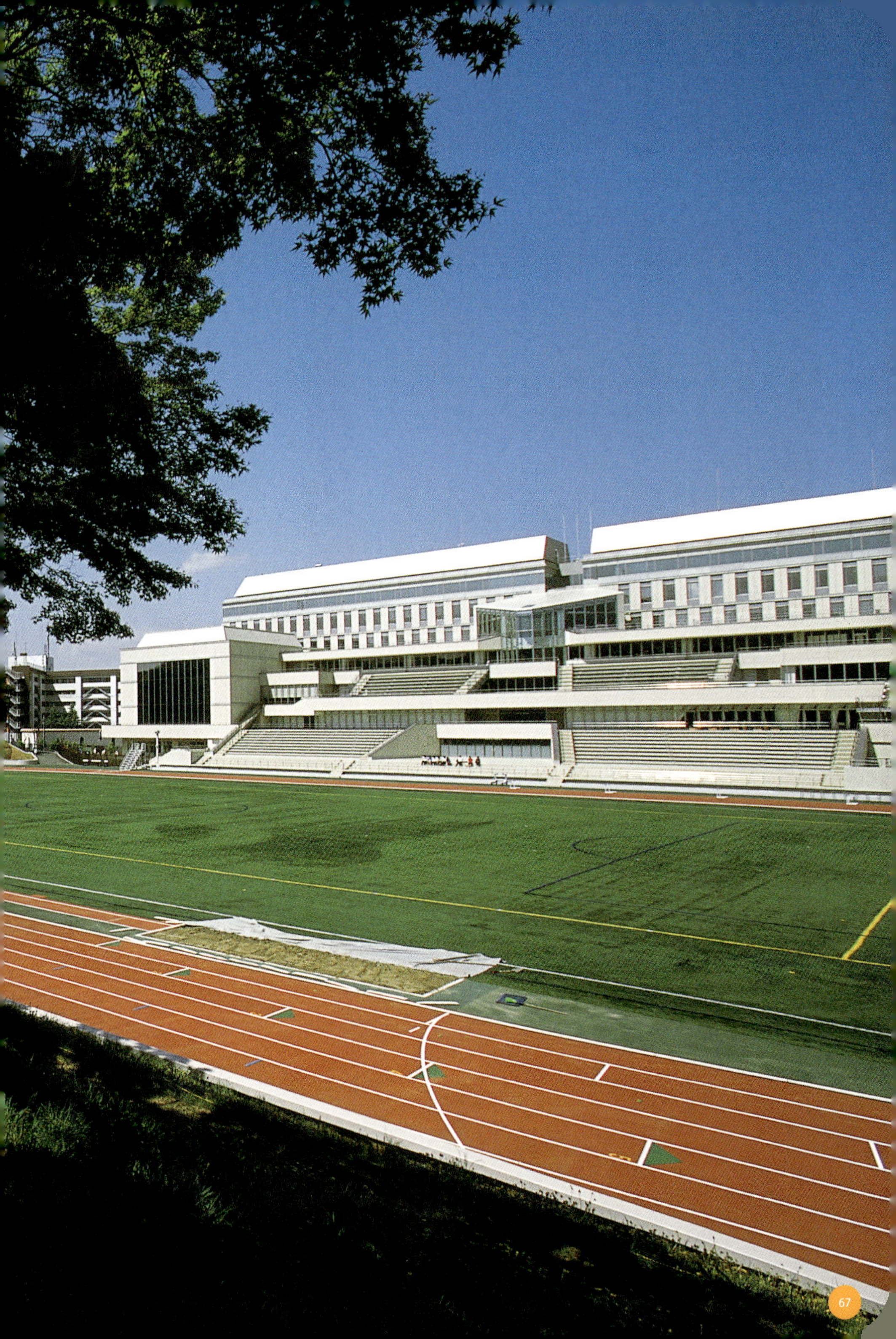

2008

慶應義塾日吉キャンパス 協生館

Keio University Collaboration Complex

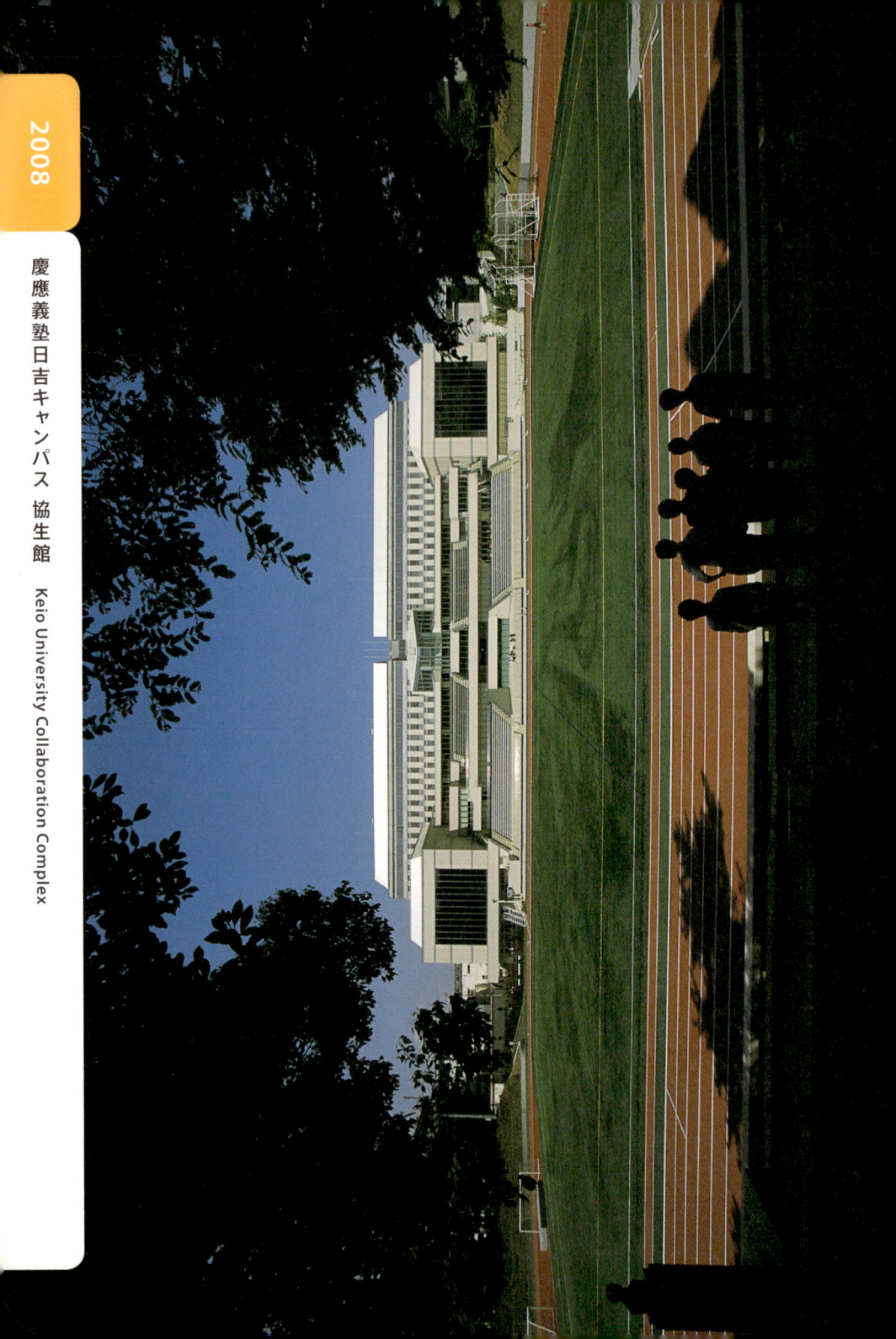

400mトラックの観覧席としての校舎
A campus building that serves as the spectator stands for the 400m tracks.

2008

慶應義塾日吉キャンパス 協生館

Keio University Collaboration Complex

横浜市営地下鉄4号線（グリーンライン）に
つながる協生館の中廊、知のパサージュ
The passage of knowledge—the central corridor connecting
the Collaboration Complex to Line 4 (Green Line)
of the Yokohama Municipal Subway

2008

50mプールは400mトラックを囲む観覧席の下に
The 50m pool is located below
the spectator stands circling the 400m tracks.

慶應義塾日吉キャンパス 協生館
Keio University Collaboration Complex

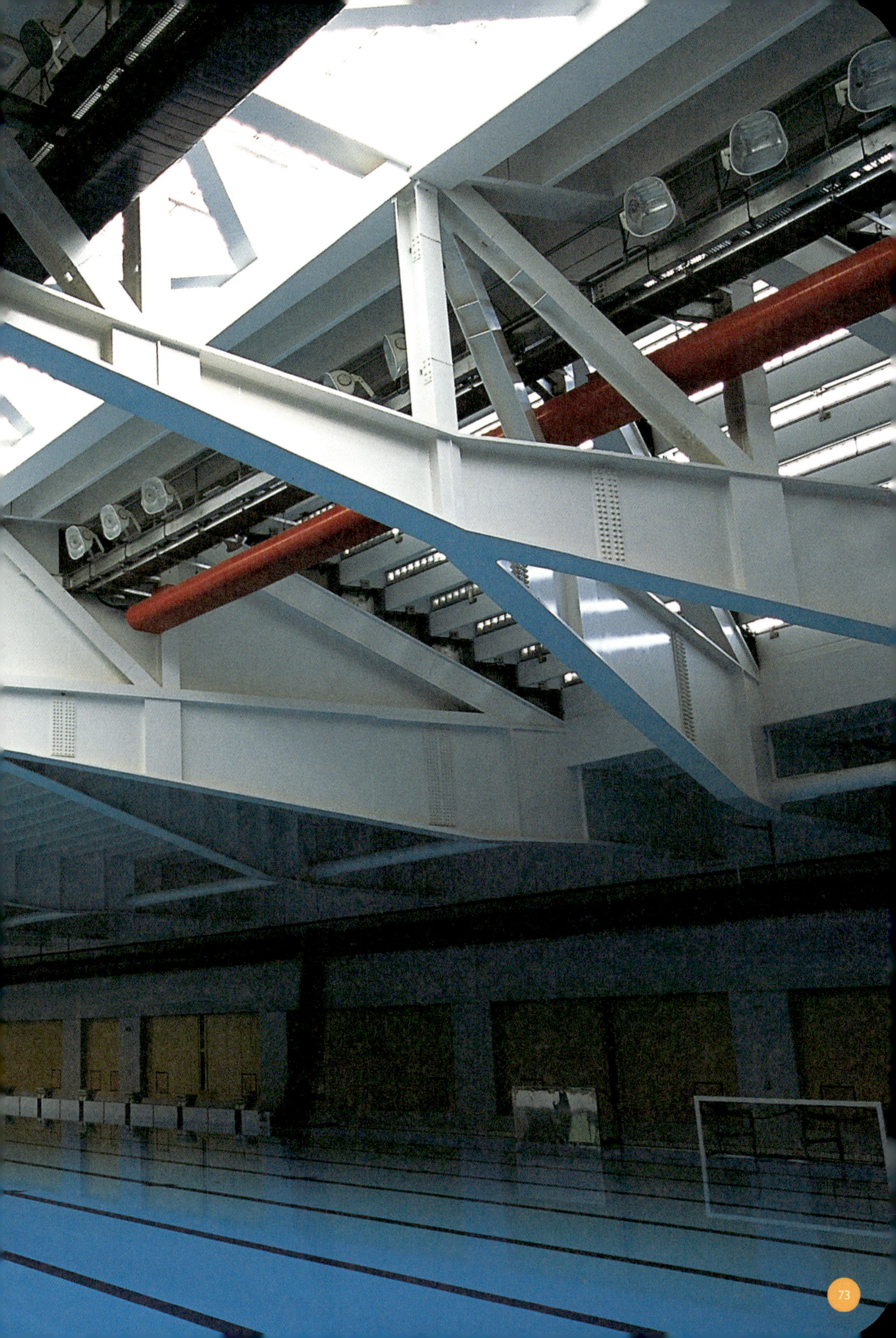

2008

慶應義塾日吉キャンパス 協生館

Keio University Collaboration Complex

500席の音楽ホールはグラウンドを望む
The 500-seat music hall looks out to the grounds.

2008

広島県立可部高等学校
Hiroshima Prefectural Kabe High School

丘の上の学び舎

広島県立可部高等学校

広島県広島市安佐北区可部東／2008
Hiroshima Prefectural Kabe High School
Kabehigashi, Asakita-ku, Hiroshima-shi, Hiroshima

広島県立可部高等学校は創立90年を超え、2万人の卒業生を持つ伝統と歴史ある学校である。その伝統を継承し、次世代の人材を育成する教育空間の形成を目指すため、生徒自身が積極的に発信できる場、多様な交流を生む場、地域の象徴となる場をコンセプトに設計された。木製デッキによる中庭を中心空間として遊環構造化された3層の建築である。

Hiroshima Prefecture Kabe High School is a school of culture and history of 90 years, and boasts 20,000 graduates. In order to pass on that tradition on, and to make a school that nurtures people of the next generation, we designed a place where the students themselves can aggressively participate, experience various exchanges, and also a place that will represent the local area in which it stands. The three-layer architecture achieves circular play system by centering the space on a garden set on a wooden deck.

2008

生徒達を迎え入れる正面
The façade that welcomes students.

広島県立可部高等学校　Hiroshima Prefectural Kabe High School

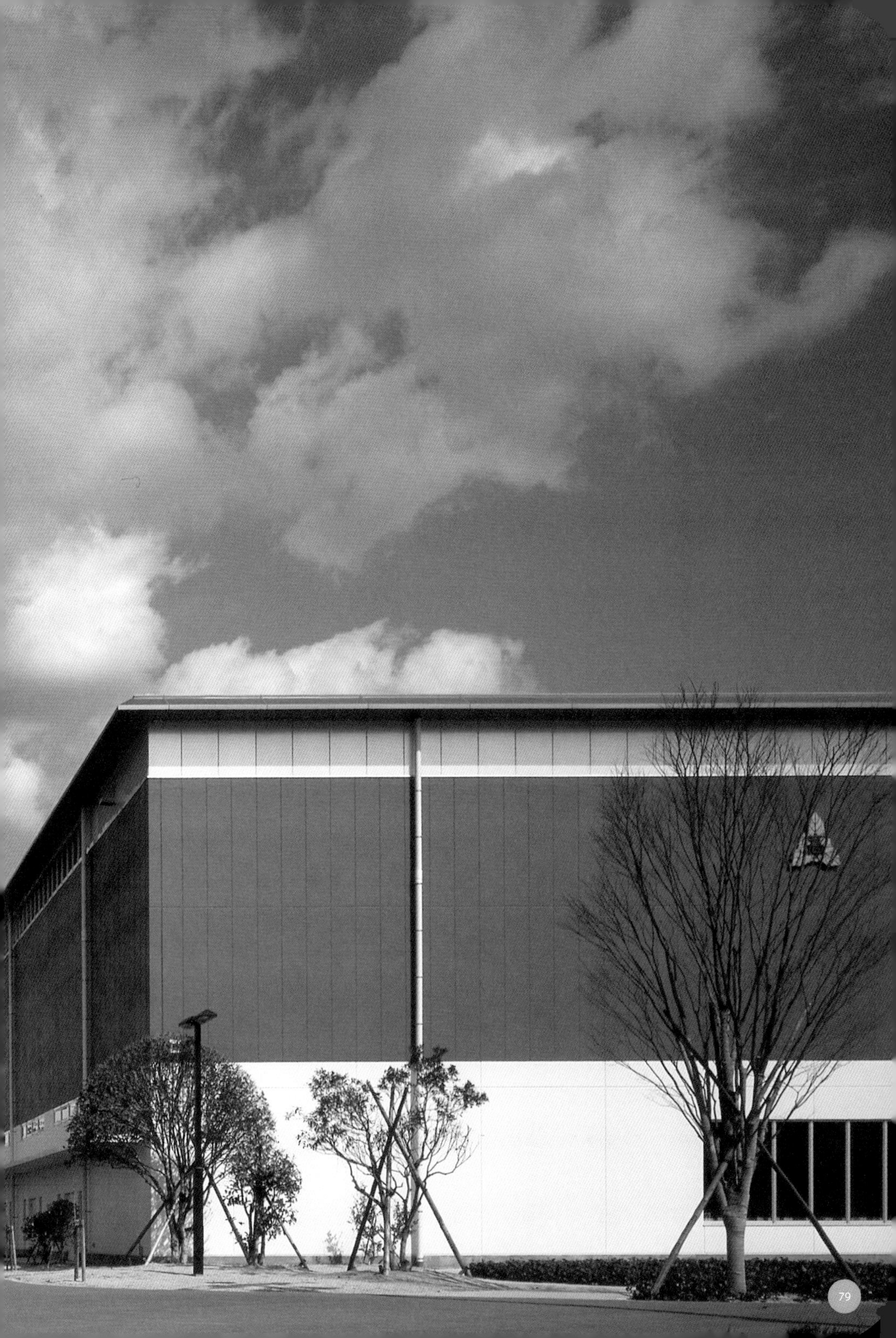

2008

広島県立可部高等学校
Hiroshima Prefectural Kabe High School

丘の上の白い校舎
The white school building standing on a hill.

81

2008

東大柏どんぐり保育園

Tokyo University Kashiwa Donguri Day Nursery

縁側建築

東大柏どんぐり保育園

千葉県柏市柏の葉／2008
Tokyo University Kashiwa Donguri Day Nursery
Kashiwanoha, Kashiwa-shi, Chiba

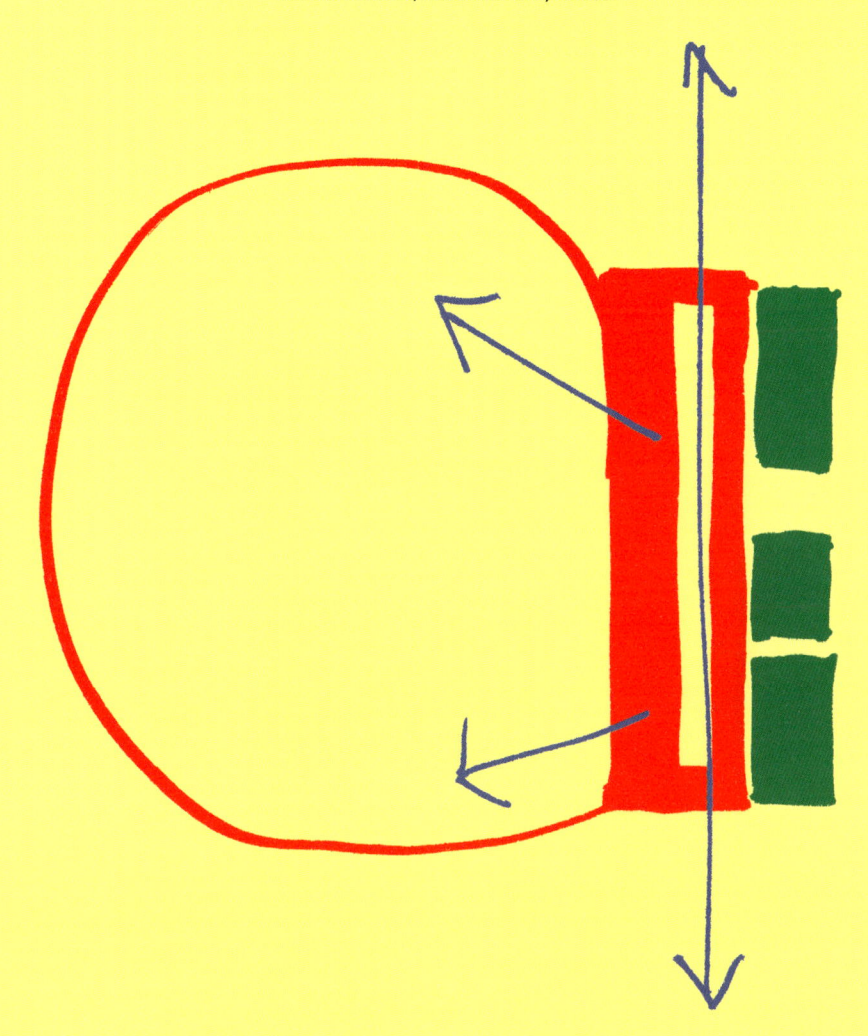

東京大学柏キャンパスの教職員・学生のための保育施設。内部空間は可動間仕切りや家具によって仕切ることのできる1層のワンルーム空間で、高い開放性によって保育室から縁側空間、そして園庭へとひとつながりとなっている。

This nursery is for the children of the faculty and students of Tokyo University, Kashiwa Campus. Inside is one spacious room that can be sectioned off by movable partitions and furniture. This highly open space leads from the nursery room, to the hallway, and out into the garden grounds.

2008

東大柏どんぐり保育園
Tokyo University Kashiwa Donguri Day Nursery

大きな杉の木の下で
Under the spreading cedar tree.

2008

岡崎げんき館
Okazaki Genkikan

元気

岡崎げんき館

愛知県岡崎市若宮町／2008
Okazaki Genkikan
Wakamiya-cho, Okazaki-shi, Aichi

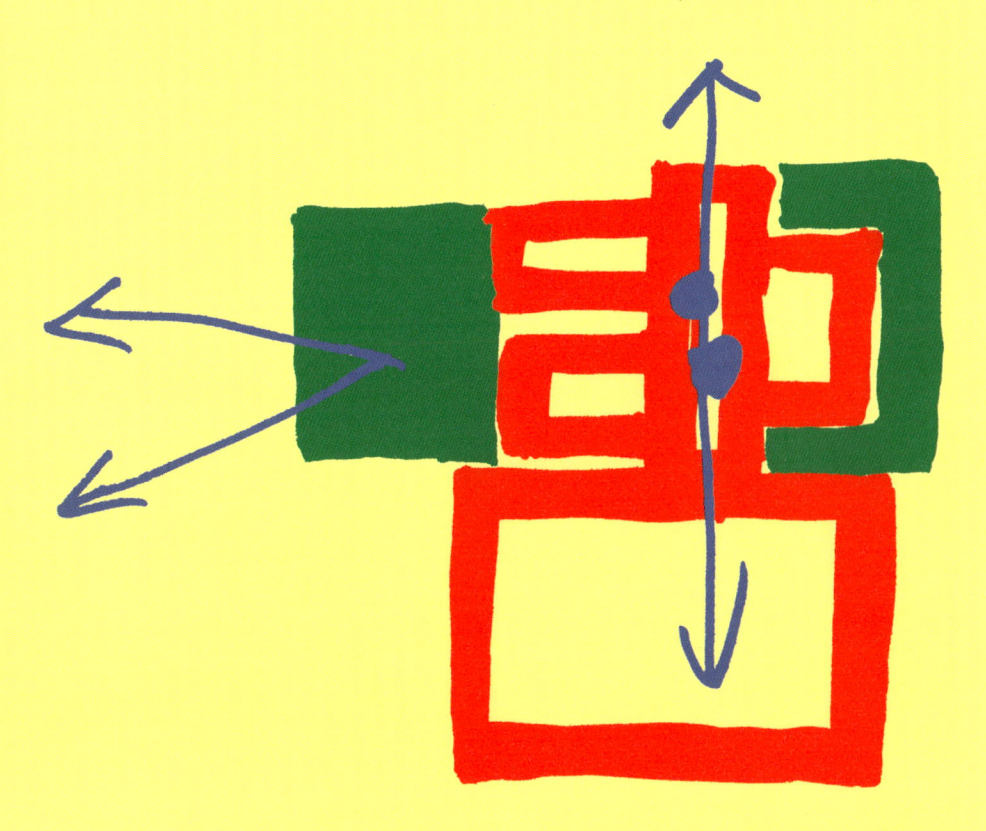

岡崎市初のPFI事業で、建物は敷地西側に残された旧市民病院の建物をコンバージョンし、新設建物と3層吹抜けのアトリウムによって一体化されている。「元気と活力を創造する拠点づくり」をコンセプトに、「市民交流」「健康づくり」「こども育成」「保健衛生」の4つのゾーンから構成されている。屋外には健康増進広場や健康回廊を設け、運営と一体となった遊環構造による賑わいづくりが図られている。

As the first PFI operation for Okazaki City, the old city hospital left on the west side of the site was converted and combined with a new building and atrium with a vaulted ceiling open three stories high. Built with the concept of "a foundation that creates healthiness and vitality", it has four zones; the "citizen's interchange" zone, "creating health" zone, "nurturing children" zone, and "health and sanitary" zone. A health promotion space and health hall were made outside to give it an overall festive mood.

2階に設けられたプールは明るく開放的
The pool on the second floor is bright and open.

2008

岡崎げんき館　Okazaki Genkikan

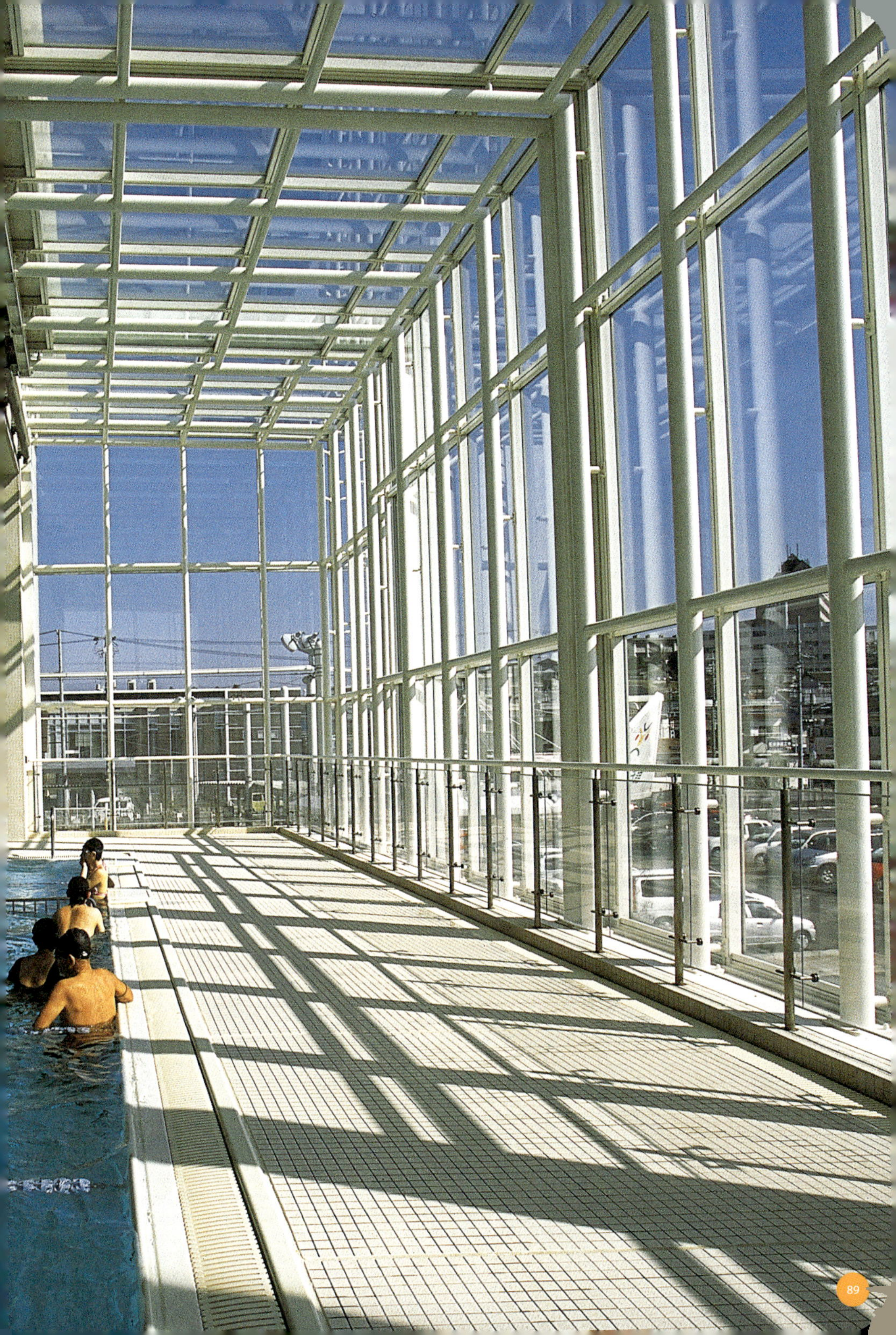

2008

岡崎げんき館　Okazaki Genkikan

こども達のあそびのための仕掛け
A mechanism built for child's play.

91

2008

あづみの公園 サテライトハウス

Alps Azumino National Government Park

大地建築

あづみの公園
サテライトハウス

長野県大町市常盤／2008
**Alps Azumino National Government Park
Tokiwa, Omachi-shi, Nagano**

北アルプスの雄大な景観と安曇野の大自然を満喫できる公園のレクリエーション施設である。体験学習・展示・休憩・遊戯・管理・便益等の機能を備えた4施設で構成されている。ゾーン全体を繋ぐ自然回廊として空中で樹間を縫うように歩く林間トレイルと園路・施設を有機的に絡み合わせている。各施設はトレイルと一体となって機能するよう計画されている。

This is a park recreation facility where visitors can enjoy the magnificent view of the Northern Alps and the vast natural surroundings of Azumino. The grounds contain four separate facilities with a full range of features, including hands-on learning, exhibits, spaces for resting, play, management, and benefits. There is also a mid-air forest trail that appears as if it was sewn between the trees. This serves as the natural corridor to connect the entire zone together, intertwining the trail with the forest path and facilities in an organic manner. Each facility is unified by the trails so as to function as one entity.

2008

あづみの公園 サテライトハウス
Alps Azumino National Government Park

あづみの高原の小さなあそびの教会
A small church for play, on the Azumino Alpine.

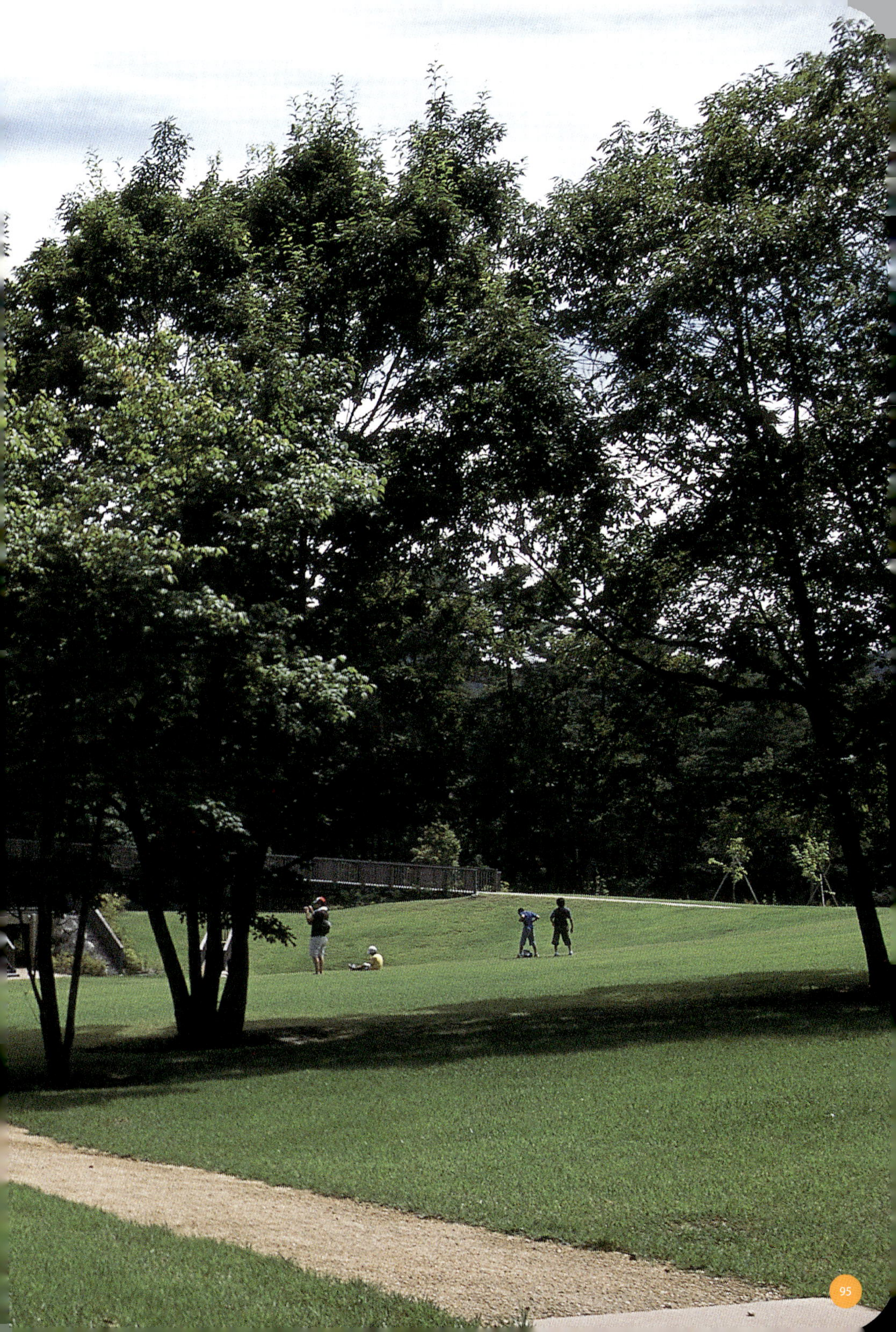

2008

あづみの公園 サテライトハウス

Alps Azumino National Government Park

木造による遊環構造をもつ内部空間
The wooden interior with circular play system.

ファイアプレイスのある大屋根広場
The large roofed square with a fireplace.

2008

あづみの公園 サテライトハウス　Alps Azumino National Government Park

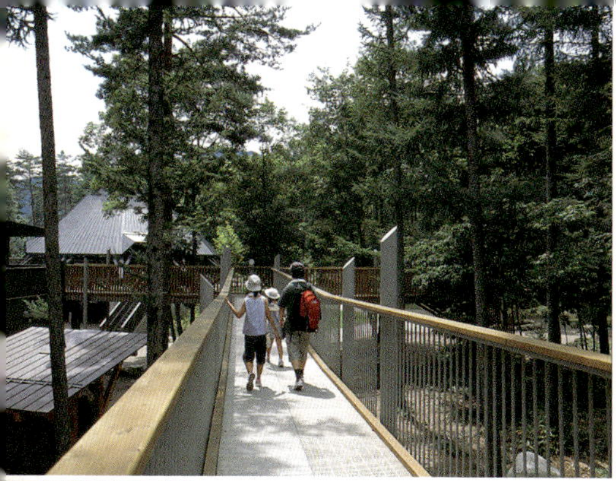
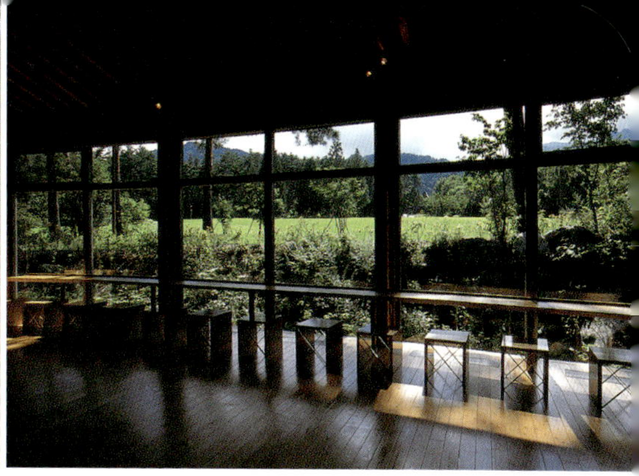
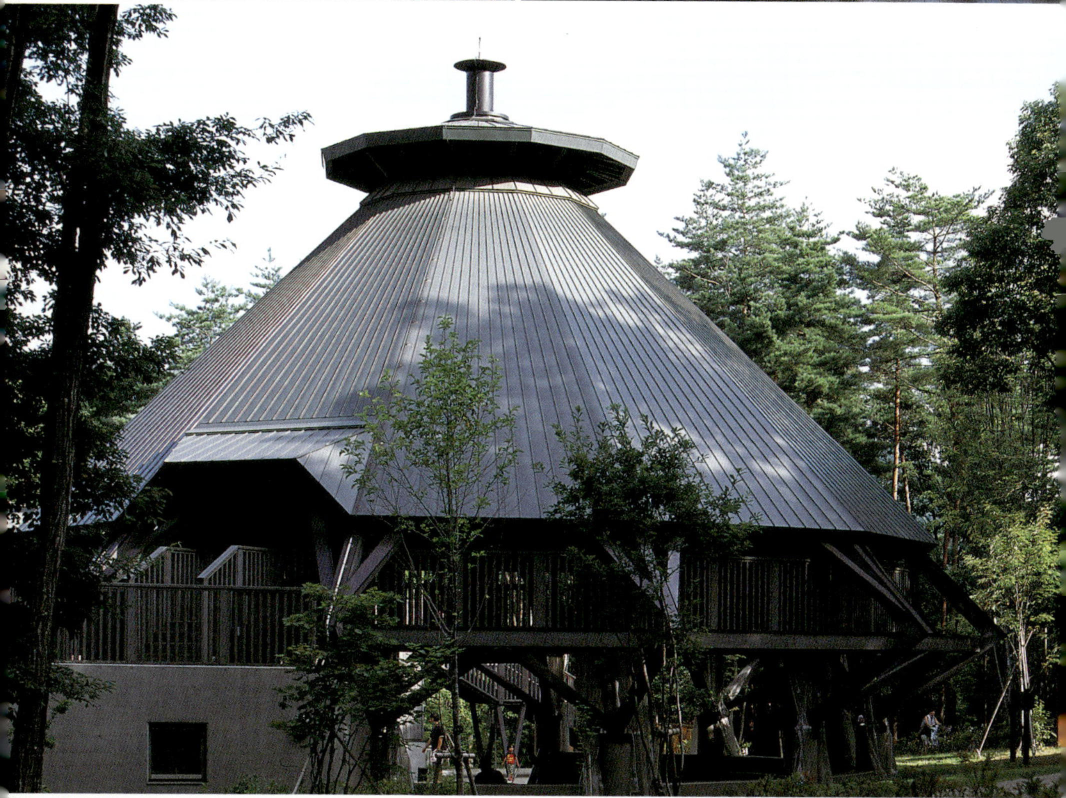
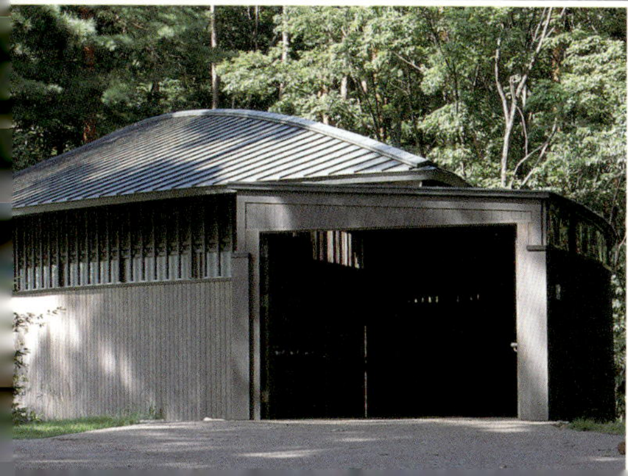
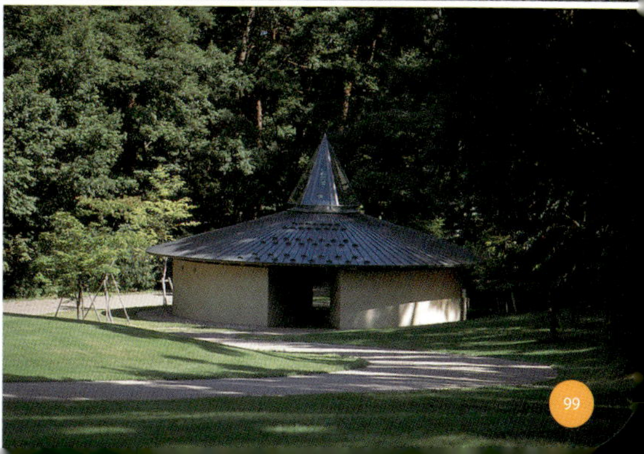

世界へ羽ばたく工場

2008
上海STEP
Shanghai STEP

上海STEP

中華人民共和国上海市／2008
Shanghai STEP
Shanghai, China

上海市の郊外である嘉定区に建設された、エレベーター等のデバイスを扱う企業の生産拠点施設。オフィス1棟、工場2棟、ゲストハウス1棟の4棟により全体を構成する。オフィス棟、工場棟については、明快でシンメトリカルな構成とし、来客の見学動線と各棟の生産動線を分離しながら魅力的な「見せる工場」ともしている。ゲストハウスの中心には静寂な光庭を設け、来館者がエントランスからいったんこの光庭に導かれ、そこから各室にアクセスできる構成としている。全体として遊環構造の平面をもつ、世界へ羽ばたく工場である。

This is a production facility for a company that manufacturers elevators and other devices. It is located in Jiading, in the suburbs of Shanghai. The entire complex comprises four buildings, including one office building, two factories, and one guest house. The office building and factories are of a clear, symmetrical structure, advertising themselves as attractive "factories open for viewing" by separating the tour corridor for customers and the production corridor of each building. The facility boasts an overall structure with circular play system plan and is a model for other such structures around the world.

2008

遊環構造の工場は見学ツアーまでもつくりだす
The factory with circular play system has even produced a tour for visitors.

上海STEP
Shanghai STEP

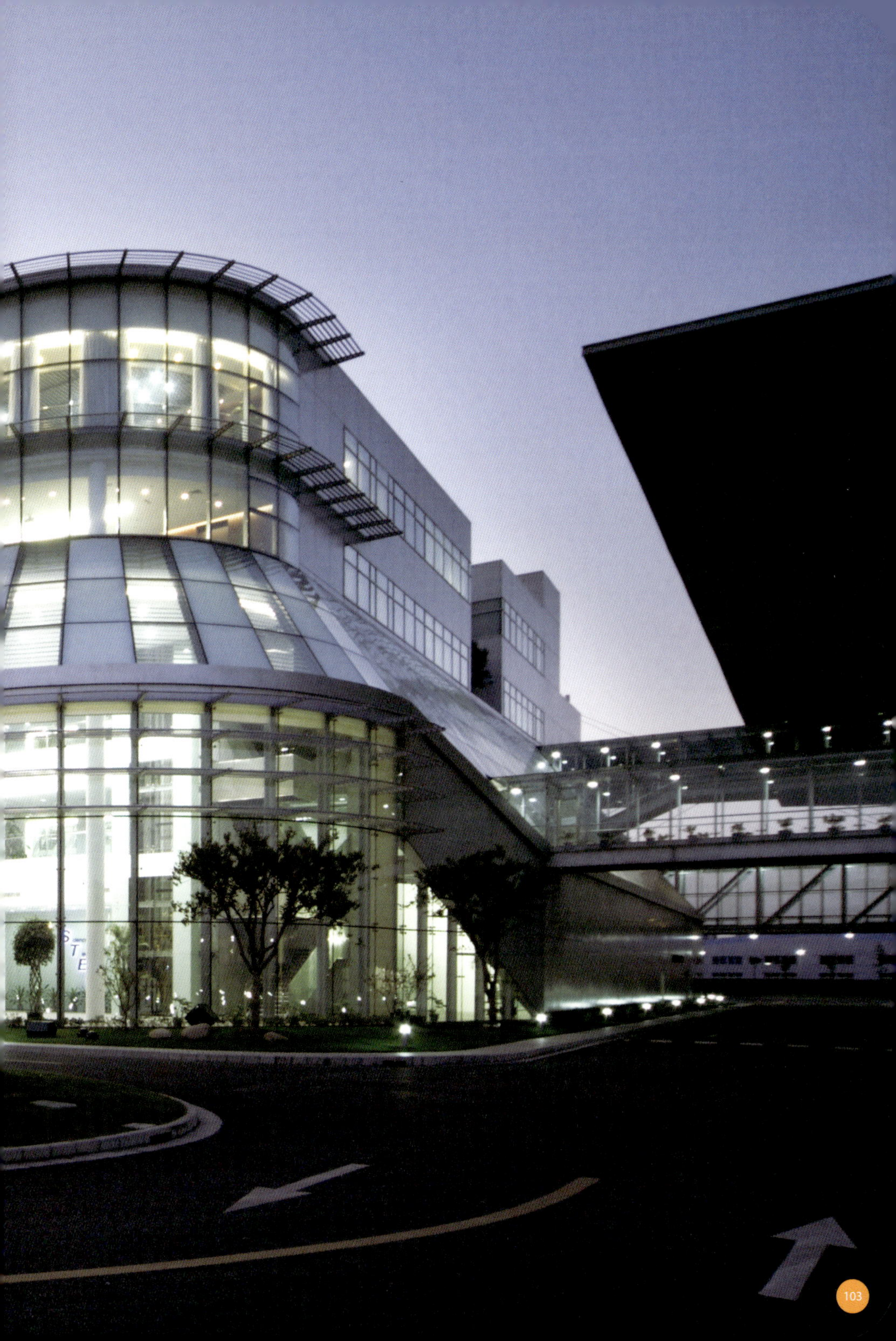

2008

上海STEP
Shanghai STEP

オフィス棟と工場棟をつなぐブリッジ群
The group of bridges linking the office and factory buildings.

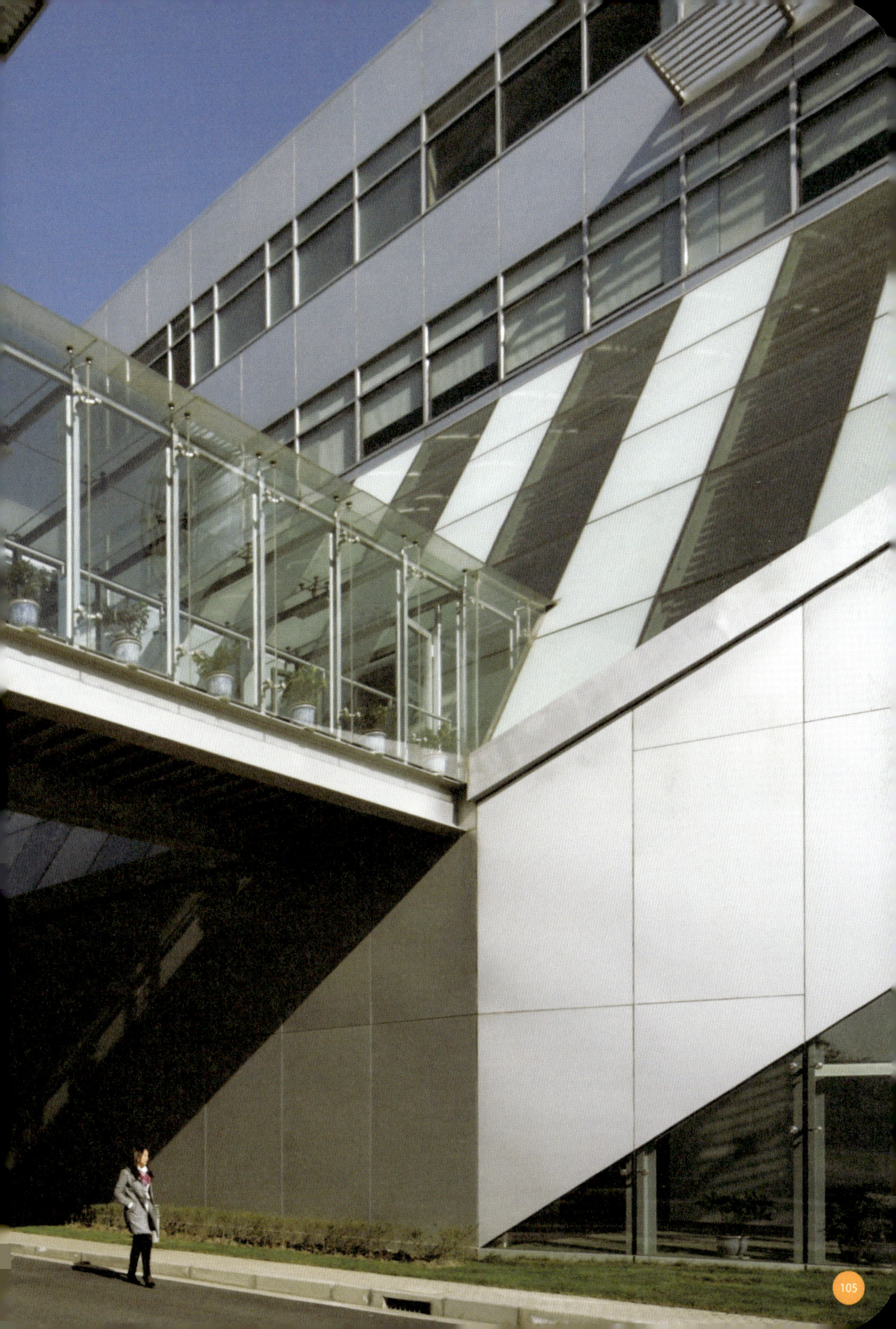

2008

上海STEP　Shanghai STEP

工場も大きなギャラリーだ
その企業コンセプト、
技術をプレゼンテーションする
The factor is also a huge gallery,
presenting the corporate concept
and technology to visitors.

2008

国際教養大学図書館棟
Akita International University, Library

ブック
コロシアム

国際教養大学図書館棟

秋田県秋田市雄和椿川／2008
Akita International University, Library
Yuwatsubakikawa, Akita-shi, Akita

閑静で豊かな森林に囲まれた国際教養大学のキャンパス整備計画の象徴として、本図書館は計画された。図書館を本と人との出合いの場所としての劇場空間「本のコロシアム」として計画され、洋書を中心とした段状の大空間「グレートホール」と、和書を中心とした1階の閲覧スペースからなっている。半円形平面のグレートホールは、中心に向かって段状に書架と閲覧席が組み合わされ、利用者は思い思いに本棚をめぐり、気に入った場所で閲覧することができる。秋田杉による濃密な木造空間と遊環構造をもつ「杜の図書館」を実現している。

The library is composed of the "book colosseum," where the library is treated as a theatrical space where books and people meet. There is the "great Hall," which is a large space with stairs and the first-floor viewing space. The half-circular shaped "great Hall" has shelves and seats combined on the floor which is layered with steps approaching the center, and people can select the book of their choice and take a seat anywhere they like. The building offers a robust wooden atmosphere with Akita cedars and a "library of trees" that provides users with a structure with circular play system.

2008

国際教養大学図書館棟

Akita International University, Library

ブックコロシアムは本と出合う場、
本に囲まれる場、本を探索する場
The book colosseum is a place
where people get in touch with books,
where they are surrounded by books,
and where they search for books.

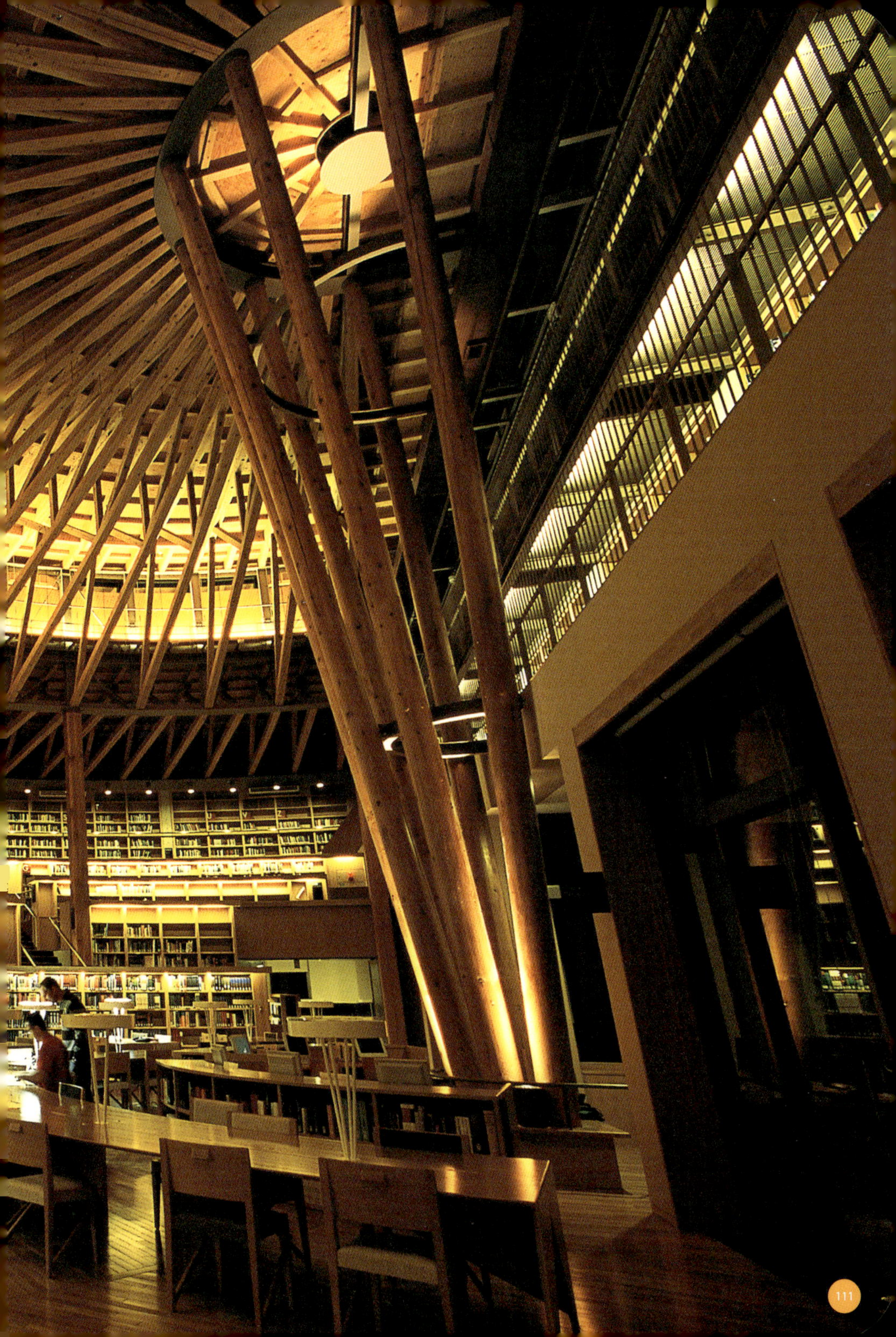

2008

国際教養大学図書館棟

Akita International University, Library

北側既存の杉林が
読書に疲れた気持ちをやわらげる

The cedar forest that had already been standing on the north side helps one to recover from the reading exhaustion.

2008

国際教養大学図書館棟
Akita International University, Library

和傘のような木の奥行
The depth of trees that bring to mind umbrellas.

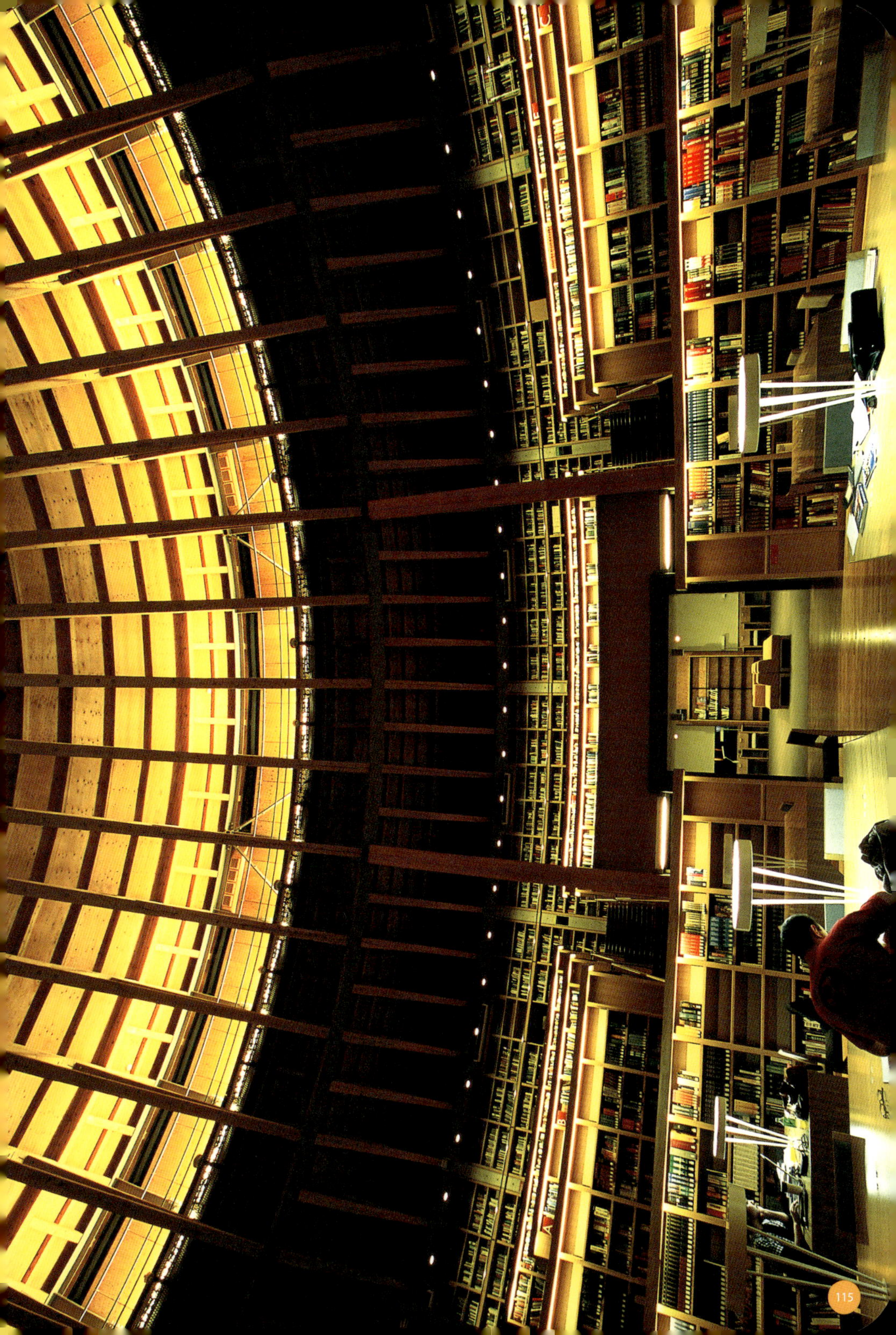

2008

国際教養大学図書館棟

Akita International University, Library

本棚の後ろの読書机の居心地の良さ
The comfort of the reading desks behind the bookshelves.

2008

国際教養大学図書館棟
Akita International University, Library

さまざまな視点からの景観の強弱
The intensity of the landscape from various viewpoints.

119

2008

国際教養大学図書館棟

Akita International University, Library

言語異文化学習センターは言語学習のラウンジ
Language Development and Intercultural Studies Center is a lounge for language learning.

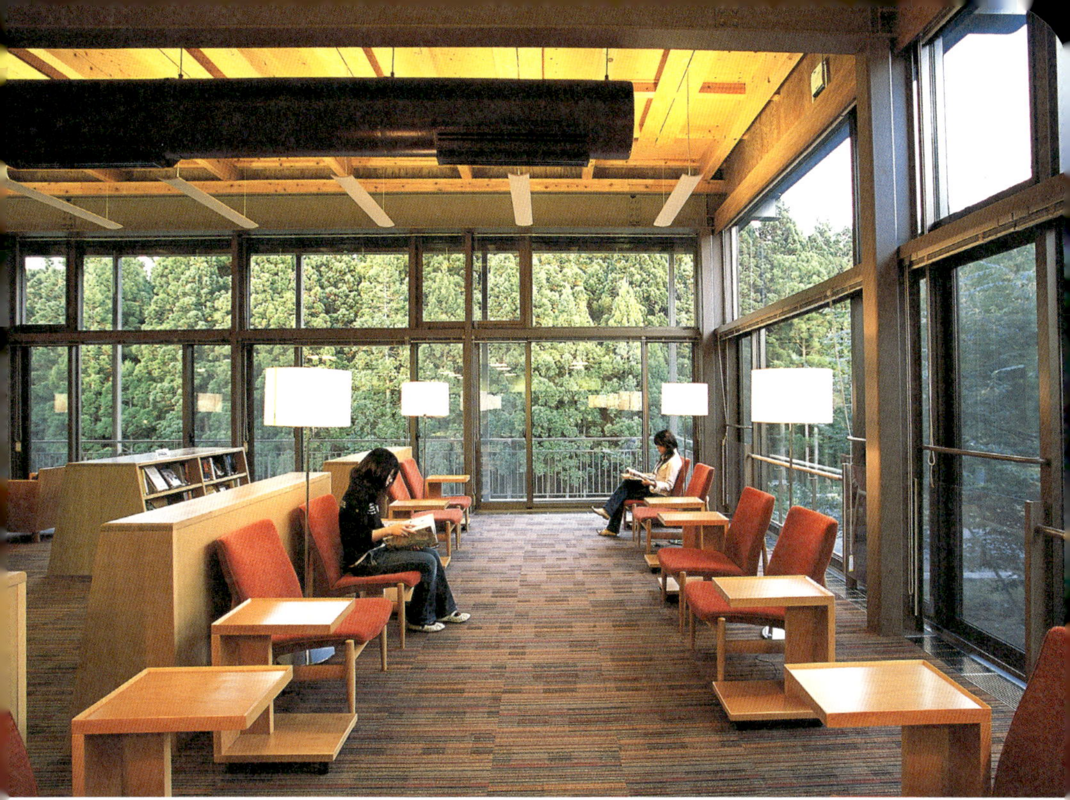

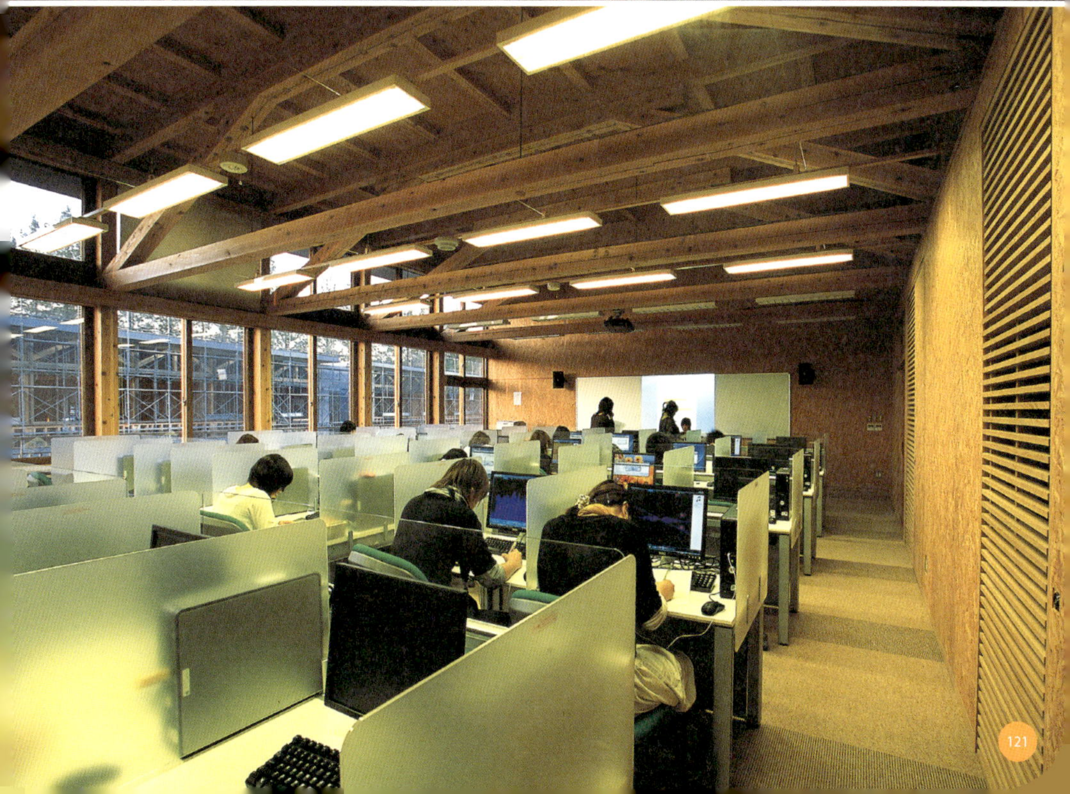

2008

国際教養大学図書館棟

Akita International University, Library

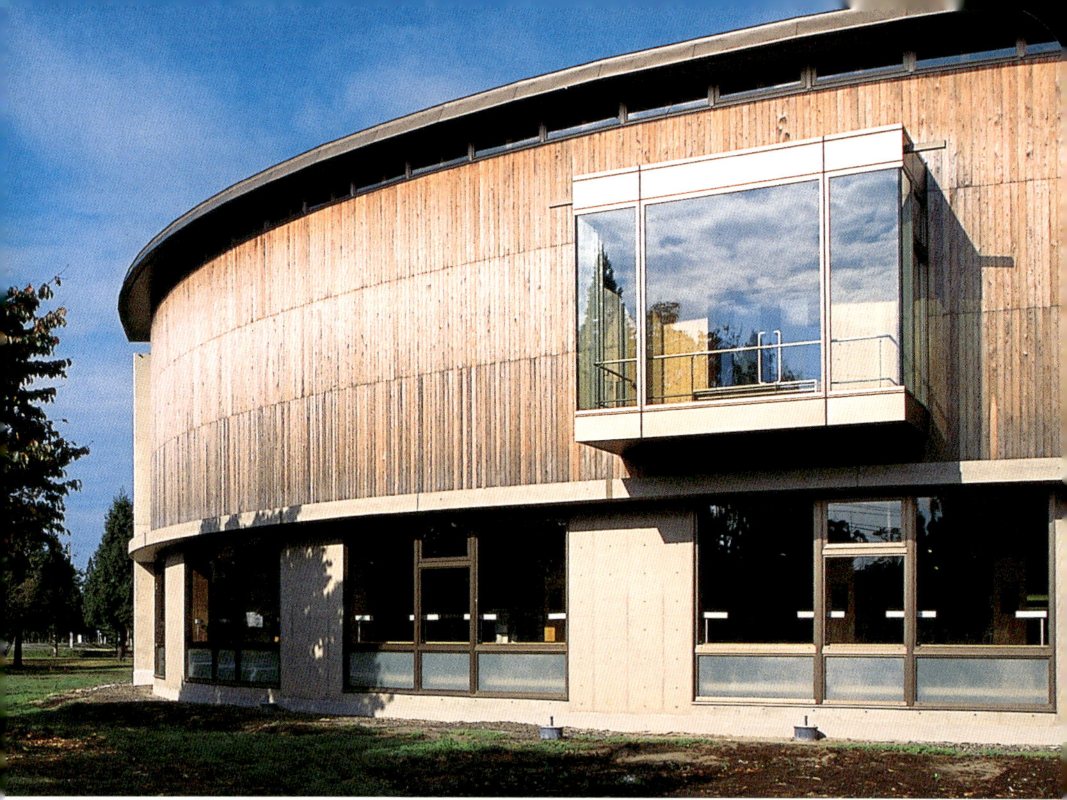

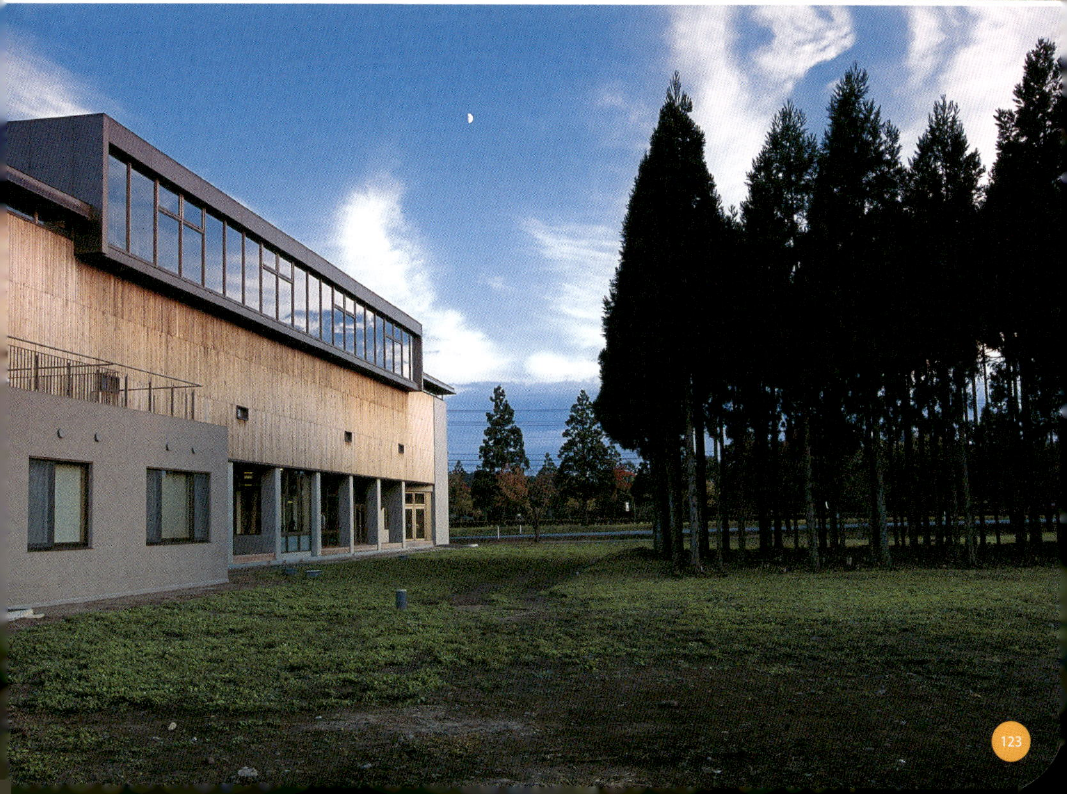

2008

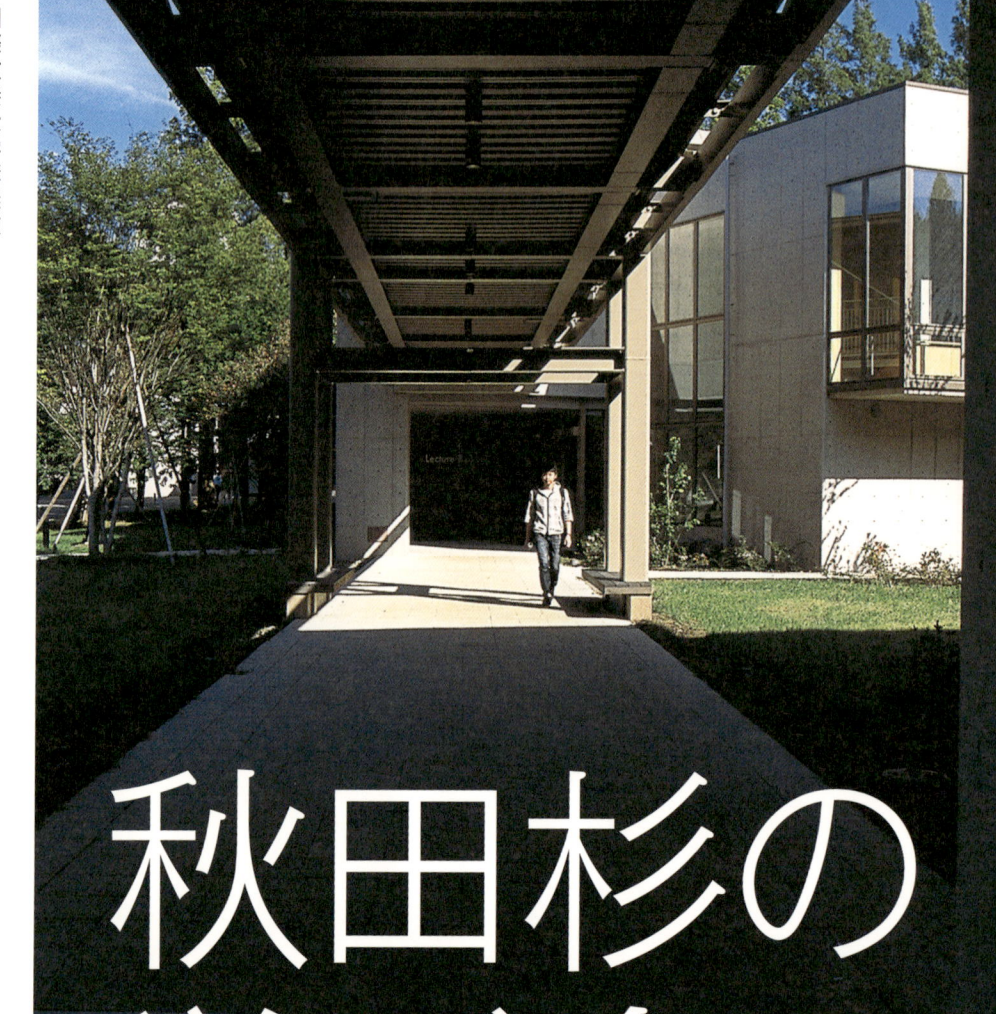

国際教養大学講義棟
Akita International University, Lecture Building

秋田杉の学び舎

国際教養大学
講義棟

秋田県秋田市雄和椿川／2008
Akita International University, Lecture Building
Yuwatsubakikawa, Akita-shi, Akita

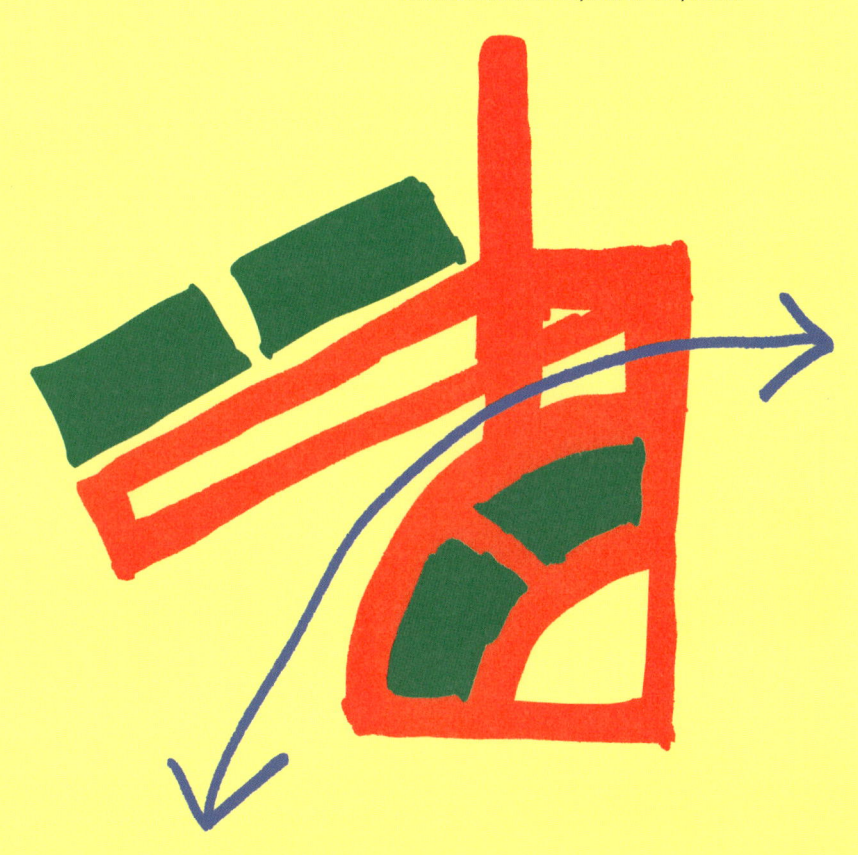

緑豊かな森林に囲まれた本施設は、300人収容可能な扇形の階段教室と一般教室、プレゼンテーションルーム、大学院研究室からなる。外殻のコンクリート造の中に、中断面集成材からなる木造を挿入した「入れ子構造」とすることで、合理的で安全な構造計画を実現した。木のぬくもりのある学習環境は、多くの学生と教職員の支持を得ている。

This building, located in the midst of a richly green forest, contains a half-circular classroom that seats 300 students, other smaller classrooms, presentation rooms, and university research rooms. A rational and safe structural plan was realized by implementing the "nested structure", where wood was inserted into the outer concrete. The learning environment receives the support of a wide range of students and teaching staff for its warm wooden feel.

2008

国際教養大学講義棟

Akita International University, Lecture Building

ブリッジが校内の遊環構造を形成する
The bridge forms circular play system within the campus compounds.

2008

国際教養大学講義棟

Akita International University, Lecture Building

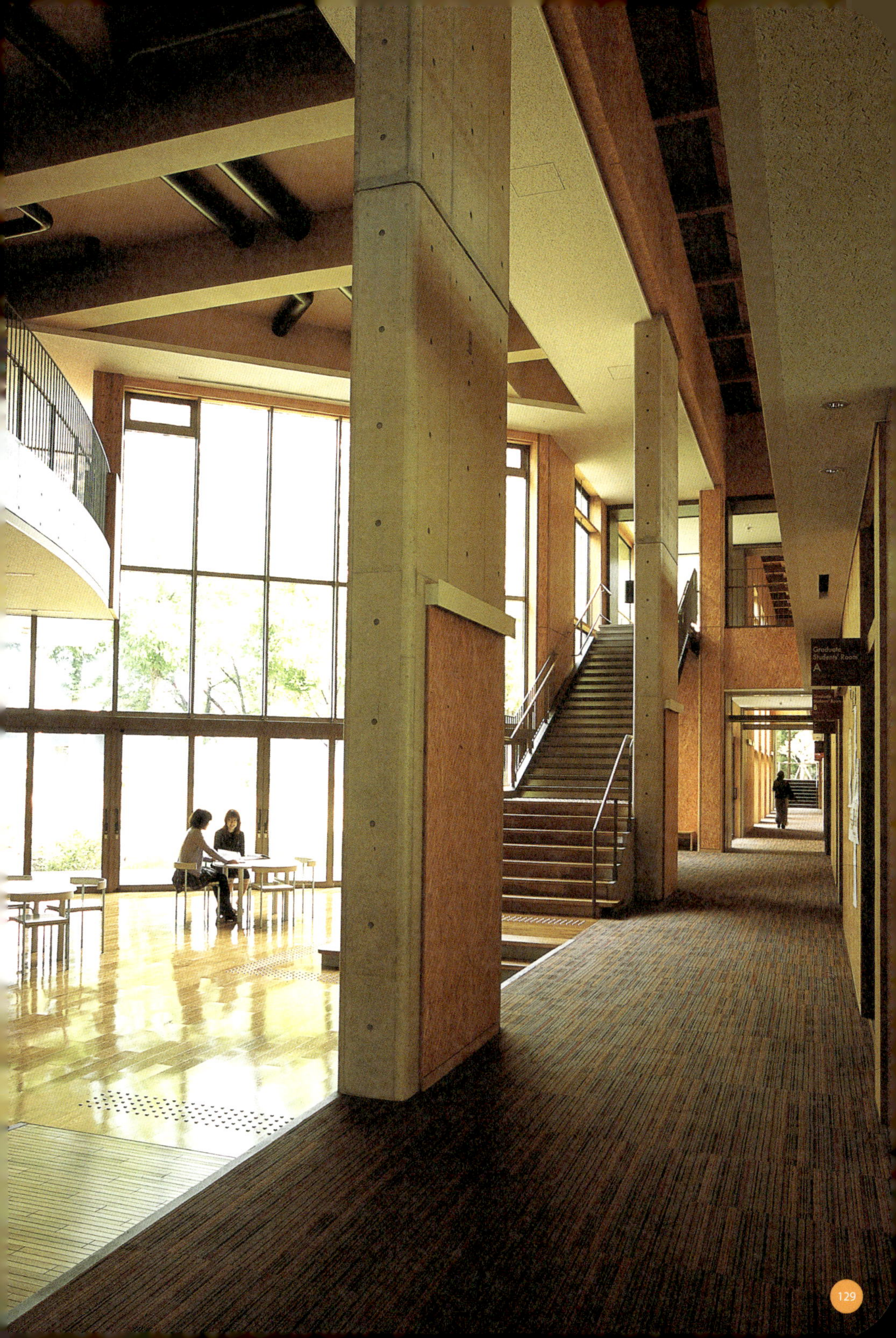
Graduate
Students' Room
A

2008

国際教養大学講義棟

Akita International University, Lecture Building

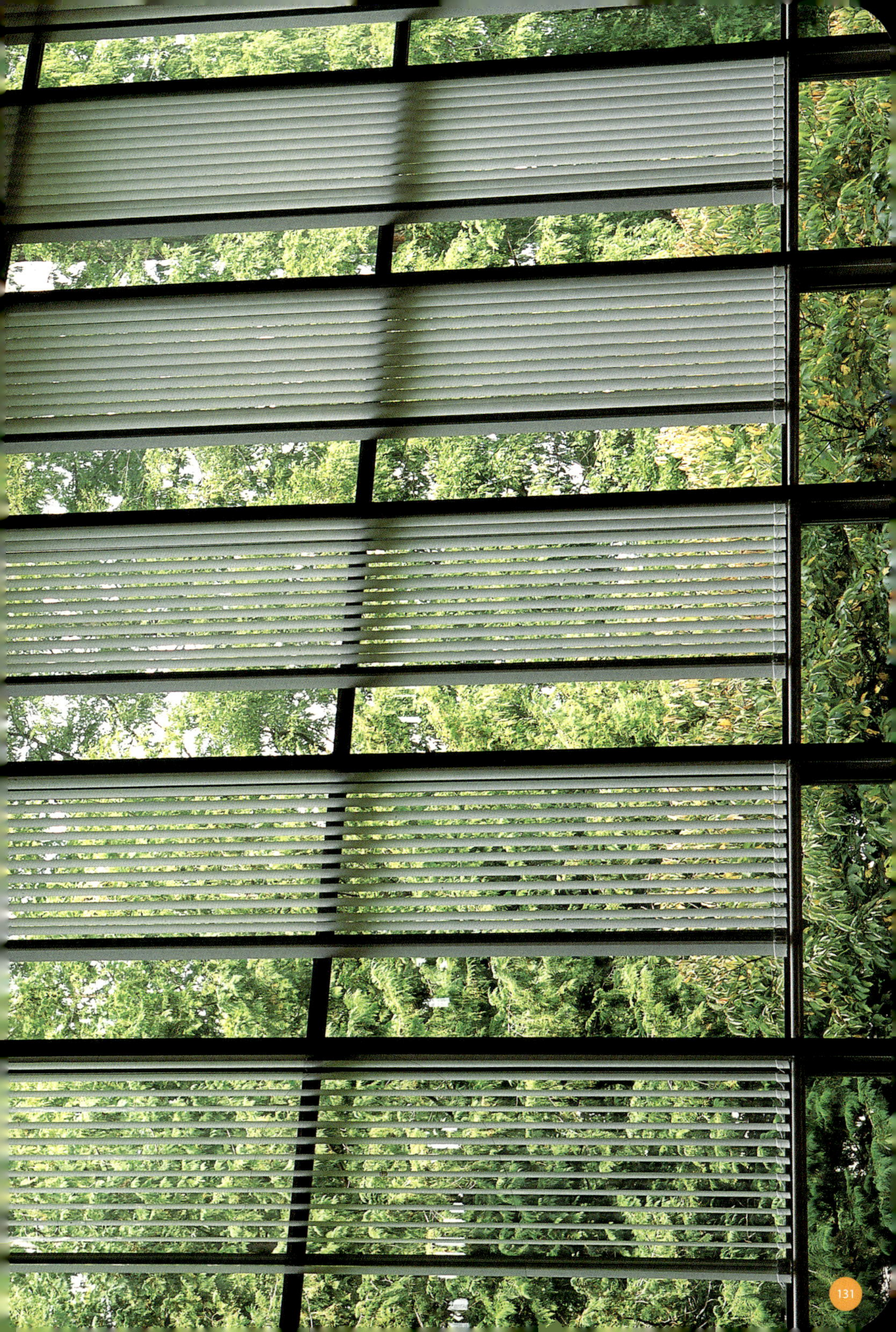

2008

国際教養大学講義棟

Akita International University, Lecture Building

133

2008

国際教養大学講義棟

Akita International University, Lecture Building

森の大学の敷地はかつて県の林業試験場
その緑を大切に継承する
The campus in the forest used to
serve as the examination hall
for the forestry examination in the prefecture,
and has inherited and cherished that greenery.

2008

国際教養大学講義棟

Akita International University, Lecture Building

木、森、静けさ、明かり、学生達のざわめき
Trees, forests, quiet, brightness, and the murmurs of students.

137

中心軸の回転

2010

国際教養大学多目的ホール

Akita International University, Multi Purpose Hall

国際教養大学
多目的ホール

秋田県秋田市雄和椿川／2010
Akita International University, Multi Purpose Hall
Yuwatsubakikawa, Akita-shi, Akita

本施設は体育館と講堂、またクラシックコンサート、現代音楽、演劇等の多様な利用が求められた。私達は中心軸を回転させて体育館、講堂、コンサートホール、コンベンションホールなどの幅広い用途に使い分けることのできる円形可変型のアリーナの提案を行った。2階の円環状ランニングコースは1周120mある。

This facility can be used for a variety of purposes, such as a gymnasium, lecture hall, and concert hall that can host classic and modern music concerts, and theater. We proposed that a circular, moveable arena model be employed that allows for rotating the central axis to use the facility differently based on a wide range of purposes, whether it be a gym, lecture hall, concert hall, or convention hall. The circular running course found on the second floor is 120 meters in length.

2010

国際教養大学多目的ホール

Akita International University, Multi Purpose Hall

体育館、音楽ホール、講堂という
3つの機能をもつ多目的ホール
A multipurpose hall that functions in three ways
—as a gymnasium, music hall, and lecture hall.

2010

2階に120mのジョギングコース
A 120m jogging course on the second floor.

国際教養大学多目的ホール
Akita International University, Multi Purpose Hall

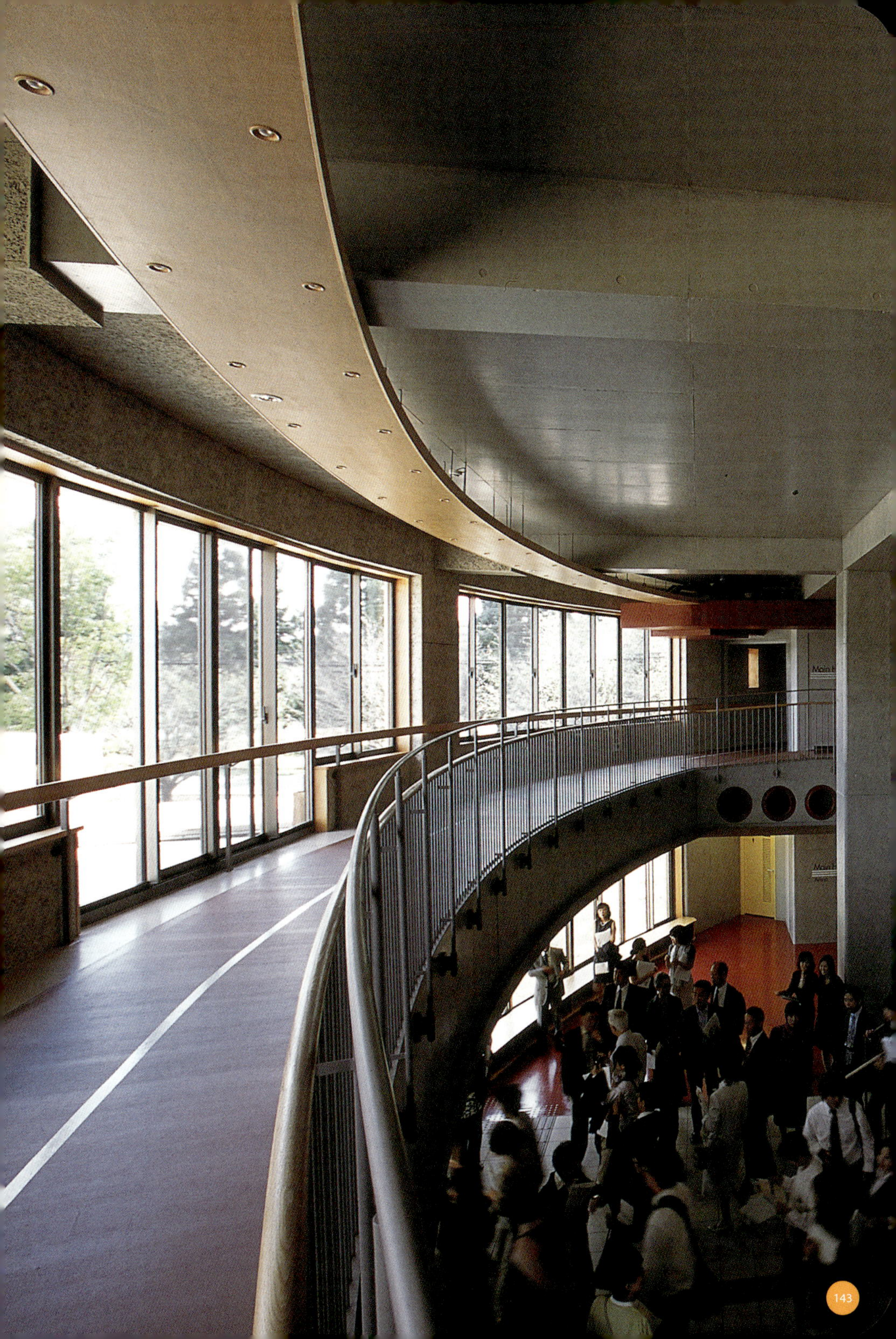

Project

探検温室

東山動植物園探検温室
Higashiyama Zoo and Botanical Gardens Adventure Glasshouse Project

東山動植物園探検温室

愛知県名古屋市千種区田代町／Project
Higashiyama Zoo and Botanical Gardens Adventure Glasshouse Project
Tashiro-cho, Chigusa-ku, Nagoya-shi, Aichi

世界の熱帯雨林や乾燥地域に生息する植物と動物を共存させた温室ドームである。植物と動物のつながりや、生き物達の多様な生活様式、人間による植物利用の歴史を、現地を探検するような感覚で体験できる遊環構造による「探検温室」として計画されている。

This is a greenhouse dome project where plants and animals of tropical rain forests and arid regions can coexist. The recreational structure was designed as an "exploration greenhouse" where visitors can explore how plants and animals live in their real local habitats by experiencing the connection between plants and animals, the diverse lifestyles of living creatures, and the history of how people have used plants.

Project

東山動植物園探検温室

Higashiyama Zoo and Botanical Gardens Adventure Glasshouse Project

ETFE膜による構造は、全体が遊環構造建築
The entire structure, created with ETFE film, makes up a building with circular play system.

広島市民球場を中心に

斎藤公男×仙田 満

出会いとこれまで

仙田 満（以下Se）　広島「広島市民球場」（2009年）の話をする前に、斎藤さんと僕のこれまであった長い付き合いの話でもしましょうか。

斎藤公男（以下Sa）　最初の出会いは、僕は仙田さんと……どのあたりからでしょうかね。

Se　仕事としては、京都「京都アクアリーナ」（2002年）ですね。最初の出会いは内田祥哉先生が建築学会の会長だった頃だから、1994年頃かな。いっしょに建築学会の理事をやりましたよね。

Sa　僕の仙田さんに対する最初の印象は、こどもの世界、特異な環境をなさっている方、という感じですね。その後1998年に、仙田さんが出された本の出版記念パーティをやりましたよね。

Se　『プレイストラクチャー』（1998年/柏書房）と『環境デザインの方法』（1998年/彰国社）の2冊を出しました。

Sa　その出版記念パーティの時、仙田さんは突然僕に「司会をやれ」っておっしゃったんです。パーティの日がどしゃぶりだったのがすごく印象的でした。

Se　そうそう、どしゃぶりか覚えていませんが、確かに雨でしたね。その時は司会ありがとうございました。

Sa　建築家の方で、2冊も本を出版されることを「すごいな」と感心したのです。そしてお客さんとしていらっしゃる人達がそうそうたるメンバーで、「何でおれが司会なんだ」って思いながらも、大変光栄なことなので、即興でやらせてもらいました。その時仙田さんの後ろ姿を見ていて、病み上がりだったのかな、とにかく細くて。

Se　そう、あのころ調子が悪かったのです、一度病気をしたのでね。

Sa　仙田さんって、細くて頼りなさそうなのに、本をつくるようなすごいエネルギーがある人なんだなあと思ったこと。そして奥さんを近くでまじまじと見たら「かくも美しい奥さんが何でこの人のところにいるのだ」ということ。当時の僕としては、この2つのことが、ものすごく印象的だったんですよね。

Se　あはははは。

Sa　それを契機に、仙田さんとはいっしょにいろいろなコンペに参加しましたよね。

Se　北京オリンピックのコンペにも出しましたね。

Sa　北京にかけたエネルギーの量も半端じゃなかったですね。オリンピックという一つのきっかけではあるけれど、鳥の巣[*1]をつくることができたあの時代に、僕達が本格的なアートとテクノロジーがちゃんと統合している建築を提案できたことは、中国にとってもよかったことだと思うんです。結局コンペに勝ったのにプロジェクトそのものがなくなってしまったことは、今となってはいい思い出ですね、残念なことだけれども。余談ですが、北京のコンペに出す最後の模型のチェックを行った時も、なぜか雨でした。

Se　ああ、雨でした。

Sa　これまで僕は「空間構造」や「構造デザイン」といったことをテーマに活動していますが、僕が関係していた「山口ドーム」と同じ頃、仙

田さんと團紀彦さん*² が手がけた、京都アクアリーナは、すごくイノベイティブでしたね。
Se 山口ドームは、もう少し前でしたよね。
Sa 山口の方が計画や設計はちょっと早いのですが、ほとんど同じ時期ですね。柱の頂部に免震を入れ、PC柱も細く設計できましたね。山口ドームはドームという形式に初めて取り入れて、京都アクアリーナはフラット屋根に初めて導入したのです。
Se 太陽熱温水パネルを3,000㎡搭載したので屋根が重くなり、斎藤さんの提案でA型柱の頂部に免震構造を埋め込んだのですね。そのためPCのA型柱そのものが、とてもスレンダーなものとなったのです。また、太陽パネルを載せた屋根以外のほとんどを覆土して屋上緑化にしたりと、画期的な手法を多く使いました。

建築家としての生きざまも
仙田さんに見せてもらった

Sa 僕はもう少し、仙田さんを押し上げる役割ができたらよかった、と反省しています。そんな中で、唯一、僕が仙田さんの役に立ったことがあって。仙田さんが建築学会の会長だった時、タイミングよく、「お前がやれ」と言われて、二つの仕事のお手伝いができたんですね。一つは「アーキテクトデザイン」。資格や他の団体のことも関係してくることではあるけど、日本の建築界が一つにまとまるようなすごい実りがあることだった、と思っています。二つ目が「建築会館のドーム」。仙田さんの改革によって、高さは20mくらいある空間が、まさに「広場」として生き返りました。仙田さんのことを、僕がタイムリーに力強く支えながら実行できたということは、本当によかったです。
Se 僕としてもあの学会の中庭は雨の日に使えるような、もっとイベンダブルな空間にしたいと考えていたのですが、当時は学会も余裕

があって斎藤賢吉事務局長も賛同してお金を出していただいて、斎藤さん達にお願いをして実現できたのですから、とても感激でした。
Sa こうしたことをさせてもらったおかげで、「アーキテクトデザイン」を日常的にもイベント的にも実現できました。そして「強い思いを出して、結びつける」という、建築家の生きざまみたいなものを見せてもらいました。
Se 建築会館のドームも、この10年間ほとんど変わらず利用されていて、建築家としてうれしいことですね。
Sa この間の月曜日もメンテナンスがあって、可動式のドーム部分はちゃんと動いていました。ああいうふうに、大事に建築物が使われている、生きているということは大事なことです。建築会館にはあそび心がある、つまり非常に堅い建築と動くドームが組み合わさっていて、多機能な建築空間になっている。強度や耐久性といったフィジカルな意味のサスティナ

斎藤公男（さいとうまさお）
1938年群馬県生まれ。工学博士。1961年日本大学理工学部建築学科卒業、1963年同大学大学院修士課程修了。1987年日本建築学会賞（業績部門）、1993年松井源吾賞、BCS賞、1997年IASS坪井賞、2007年日本建築学会教育賞、2009年E・トロハ賞受賞。主な著書に『空間構造物語』。主な作品に、出雲ドーム、山口きららドームなど。

Conversation

斎藤公男×仙田 満
Masao Saito × Mitsuru Senda

ブルだけでなく、機能や面白さといった未来的メッセージがこめられたサスティナブルがある、と思うんです。

Se　動く建築の使い方は拡大するだけではありません。地球環境建築という部分で、日本のふすま、障子のように、気候と同調していますからね。

Sa　今、一番注目したいのは、半屋外性ではないでしょうか。障子を全部開けて光が入ることも魅力的ですが、雪見障子と同じで、太陽の影が見えたり、外に何かあるという気配を感じることもいい。密閉することも必要なのだけれど、気候を感じながら屋外とルーズにつながるドームは、すごく面白いものですね。

Se　ドームというものは、閉塞感があるでしょう。僕はもともと閉所恐怖症だから、全部ふさいであると心が落ち着かないんです。

Sa　膜のドームができた時に、仙田さんが「天窓を開けろ」といったことはすごく印象的でした。ドームの膜屋根を施工していた会社は、テントをつくる業界ナンバーワンの会社で、できあがったものに穴を開けるというのは考えられなかったはず。きれいにできあがったものをカットしたら、切り傷になってしまいますからね。ところが仙田さんがそんなアイデアを提案したおかげで、彼らも新しい技術を開発して特許申請までしてしまった。今あるテクノロジーより、先に「これができるか？」というアーキテクトマインドの発想をぶつけることが、やがて広島市民球場にもつながっていったのではないでしょうか。

広島市民球場をコンペされる側と審査する側

Se　2003年頃、広島で「こどもと都市」というテーマで、僕は講演会をしたことがありました。来ていた広島市役所の人に、「先生、見てください」と野球場に連れていかれ、「これを建て直さなければいけないのですが」といわれたんですね。そういうご縁がはじまりです。

Sa　今回の「広島市民球場」で、僕は2回審査員をさせていただきました。1回目のとき、印象が薄くてよく覚えていないのですが、仙田さんはどういう形で参加されていたのでしょうか。

Se　統括建築家ですね。

Sa　最終審査まで残らなかったんですよね。

Se　全部だめでした。事業コンペだったんですが、参加したチームがほとんど失格になってしまったのですね。

Sa　そこで仕切り直して、2回目の審査をしました。その2次に残った5作品には、仙田さんの作品は残りましたよね。

Se　なんとか残りました。

Sa　審査する僕達からすると、拮抗していた他者と比べて、外観は同じようであっても、今まで発想もしなかったスタジアムだったんです。仙田さんの作品は「こういう見方もあるのか」といったような、「目からうろこ」みたいな切り口が面白かった。全体に構想されたアイデアのいくつかでも、実現できたらいいと思ったんです。「建築」という言葉や文脈ではなくて、「スポーツイベントと市民」という言葉をつかうことで、スタジアム建築が市民に寄り添っていました。そこに機能的な面白さを感じたし、使う立場からの目線もありました。そして「よくもここまで」という楽しみ方、楽しませ方も感じた反面、限られた予算の中で「果たしてどこまでできるか」というあたりの不安、期待もありました。だけどトータルで、「建築」という「枠」を外れている感じがしたんです。

Se　僕も「90億でできるか」と言われた時に、「できます」と答えたのですが、本当にすごい課題でした。1次コンペの案として出したのは鉄骨でしたが、4万㎡ある広さなので、実施設計でPCに換えたり、メインコース下部は

斎藤公男 × 仙田 満
Masao Saito × Mitsuru Senda

Conversation

RCにしたり。とにかく省けるところは省いて、部分によってつかう部材を変更させてもらいました。

Sa 結局、混構造ですが、気にならないつくりになりましたね。仙田さんの仕事ぶりを見ていると、できるところまである程度やって、あとは様子を見ながら素材を替えたり増やしていくんですね。「コンペ案通りにできてないこの部分を、どうするか、どうしたらいいのか」ということではなくて、「限られた時間の中で、変化に対応しながらつくりあげていく」ことでもいいのではないか。今回の仙田さんのやり方は、そういった新しい建築の概念、コンセプトを打ち出していったように感じます。

Se 広島市民球場のまわりの集客施設は、三井不動産がやることになったのですが、この社会情勢でテナントが集まらないんですね。僕は三井不動産に最初から完成を望まないで、できることからやっていく街づくりでいいんじゃないか、と提案したほどです。その点カープ球団は指定管理者で柔軟に対応していますね。

Sa この間、僕が見に行った時はジムをつくろうとしていました。あと、畳敷きのスタンドも新設されましたよね。グループで貸し切る時は、そういう目新しいところから、まず予約が埋まっていくようです。あの席はナイターを体験したくなるような仕組みですね。今回僕は、たまたま二度もこのコンペの審査員をやって、これまでのスタジアムや野球場は20世紀的な建築で、これからの21世紀はそうじゃないんだ、と仙田さんの案で思いました。仙田さんのおかげで、次の世代につながる建築を考えさせてもらったように感じます。建築の課題と、現状のデザインの力を感じることができたように思えます。

Se 僕は全体的にこどものための施設と同じように野球場をつくったんですね。遊環構造の野球場です。野球場としての新しい型にこだわっていたのです。材料やディテールや色は、予算の中でできるところから手をつけていったんですね。打ち放しのところも、壇上のスタンドも、正面も、本当はもっと赤く塗りたかったんです。ところが球団側に反対されてしまいました。

Sa 実際は、真っ赤じゃなくて、ベンガラ色みたいな落ち着いた赤い色でしたね。

Se 僕はもっとキビシイ赤色にしたかったんです。広島カープの松田オーナーに「真っ赤はあきあきしているんですよ」って言われてしまって、妥協したのですが。

Sa 3階のフライ席も、すごく面白いですよね。あとは広島カープがもう少し強くなればいいですね（笑）。

Se 一般的に、新しく球場をつくった場合、集客は平均として15％増らしいですが、広島の場合、60％増なんだそうです。10年前と比較すると100％増。広島カープも、売上が100億を超えたんです。これから選手に投資していけばもっと強いカープになるでしょう。そうすることで、今後広島という都市がもっと元気になると思います。

＊1 鳥の巣 北京国家体育場（ぺきんこっかたいいくじょう）／北京オリンピックのメインスタジアム。
＊2 團 紀彦（だん のりひこ）1956〜　建築家、都市計画家

About Hiroshima Municipal Baseball Stadium

Masao Saito × Mitsuru Senda

How we met and have worked together so far

Mitsuru Senda (Se): Let us talk about how we have worked together for a long time before we discuss Hiroshima Municipal Baseball Stadium (2009).

Masao Saito (Sa): How did we meet for the first time? Do you remember?

Se: We first worked together on Kyoto Aquarena (2002). I think I met you for the first time when Professor Yoshichika Uchida was the president of the Architectural Institute of Japan, so it was around 1994. I remember we worked together for the organization as board members.

Sa: My fist impression for your works was that you were dedicated to unique environments by focusing on children. Later in 1998, we held a party to commemorate the publication of your books.

Se: I published two books, "Play Structure" (1998, Kashiwashobo Publishing) and "The Method of Environment Design" (1998, Shokokusha Publishing).

Sa: You told me to work as an MC for the party all of a sudden. I clearly remember we had a very heavy rainfall on the day for the party.

Se: That's right. I do not remember whether it was a torrential rain, but it was raining. Thank you for taking the role for the party.

Sa: I thought it was fantastic that you published two books as an architect. All the guests invited there were very famous people and I felt a little out of place about working as an MC. But I took the job since it was a great commemorative occasion. As I looked at your back, I thought you were so thin. Maybe you had just recovered from illness.

Se: Yes, I used to be sick around that time. I had been taken ill for some time.

Sa: You looked so thin and fragile, but I was amazed with your energy to publish books. Also, as I gazed closely at your wife, I wondered how in the world a beautiful woman like her was with you. These two things were quite impressive for me at that time.

Se: Hahaha.

Sa: That opportunity enabled us to apply for various competitions together.

Se: We also applied for the competition related to the Beijing Olympics.

Sa: We had exceptional amount of energy to work on the Beijing project. I believe that it was also a great opportunity for China that we were able to propose the architecture integrating full-scale art and technology in the era allowing the Bird's Nest[*1] to be built based on the Olympic Games. We won the competition but the project was cancelled in the end. Looking back, I feel sorry for it but I think it was a good experience for us. By the way, it was raining when we checked the final model for the Beijing competition.

Se: Yes, I remember it was raining on that day.

Sa: I have been engaging in various activities on the themes of "spatial structure" and "structural design." Around the time when I was working on Yamaguchi Dome, I felt that working on Kyoto Aquarena together with you and Mr. Norihiko Dan[*2] was very innovative.

Se: I think you worked on Yamaguchi Dome a little earlier than that.

Sa: It was almost the same time as Yamaguchi Dome. I applied quake-resistance features on the top of columns and was able to design thin pre-stressed concrete columns. I worked on a dome structure for the first time with Yamaguchi Dome and applied a flat roof for the first time with Kyoto Aquarena.

Se: Installing 3,000-m² solar hot water panels on the roof made the top structure heavy, so we applied quake-resistance features on the top of A-shaped columns based on your proposal. This enabled the shape of pre-stressed concrete A-shaped columns to be very slender. In addition, we leveraged many unprecedented techniques by mounting soil on the most part of the roof not covered by solar panels and creating a rooftop garden there.

You showed me how an architect should live his life.

Sa: I wish I could have done more to help you. Looking back, there is one thing that I was able to help you with. When you were the president of the Architectural Institute of Japan, I was assigned to work on two projects by you. The first was "Architect Design." It was the project related to certification and other associations and was a great opportunity to integrate the whole architectural industry in Japan. The second was the dome for *Kenchiku Kaikan* (AIJ building). Your innovative design transformed 20-meter high space into a real square. It was such a great opportunity for me to be able to properly assist you in a timely manner and implement the projects.

Se: I myself wanted to change the patio into the space where a lot of activities could take place so that we could use it on a rainy day. At that time, the institute had sufficient budget to finance the project and we were able to complete the structure with assistance from various people including you. I was very glad I could work on it.

Sa: That experience enabled us to implement "Architect Design" as an on-going initiative and as an event. You showed me how an architect should live by expressing your commitment and completing your goal.

Se: The dome for *Kenchiku Kaikan* has been utilized on a continual basis for the past 10 years. I feel honored about the fact as an architect.

Sa: We did the maintenance of the structure last Monday and I found the moving dome structure was properly functioning. It is very important that structures are used with care and provide functionalities in that way. *Kenchiku Kaikan* has playful elements, creating multi-functional architectural space by integrating very hard architecture and a moving dome. Its sustainability is not only in the sense that it is physically strong or durable but also in that it is functional, interesting, and futuristic.

Se: We can use moving architecture not only to expand space. It accommodates to our climate as architecture fitted for the earth environment, just like Japanese *Fusuma* (sliding paper doors) or *Shoji* (sliding paper doors with lattice frames).

Sa: What we need to re-evaluate is the quality of semi-openness. It is nice that we have light by fully opening *Shoji* but it is also attractive that we see the shape of the sun or something existent outside through the translucent paper of Shoji. We sometimes need to tightly close space, but the dome is very interesting by letting us feel outside climate and loosely connecting us with the outside world.

Se: A dome is closed space. I am claustrophobic and do not feel comfortable in case the space is completely closed.

Sa: It was quite impressive that you told us to install a skylight as we completed the membrane dome. The company installing the membrane roof for the dome was the best company for manufacturing tents. It had no idea about opening a hole on the completed work. Cutting the beautifully completed surface would leave scars. But your proposal enabled the company to develop a new technology and apply for a patent as well. Injecting your ideas as an architect to try something new and not being limited by existing technologies should have led to the project of Hiroshima Municipal Baseball Stadium later.

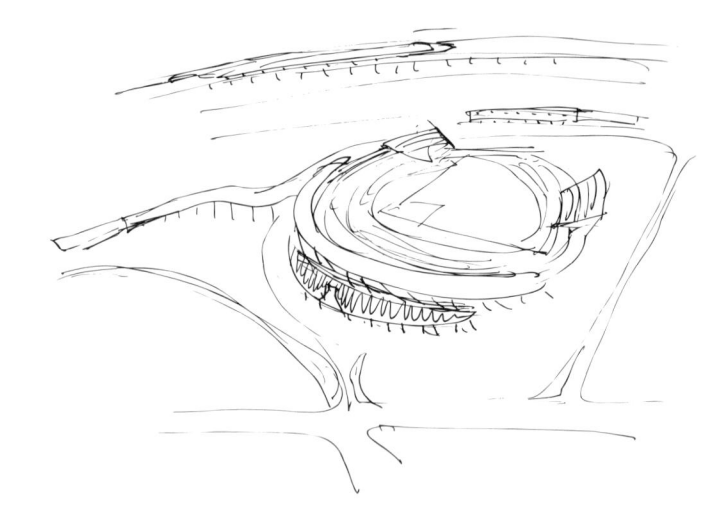

An applicant and a reviewer for the competition on Hiroshima Municipal Baseball Stadium

Se: Around 2003, I had the opportunity to give a lecture in Hiroshima on the theme of children and cities. I met people from Hiroshima City Office who took me to the ballpark to take a look at it and told me there was a plan to rebuild it. That was the beginning of the project.

Sa: I have worked as a judge for Hiroshima Municipal Baseball Stadium twice. I did not remember the first time you applied for the competition since your work did not give me a strong impression. In what capacity did you participate in the project?

Se: I worked as an architect overseeing the whole production.

Sa: Your plan did not make it to the final stage of the competition.

Se: We were not even close to it. We participated in the business idea competition and most teams were not selected.

Sa: So you worked on the project again. I also judged the competition started for the second time. Your plan was included in the five works selected for the second elimination.

Se: Yes, we made it somehow.

Sa: From the viewpoint of the judges, your plan presented a stadium nobody had ever thought about in comparison with other plans you competed against, although it looked similar from outside. You plan was very interesting since it was unprecedented and included innovative perspectives. I thought it was great if we could implement at least some of your ideas included in your plan. Your stadium architecture was completely in line with citizens not in the context or term of "architecture" but in the context of "sport events and citizens." It was interesting from the perspective of functionalities and in line with how users used the structure. I felt that you worked exceptionally hard to enjoy the structure and to make the structure enjoyable for people. On the other hand, I had some concerns and expectations for the feasibility of the plan based on the limited budget. However, at the end of the day, the work as a whole looked a little out of touch with the framework of "architecture."

Se: When I was asked if I could complete the

plan with 9 billion yen, I said yes. But it was quite a challenge. We presented the steel-frame structure for the first competition, but changed it to pre-stressed concrete and used reinforced concrete for the bottom of the main course in the execution design since the space was 40,000㎡. We did everything we could to simplify the structure and changed materials for different parts of the structure.

Sa: After all, you came up with the mixed structure but it did not have any aggravating affects on the structure. As I see how you work, you work hard on a structure to some extent and then change or add materials in line with how things proceed. You do not concentrate on how you fix some parts not in line with the competition plan, but you think it is okay to create something based on changing conditions within the limited time. I think the way you worked on this project created a new concept for architecture.

Se: Mitsui Fudosan was in charge of commercial facilities around Hiroshima Municipal Baseball Stadium, but they had a hard time to collect tenants due to the current economic conditions. So I advised Mitsui Fudosan not to target for the perfect situation from the beginning and start creating the community by doing what they could one by one. In that sense, Hiroshima Toyo Carp is flexibly dealing with situations by designating appropriate companies for various functions.

Sa: The last time I visited the site, they were trying to build a gym. They also newly created *tatami* seats. When groups reserve seats, they tell me that the first set of seats to be reserved are that sort of unique seats. Those seats make you feel like watching night games. I was blessed with having the experience of judging this competition twice and thought that conventional stadiums and ballparks were 20-century architectures and did not work in the coming 21st century. You have made me think about next-generation architecture by letting me feel the challenges of architecture and the potentials of current design.

Se: I created the whole structure of the ballpark in the same way I worked on children's facilities. It is a ballpark with Circular Play System. I focused on a new form of a ballpark. I worked on materials, details, and colors in a way I could based on the allocated budget. I originally wanted to paint exposed concrete parts, seating areas, and the facade with vivid red. But the management was opposed to my idea.

Sa: The color used there is not vivid red but a restrained color like brownish red.

Se: I wanted to use more vivid red. But the owner of the team, Mr. Matsuda, told me that he was sick of pure red. I had to make a compromise with him.

Sa: Fly seats on the third floor are also great. It will be great if Hiroshima Toyo Carp gets a little stronger (laughter).

Se: As you create a new ballpark, usually the customer base will increase by 15% on an average, but the rate increase for Hiroshima is 60%. The number has increased by 100% in comparison with 10 years ago. Hiroshima Toyo Carp will be a more formidable team if more investments are done on players. That will further revitalize Hiroshima City.

※1 The Bird's Nest of Beijing National Stadium: The main stadium for the Beijing Olympics.
※2 Norihiko Dan (1956-)**:** Architect and city planner.

Masao Saito

A doctor of engineering born in Gunma in 1938. Graduated with a degree in architecture from the Faculty of Engineering of Nihon University in 1961 and gained a master's degree from the graduate school of the same university in 1963. Prizes and awards include the Architectural Institute of Japan Prize (for Specific Contribution, 1987), Gengo Matsui Prize (1993), Building Contractors Society (BCS) Prize, Tsuboi Award Prize (IASS, 1997). Prizes and awards include the Architectural Institute of Janan Prize (2007), E. Torroja Prize (2009). Publications include "Space Structure Story" Inamain Work Izumo Dome/Yamaguchi Kirra dome.

Conversation

斎藤公男 × 仙田満

Masao Saito × Mitsuru Senda

国際教養大学図書館を中心に

内田祥哉×仙田 満

国際教養大学は素晴らしい大学

仙田 満（以下S） 内田先生は、昨年秋に見に行ってくださったんですよね。

内田祥哉（以下U） この図書館を見るために行ったのではなく、前の秋田県知事だった寺田典城さんの親せきで、小原さんという方の素晴らしい古民家のお宅に伺うために行って、偶然出合うことができたんです。それにしても秋田には非常に面白い建築がありますよね。古くてもいいものがいっぱいあるんです。例えば角館の蔵がたくさん並んでいるところもいいですし、十和田湖にある県営のホテルは、一部屋一部屋全部違っていて、リピーターも多くて、繁盛しているんです。

S 僕は若い頃から県立の児童会館など「秋田県立児童会館・こども博物館」（1980年）をお手伝いしていたのですが、秋田には昔から独特の建築文化がありますね。寺田前知事も、県の建物にはもっと秋田杉をつかってほしいといわれていたそうですね。

U 林業をされていたので、非常に木造建築に詳しい方なのです。そういう関係で僕も寺田前知事にお会いしたことがあります。話を戻しますが、ここは学校の創立主旨がすばらしいですね。

S コンセプトが非常にいいんです。学長の中嶋嶺雄[*1]先生は、東京外国語大学の学長だったのですが、日本の教育の貧しさの原因は教養教育が貧しいからだという信念にもとづいて、長年の理想のもとにこの大学をつくられたのです。

U 全国から人が集まる、と聞きました。

S まずよいのは、一年、寮生活を義務づけていることです。外国人と日本人の学生が共同生活をすることによって、共に学ぶということを体験するのです。今のこども達は個室世代ですから、個の中に閉じこもりがちですが、それを破ろうとしているのです。

U すぐそばにドミトリーもあって、ね。あれもなかなかですね。ベルゲン風で。

S そうですね。このドミトリーは、私が設計のお手伝いする前に、地元の設計事務所の方の設計でできていました。
今回の図書館棟は全国区のプロポーザルだったのですが、最後に2人残ったんです。この国際教養大学は英語で授業をしているんですが、外国からいらした先生たちが私の案を推してくださったようです。

U 英語で応募していたんですか。

S いえいえ、そうではありません、日本語でよかったのです。今回の図書館棟の仕事を機会に、全体のキャンパス計画のお手伝いもさせていただくようになりました。この大学は、アメリカの大学の日本校から、2004年に国際教養大学となって、開学したんです。それで一年の寮生活と、一年の留学を義務づけているんですね。学長の中嶋嶺雄先生が先進的な大学、理想的なリベラルアーツを重視した国際的に通用する人材の教育の場としてかかげています。

U 仙田さんが設計なさった図書館では、みんなが静かに勉強していましたよ。

S 図書館は24時間365日開館していて、県民、市民にもオープンなんですよ。

内田祥哉（うちだ よしちか）
1925年東京都生まれ。建築家、日本の建築生産学者。東京帝国大学工学部建築学科卒業後、逓信省、電気通信省を経て、日本電信電話公社建築部（現・NTTファシリティーズ）に勤務。東京大学名誉教授、明治大学教授、金沢美術工芸大学教授を歴任。1996年日本建築学会大賞受賞。2010年工学院大学建築学部特任教授就任。日本学士院会員。

こども向け施設の理想的なあり方

U　僕は、仙田さんはこどもを対象とした建築の専門家だと思っていました。

S　菊竹清訓事務所にいた時に、横浜市にある「こどもの国」を手がけたことが、こどもの施設に携わるようになった、もともとのきっかけなんです。

U　少しニュアンスが違うのかもしれないけど、こどもの施設は、社会情勢の変化、あるいはこどもの育ち具合の変化っていうのかな、そういうものと関連しているのでしょうか。10年経つと、昔のこどもと今のこどもの動き方が違うのではありませんか。

S　親が違いますね。内田先生や我々のようなあそびの時代を、親が過ごしていないんです。だからあそびの体験や、こどもへのあそびの継承性というものが欠けているのです。

U　そうなると、学校は勉強する場でよいけれど、こどものあそぶための施設をつくることは大変ですね。

S　今、都市の開発ツールとして超高層マンションが建っていますよね。あれはこどもの生活環境として、僕は最悪だと思っているんです。

U　ああいう中に、こどものあそび場はどうやって取り入れるんですか。1階に下りてあそぶわけにいかないし、屋上に行ってあそぶわけにもいかないでしょう。

S　本来は住環境の中で、多くの大人の目や手によってこどもが育まれることが必要だと思うんです。そのためにまずは住宅の接地性が重要です。また、多世代型住宅、あるいは「コレクティブハウス」[*2]のような多くのファミリーが共通のスペースをもち、こどもをみんなで見守りながら育むというような住形態を考えていかねばならないと考えています。住宅産業も戸建てか、超高層という二極分化が問題だと考えています。これからのこどもの成育環境という視点で考えると、低中層高密度の集合住宅が望ましいと考えています。日本の住宅産業が問題なのではないかと思うのです。

U　コレクティブハウスの方が、将来性がある。

S　僕はそう考えています。

U　コレクティブハウスというのは、日本にとって大変新しい概念だから、まだ親がなかなか理解しないでしょうね。

S　そうですね。若い人たちの中には「シェアハウス」と呼んで、個々の部屋は小さいけれど共通のスペースもあるようなところに住んでいる人たちも多くなってきています。そういった個のあり方、年寄りとこどもが出会ったりするような、全体で見守られながら生活する場も増えてきています。

U　そういう話を聞いていると興味が湧いてくるんですけど、こどもが減っています。例え

Conversation

内田祥哉 × 仙田満　Yoshichika Uchida × Mitsuru Senda

ば現実に起こっているのですが、団地の場合には小学校がいらなくなる。一般家庭でも高齢化してくると、こどもや孫がいっしょに住めばいいけど、そうなりそうもない。こういった社会的な居住環境の変化、家族構成の変化みたいなものに、こどもの施設はどうやって対応していけるのでしょうか。

S　例えば市役所であっても、こども連れの家族は来ます。そういったすべての空間に「こどもがあそべるスペース」「こどもがそれなりに過ごせる時間や過ごすことができる場所」が必要なのではないか、と僕は考えているんですね。「こどもがあそぶところ」と「大人がいるところ」を分けるのではなく、あらゆるところにこどもは行くわけですから。こどもがいることが中心となる社会環境にならない限り、少子化は解消しないと思います。

U　例えば「六本木ヒルズ」のように、無理につくると、無理につくった感じがしますよね。

S　こどもに向けた視点が必要なんです。僕はこどものあそぶ原空間として、自然、道、オープンスペース、アジト、アナーキー、遊具の6つのシンボルが必要だと考えています。整理整頓されてない空間が、こどもに必要だと思うんですよ。

U　それは大人もそうですね。整理整頓すると、幕張メッセみたいにちっとも面白くない場所になってしまう。むしろ入ってはいけない場所というのに、意外な魅力を感じます。

S　そういうところは、アジトになりうるんですよね。

U　僕は小さい頃この麻布辺りに住んでいて、近くに「ガマ池」というのがあるでしょう？

S　ありますね。

U　あそこは絶好のあそび場で。有栖川宮記念公園も金網があって、入ると叱られる。だからこそ「ぜひ入りたいな」と、こどもながらに思ったものです。

コンセプトは「ブックコロシアム」

S　そうなんです。こどもは柵があることで、柵の上に登りたがる、柵を越えたがる。柵という領域の境目は、あそびとしてすごく重要なんです。実はこの国際教養大学図書館棟も、考え方は同じ。基本的にあそびの場ではないし、「大人の施設だ」と先生はおっしゃったけど、あそびのスペースと同じようにつくっているんです。約1mの段床を4段設け、その背後に大きな本棚を設けています。段状にしていることによって探索したいという思いを喚起できると考えています。図書館はフラットでなくてはいけないという人もいますが、意欲を喚起するには丘が必要だと考えたのです。

U　そういう感じわかります。というのも、「図書館は静かにしなくてはいけない」ということではなくて、図書館にいた人が非常に自然に暮らしていました。

S　みんなが見える場所と、隠れ場所みたいな部分をつくったんです。そして全体的には回遊性をもたせて。

U　なんといっても、全部の本が見えるでしょう。しかもすべての本に手が届く。全体が図書館らしいというのが、一番最初に感心したところです。

S　僕は最近、こどもの施設から出発して、アリーナみたいなスポーツ施設の設計をすることが多いんですね。スポーツ施設というのは、劇場と共通した「戦う場所」だと思っています。

だからこの国際教養大学図書館棟も、本と戦う場という意味を込めて、「ブックコロシアム」をコンセプトにしているんです。

U 確かにこれはコロシアムですね。骨組みが目立たないし、大勢の人達が本を読んでいても、本に隠れて気にならない。コンペに応募した時から、このような計画だったのですか。形を半円形にしたのはなぜですか。

S プロポーザルコンペだったのですが、最初のアイデアのままできあがったんです。今まで多くのプロポーザルコンペをやってきましたが、プロポーザルに出したスケッチ通りに完成したのははじめてといっても良いと思います。建築家は、いい施主に巡りあわないと、いいものができませんから。

U そうですね、そういう意味でよかったんでしょう。

S 形については、正面にある杉林と対峙したいと思い、半円にこだわったんです。円ではなく、北側を開放するように半円で直線の部分を小堀遠州の弧蓬庵のように残された杉林を見る場としたかったんですね。とにかく木は切らないでといわれていた部分を大事にし、それを見る視線を重視しました。

U 戦後、日本はずっと木がなくて、山が裸になるのを防ぐために木を植えて、木を大事にしてきました。世界的に見ても、日本ほど木が育つところは少ないでしょう。江戸時代の伝統的な建築だけではなく、近代建築にも合うような木の種類を考えていかないといけませんよね。

S ヨーロッパの芝生と異なり、モンスーン地帯の日本は自然に放っておけば密林になってしまいます。そういった自然を管理しながら、木を大事に育てることが日本の環境として大事で、それはまた大学のキャンパスにもいえると思います。

U キャンパスというのは、一番やりがいがある仕事の一つじゃないかと思います。病院は思い出になっても二度と来たくないところだし（笑）、観光施設もなるべく違ったところへ行ってみたいはずです。学校のキャンパスというのは、建て直しても卒業生が帰ってくるし、古いものはいつまで経ってもメモリアルなものになるのでやりがいがあるものだと思いますね。

S そうですね。私たち建築家は、あまり「キャンパス」をお手伝いするチャンスがなかったので、この仕事は幸運で光栄でした。この国際教養大学の敷地は約15ヘクタールです。1学年150人の学生のキャンパスとしては十分な広さだと思います。道路を挟んで県立中央公園もあり、カジマデザインが設計したあきたスカイドームも近くにあります。市街地まで30分ぐらいかかりますが、自然環境豊かなところで勉強に打ち込むには良い環境です。秋田は雪が降るところですから各棟は空中ブリッジでつなぎ、全体としてリングになるように提案しています。その僕の遊環構造の理論に、中嶋学長が賛同してくださり、もうすぐ一回りできそうです。

U もう一つ感心していることが、図書館を壇状にして見せているのに、ワゴンが届かないところがないことです。この2つは図書館設計で両立しないと思っていましたが、この国際教養大学図書館棟はそれを両立させているので、えらく感心しました。図書館の規模にもあるでしょうが、図書館員にも利用者にもよい反応があると思います。

*1 **中嶋嶺雄**（なかじま みねお）1936〜　政治学者
*2 **多世代型住宅**（コレクティブハウス）／集合住宅において、プライベートの住戸は通常通り確保しながら、そのほかに「コモン」と呼ばれる住人共有のキッチンやリビングダイニングなどの空間をもち、生活の一部を共有する暮らし方。北欧で生まれ、北欧ではすでに暮らし方のひとつの選択肢として定着している

Conversation

内田祥哉 × 仙田満
Yoshichika Uchida × Mitsuru Senda

About Akita International University Library

Yoshichika Uchida × Mitsuru Senda

Akita International University is a wonderful college.

Mitsuru Senda (S): Professor Uchida, you were kind enough to visit the library last autumn.

Yoshichika Uchida (U): I did not go there specifically to see the library, but was able to encounter it when I visited the beautiful traditional house of Mr. Ohara, a relative of the former governor of Akita Prefecture, Sukeshiro Terata. Akita has a number of very interesting architectures, many of which are old but very intriguing. For example, I like Kakunodate where I can see many warehouses lined up and a hotel operated by the prefecture close to Lake Towada offers completely different rooms with its business booming with repeat customers.

S: I have been working on children's facilities including Akita Prefectural Children's Center and Children's Museum (1980) since young, and I think Akita has had unique architectural culture for a long time. The former governor, Mr. Terata, says that more Akita cedar should be used for buildings in the prefecture.

U: He used to be engaged in forestry and is very knowledgeable about wooden architecture. So I once met him. Coming back to our topic today, I think this school was established based wonderful principles.

S: It is based on superb concepts. President Mineo Nakajima[*1] once served as President of Tokyo University of Foreign Studies. He has created this university based on his long-held principle, believing that insufficient education in Japan comes from insufficient education in liberal arts.

U: I hear that the school collects students from across Japan.

S: What I like about the college first of all is making all students stay in the dormitory for one year. Foreign and Japanese students live together and learn from each other. Current children usually have their own rooms at home and tend to withdraw into their personal lives. The dormitory tries to change that propensity.

U: Yes, the dormitory is closely located and very good. It looks like Bergen.

S: That's right. This dormitory was designed by local designers before I was involved with the project. The competition for the library design was solicited from across the country, and two finalists were selected. Akita International University gives classes in English and teachers from overseas seem to have liked my plan.

U: You submitted your plan in English?

S: No, I could apply in Japanese. The library building project gave me the opportunity to work on the planning of the whole campus. This school used to be a Japanese branch of a U.S. college and recreated its organization as Akita International University in 2004. It requires students to stay in the dormitory for one year and study abroad for one year. Dr. Mineo Nakajima, President, advocates this school as the visionary university, or as the place to develop human resources who can exert capabilities at the international level through ideal liberal arts-based education.

U: All the students were studying silently at the library you designed.

S: The library is open 24 hours a day, 365 days

a year. It is available for the local citizens within the city and prefecture.

How children's facilities should be in their ideal form

U: I thought you were the specialist dedicated to children's architecture.
S: When I was in the office of Mr. Kiyonori Kikutake, I was involved in the project of Kodomo-no-Kuni (Children's Land) in Yokohama City. That was my origin in getting involved in children's facilities.
U: I may not be using perfectly appropriate words, but are children's facilities linked with changing social conditions or changes in how children grow? Don't you see changes in how children behave now in comparison with children of 10 years ago?
S: Parents are different. The current parents have not gone through play experiences like you or us. So they lack play experiences and cannot disseminate their experiences to their children.
U: If that is the case, schools can function as the places where children study, but it will be difficult to create play facilities for children.
S: Currently we see a lot of high-rise condominiums as the tools of urban redevelopment. I think that they are the worst living environment for children.
U: How do you incorporate play areas for children in that environment? They cannot come down to the first floor or go up to the rooftop to play.
S: Children essentially need to grow up in their living environment through the monitoring or care by adults. That environment requires the close proximity of housing to land. Also, we need to think about housing environment where multiple families share space and monitor and foster children together through Multi-Generation Housing*1 or Collective House*2. The real problem in the housing industry is the bi-polarization between stand-alone houses and super-high-rise condominiums. When we focus on future growth environment for children, I believe it is desirable to build medium-rise or low-rise apartment buildings with high density. So I think the real issue lies in the Japanese housing industry.
U: You see a brighter future with Collective House.
S: Yes, I believe so.
U: Collective House is a very new concept for Japan, so parents may still have a hard time in understanding it.
S: Yes. More young people share houses where each person occupies a small room but residents share common space. We see more living environments where the whole community monitors the life of residents and the elderly meet children through that sort of human relationships.
U: Your story makes me feel more interested, but the number of children is on the decrease. For example, we actually find that areas with huge apartment building blocks no more need elementary schools. As people age in ordinary families, it will be great if children or grandchildren could live with them, but that

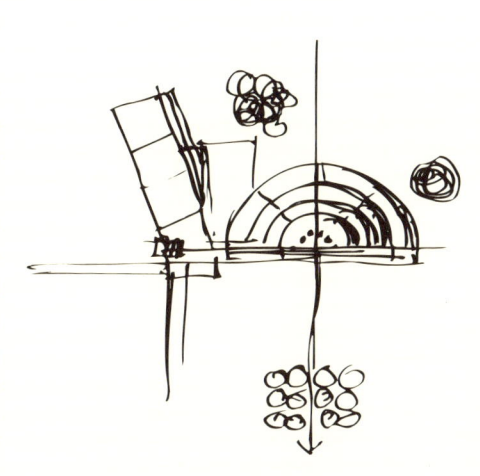

Conversation

内田祥哉 × 仙田 満　Yoshichika Uchida × Mitsuru Senda

is not happening. How can children's facilities cope with these social changes in living environment or family structure?

S: As I give you an example, even families with children visit places like a city office. So I believe that every space needs the place where children can play or the time or place allowing children to spend their time. We should not distinguish the place where children play from the place where adults stay since children go everywhere. We cannot resolve the problem of decreasing childbirth unless we can create our social environment based on children.

U: If you create an artificial building like Roppongi Hills, for example, it really feels like an artificial environment.

S: We need the perspective focusing on children. I advocate the six symbols including nature, roads, open space, secret bases, anarchy, and play equipment as the basic space where children play. Children need unorganized space.

U: That also applies to adults. If you organize your environment, you come up with a dull place like Makuhari Messe. Rather, we feel strangely attracted to places we cannot go into.

S: Those places can create secrete bases for you.

U: I used to live around this Azabu area when a child. Do you know we have Gama-Ike close by?

S: Yes.

U: That was my great play spot. Arisugawa Commemorative Park was surrounded by metal nets and I was scolded when I entered the park. That made me want to enter it all the more when I was a child.

The concept is a book colosseum.

S: That is exactly right. As children see a fence, they want to climb up and go over it. A fence proved to be a very important border for playing. In actuality, the building for Akita International University Library has the same concept. It is not basically a play spot and you said it was a facility for adults. However, I created the library just like play space. We stacked four one-meter-high elevated floors and placed large bookshelves in the background. The elevated floors make students feel like exploring books. Some people say that a library should be a flat structure, but I thought that I needed a hill to motivate students.

U: I know what you mean. At the library, students were not forced to stay silent, but they were spending their time in a very natural manner.

S: I created areas where you can see everyone and areas with secret space. And the whole structure was equipped with migratory movements.

U: The best feature of the structure is you see all the books and can reach all the books. What I was impressed with first was the whole structure looked like a proper library.

S: Recently I have often been involved in the design of sport facilities instead of children's facilities. My concept of sport facilities is the fighting place with similar qualities applied to theaters. Therefore, the basic concept of the building for Akita International University Library is "a book colosseum" as the place to fight books.

U: It is really a colosseum. The structure frameworks are not clearly visible and you do not get disturbed with so many other people reading books because they are behind books. Did you have this plan when you applied for the competition? What is the reason why you made the shape semi-circular?

S: Yes, it was a proposal competition. The initial design has turned into the completed library structure. I have created many architectures based on a proposal competition, and I can say that this project was the first experience for me to be able to build a construction exactly in line with the design I submitted for a competition. An architect cannot create good architecture without a good client.

U: I see. You had good conditions.

S: I decided to use the semi-circular shape since I wanted to make the library to face the cedar forest located across it. Instead of using the circular shape, I wanted to make the semi-circle to release the northern side and turn the straight-line part into a place to enjoy the remaining cedar forest as Kobori Enshu enjoyed nature in Koho-An. I took great care of the request not to cut down any trees and focused on how people would see trees.

U: We did not have trees for a long time after the war in Japan and planted and took great care of trees to keep mountains from getting bare. On a global scale, there are few countries like Japan that enable trees to grow to this extent. We need to think about the types of trees that fit modern architecture as well as traditional buildings in the Edo era.

S: Unlike lawns in Europe, trees in sub-tropical Japan will grow into jungles if left unmanaged. We need to manage this nature by growing trees with care. This is very important for the Japanese environment and makes sense for a college campus.

U: A college campus is one of the most rewarding projects to work on. A hospital gives you some memory but you never want to come back there (laughter). Sightseeing facilities make you want to go somewhere else. In contrast, a school campus is very valuable since students come back there after it is rebuilt and old school buildings always have memorial values. So you feel it is worthwhile to work on a school.

S: I agree. Architects including me have not had many opportunities to create a campus. So this project has been quite fortunate and rewarding for me. The campus size of Akita International University is about 15 hectares, providing ample space with the school ac-

cepting 150 students each year. The school faces Akita central Park across the street and Akita Skydome designed by Kajima Corporation is located nearby. 30 minutes away from the downtown area, the university provides a good environment for learning based on its rich natural settings.

U: One more thing I was impressed with is that the library is structured on the elevated floor but every space can be reached with wagons. I thought that these two conditions could not coexist in library design, but this Akita International University Library has made these two conditions compatible. I was amazed with this feature. I think we will be able to have good reactions from librarians and users based on the library size and other features.

✻1 **Mineo Nakajima** (1936-)**:** Political scientist.
✻2 **Multi-Generation Housing** (Collective House)**:** The way of living in apartment buildings allowing people to have private houses as usual and share a part of their life through what is called "the common," kitchen, living, or dining space shared among residents. It started in Nordic countries and has been stabilized as a choice of living there.

Yoshichika Uchida

An architect and Japanese scholar of building production, born in Tokyo in 1925. After graduating with a degree in architecture from the Faculty of Engineering of Tokyo Imperial University, worked in the Ministry of Communications and Ministry of Post and Telecommunications before joining the Architecture Division of Nippon Telegraph and Telephone Public Corporation (currently NTT Facilities). Has served as a professor emeritus of the University of Tokyo, professor of Meiji University and professor of Kanazawa College of Art. Won the Grand Prize of the Architectural Institute of Japan 1996. Was appointed as a special professor to the Faculty of Architecture of Kogakuin University in 2010. A member of the Japan Academy.

2009.03
広島市民球場

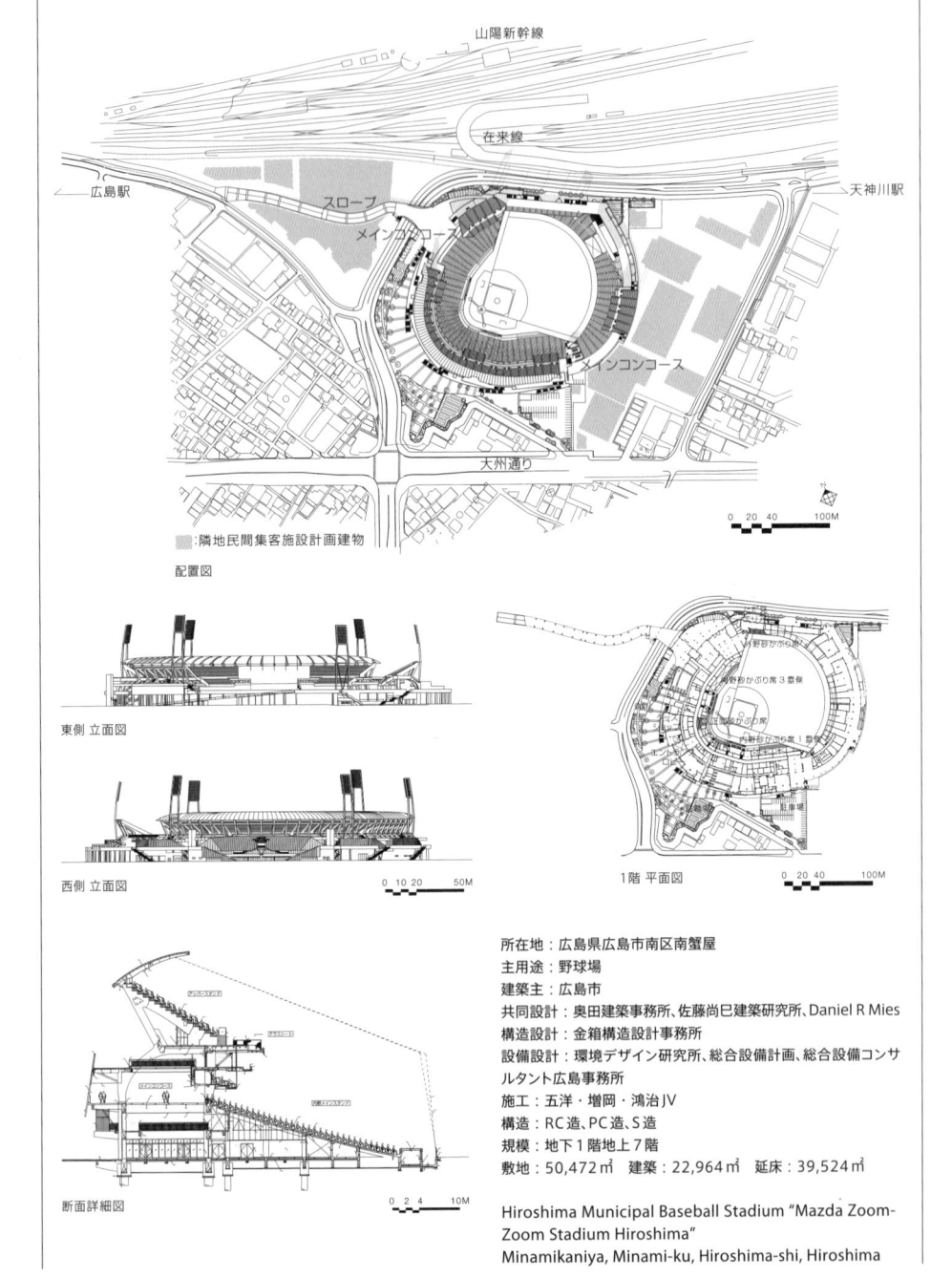

配置図

東側 立面図

西側 立面図

1階 平面図

断面詳細図

所在地：広島県広島市南区南蟹屋
主用途：野球場
建築主：広島市
共同設計：奥田建築事務所、佐藤尚巳建築研究所、Daniel R Mies
構造設計：金箱構造設計事務所
設備設計：環境デザイン研究所、総合設備計画、総合設備コンサルタント広島事務所
施工：五洋・増岡・鴻治JV
構造：RC造、PC造、S造
規模：地下1階地上7階
敷地：50,472㎡　建築：22,964㎡　延床：39,524㎡

Hiroshima Municipal Baseball Stadium "Mazda Zoom-Zoom Stadium Hiroshima"
Minamikaniya, Minami-ku, Hiroshima-shi, Hiroshima

2011.03
緑の詩保育園

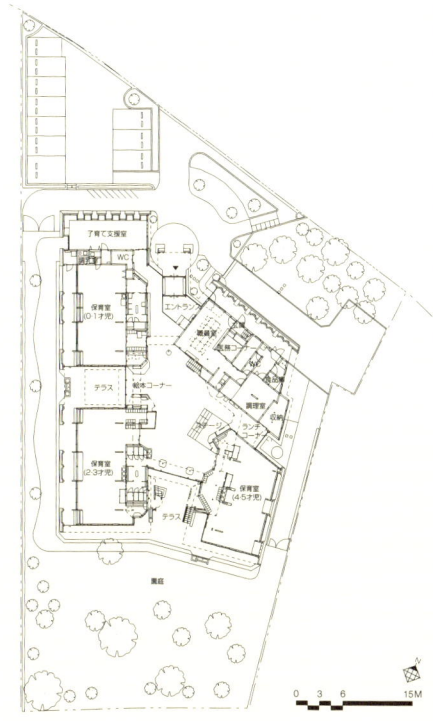

1階 平面図

断面図

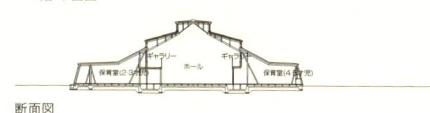

北側 立面図

所在地：埼玉県北本市深井
主用途：保育園
建築主：学校法人若山学園
構造設計：増田建築構造事務所
設備設計：ZO設計室
施工：東洋建設
構造：W造
規模：地上2階
敷地：2,893㎡　建築：911㎡　延床：971㎡

Green Note Day Nursery
Fukai, Kitamoto-shi, Saitama

2009.07
中軽井沢山荘

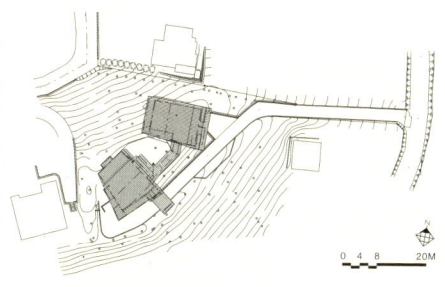

配置図

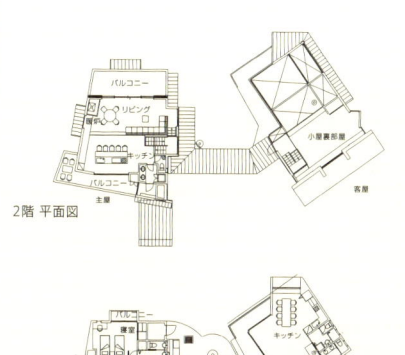

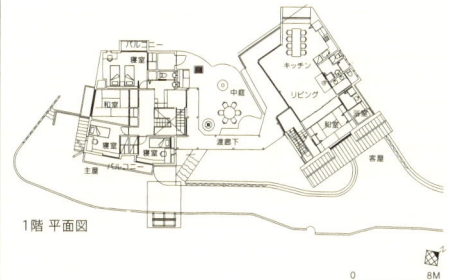

2階 平面図

1階 平面図

所在地：長野県北佐久郡軽井沢町
主用途：別荘
構造設計：増田建築構造事務所
設備設計：システムプランニング
施工：新津組
構造：RC造、W造
規模：地下1階地上2階
敷地：1,690㎡　建築：251㎡　延床：499㎡

Villa Nakakaruizawa
Karuizawa-machi, Kitasaku-gun, Nagano

2009.03
一の台幼稚園

配置パース図

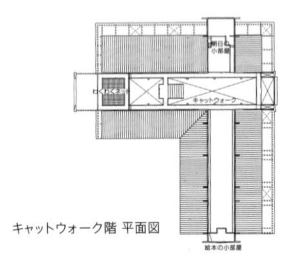

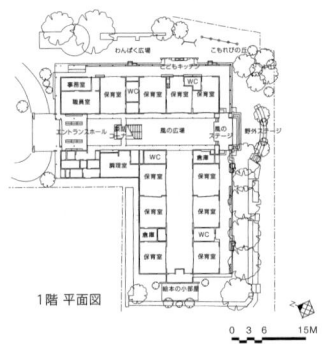

キャットウォーク階 平面図

1階 平面図

所在地：千葉県流山市東深井
主用途：幼稚園
建築主：学校法人坂巻学園
構造設計：金箱構造設計事務所
設備設計：日永設計
施工：京成建設
構造：W造
規模：地上1階
敷地：4,471㎡　建築：1,245㎡　延床：1,034㎡

Ichinodai Kindergarten
Higashifukai, Nagareyama-shi, Chiba

2009.01
勝川幼稚園

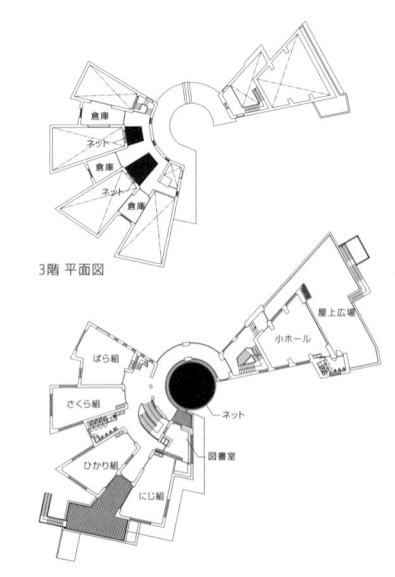

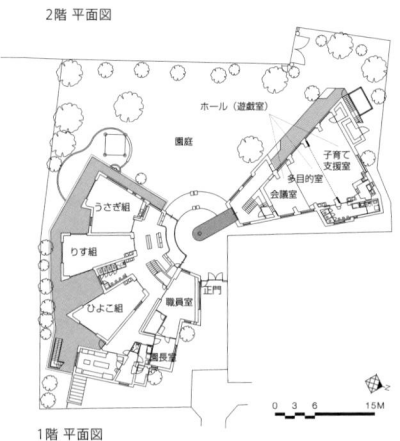

3階 平面図

2階 平面図

1階 平面図

所在地：愛知県春日井市旭町
主用途：幼稚園
建築主：学校法人勝川学園
構造設計：金箱構造設計事務所
設備設計：日永設計
施工：小原建設
構造：RC造
規模：地上3階
敷地：1,981㎡　建築：710㎡　延床：1,248㎡

Kachigawa Kindergarten
Asahi-machi, Kasugai-shi, Aichi

2008.07
慶應義塾日吉キャンパス 協生館

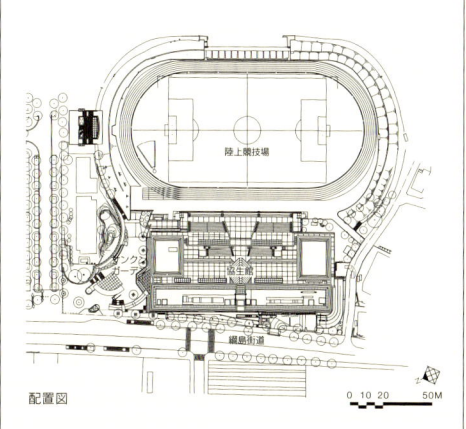

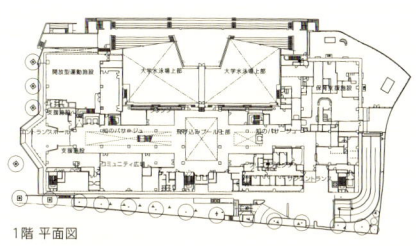

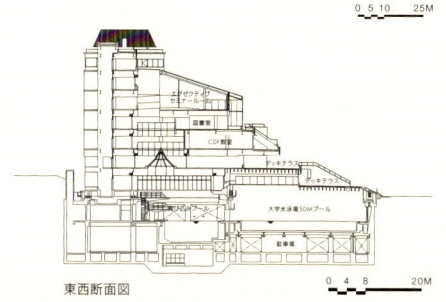

配置図

1階 平面図

東西断面図

所在地：神奈川県横浜市港北区日吉
主用途：大学施設
建築主：学校法人慶應義塾
共同設計：三菱地所設計
構造設計：金箱構造設計事務所、三菱地所設計
設備設計：三菱地所設計
施工：東急建設
構造：SRC造、S造、中間層免震構造
規模：地下2階地上7階
敷地：35,237㎡　建築：7,363㎡　延床：38,207㎡

Keio University Collaboration Complex
Hiyoshi, Kohoku-ku, Yokohama-shi, Kanagawa

2008.01
広島県立可部高等学校

配置図

2階 平面図

1階 平面図

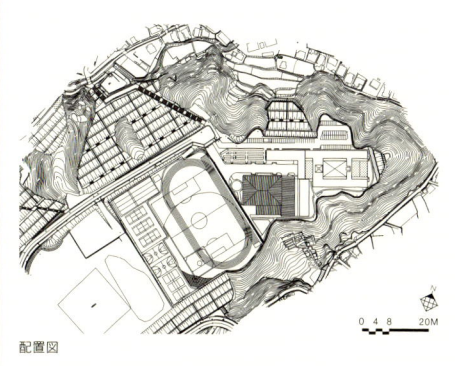

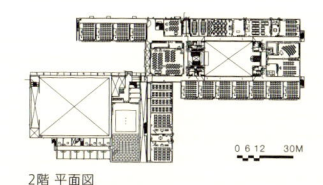

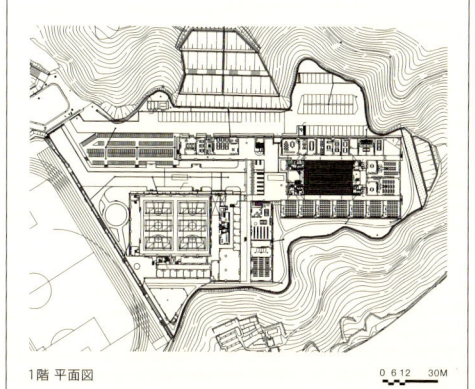

所在地：広島県広島市安佐北区可部東
主用途：高等学校
建築主：かべスクールサービス
共同設計：大成建設
構造設計、設備設計、施工：大成建設
構造：RC造、S造
規模：地上3階
敷地：88,332㎡　建築：7,063㎡　延床：12,903㎡

Hiroshima Prefectural Kabe High School
Kabehigashi, Asakita-ku, Hiroshima-shi, Hiroshima

167

2008.11
東大柏どんぐり保育園

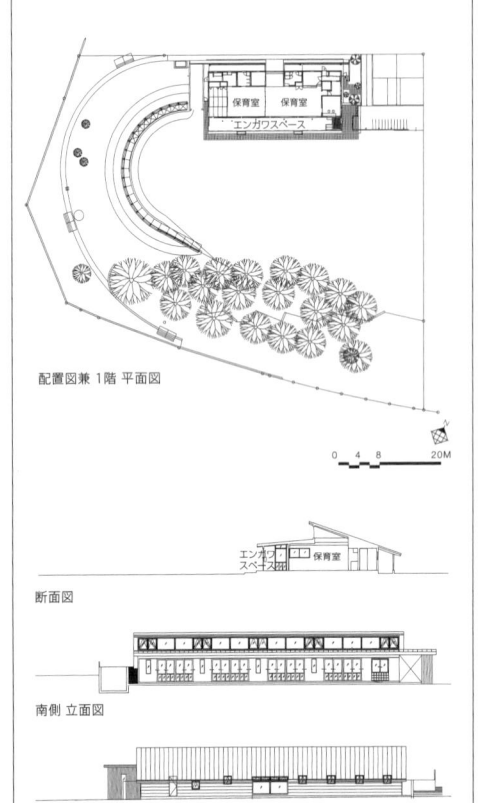

配置図兼 1階 平面図

断面図

南側 立面図

北側 立面図

所在地：千葉県柏市柏の葉
主用途：保育園
建築主：国立大学法人東京大学
構造設計：金箱構造設計事務所
設備設計：日永設計
施工：小倉建設
構造：W造
規模：地上1階
敷地：237,452㎡　建築：333㎡　延床：296㎡

Tokyo University Kashiwa Donguri Day Nursery
Kashiwanoha, Kashiwa-shi, Chiba

2008.02
岡崎げんき館

配置図

2階 平面図

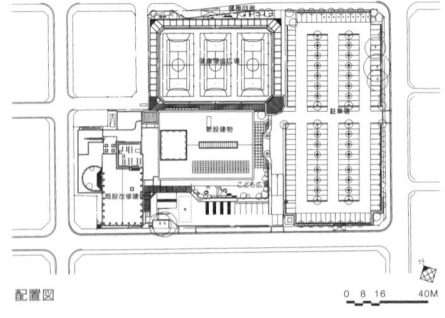

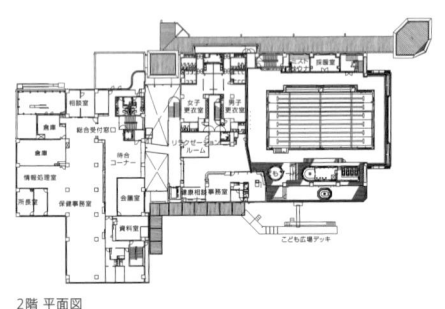

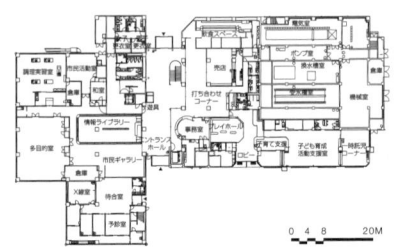

1階 平面図

所在地：愛知県岡崎市若宮町
主用途：事務所、水泳場、児童福祉施設、集会場、保健所
建築主：岡崎げんき館マネジメント
共同設計、構造設計、設備設計：大成建設
施工：大成建設・丸ヨ建設工業JV
構造：RC造、S造
規模：地上4階
敷地：13,264㎡　建築：4,214㎡　延床：8,396㎡

Okazaki Genkikan
Wakamiya-cho, Okazaki-shi, Aichi

2008.12
あづみの公園 サテライトハウス
国営アルプスあづみの公園［大町・松川地区］
林間レクリエーション公園施設

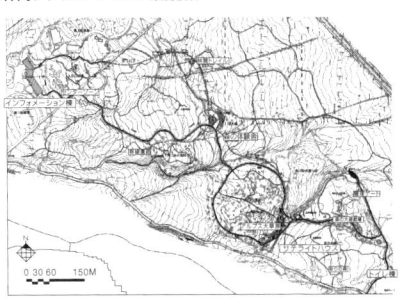

配置図

森の体験舎 1階 平面図 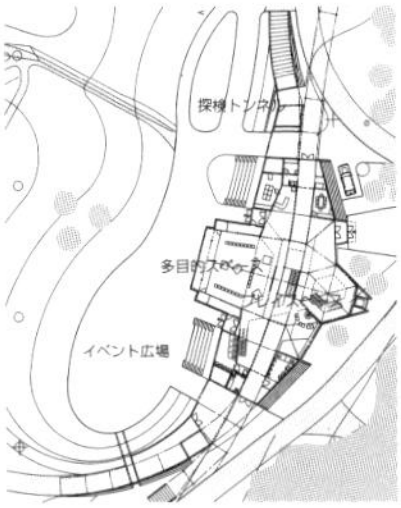　　サテライト棟 平面図

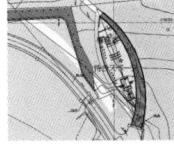

ゲート棟 1階 平面図 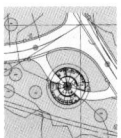　　トイレ棟 1階 平面図

所在地：長野県大町市常盤
主用途：公園施設
建築主：国営アルプスあづみの公園
構造設計：構造計画研究所
設備設計：日永設計
施工：北野建設（森の体験舎）、傳刀組・相模組JV（大草原の家）、相模組（森のゲート）、金森建設（彩の森トイレ）
構造：W造（森の体験舎、森のゲート、彩の森トイレ）、RC造・W造（大草原の家）
規模：地上2階（森の体験舎、大草原の家）、地上1階（森のゲート、彩の森トイレ）
敷地：2,530,000㎡　建築：768㎡（森の体験舎）、966㎡（大草原の家）、276㎡（森のゲート）、104㎡（彩の森トイレ）　延床：883㎡（森の体験舎）、982㎡（大草原の家）、254㎡（森のゲート）、98㎡（彩の森トイレ）

Alps Azumino National Government Park Omachi・Matsukawa area Park Facilities Recreation Area Camping
Tokiwa, Omachi-shi, Nagano

2008.10
上海STEP

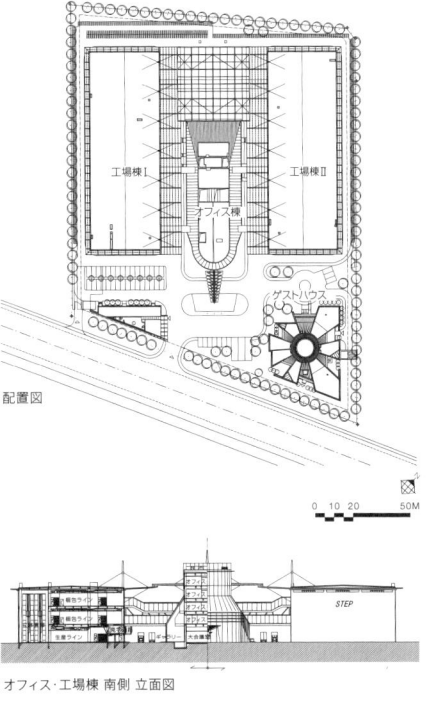

配置図

オフィス・工場棟 南側 立面図

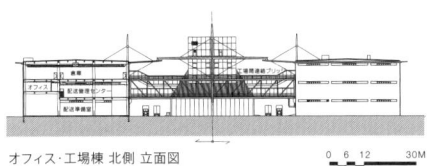

オフィス・工場棟 北側 立面図

所在地：中華人民共和国上海市
主用途：オフィス、工場、ゲストハウス
建築主：上海新時達電気有限公司
共同設計：同済大学建築設計研究院有限公司
構造設計：構造計画研究所、同済大学建築設計研究院有限公司
設備設計：総合設備計画、同済大学建築設計研究院有限公司
施工：上海開天建設集団有限公司
構造：RC造、S造
規模：地下1階地上5階
敷地：26,830㎡　建築：10,361㎡　延床：32,409㎡

Shanghai STEP
Shanghai, China

2008.02
国際教養大学図書館棟

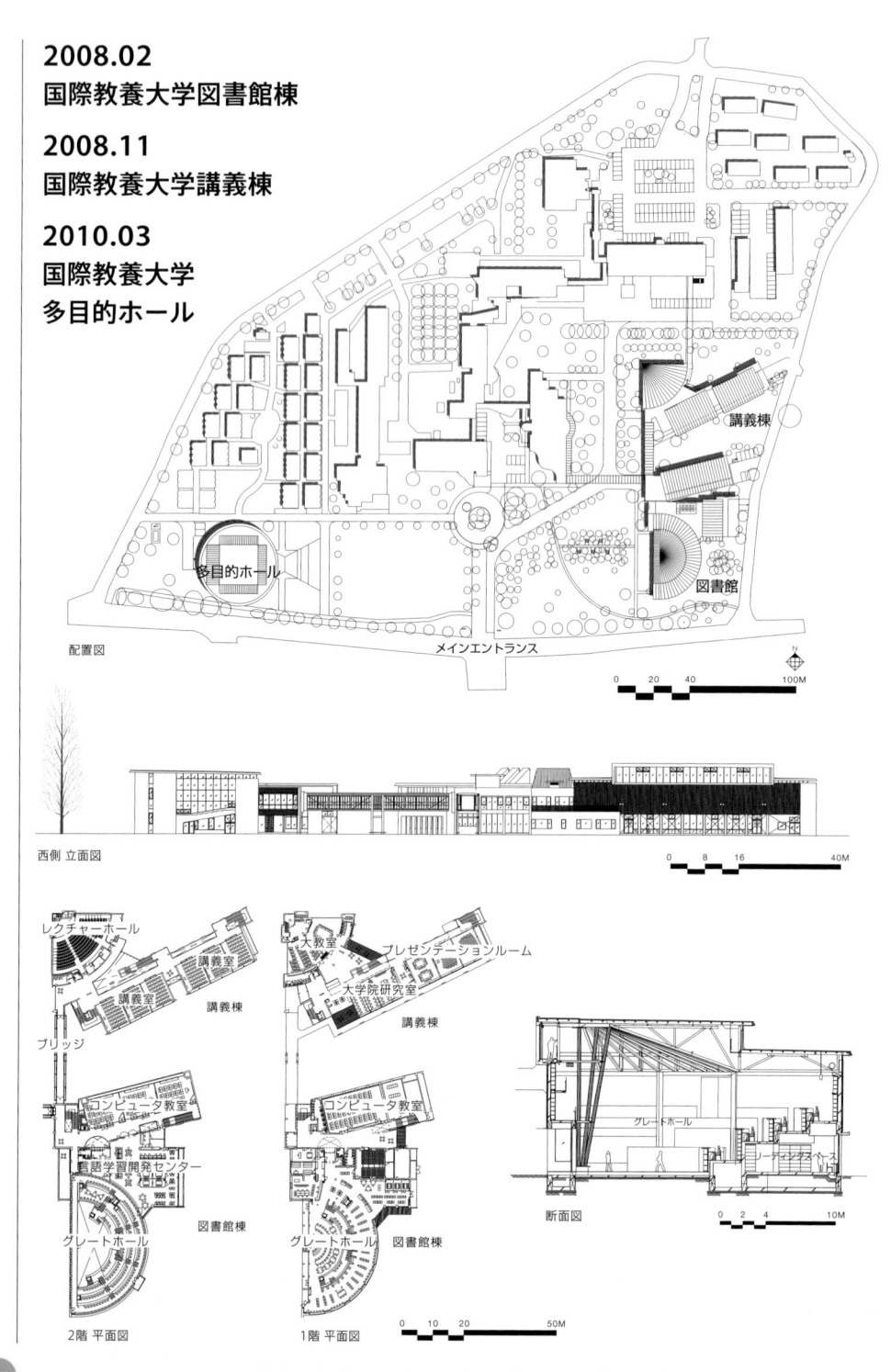

2008.11
国際教養大学講義棟

2010.03
国際教養大学
多目的ホール

配置図　メインエントランス

西側 立面図

レクチャーホール　講義室　講義棟　ブリッジ　コンピュータ教室　言語学習開発センター　グレートホール　図書館棟　2階 平面図

大教室　プレゼンテーションルーム　大学院研究室　講義棟　コンピュータ教室　グレートホール　図書館棟　1階 平面図

グレートホール　断面図

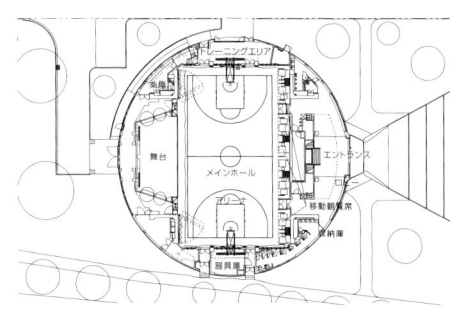

1階 平面図(体育館使用時)

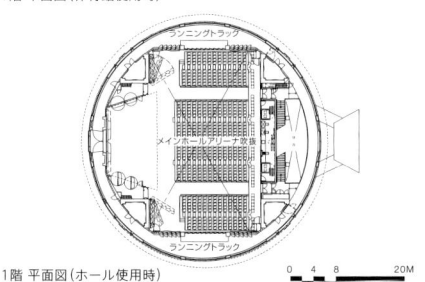

1階 平面図(ホール使用時)

所在地：秋田県秋田市雄和椿川
主用途：大学施設
建築主：公立大学法人国際教養大学
共同設計：コスモス設計

国際教養大学図書館
構造設計：増田建築構造事務所、構造計画プラス・ワン
設備設計：総合設備計画
施工：大木・沢木・足利・石郷岡・互大異業種JV
構造：RC造、W造
規模：地上2階
敷地：85,546㎡　建築：2,433㎡　延床：4,055㎡

国際教養大学講義棟
構造設計：構造計画プラス・ワン
設備設計：総合設備計画、花田設計
施工：長谷駒・三和興業・本荘電気・三和施設JV
構造：RC造、W造
規模：地上2階
敷地：65,572㎡　建築：1,579㎡　延床：2,652㎡

国際教養大学多目的ホール
構造設計：増田建築構造事務所
設備設計：総合設備計画
施工：伊藤工業・珍田・本荘電気・カミオ異業種特定建設工事JV
構造：RC造、S造
規模：地上2階
敷地：71,210㎡　建築：1,411㎡　延床：1,906㎡

Akita International University, Library, Lecture Building, Multi Purpose Hall
Yuwatsubakikawa, Akita-shi, Akita

Project
東山動植物園探検温室

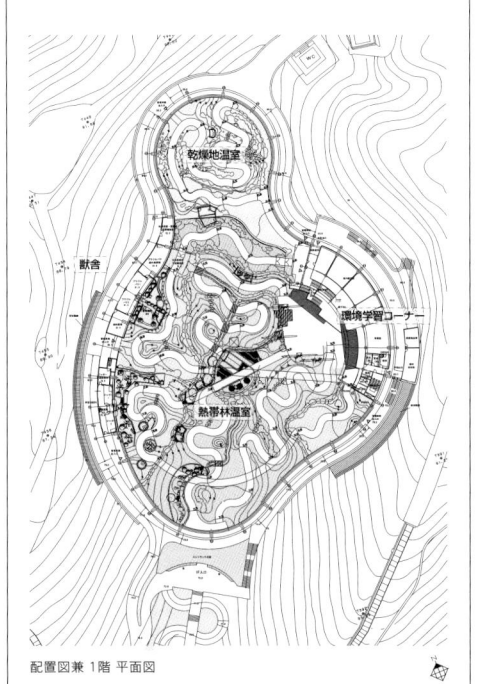

配置図兼1階 平面図

断面図

所在地：愛知県名古屋市千種区田代町
主用途：観覧温室
建築主：名古屋市
構造設計、設備設計：オーヴ・アラップ・アンド・パートナーズ・ジャパン・リミテッド
構造：S造、RC造
規模：地上4階
敷地：5,700㎡

Higashiyama Zoo and Botanical Gardens Adventure Glasshouse Project
Tashiro-cho, Chigusa-ku, Nagoya-shi, Aichi

2007

河口湖ステラシアター　Kawaguchiko Stellar Theatre

富士に開く

河口湖ステラシアター

山梨県南都留郡富士河口湖町／2007
Kawaguchiko Stellar Theatre
Fujikawaguchiko-machi, Minamitsuru-gun, Yamanashi

正面に富士山の雄姿を抱いた3,000人収容の野外シアターが斎藤義の設計により1995年に完成され、以来多くの音楽イベントの拠点として運営実績を挙げてきたが、公演が天候に左右されることを解決するため、開場13年目に「可動屋根」が設置され、催事の安定化と音響面の改善が図られた。この規模で生音のコンサートやオペラが行える施設は、国内はもとより、世界にも類を見ない存在である。

Completed in 1995, this 3,000 seat outdoors theater, which faces the great beauty of Mt. Fuji, has been the site of many musical events. In order to solve the problem of concerts being cancelled due to bad weather, an "opening roof" was installed on its 13th year, and this not only stabilized business, but improved acoustics. A facility of this scale where concerts and opera can be held is unique not only in Japan, but around the world also.

2007

河口湖ステラシアター　Kawaguchiko Stellar Theatre

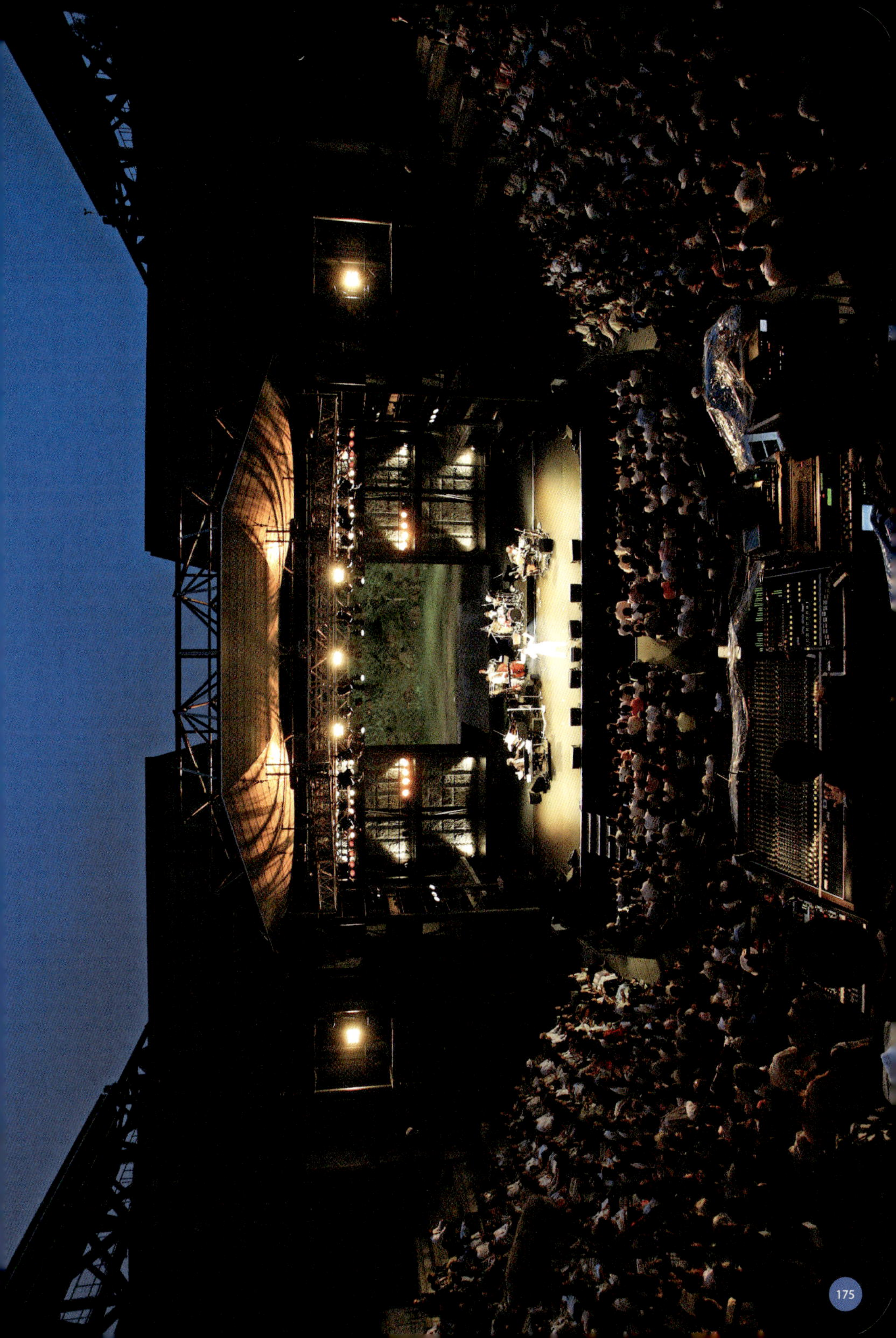

2007

港区立飯倉保育園・学童クラブ

Iigura Day Nursery, Iigura After School Club

地域を見守る塔

港区立飯倉保育園・学童クラブ

東京都港区東麻布／2007
Iigura Day Nursery, Iigura After School Club
Higashiazabu, Minato-ku, Tokyo

地階から2階までが保育園、3・4階が学童クラブからなる幼児・児童のための複合施設である。エントランスである北側全面をカーテンウォールとし、視覚的にこども達を大きく迎え入れる。公園に面する南側にはバルコニーと大きなカーテンウォールの開口を設けて、公園の豊かな緑を内部に取り込みながら、公園であそぶこども達をやさしく見守る建物となっている。

This is a multi-functional facility for small children with a nursery school from the basement level to second floor and children's club on the third and fourth floors. The entire north side is a curtain-wall that provides a large entrance for arriving children, and on the south side, facing the park, is a balcony and large opening to the curtain-wall. This allows the rich greenery from outside to filter indoors, as the building gently looks over the children as they play in the park.

2007

港区立飯倉保育園・学童クラブ
Iigura Day Nursery, Iigura After School Club

児童公園と一体となった保育園
The nursery school that has become one with the children's park.

屋上も保育室

The rooftop also serves as a nursery room.

2007

港区立飯倉保育園・学童クラブ

Iigura Day Nursery, Iigura After School Club

さまざまな場所にこども達の居場所
The children can find a spot
for themselves in various places.

2007

四街道さつき幼稚園　Yotsukaido Satsuki Kindergarten

内から外へ

四街道さつき幼稚園

千葉県四街道市下志津新田／2007
Yotsukaido Satsuki Kindergarten
Shimosizushinden, Yotsukaido-shi, Chiba

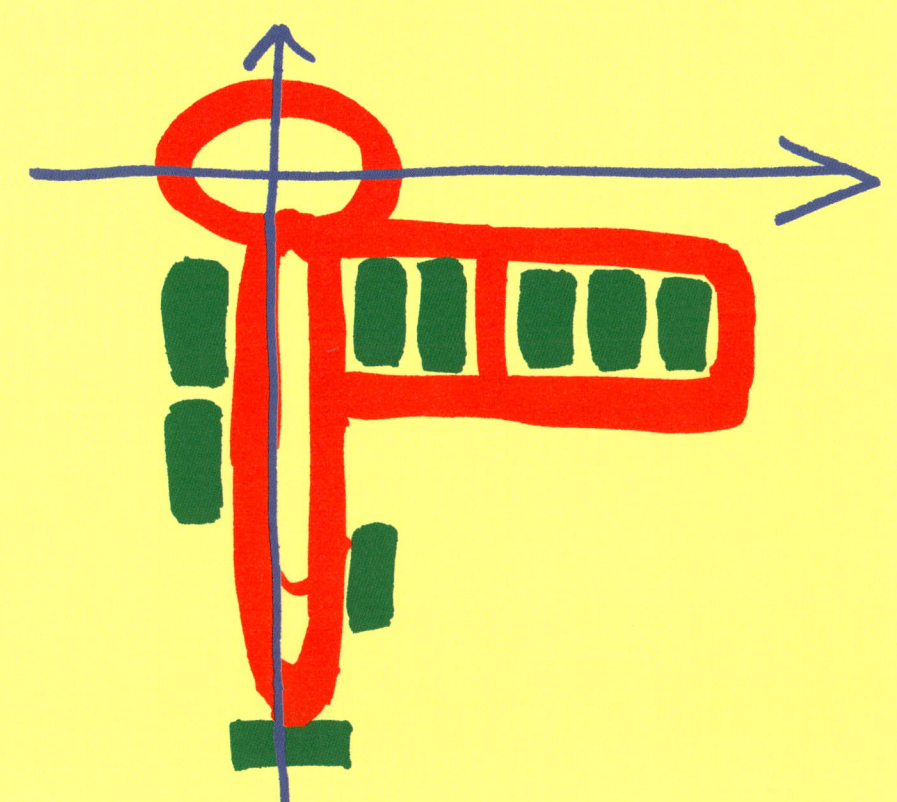

千葉県四街道市の住宅街に位置する園児数約200人の幼稚園である。園舎は南北に伸びる改築園舎部分と、東西方向の耐震補強した保育室部分に大きく分けられる。改築園舎は木造で、祈りと劇場的な空間をもつ「たけのこホール」が付属され、鉄骨造の旧園舎棟は前後に耐震補強のフレームを入れ、南側に幅3mのテラス、北側2mの廊下が新設され、全体として遊環構造が形成されている。内部は木材を多用し温かみのある室内としている。また園児達の参加により自然・農体験ができる「ふれあいの森」が整備された。

This is a 200-person kindergarten located in a residential area in Yotsukaido City. The building is composed of a renovated school house and a nursery section that has undergone earthquake-proofing construction. The school house is made of wood and is attached to "Takenoko Hall," which boasts an aura of the performing arts. Earthquake reinforcement frames were inserted to the front and back of the old steel school building, and a three-meter terrace was constructed on the southern side along with a two-meter hallway on the northern side, thus giving the structure with circular play system its form.

2007

四街道さつき幼稚園　Yotsukaido Satsuki Kindergarten

幅3mのテラスは内と外をつなぐ
The 3m-wide terrace links the indoors and the outdoors.

2007

四街道さつき幼稚園　Yotsukaido Satsuki Kindergarten

廊下も教室
The corridors also serve as classrooms.

2007

四街道さつき幼稚園　Yotsukaido Satsuki Kindergarten

裏庭は自然の教室
The backyard is a classroom set amidst the nature.

2006

多治見市立滝呂小学校

Takiro Elmentary School, Tajimi

教室毎に玄関

多治見市立滝呂小学校

岐阜県多治見市滝呂町／2006
Takiro Elmentary School, Tajimi
Takiro-cho, Tajimi-shi, Gifu

岐阜県多治見市のニュータウン地区に建設された小学校、生徒は新住民と旧住民がほぼ半々である。校舎棟・管理棟・体育館棟の3つの建物と一つの広場から構成されている。一番環境のよい南側に校舎棟を配し、北側のエントランス広場は、地域と学校をつなぐ市民の広場として計画されている。この建物の大きな特徴は、教室毎に玄関が設けられていることで、自分の家のような親しみのある場所となり、また、外へあそびに出やすく、避難上の安全性も高い学校となっている。

This is an elementary school constructed in the New Town district of Tajimi City. The facilities comprise of the school building, management building, and gymnasium. The school building stands on the best location, the south side, and the north-side entrance opening is made as a space for the local residents, connecting the district and the school. The main characteristic of the building is that there is an entrance to the outside for each classroom in the two-story building. This was done to give the school a homely atmosphere, where it is easy to go outside and play, and also provides safe passage outdoors in case of emergency.

2006

多治見市立滝呂小学校　Takiro Elmentary School, Tajimi

オープンスペースは
さまざまなあそび場になる
The open spaces serve
as a variety of play spaces.

各教室毎の出入口
The entrances and exits for each classroom.

2006

愛和病院ANNEX

Aiwa Hospital ANNEX

愛ちゃん
ワールド館

愛和病院ANNEX

埼玉県川越市古谷上／2006
Aiwa Hospital ANNEX
Furuyakami, Kawagoe-shi, Saitama

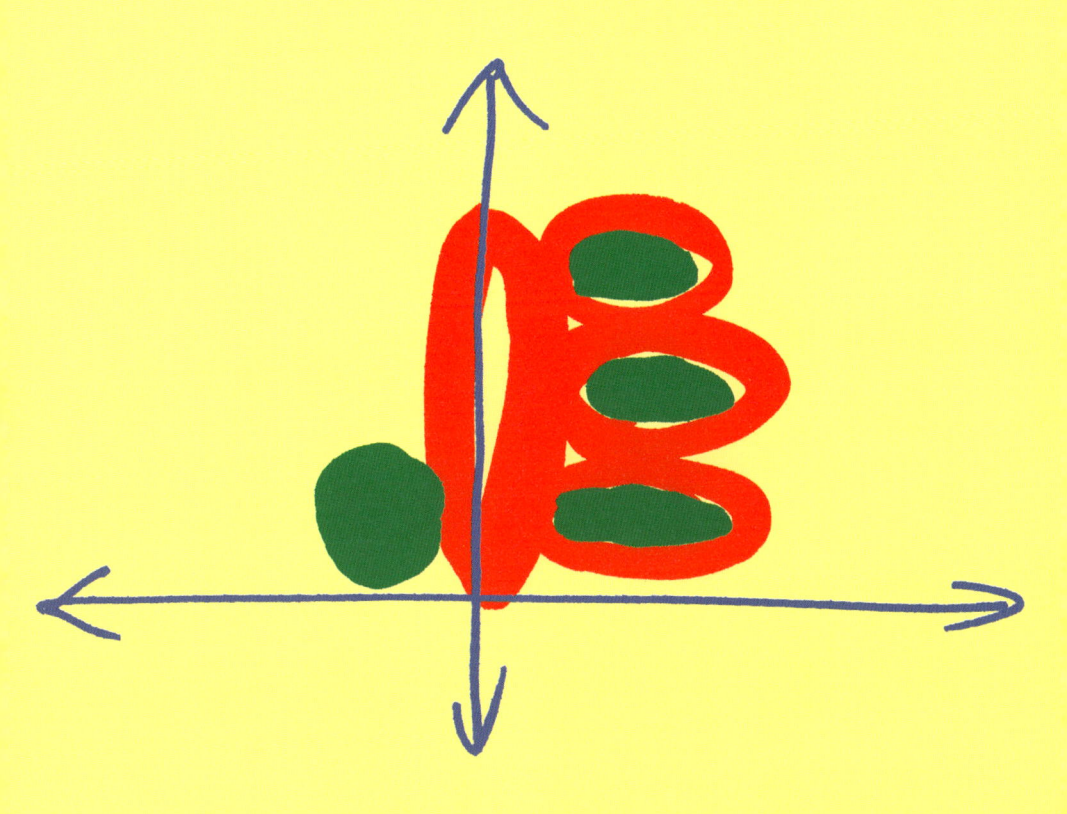

年間約2,400人を超える出産数を誇る民間病院の新館として計画された。出産直後の3カ月間、母子が社会から孤立し最もサポートを必要とするこの時期に、母親を支援する「育母支援」という新しい事業を実現する空間である。その中心となる健診センターは赤ちゃんが最もよく触れる床に無垢の桐材を使用し、暖かく柔らかな空間づくりが意図された。開放的で明るく、豊かな自然を様々な場所で感じ触れられること、癒されるだけでなく、居て楽しくなるような空間づくりが目指された。

A new wing was planned for a private hospital that boasts 2,400 births per year. Though it is when they need help most, the three months following birth is a time when both mother and the child tend to become abandoned from society and society has little to offer in terms of support. This space realizes a new operation called "ikubo shien" (aid for child-rearing mothers) which provides support to mothers with newborns. The core facility, the health inspection center, uses paulownia wood for the floor where babies touch the most, and it also creates a warm and soft atmosphere.

2006

愛和病院ANNEX

Aiwa Hospital ANNEX

小さなこども達のためのあそび場が広がる
A spacious play space for young children.

2006

愛和病院ANNEX

Aiwa Hospital ANNEX

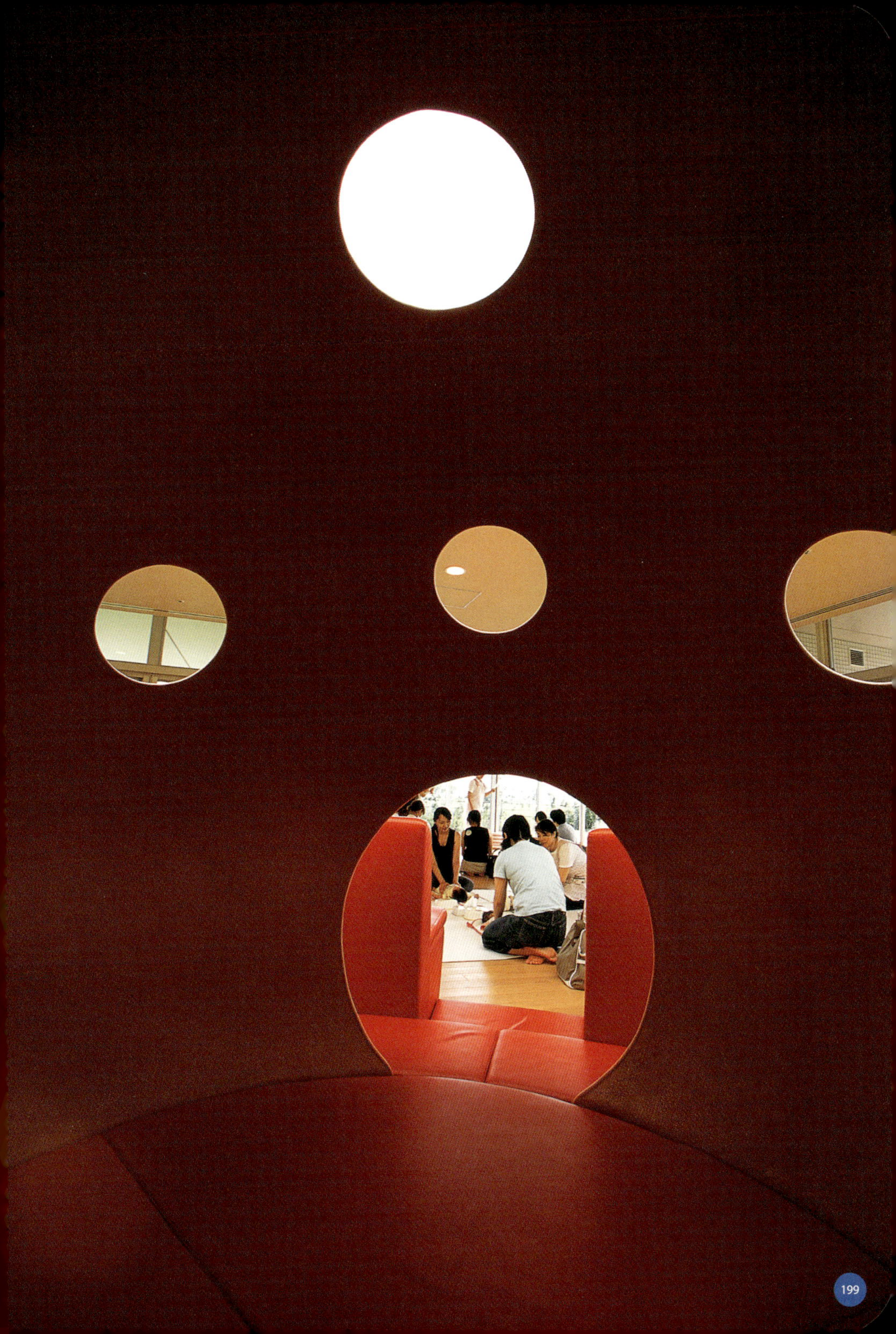

2006

猿島公園
Sarushima Park

東京自然無人島

猿島公園

神奈川県横須賀市猿島／2006
Sarushima Park
Sarushima, Yokosuka-shi, Kanagawa

「猿島」は東京湾唯一の自然の無人島で、エコロジカルな生物自然環境と歴史文化遺産をもつエコミュージアムとして重要なサイトである。ビジターセンターはここを訪れる市民のためのサービスセンターである。自然地形と一体化した木造による空間構成が図られた。エコミュージアムとしての土木遺産や豊かな自然環境のディスプレイも環境を十分に配慮した慎ましいデザインがなされた。

Sarushima is the only natural non-inhabited island in the Tokyo Bay, and it holds an important meaning that it is the site of a local eco-museum that protects the natural environment and historical culture there. It is composed so that the entire facility is a circular line of movement, in unity with the park path. We created a modest design as not to disturb the environment, with displays of the natural environment of land and trees.

2006

猿島公園

Sarushima Park

203

2006

猿島公園
Sarushima Park

斜面緑地の勾配を合わせた屋根・天井
Roofs and ceilings that match the gradient of the sloping grassland.

2006

尼崎スポーツの森　Amagasaki Sports Forest

百年の森とスポーツ

尼崎スポーツの森

兵庫県尼崎市扇町／2006
Amagasaki Sports Forest
Ogi-machi, Amagasaki-shi, Hyogo

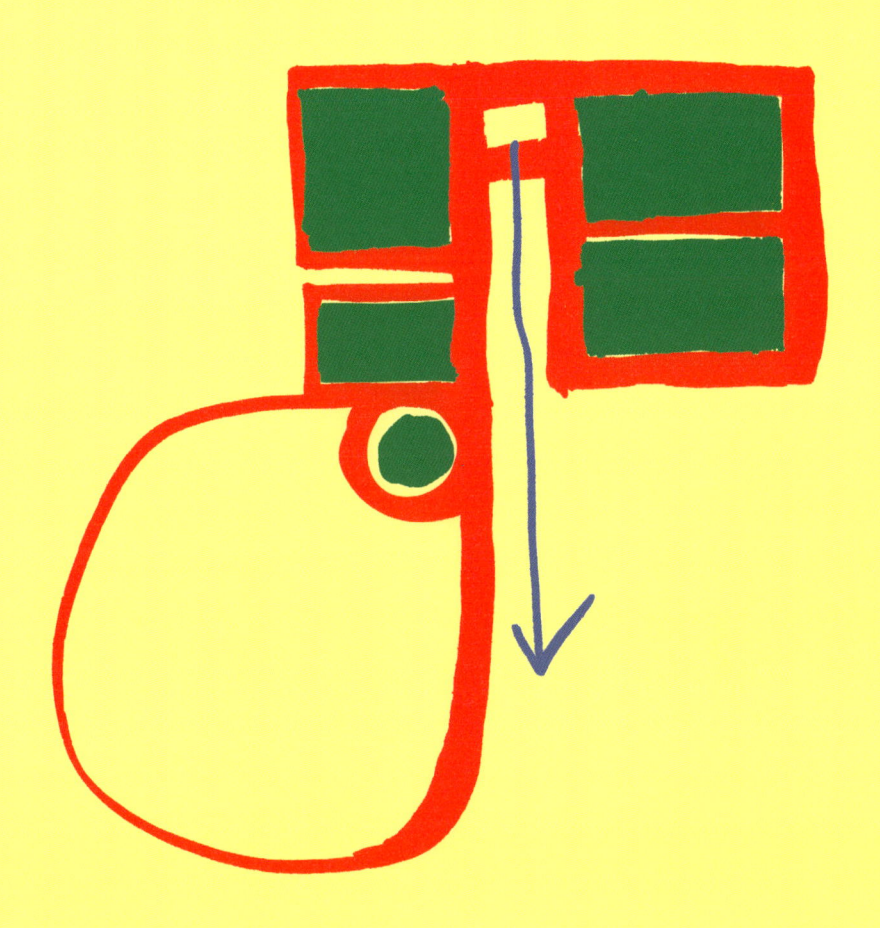

兵庫県初のPFI事業による複合健康増進施設として計画された。夏期以外はアイススケート場として使われるメインアリーナのほか、50mプール、25mプール、トレーニングルーム、フィットネススタジオ等の他、屋外にフットサルコート、グラウンドゴルフ場、レジャープールなどの多様なプログラムを有したスポーツ集客施設である。

As the first PFI operation in Hyogo Prefecture, this was designed to be a total health promotion facility. The space offers a variety of facilities, including a main arena that is used as an ice skating rink in all seasons but the summer, a 50-meter pool, 25-meter pool, training room, fitness studio, outdoor futsal court, ground golf course, and leisure pool.

2006

尼崎スポーツの森　Amagasaki Sports Forest

子育て支援機能を持つ運動レジャー公園
A sports and leisure park with functions that provide support for child rearing.

2006

尼崎スポーツの森
Amagasaki Sports Forest

できるだけ内部の気積を大きくしない屋根形状
A roof shape that minimizes the volume of the interior as far as possible.

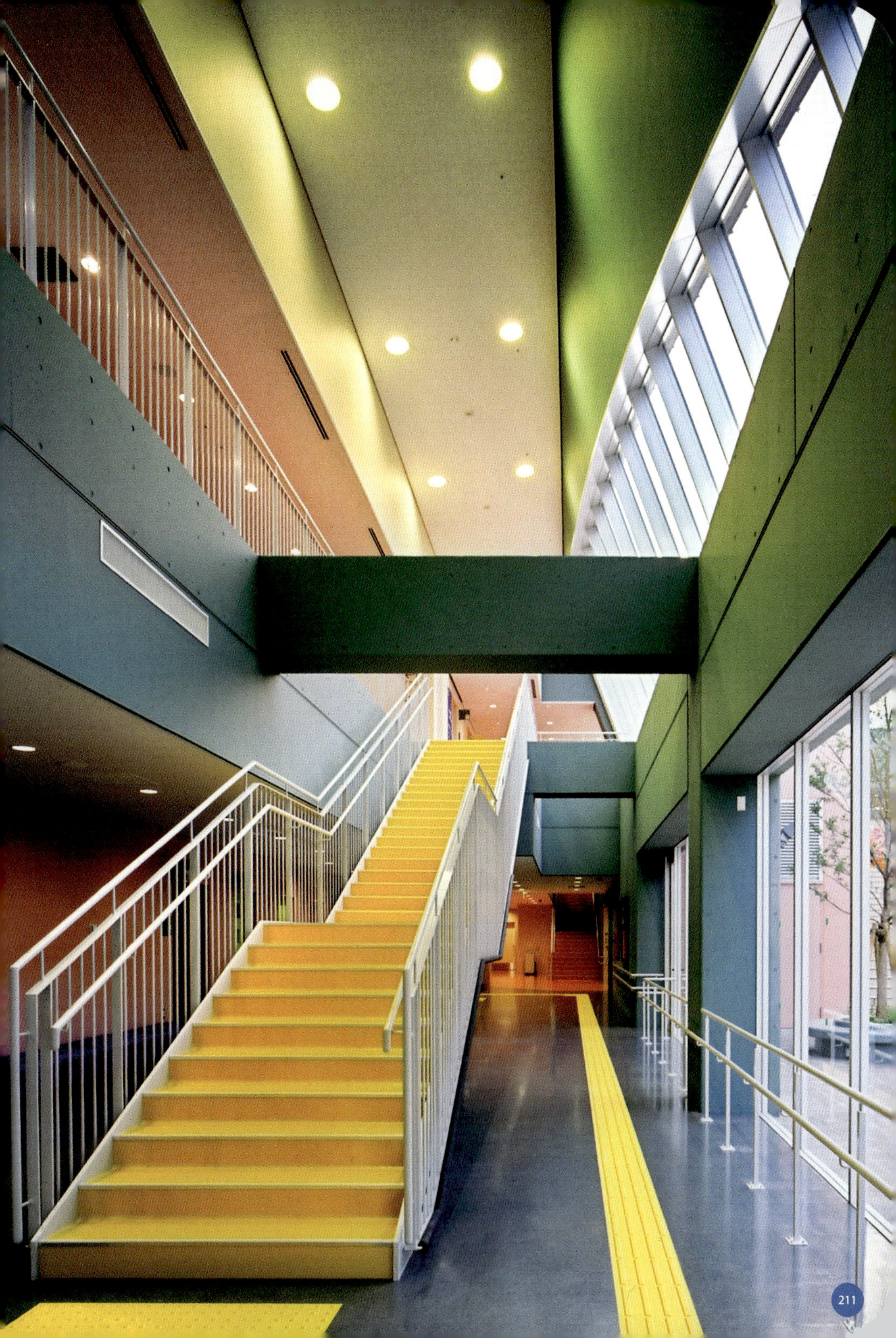

2006

佛山市岭南明珠体育館
Foshan Pearl Gymnasium

亜熱帯型
環境ドーム

佛山市岭南明珠体育館

中華人民共和国広東省／2006
Foshan Pearl Gymnasium
Guangdong, China

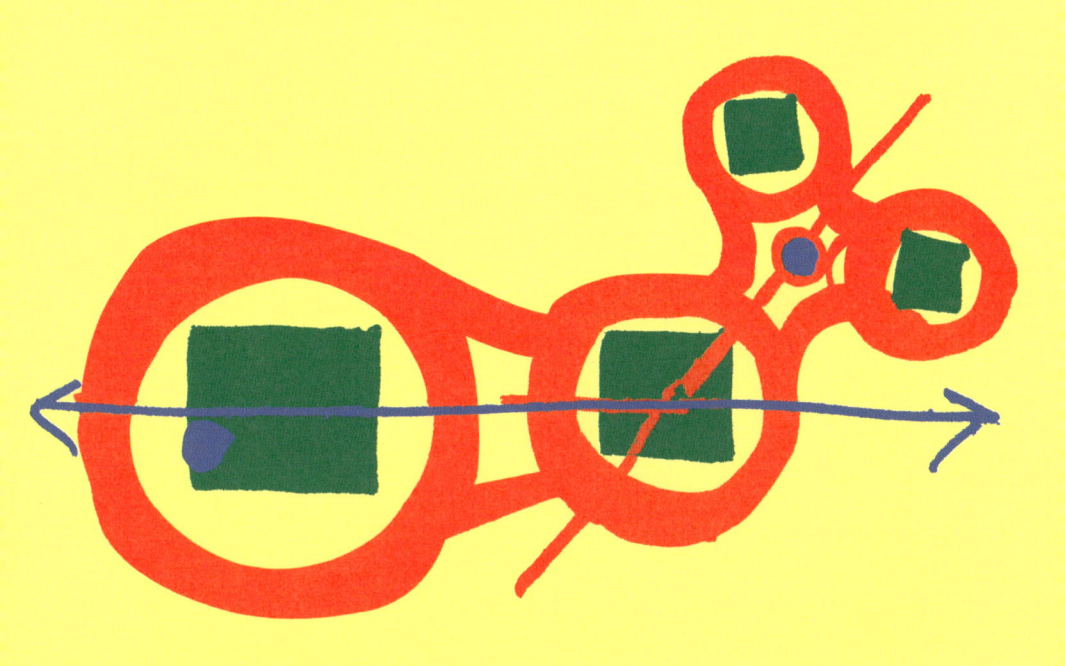

本施設は2003年9月に国際コンペが行われ、1等賞を獲得した。敷地は27ヘクタールあり、主体育館8,680席、訓練館1,500席および市民が常用する大衆館の3つの体育館が施設の中核となっている。それらをつなぐ大庁（中心ホワイエ）も含め、構造は空間構成に合致させた世界初の大空間トラス方式が採用された。体育館の西側には一周約500mの健康回廊があり、雨も多く、暑さの厳しい亜熱帯気候での屋根をもつ回廊型遊環構造建築である。また、明るさを確保しながら通風、温熱環境に配慮した地球環境建築として実現した。

On a site of 27-hectare, this project required a metropolitan facility that serves as a sports park. At the core, there are three gymnasiums; the main gymnasium that seats 8,680, the training gymnasium that seats 1,500, and a general gymnasium for the local residents. A central foyer created to connect the three facilities is a unique space for movement, and is a very creative design in the world's first large-space truss structure. This facility presents an environment-friendly architecture in a hot environment.

2006

佛山市岭南明珠体育馆

Foshan Pearl Gymnasium

無柱の内部空間をもつ３つのドームの連なり
A series of three domes with pillar-free interior spaces.

2006

佛山市岭南明珠体育馆

Foshan Pearl Gymnasium

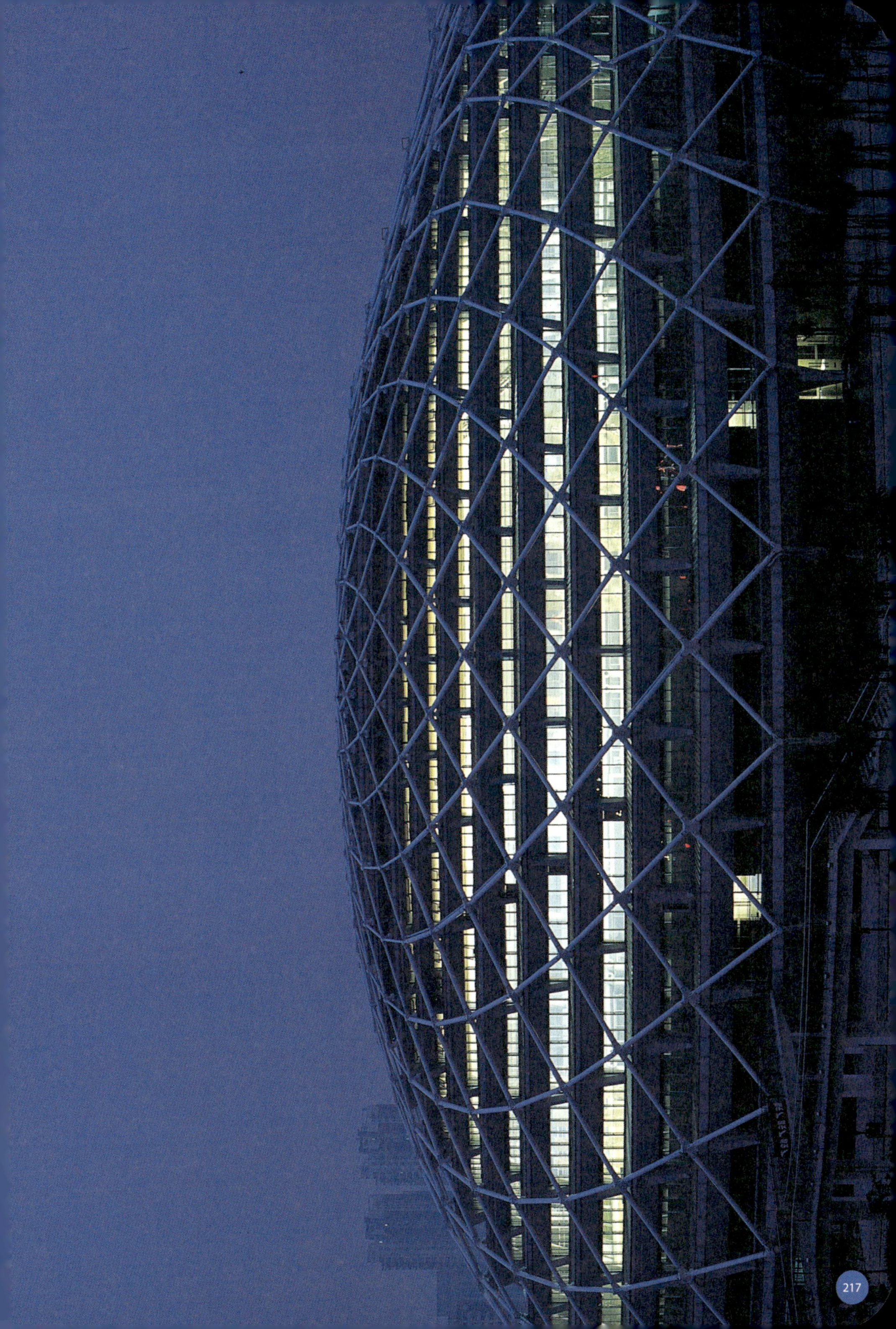

2006

佛山市岭南明珠体育館　Foshan Pearl Gymnasium

地下室の駐車場からメインフロアへ　From the basement carpark to the main floor

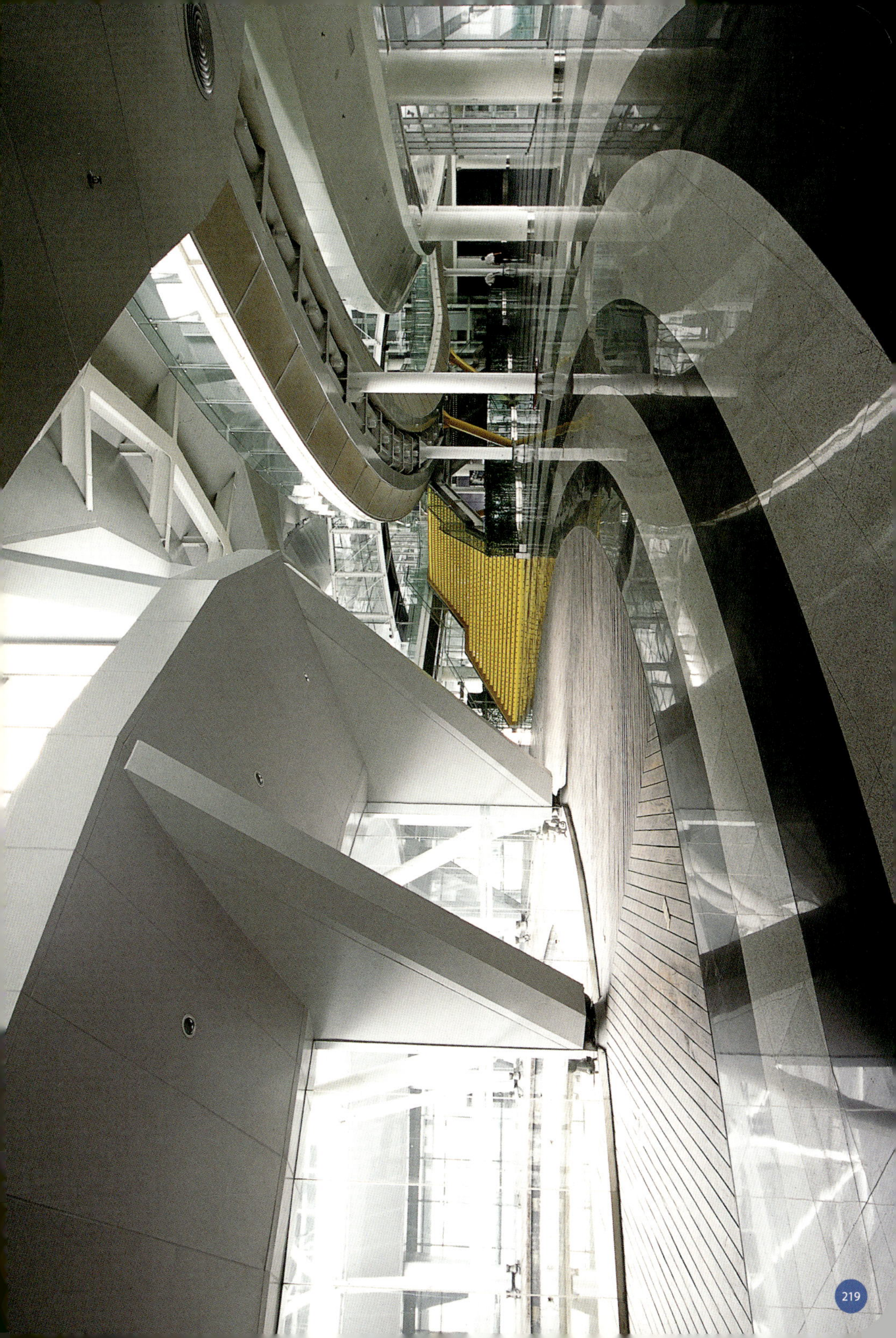

2006

佛山市岭南明珠体育馆

Foshan Pearl Gymnasium

中央部ロビーの交差する動線が空間を豊かにする

The intersecting routes in the central lobby enrich the space.

2006

佛山市岭南明珠体育馆

Foshan Pearl Gymnasium

メインアリーナは層状の屋根から昼光を採り、
省エネルギー化を図る
The layered roof of the main arena lets
in the daylight and helps to conserve energy.

2006

佛山市岭南明珠体育馆　Foshan Pearl Gymnasium

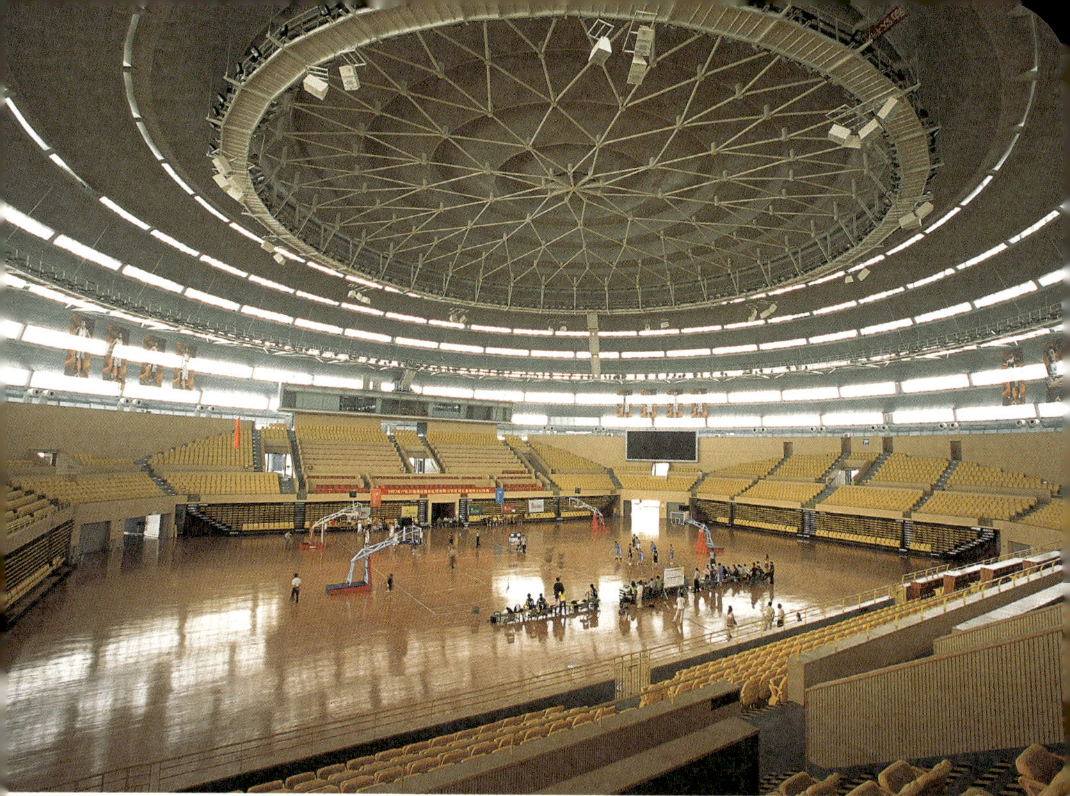

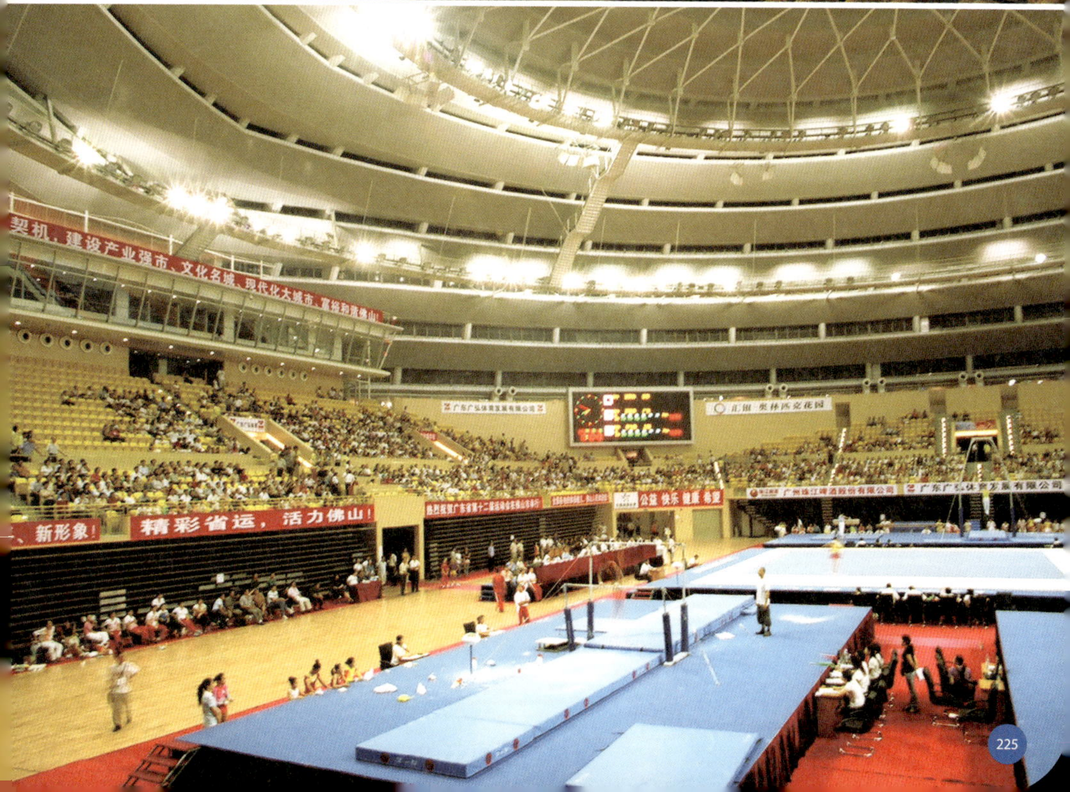

契机、建设产业强市、文化名城、现代化大城市
、新形象！
精彩省运，活力佛山！
公益 快乐 健康 希望
广东广弘体育发展有限公司

2006

佛山市岭南明珠体育馆

Foshan Pearl Gymnasium

227

空に開く花びら

2005

上海旗忠森林体育城テニスセンター

Shanghai Qizhong Forest Sports City Tennis Center

上海旗忠森林体育城テニスセンター

中華人民共和国上海市／2005
Shanghai Qizhong Forest Sports City Tennis Center
Shanghai, China

上海市閔行区に建設されたテニスセンターである。敷地面積20ヘクタール、メインスタジアムは15,000席の規模を有し、8枚の花びらのような屋根がカメラのシャッターのように開く世界初の新しいタイプの開閉屋根機構をもつ。開閉の過程において、各屋根間のクリアランス形状は刻一刻と変化し、天空からの光の表情も変化に富んだものとなり、全開したときには従来のスライド式開閉屋根にはない、高い開口率を持つ。竣工後は、多機能なイベントセンターとしての役割も果たしている。

This is a tennis center built in the Min-hang District of Shanghai. With a total area of 20 hectares, the main stadium has a capacity for 15,000 spectators. The first of its kind in the world, the roof has a new style of opening mechanism, where eight panels like petals of a flower move open and close like a camera shutter. The shape of the opening will change as the roof opens and closes, giving the light from the sky a variety of expressions. Another characteristic is that the percent that the roof opens when it is completely open is much higher than that of conventional sliding type movable roofs.

2005

リングトラスの上を
8枚の屋根パネルが滑るシャッター型開閉
Eight roof panels on top of the ring truss open
and close with sliding shutters.

上海旗忠森林体育城テニスセンター　Shanghai Qizhong Forest Sports City Tennis Center

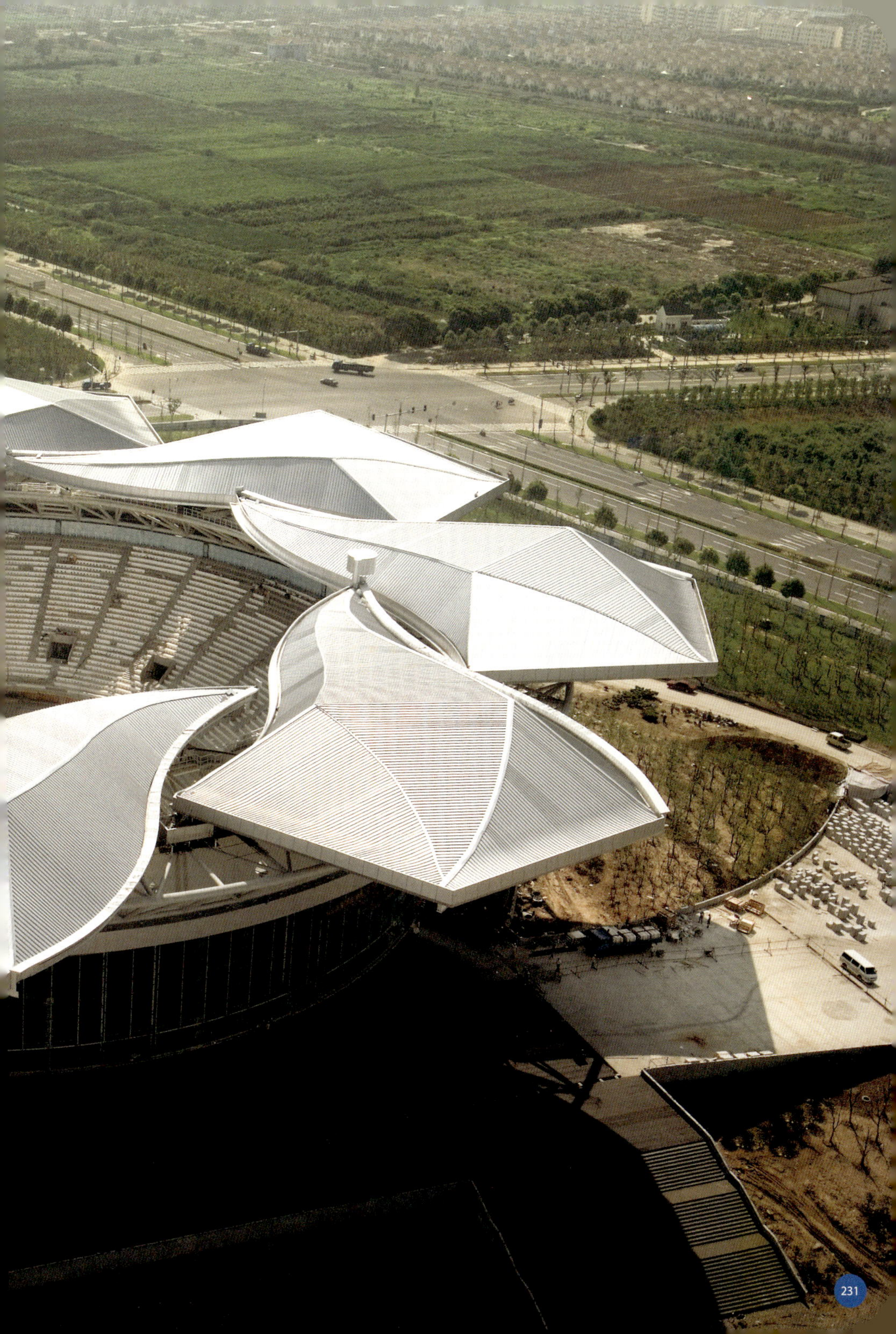

2005

上海旗忠森林体育城テニスセンター　Shanghai Qizhong Forest Sports City Tennis Center

233

2005

上海旗忠森林体育城テニスセンター　Shanghai Qizhong Forest Sports City Tennis Center

上海浦東国際空港の近く、飛行機からも見える
**Near to Shanghai's Pudong International Airport,
and is visible even from the planes.**

2005

浪速スポーツセンター　Naniwa Sports Center

スポーツ&デイケア

浪速スポーツセンター

大阪府大阪市浪速区難波中／2005
Naniwa Sports Center
Nanbanaka, Naniwa-ku, Osaka-shi, Osaka

大阪市の都心部に建設される大型市民スポーツ施設と老人デイケア施設の合築である。地階にアイスアリーナ、上階に大体育館、最上階にプールをもつブロックと多目的ホール、小体育館ブロックに分節化され、その間にクレバス状のアトリウムが設けられている。ガラスの横ルーバーの立面を持ち、明るくカジュアルな市民施設として立体的な遊環構造建築となっている。

Built in the center of Osaka, this is a combined structure that houses a large-scale citizen's sports facility and day-care facility for the elderly. The ground floor hosts an ice arena and the upper floors a large gymnasium. On the top floor visitors will find a block with a pool, as well as another block with a multi-purpose hall smaller gymnasium. In between the blocks is a crevice-like atrium. With glass horizontal louvers, the three-dimensional circular play system was designed to be a bright and casual citizen's facility.

2005

浪速スポーツセンター　Naniwa Sports Center

地下アイスアリーナは
関西で最も人気のアリーナとなっている
The underground ice arena is
the most popular arena in the Kansai region.

2005

浪速スポーツセンター　Naniwa Sports Center

最上階は25mプール
A 25m pool on the top floor.

1階2階に100台の駐車場が挿入されている
A carpark with a capacity for 100 vehicles is located on the first and second floors.

2005

よつば循環器科クリニック
Yotsuba Circulation Clinic

ハート
クリニック

よつば循環器科クリニック

愛媛県松山市南江戸／2005
Yotsuba Circulation Clinic
Minamiedo, Matsuyama-shi, Ehime

四国松山市の新空港通り沿いに立地する循環器内科を専門とするクリニック。近年、加速度的に高度化・専門化する医療に対して、安心して来訪できる親しみやすさと、心身ともに癒され、安心を与えリフレッシュする空間形成が意図された。

This is a circulatory systems clinic located near the new airport in Matsuyama-city, Shikoku. We were careful to make this an environment where medicine, which has rapidly become high-level and specialized, into a friendlier place to visit, and patients will be comforted in health and mind.

2005

よつば循環器科クリニック

Yotsuba Circulation Clinic

旧薬局の鉄骨店舗をコンバージョンし、
RC病床棟を追加したハイブリッドな構造形式
Converting the old steel-structured pharmacy into a hybrid structure with RC hospital wards.

2005

こばと幼稚園絵本館

Kobato Children's Library

ブックタワー

こばと幼稚園絵本館

岐阜県岐阜市鹿島町／2005
Kobato Children's Library
Kashima-cho, Gifu-shi, Gifu

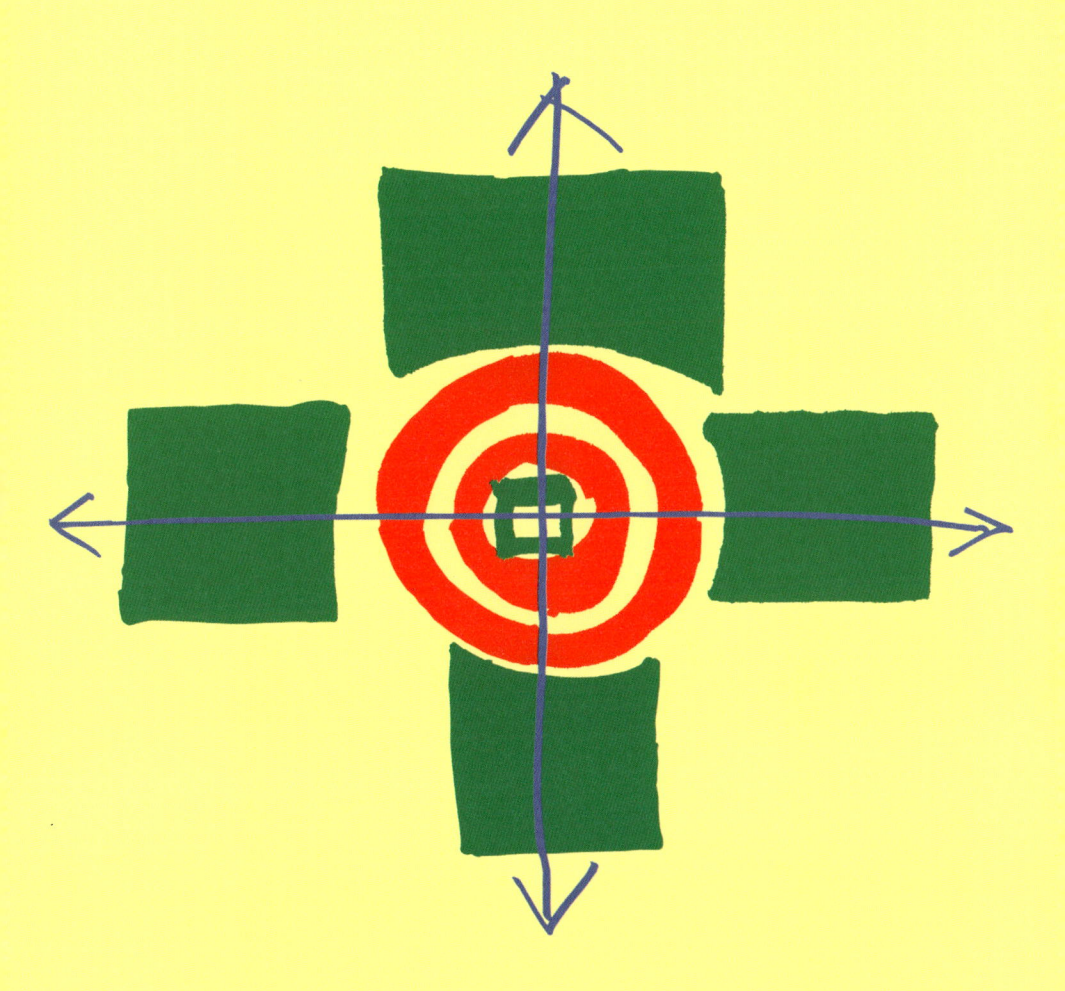

日本では珍しい幼稚園専用の絵本館である。内部すべてを桐の空間に囲まれた読書室、大量の本を陳列できるブックタワー、ふれあいの保育室、さらに屋外で本の世界を体感できるチルドレンズガーデンを備え、想像と創造する力を育む空間をテーマとした、木造の遊環構造建築である。

A very unique idea in Japan, this is a picture book house created especially for a kindergarten. This wooden recreational structure comprises a paulownia wood reading room, massive book shelves, nursery, and children's garden where children can experience the world of books outdoors.

2005

こばと幼稚園絵本館

Kobato Children's Library

ブックタワーは
隠れ家と光りに満ちた天空の読書室
The book tower is a reading room in the sky,
hidden yet filled with light.

2005

中心は巨大ネット

ゆうゆうのもり幼保園

Yuyu-no-Mori Nursery School and Day Nursery

ゆうゆうのもり幼保園

神奈川県横浜市都筑区早渕／2005
Yuyu-no-Mori Nursery School and Day Nursery
Hayabuchi, Tsuzuki-ku, Yokohama-shi, Kanagawa

横浜市の港北ニュータウン東側に位置する、幼保一元化施設。約2,400㎡の敷地は、西側が下り斜面で、丹沢連山から遠く富士山も望める緑豊かな環境である。「こども主体の保育」という保育理念をかかげ、こどもが主体的・自発的に行動したくなるような環境づくりが目指されている。吹抜け中央の空間には、2階と上部のキャットウォークをつなぐ「大ネット」があり、自由な発想でいろんなあそび方が生まれるあそびの中心空間である。また、2階には一周できるテラスが外部の園庭とつながり、内外ともに遊環構造の原理により設計されている。

This facility is a combination of a kindergarten and nursery school, located on the east side of New Town in Yokohama, with an area of 2,400㎡. To realize the ideology of "nursing children with individuality", the environment was created to induce the children's self-motivated actions. The central space is a wellhole which has a "great net" that connects the second floor and upper level, which provides space for free-style ideas for play. Moreover, the second floor has a fully compassable terrace that is connected to an outdoor garden, making both the inside and outside based on the principles of a structure with circular play system.

2005

ゆうゆうのもり幼保園

Yuyu-no-Mori Nursery School and Day Nursery

253

2005

ゆうゆうのもり幼保園

Yuyu-no-Mori Nursery School and Day Nursery

約2,400㎡の園地を徹底的に使う回遊性は、
多様な体験が可能

Through the migratory character
that makes complete use of the 2,400㎡ school site,
it is possible to enjoy a variety of experiences.

2005

ゆうゆうのもり幼保園
Yuyu-no-Mori Nursery School and Day Nursery

257

2005

ゆうゆうのもり幼保園

Yuyu-no-Mori Nursery School and Day Nursery

259

2007.06
河口湖ステラシアター

立面図
屋根閉状態
屋根開状態

所在地：山梨県南都留郡富士河口湖町
主用途：野外音楽堂
建築主：富士河口湖町
プロジェクト内容：増築
構造設計：団設計同人
設備設計：建築設備設計研究所
施工：鴻池組・早野組JV
構造：RC造、S造
規模：地下1階地上3階
敷地：24,877㎡　建築：3,936㎡　延床：4,870㎡

Kawaguchiko Stellar Theatre
Fujikawaguchiko-machi, Minamitsuru-gun, Yamanashi

2007.03
港区立飯倉保育園・学童クラブ

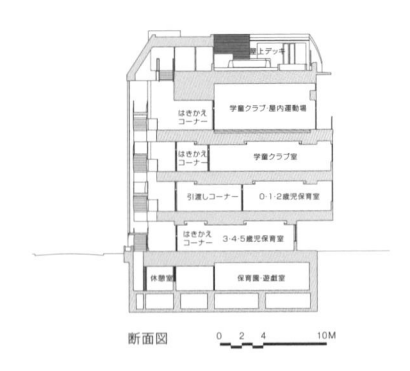

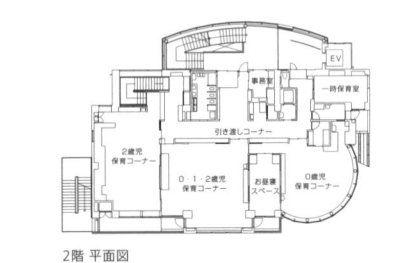

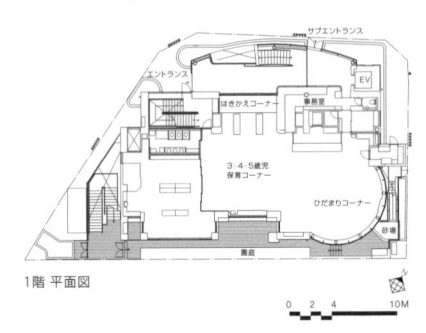

断面図
2階 平面図
1階 平面図

所在地：東京都港区東麻布
主用途：保育園、学童クラブ
建築主：港区
構造設計：金箱構造設計事務所
設備設計：日永設計
施工：合田・松鶴建設JV
構造：S造、SRC造
規模：地下1階地上5階
敷地：570㎡　建築：419㎡　延床：1,996㎡

Iigura Day Nursery, Iigura After School Club
Higashiazabu, Minato-ku, Tokyo

2007.02
四街道さつき幼稚園

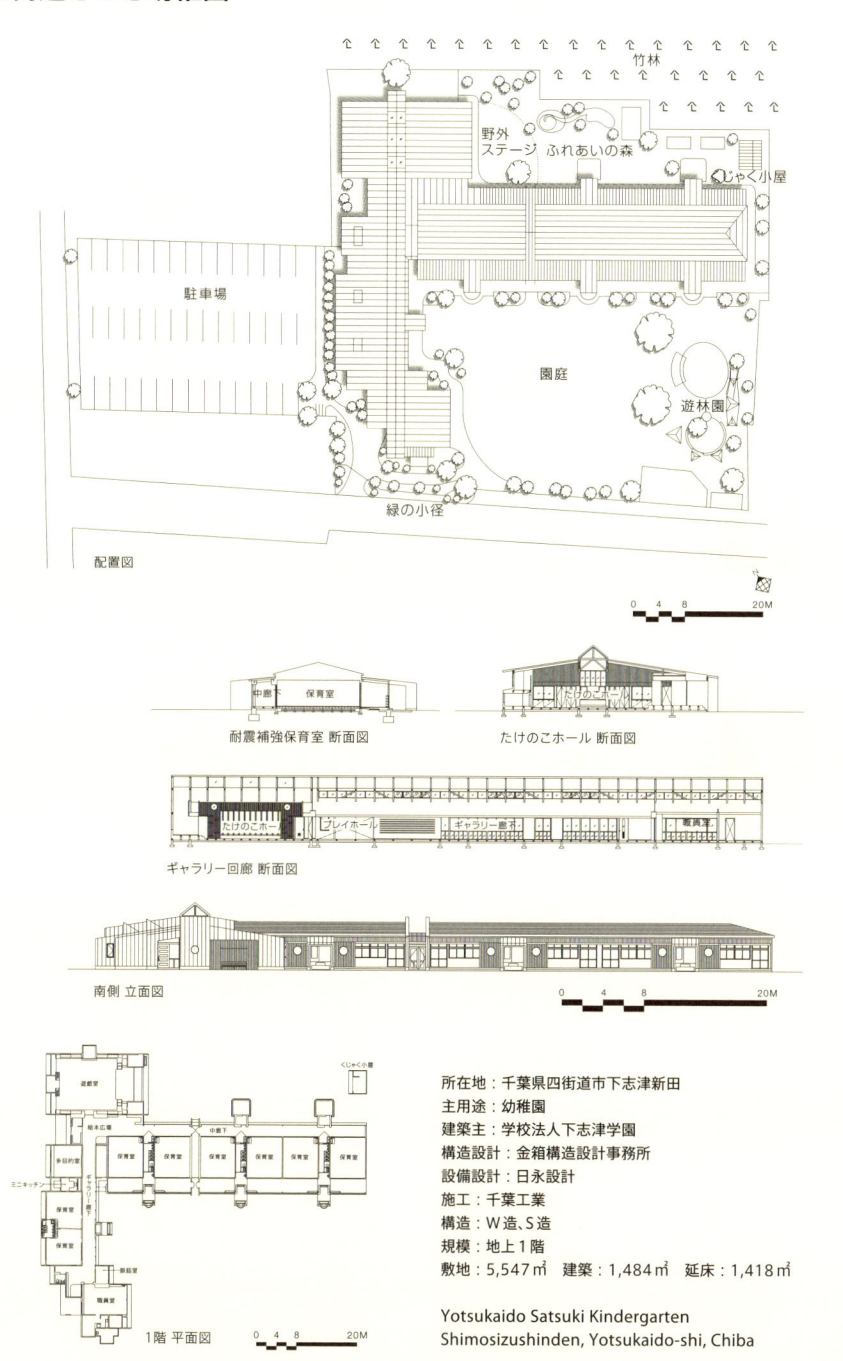

配置図

耐震補強保育室 断面図

たけのこホール 断面図

ギャラリー回廊 断面図

南側 立面図

1階 平面図

所在地：千葉県四街道市下志津新田
主用途：幼稚園
建築主：学校法人下志津学園
構造設計：金箱構造設計事務所
設備設計：日永設計
施工：千葉工業
構造：W造、S造
規模：地上1階
敷地：5,547㎡　建築：1,484㎡　延床：1,418㎡

Yotsukaido Satsuki Kindergarten
Shimosizushinden, Yotsukaido-shi, Chiba

2006.03
多治見市立滝呂小学校

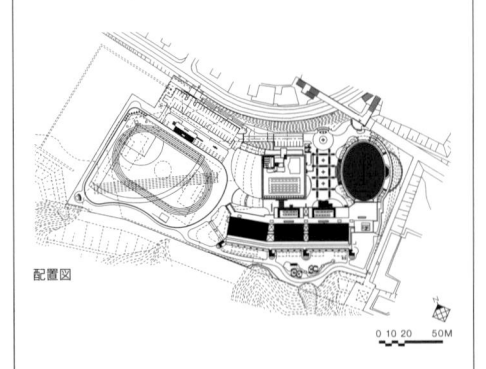

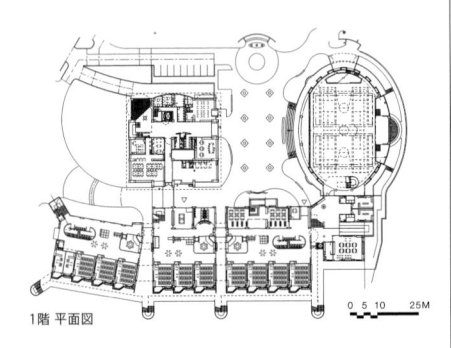

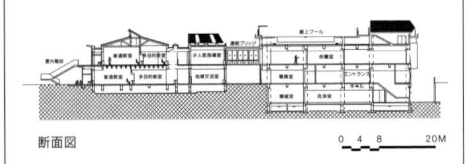

配置図

1階 平面図

断面図

所在地：岐阜県多治見市滝呂町
主用途：小学校
建築主：多治見市
教育施設計画監修：東京工業大学宮本研究室
構造設計：金箱構造設計事務所
設備設計：テーテンス事務所、設備計画
施工：宇佐美組
構造：RC造一部W造一部S造
規模：地下1階地上2階
敷地：27,891㎡　建築：5,579㎡　延床：9,651㎡

Takiro Elmentary School, Tajimi
Takiro-cho, Tajimi-shi, Gifu

2006.09
愛和病院 ANNEX

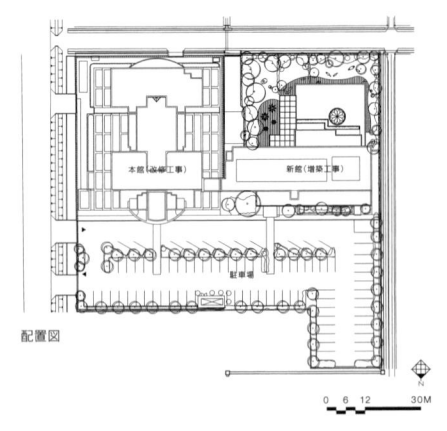

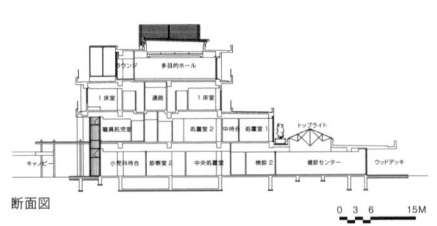

配置図

1階 平面図

断面図

所在地：埼玉県川越市古谷上
主用途：病院
建築主：医療法人愛和会
共同設計、構造設計、設備設計、施工：大成建設
構造：RC造
規模：地上4階
敷地：8,026㎡　建築：1,508㎡　延床：3,213㎡

Aiwa Hospital ANNEX
Furuyakami, Kawagoe-shi, Saitama

2006.06
猿島公園

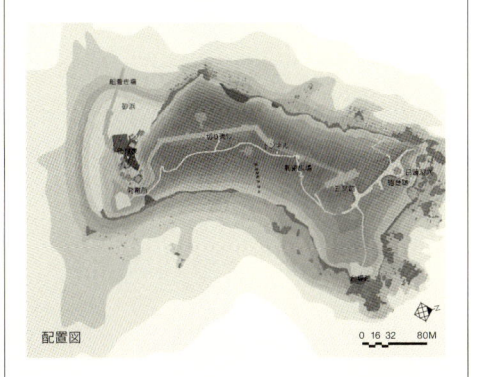

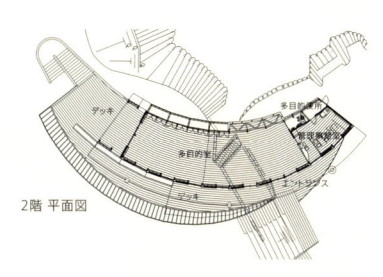

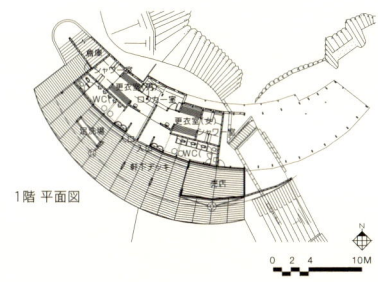

配置図

2階 平面図

1階 平面図

所在地：神奈川県横須賀市猿島
主用途：公園管理施設
建築主：横須賀市
構造設計：金箱構造設計事務所
設備設計：テーテンス事務所、設備計画
施工：小林組（管理棟）、奥山工務店（物販棟）
構造：W造一部RC造（管理棟）、W造（物販棟）
規模：地上2階（管理棟）、地上1階（物販棟）
敷地：55,871㎡　建築：373㎡（管理棟）、163㎡（物販棟）
延床：386㎡（管理棟）、163㎡（物販棟）

Sarushima Park
Sarushima, Yokosuka-shi, Kanagawa

2006.05
尼崎スポーツの森

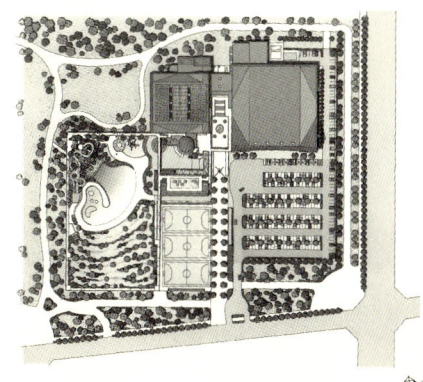

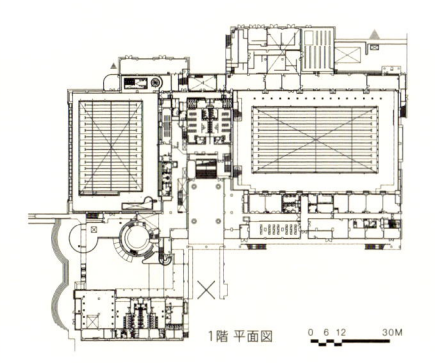

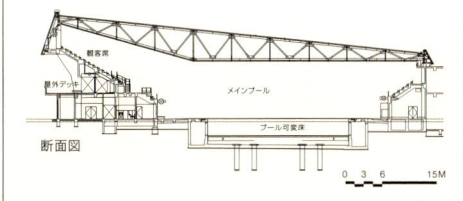

配置図

1階 平面図

断面図

所在地：兵庫県尼崎市扇町
主用途：水泳場、スケート場、観覧場
建築主：兵庫県、あまがさき健康の森（SPC）
構造設計：T&A
設備設計：設備技研、婦木建築設備事務所
施工：柄谷工務店・三菱重工業・近畿菱重興産JV
構造：RC造一部S造
規模：地下1階地上3階
敷地：34,978㎡　建築：9,300㎡　延床：12,400㎡

Amagasaki Sports Forest
Ogi-machi, Amagasaki-shi, Hyogo

2006.08
佛山市岭南明珠体育館

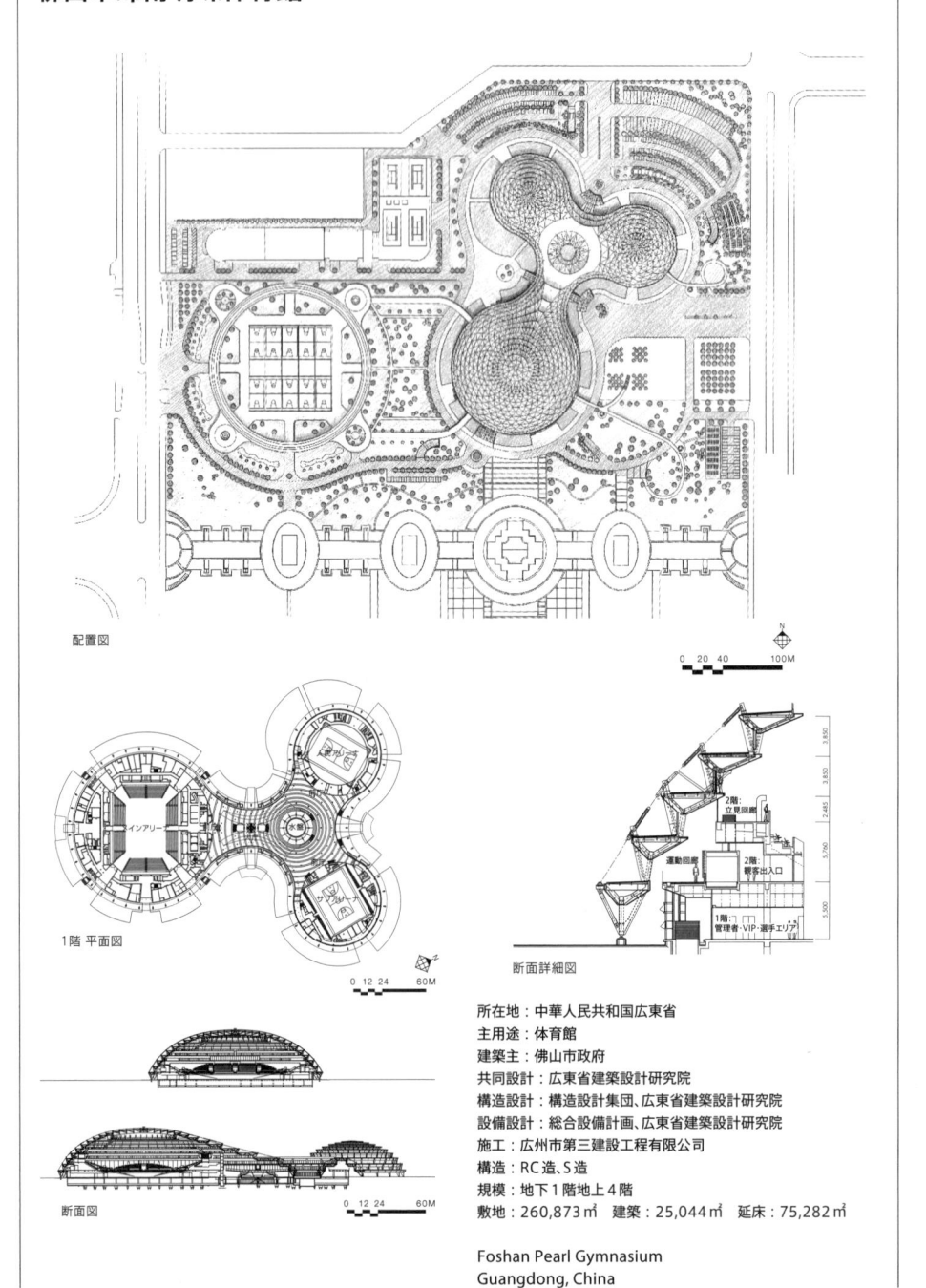

配置図

1階 平面図

断面詳細図

断面図

所在地：中華人民共和国広東省
主用途：体育館
建築主：佛山市政府
共同設計：広東省建築設計研究院
構造設計：構造設計集団、広東省建築設計研究院
設備設計：総合設備計画、広東省建築設計研究院
施工：広州市第三建設工程有限公司
構造：RC造、S造
規模：地下1階地上4階
敷地：260,873㎡　建築：25,044㎡　延床：75,282㎡

Foshan Pearl Gymnasium
Guangdong, China

2005.10
上海旗忠森林体育城テニスセンター

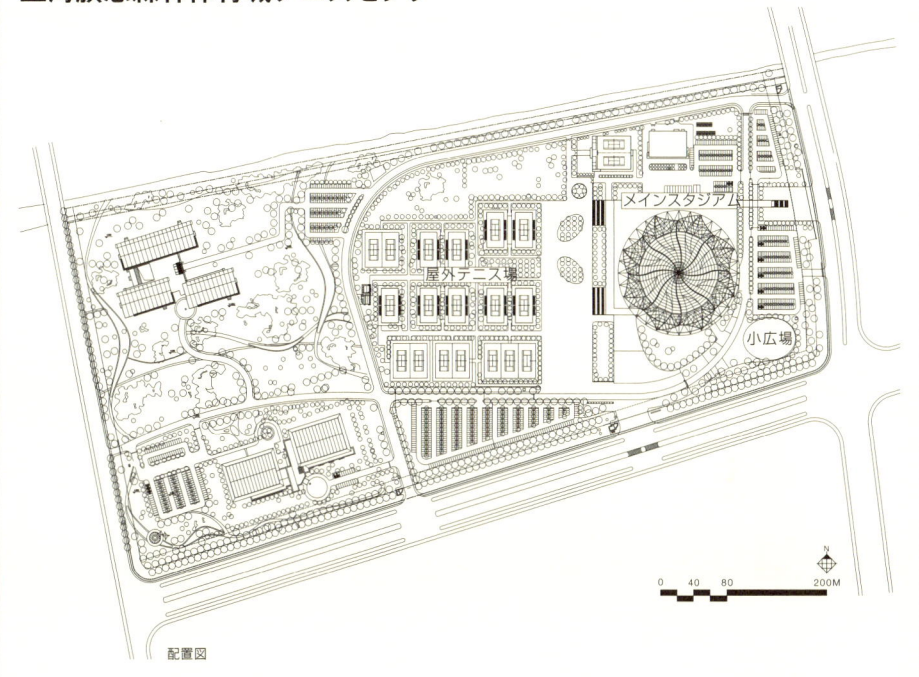

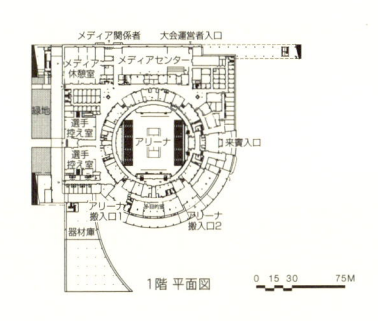

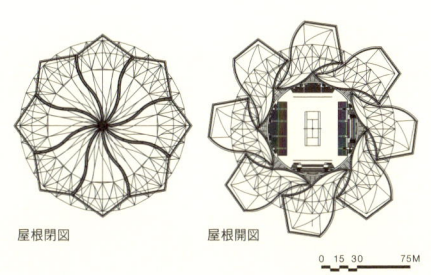

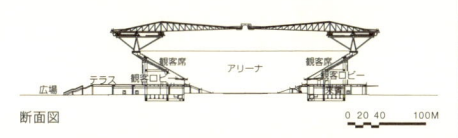

配置図

1階 平面図

断面図

屋根閉図 屋根開図

所在地：中華人民共和国上海市
主用途：可動屋根付テニス場
建築主：上海旗忠森林体育場有限公司
共同設計：佐藤尚巳建築研究所（方案及び初歩設計顧問、施工図設計：上海建築設計研究院有限公司）
構造設計：構造設計集団(SDG)、上海建築設計研究院有限公司
設備設計：総合設備計画、三菱重工業神戸造船所鉄構部（屋根開閉機構）、上海建築設計研究院有限公司
施工：中国建築第三工程局、北京特殊工程設計研究院、江南重工股分有限公司
構造：RC造、S造
規模：地上4階
敷地：202,526㎡　建築：23,880㎡　延床：36,010㎡

Shanghai Qizhong Forest Sports City Tennis Center
Shanghai, China

2005.07
浪速スポーツセンター

浪速スポーツセンター・浪速屋内プール・アイススケート場・浪速区在宅サービスセンター

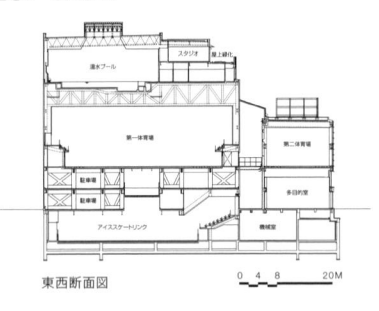

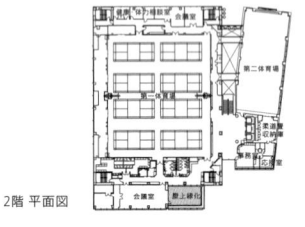

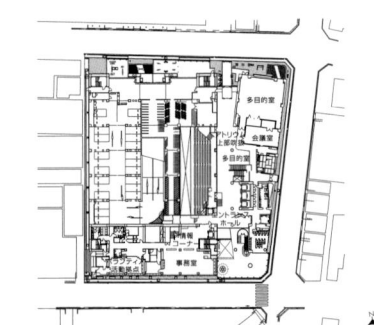

東西断面図

2階 平面図

配置図兼 1階 平面図

所在地：大阪府大阪市浪速区難波中
主用途：アイススケート場、多目的ホール、体育場、温水プール、フィットネス、マシンジム、在宅サービス
建築主：大阪市、社会福祉法人浪速区社会福祉協議会
構造設計：構造計画研究所、金箱構造設計事務所
設備設計：総合設備計画、新日本設備計画
施工：大林・三井住友・南海辰村 JV
構造：SRC造一部RC造
規模：地下1階地上7階
敷地：4,662㎡　建築：3,831㎡　延床：18,356㎡

Naniwa Sports Center, Swimming Pool, Ice Skating Link, Home Service Center
Nanbanaka, Naniwa-ku, Osaka-shi, Osaka

2005.11
よつば循環器科クリニック

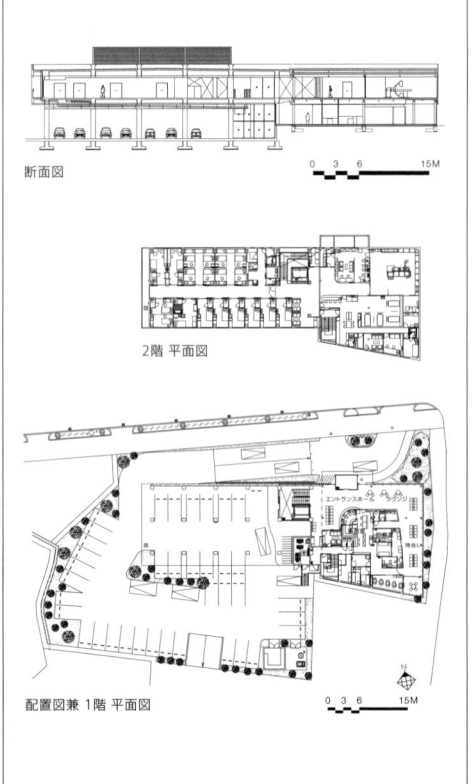

断面図

2階 平面図

配置図兼 1階 平面図

所在地：愛媛県松山市南江戸
主用途：診療所
建築主：医療法人松山ハートセンター
構造設計：構造計画研究所
設備設計：日永設計
施工：堀田建設
構造：RC造、S造
規模：地上2階
敷地：2,451㎡　建築：898㎡　延床：1,687㎡

Yotsuba Circulation Clinic
Minamiedo, Matsuyama-shi, Ehime

2005.03
こばと幼稚園絵本館

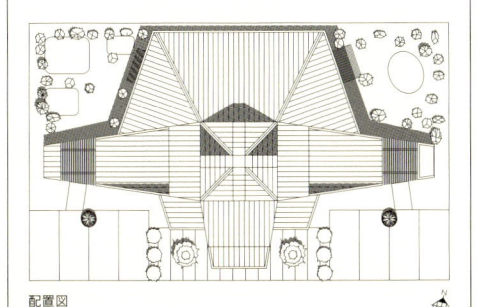

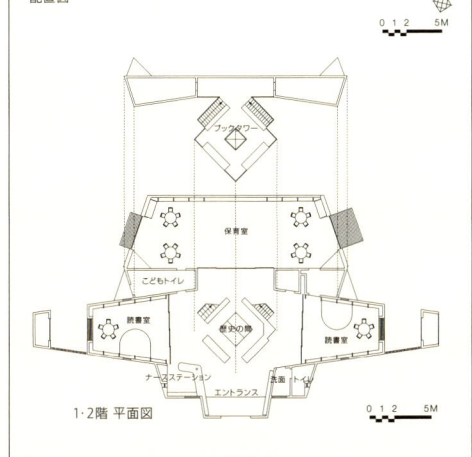

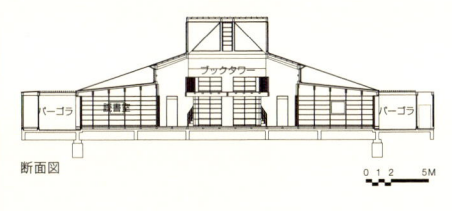

配置図

1・2階 平面図

断面図

所在地：岐阜県岐阜市鹿島町
主用途：絵本館
建築主：学校法人加納学園
構造設計：金箱構造設計事務所
設備設計：日永設計
施工：東建設
構造：W造
規模：地上2階
敷地：674㎡　建築：270㎡　延床：321㎡

Kobato Children's Library
Kashima-cho, Gifu-shi, Gifu

2005.03
ゆうゆうのもり幼保園

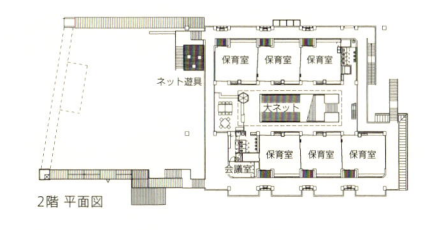

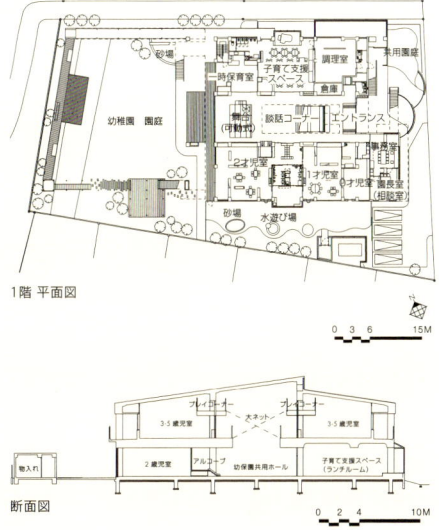

2階 平面図

1階 平面図

断面図

所在地：神奈川県横浜市都筑区早渕
主用途：こども園
建築主：社会福祉法人光と風の村、学校法人渡辺学園
構造設計：金箱構造設計事務所
設備設計：日永設計
施工：馬淵建設
構造：RC造
規模：地上2階
敷地：2,434㎡　建築：963㎡　延床：1,540㎡

Yuyu-no-Mori Nursery School and Day Nursery
Hayabuchi, Tsuzuki-ku, Yokohama-shi, Kanagawa

2004

福井まちなか文化施設［響のホール］

Fukui Cultural Complex "Hibiki Hall"

街路をつなぐ劇場

福井まちなか文化施設
［響のホール］

福井県福井市中央／2004
Fukui Cultural Complex "Hibiki Hall"
Chuo, Fukui-shi, Fukui

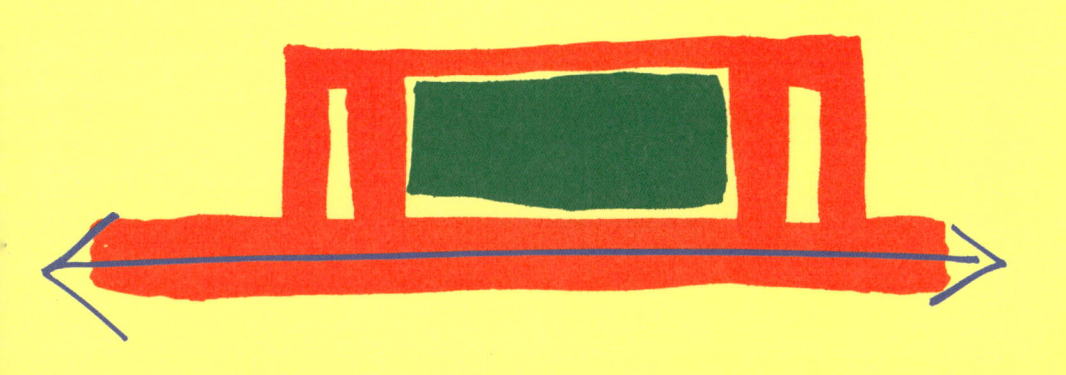

福井市の中心街活性化策として、空きビル跡地に「市民が集まり文化活動をすすめられる」新しいタイプの文化施設として、本施設は計画された。230席の高機能多目的小ホールを中心に、市民の演劇、音楽の練習場や市民ギャラリーに加えて、市民が集い、楽しみ、交流できるような溜まり場ともなるカフェが設けられた。1階は南北の大通りをつなぐ通り抜けの通路が設けられ、それにカフェとギャラリーが寄り添い、多くの市民利用でいつも賑わいをみせている。

As a measure to activate city life in the center of town, Fukui City rebuilt an unused building into a new type of cultural facility where "the citizens can gather and enjoy cultural activities". Centered on a small, 230-seat multi-functional hall, in addition to a place for citizen performances, music practice, and a citizen gallery, a café is located on the first floor so that people can gather, talk and exchange information. The outside of the building looks like a gate to the entrance of a theater, and there also is a passageway that connects the main streets on the south and north sides.

2004

福井まちなか文化施設［響のホール］

Fukui Cultural Complex "Hibiki Hall"

客席の幅8m、230席
The 8m-wide audience seats; 230 seats.

2004

福井まちなか文化施設［響のホール］

Fukui Cultural Complex "Hibiki Hall"

1階は通り抜けレストラン
The first floor is a restaurant that we can pass through.

HEALTH PARK

2004

健康パークあざい　Wellness Park Azai

健康パークあざい

滋賀県長浜市野瀬町／2004
Wellness Park Azai
Nose-cho, Nagahama-shi, Shiga

健康をテーマとした地域住民のための町立（現：長浜市）の複合施設である。町並みに合わせた切妻屋根を持ち、外壁はこの地域の伝統的民家に多く用いられる深い紅殻色としている。一部2階はあるが、ほとんど平屋で、町民のための診療所、温浴施設、屋外のスポーツ施設で構成されている。全体が遊環構造的に連携し、あらゆる世代の町民が元気で生き生きと暮らすための健康・生きがい・保健・福祉の拠点となることが目指されている。

This is a multi-functional facility run by the city that constructed for local residents with "health" as the theme. With gable roofing to match the surrounding town, the outside walls were painted a deep red, which is traditionally used on many houses in the region. There is a partial second floor, but the facility is mostly single-level, and is composed of a clinic, bathing facility, and sports facility for residents. The overall facility is connected like a circular play system, aiming to be a center to promote health, meaningful living, and welfare for townspeople of all generations so that they can live active lives.

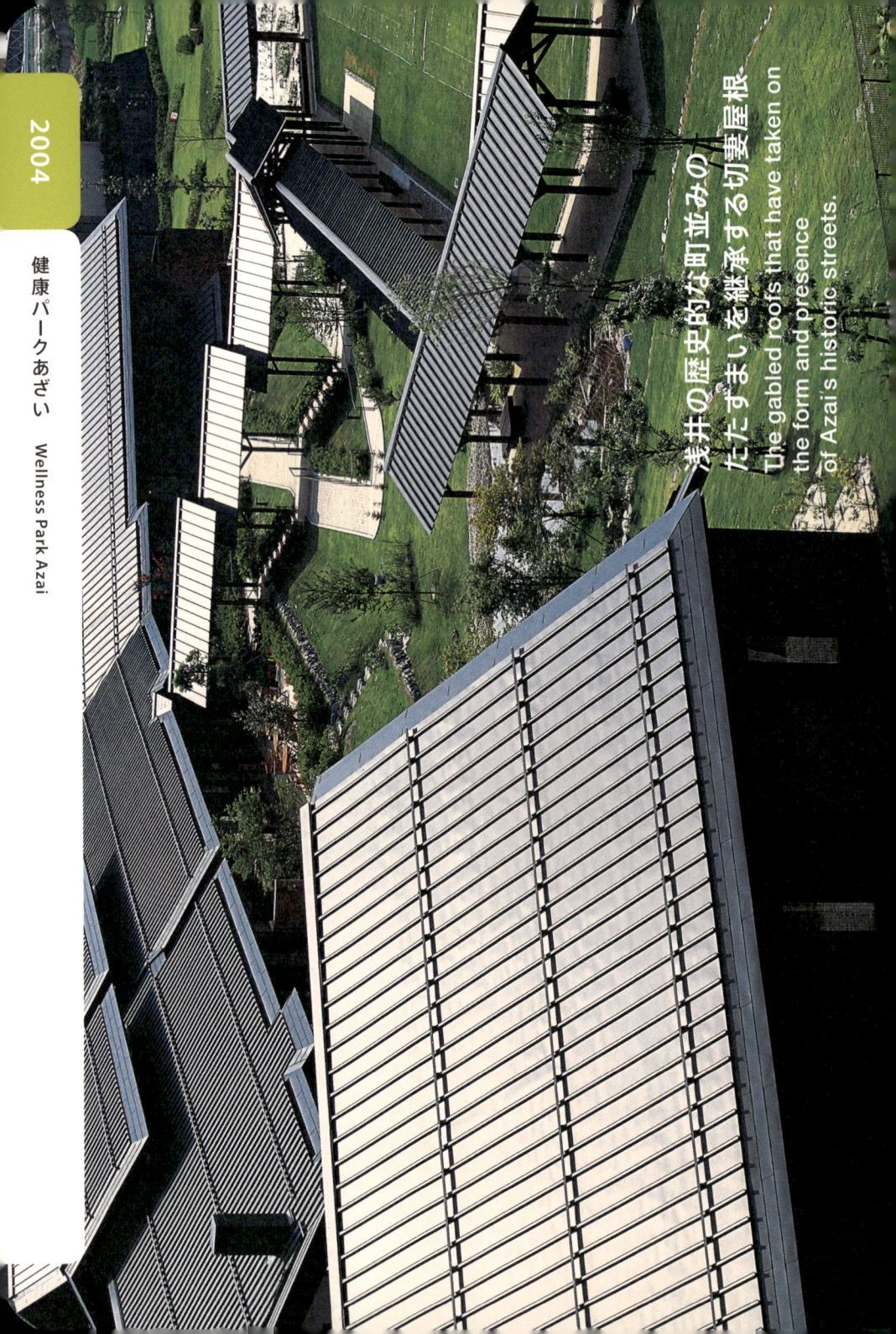

2004

健康パークあざい　Wellness Park Azai

浅井の歴史的な町並みの
たたずまいを継承する切妻屋根

The gabled roofs that have taken on
the form and presence
of Azai's historic streets.

谷あいの風景に
つくられた健康回廊

A health galleria was made in a valley landscape.

2004

健康パークあざい　Wellness Park Azai

279

2004

健康パークあざい　Wellness Park Azai

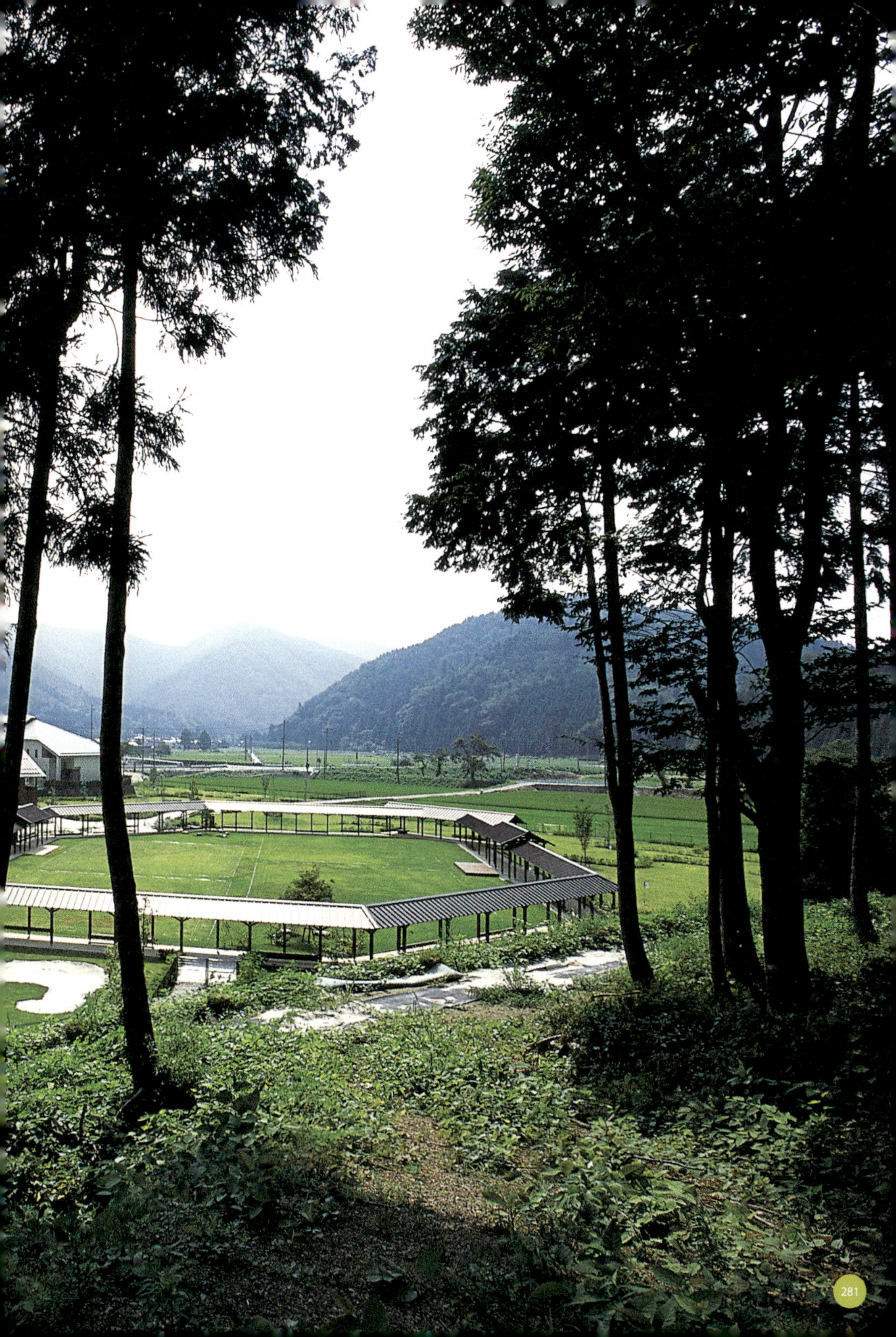

2004

やすらぎの杜
Yasuragi-no-Mori

自立のための家

やすらぎの杜

東京都練馬区関町／2004
Yasuragi-no-Mori
Seki-machi, Nerima-ku, Tokyo

閑静な住宅街に位置する、民設民営の知的障害者援護施設（入所更生・通所授産施設）である。知的障害を持つ人達に楽しく働く場所と豊かな生活を提供し、将来的に地域での自立が可能となるよう、地域に開かれた施設となっている。建築、外構、運営が一体となり、遊環構造理論が応用された新しい障害者福祉施設のモデルとして計画されている。

Located in a quiet residential area, this is a privately run facility for the intellectually challenged (rehabilitation and vocational aid center). It provides people with intellectually impairments a fun place to work and a space to lead a fruitful life. The facility was designed to be open to the community so as to assist people in becoming independent members of the community in the future. The architecture, outside construction, and operations are all linked together, making this a new model for facilities for the intellectually challenged by applying of circular play system theory.

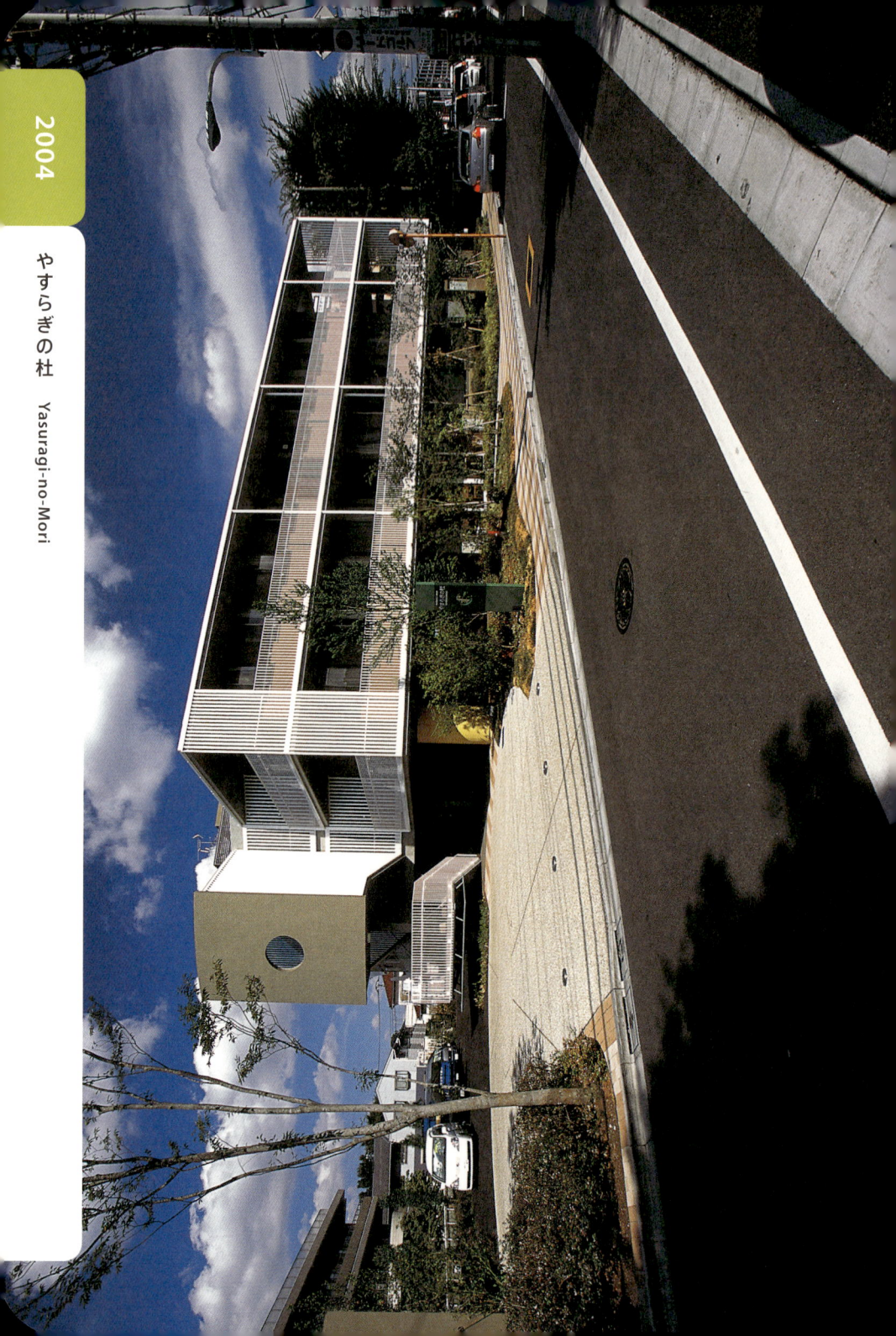

2004

やすらぎの杜

Yasuragi-no-Mori

町に張り出すテラスは、
障害者の施設としての垣根を取り外す

The terrace, which hangs over the streets, removes the barriers between this facility for the disabled and the outside world.

2004

やすらぎの杜　Yasuragi-no-Mori

楽しい空間こそが必要
An enjoyable space is all the more essential.

| 2003

ふじえだファミリークリニック
Fujieda Family Clinic

あそべる クリニック

ふじえだ
ファミリークリニック

愛媛県四国中央市中曽根町／2003
Fujieda Family Clinic
Nakazone-cho, Shikokuchuo-shi, Ehime

小児科、皮膚科の専門医による2科診療所、病後児保育施設に医師の自宅を併設した複合施設である。限られた敷地の中に広く庭を確保し、複合遊具を設置するなど、こども達が待ち時間に退屈しないような仕掛けがちりばめられている。

This facility is a combination of a pediatrics and dermatology clinic, as well as a facility for children's recovery facility, and the doctor's residence. A large garden was made in the site with a limited area, and by installing play structures, the children can wait for their turn without becoming bored.

2003

ふじえだファミリークリニック　Fujieda Family Clinic

291

2003

わかくさ保育園
Wakakusa Day Nursery

もうひとつの家、
もうひとりの父母

わかくさ保育園

東京都昭島市玉川町／2003
Wakakusa Day Nursery
Tamagawa-cho, Akishima-shi, Tokyo

昭島市の住宅街に立地する園児数約160人の保育園。「もうひとつの家、もうひとりの父・母」を保育理念に、古木の桜の木を中心として立体的で動的な活動空間となる廊下が遊環構造的にかつ連続的に配置されている。こども達の自由かつ多様な活動を可能にしている。

This is a nursery for about 160 children, located in a residential area in Akishima city. Based on the nursery ideology of it being "a home away from home, and my other father and mother", corridors are located to give the facility a continuous space to enable children to move freely and in a variety of activities.

2003

わかくさ保育園 Wakakusa Day Nursery

内部はやさしい色使いで統一され、
こども達の動きが彩りをそえる

The interior is decorated with a uniform color scheme of gentle colors, adding beauty and color to the children's movements.

295

森の大屋根広場

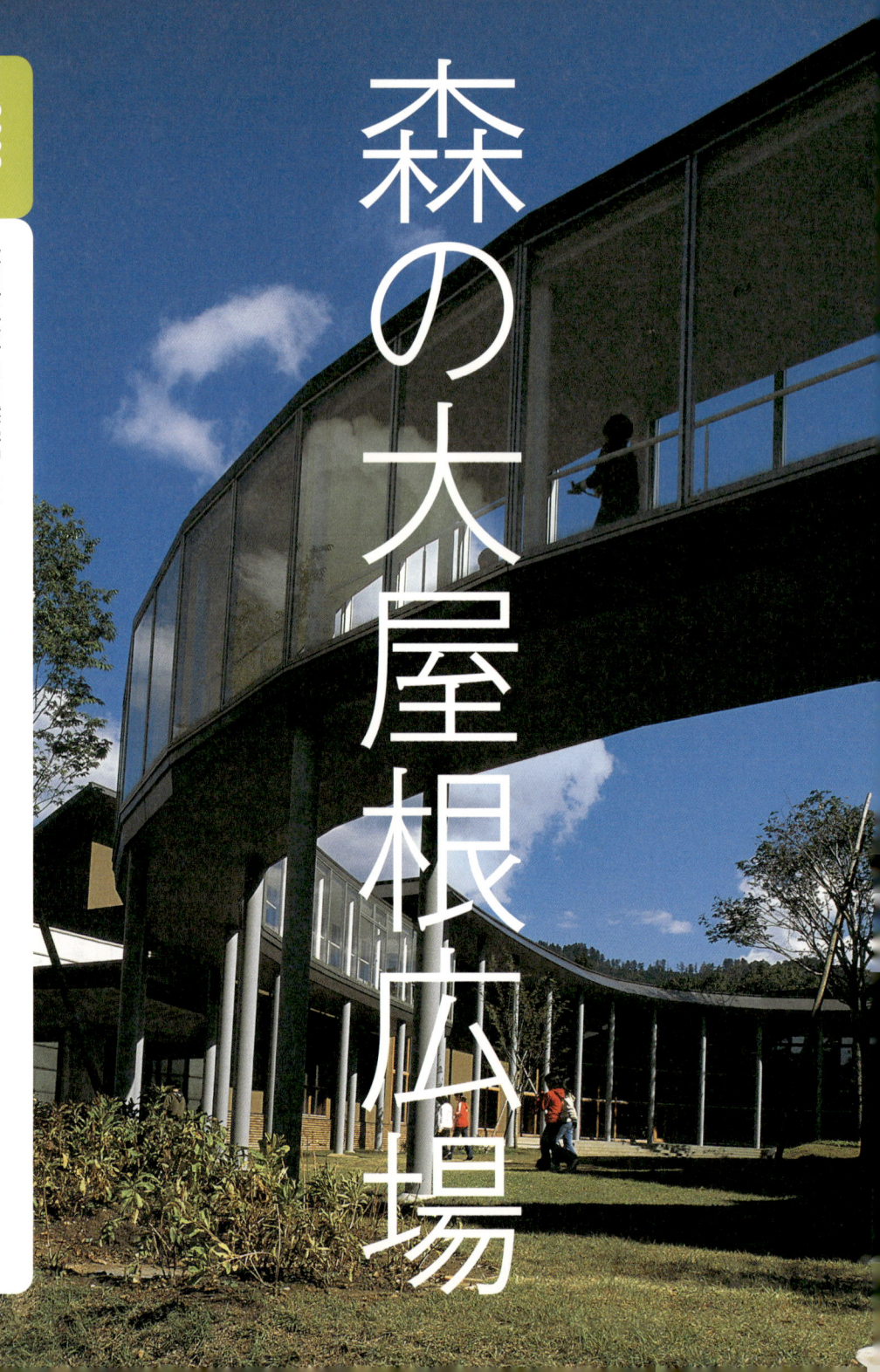

2003

秋田市太平山自然学習センター
Akita Taiheizan Nature Learning Center

秋田市太平山自然学習センター

秋田県秋田市仁別／2003
Akita Taiheizan Nature Learning Center
Nibetsu, Akita-shi, Akita

自然とのふれあいや野外活動・創作活動を通じ、青少年の健全な育成と市民のための生涯学習施設として計画された。大屋根広場をシンボル空間として設置し、宿泊・活動施設と大屋根広場を連絡ブリッジで結んで、一体的な生活空間として形成され、自然体験と共同体験の連続的な体験が意図されている。

This center was constructed with the plan of providing a space to ensure the healthy nurturing of youths and continuing education for citizens by spending time in a natural environment, doing outdoor activities, and engaging creative activities. A large space was created on the roof as a sort of symbol of the facility. The large room space is connected by a bridge to the lodging and activities facility to form a unified living space and allow for joint experiences and activities with nature.

2003

秋田市太平山自然学習センター　Akita Taiheizan Nature Learning Center

299

2003

秋田市太平山自然学習センター

Akita Taiheizan Nature Learning Center

宿泊・活動施設と大屋根、そして広場をつなぐブリッジ

A bridge connecting the dormitory, activity facilities, and large roof to the square.

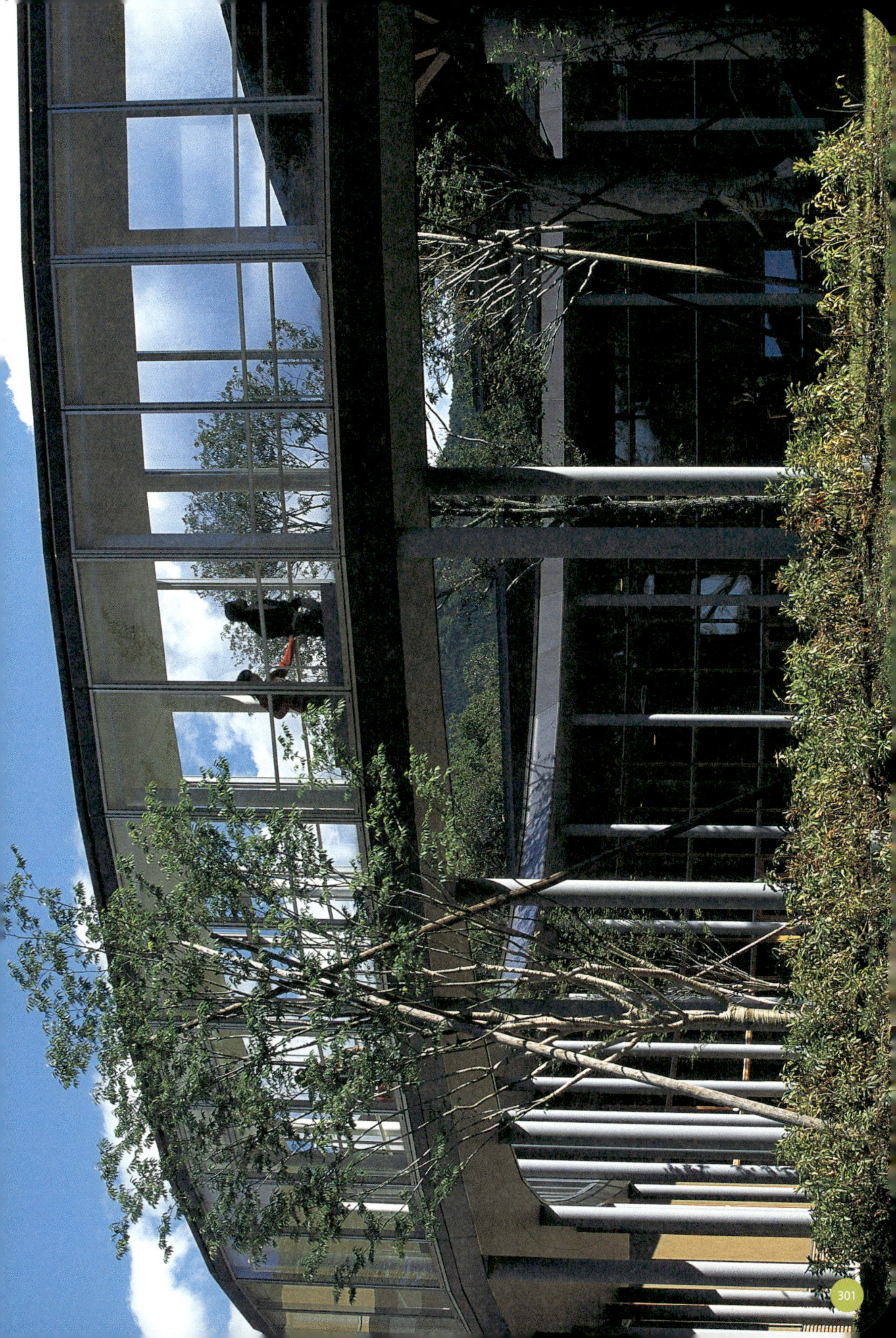

2003

秋田市太平山自然学習センター
Akita Taiheizan Nature Learning Center

縦横に積まれた３層のベッドは
こども達のわくわく感を増す
The three-layered beds laid out vertically and horizontally
make the place even more exciting for the children.

2003

関門海峡ミュージアム　Kaikyo Dramaship

海峡ドラマシップ

関門海峡ミュージアム

福岡県北九州市門司区西海岸／2003
Kaikyo Dramaship
Nishikaigan, Moji-ku, Kitakyusyu-shi, Fukuoka

関門海峡の過去・現在・未来を紹介する観光拠点機能を持つ文化施設で、2つの立体的遊環構造で構成されている。海峡側は船をモチーフとしたガラスの建築「ドラマシップ」とし、門司港の未来を象徴している。内陸側は既存の歴史的建築との連続性を意識したアールデコ調のファサード「レトロボックス」とし、門司港の過去を象徴している。入館者は中央の巨大アトリウムの周囲を巡る展示空間を、海峡の歴史ドラマを体験しながら上部へと上がっていく。歴史展示は、国内第一級の人形作家の作品で歴史上のトピックが再現され、人形の博物館としても注目されている。

This is a cultural facility as well as a tourist spot, which introduces the past, present and future of the Kanmon Straits based on the circular play system. The outside of the building has a different image depending on which side is seen. The side facing the straits is "Dramaship", a glass structure in the shape of a ship, and this characterizes the future of Moji port. The opposite land side is the "Retrobox", with an art déco façade, it is a continuum of existing historical architecture, characterizing the past of Moji port. Guests experience the drama of the history of the straits by viewing the exhibitions that surround the atrium.

2003

関門海峡ミュージアム　Kaikyo Dramaship

関門海峡はドラマの海峡
The Kanmon Straits is full of drama.

307

2003

関門海峡ミュージアム
Kaikyo Dramaship

山側のレトロボックスと海側のドラマシップ
The "Retrobox" on the side of the mountain, and the "Dramaship" on the side of the sea.

309

2003

関門海峡ミュージアム　Kaikyo Dramaship

海の中のあそび場
A playground in the sea.

2003

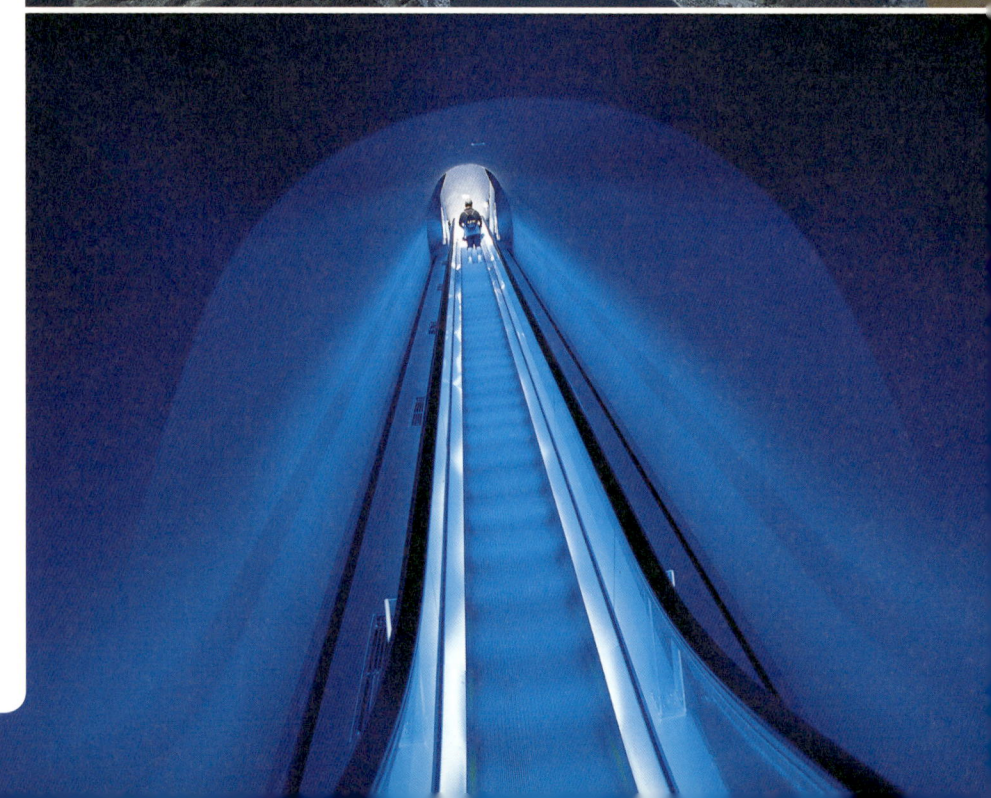

関門海峡ミュージアム
Kaikyo Dramaship

日本第一級の人形作家による歴史ドラマ展示
An exhibition showing a historical drama created by a first-class doll-maker in Japan.

2003

関門海峡ミュージアム　Kaikyo Dramaship

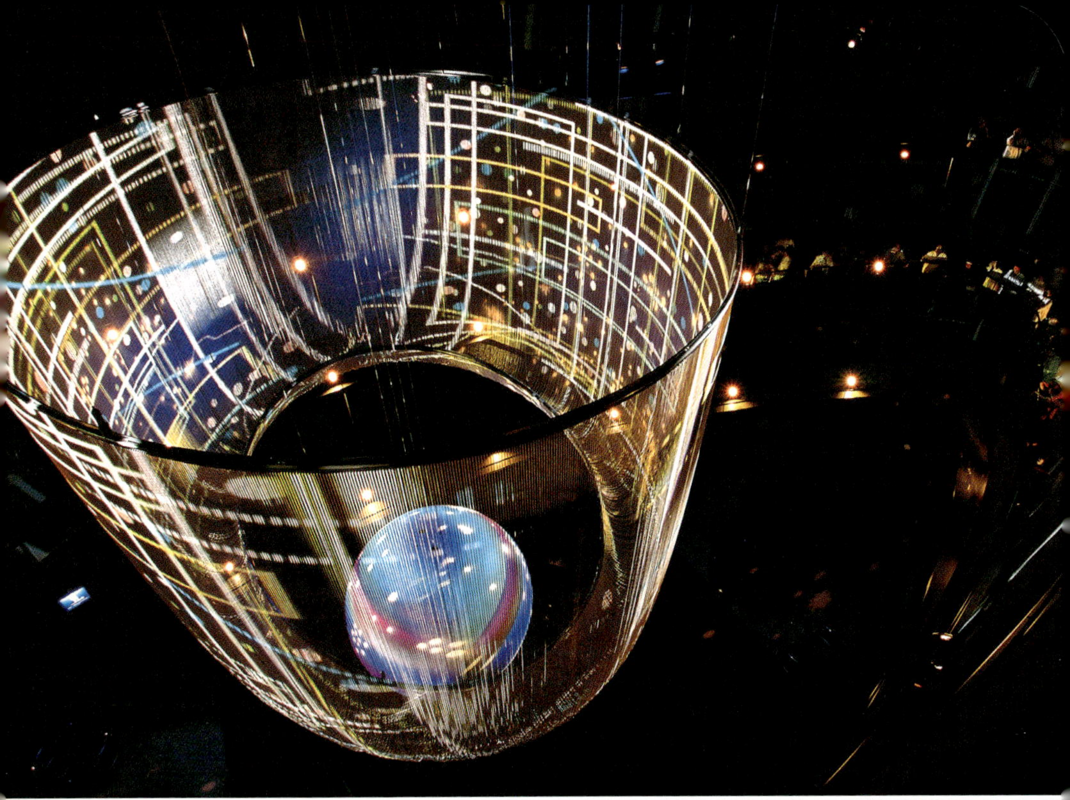

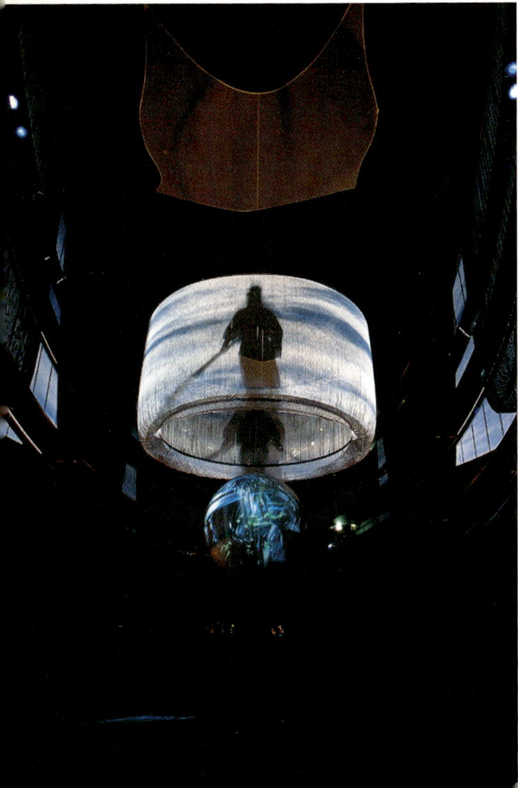

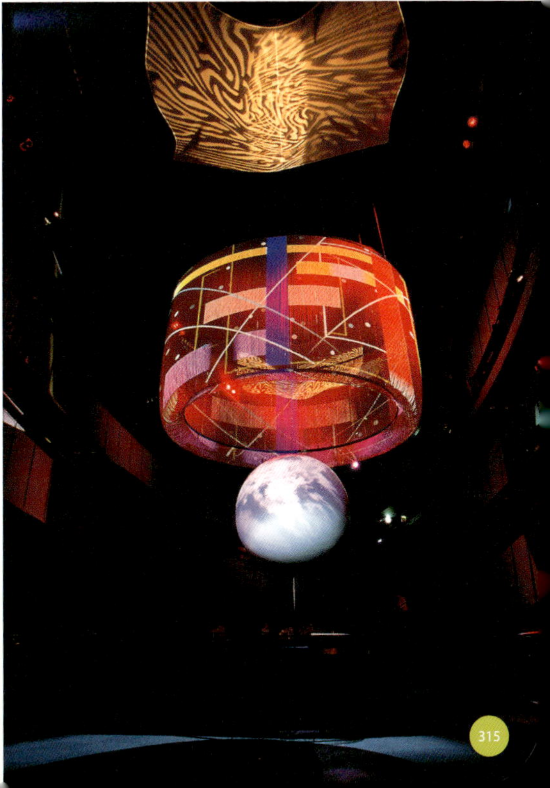

2000, 2002

タイムトンネル

きききのつりはし＋御所野縄文博物館

Bridge Kikiki + Goshono Jomon Museum

きききのつりはし＋
御所野縄文博物館

岩手県二戸郡一戸町／2000, 2002
Bridge Kikiki + Goshono Jomon Museum
Ichinohe-cho, Ninohe-gun, Iwate

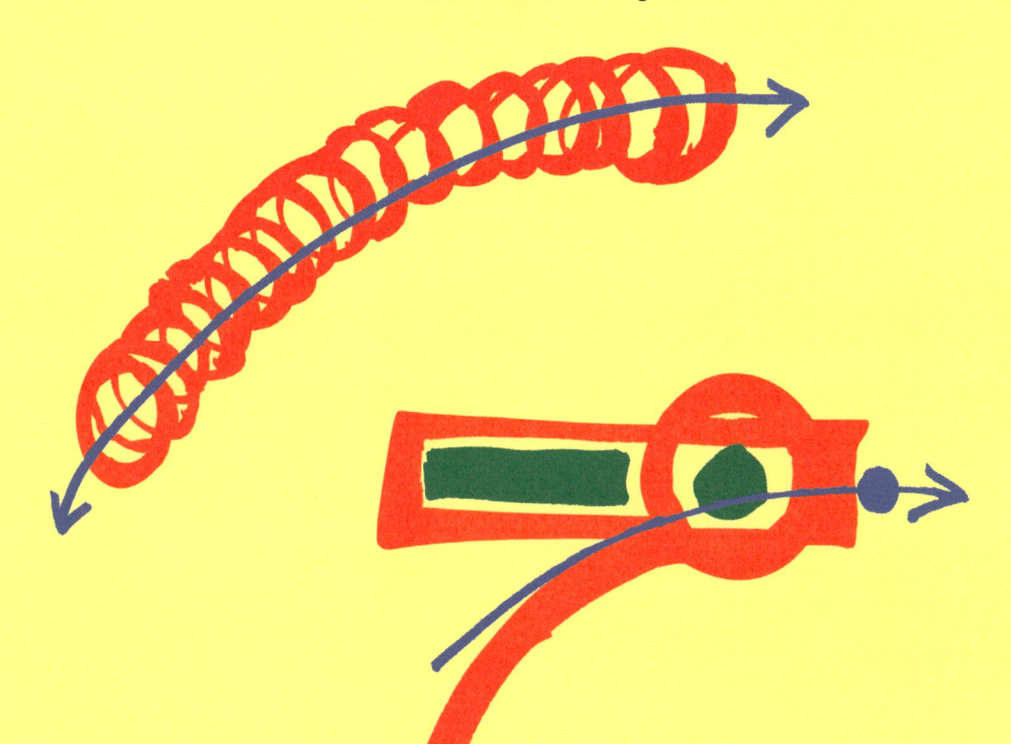

谷を挟んで立地する遺跡公園と駐車場を結ぶための歩道橋。ただ人が渡るためだけでなく、谷の向こうにある数千年前の縄文時代の景観に向かうためのタイムトリップ装置としても機能する。弧になって曲がっているため見通しのきかない不安と期待を喚起し、外光の入る明るい部分と板張りの暗い部分が交互に体験することで、時間を圧縮した感覚を味わうことができる。博物館は主にこの遺跡公園ガイドとなる展示棟と収蔵庫棟からなる遊環構造による平面計画で、公園側からなるべく姿を隠すように配置され、屋根には芝生が被せられている。

This bridge connects a park decorated with ancient ruins set across the valley from the parking lot. However, this is not a normal bridge. Rather, it is almost like a time machine that takes people across the valley to the landscapes of the Jomon Period from thousands of years ago. The museum is a flat structure based on circular play system comprising an exhibition building, which serves as a guide for the park, and a storage building. It is situated so as to conceal its presence as much as possible from the park, and there is a grass area on the roof.

2000, 2002

ききのつりはし＋御所野縄文博物館

Bridge Kikiki + Goshono Jomon Museum

319

2000, 2002

きききのつりはし＋御所野縄文博物館

Bridge Kikiki + Goshono Jomon Museum

直径2.7m、長さ86.5mの
大きく円弧を描く木のつりはし
A wooden bridge that inscribes
a large arc 2.7m in diameter and 86.5m long.

321

2000, 2002

kikiki のつりはし ＋ 御所野縄文博物館

Bridge Kikiki + Goshono Jomon Museum

博物館本館は、木々の間から復元住居を見る
The main building of the museum looks at
restored residences from among the trees.

2000, 2002

きききのつりはし＋御所野縄文博物館

Bridge Kikiki + Goshono Jomon Museum

325

2002

東京工業大学大学会館［すずかけホール］

Tokyo Institute of Technology "Suzukake Hall"

キャンパスドーム

東京工業大学大学会館
[すずかけホール]

神奈川県横浜市緑区長津田町／2002
Tokyo Institute of Technology "Suzukake Hall"
Nagatsuda-cho, Midori-ku, Yokohama-shi, Kanagawa

東京工業大学すずかけ台キャンパスの新しい核として計画、設計された。特徴的な屋根架構をもった食堂機能としてのH1棟、生協売店、会議室や多目的ホールのあるH2棟から構成されており、ラウンジ機能をもつ空中のブリッジにより連続されている。食堂棟最上部はレセプションホールで、屋根はワイヤーによるテンション構造で重層化された形式をもつ。

This facility was planned and designed as the new center of Suzukakedai Campus of the Tokyo Institute of Technology. It consists of the H1 building, which functions as a cafeteria and has a uniquely framed roof, and the H2 building, which houses the co-op, meeting rooms, and a multi-purpose hall. These two buildings are connected by a bridge that functions as a lounge. The top floor of the cafeteria is a reception hall whose roof is made to be multilayered using a wired tension structure.

2002

東京工業大学大学会館［すずかけホール］

Tokyo Institute of Technology "Suzukake Hall"

329

2002

弘法湯
Bath House "Kobo-Yu"

交流銭湯

弘法湯

石川県七尾市北藤橋町／2002
Bath House "Kobo-Yu"
Kitafujihashi-machi, Nanao-shi, Ishikawa

能登半島の入口に位置する七尾市の大衆浴場。1階部分は浴場、2階部分は経営者の住居である。浴場は更衣室部分と浴場を中庭を挟んで対置させ、中庭の美しい湧水によってゆったりとした心身の開放感を促す空間演出が意図された。

This is a public bath house in Nanao city, located at the entrance to Noto Peninsula. On the first floor is the bath, and the owner's residence is on the second floor. A courtyard is placed between the changing room and bath, and this courtyard creates a space that provides beauty and peace to the people who come to bathe.

2002

弘法湯　Bath House "Kobo-Yu"

333

2002

里山の幼稚園

ほうとく幼稚園
Houtoku Kindergarten

ほうとく幼稚園

福島県いわき市後田町／2002
Houtoku Kindergarten
Ushiroda-machi, Iwaki-shi, Fukushima

「家族といっしょ」という理念を掲げるお寺の運営による幼稚園である。その理念に配慮して新園舎と保育センターは「村」としていくつかの小さな棟に分節化し、家並みのような空間を構成させている。そして山の上のあそび場を含め、斜面いっぱいに遊環構造によるこども達の元気村「ほうとくファーム」が形成されている。

This kindergarten is run by a temple under the theme "togetherness with family." With that theme in mind, the new school building and nursery centers are dispersed throughout the grounds to form a "village," creating a space similar to a small town. There is also a playground on top of a hill, making this an area full of fun for children via its circular play system with numerous hills.

2002

ほうとく幼稚園
Houtoku Kindergarten

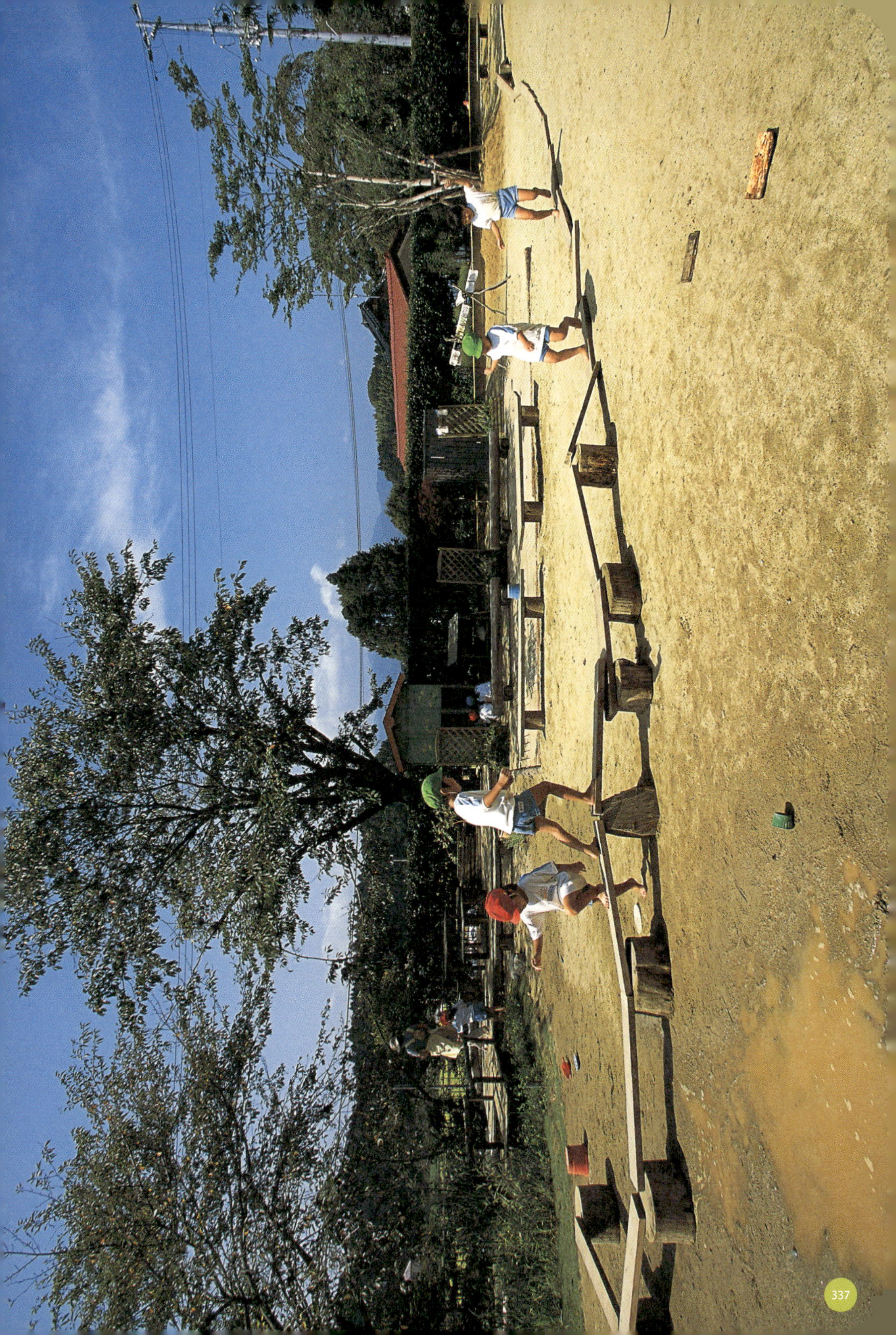

2002

ほうとく幼稚園 Houtoku Kindergarten

339

2002

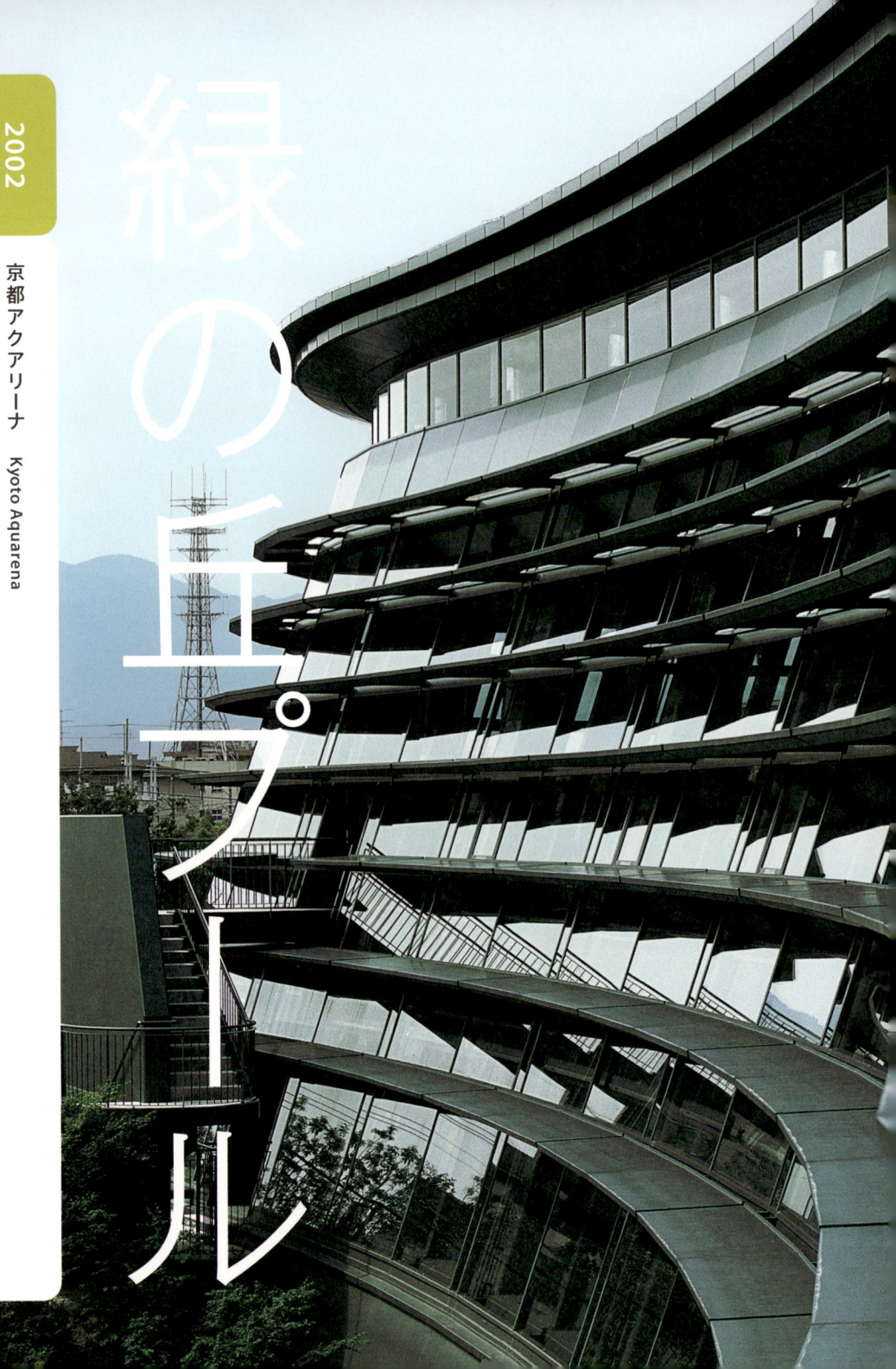

緑の丘プール

京都アクアリーナ　Kyoto Aquarena

京都アクアリーナ

京都府京都市右京区西京極徳大寺団子田町／2002
Kyoto Aquarena
Nishikyogokutokudaijidangoden-machi, Ukyo-ku, Kyoto-shi, Kyoto

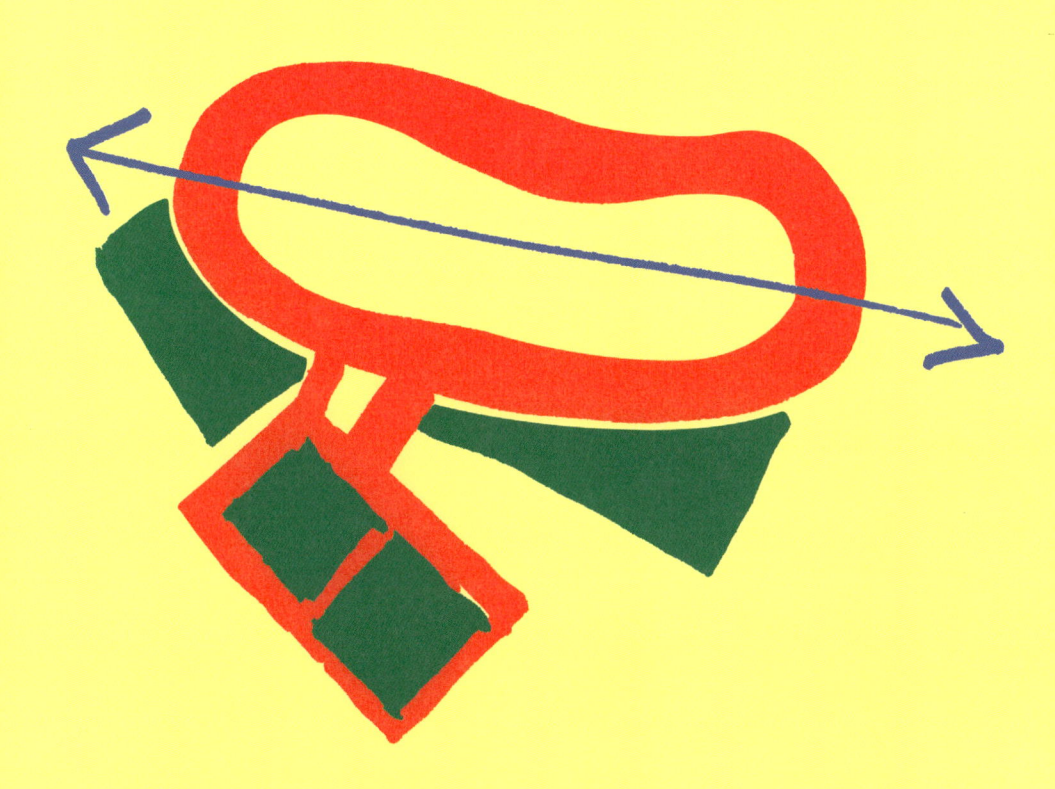

1998年京都市が行った公募型プロポーザルで最優秀案として選定された。敷地は既設西京極総合運動公園の北側、阪急電車京都線をまたいだ3.6ヘクタールの敷地に位置し、国際B級公認プールである。メインプール棟の屋上には太陽熱パネル、サブプール棟には太陽光パネルが装備され、それ以外の屋根部分は緑の丘と称して全面的に緑化されている。重い屋根は免震構造が搭載され、自然エネルギーの徹底活用と同時に公園部分との一体化が図られている。平面的にも立体的にも遊環構造建築であると同時に、21世紀最初の地球環境建築として位置づけられている。

It is an international B-grade certified pool in Kyoto. The roof of the main pool is covered with solar heat paneling and the roof of the sub pool is covered with solar light paneling. All of the other rooftops have been totally covered with greenery and are called the "green hill." The heavy roofing provides earthquake absorbing function, serves as an energy-saving measure, and also appears as if it is a part of the park. The structure with circular play system exists on both a flat and three-dimensional planes, and is one of the first global environment architecture pieces of the 21st century.

2002

京都アクアリーナ　Kyoto Aquarena

多重な庇は伝統的な環境調整装置
The multiple eaves are traditional devices that help us to regulate the environment.

2002

京都アクアリーナ　Kyoto Aquarena

345

2002

京都アクアリーナ　Kyoto Aquarena

メインアリーナとサブアリーナをつなぐ空中ブリッジ
Bridges suspended in mid-air, linking the main and sub-pools.

347

2002

メインプールの屋根には
3,000m²の太陽熱パネルと屋根免震を装備
The roof of the main pool is seismic isolated and equipped with 3,000m² of solar panels.

京都アクアリーナ　Kyoto Aquarena

サブプールにはこどものあそびプールが付属する
A play pool for kids is attached to the sub-pool.

2002

京都アクアリーナ　Kyoto Aquarena

サブプールの屋根には500㎡の太陽光パネルを搭載

500㎡ of solar panels have been installed on the roof of the sub-pool.

出会いの海

2001

アクアワールド大洗水族館

Oarai Aquarium "Aqua World"

アクアワールド大洗水族館

茨城県東茨城郡大洗町／2001
Oarai Aquarium "Aqua World"
Oarai-machi, Higashiibaraki-gun, Ibaraki

大洗の海＝出会いの海を中心テーマに、動線のストーリーに沿った水槽テーマを建築空間の中に立体的に組み込み、目前に広がる大洗の海から鹿島灘、世界の海、水源をたどり、再び大洗の海へ戻る空間構成を実現させ、それを空間の明暗の変化の演出とも整合させている。
また、参加性の高い演出要素やワークショップを取り込み、こども・ファミリーのための魚の遊具ゾーン、魅力的な物販・飲食ゾーンを持つ遊環構造総合水族館として高い集客力を誇っている。

Based on the theme "the ocean of Oarai is an ocean of encounters," fish tanks that proceed according to a story are lined in the architectural space. The aquarium's theme follows the movement of water from the Oarai, to Kashima, to the seas of the world, and back to Oarai, illustrating the journey by changing the presentation's lighting throughout.
Also, we incorporated events that visitors can participate in as well as workshops, a fish play zone, and an shop and food court. This circular play system serves as a comprehensive aquarium and attracts large amounts of visitors regularly.

2001

アクアワールド大洗水族館

Oarai Aquarium "Aqua World"

大洗の海は波高い太平洋で、
サーファーという生物を観察できる

The high waves of the Oarai seas in the Pacific Ocean
allows one to observe a species
of living thing known as "surfer."

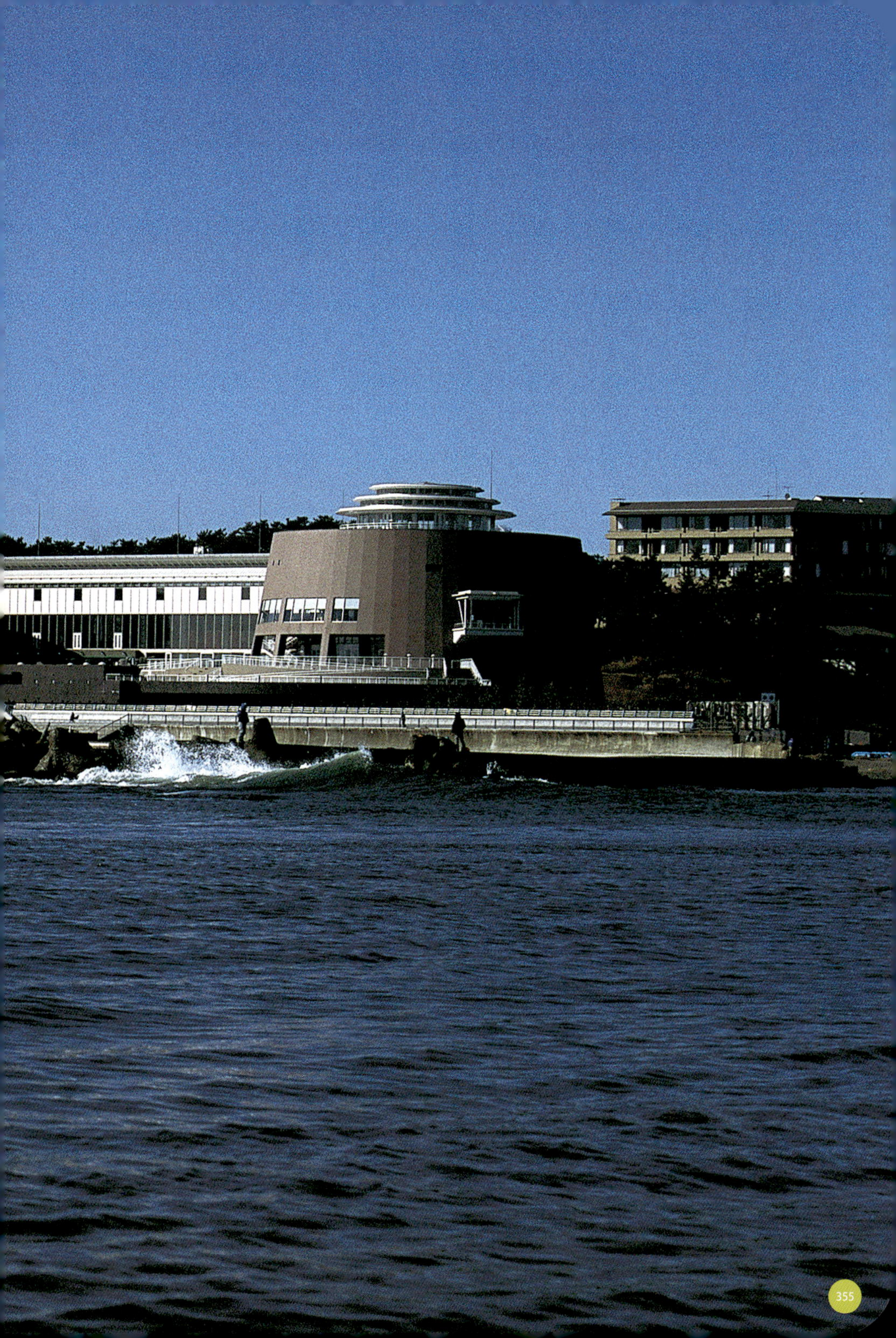

2001

大洗の海に開放する水族館
An aquarium that opens into the Oarai seas.

アクアワールド大洗水族館

Oarai Aquarium "Aqua World"

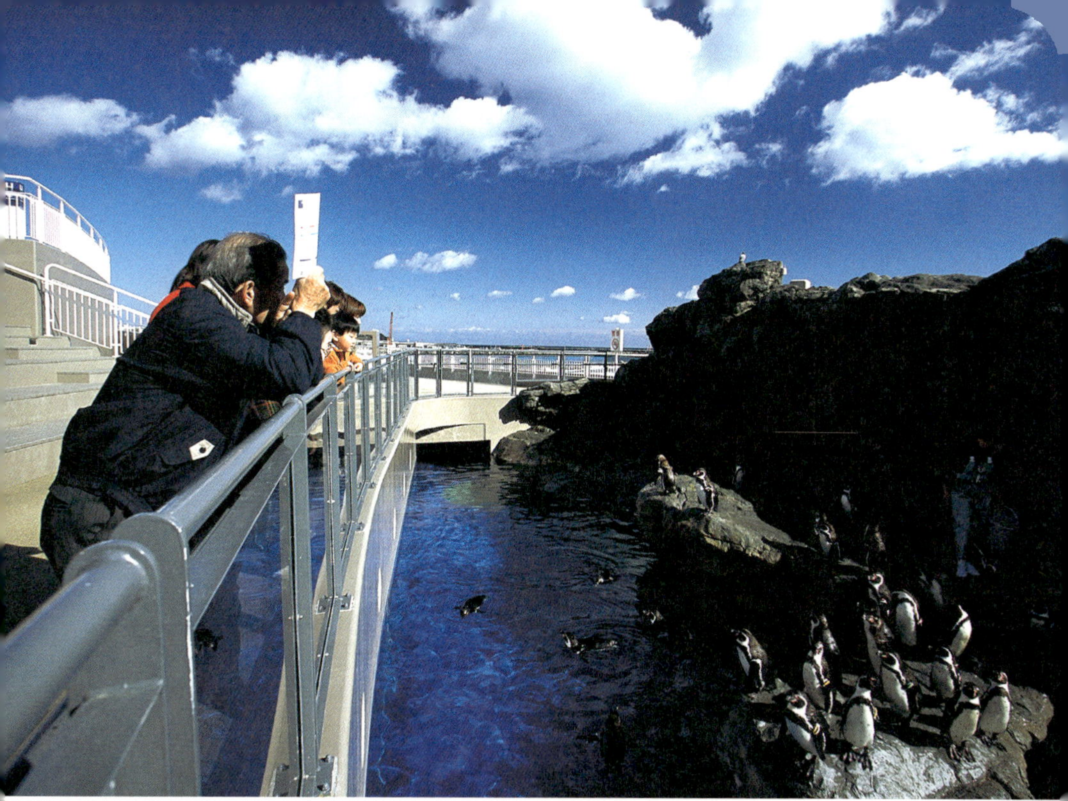

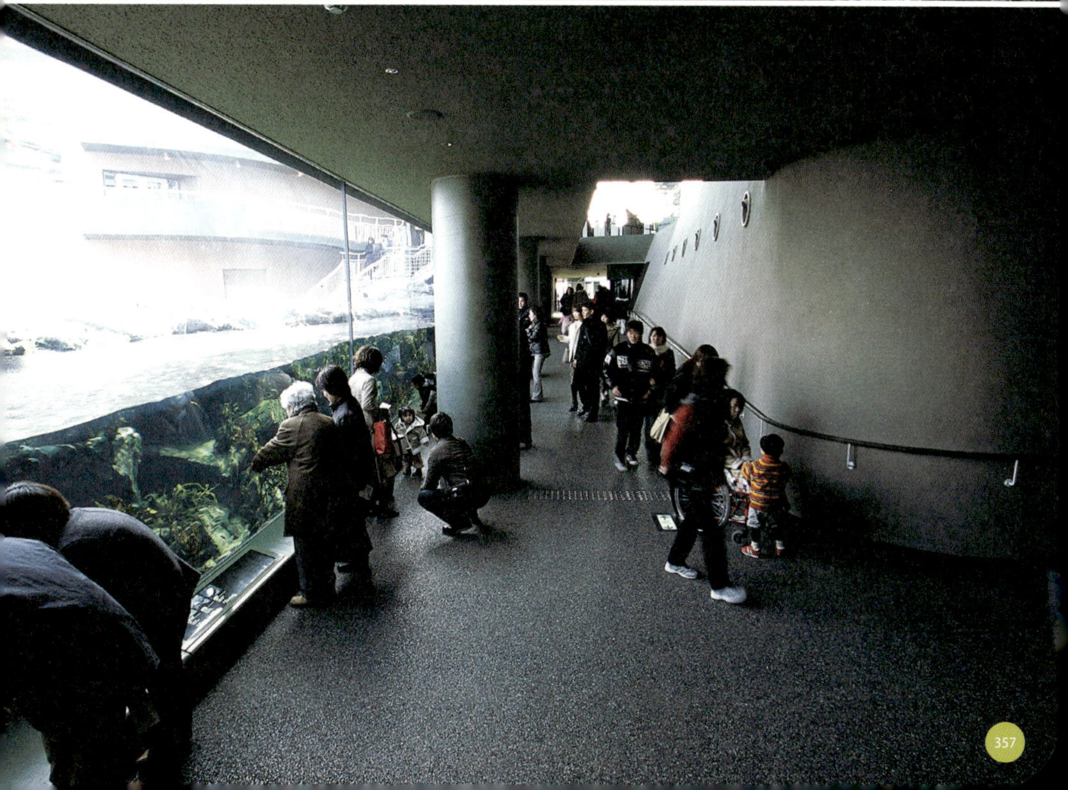

2001

アクアワールド大洗水族館

Oarai Aquarium "Aqua World"

ここの目玉は水量4,000トンのサメの大水槽
The key attraction here is the large shark tank that has a 4,000t water capacity.

2001

アクアワールド大洗水族館
Oarai Aquarium "Aqua World"

イルカのショープールは海を背景としている
The sea forms a background to the dolphin show pool.

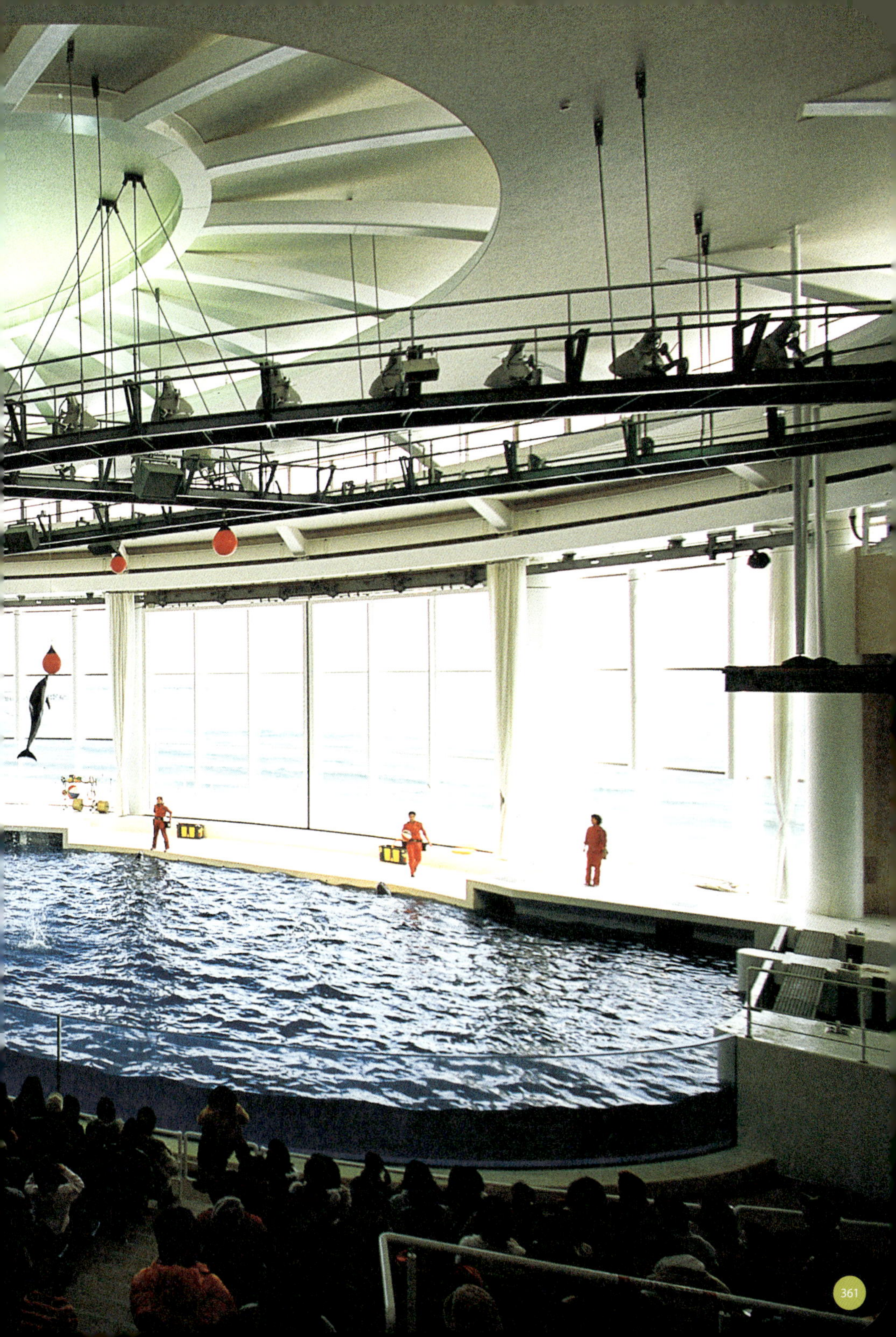

2001

アクアワールド大洗水族館
Oarai Aquarium "Aqua World"

さまざまな視点からの発見
Discoveries from various differing viewpoints.

363

2001

アクアワールド大洗水族館

Oarai Aquarium "Aqua World"

お魚発見教室
Discovery Room

2001

佐久市子ども未来館

Saku Children's Science Dome for the Future

円盤形建築

佐久市子ども未来館

長野県佐久市岩村田／2001
Saku Children's Science Dome for the Future
Iwamurata, Saku-shi, Nagano

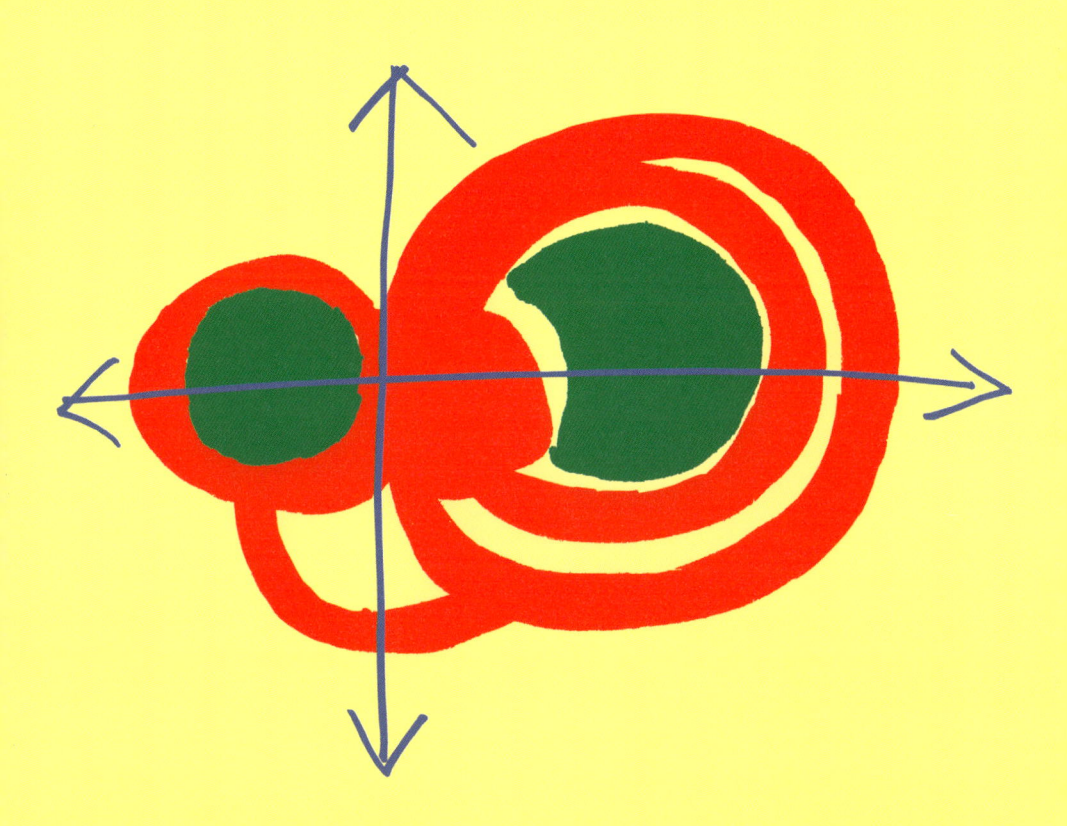

長野県佐久市のこどものための科学館である。外観はこども達の未来を象徴して、円盤のような形状で、大小2つのドームは、展示棟とプラネタリウムである。建物内部は「未来への創造」－進化する宇宙・地球・生命をテーマに、3層構造のフラクタルタワーを巡り、遊環構造による計画理論により展開されている。

This is a science museum for children located in Saku City in Nagano Prefecture. Symbolizing the future of children, the outer structure was constructed in a disk-like shape. There are two domes, large and small, one for the exhibition arena and one for the planetarium. Exhibits are arranged to revolve around the three layer "fractal tower" inside the building, based on the theme "Creation for the Future: Furthering the universe, earth and life."

2001

佐久市子ども未来館
Saku Children's Science Dome for the Future

立体的な科学迷路であそぶ。
こども達は迷路が好きだ。
Play in the three-dimensional science maze.
Children love mazes.

369

2001

佐久市子ども未来館

Saku Children's Science Dome for the Future

371

2001

浜松こども館

Hamamatsu Children's Center

空中トンネル
全長85m

浜松こども館

静岡県浜松市中区鍛冶町／2001
Hamamatsu Children's Center
Kaji-machi, Naka-ku, Hamamatsu-shi, Shizuoka

中心市街地の活性化に向けた大型商業施設の6、7階に設けられた、都市型の児童施設・子育て支援施設である。全長85mのあそび機能を持った空中トンネルが巡らされ、6階と7階、室内と屋上を有機的に連続させている。

Established on the 6th and 7th floors of the large-scale commercial building, made to promote activity in the center of the city, this facility is a children's facility to aid the nurturing of children. The 85-meter long tunnel for play is suspended in space, and other play structures are placed on the 6th and 7th floors in a continuous movement line.

2001

浜松こども館　Hamamatsu Children's Center

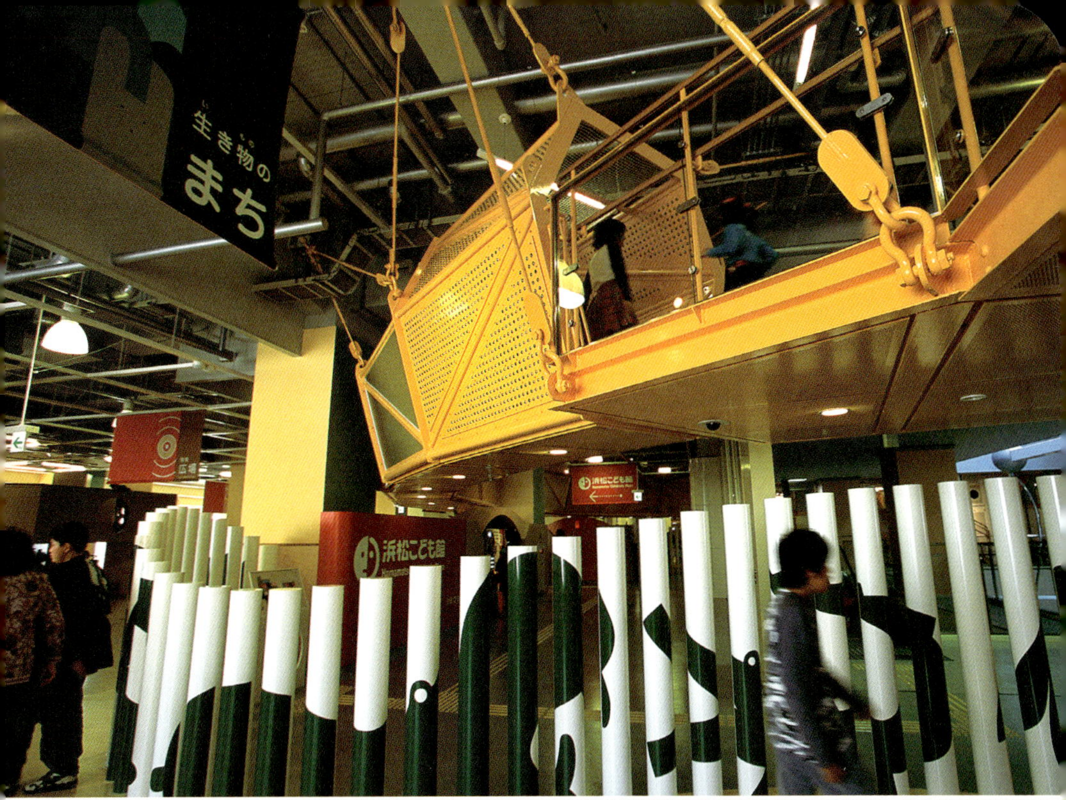
生き物の
まち
浜松こども館

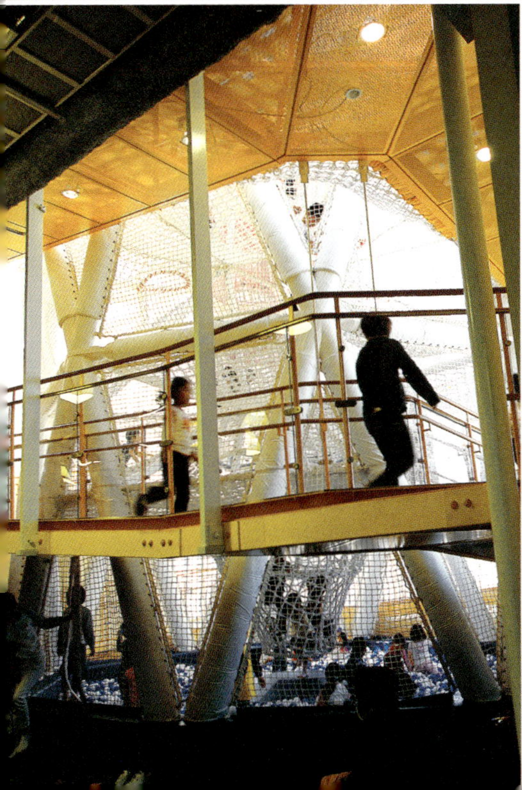

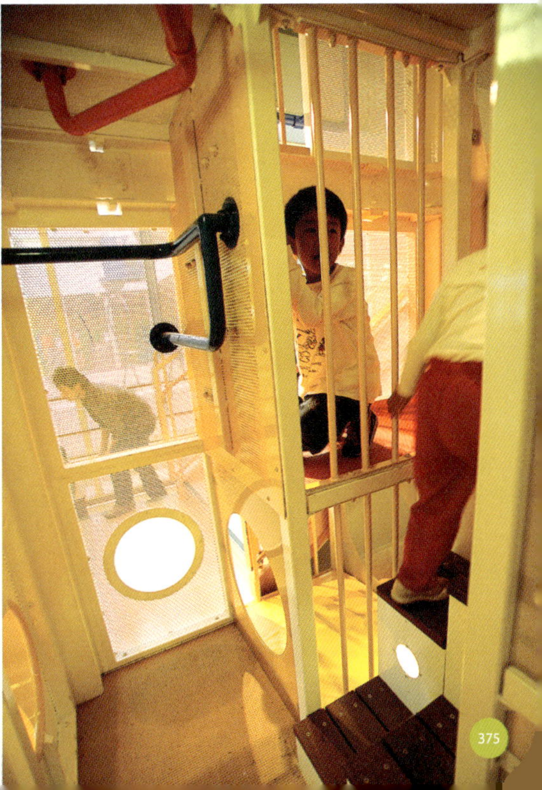

2001

浜松こども館　Hamamatsu Children's Center

もぐる、のぞく、とぶ、はしる、ぶらさがる、
なんでもやってみよう
Dive, peep, jump, run, hang upside-down
—try anything you wish to.

2001

国立成育医療センター　National Center for Child Health and Deveropment

成育医療デザイン

国立成育医療センター

東京都世田谷区大蔵／2001
National Center for Child Health and Deveropment
Okura, Setagaya-ku, Tokyo

国立大蔵病院と国立小児科病院が統合され、妊娠から出産、新生児、小児、思春期、成人へという総合的、継続的な医療を実践する国立成育医療センターとして再生された。病気のこども達の治療・回復には、あそびが重要な役割を果たすとの考えにもとづき、病棟、外来および成育庭園を中心にあそび機能をもった癒しの環境デザインが提案された。日本を代表する小児病院である。

Due to the unification of the National Okura Hospital and National Children's Hospital, this new National Center for Child Health and Development was created to execute a total and continuous medical care from conception to birth, for children as they grow into puberty, then to adults. Based on the idea that play is an important factor in the treatment and recovery of ill children, we proposed an environmental design that has playful features in the hospital wing, visiting patient's wing, and nurturing garden. This is a representative children's hospital of Japan.

2001

国立成育医療センター　National Center for Child Health and Deveropment

チルドレンズミュージアムのような病院
A hospital that resembles a children's museum.

2001

国立成育医療センター　National Center for Child Health and Deveropment

こどもの居場所が
さまざまなところに用意されている
Spots have been created
for children in various places.

383

2001

国立成育医療センター
National Center for Child Health and Deveropment

通り抜けをする人々にも安らぎを与える環境
An environment that is also soothing
for people passing through.

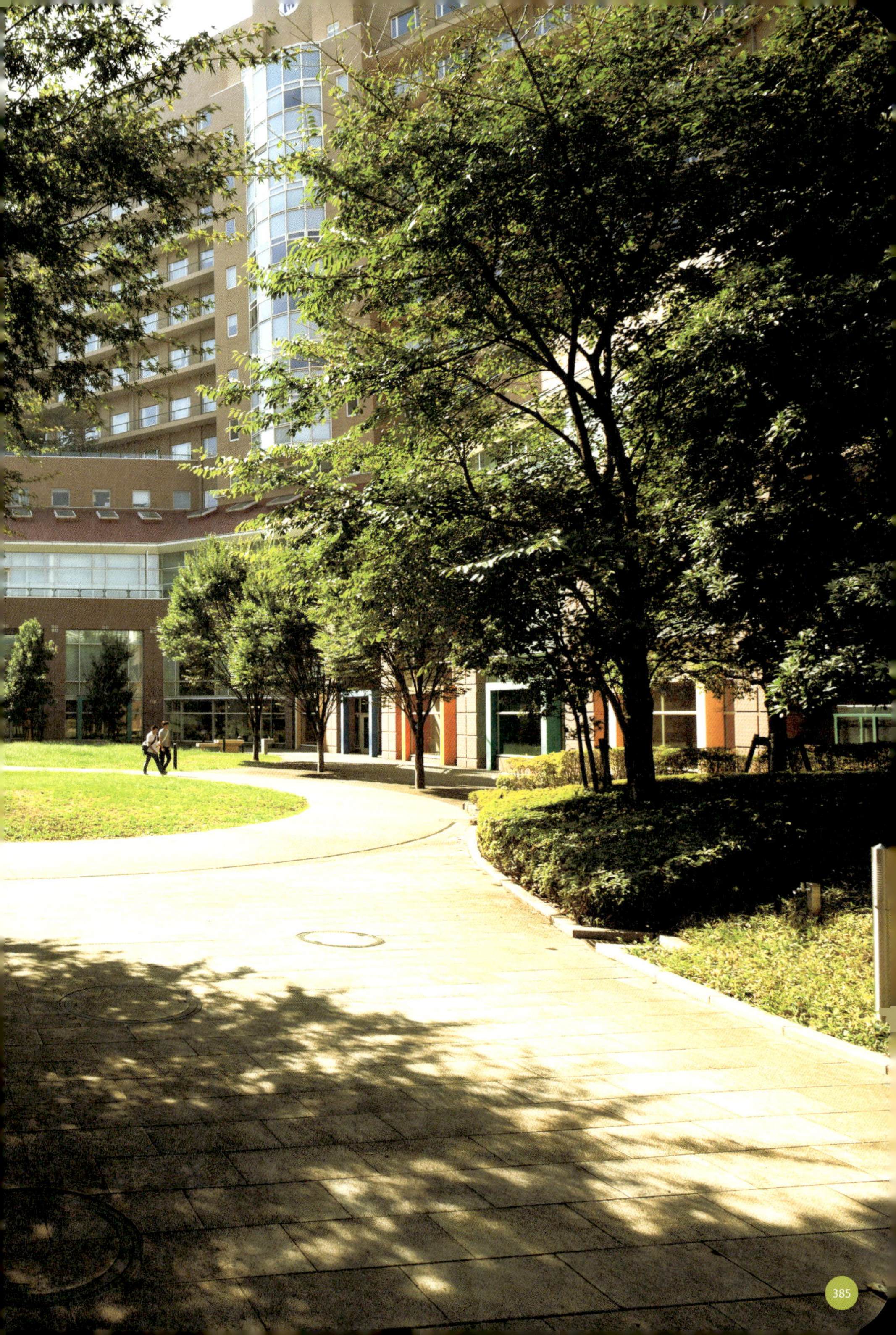

2001

七尾希望の丘公園［ブリッジ遊具］

巨大遊具ブリッジ

Nanao Bridge Play Structure

七尾希望の丘公園
［ブリッジ遊具］

石川県七尾市万行町／2001
Nanao Bridge Play Structure
Mangyo-machi, Nanao-shi, Ishikawa

公園内の通路や水路の上空に架かるブリッジ遊具は、遊具と歩道橋の2つの機能をあわせ持つ。橋の内部には様々な遊具が組み込まれているが、床面に段差がないので車椅子でも通ることができる。また、屋根が付いているので、雨天時の避難場所にもなる。

The bridge play area suspended above the park's walkway and waterway can be used for playing or simply crossing. The bridge contains various different play equipments, and it is even possible to pass over the bridge in a wheelchair as the flooring is an even, flat surface. In addition, the bridge is roofed, so it can also be used to hide from bad weather on rainy days.

2001

七尾希望の丘公園［ブリッジ遊具］

Nanao Bridge Play Structure

２つの公園の丘をつなぐ
Links the hills in the two parks.

2001

桜山の家
Sakurayama House

世界を望む家

桜山の家

神奈川県逗子市桜山／2001
Sakurayama House
Sakurayama, Zushi-shi, Kanagawa

湘南の海を愛し、山を愛するクライアントの別邸である。敷地は逗子の海岸から近く、急峻な斜面に囲まれた細い谷戸の最奥部に位置し、北西の方向には江の島、相模湾、富士山を望むことができる。107㎡という限られた建築面積と周辺の環境を利用して、空間の豊かさを最大限に獲得する空間形態が求められた。

This cottage is for the client who loves the oceans and mountains of Shonan. The plot is close to Zushi beach, located in the farthest rear of a valley surrounded by steep hills. Enoshima, Sagami Bay, and Mt. Fuji can be seen to the northwest. Considering the small area of the land, only 107㎡, we sought out a form of space that fully utilizes the richness of the surrounding environment.

2001

谷戸に建ち ここから富士山と江ノ島を望む
Built in a valley, one can look out to
Mt. Fuji and Enoshima from here.

桜山の家
Sakurayama House

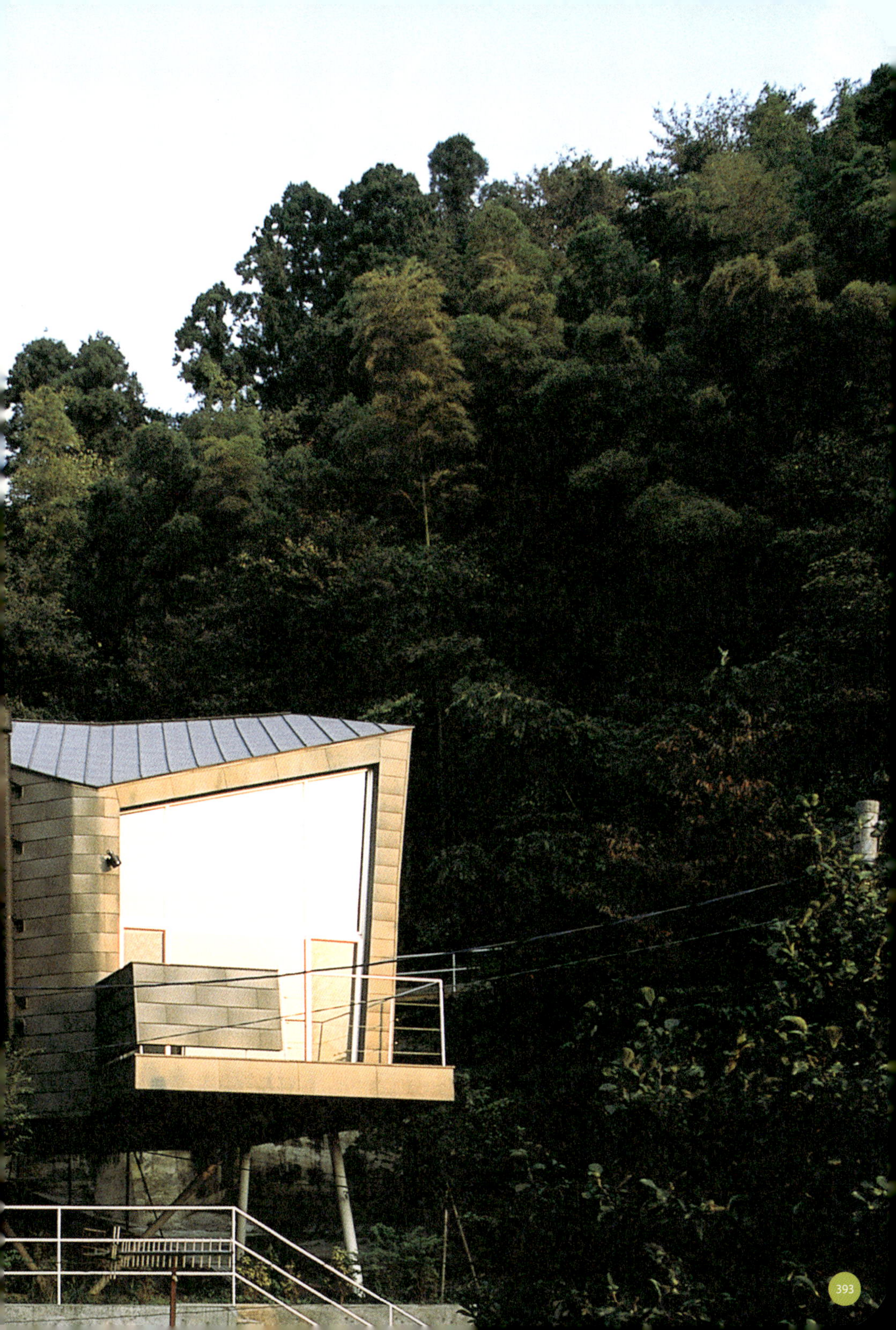

2001

桜山の家

Sakurayama House

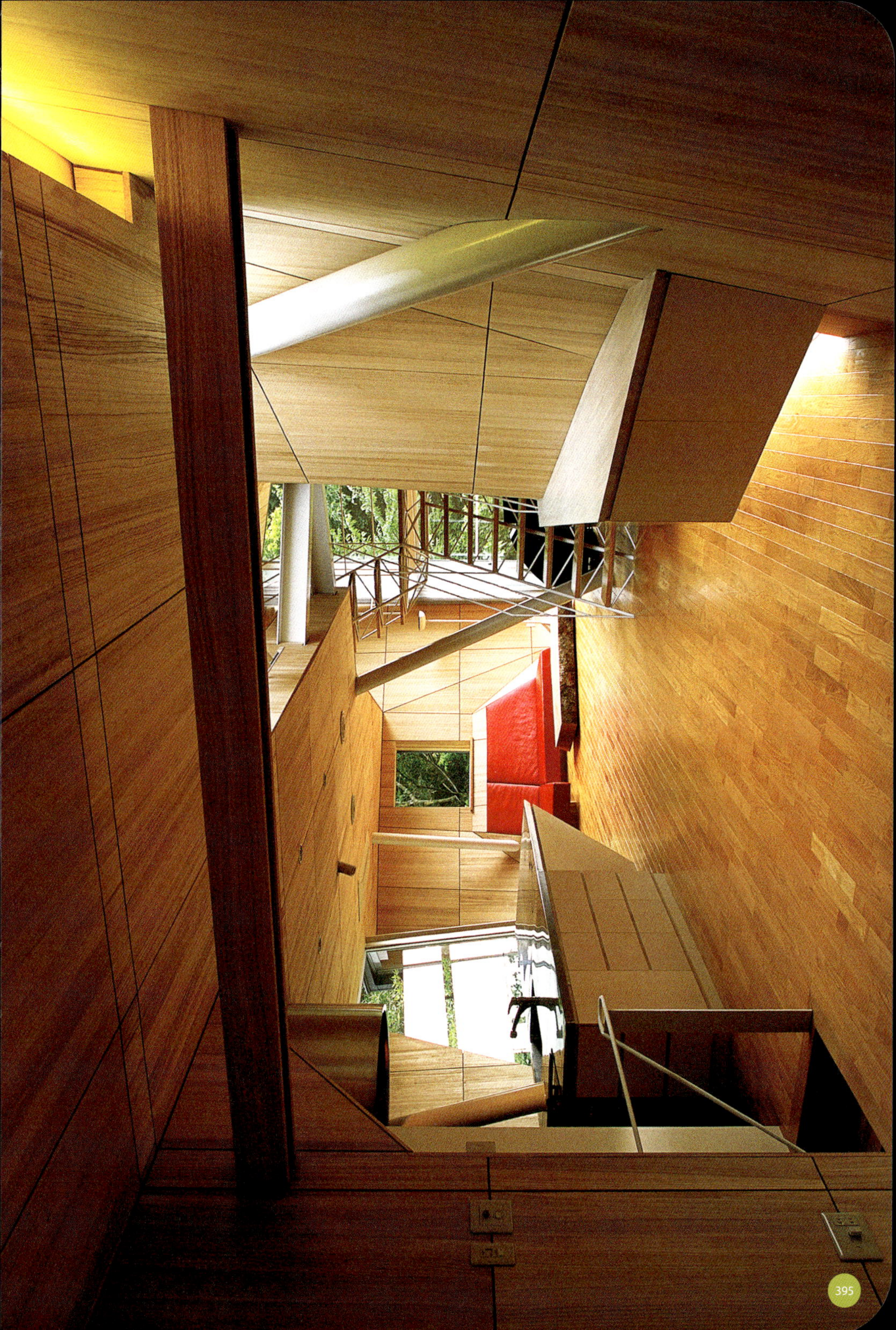

2001

桜山の家
Sakurayama House

397

2000

海南市わんぱく公園

Kainan Wanpaku Park

トルネード

海南市わんぱく公園

和歌山県海南市大野中／2000
Kainan Wanpaku Park
Ononaka, Kainan-shi, Wakayama

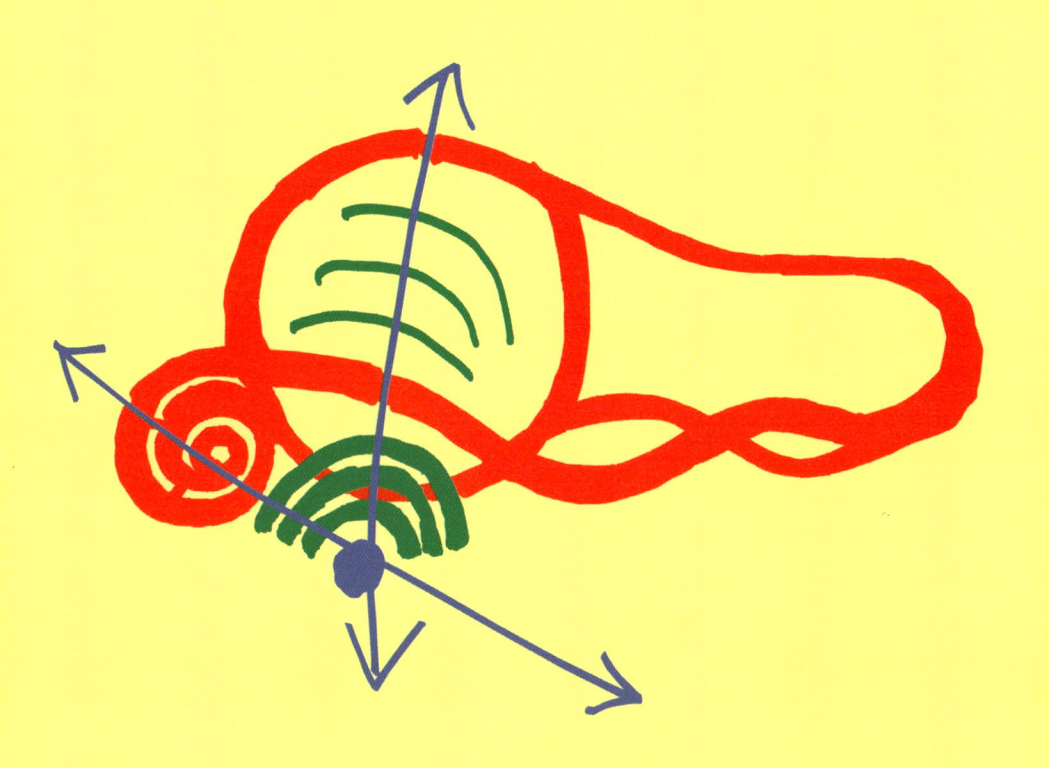

和歌山県海南市の元みかん畑に計画された、こどもとそのファミリーのための敷地9ヘクタールの公園である。この中心施設である風の子館は、大きならせん状のネット遊具で構成された屋根をもつ。下部には集会室や工房等の機能をもつ諸室が内包されている。全体に屋根付き回廊により遊環構造が形成され、敷地全体の回遊性と多様性が意図されている。

This is a 9-hectare park created for children and families at an old tangerine orchard in Kainan City in Wakayama Prefecture. The park's central facility, Kazenoko Hall, has a roof constructed of netted play equipment shaped like a large spiral. In the lower portion of the facility one will find various rooms that fill the function of meeting rooms and craft centers. The circular play system gets its shape from the corridor, which is completely roofed, aiming to achieve an overall sense of playfulness and diversity for the park.

2000

海南市わんぱく公園 Kainan Wanpaku Park

芝すべりがハイライト
Grass-surfing is a highlight.

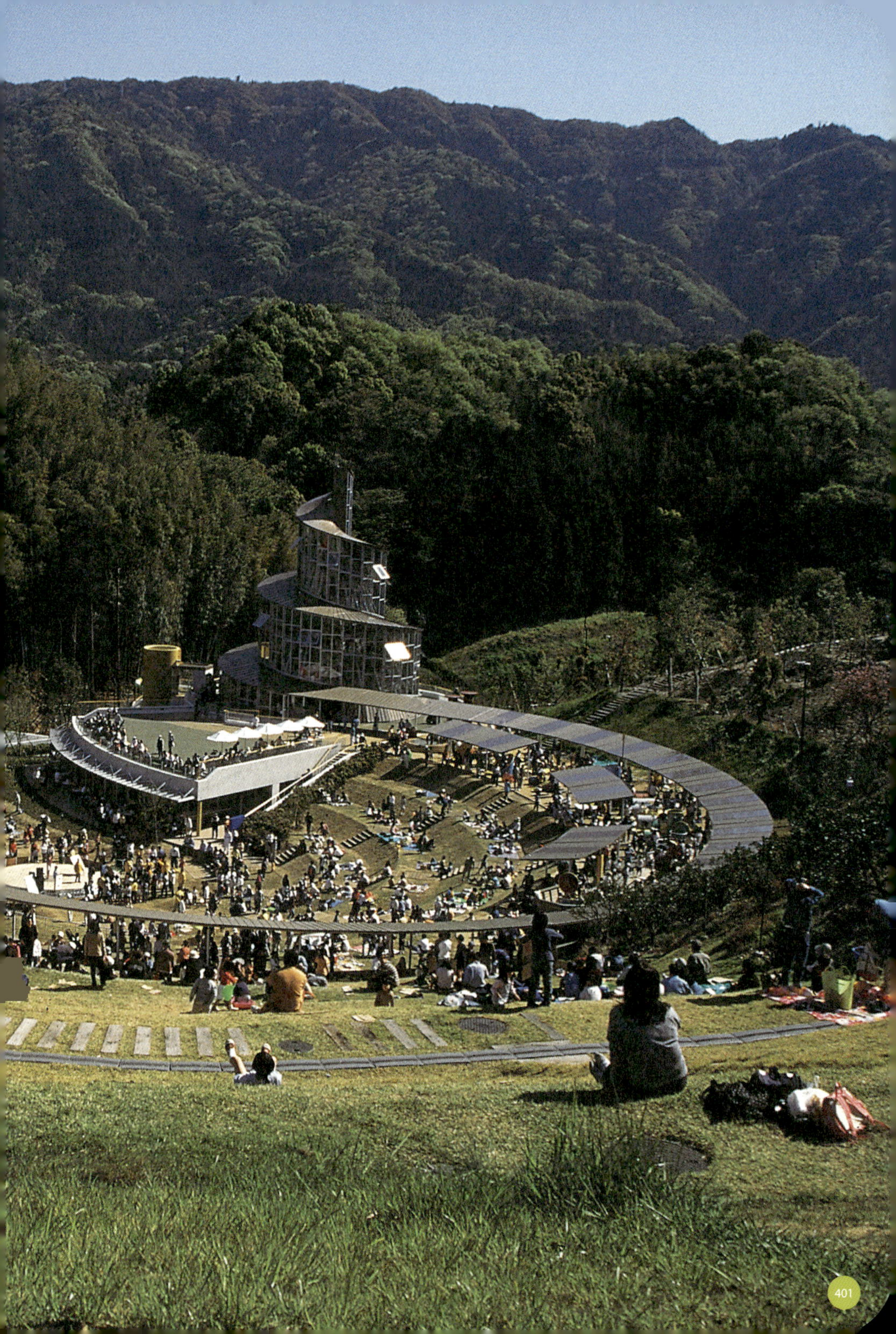

2000

海南市わんぱく公園　Kainan Wanpaku Park

403

2000

海南市わんぱく公園

Kainan Wanpaku Park

風の子館天井の巨大ネットは、
わんぱく公園のあそびステーション
The giant net on the ceiling of the children's center is
the play area in the Wanpaku Park.

2000

海南市わんぱく公園

Kainan Wanpaku Park

407

2000

海南市わんぱく公園　Kainan Wanpaku Park

ホップ、ステップ、ジャンプ、
年齢別あそび場に挑戦

Hop, step, jump!
Try out the play spaces
for different age groups.

2000

和歌山県動物愛護センター
Wakayama Prefectural Animal Welfare Center

ふれあいパーク

和歌山県動物愛護センター

和歌山県海草郡紀美野町／2000
Wakayama Prefectural Animal Welfare Center
Kimino-cho, Kaiso-gun, Wakayama

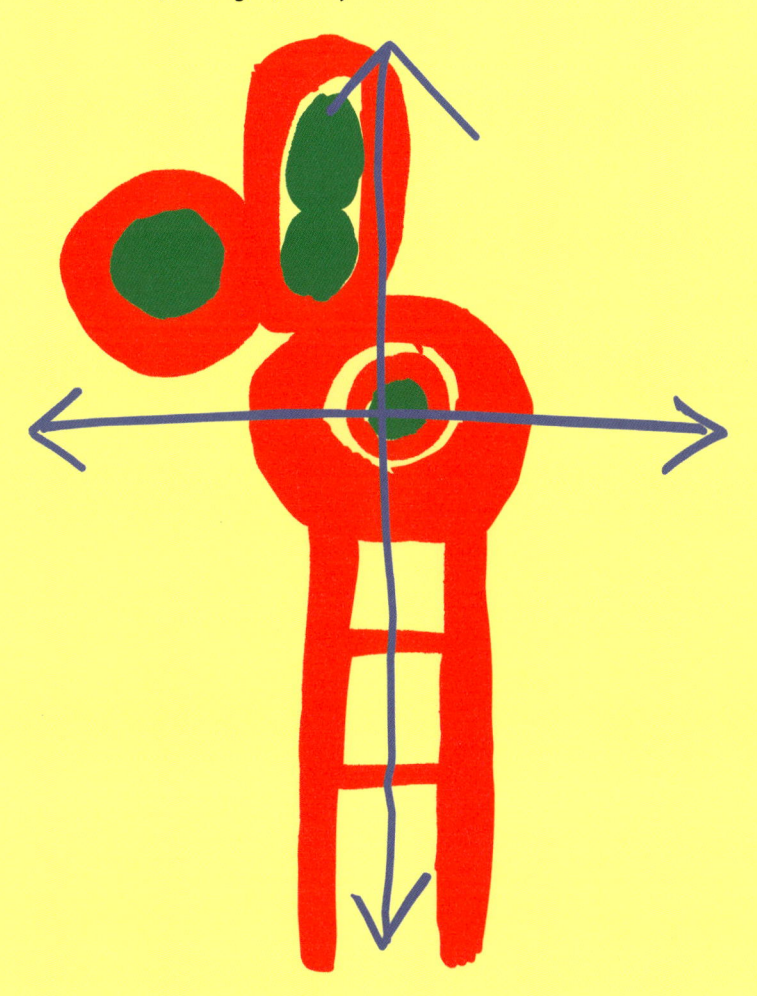

和歌山県の公共施設で、動物に接するのに必要な知識と飼い方の普及啓発をするための施設として計画された。管理動物に対する個別犬房の全面的採用も全国で初めての試みであり、博物館的要素とあそび場的要素を両立させ、動物愛護の精神を十分に学べる施設となっている。

A public facility in Wakayama Prefecture, this was planned to serve as a place to teach people the knowledge necessary to handle animals and how to feed them. In the nation's first attempt to use individual kennels for managed animals, it offers both museum-like and recreational elements and is a place where people can learn the spirit of animal care.

2000

和歌山県動物愛護センター　Wakayama Prefectural Animal Welfare Center

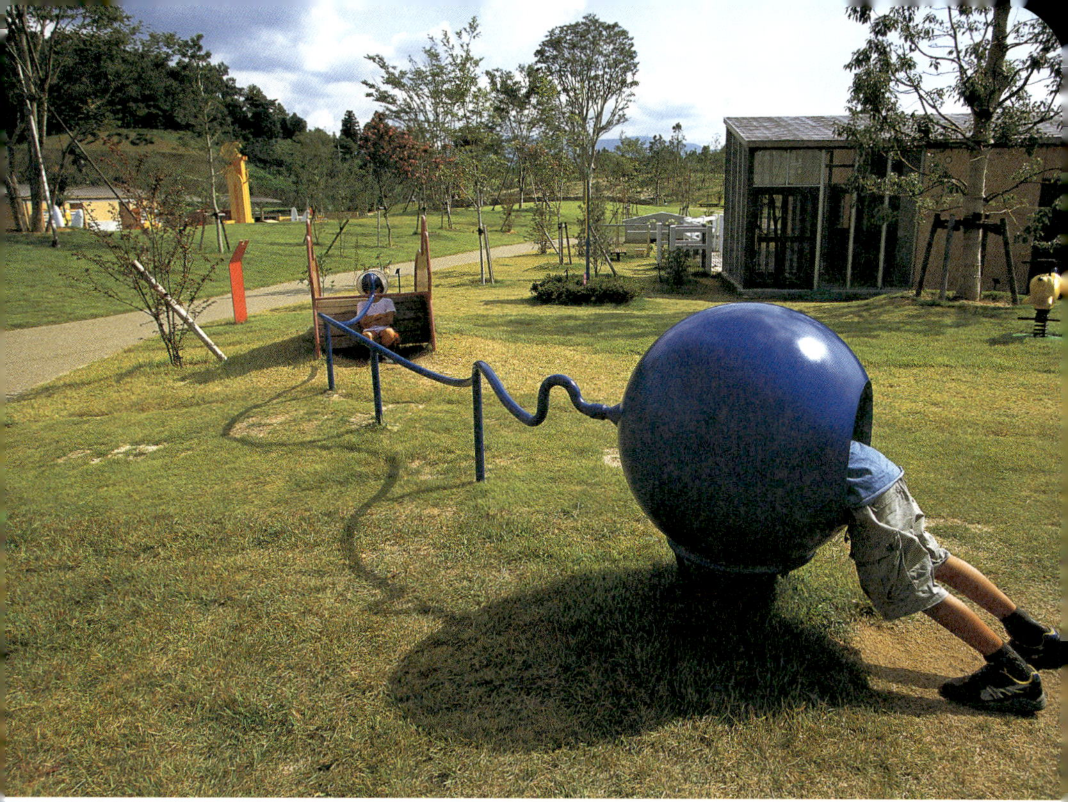

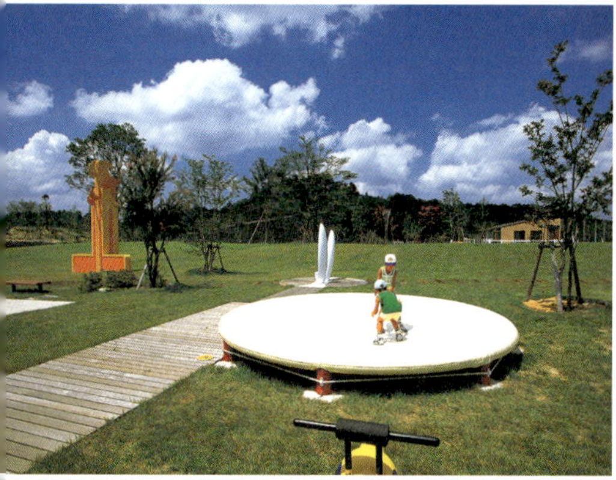

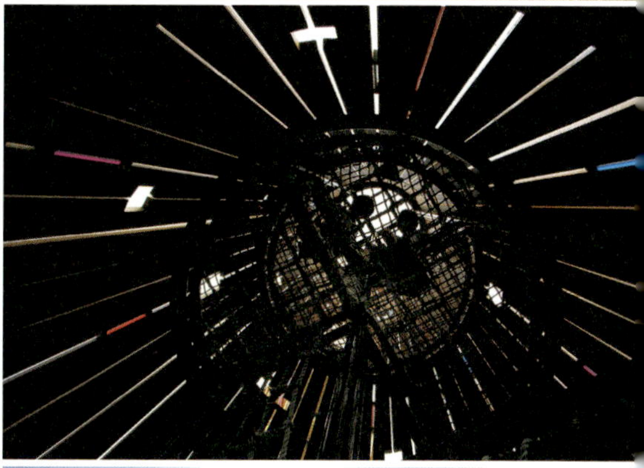

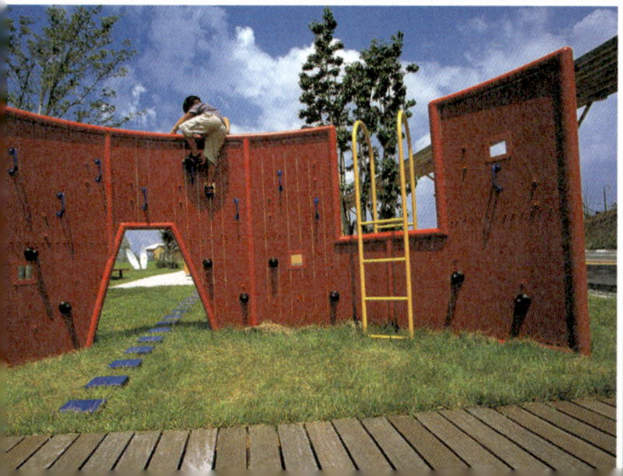

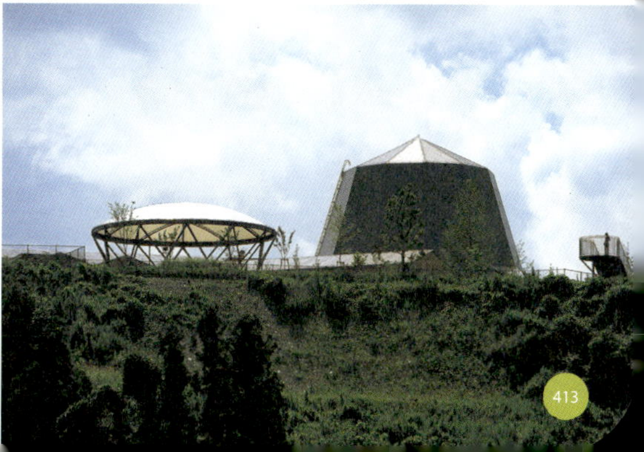

2004.03
福井まちなか文化施設
［響のホール］

断面パース図

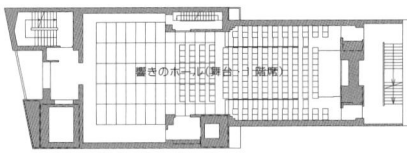

3階 平面図

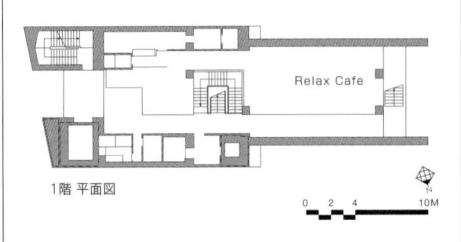

1階 平面図

所在地：福井県福井市中央
主用途：劇場、飲食、スタジオ
建築主：まちづくり福井
構造設計：金箱構造設計事務所
設備設計：日永設計
施工：大成建設・村中建設JV
構造：S造一部SRC造
規模：地下1階地上9階
敷地：448㎡　建築：382㎡　延床：2,478㎡

Fukui Cultural Complex "Hibiki Hall"
Chuo, Fukui-shi, Fukui

2004.04
健康パークあざい

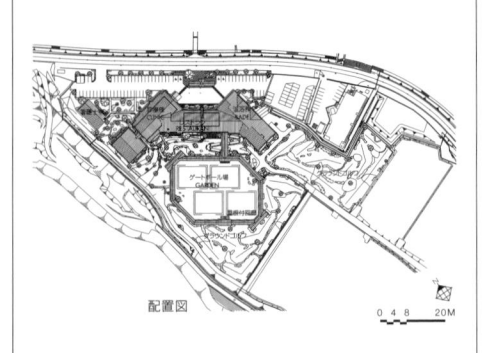

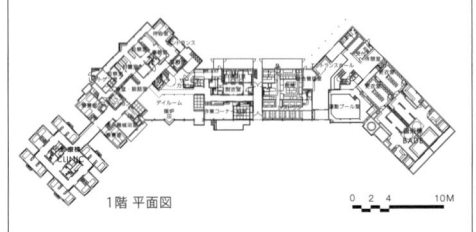

配置図

1階 平面図

診療棟 東側 立面図　診療棟 北側 立面図　療養棟 北側 立面図

所在地：滋賀県長浜市野瀬町
主用途：診療所、温浴施設、レストラン
建築主：浅井町（現長浜市）
構造設計：金箱構造設計事務所
設備設計：総合設備計画
施工：塩浜工業
構造：RC造、S造
規模：地下1階地上2階
敷地：20,835㎡　建築：2,825㎡　延床：3,550㎡

Wellness Park Azai
Nose-cho, Nagahama-shi, Shiga

2004.02
やすらぎの杜

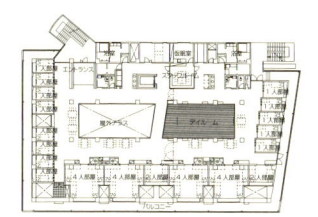

2階 平面図

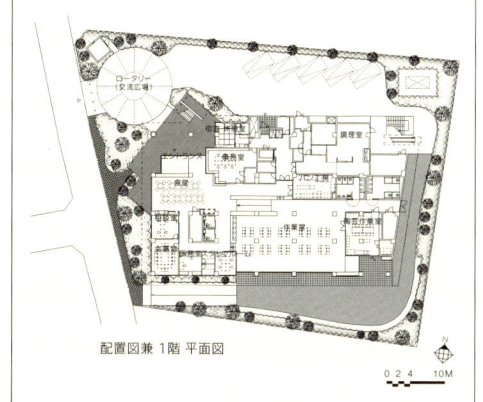

配置図兼 1階 平面図

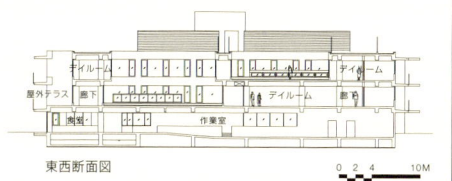

東西断面図

所在地：東京都練馬区関町
主用途：知的障害者厚生・授産施設
建築主：社会福祉法人章佑会
設備設計：システムプランニング
施工：東急建設
構造：RC造
規模：地上3階
敷地：2,752㎡　建築：1,238㎡　延床：2,749㎡

Yasuragi-no-Mori
Seki-machi, Nerima-ku, Tokyo

2003.11
ふじえだファミリークリニック

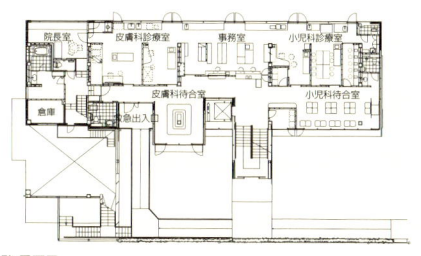

2階 平面図

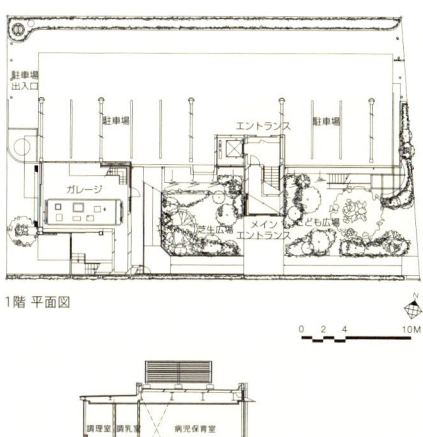

1階 平面図

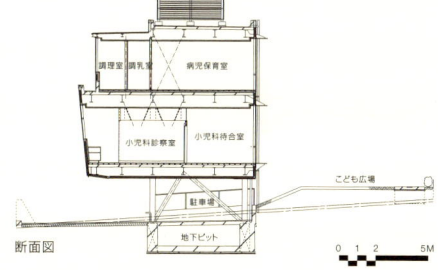

断面図

所在地：愛媛県四国中央市中曽根町
主用途：診療所
建築主：医療法人周水舎
構造設計：金箱構造設計事務所
設備設計：RS設備計画
施工：清水建設
構造：S造
規模：地上3階
敷地：840㎡　建築：385㎡　延床：941㎡

Fujieda Family Clinic
Nakazone-cho, Shikokuchuo-shi, Ehime

415

2003.09
わかくさ保育園

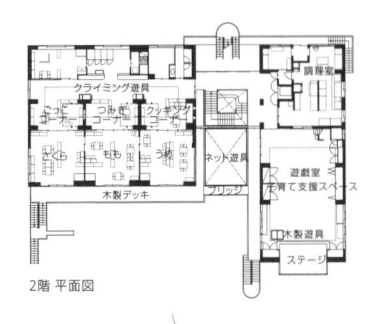

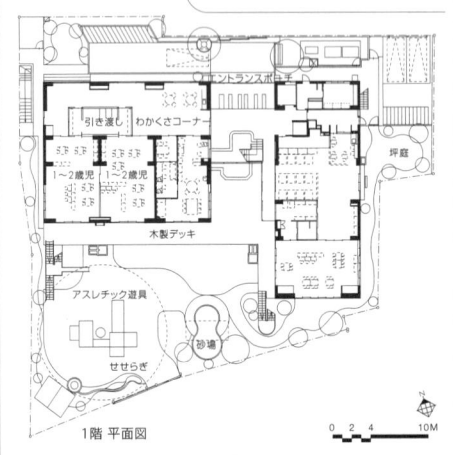

2階 平面図

1階 平面図

所在地：東京都昭島市玉川町
主用途：保育園
建築主：社会福祉法人みきの家
構造設計：金箱構造設計事務所
設備設計：石井建築事務所
施工：カトービルドシステム
構造：RC造一部S造
規模：地上3階
敷地：1,437㎡　建築：547㎡　延床：1,125㎡

Wakakusa Day Nursery
Tamagawa-cho, Akishima-shi, Tokyo

2003.07
秋田市太平山自然学習センター

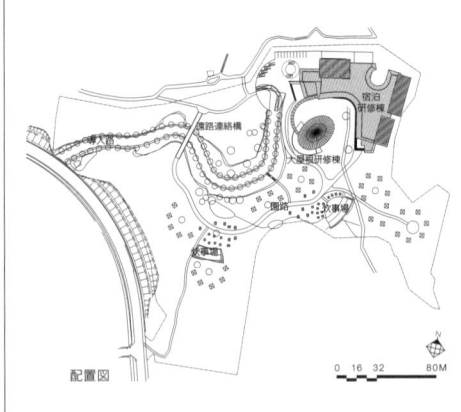

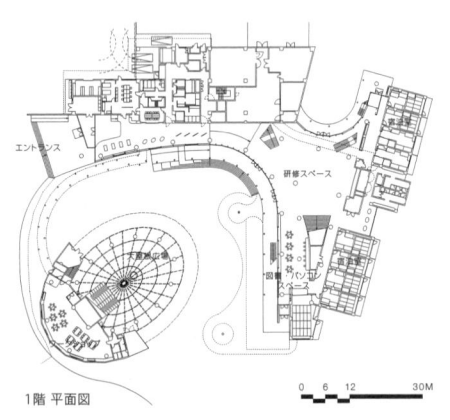

配置図

1階 平面図

所在地：秋田県秋田市仁別
主用途：野外活動宿泊研修施設
建築主：秋田市
共同設計：松橋設計
構造設計：構造計画研究所
設備設計：総合設備計画
施工：中田・日本海・加賀伊JV
構造：RC造一部S造、W造
規模：地下1階地上3階
敷地：42,210㎡　建築：4,099㎡　延床：5,285㎡

Akita Taiheizan Nature Learning Center
Nibetsu, Akita-shi, Akita

2003.04
関門海峡ミュージアム

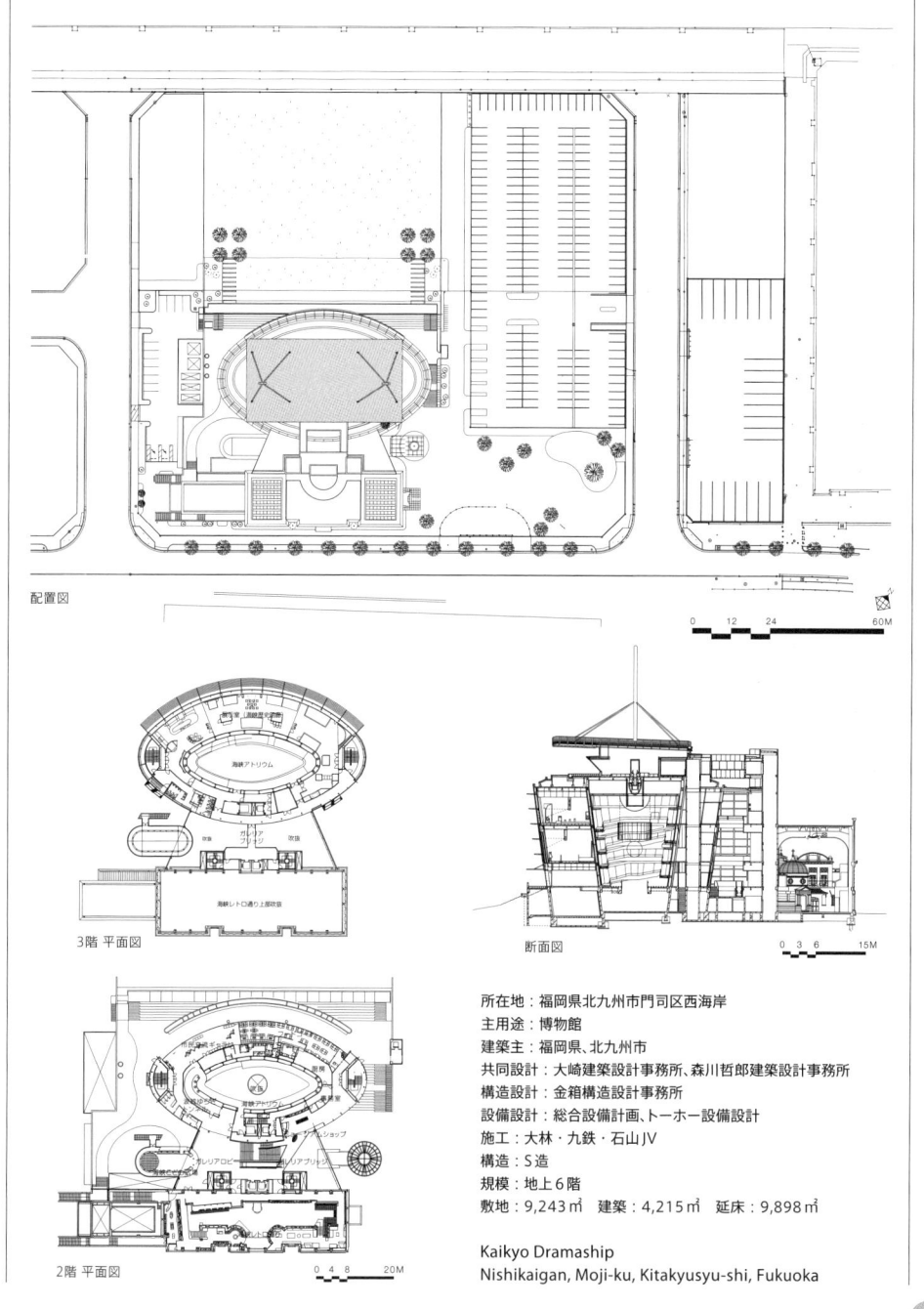

配置図

3階 平面図

断面図

2階 平面図

所在地：福岡県北九州市門司区西海岸
主用途：博物館
建築主：福岡県、北九州市
共同設計：大崎建築設計事務所、森川哲郎建築設計事務所
構造設計：金箱構造設計事務所
設備設計：総合設備計画、トーホー設備設計
施工：大林・九鉄・石山JV
構造：S造
規模：地上6階
敷地：9,243㎡　建築：4,215㎡　延床：9,898㎡

Kaikyo Dramaship
Nishikaigan, Moji-ku, Kitakyusyu-shi, Fukuoka

2000.05, 2002.03
きききのつりはし＋
御所野縄文博物館

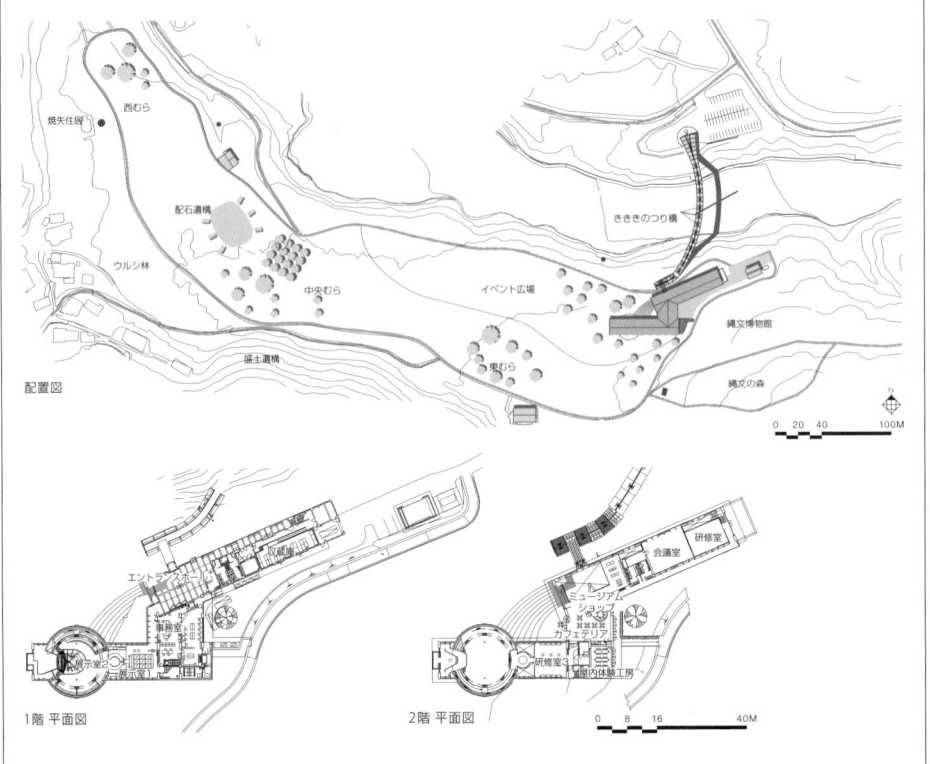

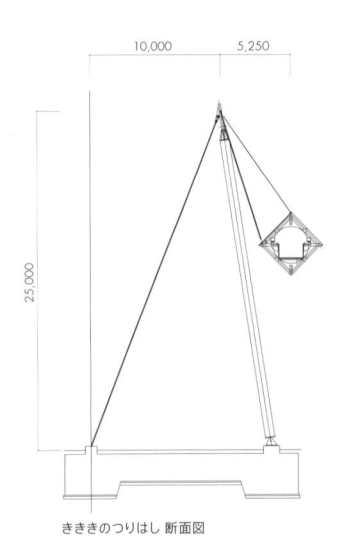

配置図

1階 平面図　　　2階 平面図

きききのつりはし 断面図

所在地：岩手県二戸郡一戸町

きききのつりはし
主用途：木橋
建築主：一戸町
共同設計：長内建築設計事務所
構造設計：金箱構造設計事務所
施工：一戸建設・斎藤木材工業JV
構造：木造
規模：中央部の高さ14.1m、全長86.5m（円周距離）

御所野縄文博物館
主用途：博物館
建築主：一戸町
構造設計：金箱構造設計事務所
設備設計：建築設備設計研究所、東北事務所
施工：田中建設・一戸建設JV
構造：RC造
規模：地上2階
敷地：16,105㎡　建築：1,719㎡　延床：2,637㎡

Bridge Kikiki + Goshono Jomon Museum
Ichinohe-cho, Ninohe-gun, Iwate

2002.03
東京工業大学大学会館
［すずかけホール］

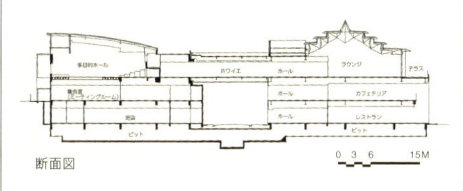

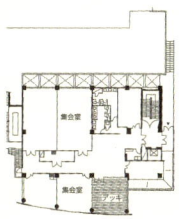

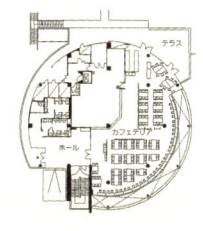

断面図

2階 平面図

1階 平面図

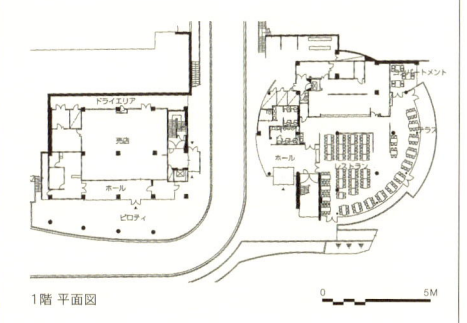

所在地：神奈川県横浜市緑区長津田町
主用途：大学施設
建築主：東京工業大学
プロジェクト内容：基本設計及び実施設計指導
構造設計指導：和田章
構造設計：教育施設研究所
設備設計：桜井システム
施工：鴻池組
構造：SRC造
規模：地上4階
敷地：177,320㎡　建築：1,367㎡　延床：3,330㎡

Tokyo Institute of Technology "Suzukake Hall"
Nagatsuda-cho, Midori-ku, Yokohama-shi, Kanagawa

2002.10
弘法湯

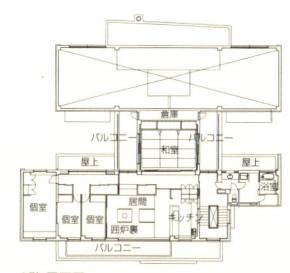

断面図

2階 平面図

1階 平面図

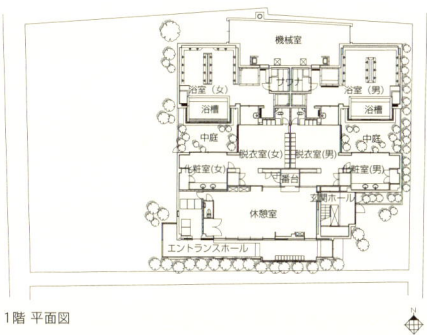

所在地：石川県七尾市北藤橋町
主用途：公衆浴場、住宅
構造設計、設備設計、施工：大林組
構造：RC造
規模：地上3階
敷地：821㎡　建築：431㎡　延床：688㎡

Bath House "Kobo-Yu"
Kitafujihashi-machi, Nanao-shi, Ishikawa

2002.07
京都アクアリーナ

配置図

断面図

1階 平面図

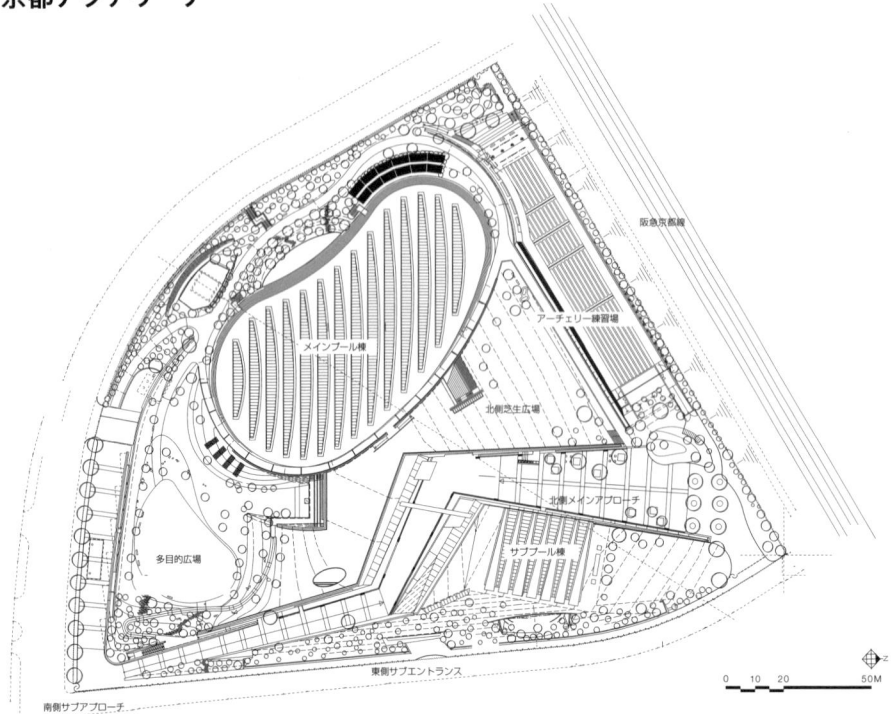

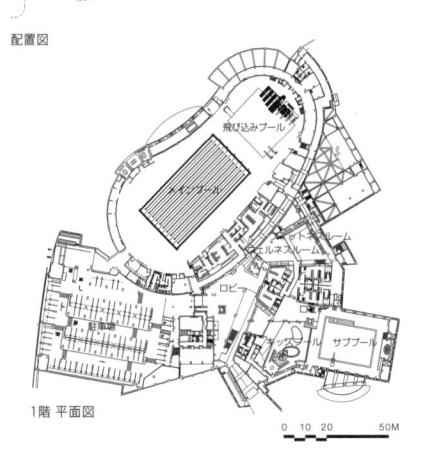

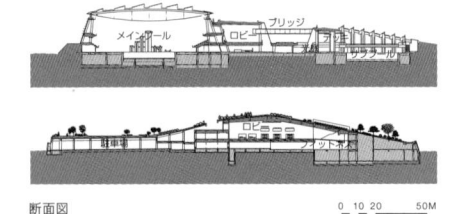

所在地：京都府京都市右京区西京極徳大寺団子田町
主用途：観覧場併設水泳場
建築主：京都市
共同設計：團紀彦建築設計事務所
構造設計：構造計画研究所、構造計画プラス・ワン
設備設計：設備技研、テーテンス事務所
施工：清水・東急・竹島・岡野 JV
構造：RC造、S造
規模：地下1階地上3階
敷地：36,000㎡　建築：7,917㎡　延床：30,586㎡

Kyoto Aquarena
Nishikyougokutokudaijidangoden-machi, Ukyo-ku,
Kyoto-shi, Kyoto

2001.10
アクアワールド大洗水族館

3階 平面図

断面図

配置図

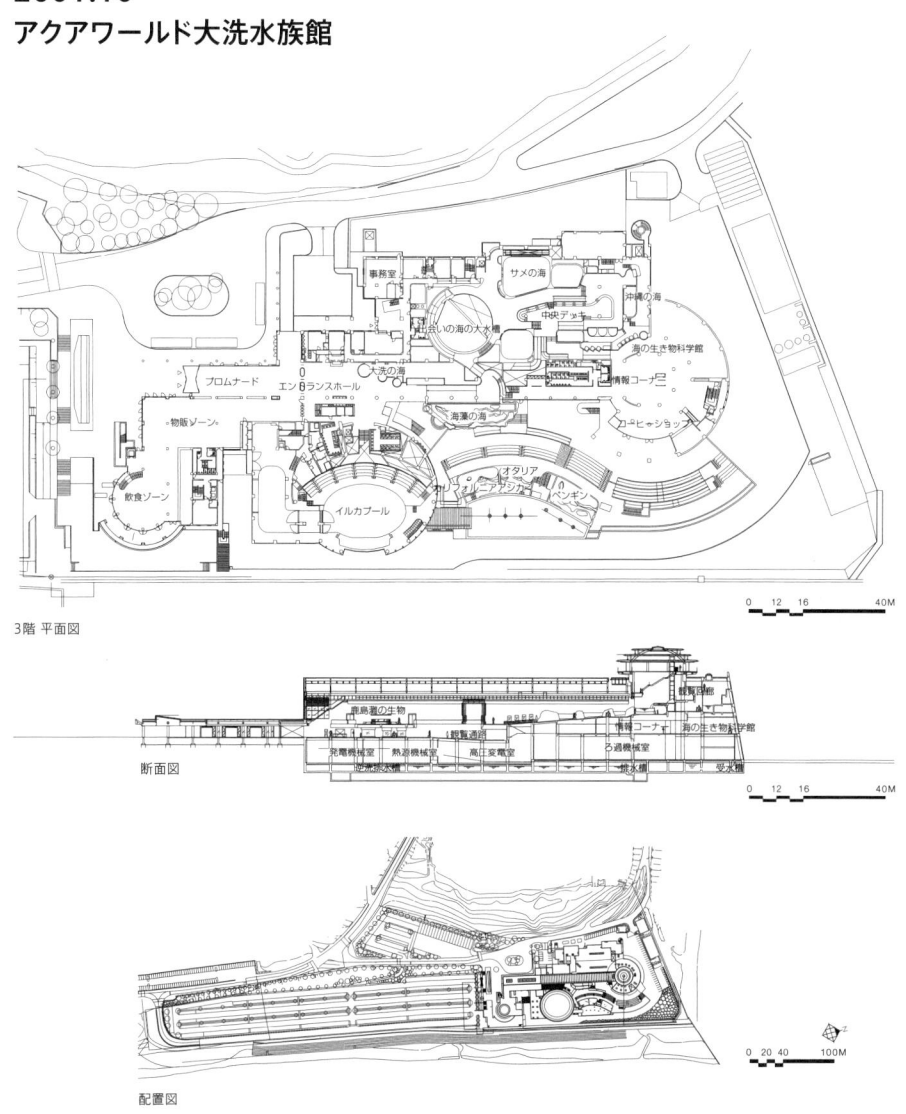

所在地：茨城県東茨城郡大洗町
主用途：水族館
建築主：茨城県
構造設計：構造計画研究所
設備設計：森村設計
施工：清水・日産・武藤・鈴木良JV
構造：SRC造、RC造一部S造
規模：地上7階
敷地：59,246㎡　建築：11,065㎡　延床：19,782㎡

Oarai Aquarium "Aqua World"
Oarai-machi, Higashiibaraki-gun, Ibaraki

2002.06
ほうとく幼稚園

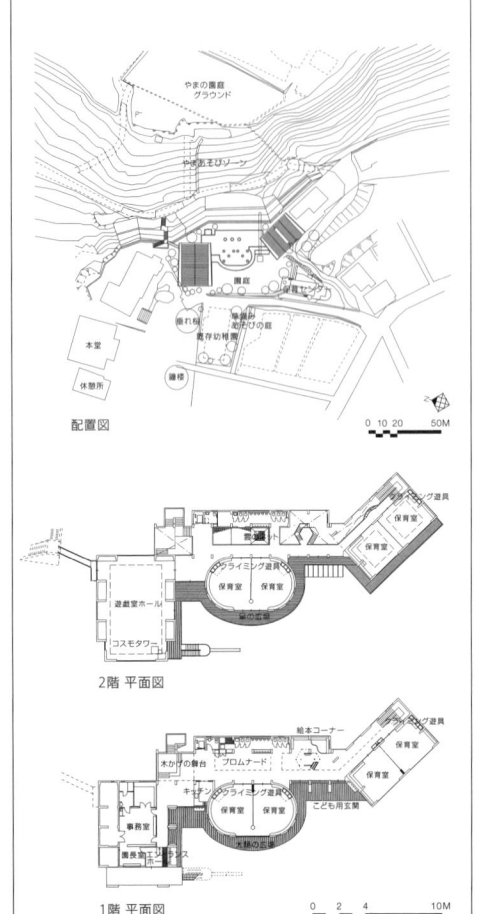

配置図

2階 平面図

1階 平面図

所在地：福島県いわき市後田町
主用途：幼稚園
建築主：学校法人宝徳学園
構造設計：金箱構造設計事務所
設備設計：日永設計
施工：西松建設(本館)、常磐開発(保育センター)
構造：RC造一部S造(本館)、W造(保育センター)
規模：地上2階
敷地：7,159㎡　建築：815㎡(本館)、102㎡(保育センター)
延床：1,110㎡(本館)、159㎡(保育センター)

Houtoku Kindergarten
Ushiroda-machi, Iwaki-shi, Fukushima

2001.02
佐久市子ども未来館

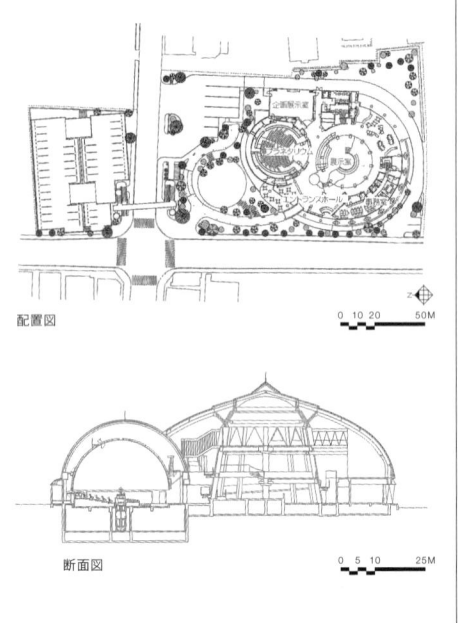

配置図

断面図

所在地：長野県佐久市岩村田
主用途：児童科学館
建築主：佐久市
構造設計：構造計画研究所
設備設計：日永設計
施工：西松・田中住建JV
構造：RC造一部S造
規模：地下1階地上3階
敷地：5,539㎡(本館)、1,572㎡(立体駐車場)　建築：2,117㎡(本館)、986㎡(立体駐車場)　延床：3,507㎡(本館)、986㎡(立体駐車場)

Saku Children's Science Dome for the Future
Iwamurata, Saku-shi, Nagano

2001.11
浜松こども館

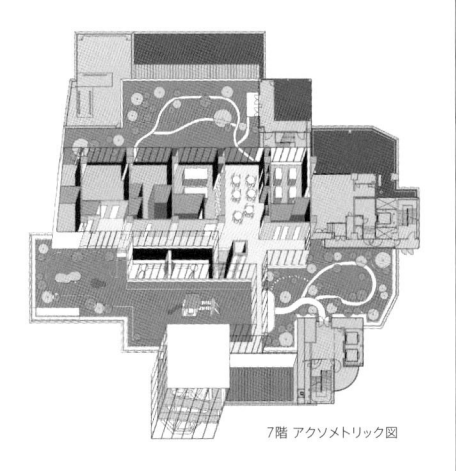

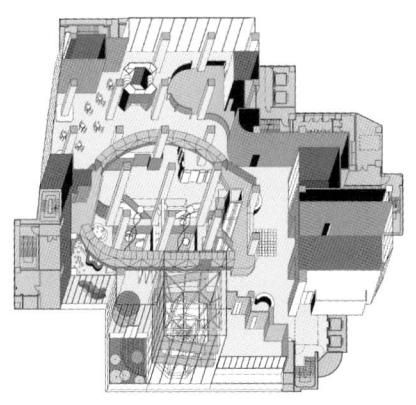

7階 アクソメトリック図

6階 アクソメトリック図

所在地：静岡県浜松市中区鍛冶町
主用途：児童館
建築主：浜松市
構造設計：構造計画研究所
設備設計：日永設計
施工：中村組
構造：RC造一部S造
規模：地上15階のうち6-7階部分
敷地：4,673㎡　延床：3,004㎡

Hamamatsu Children's Center
Kaji-machi, Naka-ku, Hamamatsu-shi, Shizuoka

2001.11
国立成育医療センター

配置図

1階 平面図

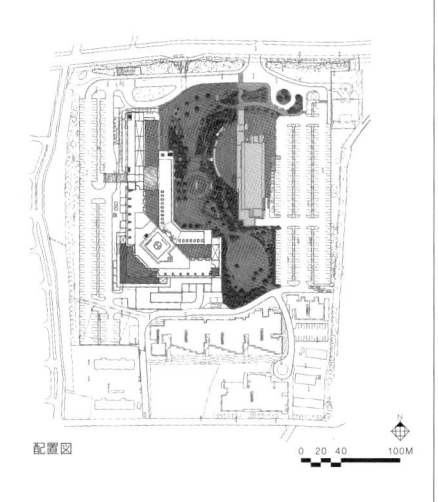

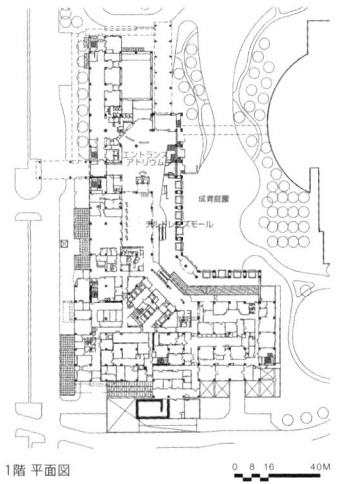

所在地：東京都世田谷区大蔵
主用途：病院
建築主：厚生労働省
共同設計：厚生労働省健康局国立病院部経営指導課、日建設計
構造設計、設備設計：日建設計
施工：大成・奥村・安藤JV
構造：SRC造
規模：地下2階地上12階
敷地：75,470㎡　建築：9,662㎡　延床：64,662㎡

National Center for Child Health and Deveropment
Okura, Setagaya-ku, Tokyo

423

2001.10
七尾希望の丘公園
[ブリッジ遊具]

パース図

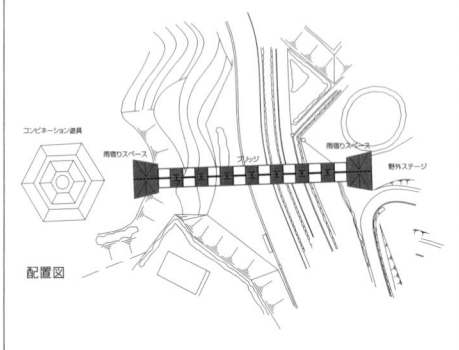

配置図

所在地：石川県七尾市万行町
主用途：歩道橋、遊具
建築主：七尾市
構造設計：金箱構造設計事務所
施工：一戸建設・斎藤木材工業JV
構造：W造
規模：全長64.6m

Nanao Bridge Play Structure
Mangyo-machi, Nanao-shi, Ishikawa

2001.07
桜山の家

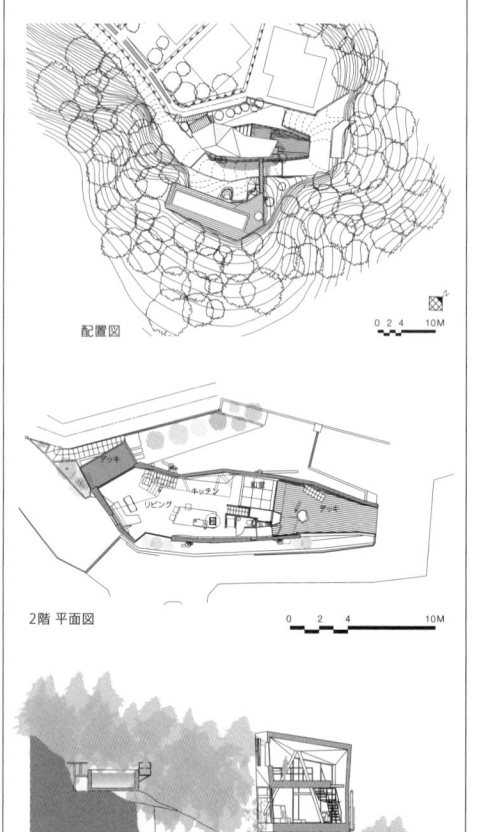

配置図

2階 平面図

断面図

所在地：神奈川県逗子市桜山
主用途：住宅
共同設計：東京工業大学仙田満研究室
構造設計：金箱構造設計事務所
設備設計：日永設計
施工：平成建設
構造：S造
規模：地上3階
敷地：3,462㎡　建築：107㎡　延床：159㎡

Sakurayama House
Sakurayama, Zushi-shi, Kanagawa

2000.03
海南市わんぱく公園

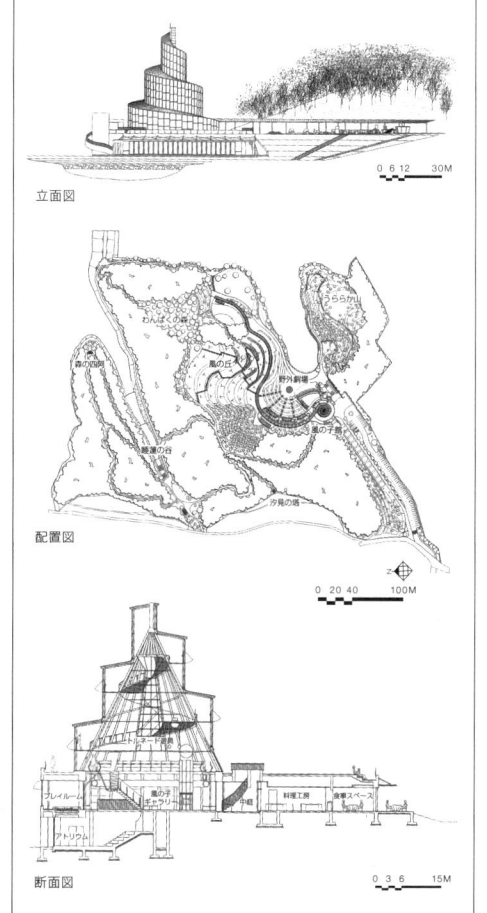

立面図

配置図

断面図

所在地：和歌山県海南市大野中
主用途：公園、児童館
建築主：海南市
構造設計：構造計画研究所
設備設計：システムプランニング
施工：丸山組
構造：壁式構造一部S造
規模：地上2階塔屋1階
敷地：91,060㎡　建築：925㎡（風の子館）、414㎡（風の回廊・屋外トイレ）　延床：1,047㎡（風の子館）、52㎡（風の回廊・屋外トイレ）

Kainan Wanpaku Park
Ononaka, Kainan-shi, Wakayama

2000.03
和歌山県動物愛護センター

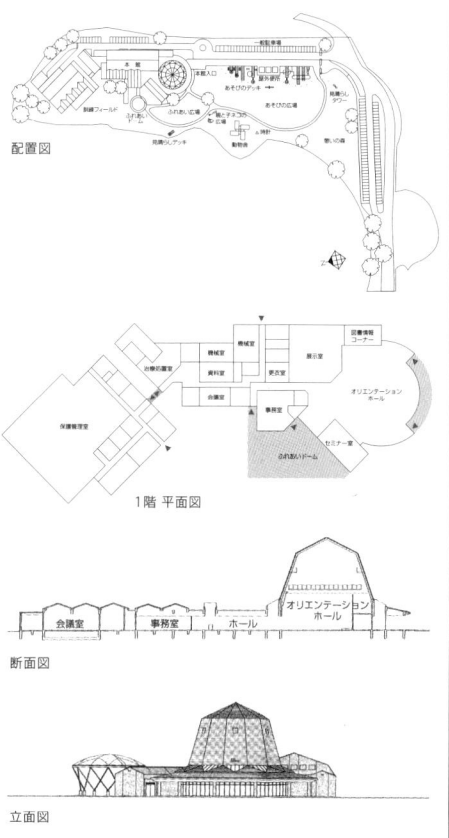

配置図

1階 平面図

断面図

立面図

所在地：和歌山県海草郡紀美野町
主用途：動物愛護施設
建築主：和歌山県
共同設計、構造設計、設備設計：大建設計
施工：前田建設工業・森組・丸山組JV
構造：S造、RC造
規模：地下1階地上2階
敷地：31,750㎡　建築：4,255㎡　延床：4,057㎡

Wakayama Prefectural Animal Welfare Center
Kimino-cho, Kaiso-gun, Wakayama

1999

世界淡水魚園オアシスパーク　Oasis Park

ハイウェイ
オアシス

世界淡水魚園
オアシスパーク

岐阜県各務原市川島笠田町／1999
Oasis Park
Kawashimakasada-machi, Kakamigahara-shi, Gifu

国営木曽三川公園の一部、河川環境楽園と高速道路川島サービスエリア及び、ハイウェイオアシスと複合した新しいタイプの官民共同プロジェクトである。敷地面積は3ヘクタール、第一期の商業エリアと第二・三期の水族館エリアに分かれており、第一期商業エリアを担当した。商業施設エリアは、物販、ゲーム、バーチャルレストラン等からなっており、水辺空間の賑わいをつくりだし、商業的にも成功している。

This is new type joint public and private project in which Kasen Kankyo Rakuen, a part of Kiso Sansen National Government Park and Kawashima Highway Service Area and highway rest stop are merged. The site is on 3-hectare, and is divided into a first stage commercial area and second and third stage aquarium areas. We were in chare of the first stage commercial area. The commercial facilities area, composed of merchandising, gaming and virtual restaurant area, etc., and which a lively waterfront space, has been a commercial success.

1999

世界淡水魚園オアシスパーク
Oasis Park

429

1999

世界淡水魚園オアシスパーク
Oasis Park

こどもは水が好きだ、
水が人を集める
Children like water,
and people gather around water.

1999

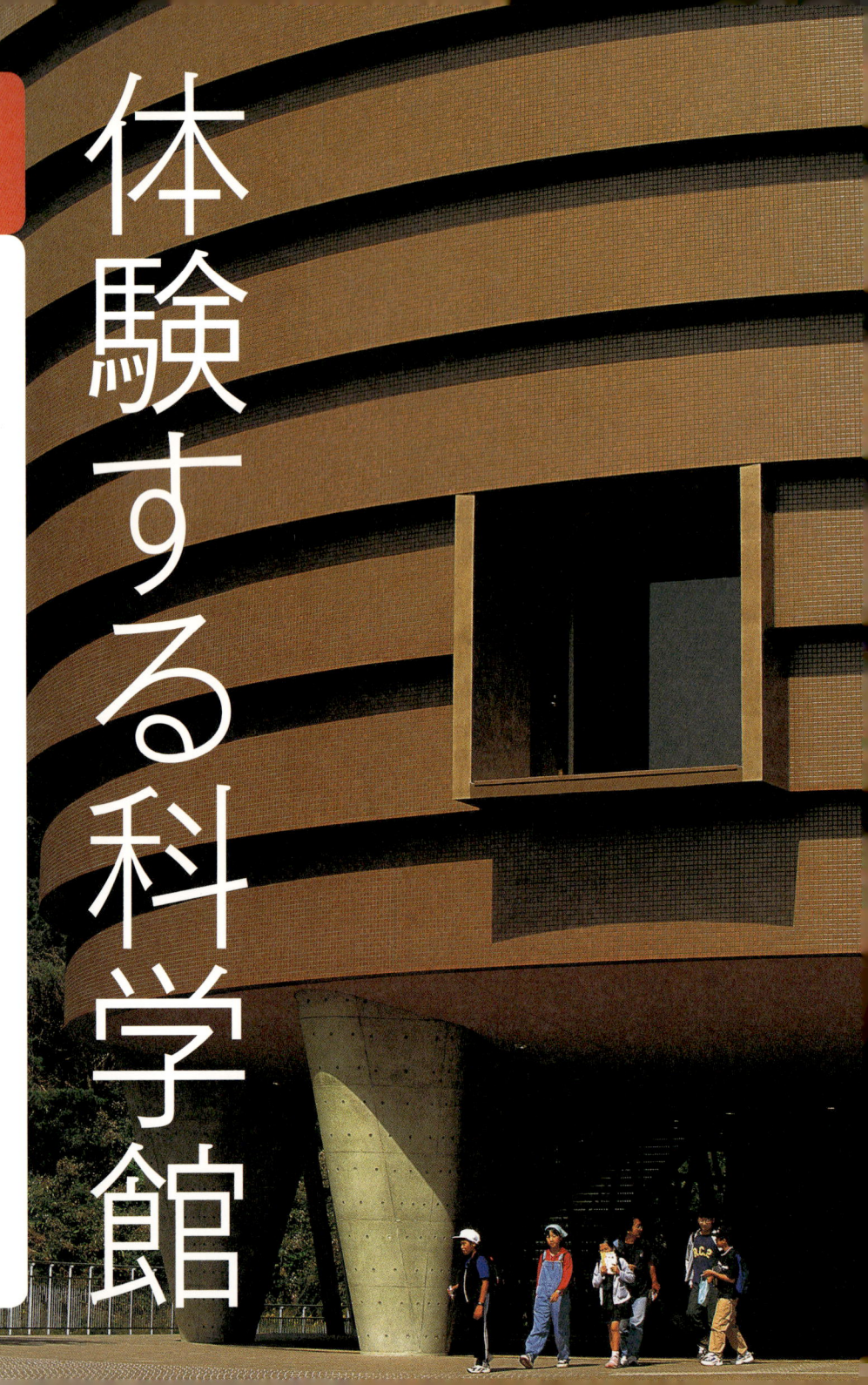

岐阜県先端科学技術体験センター
Gifu Advanced Science and Technology Experience Center

体験する科学館

岐阜県先端科学技術体験センター

岐阜県瑞浪市明世町／1999
Gifu Advanced Science and Technology Experience Center
Akiyo-cho, Mizunami-shi, Gifu

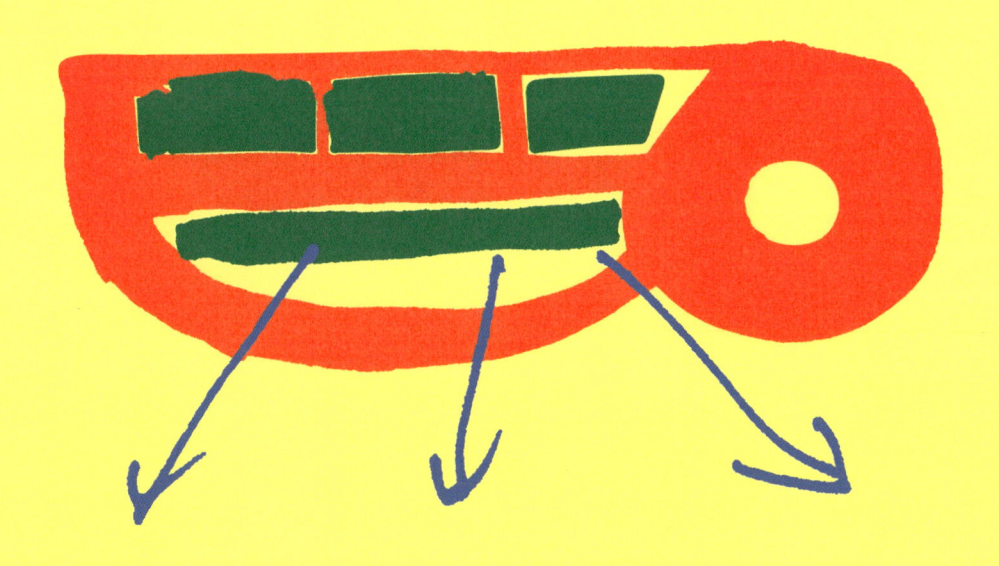

本施設は、従来の科学館とは異なり展示物を見せるのが目的ではなく体験する科学館として計画され、展示物がないのが最大の特徴である。さまざまな実験室が中心的な空間となり、全体の構成は遊環構造に基づいている。エントランス上部に位置する実験ショーを行なうレクチャーラボの形態は、遠心分離機をモチーフにしたものである。

Different from conventional science museums that simply exhibit items, this facility was designed as a hands-on science hall, and its main feature is the lack of objects for display only. The central space is taken up by various experiment rooms with an overall construction based on the concept of recreational structures. The shape of the lecture lab, located above the entrance and serving as a place for hands-on shows, is based on a centrifuge motif.

1999

岐阜県先端科学技術体験センター
Gifu Advanced Science and Technology Experience Center

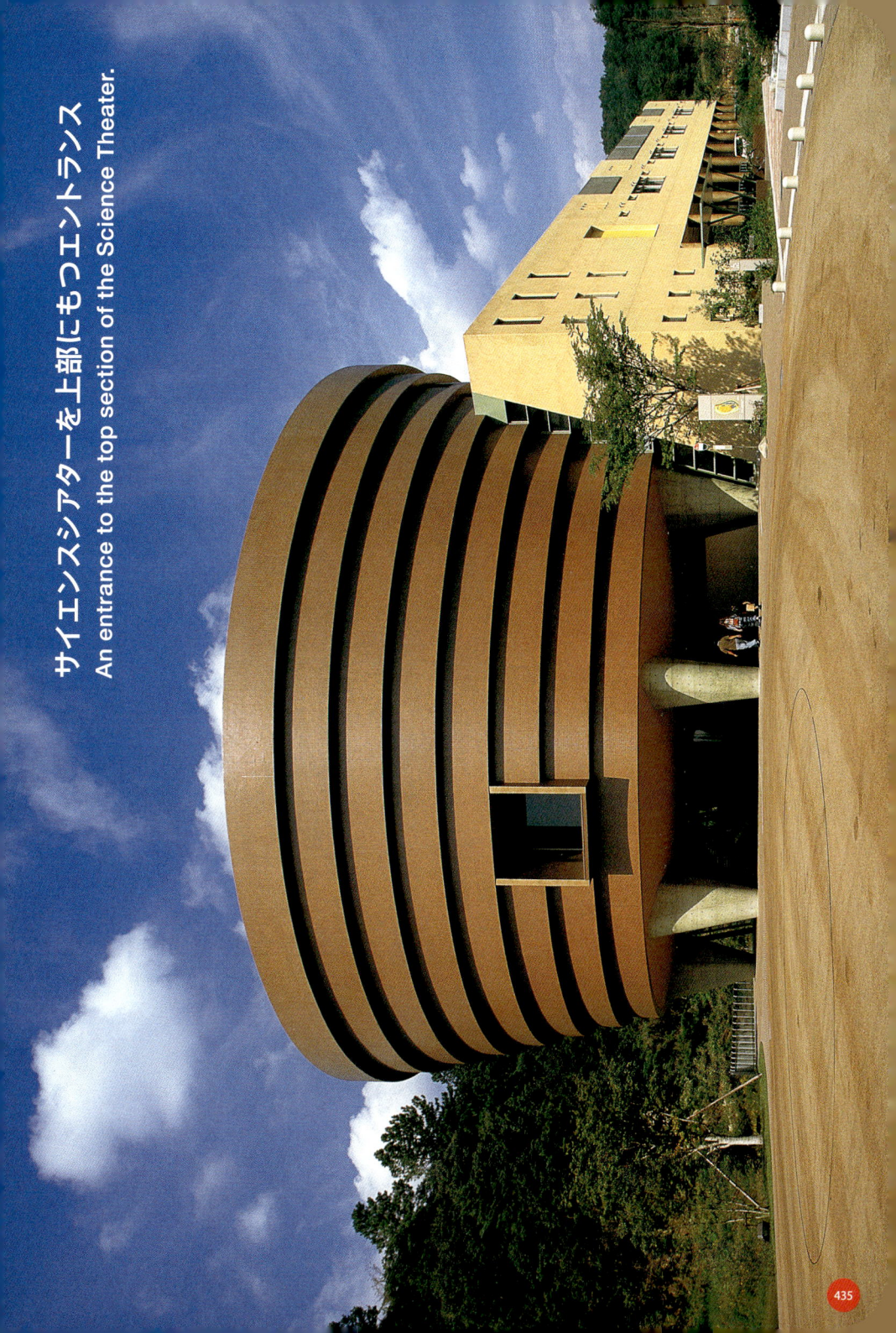

サイエンスシアターを上部にもつエントランス
An entrance to the top section of the Science Theater.

1999

岐阜県先端科学技術体験センター　Gifu Advanced Science and Technology Experience Center

437

1999

岐阜県先端科学技術体験センター　Gifu Advanced Science and Technology Experience Center

実験するだけの科学館が
日本にもっと増えれば良い

It would be good if there were
more science centers in Japan
that are used solely
for experiments.

1999

都市の親水空間

富岩運河環水公園　Fugan Canal Park

富岩運河環水公園

富山県富山市湊入船町／1999
Fugan Canal Park
Minatoirifune-machi, Toyama-shi, Toyama

産業的には役目を終わった富岩運河を中心として富山駅北側を再開発する目的で、1989年富山県カナルパーク指名設計競技が行われ、本提案は最優秀案として選定された。富岩運河の最終的なエッジは、直径35mの美しい水盤によってよみがえった。約20年間にわたり天門橋、小運河、野外劇場、コーヒーショップ等が連続的に建設され、また、隣接した県立施設、市立体育館ができ、多くの市民に利用されている。新しい副都心の核を形成している。

In 1989, a design contest was held with the purpose of redeveloping the northern side of Toyama Station centered around Fugan Canal, which had industrially concluded its services. The edge of Fugan Canal has been reborn in the form of a beautiful 35-meter diameter basin. There have been a series of developments over a period of nearly 20 years, including Tenmon Bridge, small canals, outside theaters, and coffee shops used by a large number of residents. The park is forming the center of a new city center.

1999

歩道橋と塔状ギャラリーという機能を持つ天門橋
Tenmonbashi bridge serves the functions
of a pedestrian bridge and a tower-structure gallery.

富岩運河環水公園　Fugan Canal Park

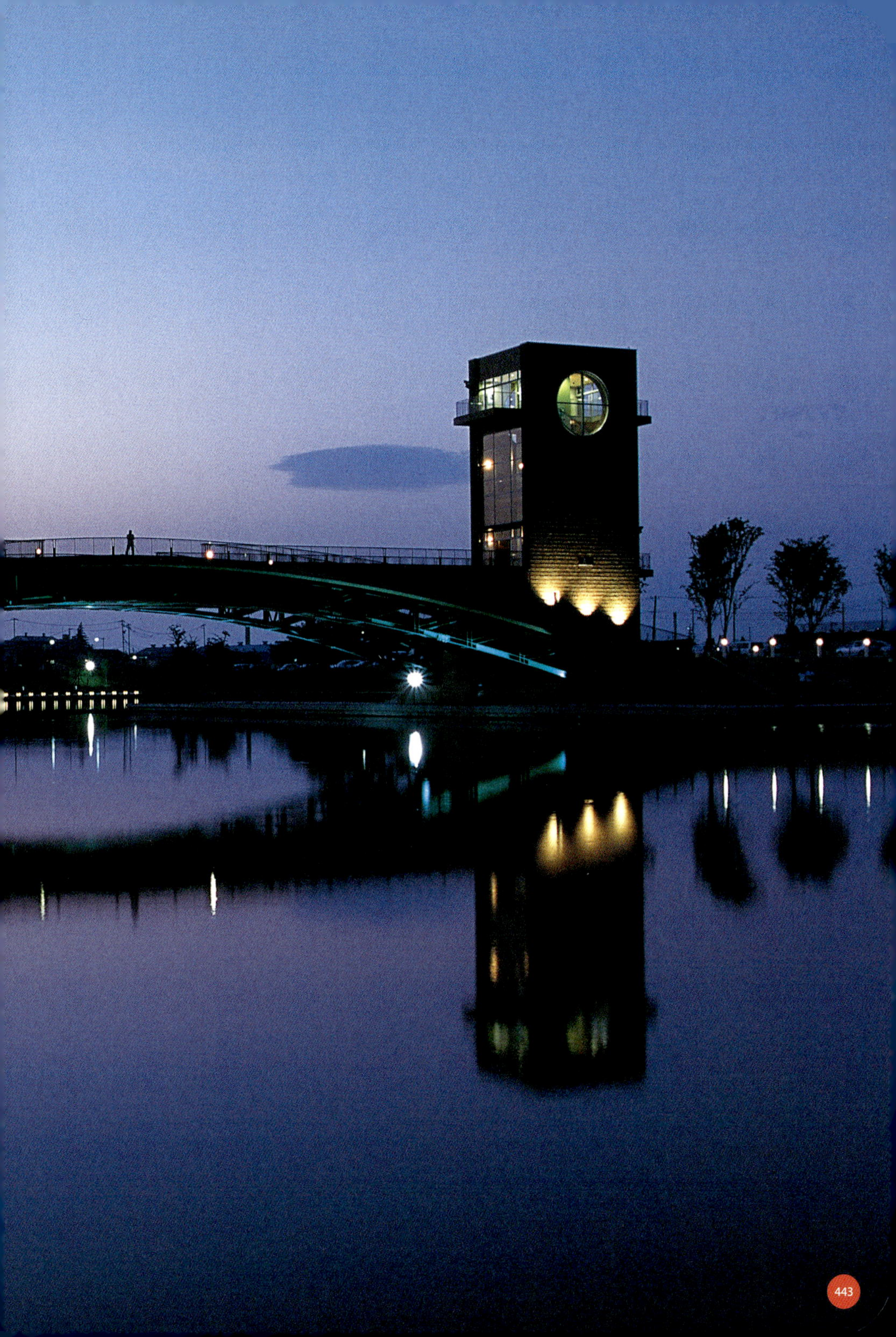

1999

富岩運河環水公園　Fugan Canal Park

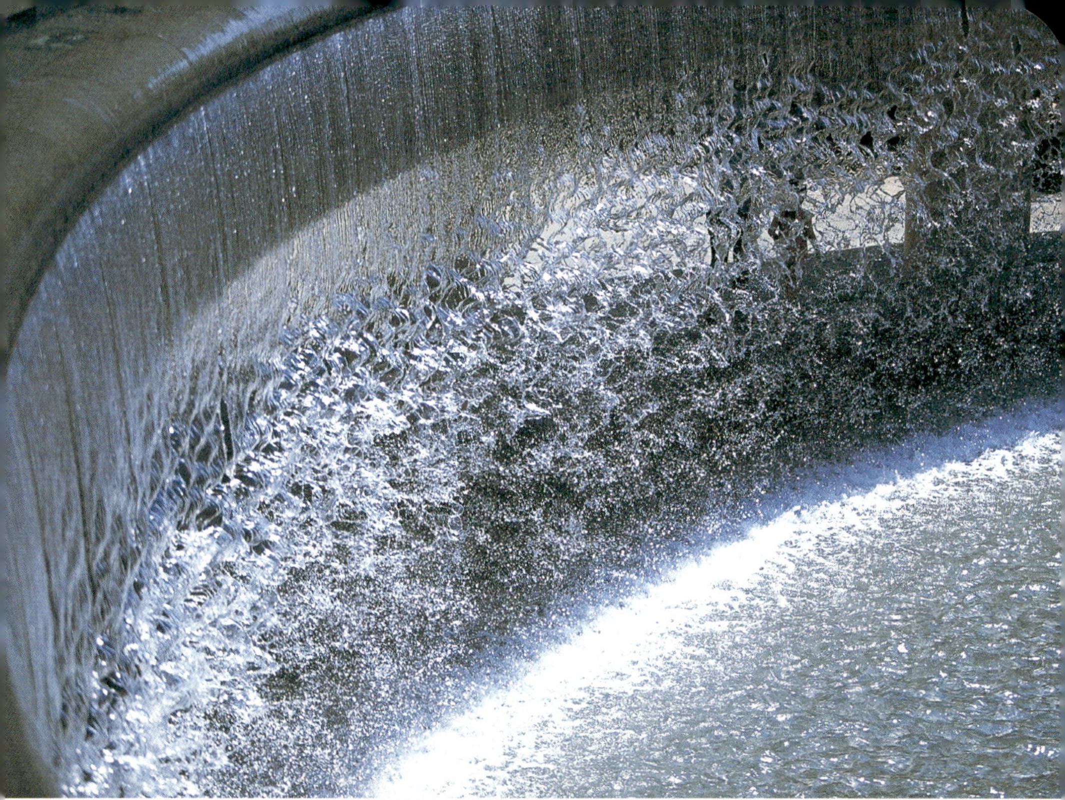

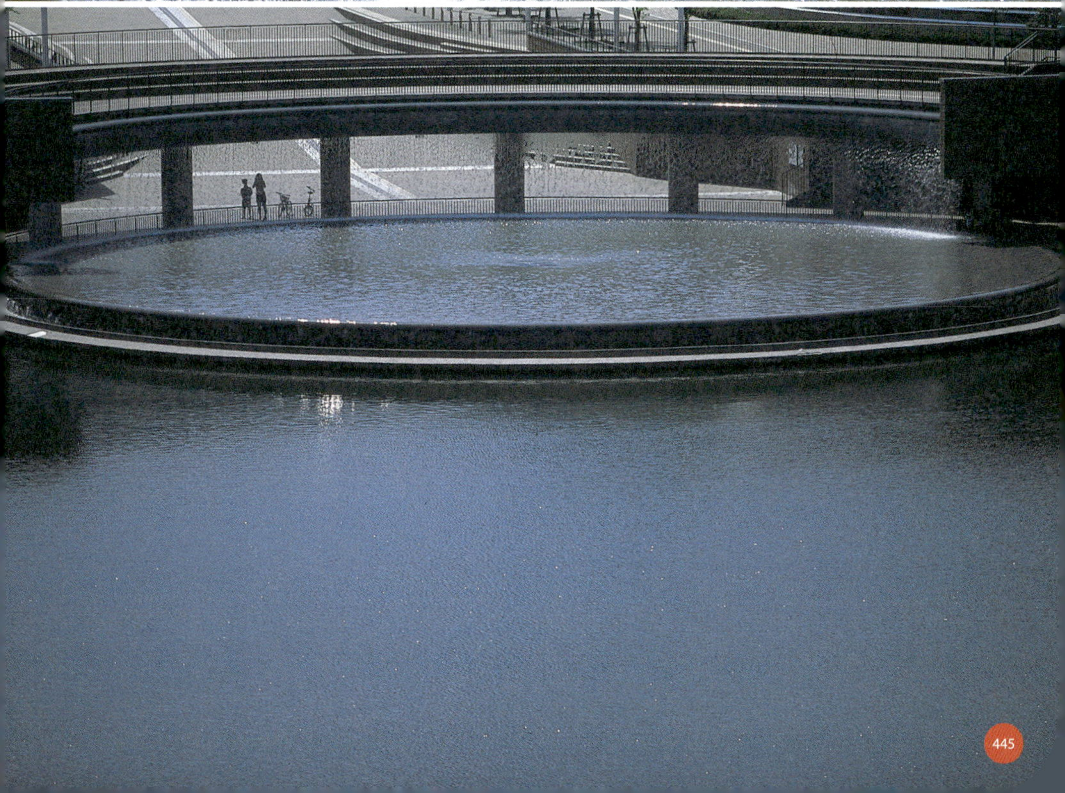

1999

富岩運河環水公園　Fugan Canal Park

天門橋より富山新都心を望む
Look over the new city center of Toyama from the Tenmonbashi bridge.

1999

富岩運河環水公園　Fugan Canal Park

Starbucks Coffeeが出店して水際の賑わいが増した
The Starbucks Coffee store has contributed to the bustle at the waterfront.

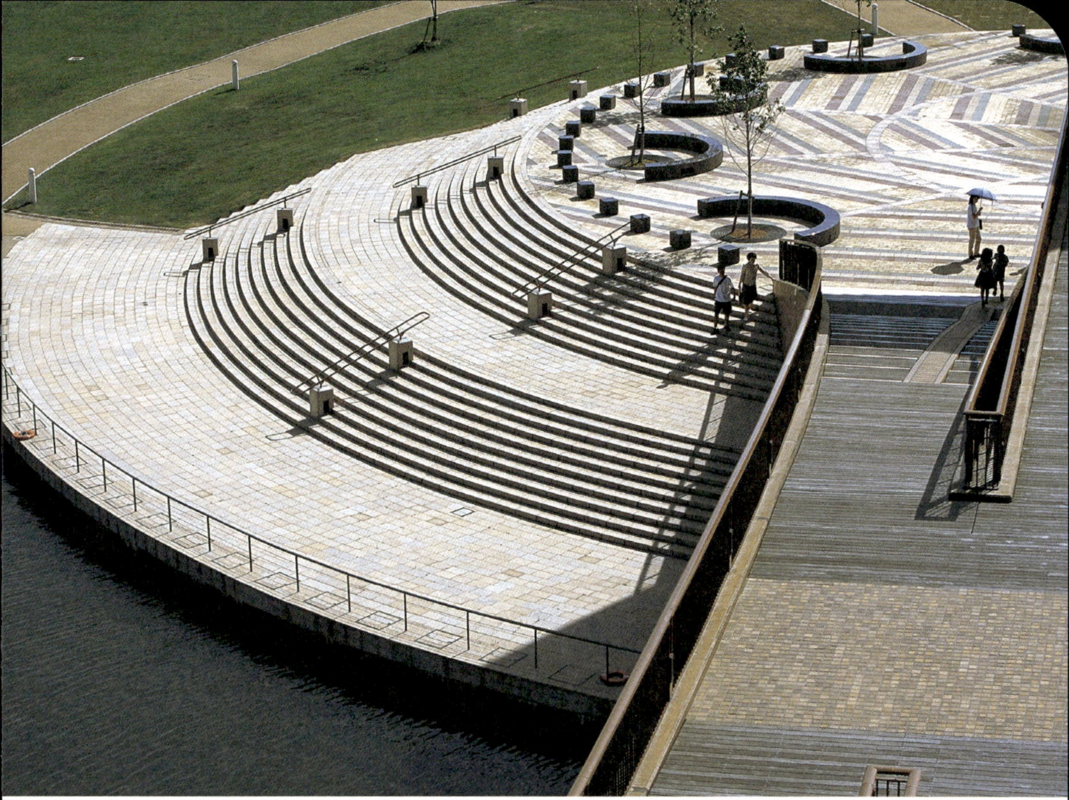

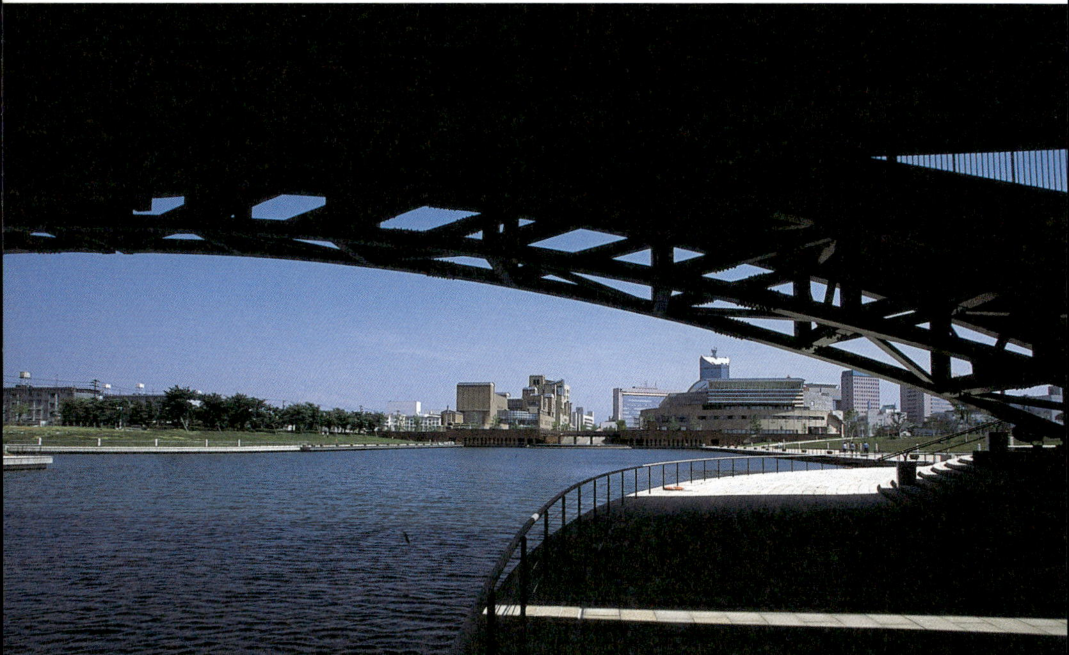

やすらぎの環

1999

やすらぎミラージュ
Yasuragi Mirage

やすらぎミラージュ

東京都練馬区大泉町／1999
Yasuragi Mirage
Oizumi-machi, Nerima-ku, Tokyo

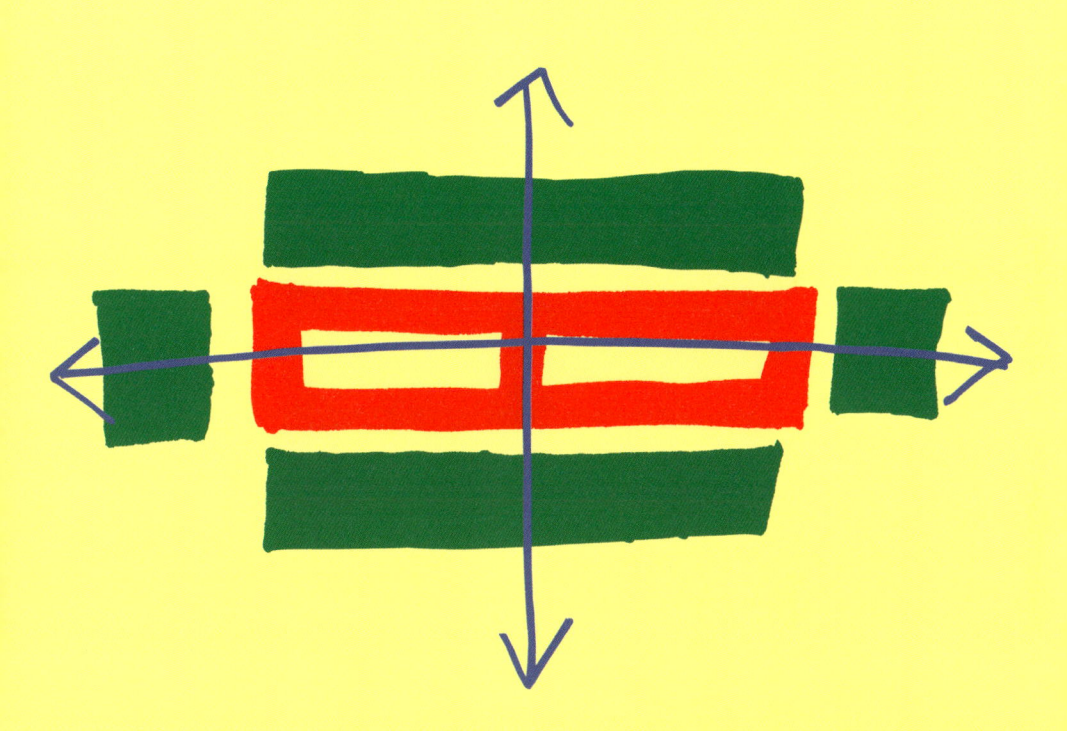

敷地は東京郊外の閑静な住宅地である。東西に長い敷地の中央にクスノキのある中庭を設け、回遊性と安らぎのある遊環構造理論に基づく老人福祉施設として計画された。規模は、24室・84床である。

Sited in a quiet residential area, with its longitudinal axis from east to west, and centered on a courtyard with a kusunoki tree at its heart, this is a welfare facility for the elderly constructed based on circular play system theory that boasts the elements of circulation and serenity. Capacity is 24 rooms and 84 beds.

1999

やすらぎミラージュ　Yasuragi Mirage

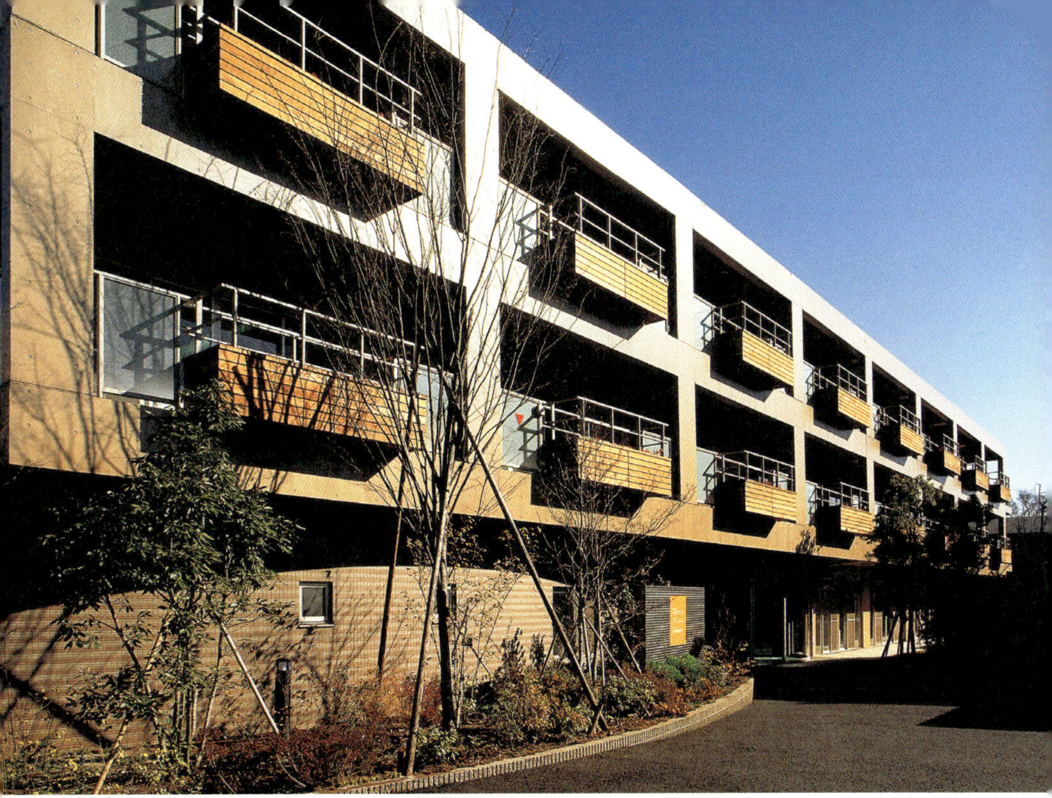

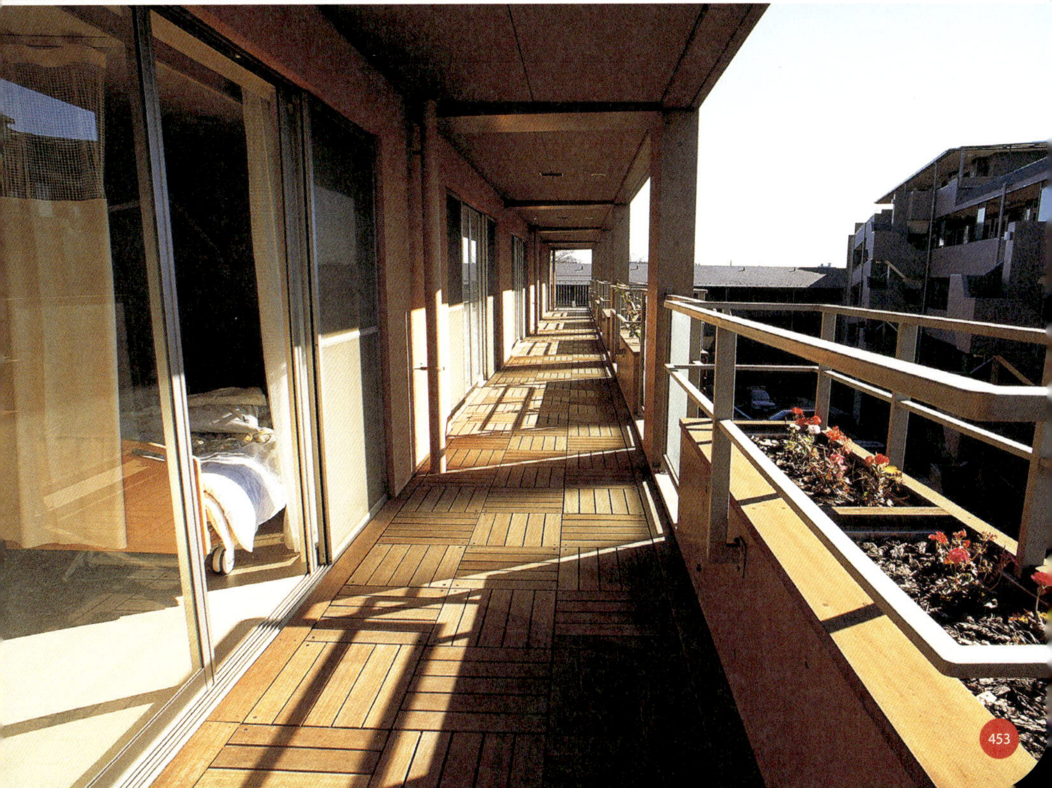

1999

大森の家
Omori House

2.5m × 10mプール

大森の家

東京都大田区大森東／1999
Omori House
Omorihigashi, Ota-ku, Tokyo

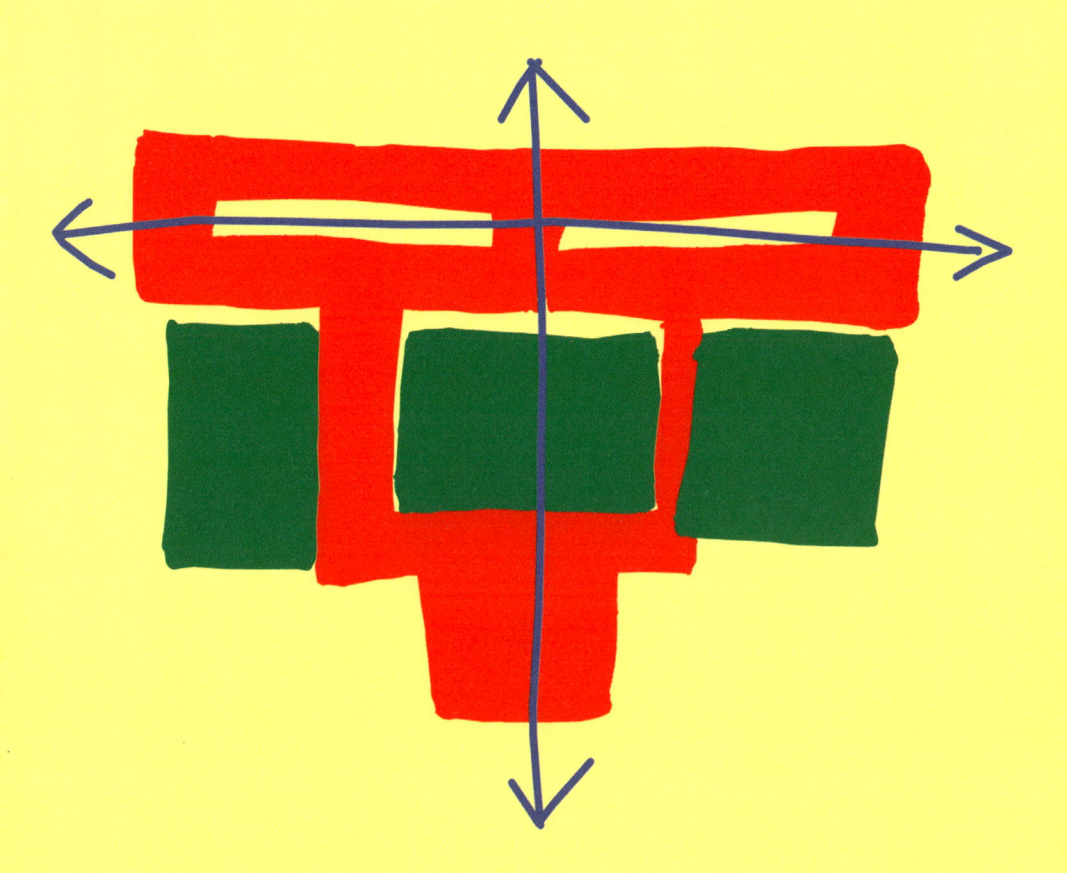

施主は当時30代前半と若く、2人のこどもも幼児であった。下町の比較的狭い敷地に両親と住む予定で2世帯住宅として計画された。1階に両親の部屋、2階はリビングとダイニング、キッチン、3階は寝室階である。屋上には2.5m×10mのプールがある。十字式設計法により、四隅に緑が配され、近隣との関係が考慮された。

At the time it was built, the owner was in his early thirties, and his two children were small children. It was designed as a duplex on a relatively small plot in the downtown area so that he can live with his parents. His parents' room was on the first floor, living room, dining room and kitchen on the second floor, and bedrooms on the third floor. On the roof is a 2.5m × 10m pool. The criss-cross design method allows for placing green in each of the four corners in consideration of the structure's relationship with the neighborhood.

1999

大森の家　Omori House

屋上のプールは展望台
The roof-top pool is a viewing platform.

風と光が家のすみずみまで行き渡る
Wind and natural light penetrate each and every corner of the house.

1999

大森の家
Omori House

プレイステーションはこどもの基地だ、
居間の中心に対峙する

The playstation is a cemetery for children;
it takes a confronting stance
in the heart of the living room.

1998

春日部の家
Kasukabe House

廊空間住宅

春日部の家

埼玉県春日部市／1998
Kasukabe House
Kasukabe-shi, Saitama

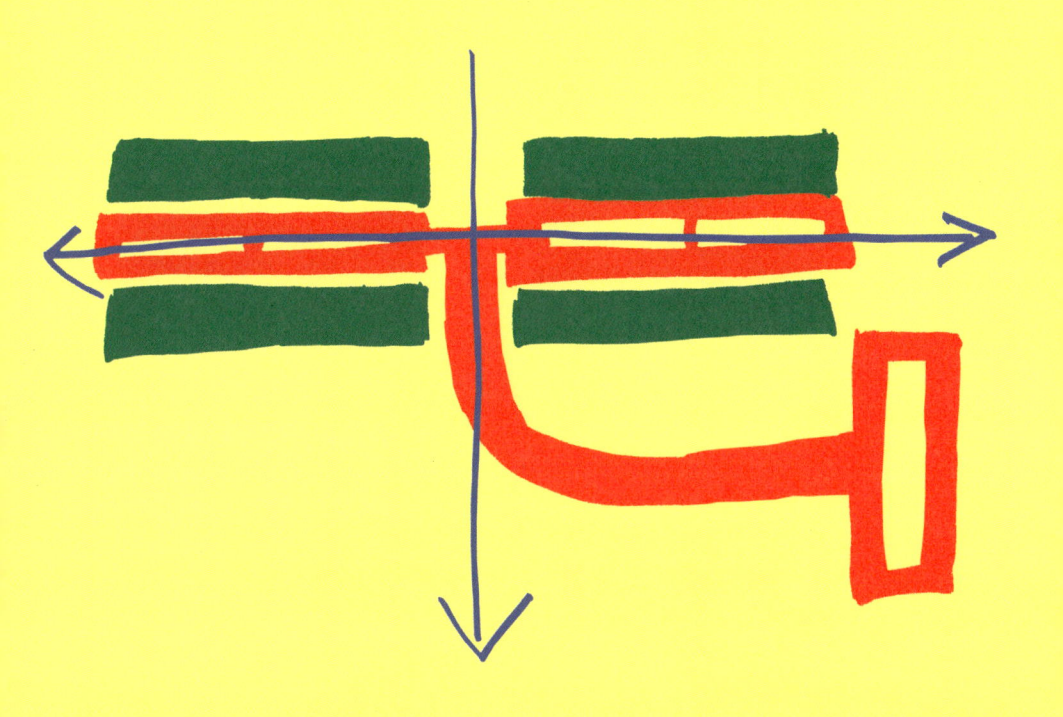

埼玉県郊外につくられた3世代、2世帯のための住宅である。敷地は旧地主で庭を囲む母屋、客屋、門屋という伝統的な佇まいをもちながら、全体としては現代的で快適な楽しさのある住生活が営まれるような空間構成が意図されている。

This house is a duplex for a family of three generations built in the suburbs of Saitama Prefecture. It is a traditional style house with the main house surrounding the garden, with a guest house and gate house. Overall it is a modern space that provides comfortable pleasure to those who live there.

1998

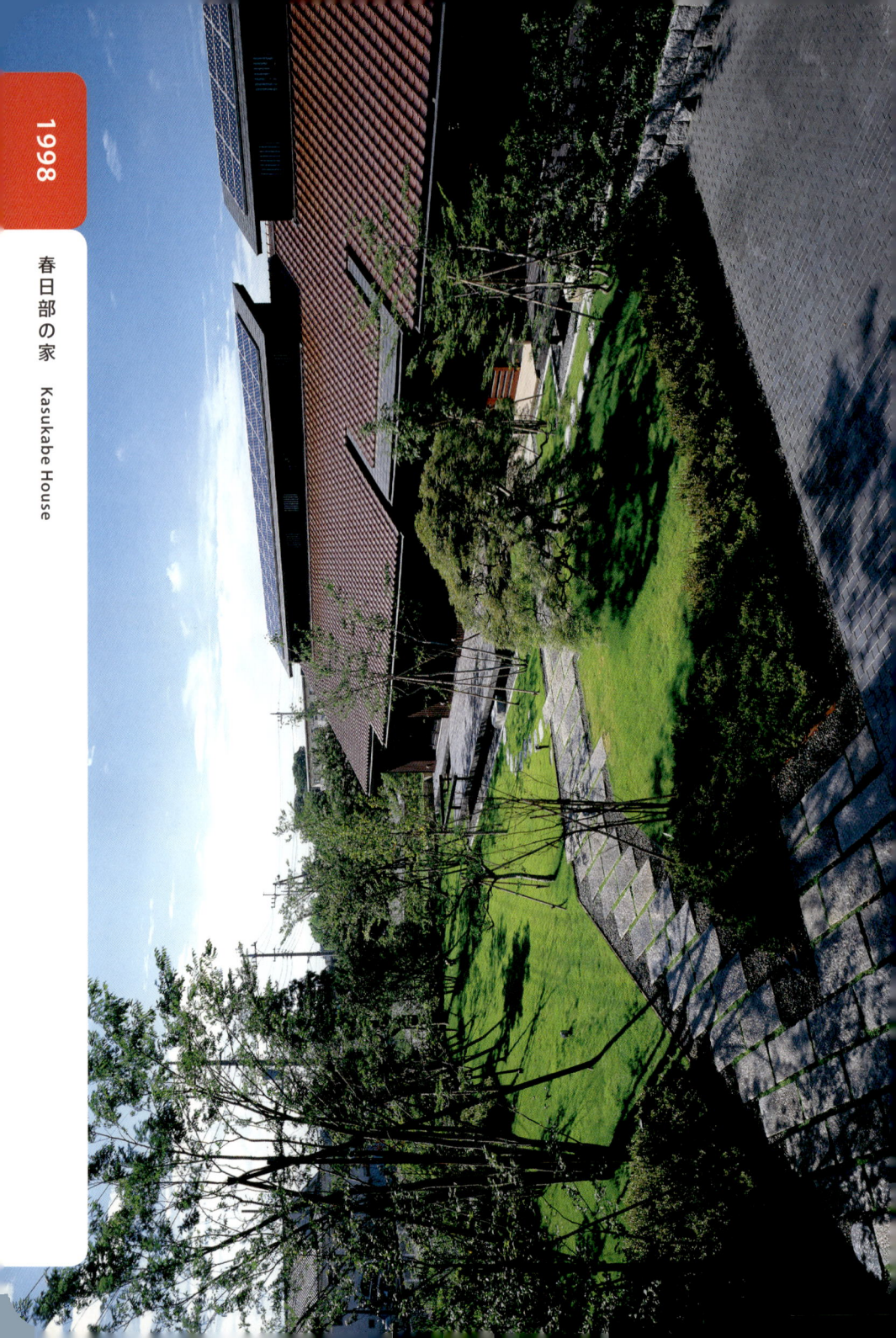

春日部の家　Kasukabe House

和室の原型は庭との関係によって決まる

The form of the Japanese room is decided based on its relationship with the garden.

サイエンスシップ

1998

山梨県立科学館
Yamanashi Prefectural Science Center

山梨県立科学館

山梨県甲府市愛宕町／1998
Yamanashi Prefectural Science Center
Atago-machi, Kofu-shi, Yamanashi

甲府を一望できる丘の上に建設された科学館である。風致地区である敷地の等高線に緩やかに沿った曲面形状を持ち、展示ストーリーの効果的な展開ができる一体型の展示空間が構想された。施設は遊環構造による空間構成が展開されている。木の大断面集成材により船の構造を引用し、未来へ夢を広げる「科学の船」をイメージさせるシンボリックな形態である。

This is a science museum constructed on the top of a hill with a panoramic view of Kofu. With a curved surface that loosely follows the contours of the scenic site, the center has an integrated exhibition space capable of effectively developing the exhibition narrative. The facility's architectural space is composed of a circular play system. Using large-surface laminated wood to create a ship's structure architecturally, the facility takes on a symbolic shape that incites visualization of a "Science Ship" inspiring dreams of the future.

1998

山梨県立科学館
Yamanashi Prefectural Science Center

467

1998

山梨県立科学館
Yamanashi Prefectural Science Center

屋外もサイエンス遊具であふれている
The outdoor area is also filled with science play structure.

469

1998

福井県児童科学館
Fukui Children's Science Center

サイエンス＆プレイ

福井県児童科学館

福井県坂井郡春江町／1998
Fukui Children's Science Center
Harue-cho, Sakai-gun, Fukui

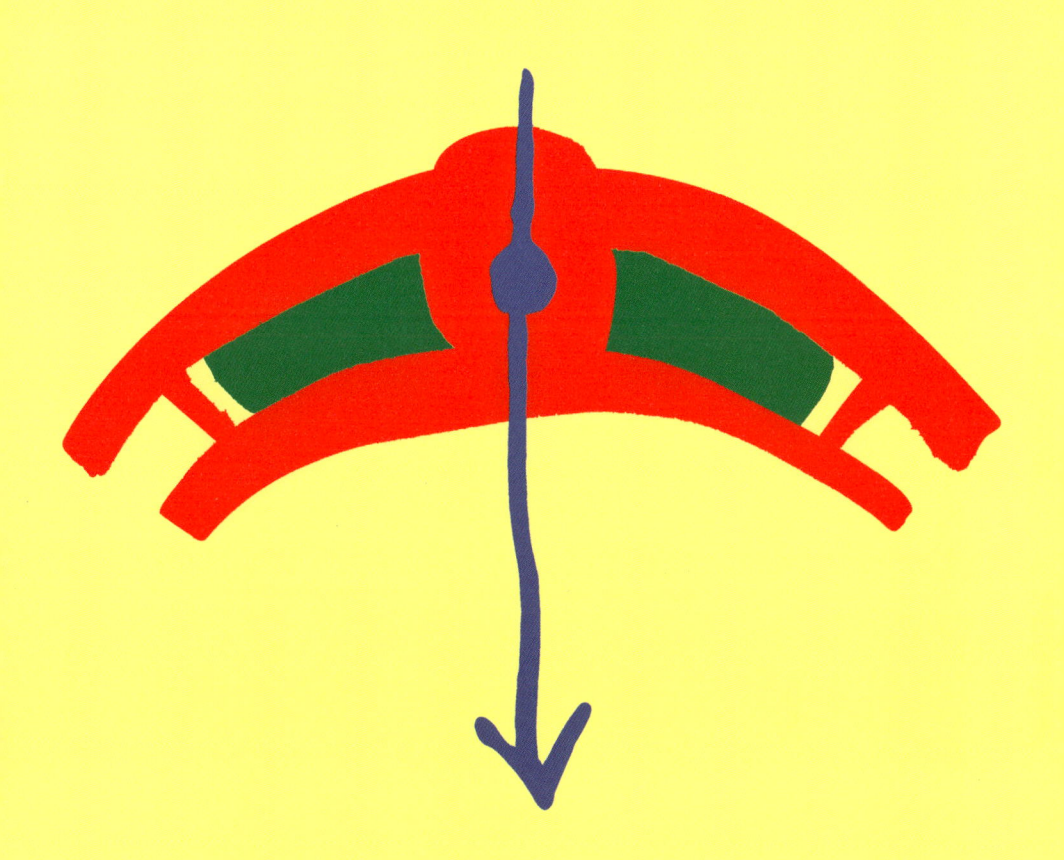

福井県の中央部福井市の北に位置するベッドタウン春江町に建設された。大きな翼状の平面をもち、中央にホール、両翼に科学ゾーンとあそびゾーンにより構成されている。あそびゾーンには恐竜広場と呼ばれる室内あそび場、絵本のコーナー、乳児コーナーなども設けられている。敷地は5.5ヘクタール、全体として「環境」をテーマとした内外ともに遊環構造にもとづく科学公園としてデザインされている。

This facility was constructed in the town of Harue, a bed town north of Fukui City, in the center of Fukui Prefecture. Shaped like a large pair of wings, there is a hall in the center with a science zone and play zone on each respective wing. The play zone wing includes an indoor play area called "Dinosaur square," along with a picture book corner, infants corner, and more. The 5.5-hectare area is designed as an indoor-outdoor science park based on circular play system theory under the theme of "the environment."

1998

福井県児童科学館

Fukui Children's Science Center

あそびと発見を喚起する環境は、5.5ヘクタールの敷地に科学館とサイエンス遊具が展開する

An environment that play and exploration is created in the 5.5-hectare grounds, where a science center (main building and annex) and science play structure can be found.

1998

福井県児童科学館　Fukui Children's Science Center

475

1998

福井県児童科学館　Fukui Children's Science Center

477

1998

但馬の山並みを望む開閉ドーム

兵庫県立但馬ドーム　Hyogo Prefectural Tajima Dome

兵庫県立但馬ドーム

兵庫県豊岡市日高町／1998
Hyogo Prefectural Tajima Dome
Hidaka-cho, Toyooka-shi, Hyogo

本プロジェクトは1995年のオープンコンペで最優秀案となり、採用された開閉ドームである。左右150m、最高高さ60mの巨大な空間で、観客席は3層構造になっている。上階からは但馬地方の雄大な景観が楽しめる。スポーツミュージアムというコンセプトによってドーム自体が展望、観覧、休息、学習機能を楽しめる立体的な遊環構造を持っている。外観は開閉部分のテフロン膜の部分と北側の山小屋風の多重屋根の金属部分に大きく分けられ、南側は白、北側は渋茶というように色彩的にも様々な表情、様々な景観をもつドームである。

This retractable dome has a huge space, 150m from side to side, and 60m at the highest point, with three tiers of seating. Created with the concept of a "sports museum", the dome is itself a three-dimensional circular play system where one can enjoy the play, view, rest, or even study. This dome has various faces. The outside appearance has two different scenes, which are Teflon membrane area which can be opened and metal area of multiplex roofs like mountain villa, as well as various different expressions created by using white on the south side and a dark brown on the north side.

1998

兵庫県立但馬ドーム　Hyogo Prefectural Tajima Dome

高さ60m、幅150mの開閉ドームの目前には但馬の山々が広がる

The mountains of Tajima spread out before one's eyes from the open-shut dome 60m high and 150m wide.

1998

兵庫県立但馬ドーム　Hyogo Prefectural Tajima Dome

15分間で開き、15分間で閉じる
It opens and closes for about 15 minutes respectively.

1998

兵庫県立但馬ドーム　Hyogo Prefectural Tajima Dome

閉じられたドームは大きな和傘の中にいるようだ
The closed dome makes one feel
as if one were standing inside a giant umbrella.

1998

兵庫県立但馬ドーム　Hyogo Prefectural Tajima Dome

こどものための
スポーツミュージアム
A sports museum for children.

1998

運動意欲、交流意欲を喚起する自然発見遊具
Play equipment for discovering nature, which stimulate the desire to exercise and to mingle with others.

兵庫県立但馬ドーム　Hyogo Prefectural Tajima Dome

489

1998

兵庫県立但馬ドーム

Hyogo Prefectural Tajima Dome

緑の中に大きな白い鳥が舞い降りた

As if a large, white bird is descending onto the greenery.

1998

兵庫県立但馬ドーム

Hyogo Prefectural Tajima Dome

美しい建築は往々にして対称形だ
Beautiful architectural structures are often symmetrical.

1998

山並みと連続する大きな山小屋
A large mountain lodge
that continues on from the mountain range.

兵庫県立但馬ドーム　Hyogo Prefectural Tajima Dome

495

∞小学校

1997

川崎市向丘小学校
Mukaigaoka Elementary School, Kawasaki

川崎市向丘小学校

神奈川県川崎市宮前区平／1997
Mukaigaoka Elementary School, Kawasaki
Taira, Miyamae-ku, Kawasaki-shi, Kanagawa

建物内をぐるりと一周できるような廊下と、外廊の空間により多年齢の交流をテーマとして計画された小学校。行き止まりをつくらず、こども達の行動を制限しない動線計画や教室棟と体育館の間のガレリアと呼ぶ半野外広場等の形成により、こども達が友達や先生と交流し、日々変化する自然との新たな出会いを体験することが意図されている。

Inside the elementary school, the corridor allows one to make a complete loop with no dead ends, a plan based on the concept of promoting exchanges between multiple generations via the outer corridor. The design eliminates boundaries on children's movement and includes an indoor-outdoor plaza between the school building and the gymnasium, known as the "Galleria." These allow children to interact with other friends and teachers and to experience new encounters with the daily changing nature.

1997

川崎市向丘小学校

Mukaigaoka Elementary School, Kawasaki

499

1996

愛知県児童総合センター
Aichi Children's Center

斜塔と二重らせん

愛知県児童総合センター

愛知県愛知郡長久手町／1996
Aichi Children's Center
Nagakute-cho, Aichi-gun, Aichi

愛知県長久手青少年公園の中に建設された、日本国内最大規模の大型児童施設である。プレイアトリウム上部には建築的な廊下以外に遊具的廊下が巡らされている。中央部にはチャレンジタワーと呼ぶ二重らせん動線をもつ塔状の遊具建築がテフロンの大屋根を支えている。全体として大きな遊環構造を形成する遊具的建築である。県内の児童施設のセンター機能をもつと同時に、県内のこどものあそび環境の研究・研修機能をもっている。大ホール及び研修実験設備も充実している。

Constructed inside Aichi Prefectural Park, this is one of the Japan's largest children's facility. The "play atrium" is encircled at its top part by a corridor for play equipment, in addition to an architectural corridor. At the center part, a tower-like construction of play equipment called the "Challenge Tower" sustains the large Teflon roof with a double helical flow line. Overall, it comprises a play equipment assembly that forms a great circular play system. It functions as a research and training facility for children's play environments as well as the central function of children's facilities in the prefecture.

1996

愛知県児童総合センター　Aichi Children's Center

中央部のチャレンジタワーには
二重らせんのスロープが取りつき、
それに向かってショートカットのブリッジがからむ
The Challenge Tower in the center has a double-helical flow line; facing that, a bridge serving as a short-cut is entwined.

1996

愛知県児童総合センター

Aichi Children's Center

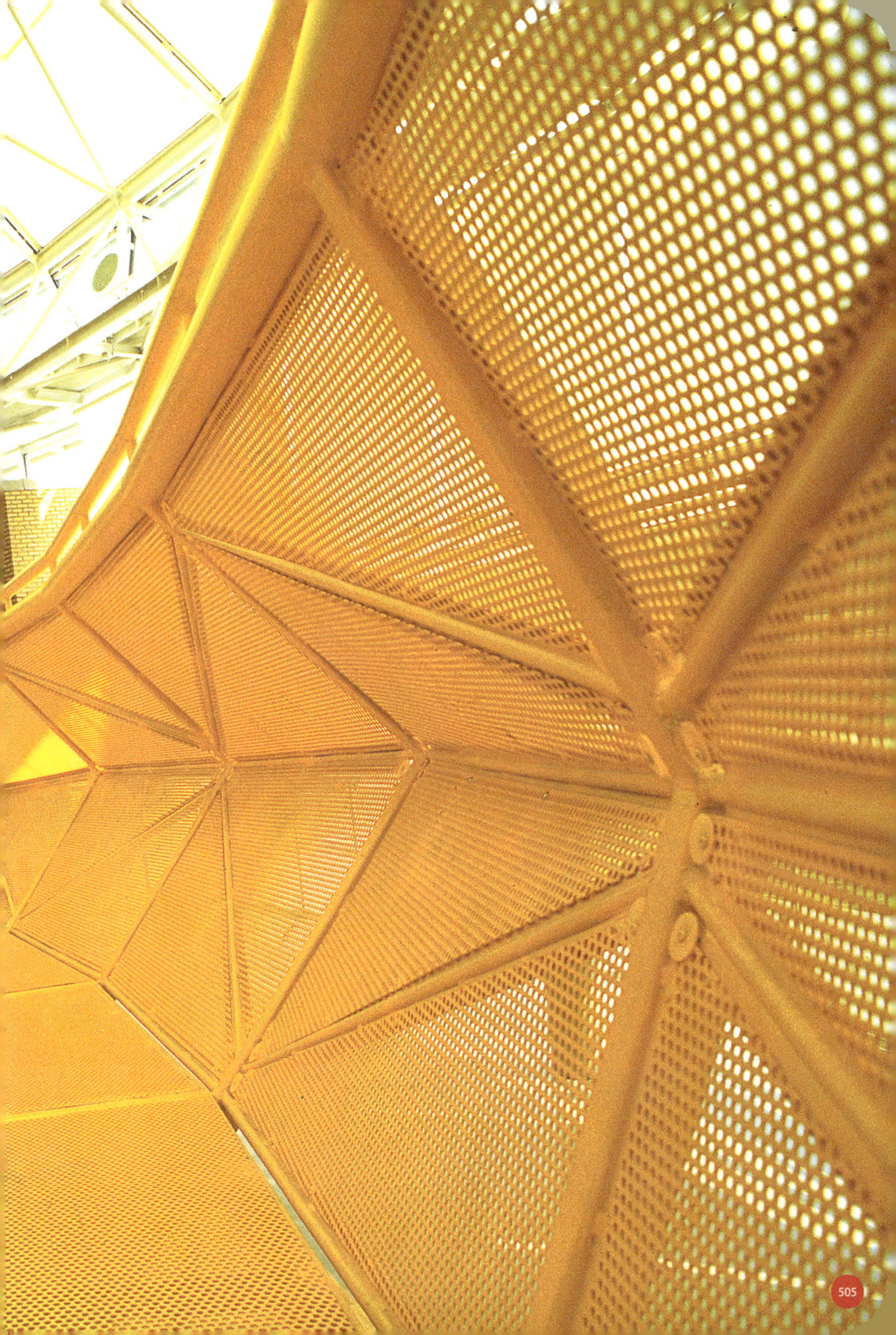

1996

愛知県児童総合センター
Aichi Children's Center

チャレンジタワー内部は、天井の暗転装置により光量が変化する
Inside the Challenge Tower, a dimming unit on the ceiling adjusts the degree of light in the space.

507

1996

愛知県児童総合センター　Aichi Children's Center

509

1996

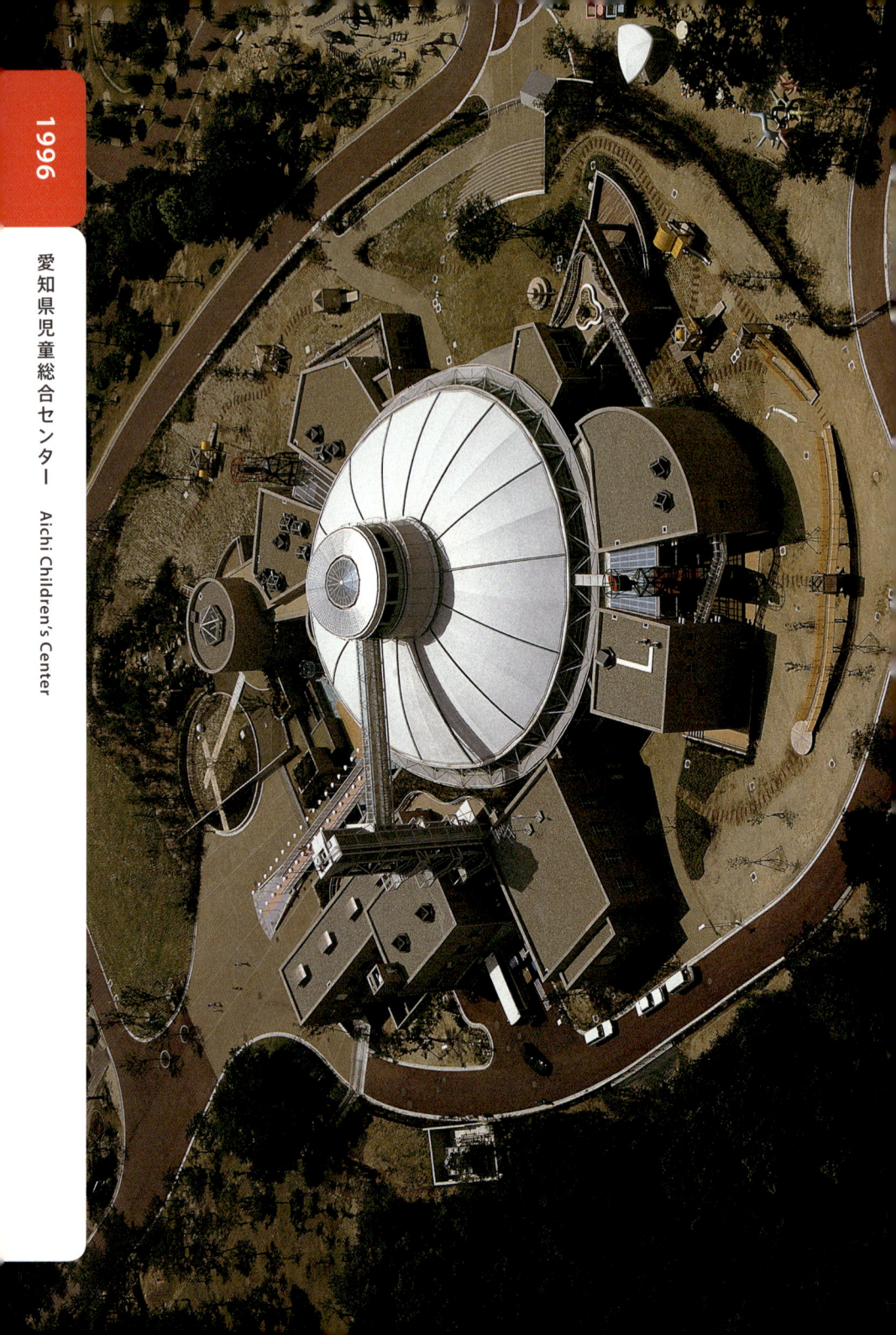

愛知県児童総合センター　Aichi Children's Center

大屋根はテフロン膜で透過率16％
The degree of light penetration through the large roof, with its Teflon film, is 16%.

1996

五藤光学研究所山梨工場
Goto Optical MFG. Yamanashi Factory

光学研究

五藤光学研究所山梨工場

山梨県南アルプス市下市之瀬／1996
Goto Optical MFG. Yamanashi Factory
Shimoichinose, Minamialps-shi, Yamanashi

山梨県につくられたプラネタリウム制作工場である。施設は大きく2つのゾーンに分けられ、エントランス・食堂・更衣室は外部の恵まれた自然に対して、開放的で明るい、くつろげる空間である。それに対して監理・設計・開発・研究部門は、機能的欲求から自然光が入りにくい空間である。外部には芝生のオープンスペースが設けられ、従業員のためのレクリエーションスペースとして利用されている。

This is a planetarium factory built in Yamanashi Prefecture. This facility is divided into two primary zones, with the entrance, dining room and changing room created as open, bright and relaxing spaces oriented to the luxuriant nature outside. The control, design, development and research section, due to functional requirements, is created as structure into which natural light does not readily penetrate. There is an open lawn space created outside that is used as a recreation space.

1996

五藤光学研究所山梨工場

Goto Optical MFG. Yamanashi Factory

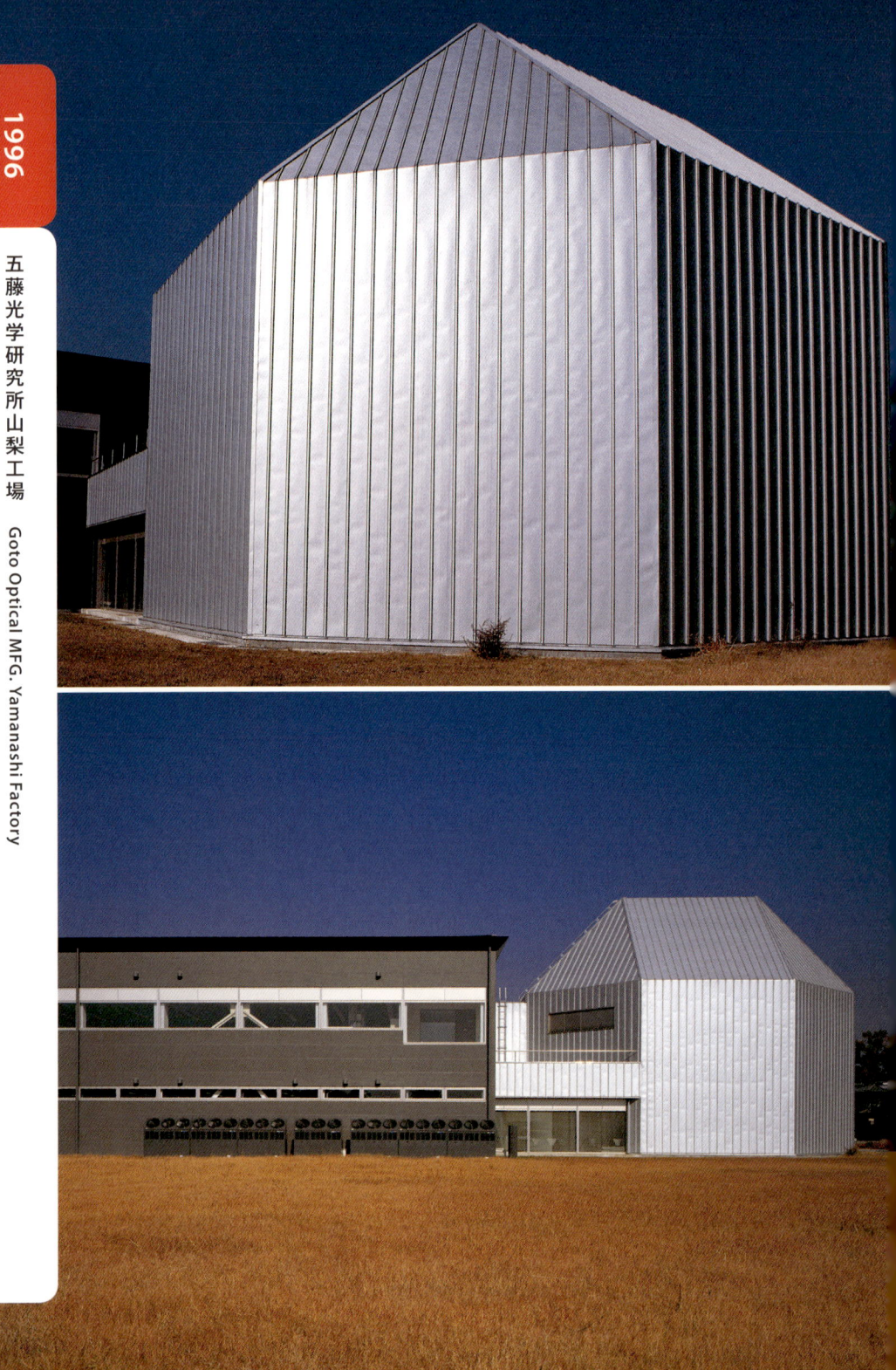

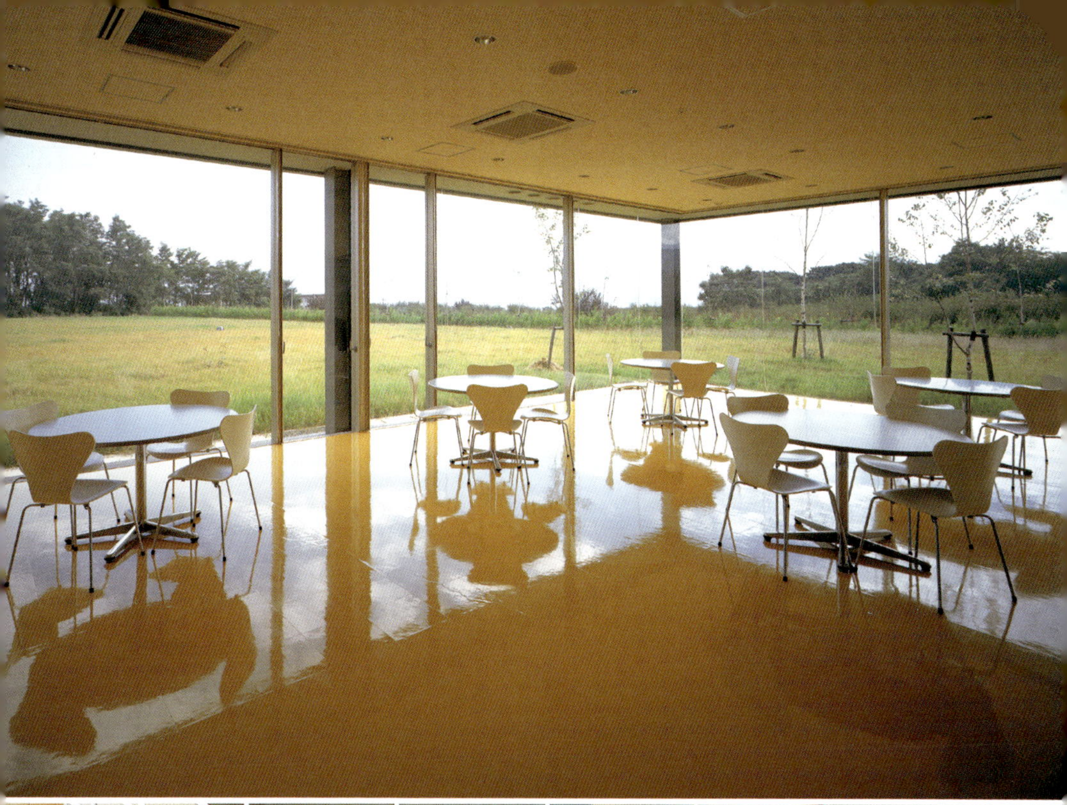

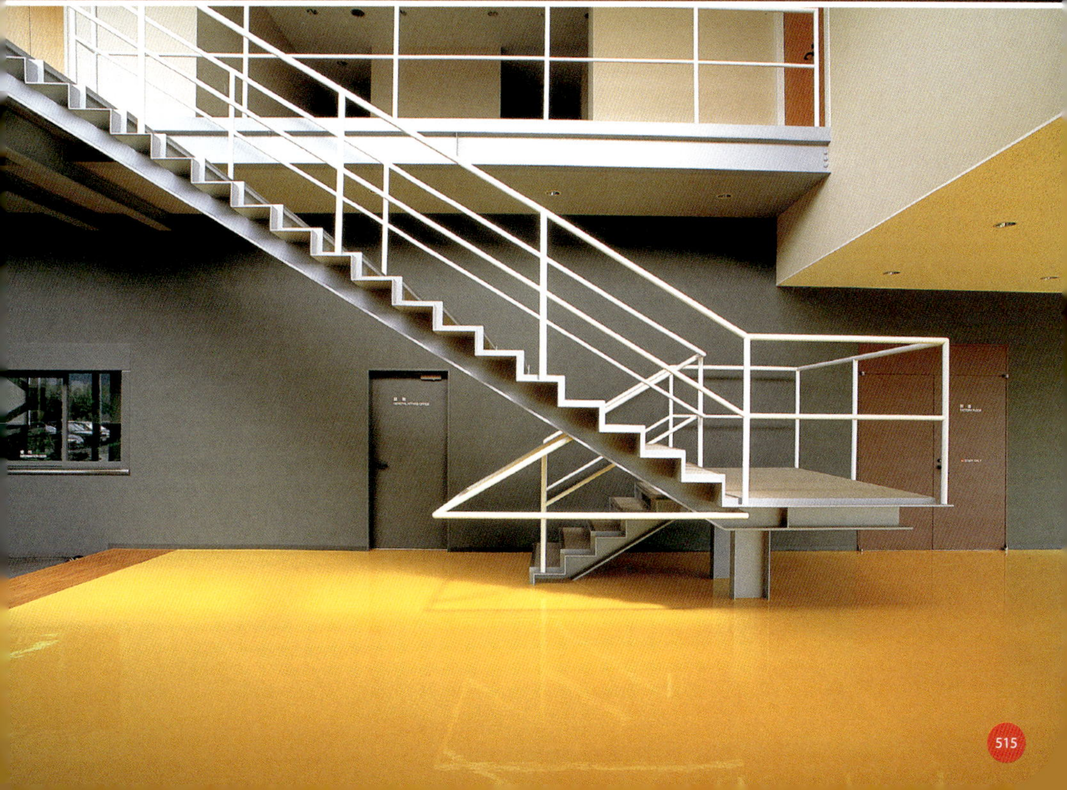

1996

珠洲ビーチホテル
Suzu Beach Hotel

ペントハウス

珠洲ビーチホテル

石川県珠洲市蛸島町／1996
Suzu Beach Hotel
Takojima-machi, Suzu-shi, Ishikawa

能登半島の周遊観光客を対象としたリゾートホテル機能と、地域住民を対象としたウェルネス機能を組み合わせた総合的なレクリエーション施設である。海に向かってまっすぐに伸びる700mのアプローチをもち、細長い平面形と客室の最上部にプールを載せた断面構成が特徴的である。海の景観がすばらしいペントハウスプール、珠洲特産の珪藻土を用いた内装壁、どの部屋からも富山湾を望める客室など、訪れる人が思い出をもって帰れるような空間体験が意図された。

This is a comprehensive recreation facility that combines the features of a resort hotel targeting sightseers visiting the Noto Peninsula and the features of a wellness center for local residents. The facility has a 700-meter approach that stretches straight out into the ocean, and presents a unique cross-sectional construction that has an elongated, flat guest room space with a pool set on the top floor. The facility was built so that visitors would be able to take home memories from their stay. There is a penthouse with a breathtaking view of the ocean and a pool.

1996

珠洲ビーチホテル　Suzu Beach Hotel

519

1996

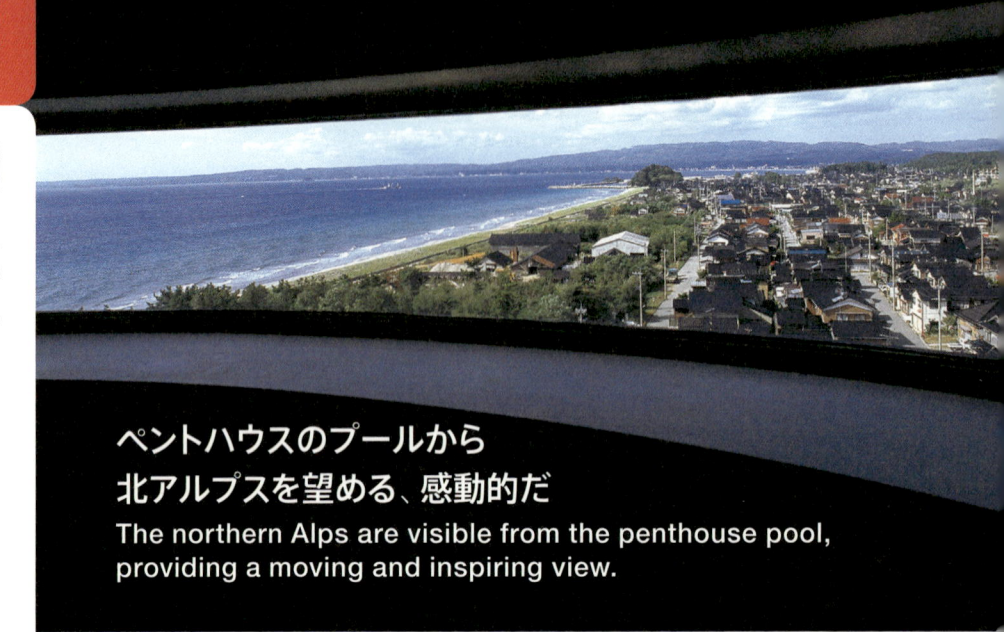

珠洲ビーチホテル
Suzu Beach Hotel

ペントハウスのプールから
北アルプスを望める、感動的だ
The northern Alps are visible from the penthouse pool, providing a moving and inspiring view.

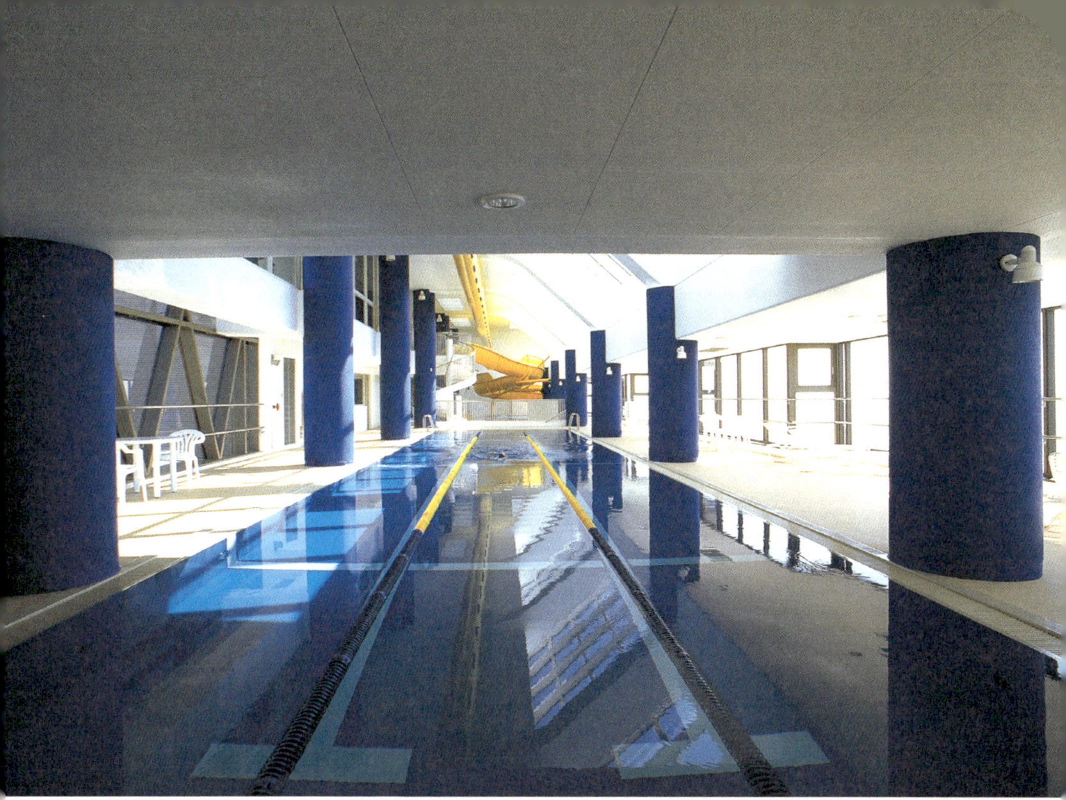

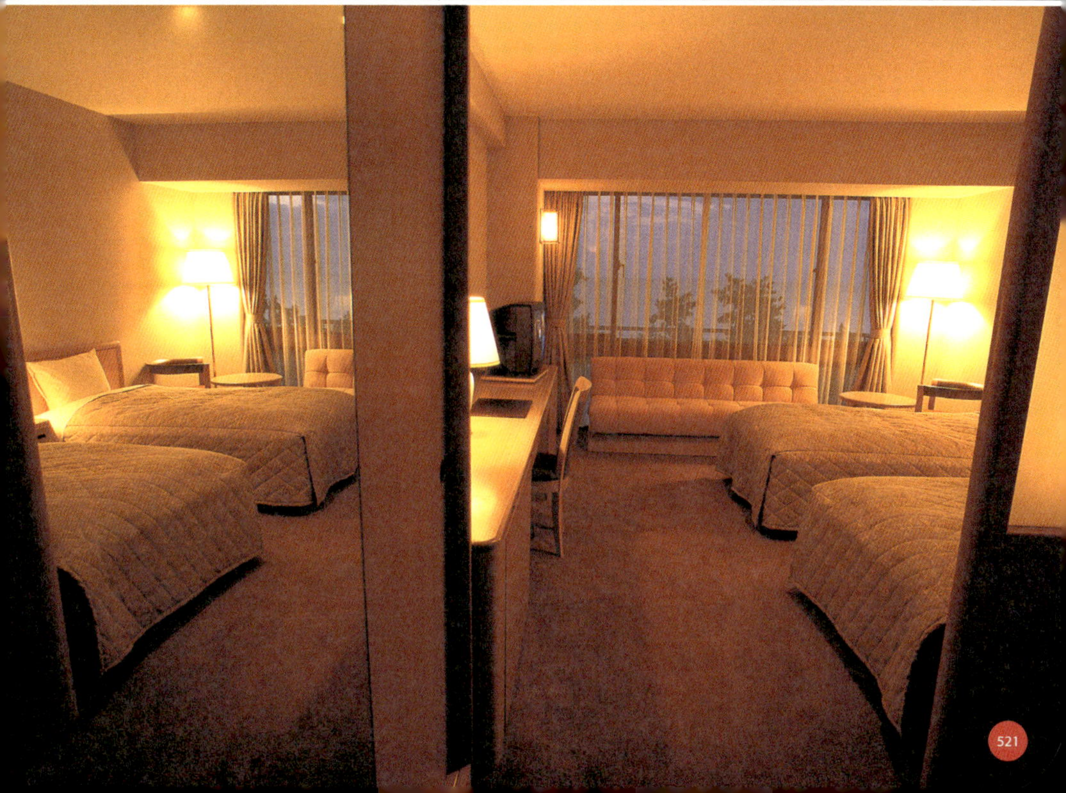

長崎の町に

1996

長崎市科学館
Nagasaki Science Museum

長崎市科学館

長崎県長崎市油木町／1996
Nagasaki Science Museum
Aburagi-machi, Nagasaki-shi, Nagasaki

坂の町、長崎に建つ科学館である。建築全体のボリュームを抑えつつ、町のシンボルとなり利用者にも分かりやすい施設として展示棟・プラネタリウム・天文台はそれぞれ特徴ある形態・仕上げで構成された。全体として船の町長崎が象徴されている。展示室内部では長崎の町並みをイメージし、ひな壇状に6つのレベルに分節化した。遊環構造による変化のある空間の連続的な体験を可能とし、遠近感の錯覚を利用して変化あるダイナミックな展示空間としている。

This is a science museum constructed in the "city of hills," Nagasaki. To make this facility into a symbol of the city that is easy for visitors to understand, while holding down the total architectural volume, the exhibition hall, planetarium, and observatory have all been composed with characteristically shaped external appearances and finishes. Overall, the facility portrays the city as a "city of ships." The exhibition hall has an interior that draws on the cityscape of Nagasaki, and this is divided into the six levels. The hall gives it a continuously changing space with circular play system.

1996

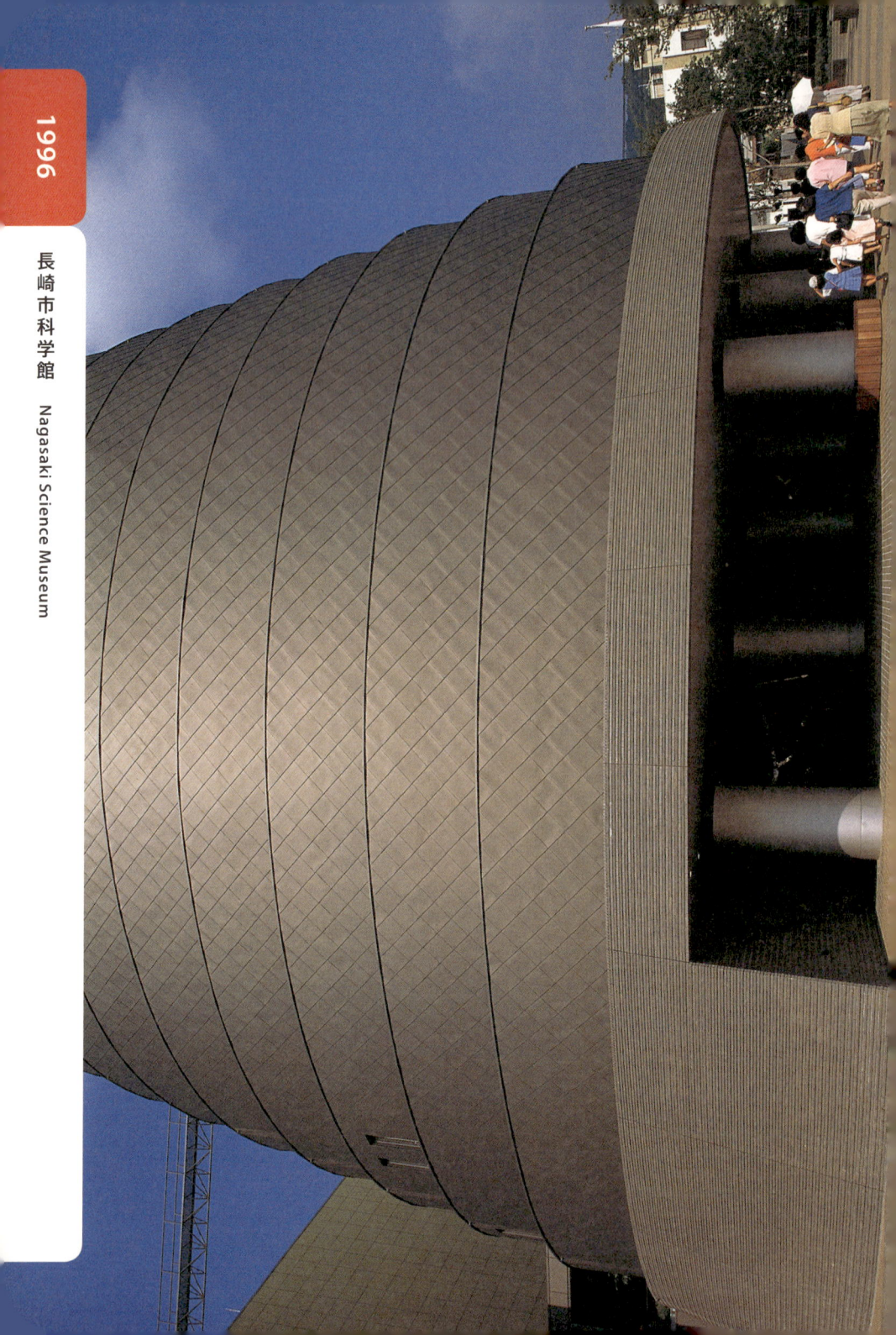

長崎市科学館

Nagasaki Science Museum

525

1996

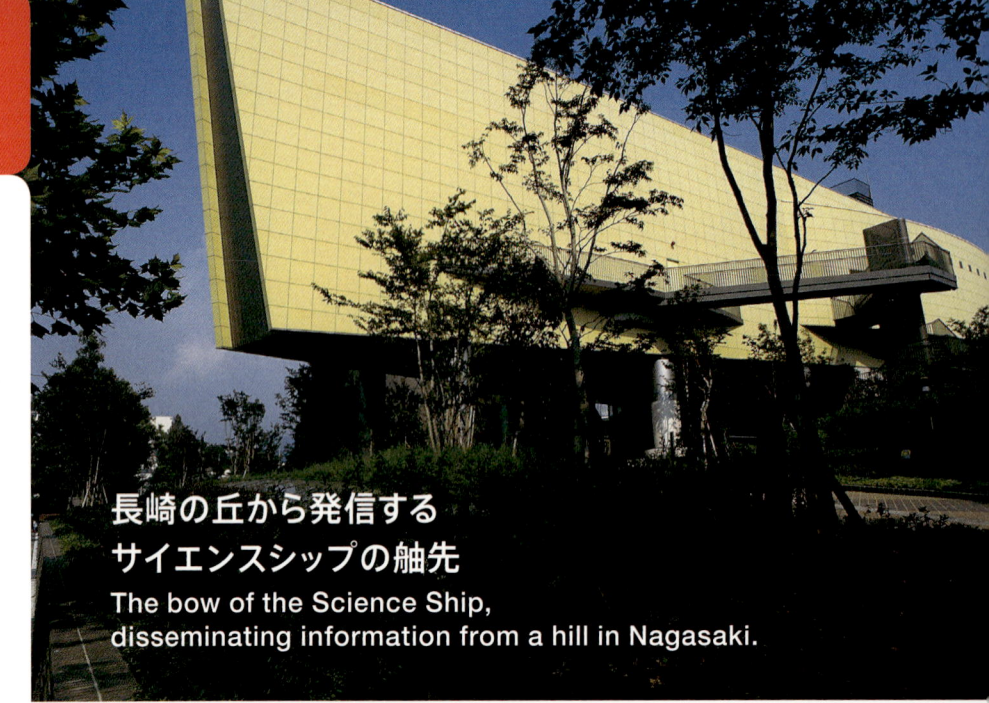

長崎市科学館
Nagasaki Science Museum

長崎の丘から発信する
サイエンスシップの舳先
The bow of the Science Ship,
disseminating information from a hill in Nagasaki.

527

1996

魚・水・技

鈴廣かまぼこ博物館
Suzuhiro Kamaboko Museum

鈴廣かまぼこ博物館

神奈川県小田原市風祭／1996
Suzuhiro Kamaboko Museum
Kazamatsuri, Odawara-shi, Kanagawa

本プロジェクトは小田原市につくられた企業博物館である。伝統的な技の伝承と手作りの味へのこだわりから、旧見学工場を体験型の手作りコミュニケーションプレイスへと再生した。「魚・水・技」という3つを展示テーマとし、「作る・見る・遊ぶ」体験ができるライブミュージアムが目指された。

This project was a corporate museum located in Odawara City. In respect of the transmission of traditional techniques and out of the loyalty for the feel of handmade goods, the old tour-based factory was revamped into a hands-on museum where people can communicate about hand-made products. There are three exhibition themes, fish, water, and techniques, and a lively museum where people can experience creating, watching, and playing.

1996

鈴廣かまぼこ博物館　Suzuhiro Kamaboko Museum

かまぼこのぞきカラクリ

1996

鈴廣かまぼこ博物館

Suzuhiro Kamaboko Museum

美しい水、美しい木をみせる
Showing off beautiful waters and trees.

1995

由比ヶ浜の家
Yuigahama House

海岸から
200m

由比ヶ浜の家

神奈川県鎌倉市／1995
Yuigahama House
Kamakura-shi, Kanagawa

鎌倉の由比ヶ浜の海岸から200ｍほど入った住宅地に立地している。1階は個室、2階に居間・食堂・和室があり、それをつなぐ踊り場に便所・浴室が配されている。小規模だが、快適で気持ちのよい住まいの空間が意図されている。

This house stands in a residential area about 200 meters from the Yuigahama beach in Kamakura. Private rooms are on the 1st floor, with the living room, dining room, and Japanese style room on the second floor, with a restroom and bath along the hall that connects them.

1995

由比ヶ浜の家　Yuigahama House

幸せな家庭の器
The happy family vessel.

1995

藤野芸術の家
Fujino Workshop for Art

芸術と自然

藤野芸術の家

神奈川県相模原市緑区牧野／1995
Fujino Workshop for Art
Makino, Midori-ku, Sagamihara-shi, Kanagawa

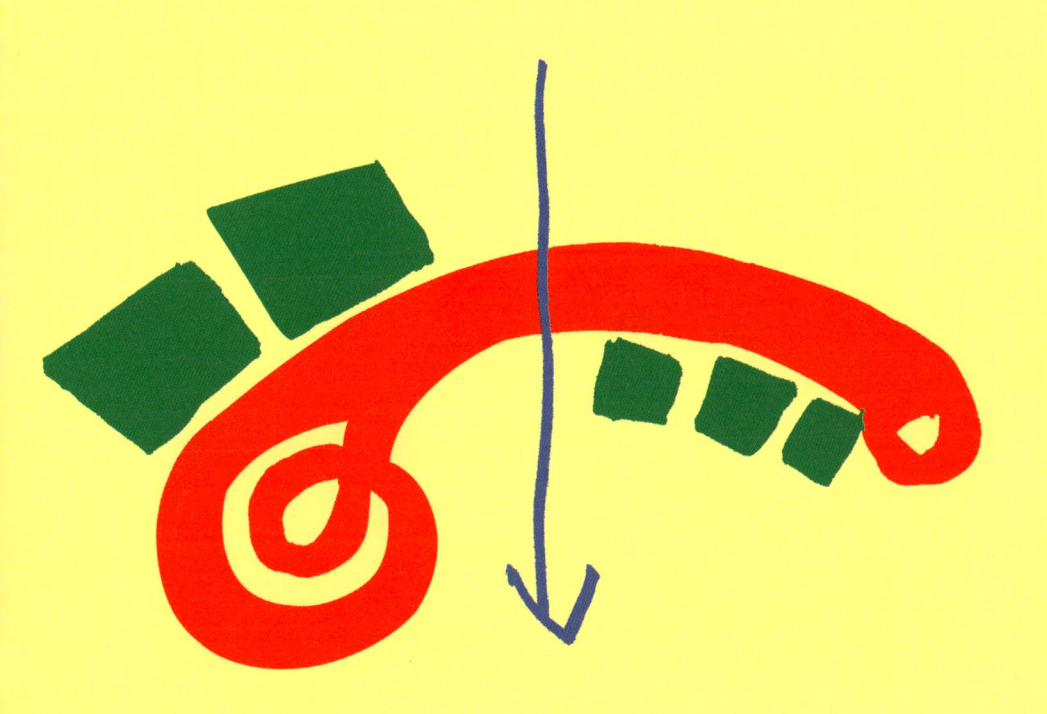

藤野町は、戦時中東京の芸術家達が疎開し、芸術村をつくったことで有名で、現在も約50人の芸術家達が在住している。芸術による町おこしを掲げる藤野町のシンボル施設として本プロジェクトは計画された。宿泊しながら様々な芸術体験や自然体験を通して、豊かな感性と創造性を育める施設として知られ、若いファミリーから熟年グループまで、人気の施設となっている。

Fujino Town is famous for being an artists' colony created by artists who evacuated Tokyo during wartime, and at present 50 artists are in residence, The town had been developed economically through art and the Fujino Workshop for Art was planned as a facility symbolic of this. Known as a facility in which profuse sensitivity and creativeness can be nurtured during stays through the experience of art and nature, it is very popular with all, from young families to groups of senior citizens.

1995

藤野芸術の家
Fujino Workshop for Art

541

1995

藤野芸術の家
Fujino Workshop for Art

楽しさ、豊かさ、心地よさ、
集い、語らい、笑い合い
Enjoyment, richness, comfort,
gathering, talks, laughing together.

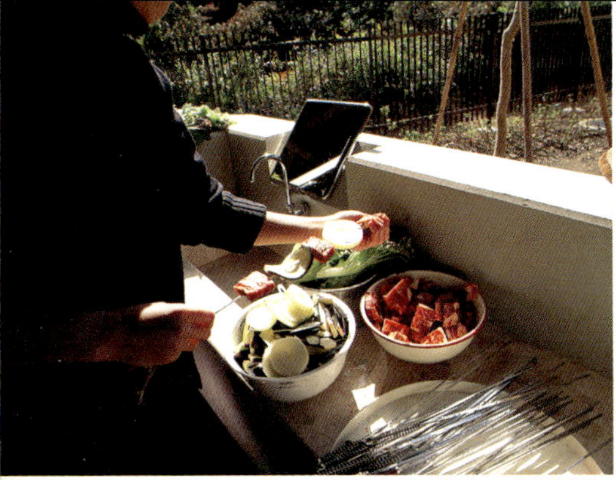
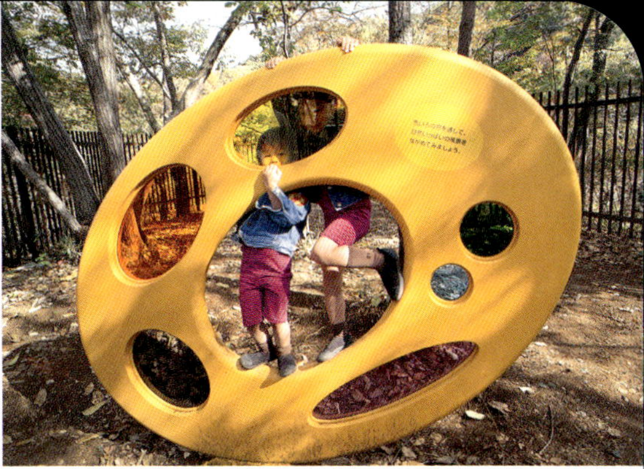
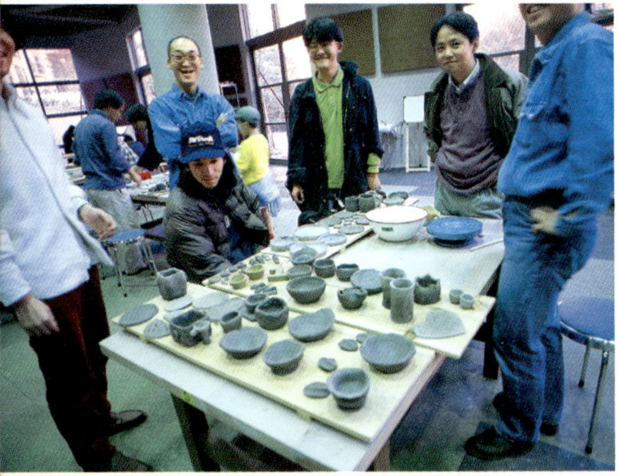
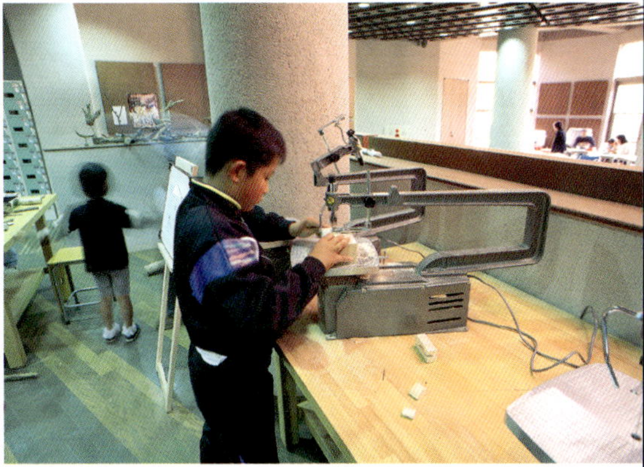
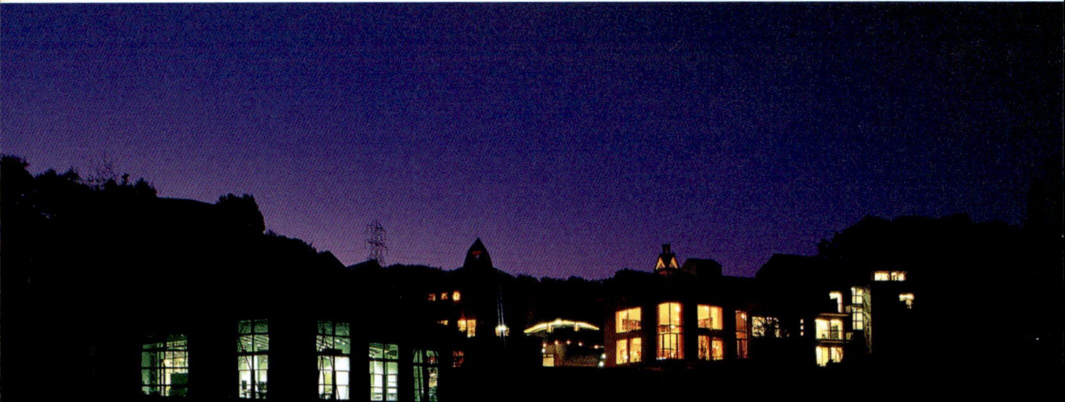

但馬ドームを中心に

植田 実×仙田 満

仙田作品には一貫性がある

仙田 満（以下S） 最近スポーツ施設を手がけることが多いんですけど、その中でも、1993年の東京辰巳国際水泳場に次いで、兵庫県立但馬ドームを設計したのは98年でした。

植田 実（以下U） 日本建築学会賞を受賞した愛知県児童総合センターが、その間の96年ですか。この頃から大きな規模のものを手がけられるようになったという印象がありますが。

S そうです。あの時代、けっこうドームがつくられはじめて、それはワールドカップがあったことも大きい。時代として、スポーツ振興や健康志向が流行だったのかもしれません。

U 各自治体も「市庁舎や町役場の代わりに、今度はドームだ」みたいな風潮でしたよね。
但馬ドームの話を伺って、いろいろ思い出したことがあるのですが、仙田さんは一番ちっちゃい建築、いわゆる遊具を徹底してつくってこられましたね。そのなかでも傑作は「キシャコゾウ」（1975年）。娘が幼い頃使っていたのですが、個室であり、あそび場でもあり、勉強したり、ものをしまう生活の場でもある。同時に親と話し合える開かれた家具でもある。最小限の形にまとめられた総合的な建築です。文字通り最大で総合的な建築の一つが、但馬ドームだと思いますが、仙田さんはそこでは逆に「土と空を見てくれるだけでいい」という、極度に単純な発想で建築物になっているんですね。

S 但馬ドームは確かにキシャコゾウの大きなものなのですね。キシャコゾウの特徴は45cm上がった高い床です。但馬ドームは高さ20mのところに床を設けていて、こども達が上から眺望できるようになっています。意識を向こうの日高の山々まで届くようにしているのです。2010年に日本建築家協会賞を受賞した「国際教養大学図書館棟」（2008年）がありますが、但馬ドームと同じように平面形が半円形で、断面的に階段状の本棚とその後ろ側に机がしつらえられていて、キシャコゾウの図書館版なのです。

U 仙田さんのお仕事は、一人のこどもが使う遊具から大勢の人が参加する大ドームまで、発想が一貫している。但馬ドームを拝見して、そのことに気がつき驚きました。確かに、バックヤードもあり、外に開かれてもいる。キシャコゾウの机の上を広げて、大人の領域に行くと但馬ドームになる。

S まさか植田さんのお嬢さんにあげたキシャコゾウと但馬ドームが共通しているなんて、指摘されるまで気がつきませんでした。広島市民球場（2009年）も、僕としては幼稚園と同じようにつくっているつもりなのですが。

U あそびというか楽しみ方が一義的ではなく、多方向になっている。球場も野球観戦だけでなく、そこでいろいろと楽しめばいい。そういうユニークな考え方ですね。

S そう考えると、僕のアイデアは単純で、あんまり進歩してない、あんまり変わってないんだなあ。

U いやいや、いいかえれば規模の大小や建築内容に関係なく、仙田さんの初々しい感性はすり減っていないということですよ。僕は仙田さんのこどもの施設の代表作はだいたい拝

見していて、いつも驚くべき面白い空間ばかりだし、予想を大きく裏切られるような楽しみがあります。児童館にしろ、プールにしろ、40年前と同じようにこどもを中心にしてちゃんと考えておられる。本当に感心してしまいます。

但馬ドームのこと

S　僕は閉所恐怖症なんです。

U　それは知らなかった。何か関係しているのかもしれませんね。但馬ドームの天井の開けかたも尋常ではなく、突然建築そのものが消えて自然が現れるような、単なる解放感じゃない。

S　閉じこもったところは、どうしても苦手ですね。

U　今回、拝見する前に準備として資料をいろいろ読みこんでから行ったんです。だけどあんなに土の部分が違うと思わなかった。ドームが開いたところを見ると、真っ平らの土と外の自然が連続していて、あれはすばらしかった。例えば、ゴルフコースというのは、自然を素材にしながら、自然をねじまげている。だけど但馬ドームは自然をストレートに感知させてしまう。コンセプトが建築物として目に見えるんですね。しかも野球だけでなく、ゲートボールの面が10面以上取れるとか、多様な使い方のパターンを見ても不思議な広がりを感じました。

S　ドームを開くと、山と観客席にいる人の高さの対比が、極端に出るんですよ。

U　ドームの天井が開く側には、基本的に観客席を置いていない。今までのスタジアムには、ああいうプランはなかったと思いますが。

S　ないわけではないけれども、一般的にはスタジアムとかアリーナって、線対称なんですね。場所のもっている重さが変わらないほうがいい、と。僕のコンセプトで「世界を望む家」という、建築を外観から見るというベクトルよりも、内側から外側を見るというベクトルとか視点が重要だ、という考え方があるんですよ。但馬ドームも、使う視線や方向性を気にしていて、できれば向こう側(奥側)に開けたいと思ったんです。

U　まず使う側の視点から建築をとことん構成していく、ほかは考えないというくらいに。

S　座った時に何が見えるか、というような内側から外側に対するエネルギーをけっこう気にしています。

U　仙田さんの作品の多くは、こどもが使うものが多いわけだけど、野中保育園の「野中ザウルス」(1972年)、「野中丸」(1981年)などはうまく使いこなすという以上に、容赦なく使いこんでいるというか、仙田さんの建築と取っ組み合いをしている。いわば建築を超えた超建築のような、すごいイメージです。但馬ドームも、きれいに使われているようだけど、やはり皆さん容赦なく使っていて、そこが

Conversation

植田 実 × 仙田 満

Makoto Ueda × Mitsuru Senda

植田 実（うえだ まこと）
1935年東京都生まれ。建築評論家。早稲田大学第一文学部フランス文学専攻卒業。「建築」編集スタッフ、「都市住宅」(1968年創刊)編集長、「GA HOUSES」編集長などを経て、現在、住まいの図書館出版局編集長。2003年度日本建築学会文化賞受賞。主な著書に「集合住宅物語」「都市住宅クロニクル」1、2巻。

対談 但馬ドームを中心に　About Tajima Dome

やっぱり面白い。沖縄の「石川少年自然の家」（1975年）も、僕の好きな仙田作品の一つですが、壇段と屋根だけで建築になっている。但馬ドームも同じようにシンプルで、屋根が閉じている時も、開いている時も、グラウンドを強く見せています。

仙田建築がこども達に伝えていくこと

S　僕は、大学での建築教育も、もう少し考えなくてはと思うんです。

U　ぜひやってほしいですよね。どこの大学でも、1年生は家具をやり、有名住宅のコピーをやり、2年生で住宅設計、3年生で集合住宅という順序が同じだったりしている。最近はいろいろと工夫もされているようですが。

S　僕も大学では建築を学んだでしょう？卒業してから、菊竹清訓*1さんの事務所で働き始めて、造園家に出会ったり、イサム・ノグチ*2の仕事に出合ったことで、「すごいな、大地をデザインしているんだ」って知りました。菊竹さんのところで「日本建築展」の仕事をして、粟津潔*3さんに出会ったことも、僕にとってはとても大事な経験だった。

U　「日本建築展」はいつでしたか。

S　1964年か5年くらいで、100枚くらいのパネルをつくって、それを世界中に紹介する、という仕事でした。大学を出たばかりの僕が、川添登*4さんや、菊竹さん、粟津さんの指示で、レイアウトや翻訳作業、校正作業といった編集的なことから、紹介用のパネルをつくって、梱包するパッケージデザインまでやったのです。企画、デザイン監理、予算、制作スケジュール管理まで一人でしました。すごく面白かったし、勉強になった。その後独立して、倉俣史朗*5さんや、伊原通夫*6さんといった、いろんな分野の人と大阪万博で出会ったことがよかった。建築以外のアート、デザインの世界を早い段階で知ったのがとてもよかったと思います。

最近の政治家もそうですけど、日本の大学の法学とか経済の出身で、政治家になるじゃないですか。ぜひ都市計画やデザインを勉強して、政治家になってほしい。昔に比べれば専門分化しているのだろうけど、大学に入学してすぐに専門分化するのもどうかと思う。総合的なもの、教養を身につけてから、専門に入ってほしいですよね。今の大学の建築教育では、グラフィックから、照明から、さまざまな分野のデザインを教養として学んだうえで、建築を勉強した方がいいと思うんですよ。

U　今まで仙田さんは、外から見ると遊具やこどもの施設の専門家という印象が強すぎたのですが、これからはもっと大人や高齢者が使うものに結びつく可能性を私も見て行きたいと思っています。

S　僕はいま必要なのは「意欲」だと思うのです。体育館に入ったら、思わず走ってみたくなるとか、スポーツをしたくなるとか、図書館に入ったら本を読みたくなるといったように、環境が人間の意欲にどう働きかけるか、という意識をかきたてる建築や環境を考えています。日本のこども達に元気がないのは、日本の都市、建築、環境に元気を喚起するものがないのでは、と反省しています。僕は建築によって意欲という力をもたせたいんです。

U　体を動かしたくなるだけではなく、自分でもびっくりするくらいその場所に長い間座っていた、という建築との関係もありますからね。

S そうそう、非常に安定した気持ちになれる、とか。

U それは現代建築に欠けていたことじゃないでしょうか。くつろぐこと、休めること、おいしく何かを食べること、楽しく料理ができること、というのが「ほどほどにできる」ようにつくられているものが多すぎるんですよね。仙田さんの「バナナハウス」(1982年)などは、別荘の通念とは違った行動を誘い出すような仕掛けになっている。

S そこにいる人を元気にするような、建築が人に与える影響はいつも考えています。こどものための建築や環境をやっているせいかもしれません。

U こどもについてだけども、いろいろな問題点が広がってくるわけでしょう。

S この40年間僕がやってきた、「こども達の成育環境のデザイン」という視点での仕事や活動の場は失っていないですが、日本の都市全体がだんだんと、こども達が生活しにくい場所になりつつあると感じるのは残念なことです。アルヴァ・アアルト[*7]は1920年代に「高層住居をつくらない」といっているのですが、今の日本では超高層マンションが再開発のツールになってきている。
僕も2004年から「こども環境学会[*8]」というのをつくって活動していますが、大人とこどものための町づくりという視点で変えていきたいと思っています。

U 大人からこどもを見る町づくりではなく、こどもから見ていく町づくりができると面白い。

S 「コンクリートから人へ」といわれていますが、僕はあそび場には空間よりこどもの成長に寄り添うような人が必要だ、と思っています。プレーリーダーのいるプレーパークは全国に200カ所くらいあるのですが、一方でこれまであった旧児童公園の(現街区公園)利用率は、30年前に比べて6分の1になっています。

U 今防犯上の問題として、公園といいながら、半ば閉ざされた場所にもなっている、こども達を自然に見守っている人がいつもいるような仕組みがあるといいのですが。

S 「公園は犯罪に遭う場所」と認識している母親も多いのです。病院でも、入院しているこども達をどうあそばせるか、あそびというサポートをしている病院の方が、入院期間が短いのだそうです。だからあそびのシステムづくり、場所づくりを考えていきたいんですよ。僕にとって、それがこれからの課題ではないかな、と思っています。

U ずいぶん話題が大きな重要なところに広がってきましたが、改めて但馬ドームの、外の線が山と地続きになっているようなグラウンドで皆さんが思い思いに楽しんでいた様子を思い出してみると、あれは人と場所との関係の原イメージのような、鮮烈なシーンだったと思うんです。だから、仙田さんが言われた場所づくり、システムづくりにも、すでにはっきりとしたイメージがあるに違いない。今日はそのことをこれまでになく確認した気持です。

[*1] **菊竹清訓**(きくたけ きよのり) 1928〜　建築家(工学博士)
[*2] **イサム・ノグチ**(Isamu Noguchi、日本名:野口 勇) 1904〜1988　彫刻家、画家、インテリアデザイナー、造園家
[*3] **粟津 潔**(あわづ きよし) 1929〜2009　グラフィックデザイナー
[*4] **川添 登**(かわぞえ のぼる) 1926〜　建築家、建築評論家
[*5] **倉俣史朗**(くらまた しろう) 1934〜1991　インテリアデザイナー
[*6] **伊原通夫**(いはら みちお) 1928〜　彫刻家
[*7] **アルヴァ・アアルト**(Hugo Henrik Aalto) 1898〜1976　建築家、都市計画家、デザイナー
[*8] **こども環境学会**／(英名 Association for Children's Environment)は、こども達が明るい地球の未来を築いていけるように、様々な学問分野が連携して、「こどものための環境づくり」をめざして2004年に設立された学会

Conversation

植田 実 × 仙田 満
Makoto Ueda × Mitsuru Senda

About Tajima Dome

Makoto Ueda × Mitsuru Senda

Works by Mitsuru Senda have a consistent quality.

Mitsuru Senda (S): I have recently been working on many sports facilities. It was in 1998 that I designed Hyogo Prefectural Tajima Dome followed by Tokyo Tatsumi International Center in 1993.

Makoto Ueda (U): So Aichi Children's Center that was awarded an Architectural Institute of Japan Prize was designed in 1996 between the two projects. I have an impression that you began to work on large-scale architecture around that time.

S: That's right. In those days, many domes began to be constructed due to the World Cup. I suppose sports and healthy lifestyles were in as the trend of the era.

U: I remember that in those days various municipal governments tried to create domes instead of city or town offices.
The story about Tajima Dome reminded me of many things. You have been focusing on the creation of the smallest architecture or so-called play equipment. The masterpiece you created among your works is *Kishakozo*(1975). My daughter used to use it when she was small. It was where she stayed, played, studied, or stored things in her daily life. It was also a piece of furniture open to discussion with parents. It includes every aspect of architecture in a minimal format. In contrast, the largest and most comprehensive architecture you have worked on is Tajima Dome. However, you completed this architecture with the exceptionally simple idea that we have only to enjoy the ground and sky.

S: Tajima Dome is actually like *Kishakozo* made larger. *Kishakozo* features a floor elevated 45 centimeters high. Tajima Dome has the floor at 20 meters high, enabling children to look over the space from above. I designed the space so that you can look over at Hidaka mountains.
The building for Akita International University Library (2008) was awarded a Japan Institute of Architects award in 2010. The library is similar to *Kishakozo* in that it has a semicircular shape horizontally like Tajima Dome, with bookshelves placed on a slope and desks located behind them vertically.

U: You have embedded the same idea into your various works from a toy used by a child to a dome housing many people. I came to notice it by taking a look at Tajima Dome.

S: It is basically the same structure as *Kishakozo*.

U: It has a backyard and is open to the outside world. As you expand the desk of *Kishakozo* and transition it to the adult space, you come up with Tajima Dome.

S: I didn't notice myself that *Kishakozo* which I gave to your daughter had something in common with Tajima Dome until you pointed it out. I also designed Hiroshima Municipal Baseball Stadium (2009) in the same way I designed a kindergarten.

U: You injected multiple ideas to the way to play or have fun, not bound by a single conviction. At the ball park, you can enjoy many things in addition to watching baseball. You have such a unique idea.

S: In a nutshell, my idea is very simple and I have not made much progress through my works.

U: Oh no, I do not think so at all. To put it another way, your fresh sensitivities are still very much alive irrespective of the size or type of your architecture. I have seen most of the facilities you have designed for children. Every space is quite interesting and greatly betrays my expectations in a good sense. As you work on a children's center or a swimming pool, you always focus on children as you did 40 years ago. I am really impressed.

On Tajima Dome

S: I am a claustrophobic.
U: I never knew that. Maybe that has something to do with your works. The way the ceiling of Tajima Dome opens up is extraordinary, showing nature all of a sudden by making the architecture disappear. It is not simple openness you feel there.
S: I cannot stand being confined to closed space.
U: I read various materials before I visited the site this time. However, I never expected to see the totally different ground space like that. As I saw the dome open, the flat ground and outside nature were connected into one and gave me a breath-taking view. In a golf course, you use nature as a material, but you totally twist it. However, Tajima Dome makes you feel nature as it is. You clearly see the concept in the architecture. Besides, the dome can provide 10 gateball courts in addition to a baseball field. The space has wonderful potentials through various ways to use it.
S: As you open the dome, you see a great contrast of height between the mountains and people sitting in their seats.
U: You basically do not place any seats on the side where the ceiling opens. I think there are no plans like that in conventional stadiums.
S: Some stadiums do have that structure. In principle, however, stadiums and arenas are line-symmetric. You try to make the whole place well-balanced in every part of it. I have a concept I call "the house looking over the world," where I treat the direction of looking over from inside to outside more importantly than the direction of looking at the building from outside. I took great care of the line of vision or direction used at Tajima Dome and I wanted to direct the vision from inside to outside.
U: You create the architecture from scratch based on the viewpoint of users and do not think about anything else.
S: I care about how the energy flows from inside to outside by focusing on what you see as you are seated.
U: Many of your works are related to children. In the case of Nonaka Day Nursery (Nonaka-Saurus in 1972 and Nonaka-Maru in 1981), users more than use the architecture to the extent that they overuse it or fight against your architecture head-on. It has transformed into super-architecture that has exceeded the functionalities of usual architecture. Tajima Dome seems to be in a good condition but people are using it in various ways they like, which is pretty good. Ishikawa Children's Natural School (1975) in Okinawa is another Senda work I like. Its architecture is mainly composed of its elevated setting and roof. Similarly, Tajima Dome is also simple, impressively showing the ground with its roof closed or open.

Messages are disseminated to children through the architecture by Mitsuru Senda.

S: I think we need to revisit the architecture education at college.
U: You have a point there. Each college goes through the same process by making freshmen work on furniture and copy famous houses, sophomores design houses, and juniors work on apartments. These days some creative programs seem to be in place, through.

Conversation

植田 実 × 仙田 満

Makoto Ueda × Mitsuru Senda

S: I also studied architecture in college. After I finished college, I worked at the office of Kiyonori Kikutake[*1], meeting garden designers and encountering the works by Isamu Noguchi[*2]. I got to know that some people were designing the earth. As I worked for Mr. Kikutake, I was involved in Exhibition of Japanese Architecture and met Kiyoshi Awazu[*3] which was a very important experience for me.

U: When was Exhibition of Japanese Architecture?

S: It was in 1964 or 1965. We created about 100 panels and showed them across the world. I was fresh from college but was able to work on editing tasks such as layout, translation, and proofreading as well as the production of introductory panels and the design of packing materials under the tutelage of Noboru Kawazoe[*4], Mr. Kikutake, and Mr. Awazu. I was also in charge of planning, design management, budgeting, and production scheduling all on our own. It was very interesting and instructive. After that I created my own business and luckily met people in various fields including Shiro Kuramata[*5] and Michio Ihara[*6] at the Osaka Expo. I was lucky enough to be able to be exposed to the world of art and design outside the boundary of architecture at an early stage.

S: Recently many people who studied law or economy at college turn into politicians. I definitely want them to study city planning or design at college before they become politicians. The current curriculum seems to be more specialized but I doubt the validity of giving highly specialized education to freshmen. Gaining comprehensive knowledge in liberal arts education should be required before moving into specialized fields. In the current architecture education at college, the knowledge on graphic design, lighting, and other types of design should be obtained for students who want to study architecture.

U: I have a strong impression that you have worked on play structure and facilities for children as a specialist. But I want to see how you will work on things for adults and elderly people going forward.

S: I believe people now need motivation more than anything else. You feel like running or playing some sport as you enter a gymnasium. You want to pick up books as you enter a library. I am working on the architecture or environment that will prompt people to do something. As I find Japanese children not motivated, I am wondering if we are not providing motivation through Japanese cities, architecture, or environment. I want to enable architecture to motivate people.

U: Architecture can enable you to feel like exercising. In addition, it also enables you to sit for a surprising long time in a certain place.

S: Right. It can make you feel very stable.

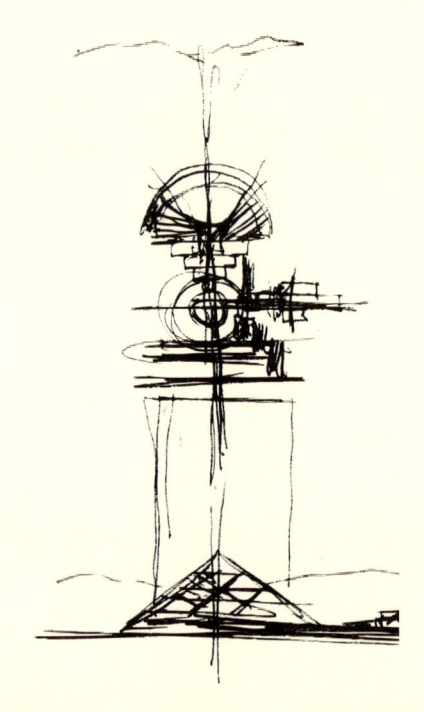

U: I think this is something Japanese architecture has not provided. Most architectures are based on moderate comfort, allowing us to get comfortable, have a rest, eat something good, or enjoy cooking. Another work of yours, "Banana House (1982)," is not confined to the traditional concept of a second house and incites people to do something.

S: I am always thinking about the revitalizing effects of architecture. My involvement in the architecture or environment for children can have something to do with this.

U: As you work on children, you probably have come up with various issues you need to tackle.

S: I still have a firm basis of working on the environment that assists the growth of children, something I have been working on for the last 40 years. However, it is such a pity that Japanese cities have been becoming less comfortable for the lives of children. Alvar Aalto[7] said in the 1920s that he would never work on high-rise apartments, but high-rise apartments are tools for area redevelopments in current Japan.

I have been implementing activities based on the Association for Children's Environment[8] since 2004. I want to work on the change of environment from the viewpoint of city planning for adults and children.

U: It will be great if you can work on city planning from the viewpoint of children instead of seeing children from the viewpoint of adults.

S: Many people advocate the transition from concrete to people. What I think we need for play areas is people who assist the growth of children and not the space. We have around 200 play parks with play leaders across Japan, but the utilization rate of conventional children's parks (i.e. current city-area parks) has decreased to one sixth in comparison with 30 years ago.

U: To counter crimes, parks are becoming half-closed spaces. We need the mechanism by which people are always monitoring children in a natural manner.

S: Many mothers consider that parks are crime spots. Hospitals offer shorter hospitalization periods in case they assist hospitalized children in their play activities. So I want to work on the creation of play systems or spots. This is the challenge I need to tackle going forward.

U: Out topics have grown into very important areas. As I remember the people enjoying their time in their own ways on the ground connecting the outer lines with the mountains at Tajima Dome, I believe it was the vivid scene that connected people with their environment in a very pure and original sense. Thus, I think you have already come up with a clear image on how you will work on play spots or systems. I was happy to be able to reconfirm that very clearly today.

*1 **Kiyonori Kikutake** (1928-): Architect.
*2 **Isamu Noguchi** (1904-1988): Sculptor, painter, interior designer, and garden designer.
*3 **Kiyoshi Awazu** (1929-2009): Graphic designer.
*4 **Noboru Kawazoe** (1926-): Architect and civilization specialist.
*5 **Shiro Kuramata** (1934-1991): Interior designer.
*6 **Michio Ihara** (1928-): Sculptor.
*7 **Alvar Aalto** (Hugo Henrik Aalto, 1898-1976): Architect, city planner, and designer.
*8 **The Association for Children's Environment:** An academic association established in 2004 based on the collaboration among multiple academic domains to create children-friendly environments and help children unfold a brighter future on a global scale.

Makoto Ueda

An architecture critic born in Tokyo in 1935. Graduated with a degree in French Literature from the First Faculty of Letters of Waseda University. Worked as editorial staff member on "Architecture," as editor-in-chief of "Toshi Jutaku" (established in 1968), and editor-in-chief of "GA HOUSES" before being appointed editor-in-chief of SUMAI Library Publishing Company. Won the Appreciation Prize of the Architectural Institute of Japan in 2003. Publications include.

Conversation

植田 実 × 仙田 満
Makoto Ueda × Mitsuru Senda

1999.07
世界淡水魚園オアシスパーク

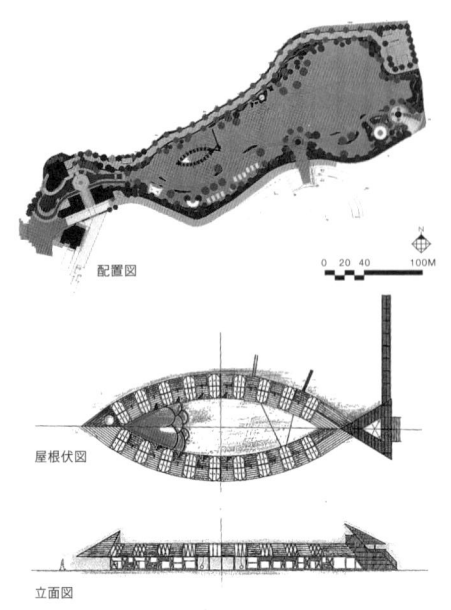

配置図
屋根伏図
立面図
基準断面図
断面図

所在地：岐阜県各務原市川島笠田町
主用途：商業施設、公園遊具
建築主：岐阜県、セガ・エンタープライゼス
構造設計：構造計画研究所
設備設計：エース設計事務所
施工：協和建設・大武建設・鷲見建設・富国建設JV
構造：S造
規模：地上1階（オアシスカフェ・オアシスマート、ギフベスト、セガワールド）、地上2階（ガレリア・大屋根、フィッシュオンチップス）
敷地：34,000㎡　建築：419㎡（オアシスカフェ・オアシスマート）、351㎡（ギフベスト）、314㎡（セガワールド）、399㎡（ガレリア・大屋根）、588㎡（フィッシュオンチップス）　延床：384㎡（オアシスカフェ・オアシスマート）、307㎡（ギフベスト）、286㎡（セガワールド）、460㎡（ガレリア・大屋根）、889㎡（フィッシュオンチップス）

Oasis Park
Kawashimakasada-machi, Kakamigahara-shi, Gifu

1999.03
岐阜県先端科学技術体験センター

岐阜県先端科学技術体験センター［サイエンスワールド］

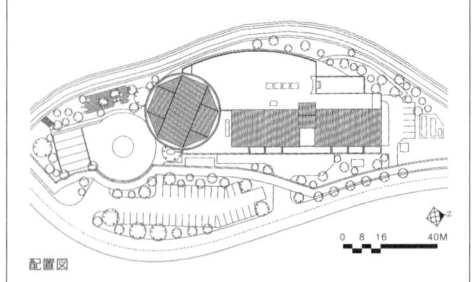

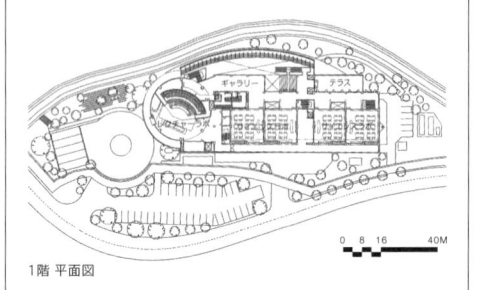

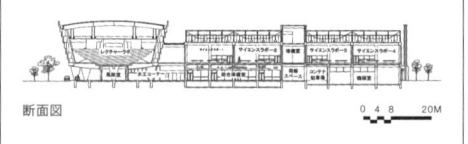

配置図
1階 平面図
断面図

所在地：岐阜県瑞浪市明世町
主用途：科学実験体験施設
建築主：岐阜県
構造設計：構造計画研究所
設備設計：日永設計
施工：大日本・野甲JV
構造：RC造一部S造
規模：地上3階
敷地：7,106㎡　建築：3,489㎡　延床：5,970㎡

Gifu Advanced Science and Technology Experience Center "Science World"
Akiyo-cho, Mizunami-shi, Gifu

1999.11
富岩運河環水公園

配置図

イメージパース図

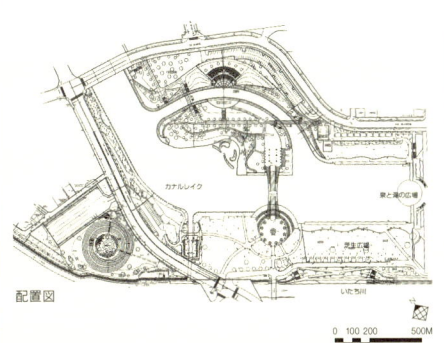

所在地：富山県富山市湊入船町
主用途：公園施設
建築主：富山県
構造設計：飯島建築設計事務所
設備設計：中部設計
施工：竹田工務店・村松建築JV（泉と滝の広場）、川田工業・水島工業・日本海建興JV（天門橋）、村松建築・牧野工業（展望塔）
構造：SRC造（天門橋・展望塔）、RC造（泉と滝の広場）
規模：地上3階（天門橋・展望塔）、地上1階（泉と滝の広場）
敷地：97,000㎡　建築：121㎡（天門橋・展望塔）、775㎡（泉と滝の広場）　延床：289㎡（天門橋・展望塔）、775㎡（泉と滝の広場）

Fugan Canal Park
Minatoirifune-machi, Toyama-shi, Toyama

1999.03
やすらぎミラージュ

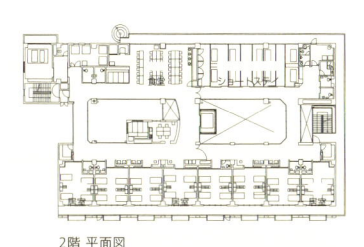

2階 平面図

1階 平面図

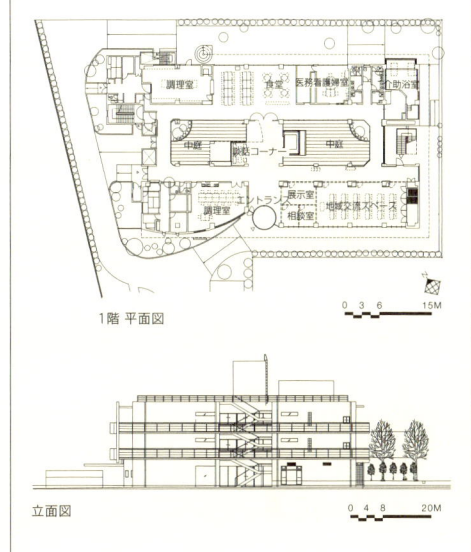

立面図

所在地：東京都練馬区大泉町
主用途：特別養護老人ホーム
建築主：社会福祉法人章佑会
構造設計：構造計画研究所
設備設計：システムプランニング
施工：太平工業
構造：RC造一部SRC造
規模：地下1階地上3階
敷地：3,150㎡　建築：1,259㎡　延床：3,650㎡

Yasuragi Mirage
Oizumi-machi, Nerima-ku, Tokyo

1999.02
大森の家

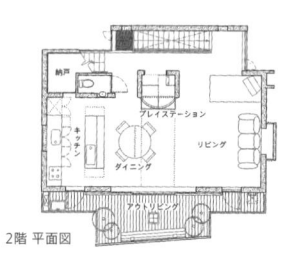

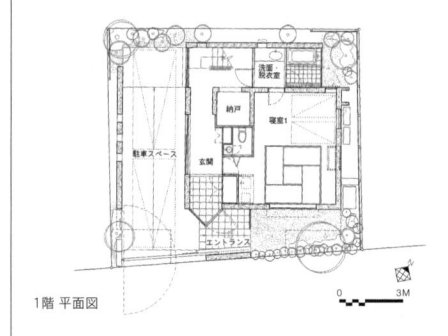

断面図

2階 平面図

1階 平面図

所在地：東京都大田区大森東
主用途：住宅
共同設計：東京工業大学仙田満研究室
構造設計：構造計画研究所
設備設計：テーテンス事務所
施工：平成建設
構造：RC造
規模：地上3階
敷地：122㎡　建築：70㎡　延床：192㎡

Omori House
Omorihigashi, Ota-ku, Tokyo

1998.03
春日部の家

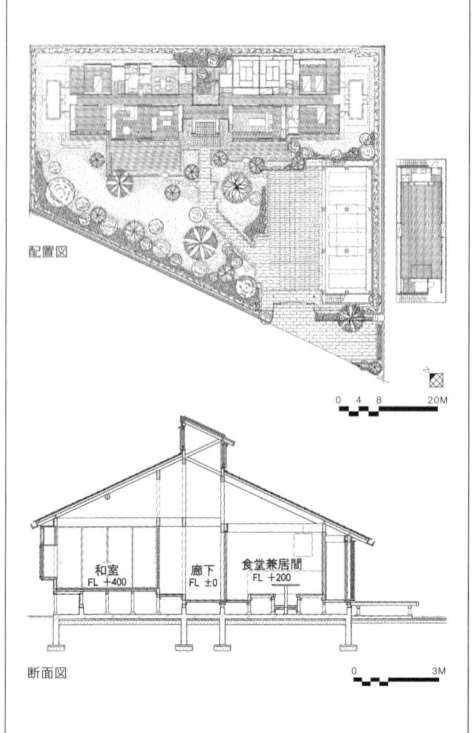

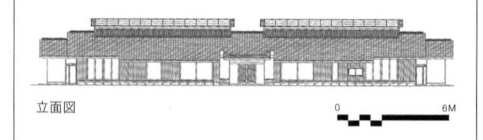

配置図

断面図

立面図

所在地：埼玉県春日部市
主用途：住宅
構造設計：構造計画研究所
設備設計：ユニ設備設計
施工：五十嵐組
構造：W造(母屋)、S造、W造(客屋)
規模：地上1階(母屋)、地上2階(客屋)
敷地：1,576㎡　建築：480㎡　延床：603㎡

Kasukabe House
Kasukabe-shi, Saitama

1998.07
山梨県立科学館

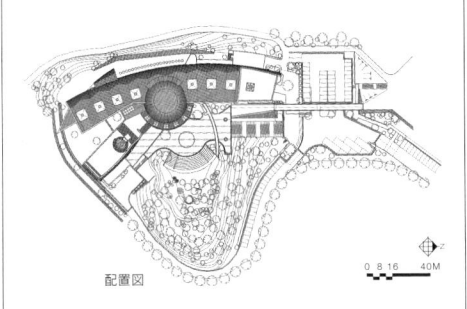

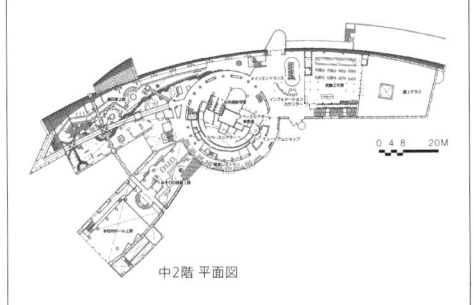

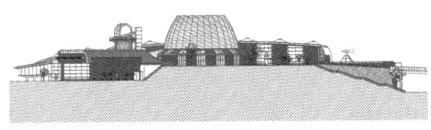

配置図

中2階 平面図

立面図

所在地：山梨県甲府市愛宕町
主用途：科学館
建築主：山梨県
構造設計：構造計画研究所
設備設計：愛住設計
施工：鴻池組・日経工業・佐野工務店JV
構造：RC造一部S造、W造
規模：地下1階地上3階
敷地：152,386㎡　建築：4,725㎡　延床：6,785㎡

Yamanashi Prefectural Science Center
Atago-machi, Kofu-shi, Yamanashi

1998.07
福井県児童科学館

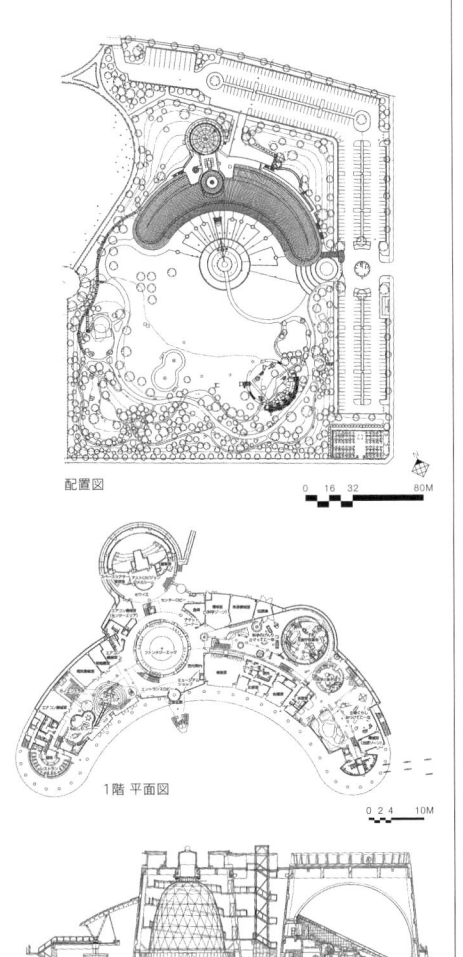

配置図

1階 平面図

断面図

所在地：福井県坂井郡春江町
主用途：児童科学館
建築主：福井県
構造設計：構造計画研究所
設備設計：テーテンス事務所、設備計画
施工：西松建設・飛島建設・石黒JV
構造：RC造一部SRC造、S造
規模：地上3階
敷地：55,826㎡　建築：5,615㎡　延床：6,874㎡

Fukui Children's Science Center
Harue-cho, Sakai-gun, Fukui

1998.10
兵庫県立但馬ドーム

配置図

断面図

1階 平面図

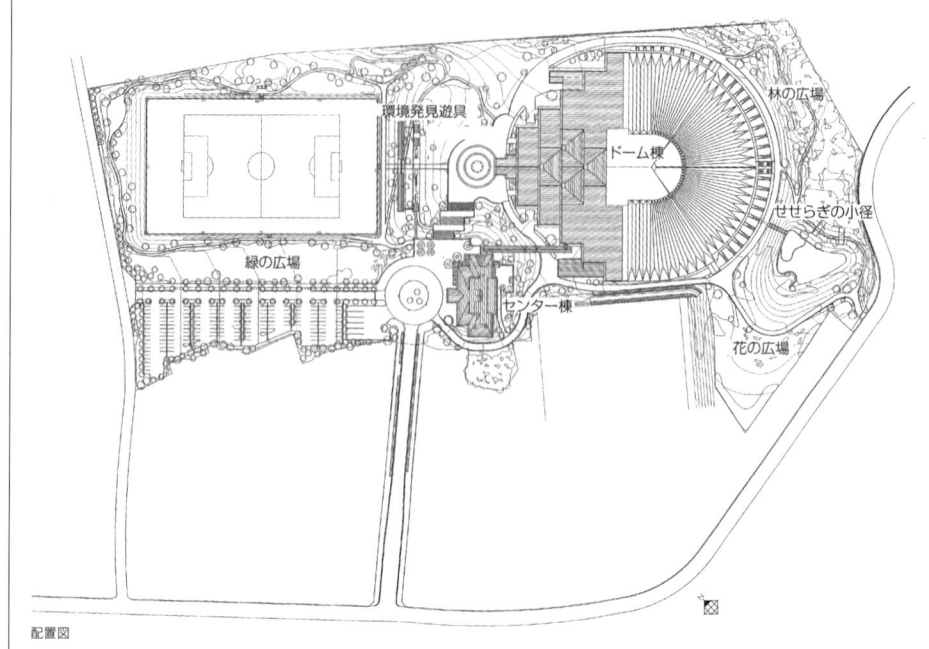

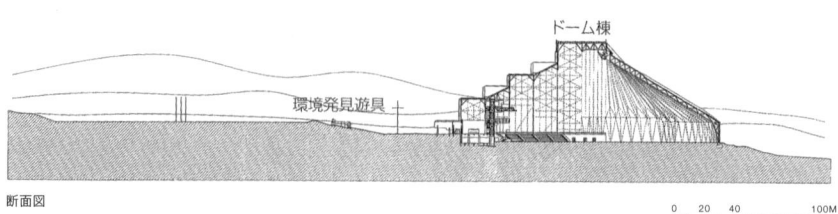

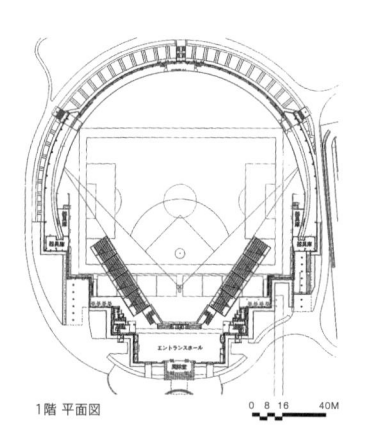

所在地：兵庫県豊岡市日高町
主用途：スポーツ施設、集会施設
建築主：兵庫県、日高町
共同設計：大建設計
構造設計指導：斎藤公男
構造設計、設備設計：大建設計、三菱重工業
施工：三菱重工業
構造：S造一部RC造
規模：地下1階地上3階
敷地：99,134㎡　建築：19,006㎡（ドーム棟）、1,380㎡（センター棟）　延床：21,812㎡（ドーム棟）、1,139（センター棟）

Hyogo Prefectural Tajima Dome
Hidaka-cho, Toyooka-shi, Hyogo

1997.03
川崎市向丘小学校

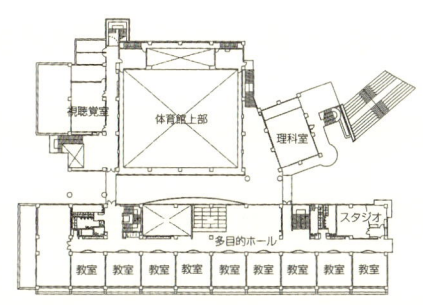

配置アクソメトリック図

2階 平面図

1階 平面図

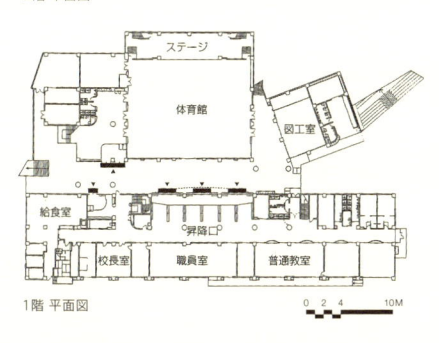

所在地：神奈川県川崎市宮前区平
主用途：小学校
建築主：川崎市まちづくり公社
構造設計：構造計画研究所
設備設計：都市設備
施工：北島・オクアキ・渡辺JV
構造：RC造一部SRC造
規模：地上4階塔屋1階
敷地：9,646㎡　建築：3,441㎡　延床：8,352㎡

Mukaigaoka Elementary School, Kawasaki
Taira, Miyamae-ku, Kawasaki-shi, Kanagawa

1996.12
五藤光学研究所山梨工場

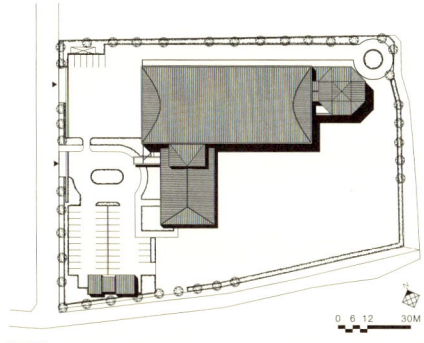

配置図

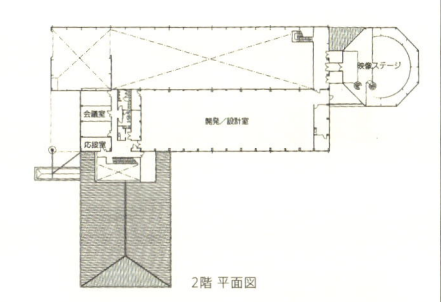

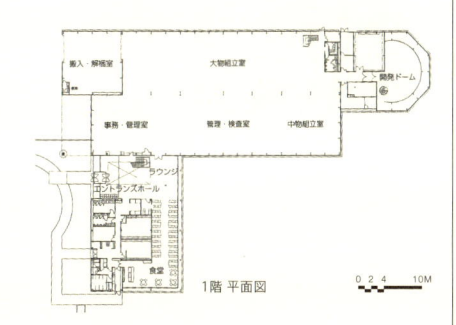

2階 平面図

1階 平面図

所在地：山梨県南アルプス市下市之瀬
主用途：研究施設、プラネタリウム製作工場
建築主：五藤光学研究所
構造設計：構造計画研究所
設備設計：システムプランニング
施工：フジタ
構造：S造
規模：地上2階
敷地：14,373㎡　建築：3,352㎡　延床：4,355㎡

Goto Optical MFG. Yamanashi Factory
Shimoichinose, Minamialps-shi, Yamanashi

1996.07
愛知県児童総合センター

配置図

断面図

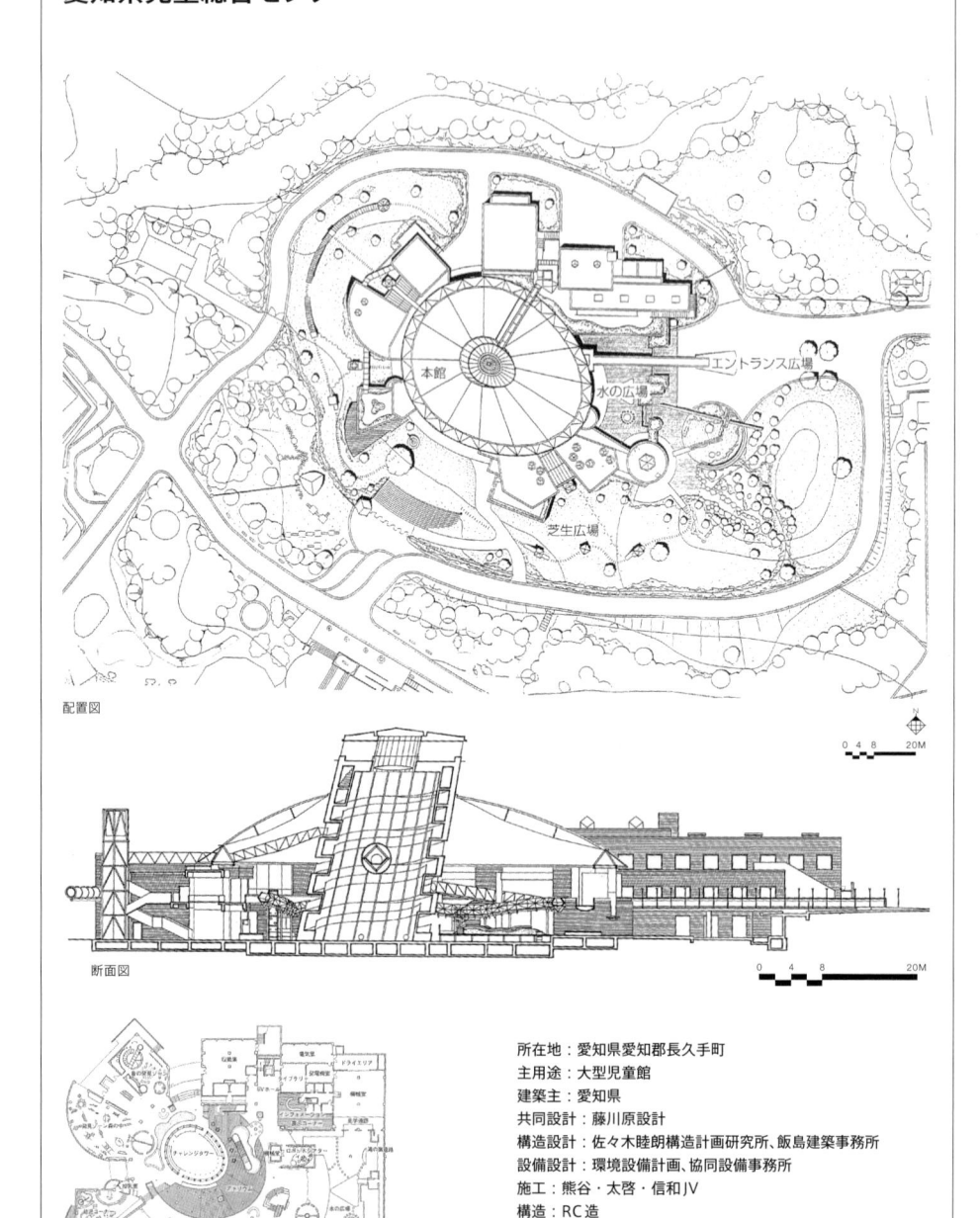

1階 平面図

所在地：愛知県愛知郡長久手町
主用途：大型児童館
建築主：愛知県
共同設計：藤川原設計
構造設計：佐々木睦朗構造計画研究所、飯島建築事務所
設備設計：環境設備計画、協同設備事務所
施工：熊谷・太啓・信和JV
構造：RC造
規模：地上3階塔屋2階
敷地：2,056㎡　建築：4,673㎡　延床：7,600㎡

Aichi Children's Center
Nagakute-cho, Aichi-gun, Aichi

1996.03
珠洲ビーチホテル

配置図

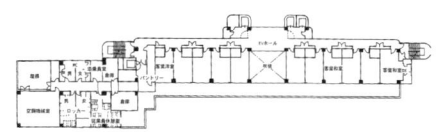

3階 平面図

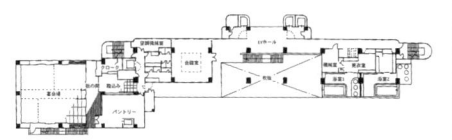

2階 平面図

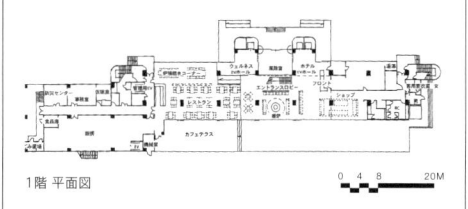

1階 平面図

所在地：石川県珠洲市蛸島町
主用途：ホテル
建築主：石川県
構造設計：構造計画研究所
設備設計：システムプランニング
施工：竹中・治山・林JV
構造：RC造一部SRC造
規模：地上8階
敷地：7,295㎡　建築：1,311㎡　延床：6,712㎡

Suzu Beach Hotel
Takojima-machi, Suzu-shi, Ishikawa

1996.11
長崎市科学館

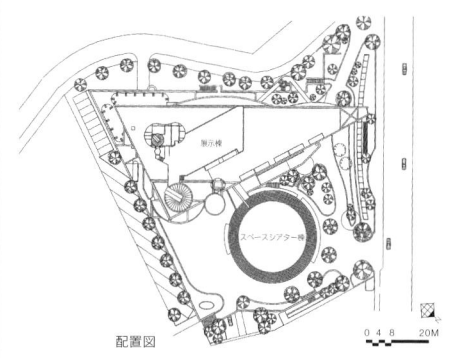

配置図

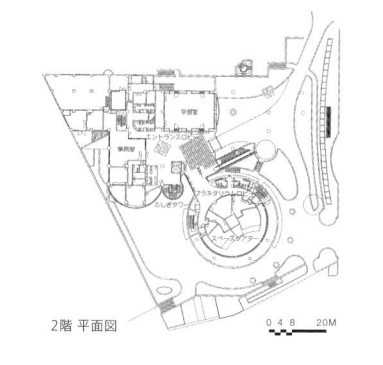

2階 平面図

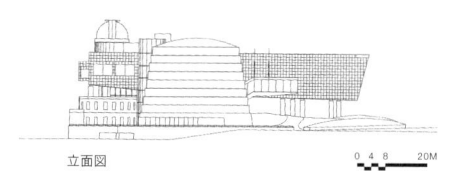

立面図

所在地：長崎県長崎市油木町
主用途：科学館
建築主：長崎市
共同設計：三建設計総合事務所
構造設計：構造計画研究所
設備設計：三建設計総合事務所
施工：奥村・豊・協大JV
構造：RC造一部S造
規模：地下1階地上4階
敷地：7,788㎡　建築：5,053㎡　延床：13,299㎡

Nagasaki Science Museum
Aburagi-machi, Nagasaki-shi, Nagasaki

1996.11
鈴廣かまぼこ博物館

1階 平面図

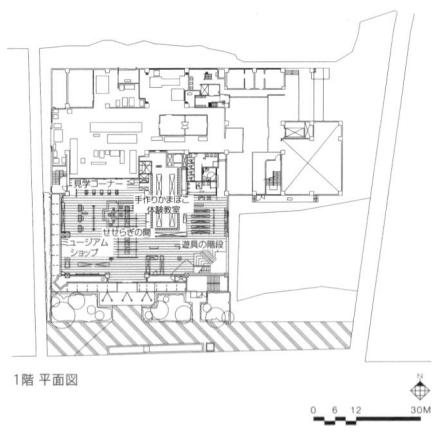

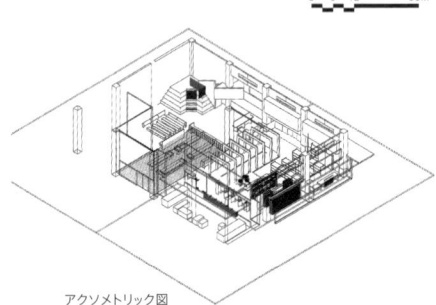

0　6　12　30M

アクソメトリック図

所在地：神奈川県小田原市風祭
主用途：企業博物館
建築主：鈴廣蒲鉾
プロジェクト内容：内装デザイン、耐震改修
共同設計：高取空間計画
施工：東急建設
構造：RC造、S造
規模：地下1階地上3階
敷地：2,624㎡　建築：1,547㎡　延床：4,538㎡

Suzuhiro Kamaboko Museum
Kazamatsuri, Odawara-shi, Kanagawa

1995.04
由比ヶ浜の家

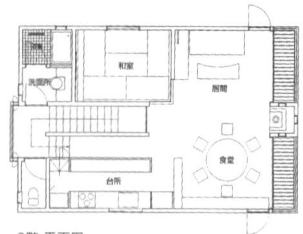

2階 平面図

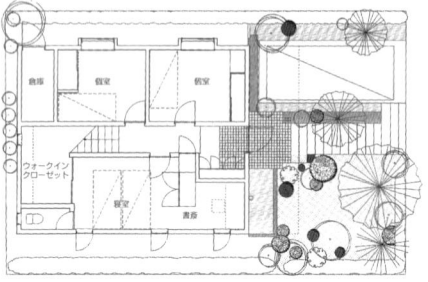

配置図兼 1階 平面図

0　　　3M

断面図

0　　　3M

所在地：神奈川県鎌倉市
主用途：住宅
共同設計：東京工業大学仙田満研究室
構造設計：構造計画研究所
設備設計：ユニ設備設計
施工：第一建設工業
構造：W造
規模：地上2階
敷地：124㎡　建築：49㎡　延床：98㎡

Yuigahama House
Kamakura-shi, Kanagawa

1995.08
藤野芸術の家

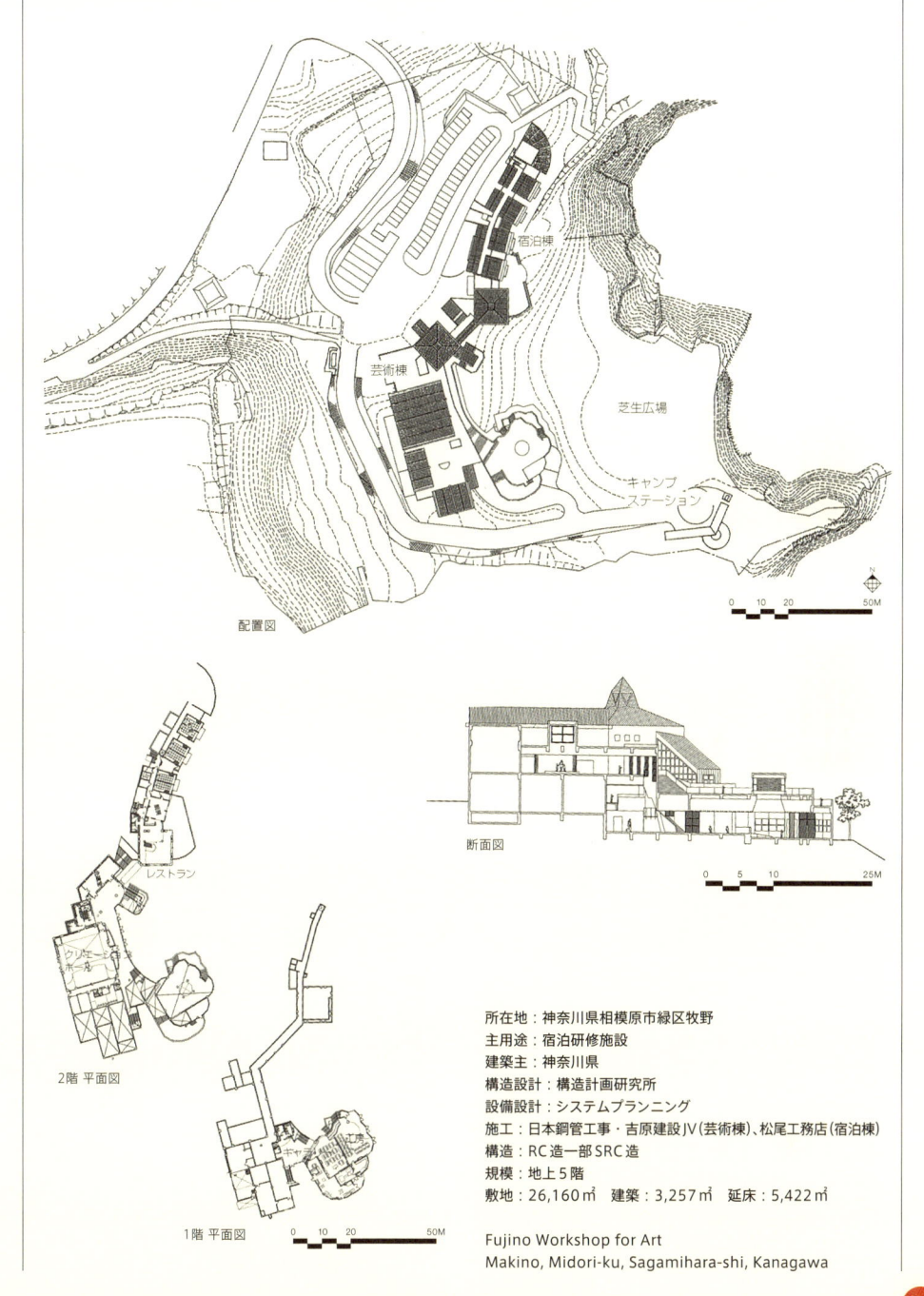

配置図

断面図

2階 平面図

1階 平面図

所在地：神奈川県相模原市緑区牧野
主用途：宿泊研修施設
建築主：神奈川県
構造設計：構造計画研究所
設備設計：システムプランニング
施工：日本鋼管工事・吉原建設JV（芸術棟）、松尾工務店（宿泊棟）
構造：RC造一部SRC造
規模：地上5階
敷地：26,160㎡　建築：3,257㎡　延床：5,422㎡

Fujino Workshop for Art
Makino, Midori-ku, Sagamihara-shi, Kanagawa

1994

旭川春光台［風の子館］

Asahikawa Shunkodai Park "Kaze no Ko Kan"

雪の日でも

旭川春光台
［風の子館］

北海道旭川市近文町／1994
Asahikawa Shunkodai Park "Kaze no Ko Kan"
Chikabumi-cho, Asahikawa-shi, Hokkaido

旭川市の新しい住宅開発地・春光台に建設された、日本ではじめて構想された木製屋根付き遊具である。冬の長い雪国のあそび場として大きな屋根を持ち立体的遊環構造建築で、オールシーズンあそべる遊具として開発された。

This is the first roofed wooden play structure designed in Japan, located in the new residential development of Shunkodai in Asahikawa City. In an area known for its heavy winter snowfall, this three-dimensional circular play system was developed as a play structure with a large roof to make it usable throughout all seasons.

1994

旭川春光台［風の子館］

Asahikawa Shunkodai Park "Kaze no Ko Kan"

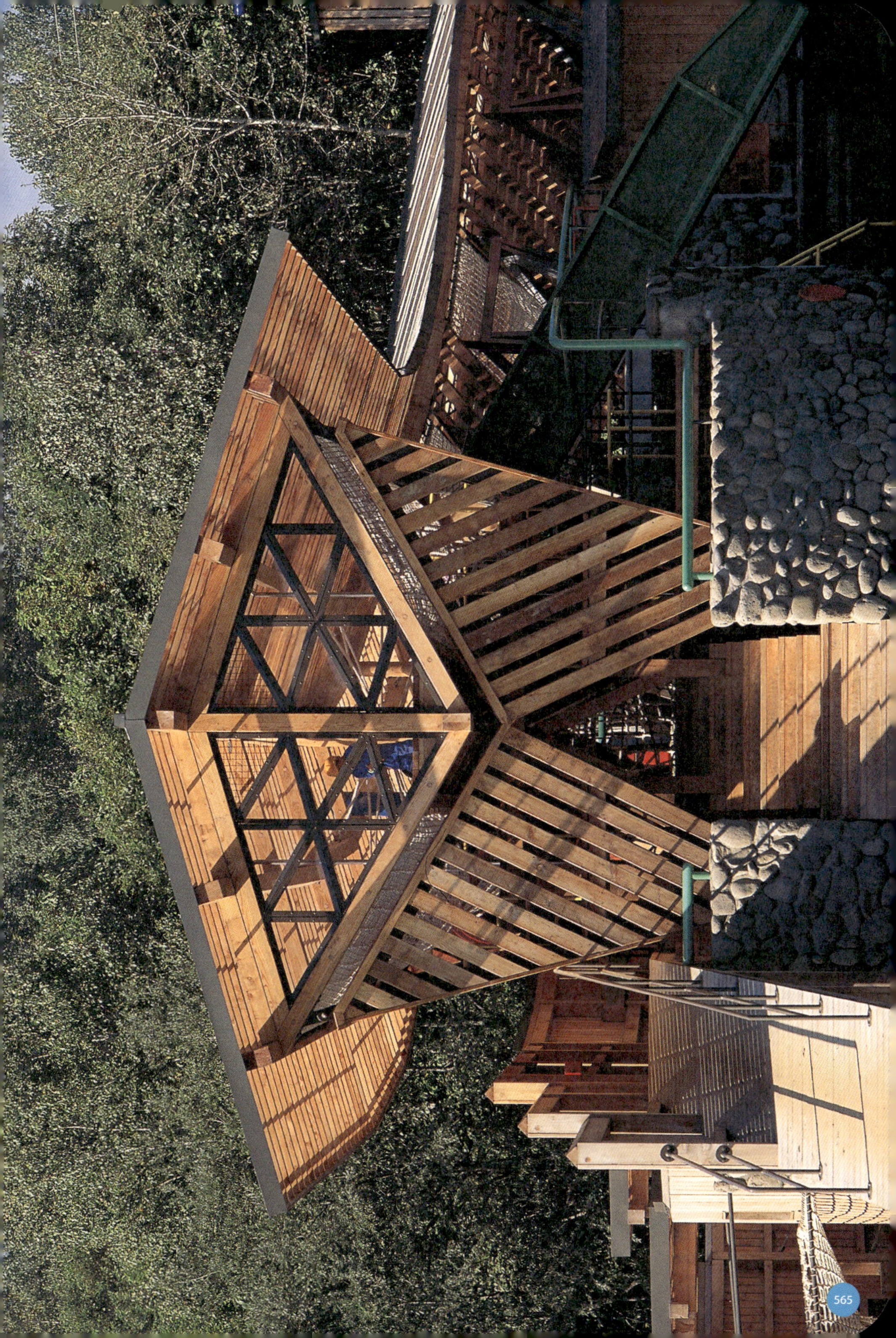

1994

旭川春光台［風の子館］

Asahikawa Shunkodai Park "Kaze no Ko Kan"

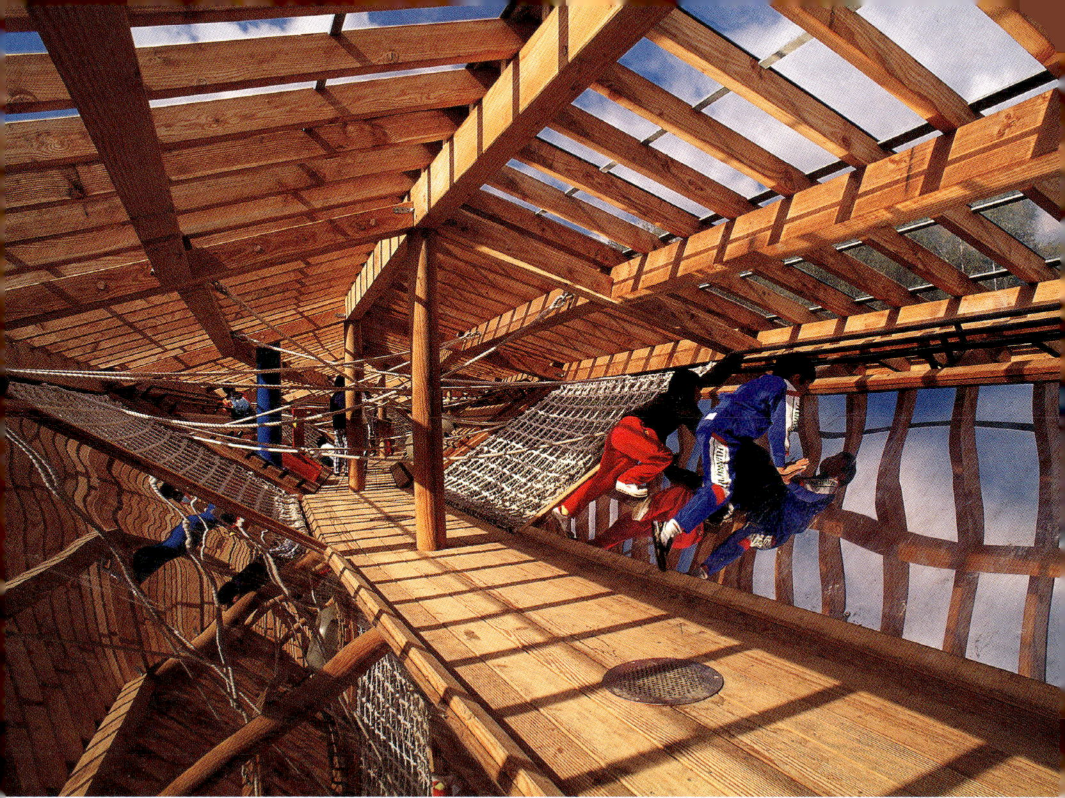

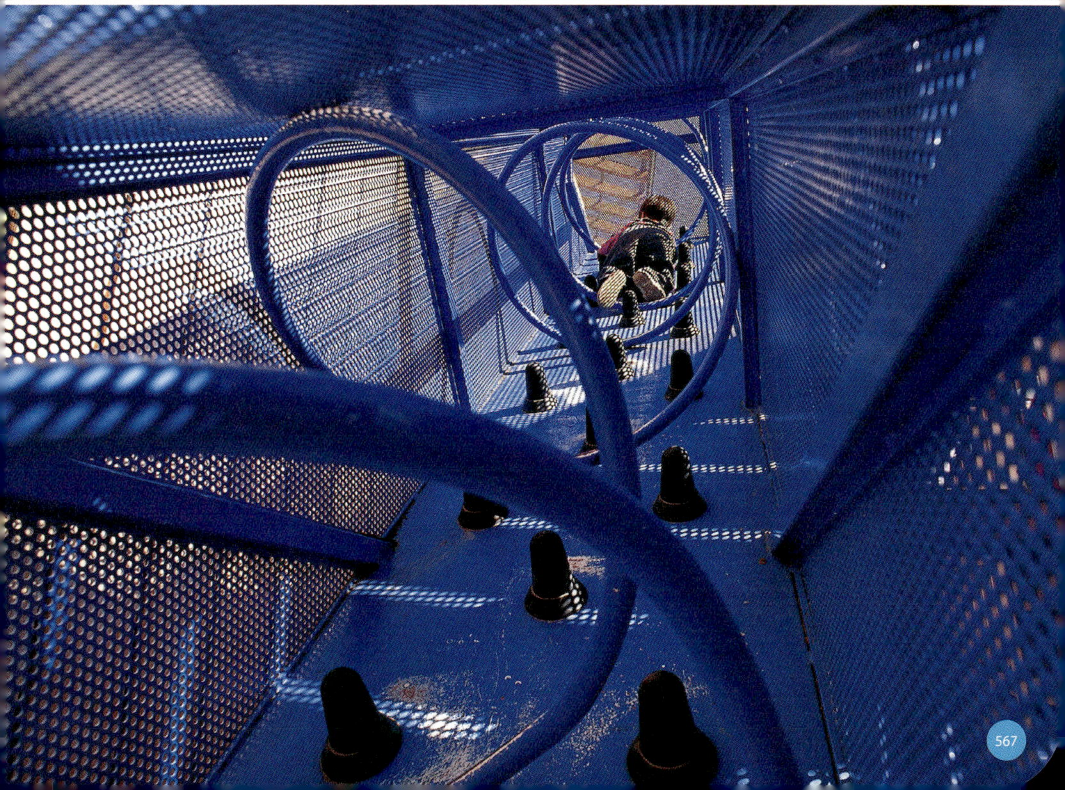

1994

旭川春光台［風の子館］

Asahikawa Shunkodai Park "Kaze no Ko Kan"

うしろの森も交わり、
リニアーだが立体的遊環構造が
形成されている
**The forests behind intersect,
forming a linear yet three-dimensional
circular play system.**

5泊6日

1994

兵庫県南但馬自然学校

Minami Tajima Nature School, Hyogo

兵庫県南但馬自然学校

兵庫県朝来郡山東町／1994
Minami Tajima Nature School, Hyogo
Santon-cho, Asago-gun, Hyogo

兵庫県は県下の小学校5年生全員に、5泊6日の自然学習体験のできる自然学校の整備を進めている。本施設はそのモデル校として計画された。こども達の宿泊する棟は従来の宿泊するための"宿泊棟"という形式ではなく、活動的な"生活棟"という形式をとり、広い吹き抜け空間をもった木造の建物である。施設の配置とその空間は全体的に寺院の構成が引用されている。

Hyogo Prefecture is promoting facilities in non-urban areas where all fifth grade children from elementary schools in the prefecture can stay for up to five nights, in order to learn from nature what they cannot gain in the classroom, and this was built as a model facility. Unlike conventional dormitory-like buildings for children, a residential form of building was adopted for the main building, where the children can learn while engaged in various activities, and this timber building was given a large open well.

1994

兵庫県南但馬自然学校

Minami Tajima Nature School, Hyogo

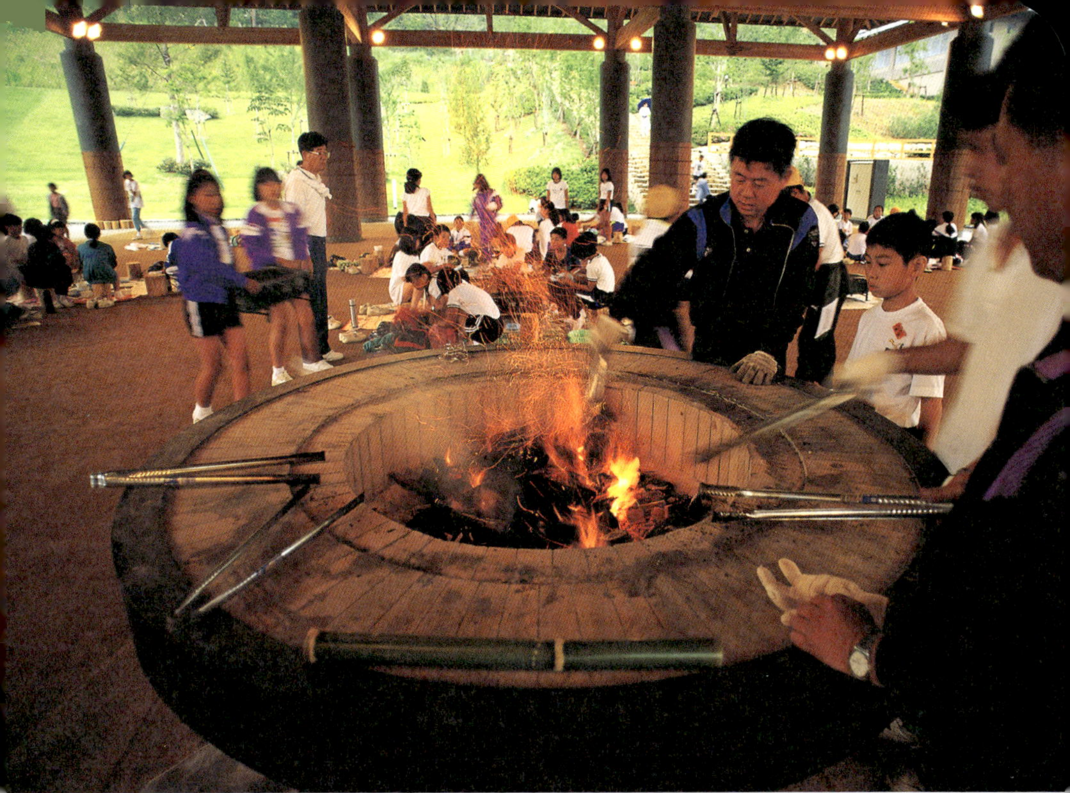

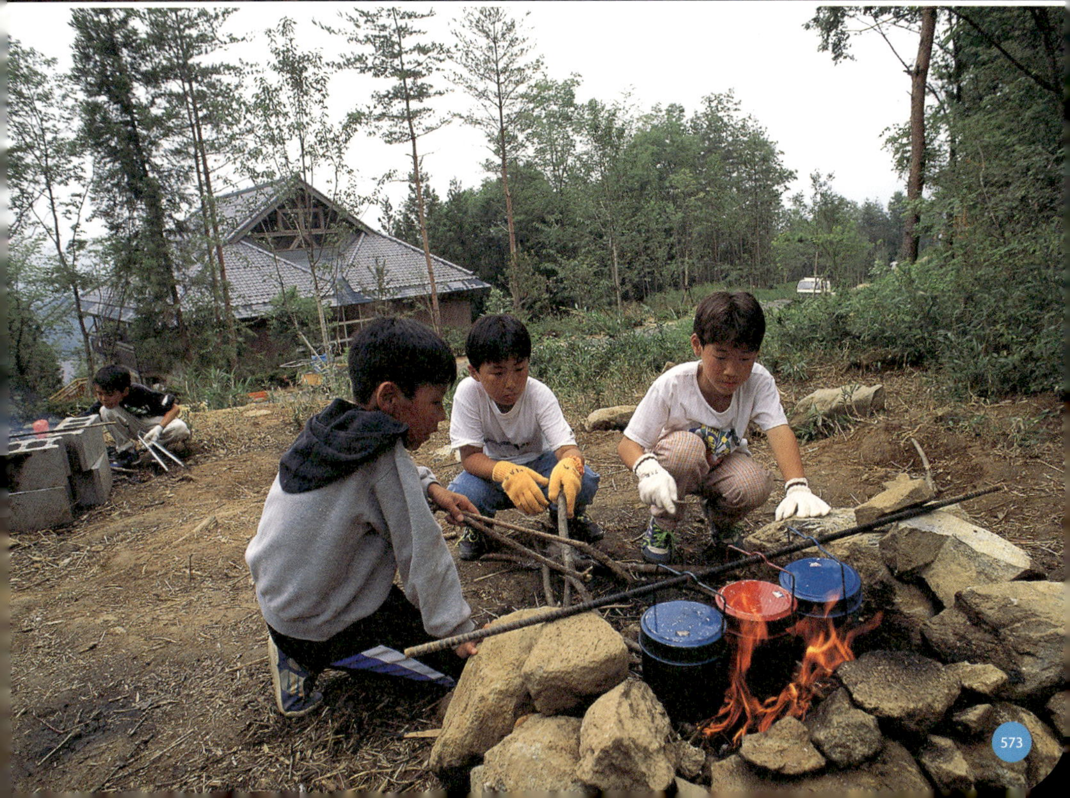

1994

お寺の伽藍配置にも似た野外活動センターの構成
The outdoor activity center
with a layout resembling that of a temple's.

兵庫県南但馬自然学校
Minami Tajima Nature School, Hyogo

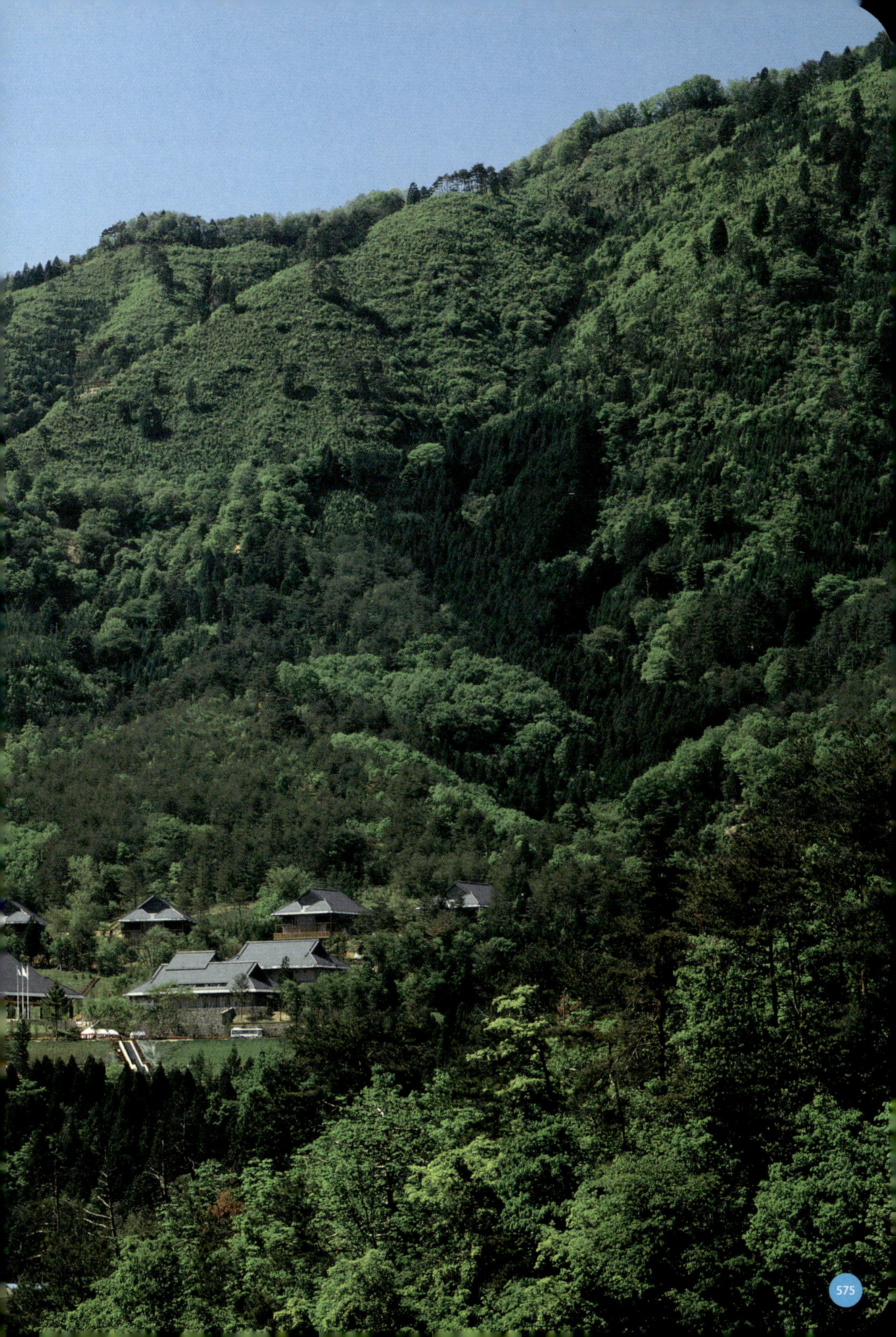

1994

ミュージアムパーク茨城県自然博物館

菅生沼が
展示室

Ibaraki Nature Museum

ミュージアムパーク茨城県自然博物館

茨城県坂東市大崎／1994
Ibaraki Nature Museum
Osaki, Bando-shi, Ibaraki

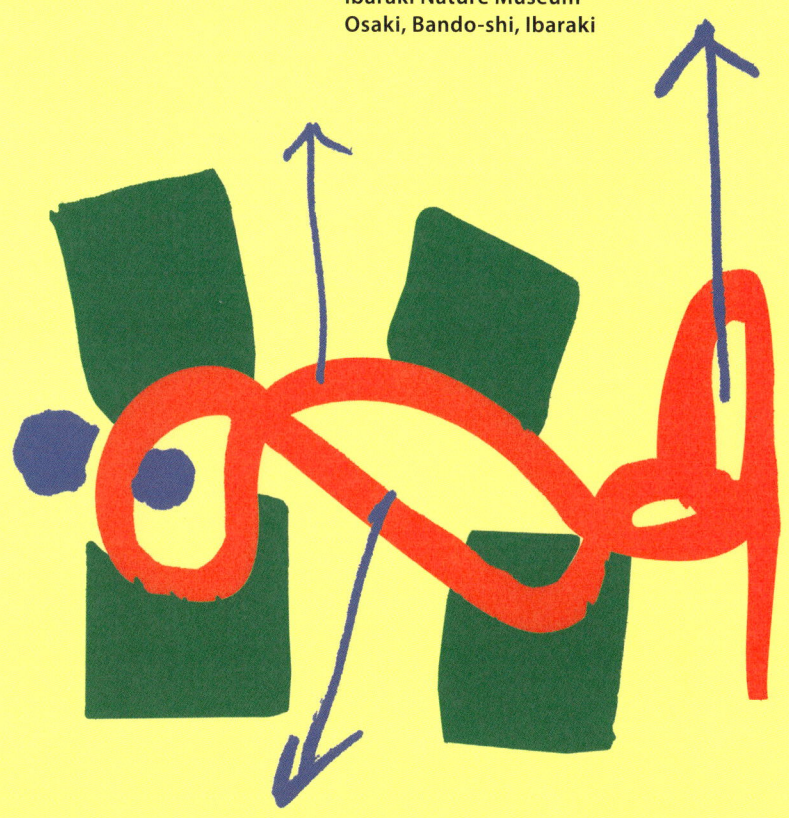

東京から車で1時間、南茨城に位置する利根川流域の菅生沼のほとりに本博物館は建設された。敷地は16.3ヘクタールあるが、約232ヘクタールの菅生沼との一体的な景観が意図された。展示空間は大きく6つの展示テーマに対応して分けられており、それぞれの展示空間は曲線を描く回遊路によって結ばれている。その中心は目次空間と呼ぶ約70mの廊空間として形成されている。建物はもちろん、園地全体が遊環構造としてデザインされている。

Located just one hour drive from Tokyo, the museum was built near Sugaonuma in the drainage basin of the Tonegawa. The site is 16.3-hectare, but the scenery as a whole, encompassing the 232-hectare Sugaonuma, is fantastic. There are basically six exhibition spaces, connected by a deck following a curve. This is known as "Contents Space" and forms a corridor of approximately 70m. In addition to the building, the entire site has been designed as a circular play system.

1994

ミュージアムパーク茨城県自然博物館

Ibaraki Nature Museum

動線が遊環構造としてうねる、
人々を引き込み、誘導する
The route is a meandering one,
forming a circular play system
that pulls in people and guides them through.

1994

ミュージアムパーク茨城県自然博物館　Ibaraki Nature Museum

博物館の目次空間
博物館という本には目次とグラビアがあるべきだ
The "Contents Space"
—the book that museums really are
should have contents and gravure spaces.

8m

6m

581

← 1

1994

ミュージアムパーク茨城県自然博物館

Ibaraki Nature Museum

多様な展示体験、明るい空間、暗い空間、
チューブのような空間、森のような空間
A diverse exhibition experience, bright spaces, dark spaces,
spaces that are like tubes, spaces that resemble forests.

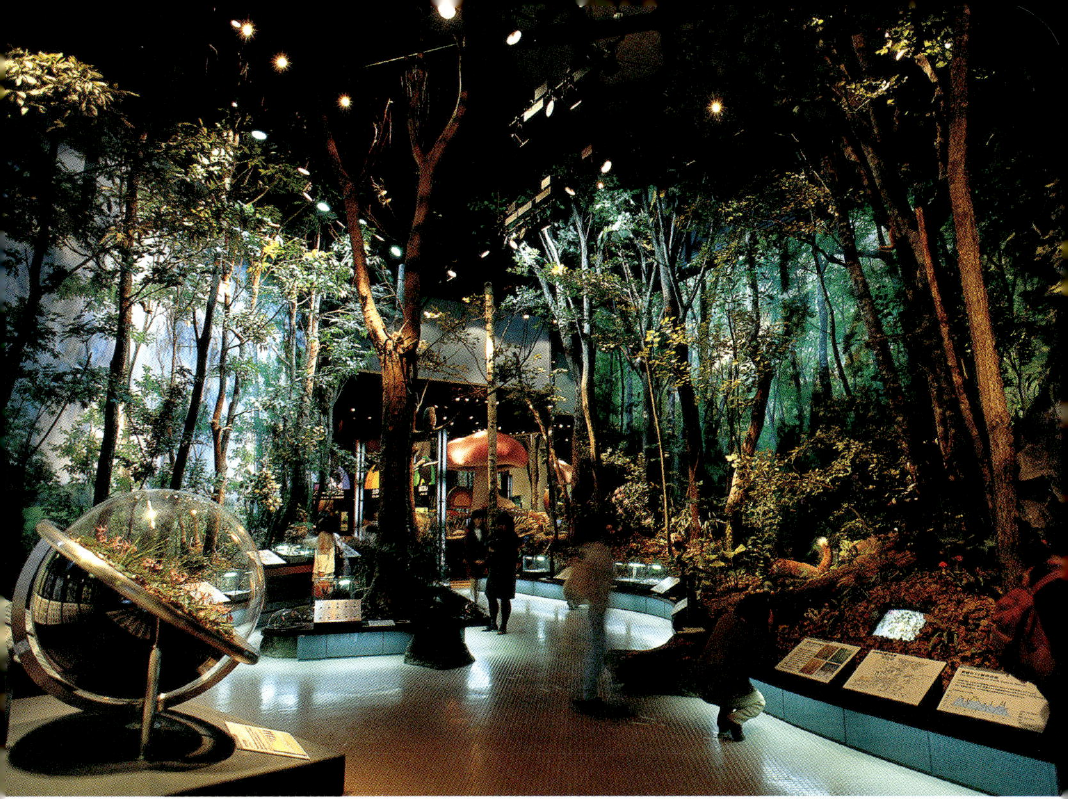

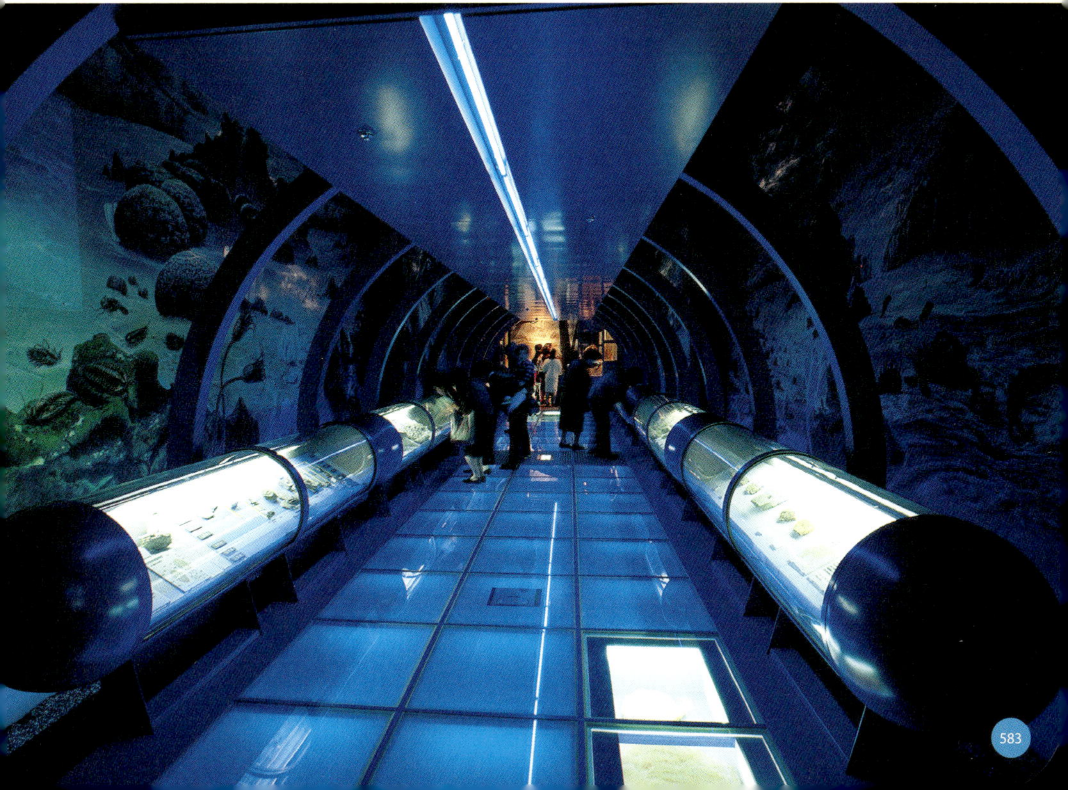

1994

ミュージアムパーク茨城県自然博物館

Ibaraki Nature Museum

菅生沼は最大の展示だ、
人々はその姿に感動する

Sugao-numa is the exhibition with the largest scale;
people are moved and inspired by it.

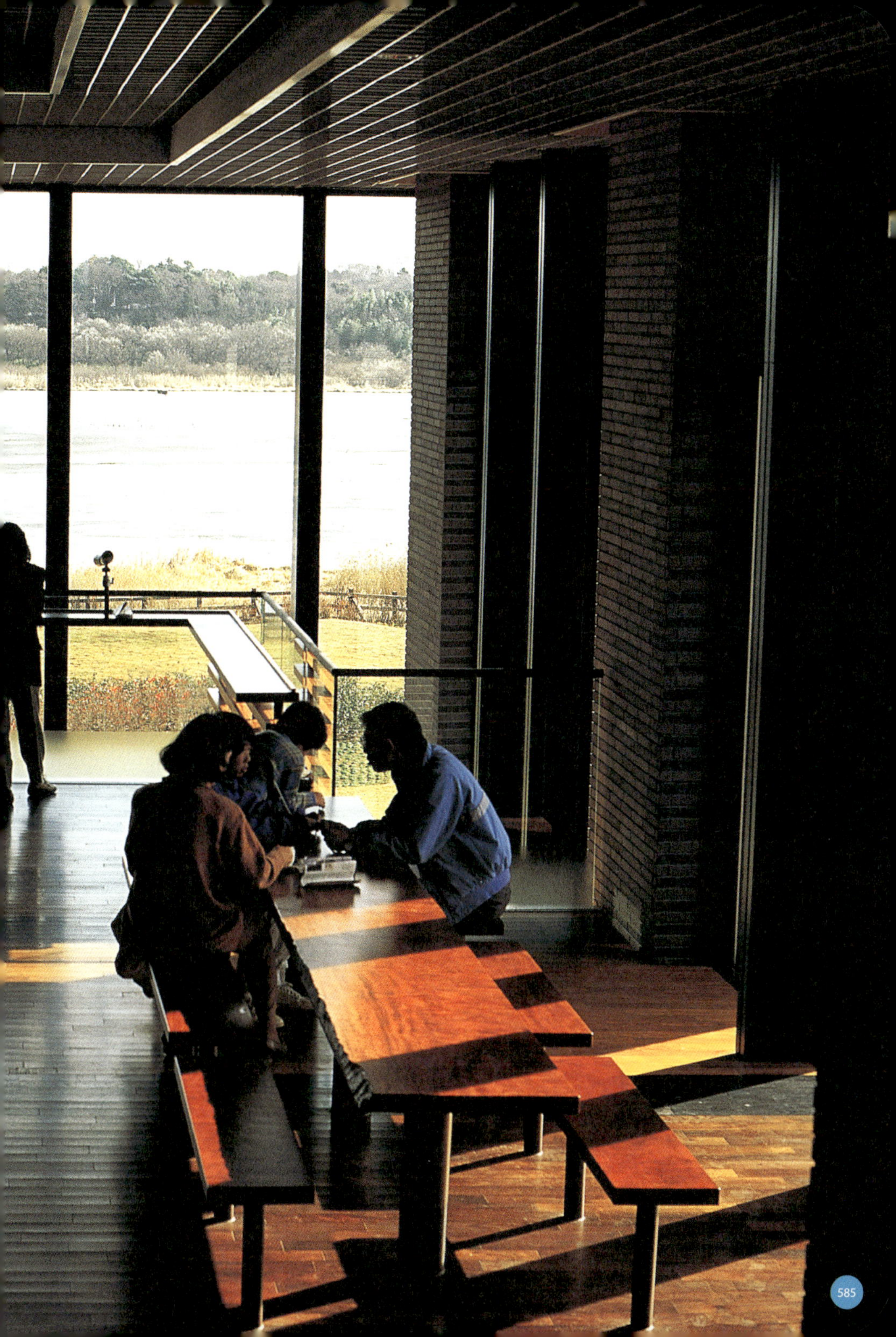

1994

ミュージアムパーク茨城県自然博物館

Ibaraki Nature Museum

動物ゴッコをする自然発見器

Nature exploration equipment, allowing people to play at pretending to be animals.

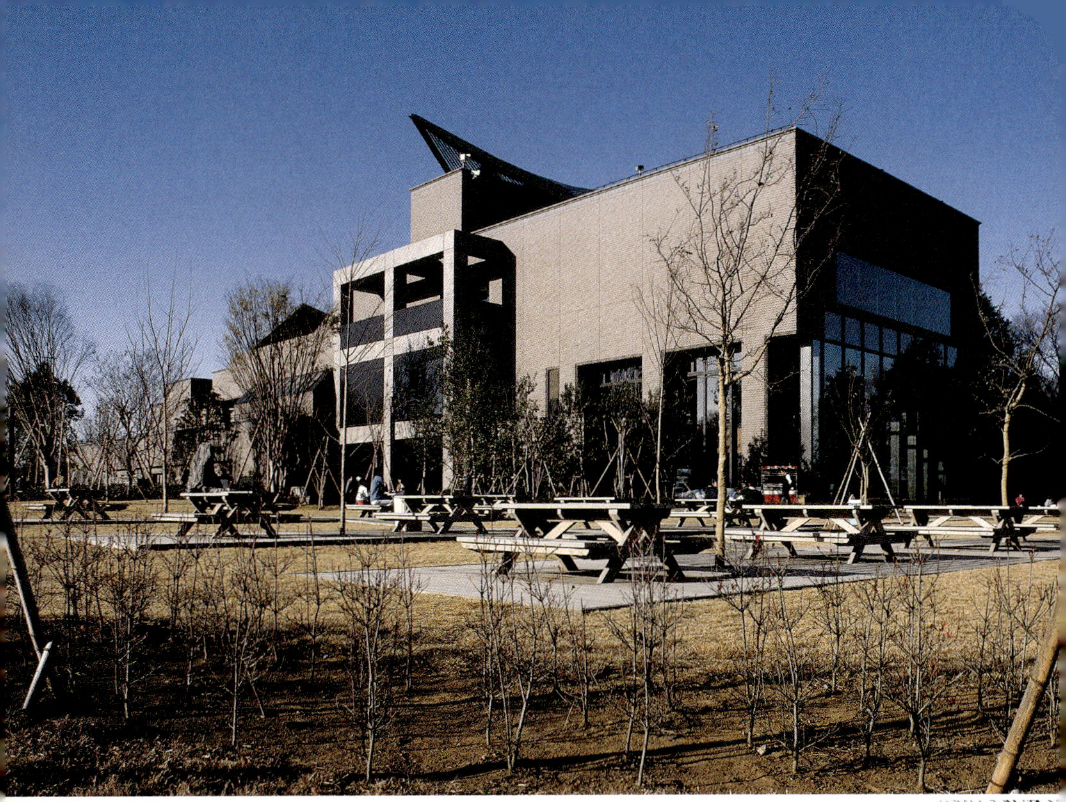

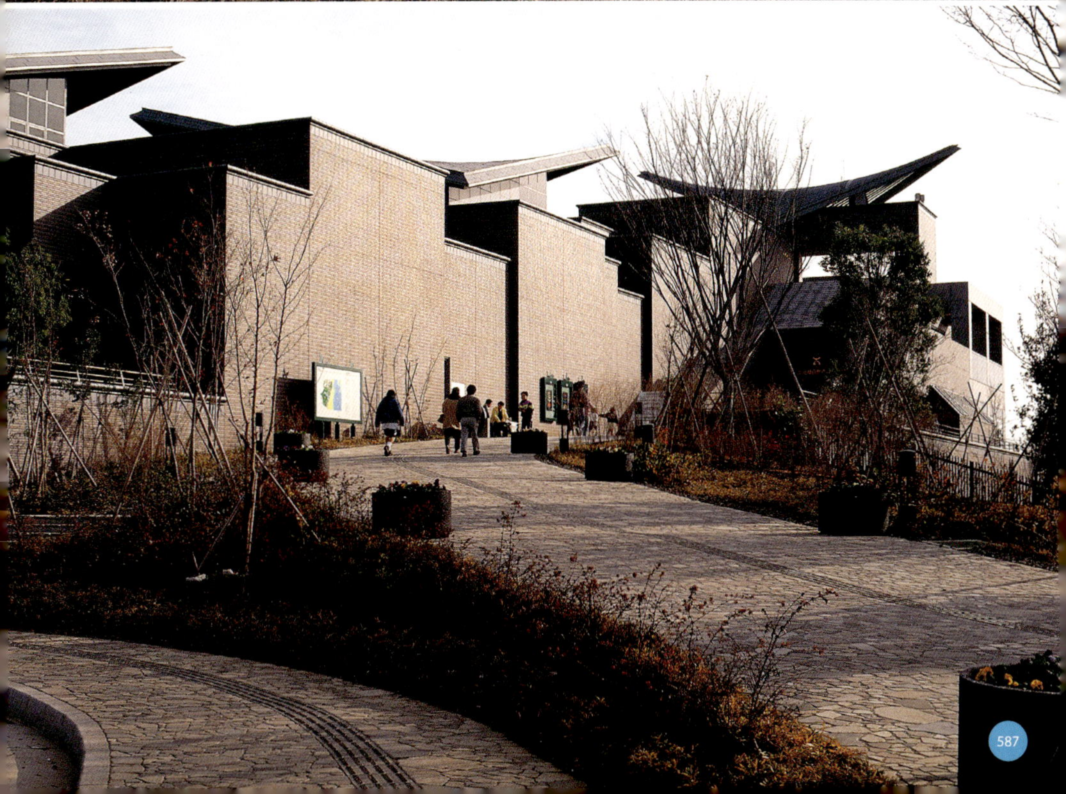

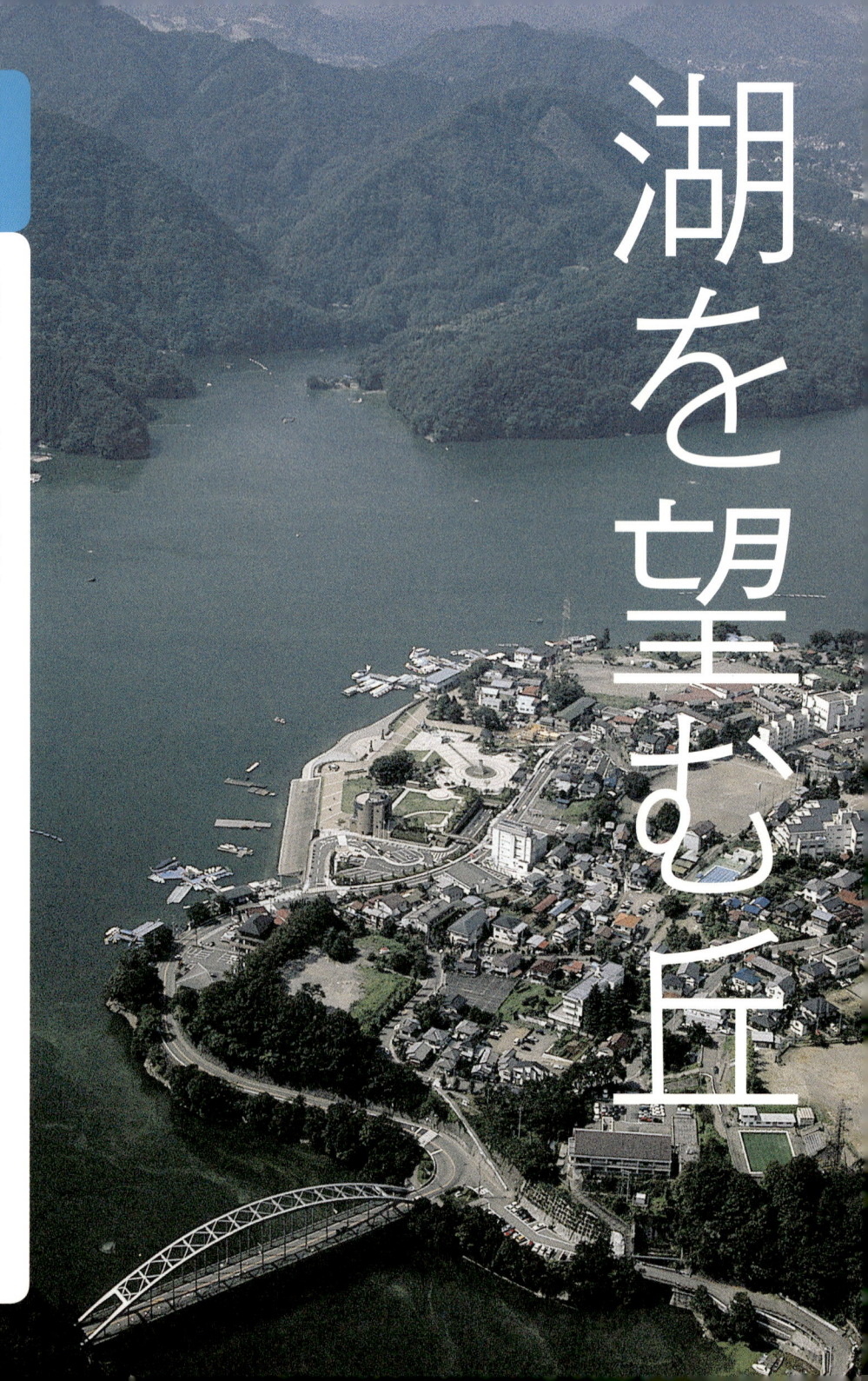

1993

相模湖カルチャーパーク［漕艇場］

Lake Sagami Culture Park, "Rowing space"

湖を望む丘

相模湖カルチャーパーク
［漕艇場］

神奈川県相模原市緑区与瀬／1993
Lake Sagami Culture Park, "Rowing space"
Yose, Midori-ku, Sagamihara-shi, Kanagawa

県立相模湖公園は広域観光レクリエーションの拠点として、相模湖とダムの歴史を象徴し、森と湖の景観を生かした公園である。湖畔には「ふるさと芸術家村」（相模原市）に至る「歩く美術館ルート」につながる湖畔プロムナードが配されている。湖とのふれあいとイベントをダイナミックに演出する大階段の背後は、駐車場を地下化し、上部を相模ダム発電所第1号発電機のモニュメントとカルチャーパーク情報センターを中心とする広場となっている。

As a base of tourism and recreation, the Lake Sagami Prefectural Park symbolizes the history of the lake and dam, and underscores the beauty of its lake and forest. On the shores of the lake is the Old Craftsmen's Village (Sagamihara City), a destination of the Open-air Art Museum route, off of which is the Lakeshore Promenade. Against the background of a grand staircase emphasizing the beauty of the lake and lending dynamism to events held there, cars are kept below ground and above is a plaza with a monument to the Sagami Dam Electric Plant's first generator and the culture park's information center.

1993

相模湖カルチャーパーク ［漕艇場］

Lake Sagami Culture Park, "Rowing space"

591

1993

自然発見

信州博アルピコ広場 [円環遊具]

"Circular Play Structure" in the Shinshu Expo Alpico Plaza

信州博アルピコ広場
［円環遊具］

長野県松本市今井／1993
"Circular Play Structure" in the Shinshu Expo Alpico Plaza
Imai, Matsumoto-shi, Nagano

一周80ｍの円環状の建築的な屋根付き遊具である。あそびながら風の音、鳥の声を聞き、松本の四季の星空をオープンプラネタリウムで見たりというように、自然発見遊具として構想された。博覧会後、恒久施設として残された。

This is a circular piece of roofed play equipment that is 80 meters in circumference. It was planned as a play structure to help children discover the fun of nature, letting them play to the sound of the wind, listen to the birds singing, and to be able to recognize the changing seasons in and around Matsumoto both during the day and at night using the open planetarium. After the expo closed, the site was maintained as a permanent facility.

1993

信州博アルピコ広場［円環遊具］

"Circular Play Structure" in the Shinshu Expo Alpico Plaza

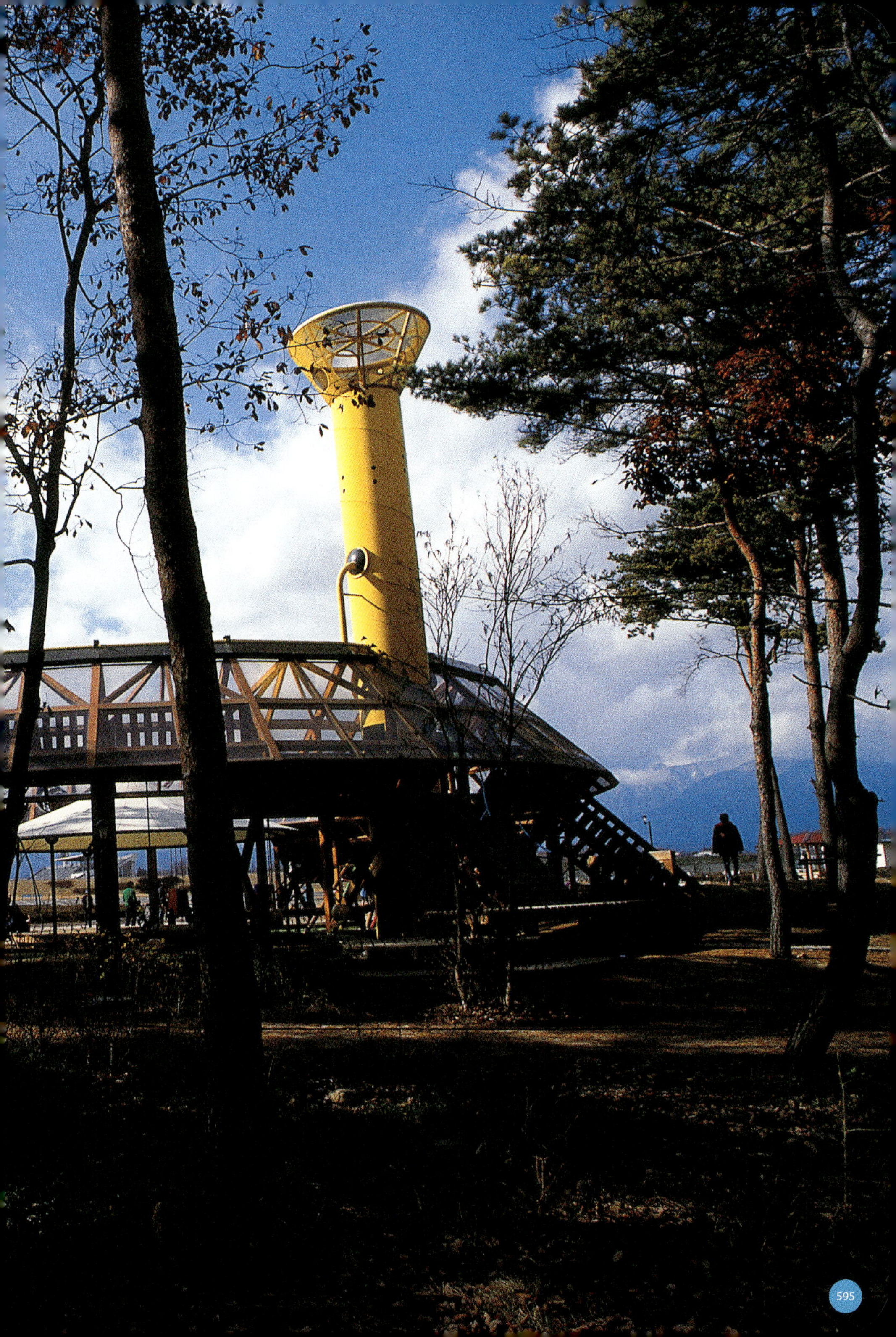

1993

信州博アルピコ広場［円環遊具］

"Circular Play Structure" in the Shinshu Expo Alpico Plaza

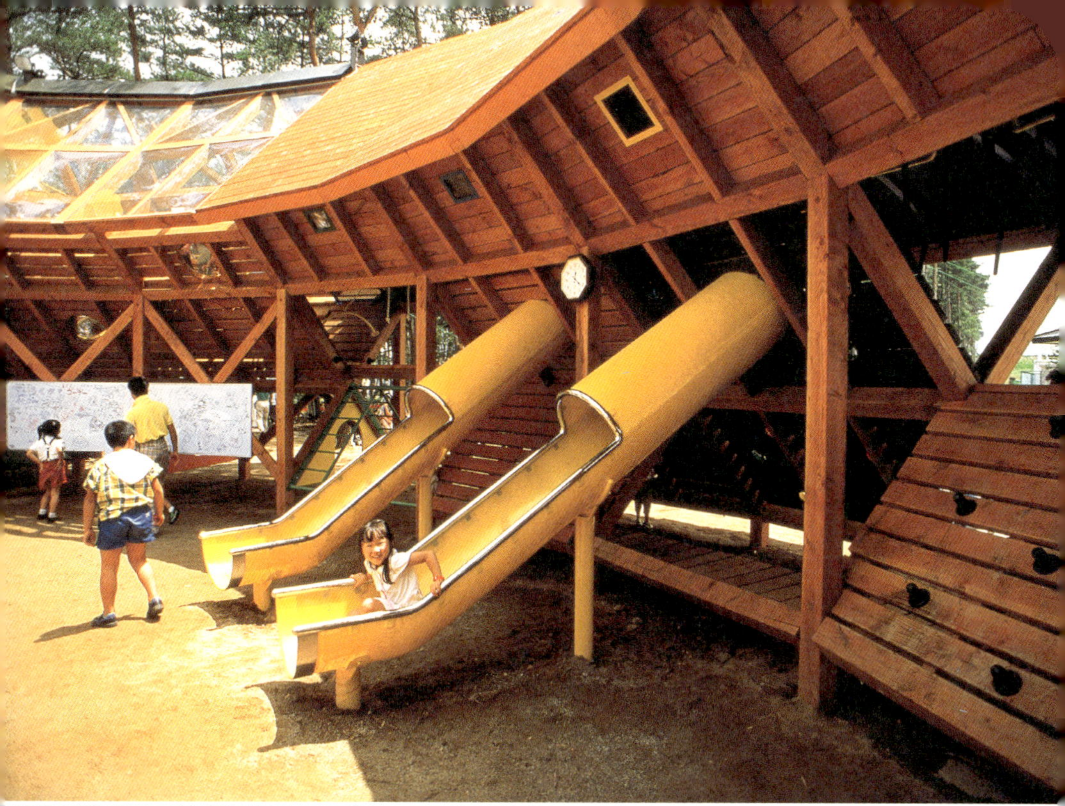

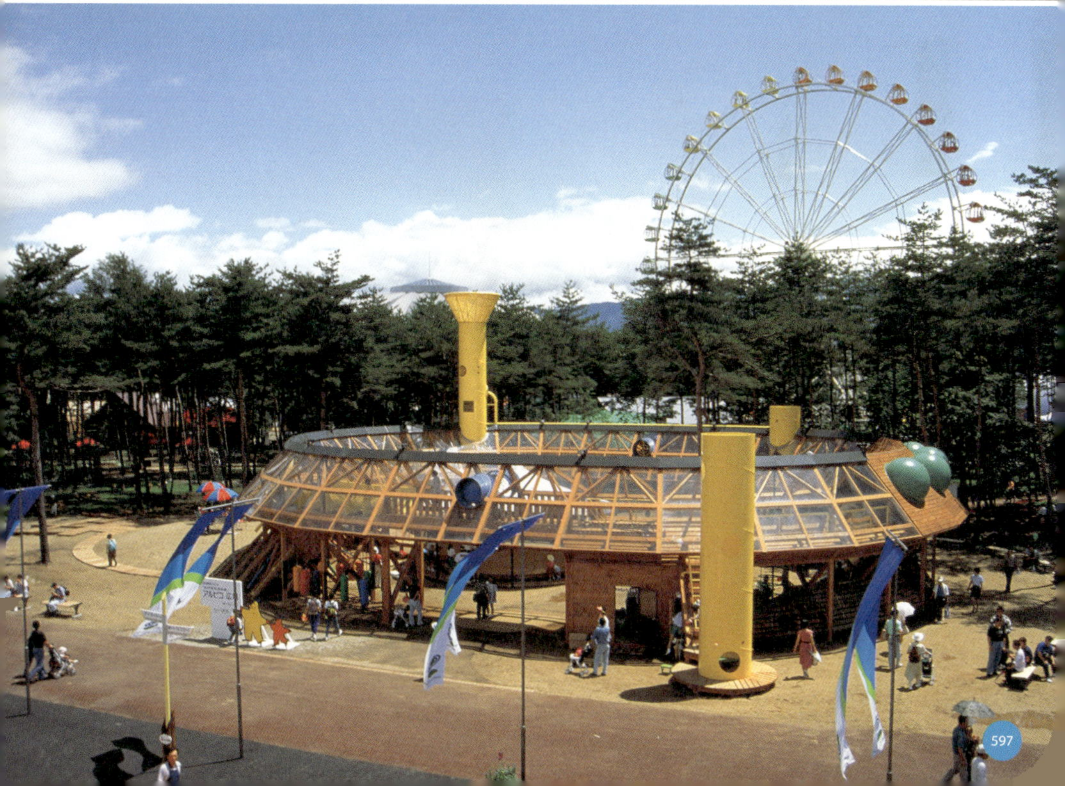

1993

姫路御立公園［たつまきロード］

Himeji Mitate Park "Tornado Road"

あそびの起爆

姫路御立公園
［たつまきロード］

兵庫県姫路市御立西／1993
Himeji Mitate Park "Tornado Road"
Mitatenishi, Himeji-shi, Hyogo

姫路市の郊外交通公園である御立公園に設置された巨大遊具である。広場にたつまきが起こったような、動的な造形がシンボリックに展開され、リニアな遊環構造としてこども達のあそびの起爆剤となるように動線がデザインされている。

This large play equipment was constructed in Mitate Park, which was built as a "transportation park" to teach children traffic rules in the suburbs of Himeji. The dynamic, symbolic structure appears as if it was awoken by a tornado that cut through the open space. The linear circular play system was designed to stimulate play.

599

1993

姫路御立公園[たつまきロード]

Himeji Mitate Park "Tornado Road"

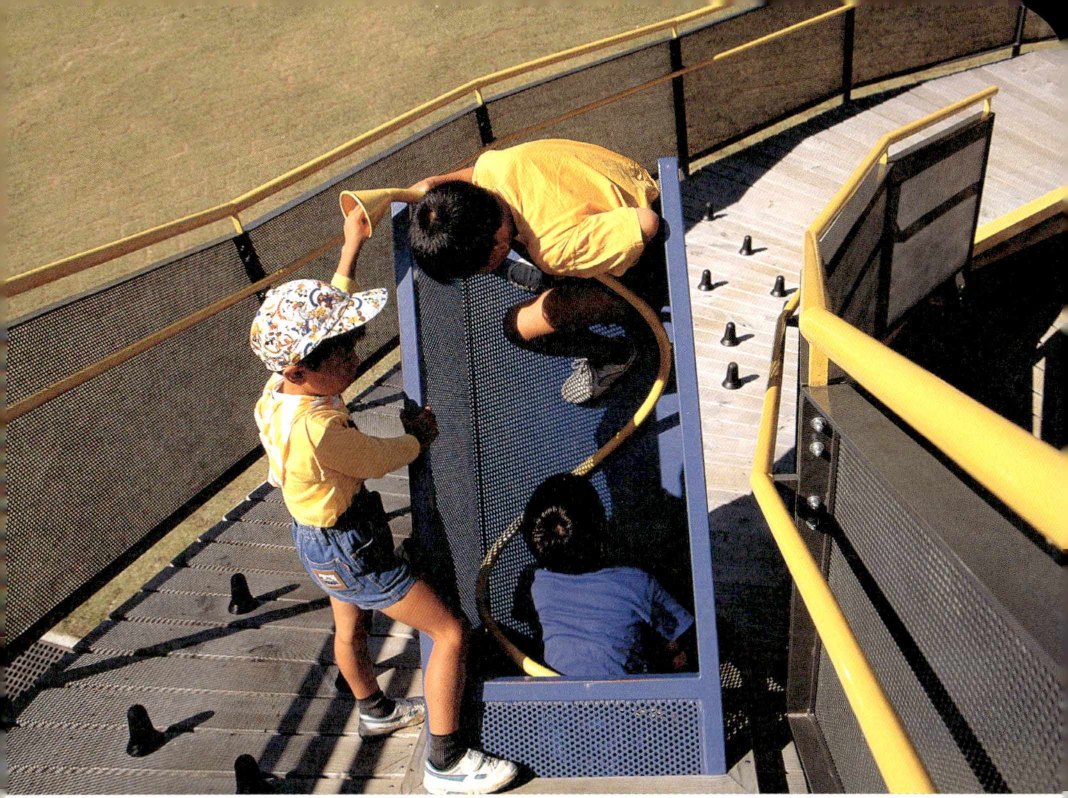

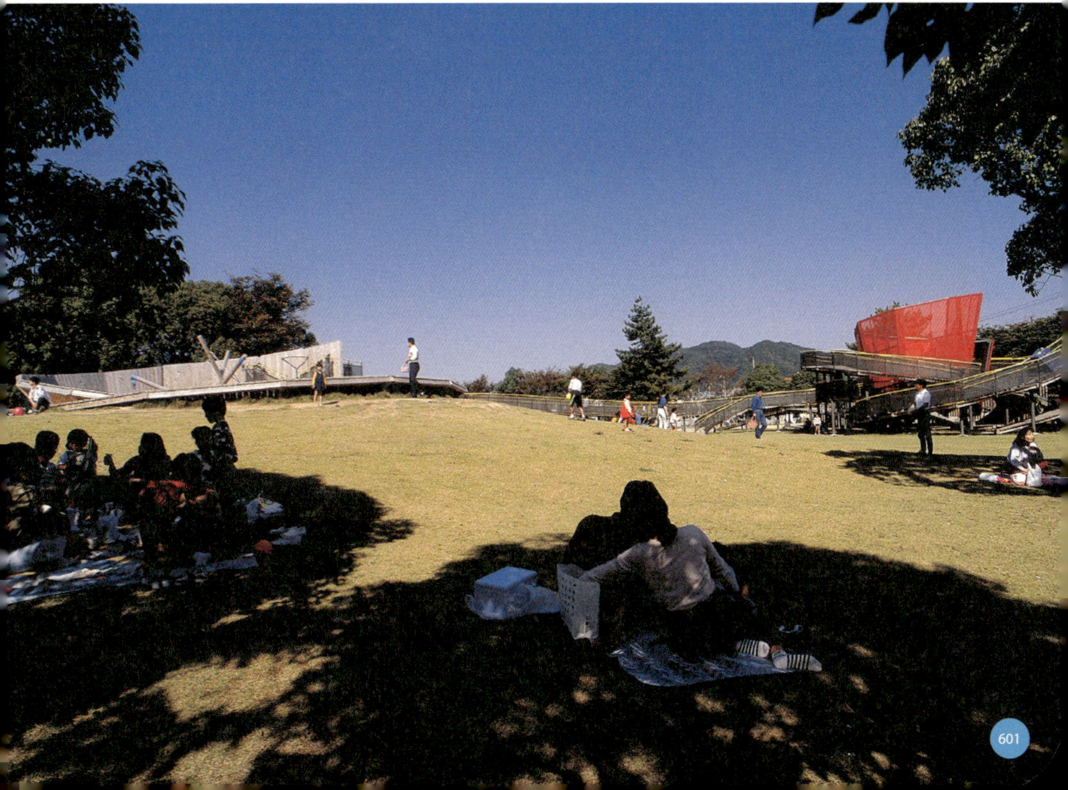

たまごの森

1993

国営ひたち海浜公園［たまごの森］

"Tamago no Mori" in Hitachi Seaside Park

国営ひたち海浜公園
［たまごの森］

茨城県ひたちなか市馬渡／1993
"Tamago no Mori" in Hitachi Seaside Park
Mawatari, Hitachinaka-shi, Ibaraki

茨城県東部、ひたち海浜公園に設置された幼児のあそびと休憩のためのエリア。たまごをイメージした造形物が森の中に物語の語りべの小道具として点在している。

This is a rest and play area for children located in Hitachi Seaside Park in eastern Ibaraki Prefecture. Structures shaped like eggs have been placed around the forest as small play equipment to tell a story.

1993

国営ひたち海浜公園［たまごの森］

"Tamago no Mori" in Hitachi Seaside Park

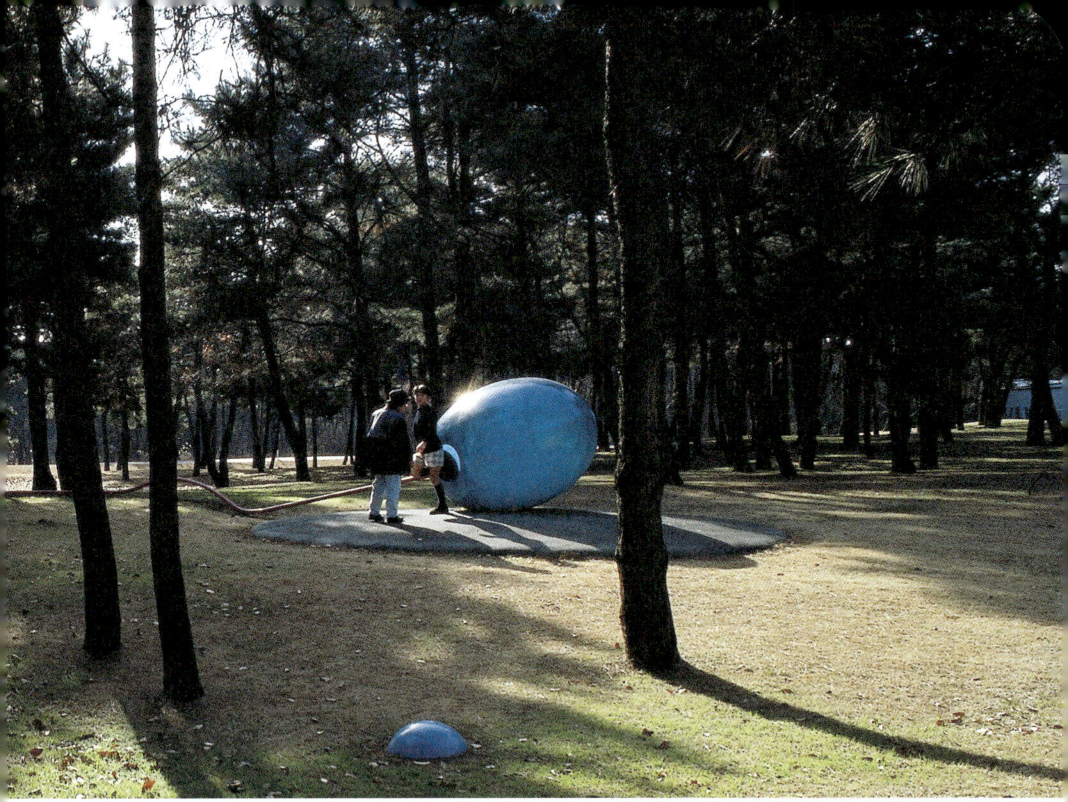

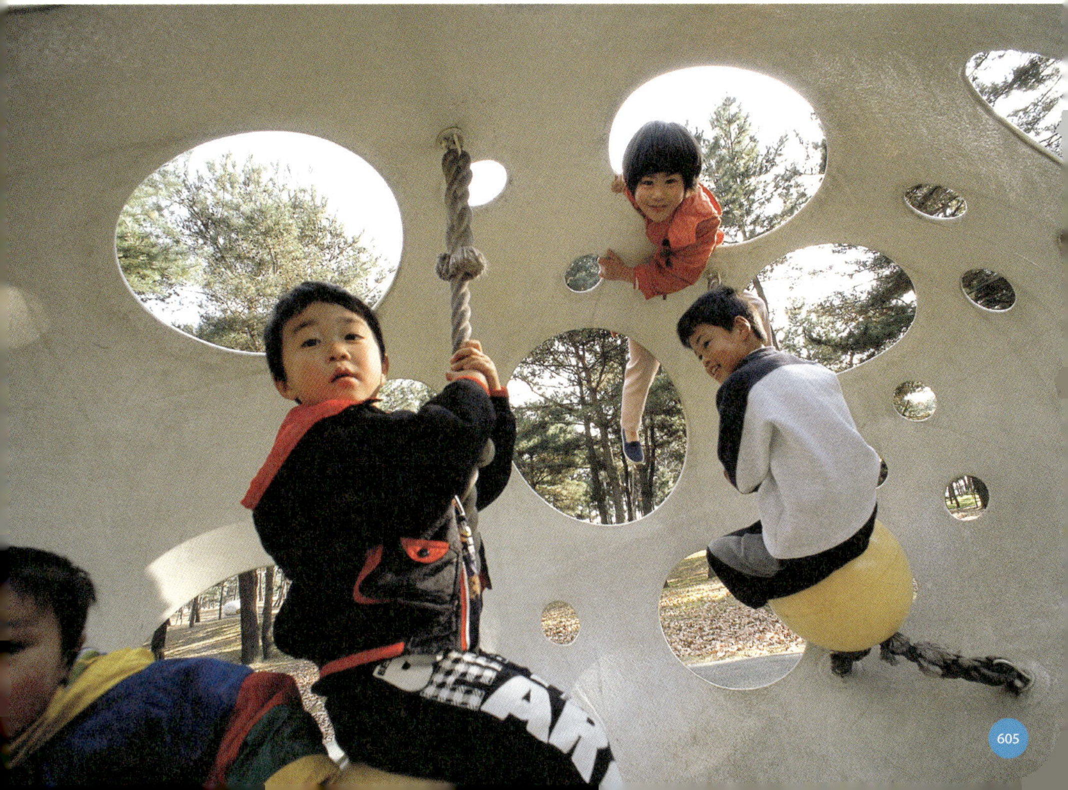

屋上プール付遊環建築

1993

相模原市星が丘こどもセンター
Sagamihara Municipal Hoshigaoka Children's Center

相模原市星が丘こどもセンター

神奈川県相模原市中央区星が丘／1993
Sagamihara Municipal Hoshigaoka Children's Center
Hoshigaoka, Chuo-ku, Sagamihara-shi, Kanagawa

相模原市内の53校の小学校に1校ずつ児童センターをつくる計画の基に本施設はそのモデルとして建設された。この児童センターは1日約200人のこども達が来館する。中央にある遊戯室を中心として、らせん状に図書コーナーをはじめ、様々なコーナーがとりついている。遊具の橋が遊戯室の空中を走り、全体として遊環構造建築となっている。屋上にはプールが搭載されている。

Individual children's centers are planned for the city's jurisdiction, and this particular facility was built as a model for these. Approximately two hundred children visit the center in one day. It has a playroom at its center with various other activity areas including a library wrapping around it. A bridge with play features runs through the playroom and it is based on circular play system. There is also a pool located on the roof.

1993

相模原市星が丘こどもセンター
Sagamihara Municipal Hoshigaoka Children's Center

入口は巻貝の中に入っていくよう
The entrance makes one think of entering the inside of a snail's shell.

小さな遊環構造建築
A small circular play system building.

1993

相模原市星が丘こどもセンター
Sagamihara Municipal Hoshigaoka Children's Center

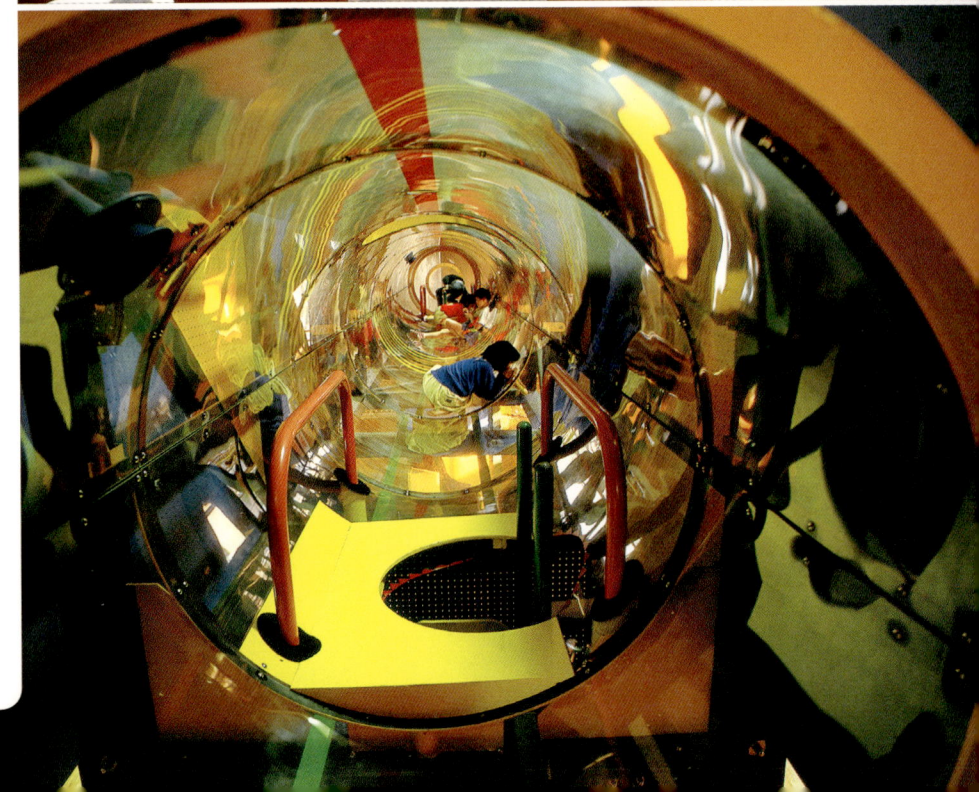

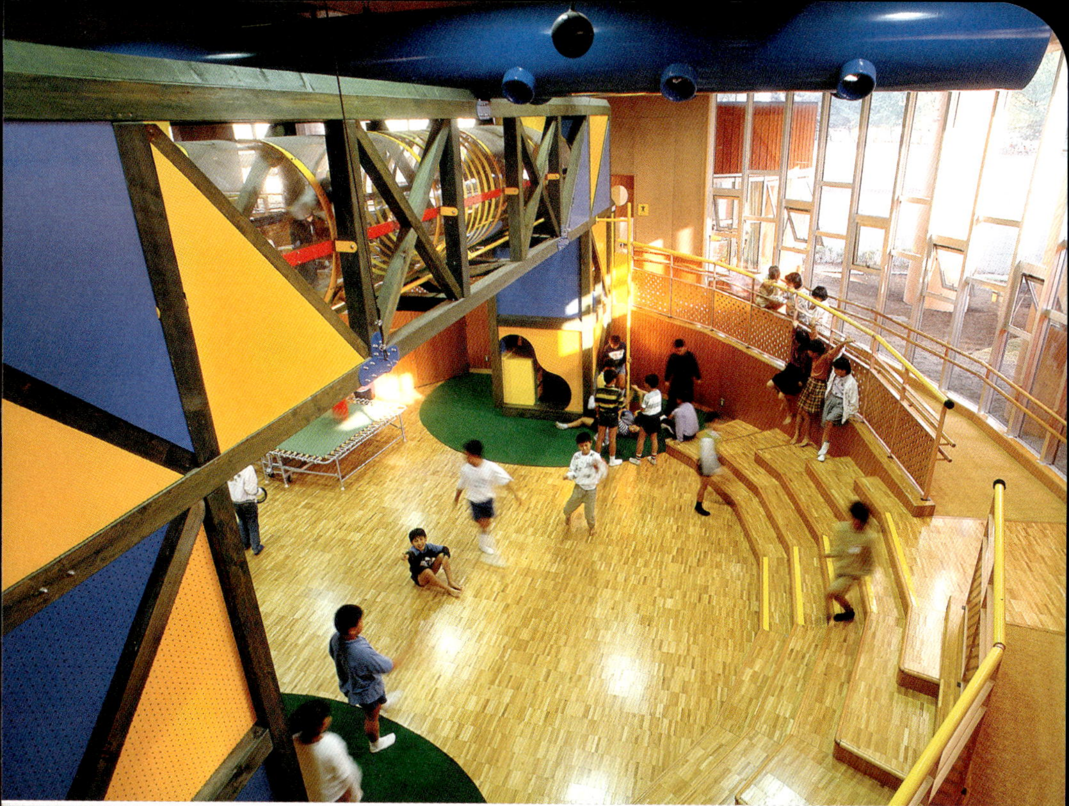

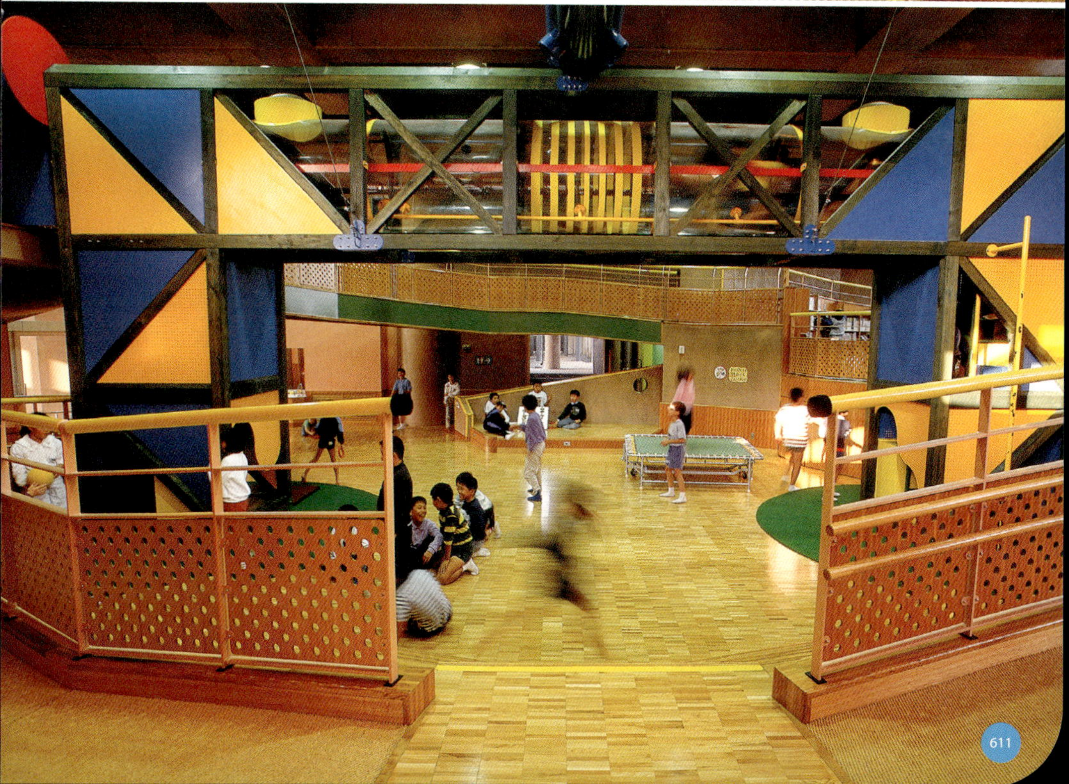

1993

多摩六都科学館

Tama Rokuto Science Museum

27mの
サイエンス・
エッグ

多摩六都科学館

東京都西東京市芝久保町／1993
Tama Rokuto Science Museum
Shibakubo-cho, Nishitokyo-shi, Tokyo

本施設は、東京都北部多摩地区の6市共同で建設運営される科学館である。テーマは、宇宙から地域の自然科学まで多岐にわたっている。雑木林を残すため、5つの展示室は3つの10mの立方体におさめられ、平面的に鎖状につながっている。その立方体の間のスリットから雑木林が楽しめる。雑木林に面した外壁は存在感を消すためにステンレスの鏡面仕上げである。

Tama Rokuto Science Museum was created by six cities of northern Tama area in Tokyo. The display themes broadly cover from the space to natural science in the area. There are five exhibition spaces within the three 10 meter cubes, which are linked on plane, but they have been arranged interestingly so that it is still possible to catch glimpses of the trees outside through slits left between them. The exterior of the building facing the trees is finished in polished stainless steel, in order to reduce its presence.

1993

多摩六都科学館

Tama Rokuto Science Museum

森の中の科学の卵
A science egg in the heart of the forest.

1993

多摩六都科学館　Tama Rokuto Science Museum

617

1993

多摩六都科学館

Tama Rokuto Science Museum

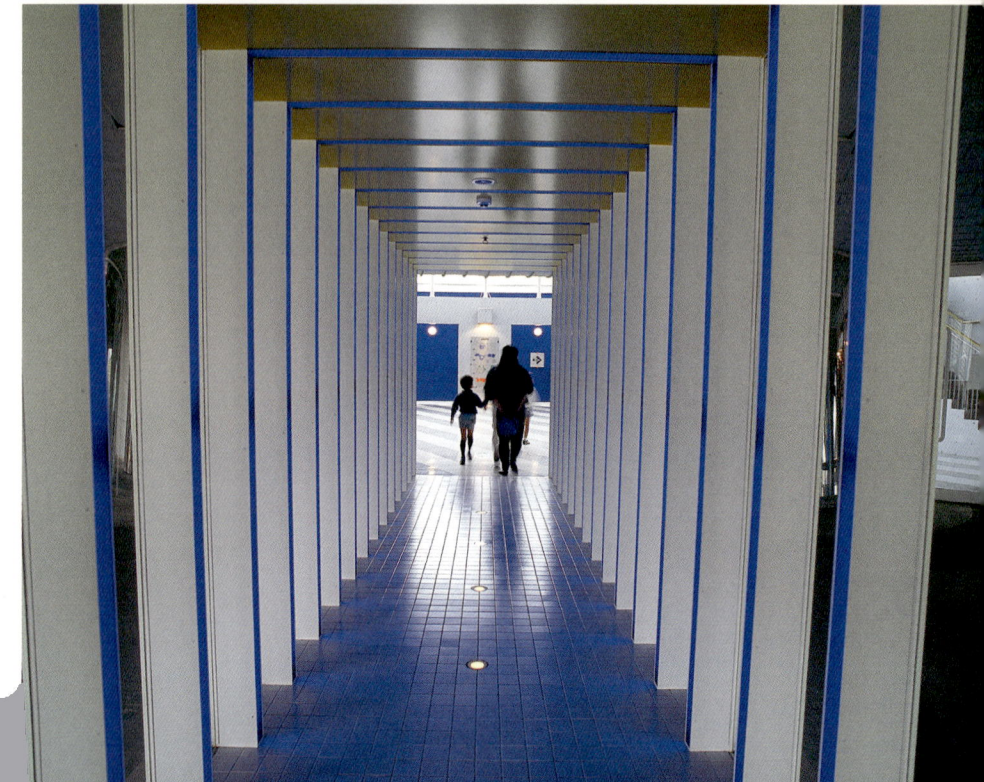

敷地の樹林も展示室
The forests on the grounds are also exhibition halls.

浮かぶスポーツの箱

1993

常滑市体育館
Tokoname Municipal Gymnasium

常滑市体育館

愛知県常滑市金山／1993
Tokoname Municipal Gymnasium
Kanayama, Tokoname-shi, Aichi

本体育館は、愛知国体の会場として新設された常滑公園の中に計画された。メインアリーナとサブアリーナを2階に、観客席を3階にし、1階は一般利用者エントランス、事務室、更衣室、トレーニング室、会議室等が配置されている。屋根は立体パイプトラスであり、それを外縁で耐候性耐火性鋼管斜め格子と逆V字型コンクリート支柱で支えるというダイナミックでシンプルな構造である。全体をハーフミラーで覆い、明るく開放的で遊環構造をもつカジュアルな体育館として設計された。

Planned for the newly constructed Tokoname Park, the venue for the National Athletics Meet in Aichi. There are the main arena and sub-arena on the second floor, seating on the third, and the main entrance, administration room, changing room, training room, meeting room on the first. With a tree-dimensional pipe truss roof sustained by a skew lattice of weatherproof and fireproof copper pipes and reverse V shaped concrete at the outer edge, it has a dynamic and simple structure. Completely enveloped in mirrored glass, the intention here was to create a sports facility with a feeling of lightness and openness.

1993

常滑市体育館　Tokoname Municipal Gymnasium

サブアリーナからは
中部国際空港と伊勢湾が一望できる
The sub-arena looks out to
Central Japan International Airport and Ise Bay.

1993

常滑市体育館
Tokoname Municipal Gymnasium

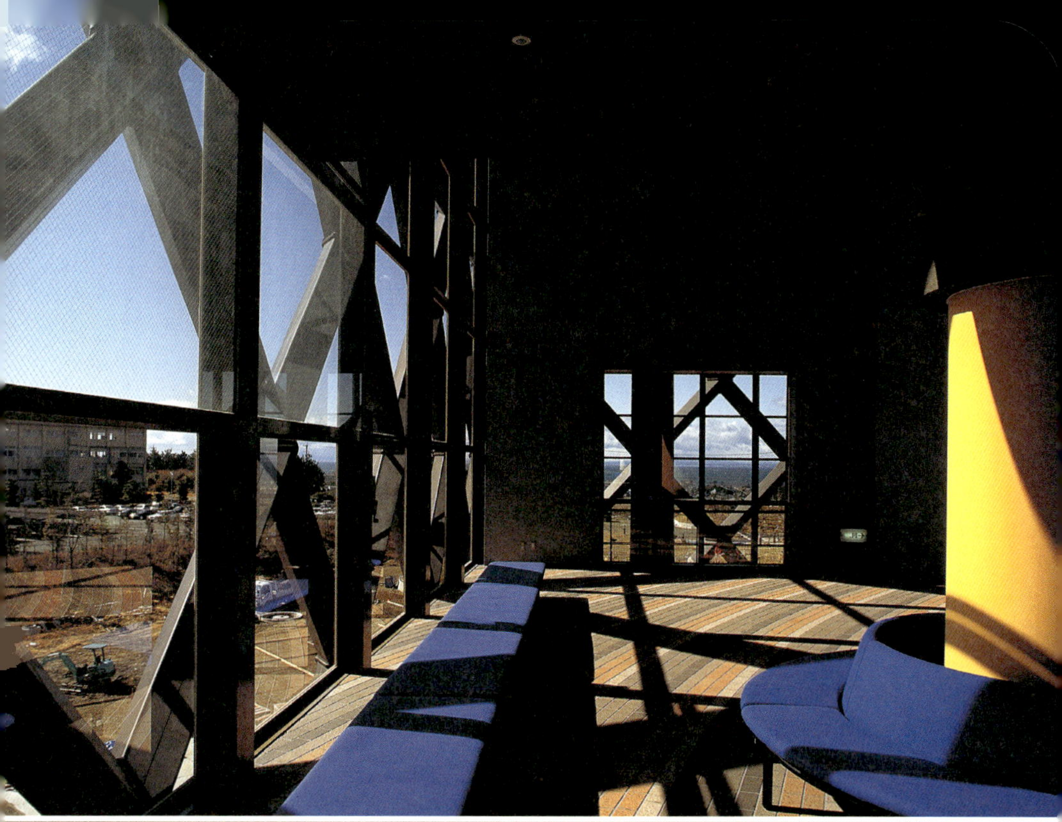

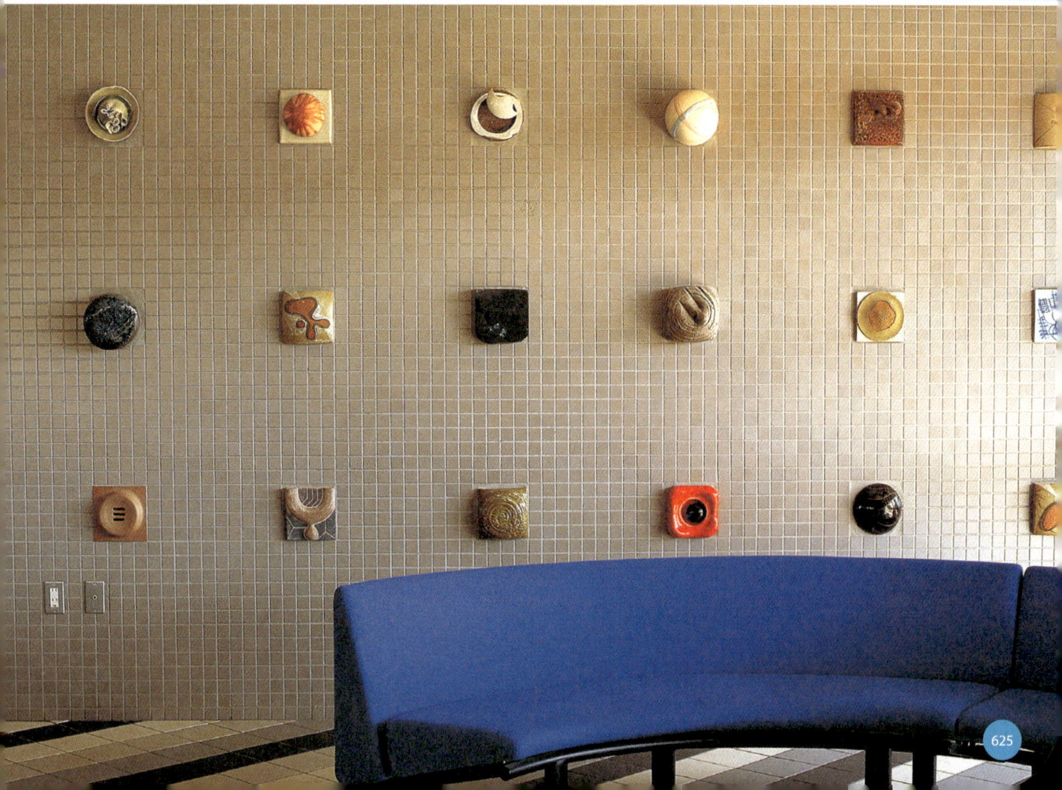

1993

空中に浮かぶ体育館
A gymnasium that is suspended in mid-air.

常滑市体育館
Tokoname Municipal Gymnasium

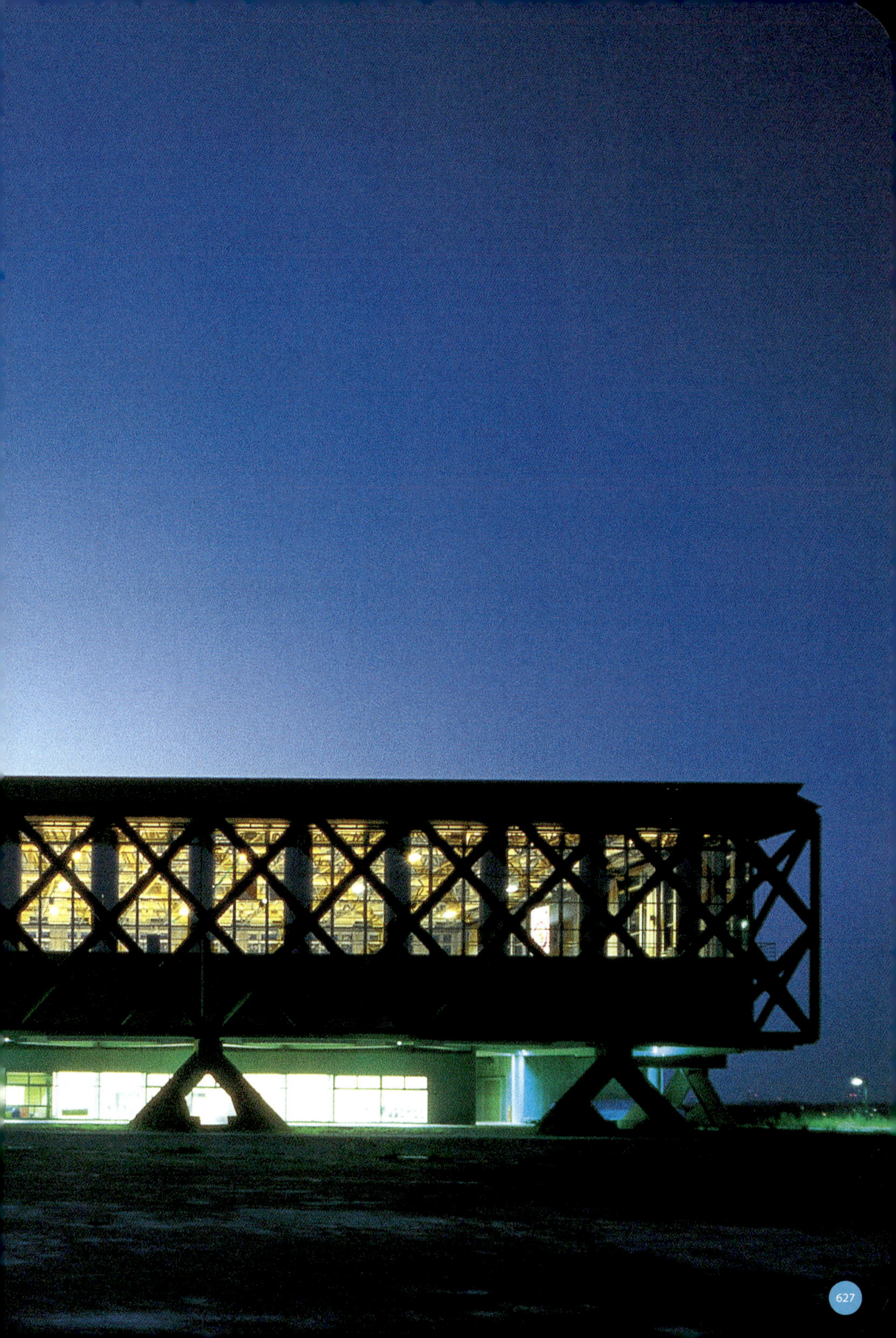

1993

東京辰巳国際水泳場

Tokyo Tatsumi International Swimming Center

水面に羽ばたく

東京辰巳国際水泳場

東京都江東区辰巳／1993
Tokyo Tatsumi International Swimming Center
Tatsumi, Koto-ku, Tokyo

東京都の臨海地にある辰巳臨海公園の一角に位置している。国際的な水泳競技大会ができるとともに、一般都民のスポーツレクリエーションの場として計画されている。北側に運河の大きな水面があるため観客席を南側のみに設け、メインプールとダイビングプールの水面と運河の水面が連続するような空間構成がとられた。水面に羽ばたく水鳥をイメージした5枚のヴォールト状の屋根は立体トラスによって形作られている。全体的に平面的・立体的遊環構造が応用されながら周囲の環境と調和し、泳ぐ人、見る人にとってもやさしい環境となるよう意図されている。

Located in Tokyo's Tatsumi Seaside Park. The facility was planned for international swimming events as well as sports recreation of the citizens of Tokyo. The main diving and swimming pools were planned to be a continuation of the open tract of water located on the north side of building and have a consistent water level. Centrally located and at the focus of the five roof-shells designed as an impression of a bird beating its wings on the water. Harmonizing as a whole with the surrounding environment, the intention here was to create an environment which was both swimmer and spectator friendly.

1993

東京辰巳国際水泳場

Tokyo Tatsumi International Swimming Center

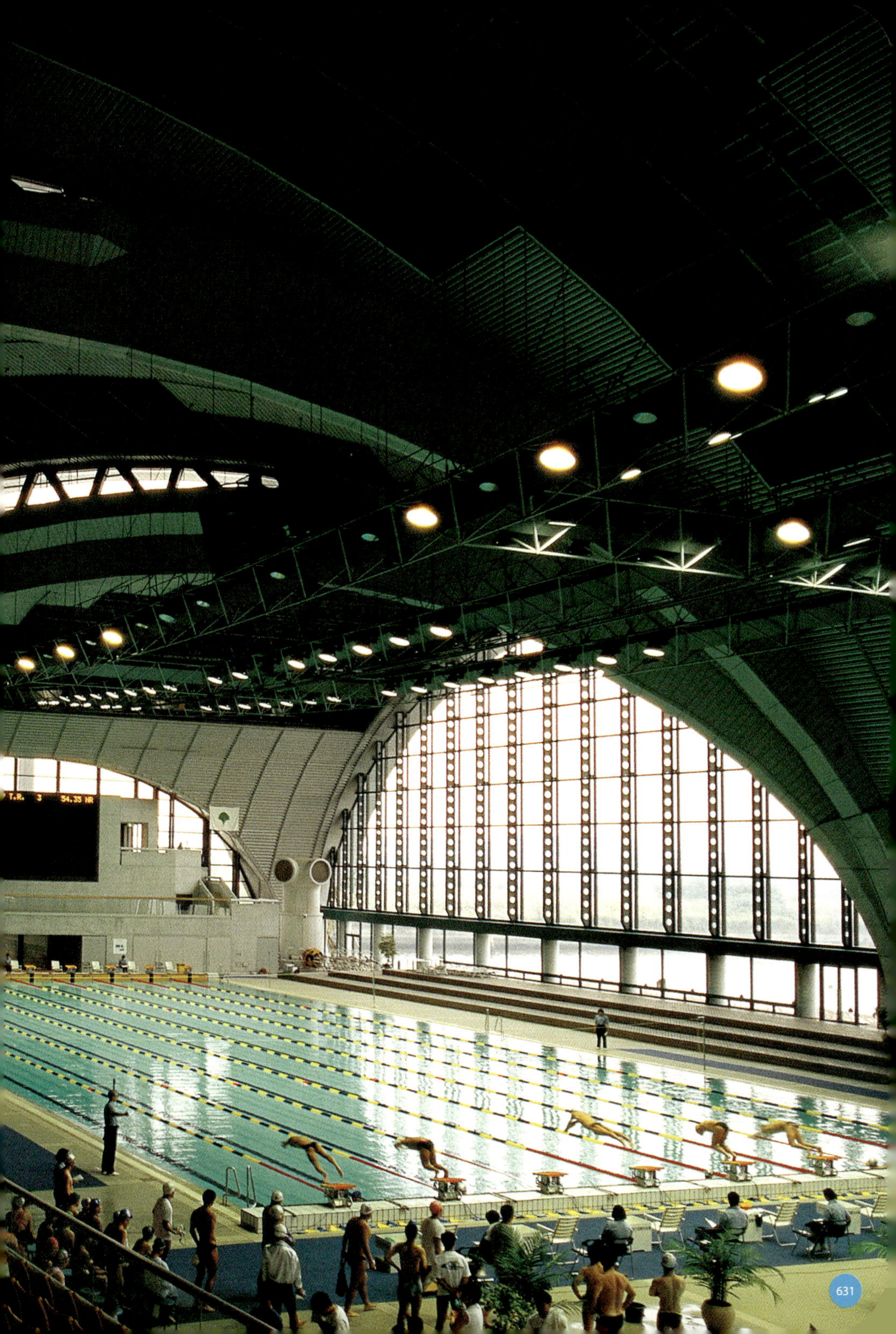

T.R. 3 54.35 NR

1993

東京辰巳国際水泳場　Tokyo Tatsumi International Swimming Center

水鳥が飛び立つ瞬間、
バタフライの水泳者の水しぶき

In the instant that waterfowls stand,
the water sprays upwards as if swimmers are
doing the butterfly stroke.

633

1993

京葉線から今度の土曜はここで泳ごうと叫ぶ
Shout from the Keiyo Line,
"Let us swim here next Saturday!"

東京辰巳国際水泳場　Tokyo Tatsumi International Swimming Center

635

1993

東京辰巳国際水泳場　Tokyo Tatsumi International Swimming Center

中央の赤いアイコンは
彫刻家・脇田愛二郎の作品『ヘリックス』
The red icon in the center is "Helix,"
a piece of work by sculptor Aijiro Wakita.

1992

稲荷公園わんぱく広場

Inari Park Wanpaku Plaza

丘を走る

稲荷公園わんぱく広場

富山県富山市稲荷町／1992
Inari Park Wanpaku Plaza
Inari-cho, Toyama-shi, Toyama

富山市の中心部の工場跡地が稲荷公園として整備され、その一角にこどもの広場が設けられた。小さな丘を造成し、景観的なシンボル遊具とした3本の黄色い塔がつくられている。塔を起点として、長さ120mの線型の巨大遊具が丘の上を走っている。その遊具には2重の動線があり、全体としては遊環構造を形成している。便所も遊具の一環として造形されている。

This children's space was planned for part of an improvement scheme for Inari Park, utilizing a former factory site in the center of Toyama. Acting as landscape elements, three yellow, symbolic play towers were erected on a manmade hill. Then, focusing on there towers, a giant, 120 meter-long piece of play apparatus was arranged to run around the hill. Having an overlapping pattern of circulation, the whole thing forms a circular play system, with the toilets forming an integral part of it.

1992

稲荷公園わんぱく広場　Inari Park Wanpaku Plaza

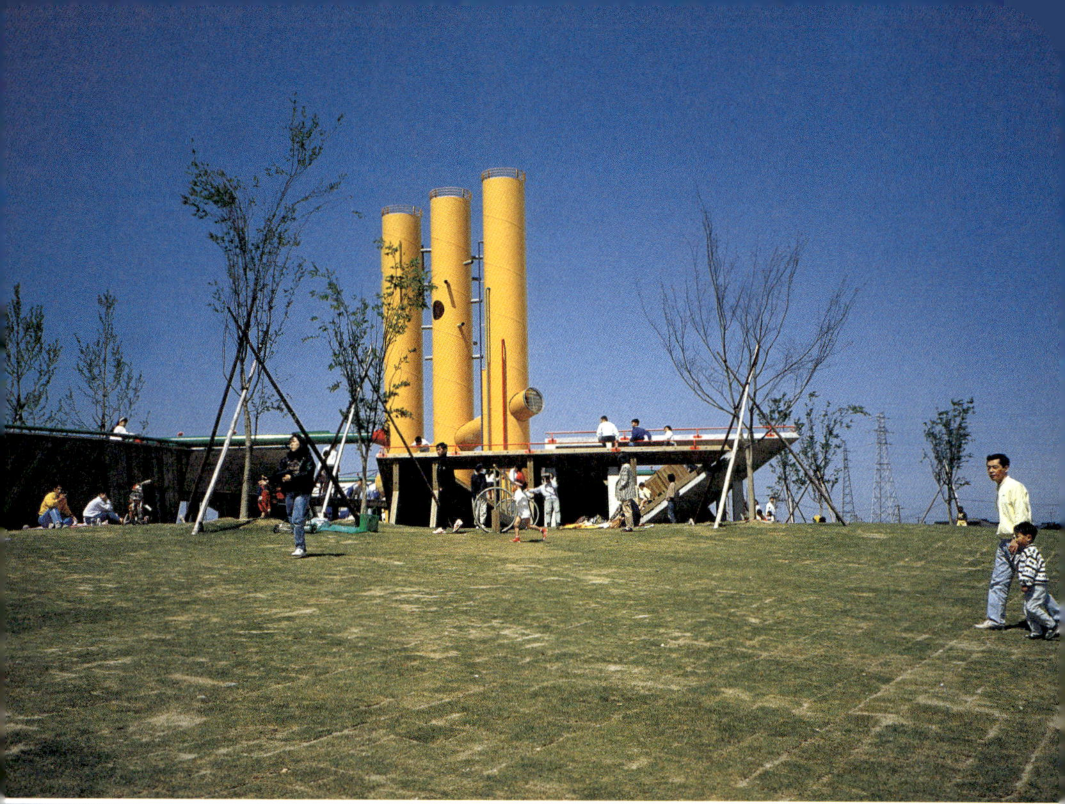

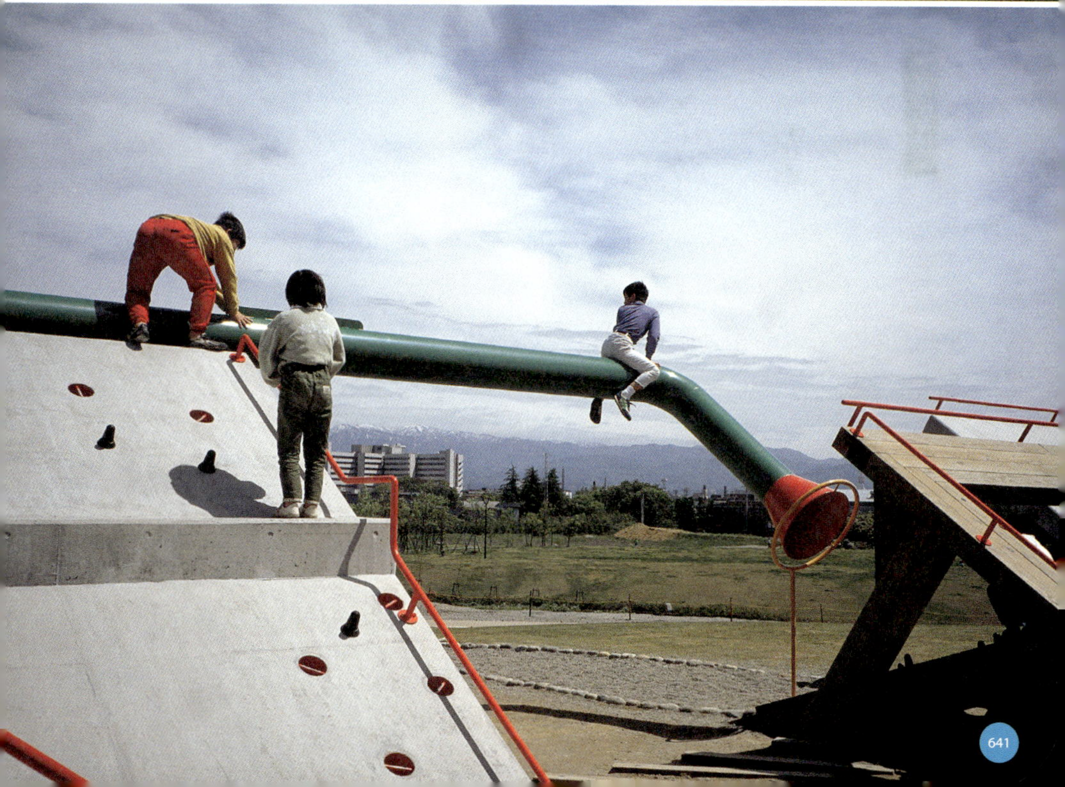

1992

スターズ・アート 23

Stars Art 23

ART BASE

スターズ・アート23

神奈川県横浜市金沢区／1992
Stars Art 23
Kanazawa-ku, Yokohama-shi, Kanagawa

施主がアーティストであるこの家は、作家のギャラリーであり、スタジオであり、住まいでもある。大きな吹抜けのあるギャラリー、創作室、ジャグジーのある居室等がスロープとスリリングな階段によってつなげられ、空間構成として遊環構造が形成されている。

This house, built for an artist, comprises gallery space, a studio as well as private accommodation. The gallery with its high ceiling, workroom and living areas where there is a Jacuzzi are linked by a slope and excitingly planned stairs, making the whole spatial composition a true piece of circular play system architecture.

1992

スターズ・アート 23

Stars Art 23

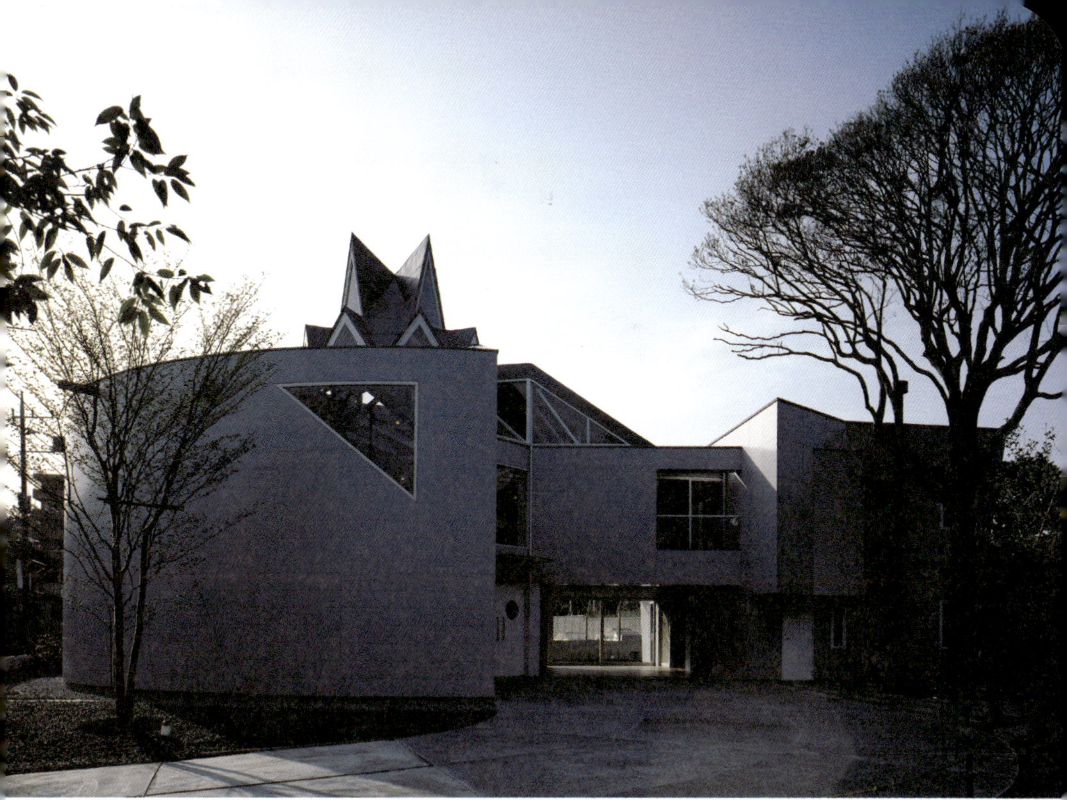

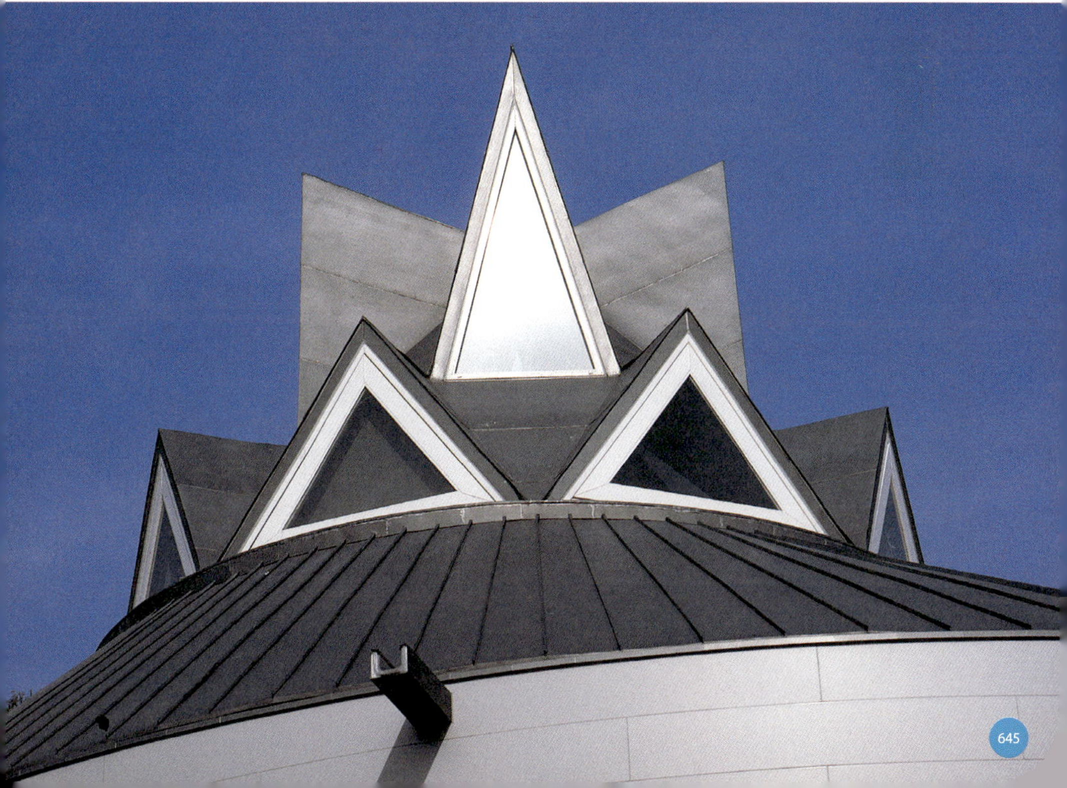

1992

滋賀県立びわ湖こどもの国　Lake Biwa Children's Land

遊具の建築と道

滋賀県立びわ湖こどもの国

滋賀県高島市安曇川町／1992
Lake Biwa Children's Land
Adogawa-cho, Takashima-shi, Shiga

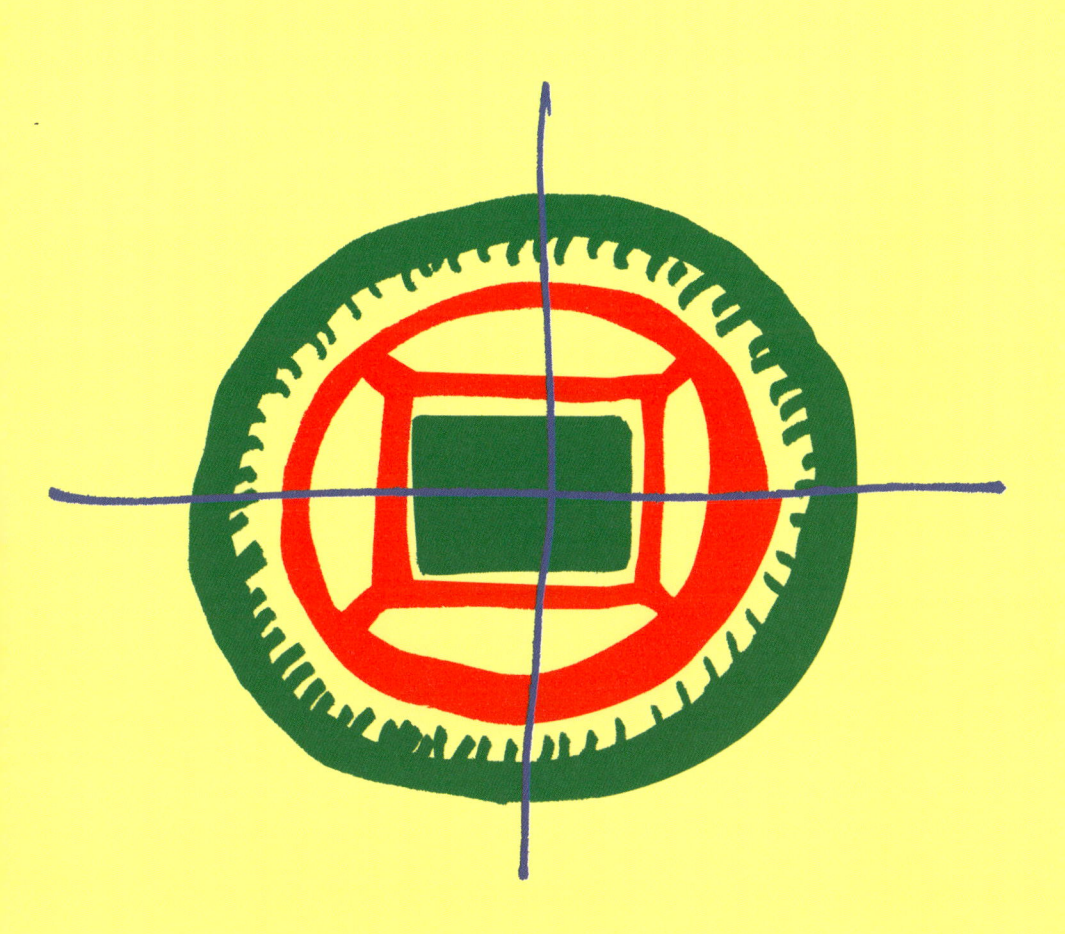

宿泊型の児童施設と180ｍの遊具の道、キャンプ場等で構成されている。中心施設である"虹の家"と名付けられた宿泊施設は中央にイベント広場を持つ円形の建物であり、遊環構造にもとづく平面を持つ。180ｍの遊具の道は利用者のあそびの動線の役割を果たしている。

The facility itself is composed of children's lodgings, a 180 meter undulating "Adventure Road", and a camping site. The round, residential facility called "Rainbow House" has an event space at its center and is therefore structured as a circular play system. The 180-meter equipment course is designed to stimulate play among users.

1992

滋賀県立びわ湖こどもの国
Lake Biwa Children's Land

人の環を象徴する円環状の宿泊棟
The circular dormitory block, symbolizing a ring of people.

649

1992

滋賀県立びわ湖こどもの国　Lake Biwa Children's Land

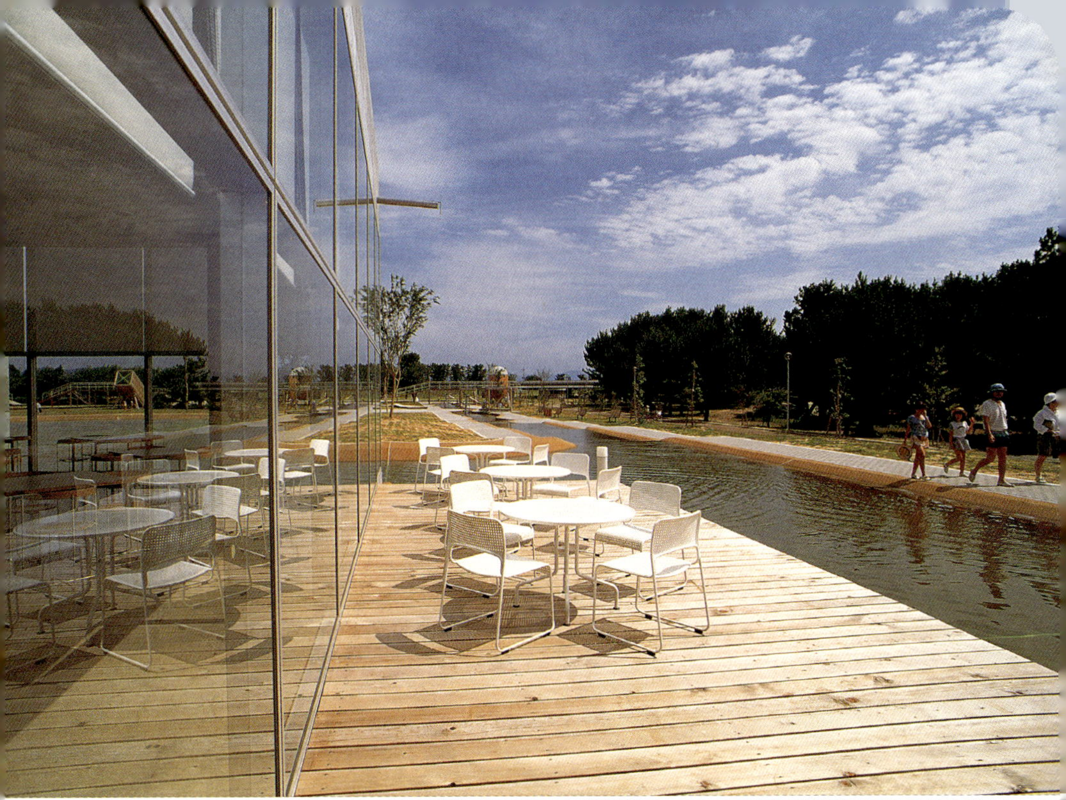

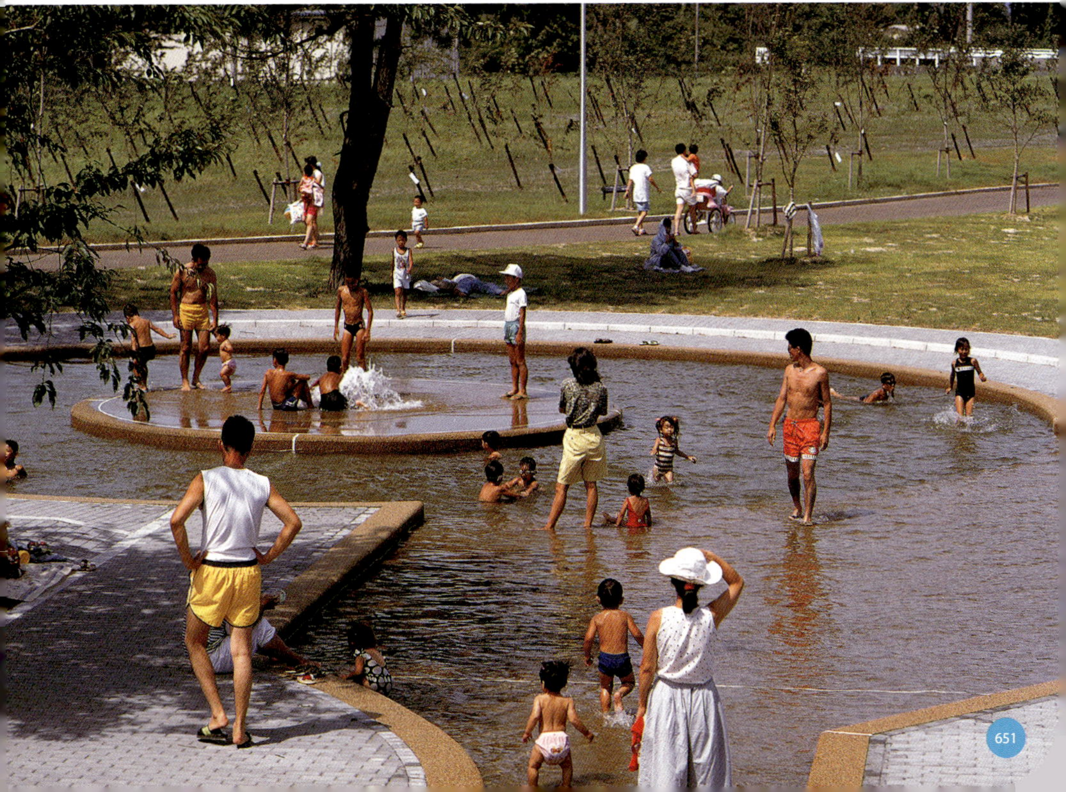

1992

富山県こどもみらい館
Toyama Children's Center

8の字遊環建築

富山県こどもみらい館

富山県射水市黒河／1992
Toyama Children's Center
Kurokawa, Imizu-shi, Toyama

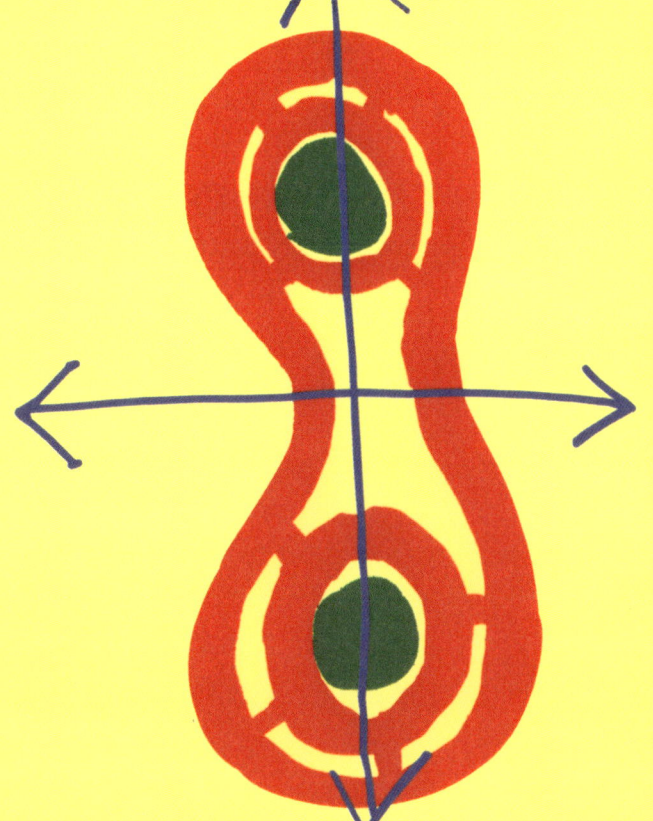

富山市と高岡市の中間に位置する95ヘクタールの太閤山ランドという総合公園の中央部に建設された。アメリカのチルドレンズミュージアム型の展示機能をもった日本最初の児童施設である。3層に分かれており、1層部分は創作活動スペース、2階部分は展示・体験スペース、3層部分はあそびのスペースとして100mの遊具が走り回っている。全体として8の字型の遊環構造の平面計画がなされ、こども達のあそびやすい空間構成が目指されている。屋上も展望機能を持ったあそび広場としてつくられている。

Located between Toyama City and Takaoka City, this structure is set in the center of a 95-hectare comprehensively planned park. This is the first facility in Japan to combine the kind of "hands-on" exhibition space found in children's museums. Divided into three levels, the first comprises an activity space fostering creativity, the second is as a "hands-on" exhibition space, and the third is for a play space with a 100-meter long play structure. Aiming to create a space where children would find it easy to play, the space is designed in the form of a figure eight with circular play system.

1992

富山県こどもみらい館
Toyama Children's Center

天井に100mのチューブ型遊具が走る
A 100m long tubed play structure runs on the ceiling.

工 房

1992

富山県こどもみらい館

Toyama Children's Center

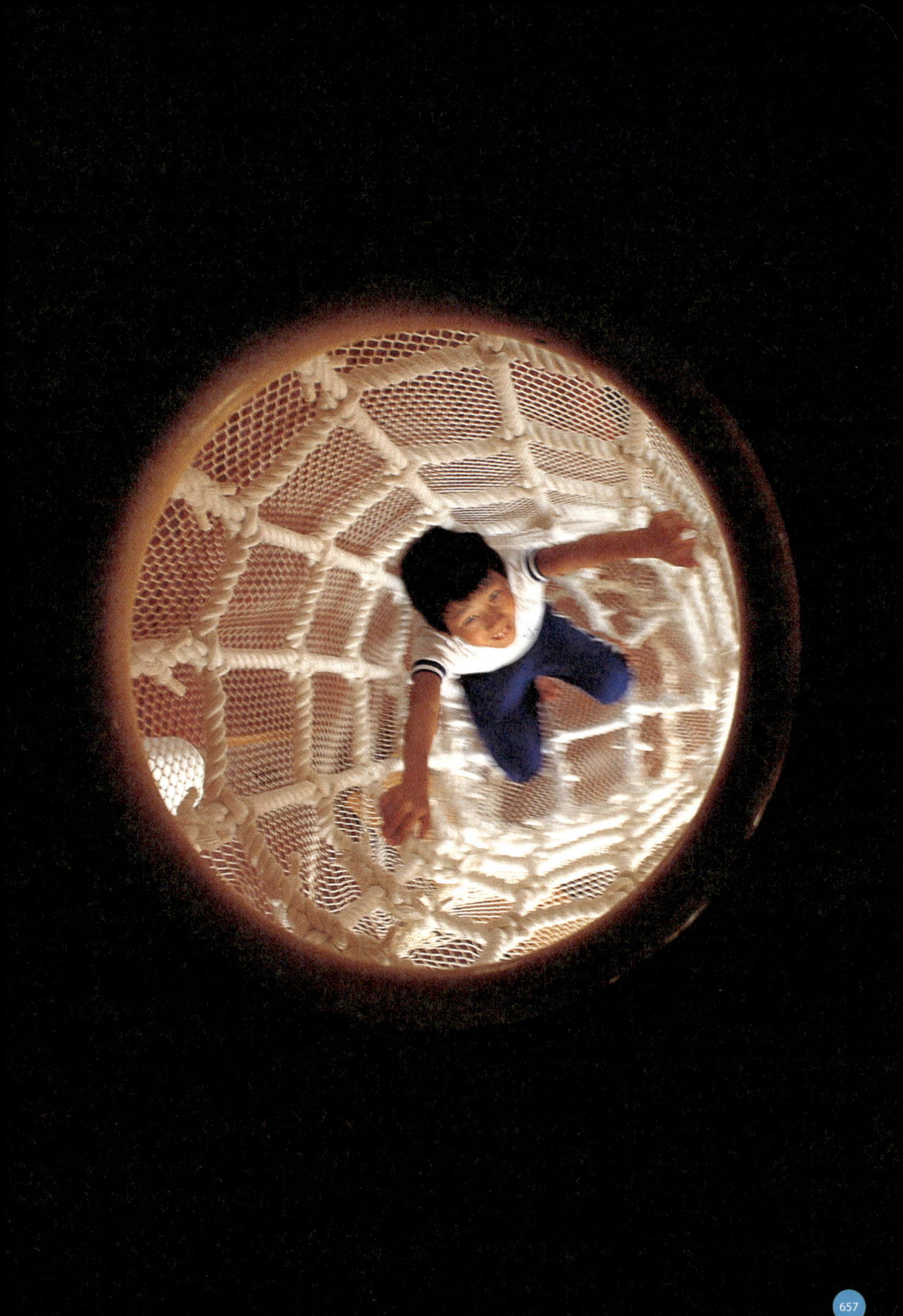

1992

富山県こどもみらい館　Toyama Children's Center

トンネルはこども達のあそびの原点
Tunnels are the origin of play areas for children.

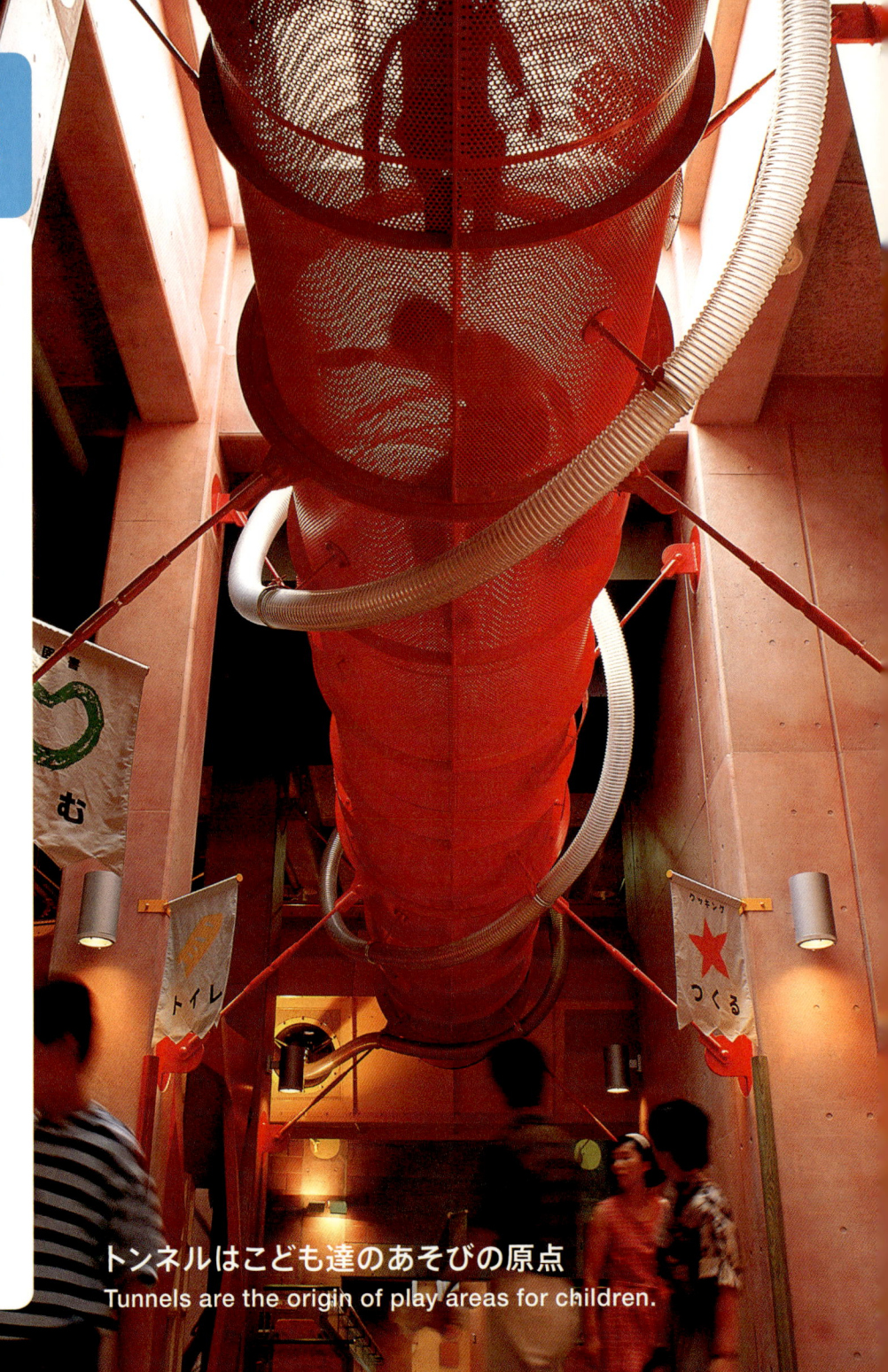

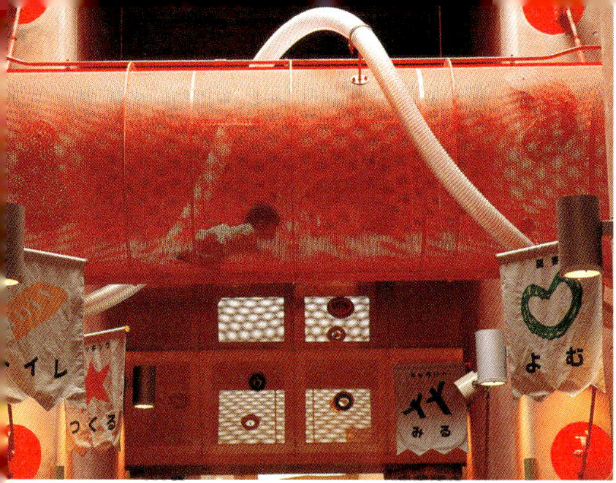
つくる
よむ
みる
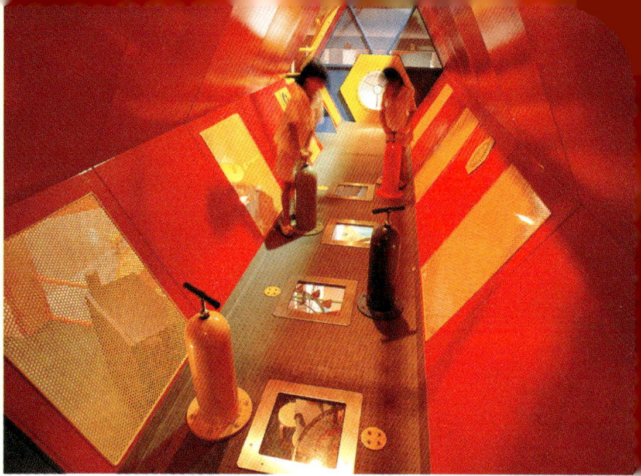
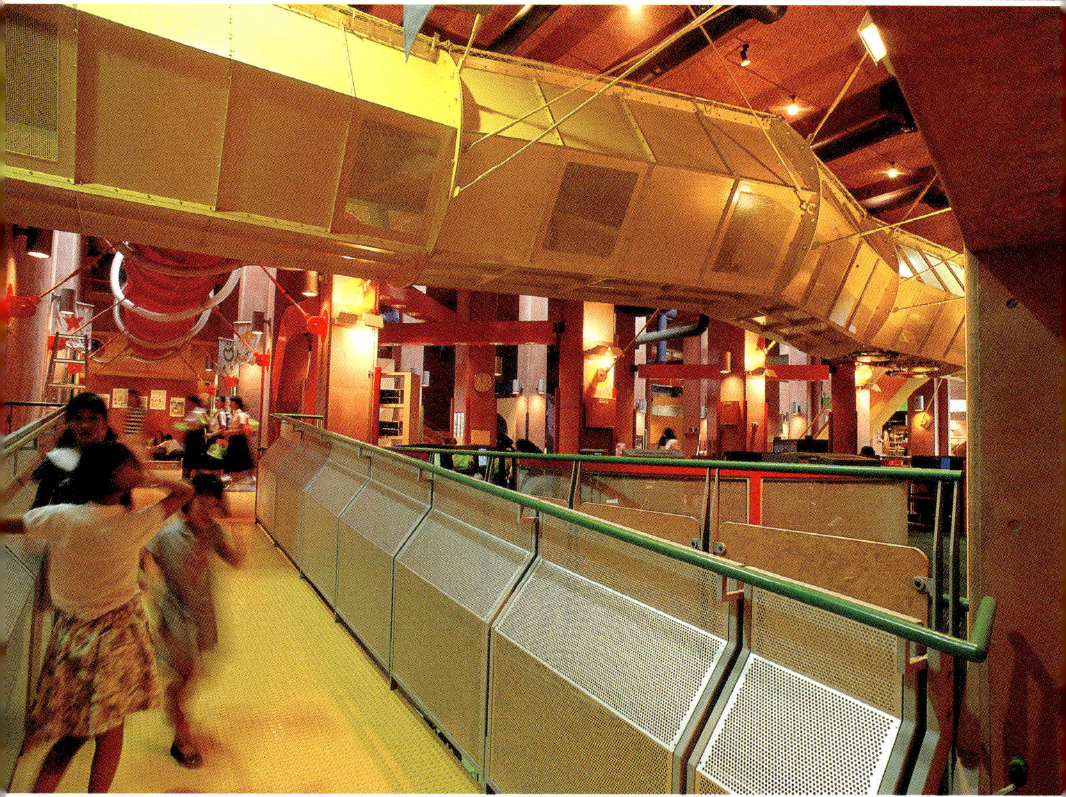
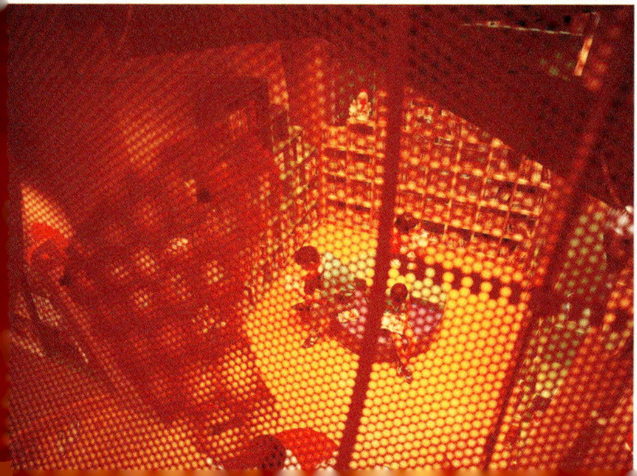
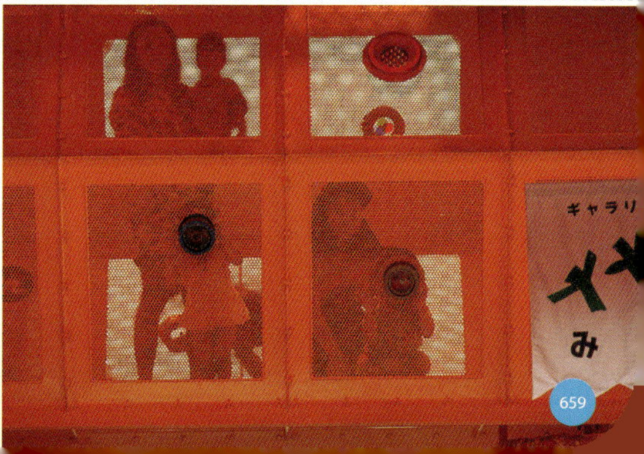

1992

富山県こどもみらい館

Toyama Children's Center

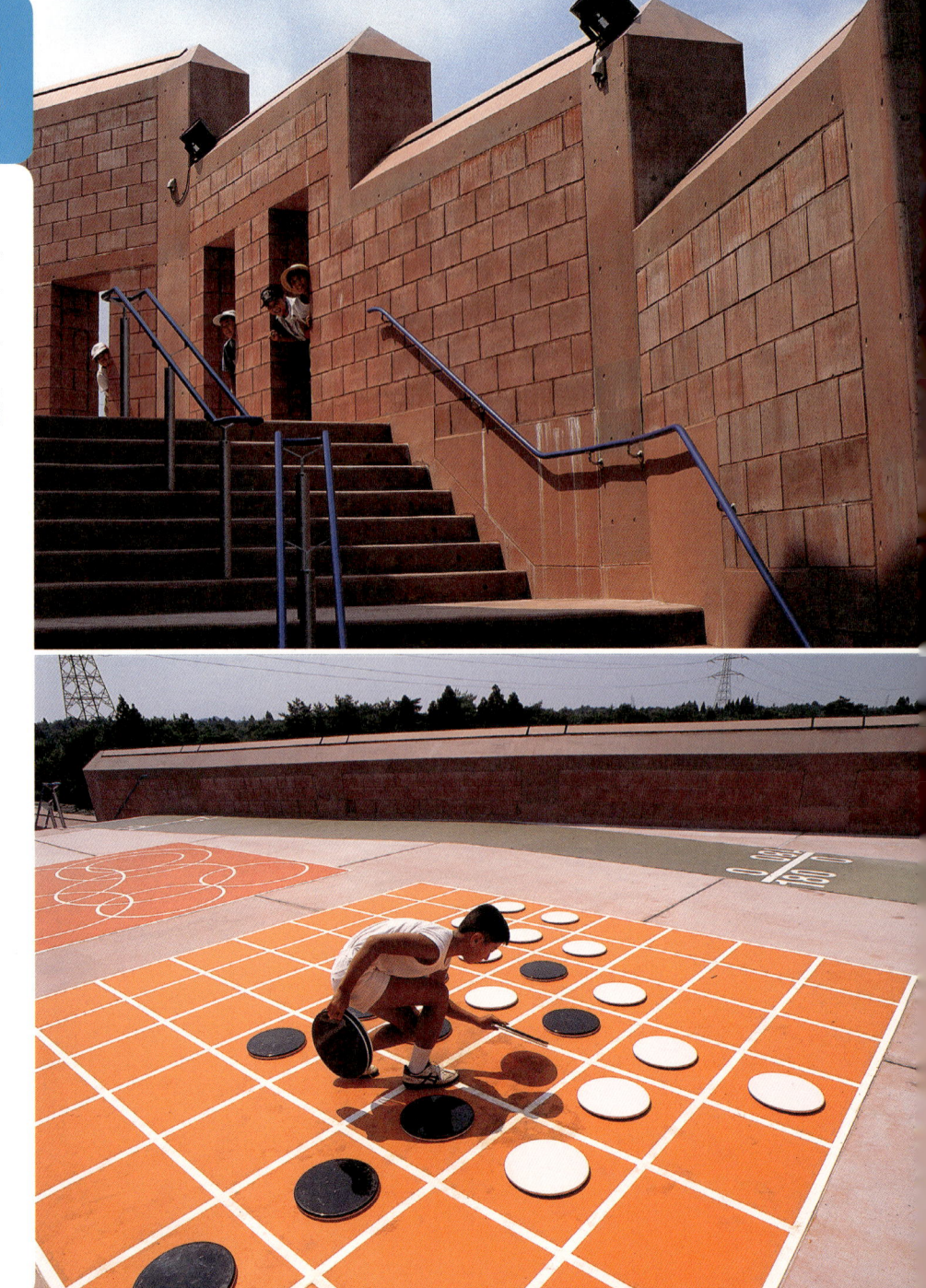

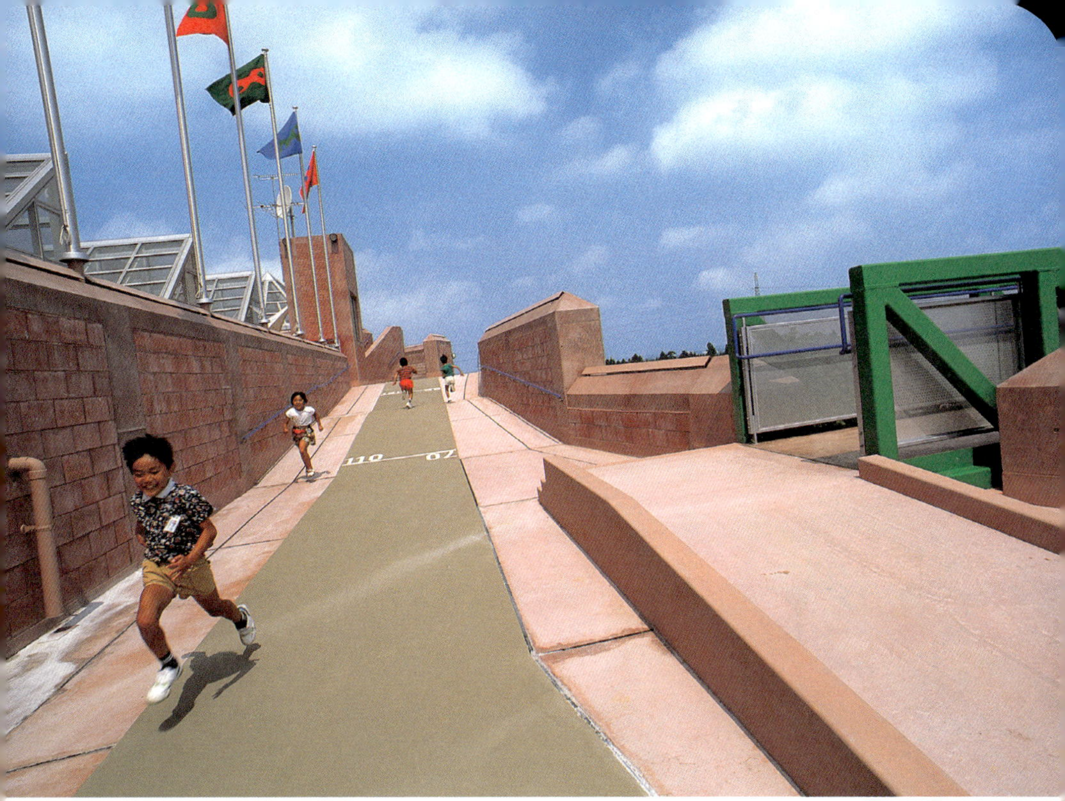

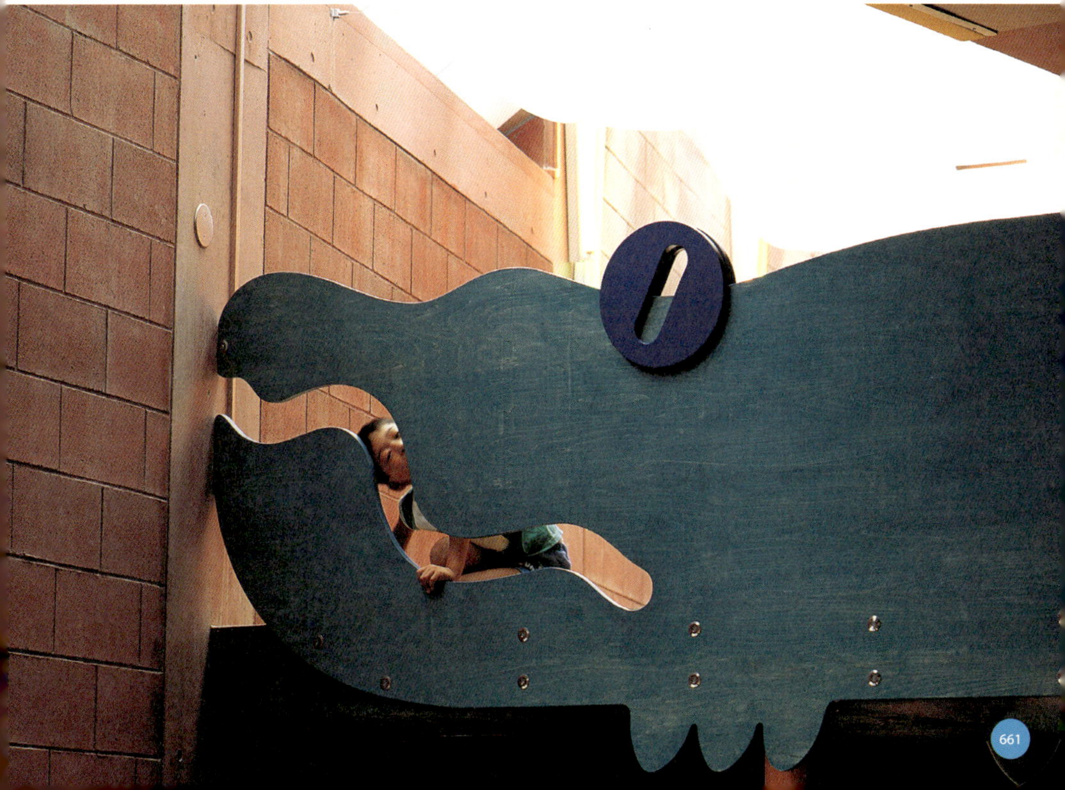

1992

富山県こどもみらい館　Toyama Children's Center

屋上も遊環構造
The rooftop area is also circular play system.

663

1991

中国北京科普楽園　Beijing Children's Science Park

錯覚の森

中国北京科普楽園

中国北京市／1991
Beijing Children's Science Park
Beijing, China

北京宋慶齢児童科学館に隣接した敷地約1,000㎡に8つの科学的な遊具が配置された。錯覚のゲート等、様々な視覚的な変化をテーマとし、あそびながら、科学の原理やおもしろさが体験できる場として計画された。

Eight pieces of play equipment to help explain scientific effects and principles were planned for this 1,000㎡ adjusting Beijing Song-Qing-Ling Children's Science Museum, with the idea of getting children to actually experience some of the principals of science while they play based on a theme of various visual changes such as a gate of hallucination. It is therefore representative of a piece of scientifically orientated play equipment.

1991

中国北京科普楽園　Beijing Children's Science Park

667

1991

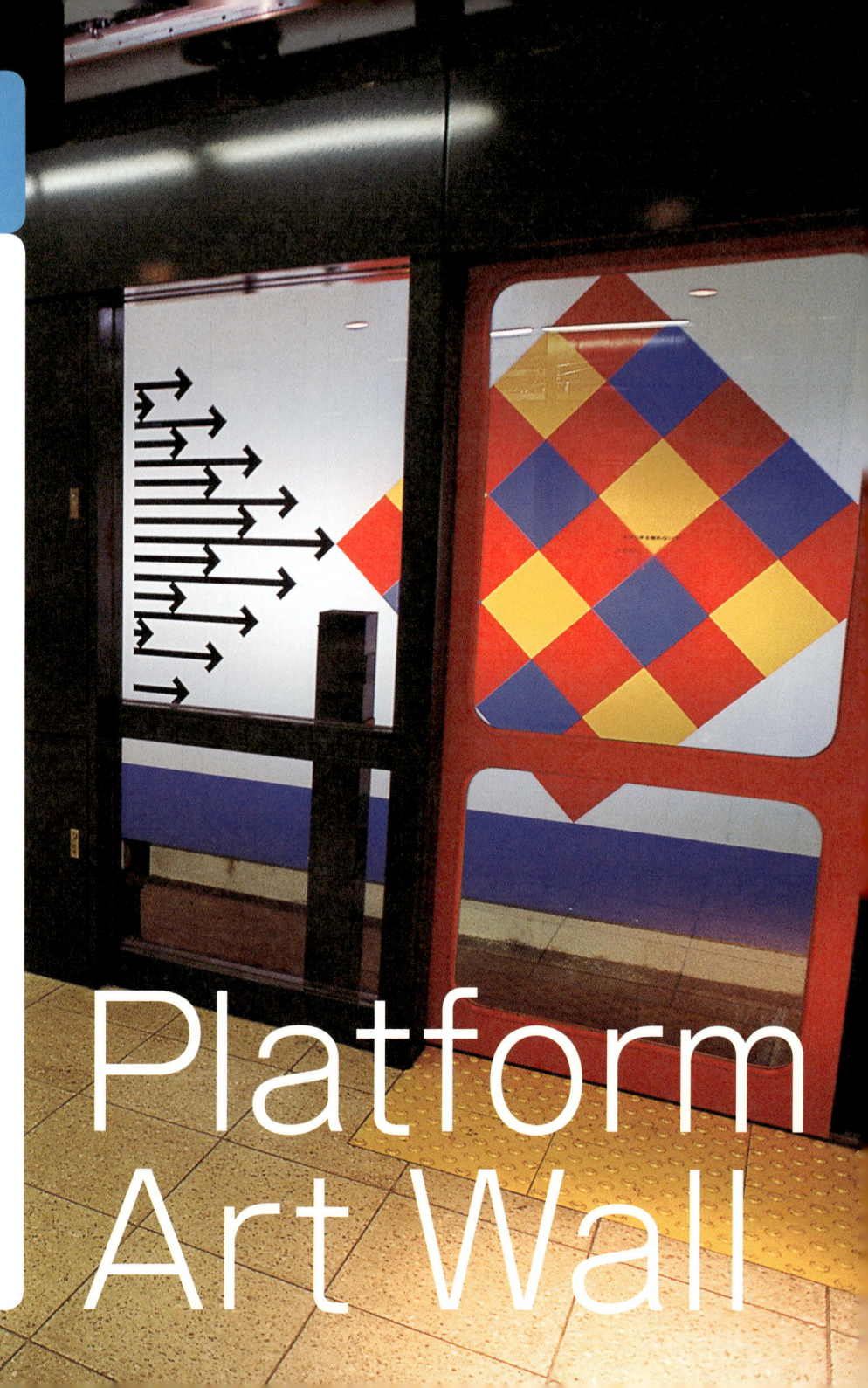

営団地下鉄南北線

Eidan Subway, Nanboku Line

Platform Art Wall

営団地下鉄南北線

南北線駒込駅－赤羽岩淵駅間／1991
Eidan Subway, Nanboku Line
Nanboku Line between Komagome Station
and Akabane Iwabuchi Station

南北線は日本ではじめて地下鉄にホームドアが採用された。そのため、ホームの人々にとって閉塞感を増す心配が持たれた。私達はホームの対向面にアートウォールというシステムを提案し、採用された。色彩豊かな連続した芸術的にスポンサードされた壁面である。地上部の上屋はパンタグラフをモチーフにして空中に浮かび、都市景観的に軽い存在感の屋根をもつ。

The Namboku Line was the first example of in Japan where platform doors were adopted for use in subways. However, because the use of such doors creates a rather claustrophobic atmosphere on the platforms, we proposed a scheme for decorating the tunnel walls beyond the doors to try and alleviate this. Companies were asked to sponsor the production of richly colorful murals. For the station roof, a suspended train pantograph motif was used to create the image of a light cityscape.

1991

営団地下鉄南北線

Eidan Subway, Nanboku Line

駅毎に異なるテーマカラーは
乗越防止にも役立つ

A different theme color for each station is
also useful in keeping people
from alighting at the wrong stations.

1990

Sky River

弁天町ウォーターランド［プールズ］

Bentencho Waterland "Pools"

弁天町ウォーターランド ［プールズ］

大阪府大阪市港区弁天／1990
Bentencho Waterland "Pools"
Benten, Minato-ku, Osaka-shi, Osaka

大阪市弁天町の再開発ブロックの一角に立体的アミューズメント施設として計画された。平面的に長さ150m、幅75mの広さで、屋内では国内最大規模の水のプレイランドである。中央部が低く、両端部が丘状となっており、それをスカイリバーという透明な水の橋によって連結している。水の遊環構造建築である。

This amusement facility built as part of the development taking place in the Bentencho district of Osaka, is 150 meters long and 75 meters wide, making it the largest indoor water amusement facility in Japan. The central area is lower than the two ends which are terraced and they are connected by what is called the "Sky River." This is a circular play system that makes use of water.

1990

弁天町ウォーターランド［プールズ］

Bentencho Waterland "Pools"

水の巨大遊環構造 50m × 100m
A giant water circular play system 50m×100m

675

1990

弁天町ウォーターランド［プールズ］

Bentencho Waterland "Pools"

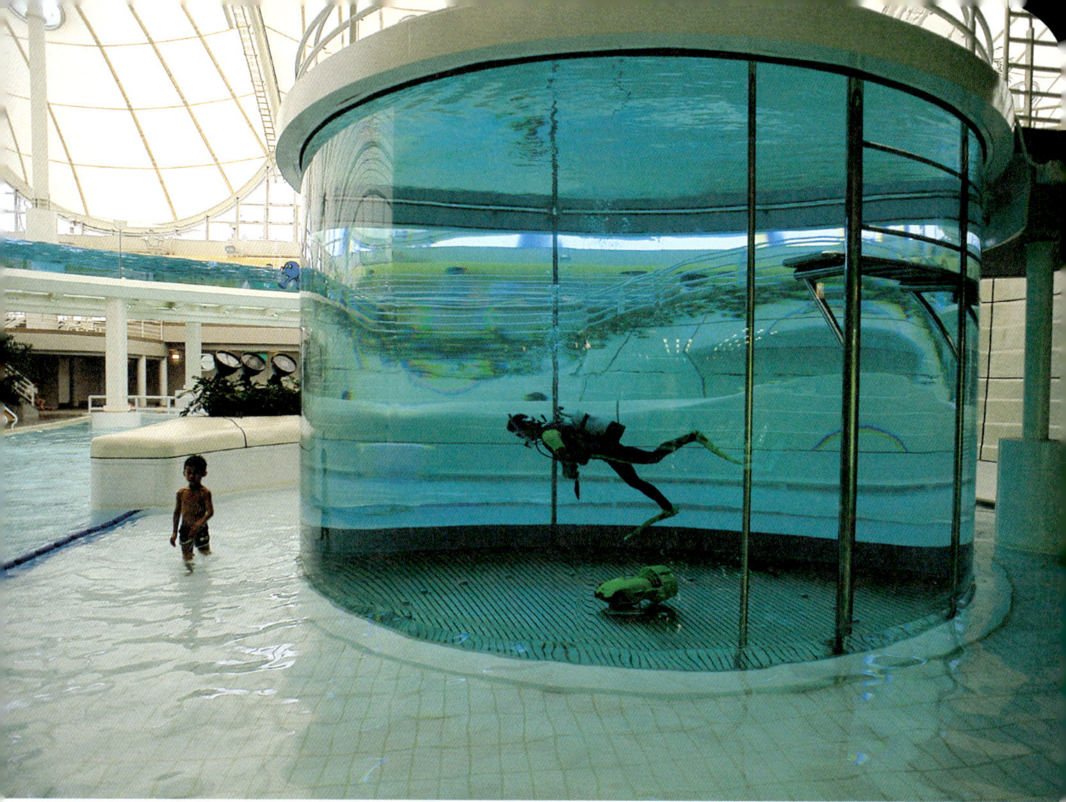

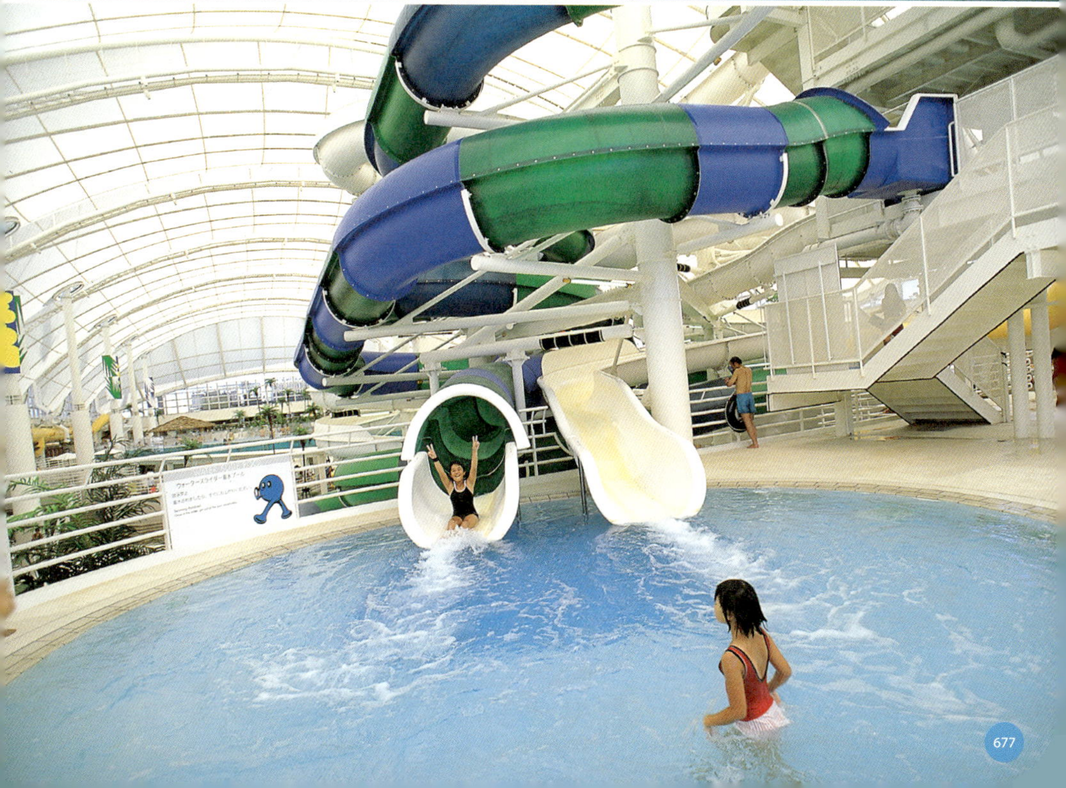

1990

鳥の家
Bird House

望楼の書斎

鳥の家

長野県南佐久郡南牧村／1990
Bird House
Minamimakimura,
Minamisaku-gun, Nagano

八ヶ岳の中腹に建てられた山荘である。3階部分は1.5m四方のガラス張りの書斎である。この部屋から八ヶ岳の山頂を望むことができる。平面形が鳥の羽を広げたような形から"鳥の家"と名付けられているが、立体的遊環構造住宅である。

This mountain cabin built on the slopes of the range of eight peaks, "Yatsugatake". The "rookery" is a 1.5 meter square study at third floor level, with glass on all sides, from where there are wonderful views of Yatsugatake. The three-dimensional, circular play system house was named "Bird House" because of the building shape as if a bird is spreading the wings.

1990

鳥の家　Bird House

森を見下ろす1.8m角の書斎
A 1.8m study room that looks down on the forests.

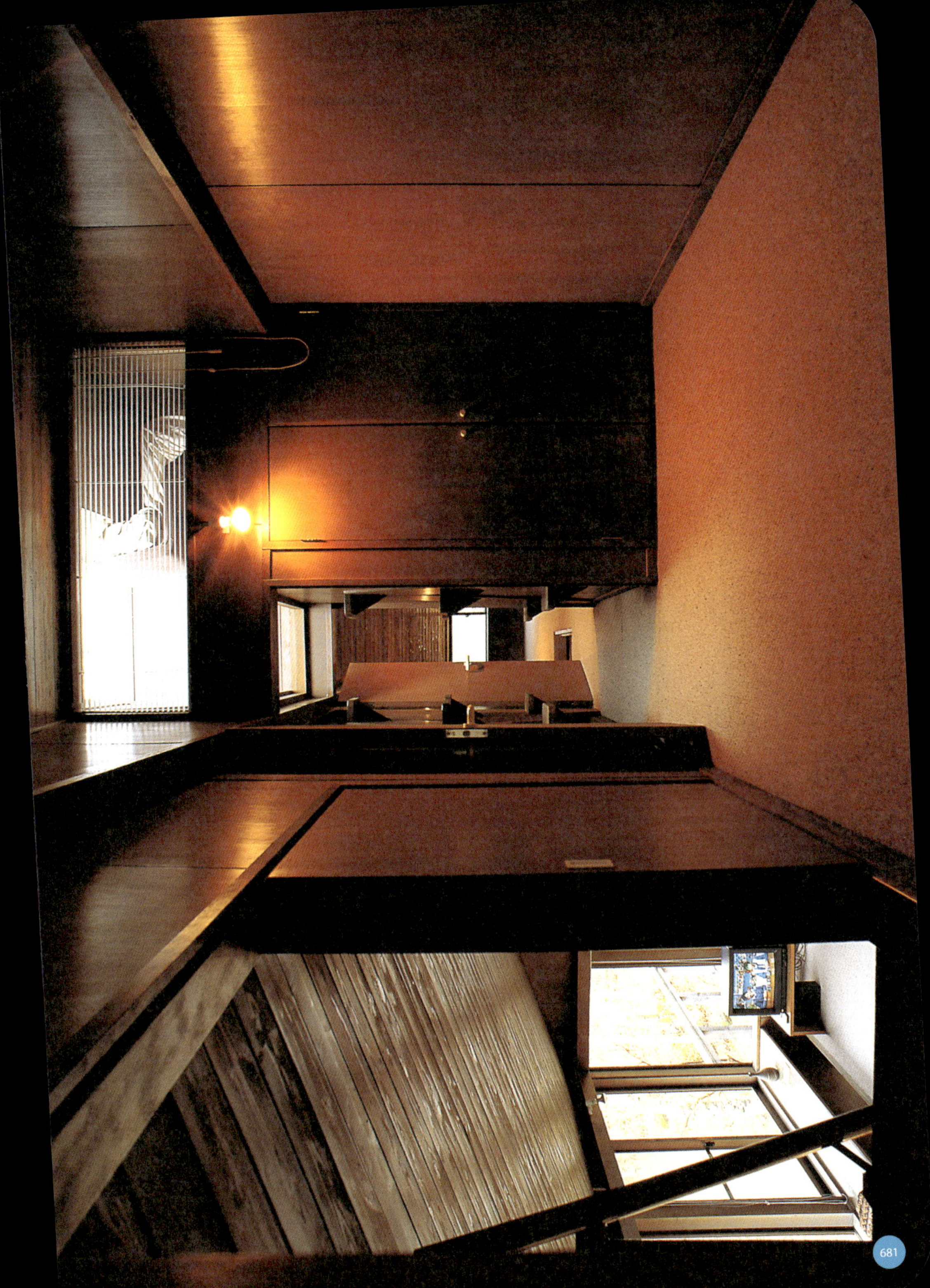

1990

鵠沼の家
Kugenuma House

2階居間居住

鵠沼の家

神奈川県藤沢市鵠沼／1990
Kugenuma House
Kugenuma, Fujisawa-shi, Kanagawa

海浜都市の住宅地に建てられた小住宅である。変形した十字型平面をもち、周辺にできるだけ多くの緑を配した。2階は居間・台所のワンルーム形式で、1階に個室、寝室、浴室がある。垂木構造が採用され、明るくリラックスできる住空間である。

This small house is located in a residential area of a seaside city. The house is in the shape of a deformed cross with as much green as possible placed in the surrounding area. The second floor is a single room comprising a living area and kitchen, and the first floor a private room, bedroom, and bathroom. The house makes use of rafters and is a bright, yet relaxing, living space.

1990

鵠沼の家　Kugenuma House

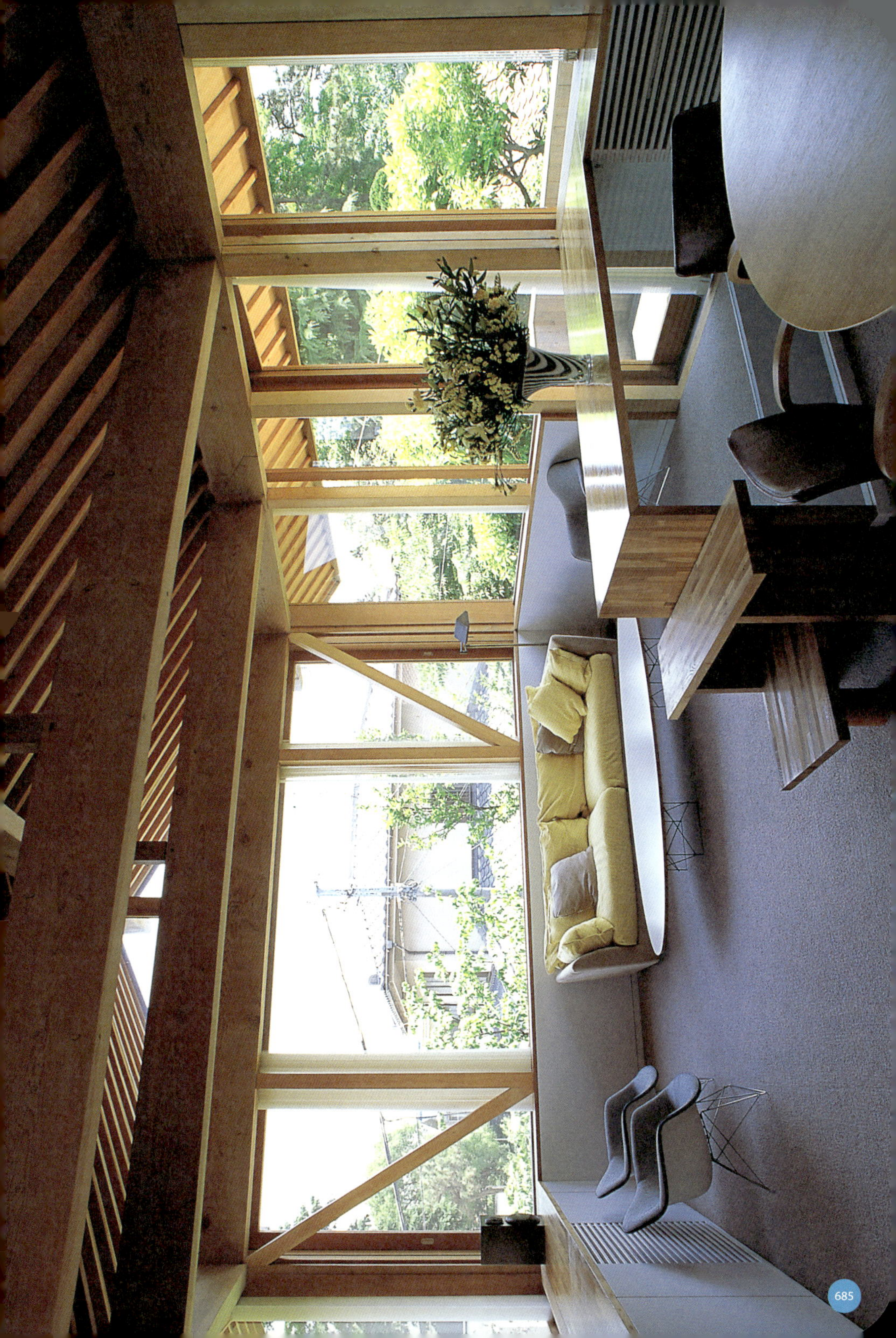

1990

鵠沼の家　Kugenuma House

687

1990

松庵の家
Shoan House

十字式設計法

松庵の家

東京都杉並区松庵／1990
Shoan House
Shoan, Suginami-ku, Tokyo

東京の住宅地である杉並区の松庵につくられた敷地約200㎡の住宅である。平面は十字型をし、四角（よすみ）に緑を配している。こうすることによって、どの室からも緑を楽しむことができ、また、隣地との視覚的距離も確保できる。

This house stands on a 200 square meter plot of land in the Shoan district of Suginami Ward in Tokyo, a predominantly residential neighborhood. The house is shaped in cross form with plants in the four open corners of the site, meaning that views of the garden can be enjoyed from every room, while visual distance is secured from the adjoining sites.

1990

松庵の家
Shoan House

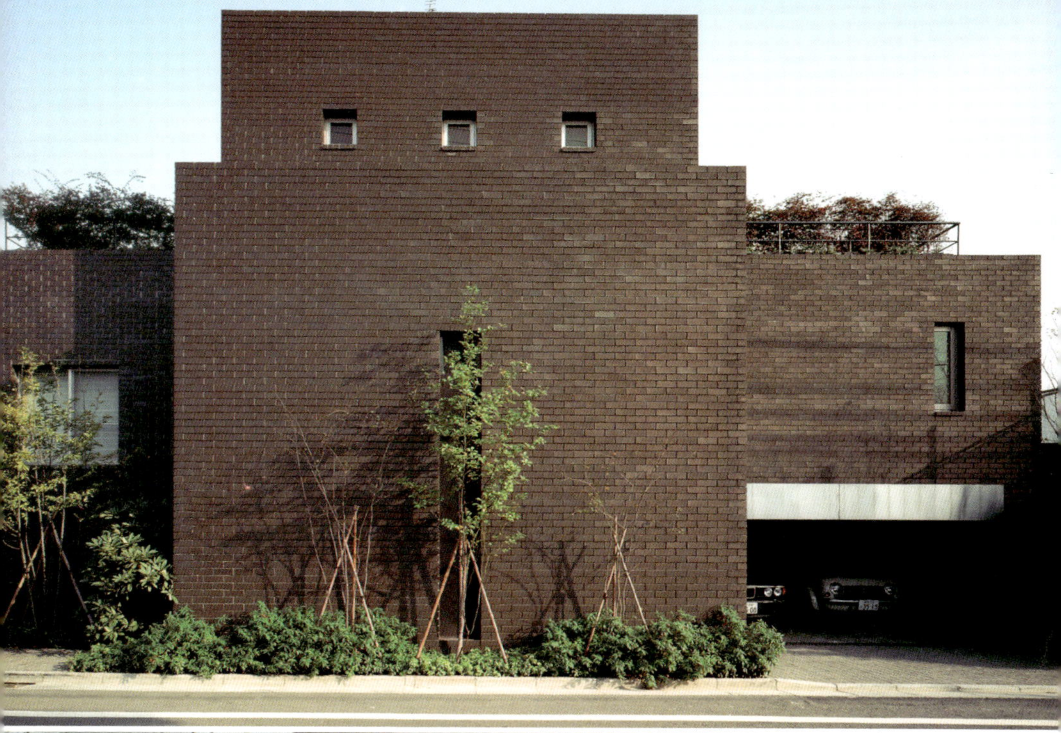

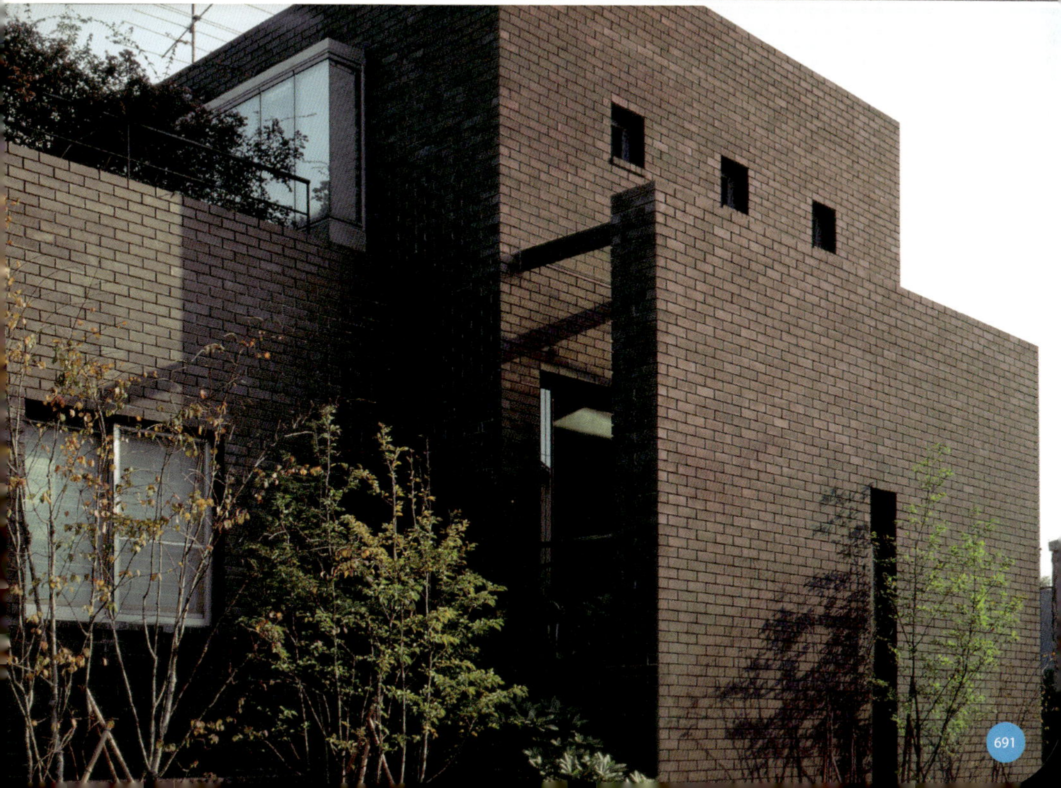

1994.07
旭川春光台
[風の子館]

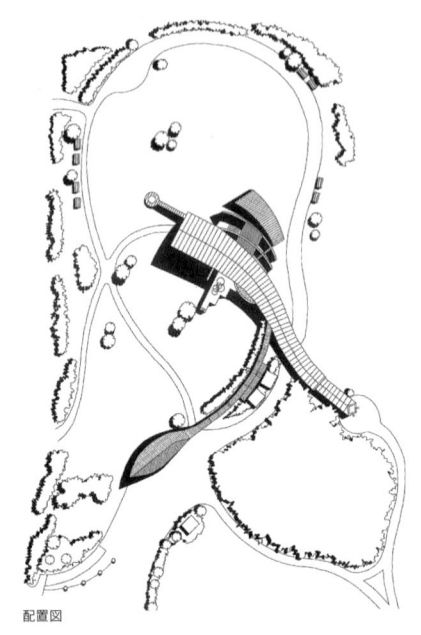

立面図

配置図

所在地：北海道旭川市近文町
主用途：公園施設
建築主：旭川市
構造設計：構造計画研究所
施工：岡部
構造：W造、S造
敷地：8,000㎡　延床：485㎡

Asahikawa Shunkodai Park "Kaze no Ko Kan"
Chikabumi-cho, Asahikawa-shi, Hokkaido

1994.05
兵庫県南但馬自然学校

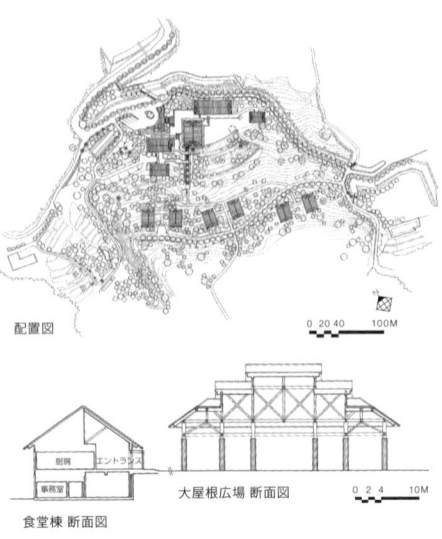

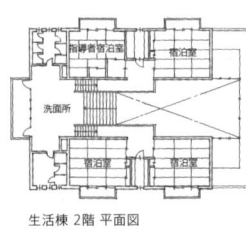

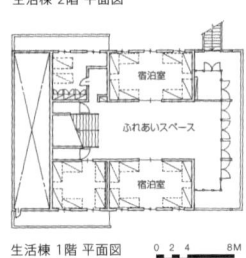

配置図

食堂棟 断面図　　大屋根広場 断面図

生活棟 2階 平面図

生活棟 1階 平面図

所在地：兵庫県朝来郡山東町
主用途：野外活動施設
建築主：兵庫県
構造設計：構造計画研究所
設備設計：システムプランニング
施工：竹中・新井・明生JV
構造：RC造
規模：地上2階
敷地：1,200,000㎡　延床：6,429㎡

Minami Tajima Nature School, Hyogo
Santon-cho, Asago-gun, Hyogo

1994.03
ミュージアムパーク茨城県自然博物館

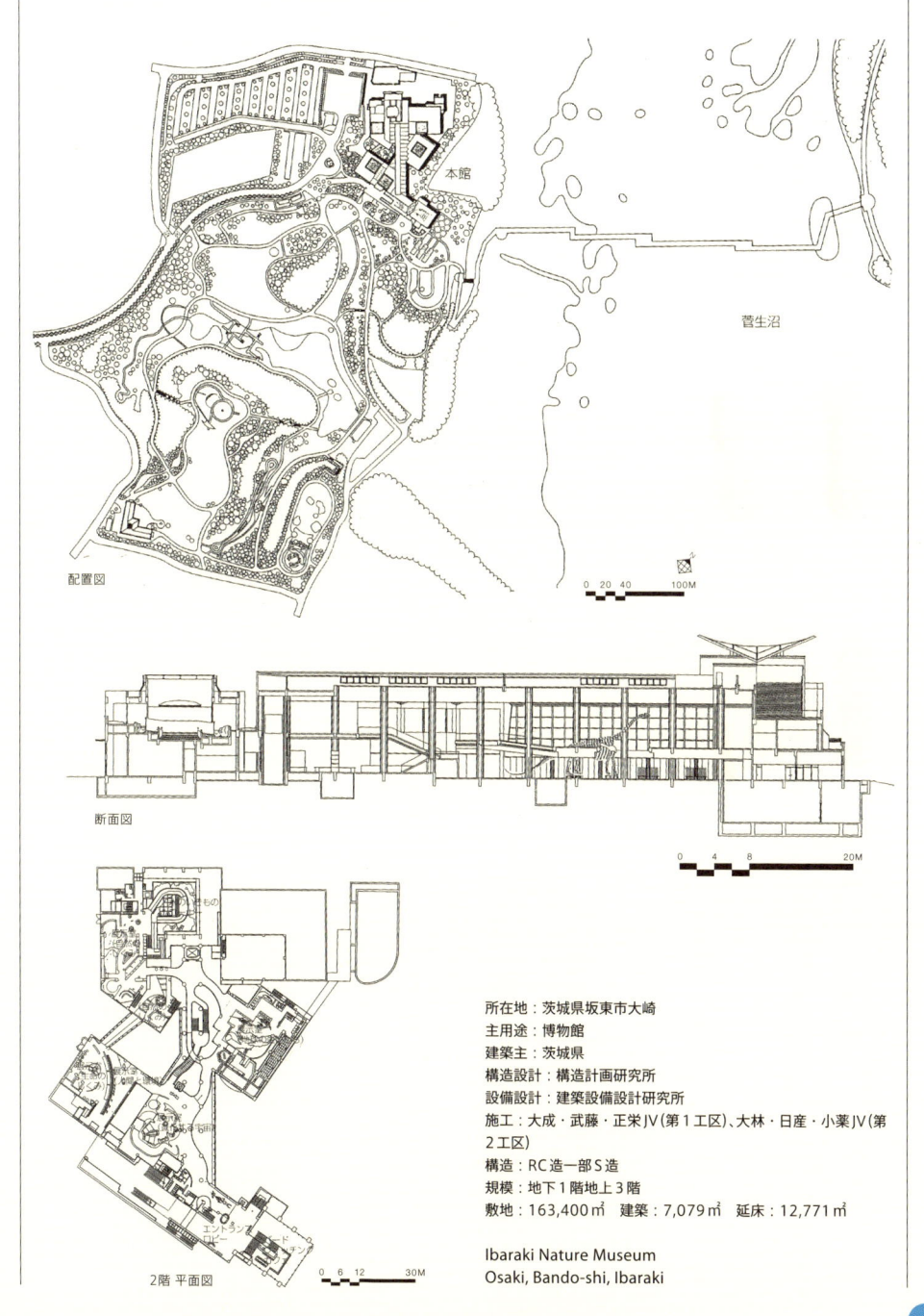

配置図

菅生沼

本館

断面図

2階 平面図

所在地：茨城県坂東市大崎
主用途：博物館
建築主：茨城県
構造設計：構造計画研究所
設備設計：建築設備設計研究所
施工：大成・武藤・正栄JV(第1工区)、大林・日産・小薬JV(第2工区)
構造：RC造一部S造
規模：地下1階地上3階
敷地：163,400㎡　建築：7,079㎡　延床：12,771㎡

Ibaraki Nature Museum
Osaki, Bando-shi, Ibaraki

1993.12
相模湖カルチャーパーク
[漕艇場]

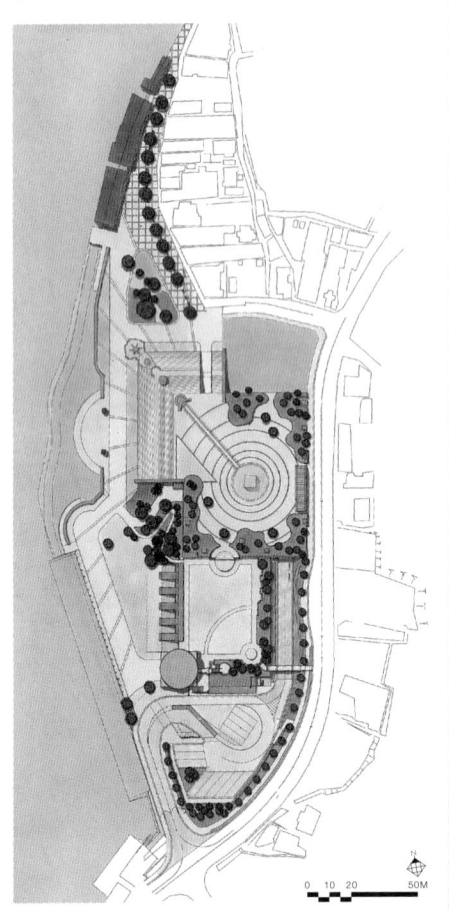

配置図

所在地：神奈川県相模原市緑区与瀬
主用途：漕艇場、艇庫
建築主：神奈川県
施工：松尾工務店
構造：RC造
規模：地下1階地上3階
敷地：26,000㎡　建築：282㎡　延床：3,214㎡

Lake Sagami Culture Park, "Rowing space"
Yose, Midori-ku, Sagamihara-shi, Kanagawa

1993.07
信州博アルピコ広場
[円環遊具]

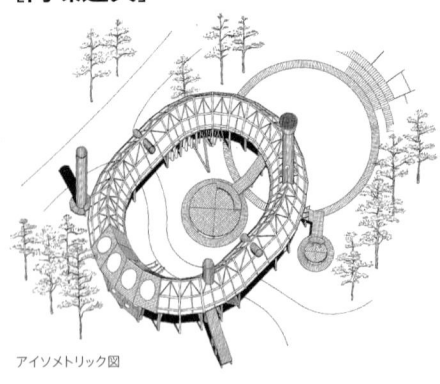

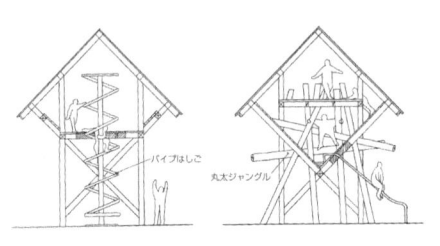

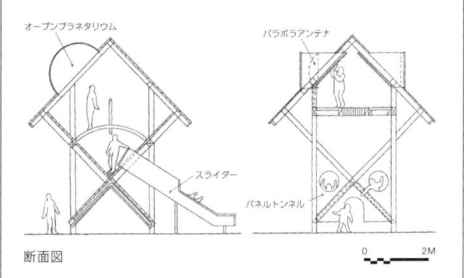

アイソメトリック図

断面図

所在地：長野県松本市今井
主用途：遊具
建築主：松電建設
施工：アルピコグループ松本電気鉄道
構造：W造一部S造
規模：一周80m

"Circular Play Structure" in the Shinshu Expo Alpico Plaza
Imai, Matsumoto-shi, Nagano

1993.03
姫路御立公園
［たつまきロード］

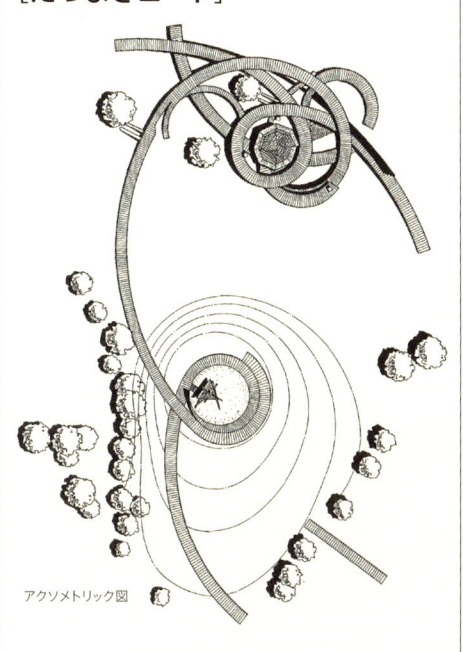

アクソメトリック図

1993.10
国営ひたち海浜公園
［たまごの森］

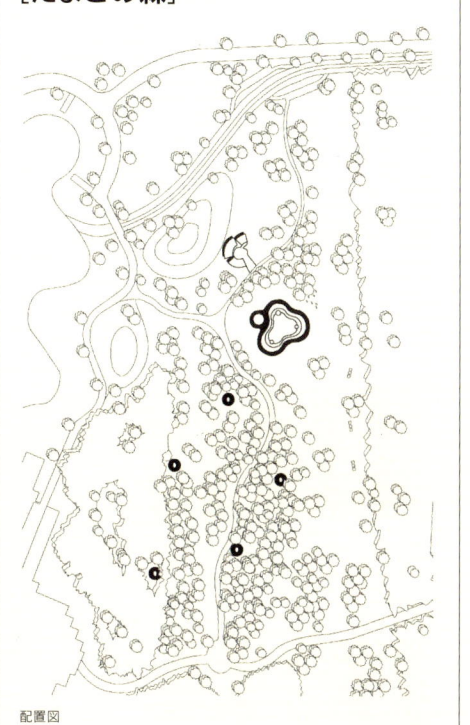

配置図

所在地：兵庫県姫路市御立西
主用途：遊具
建築主：宝企画
施工：岡部
構造：S造、W造
敷地：6,300㎡

Himeji Mitate Park "Tornado Road"
Mitatenishi, Himeji-shi, Hyogo

所在地：茨城県ひたちなか市馬渡
主用途：遊具
建築主：国土交通省関東地方建設局
施工：コトブキ
構造：W造一部S造
敷地：10,000㎡

"Tamago no Mori" in Hitachi Seaside Park
Mawatari, Hitachinaka-shi, Ibaraki

1993.07
相模原市星が丘こどもセンター

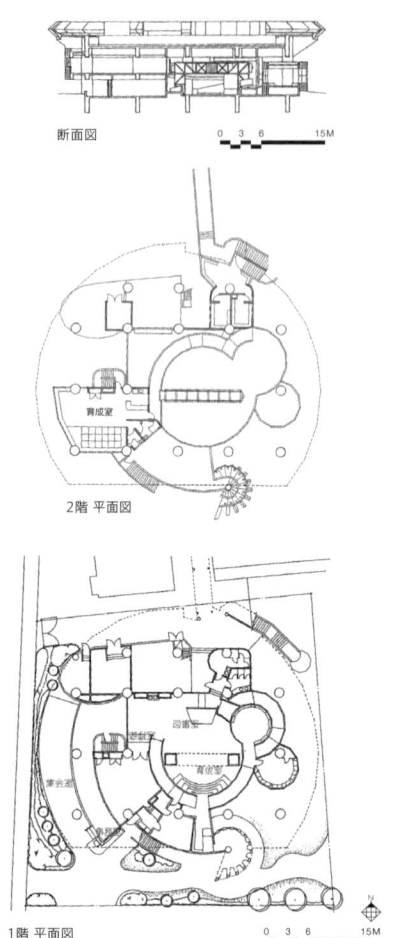

断面図

2階 平面図

1階 平面図

所在地：神奈川県相模原市中央区星が丘
主用途：児童館
建築主：相模原市
構造設計：飯島建築設計事務所
設備設計：システムプランニング
施工：西野工務店
構造：SRC造
規模：地上3階
敷地：1,629㎡　延床：706㎡

Sagamihara Municipal Hoshigaoka Children's Center
Hoshigaoka, Chuuou-ku, Sagamihara-shi, Kanagawa

1993.12
多摩六都科学館

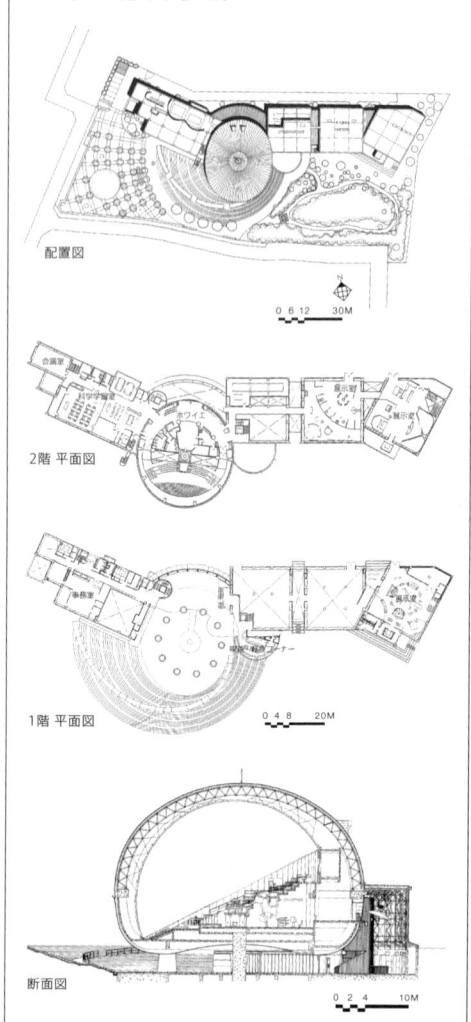

配置図

2階 平面図

1階 平面図

断面図

所在地：東京都西東京市芝久保町
主用途：科学館
建築主：多摩北部広域子供科学博物館組合
構造設計：構造計画研究所
設備設計：建築設備設計研究所
施工：大成・村本JV
構造：RC造一部S造
規模：地下2階地上3階
敷地：11,083㎡　建築：3,269㎡　延床：6,497㎡

Tama Rokuto Science Museum
Shibakubo-cho, Nishitokyo-shi, Tokyo

1993.03
常滑市体育館

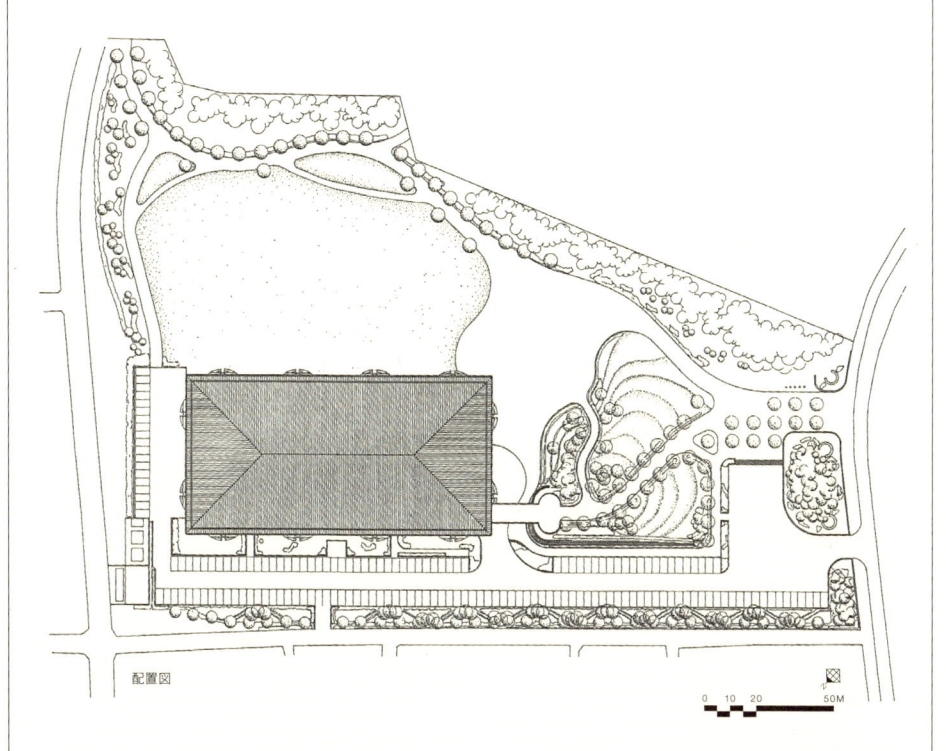

配置図

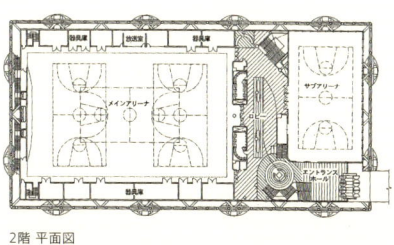

2階 平面図

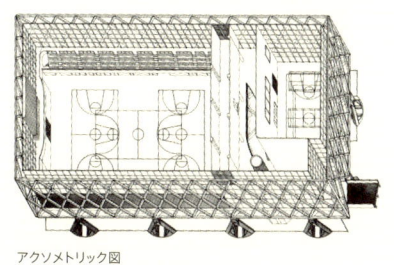

アクソメトリック図

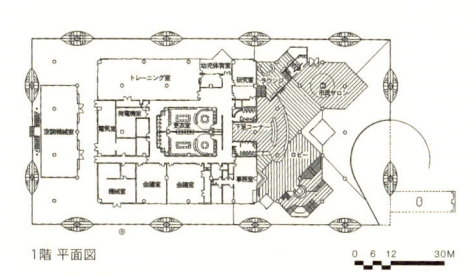

1階 平面図

所在地：愛知県常滑市金山
主用途：体育館
建築主：住宅・都市整備公団
構造設計：構造計画研究所
設備設計：建築設備設計研究所
施工：西松・矢作・兵善組JV
構造：RC造一部SRC造
規模：地上4階
敷地：35,180㎡　建築：5,099㎡　延床：9,052㎡

Tokoname Municipal Gymnasium
Kanayama, Tokoname-shi, Aichi

1993.03
東京辰巳国際水泳場

断面図

配置図

1階 平面図

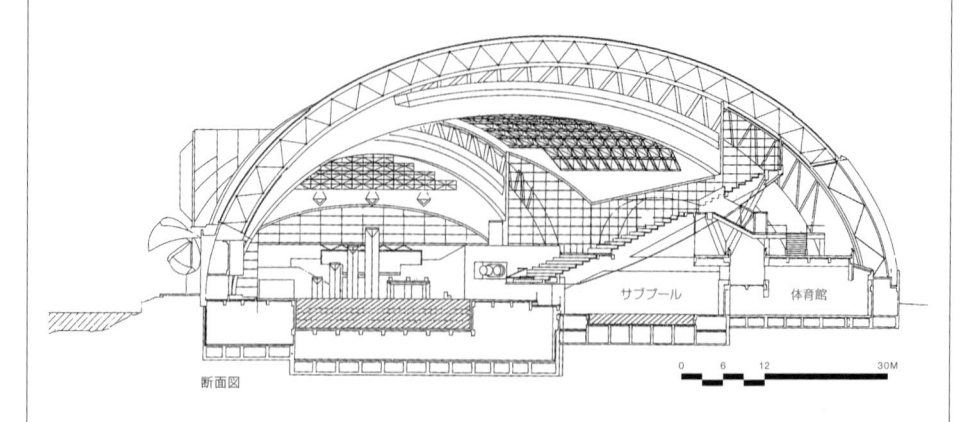

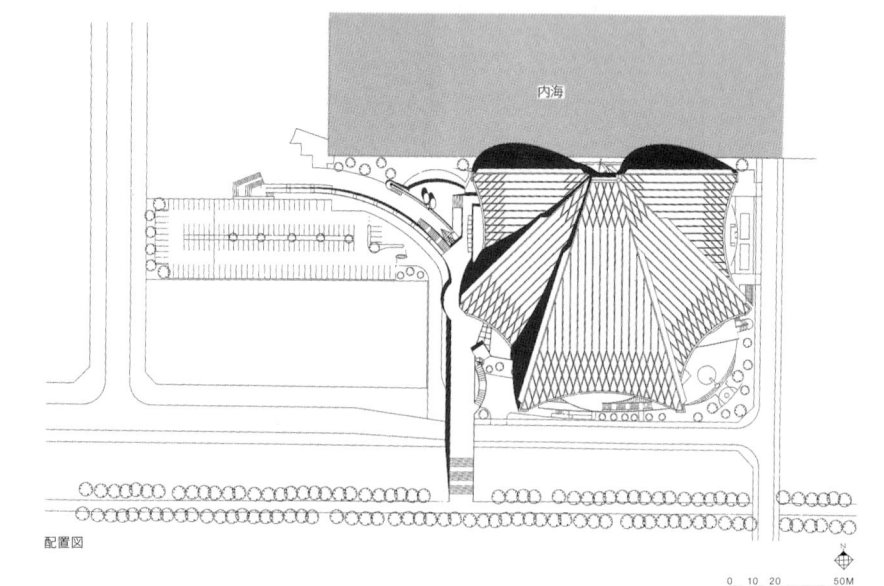

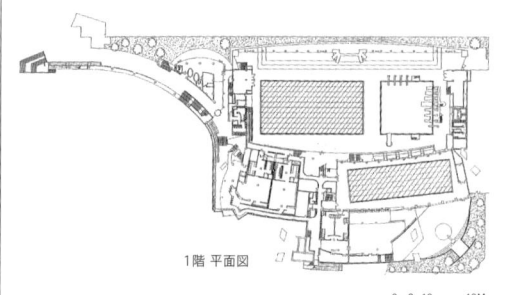

所在地：東京都江東区辰巳
主用途：観覧場併設水泳場
建築主：東京都
構造設計：構造計画研究所
設備設計：森村設計
施工：清水・大日本・勝村・丸石JV
構造：RC造一部SRC造
規模：地下2階地上3階
敷地：22,772㎡　建築：12,319㎡　延床：22,319㎡

Tokyo Tatsumi International Swimming Center
Tatsumi, Koto-ku, Tokyo

1992.03
稲荷公園わんぱく広場

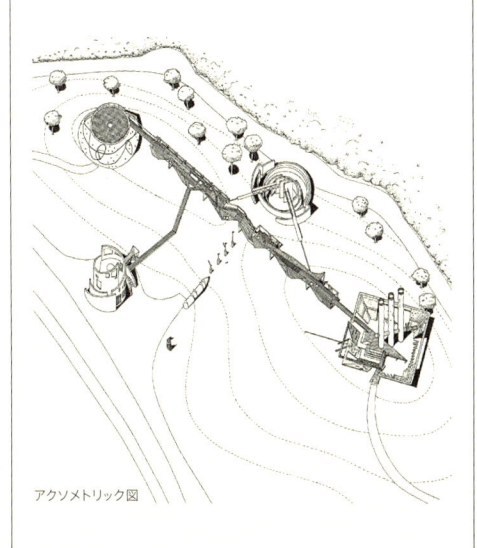

アクソメトリック図

所在地：富山県富山市稲荷町
主用途：児童公園
建築主：宝企画
構造設計：構造計画研究所
施工：岡部
構造：W、S製塔
規模：長さ120m

Inari Park Wanpaku Plaza
Inari-cho, Toyama-shi, Toyama

1992.04
スターズ・アート 23

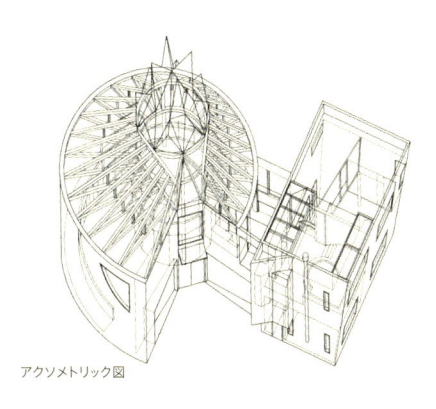

アクソメトリック図

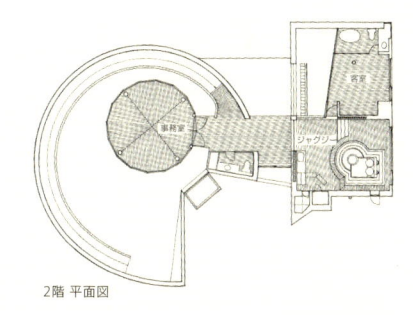

2階 平面図

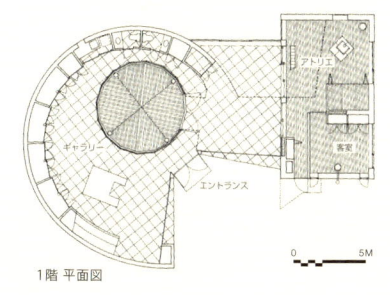

1階 平面図

所在地：神奈川県横浜市金沢区
主用途：ギャラリー、アトリエ
構造設計：構造計画研究所
設備設計：ユニ設備設計
施工：第一建設工業
構造：S造
規模：地上2階
敷地：893㎡　建築：283㎡　延床：412㎡

Stars Art 23
Kanazawa-ku, Yokohama-shi, Kanagawa

1992.05
滋賀県立びわ湖こどもの国

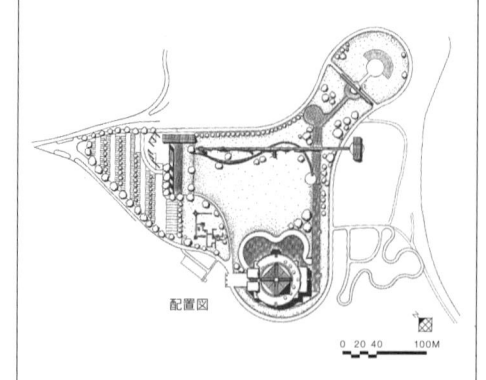

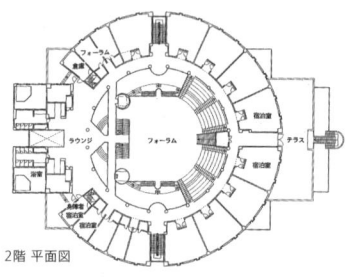

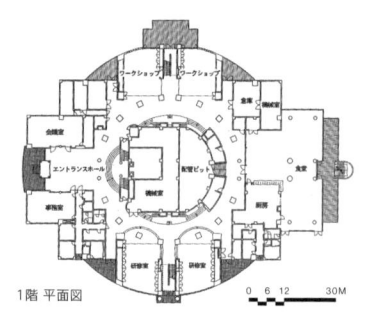

配置図

2階 平面図

1階 平面図

所在地：滋賀県高島市安曇川町
主用途：野外活動施設
建築主：滋賀県
構造設計：構造計画研究所
設備設計：愛住設計
施工：桑原・澤村建設JV
構造：RC造、S造
規模：地下1階地上2階塔屋1階
敷地：77,000㎡　建築：3,752㎡　延床：6,144㎡

Lake Biwa Children's Land
Adogawa-cho, Takashima-shi, Shiga

1992.07
富山県こどもみらい館

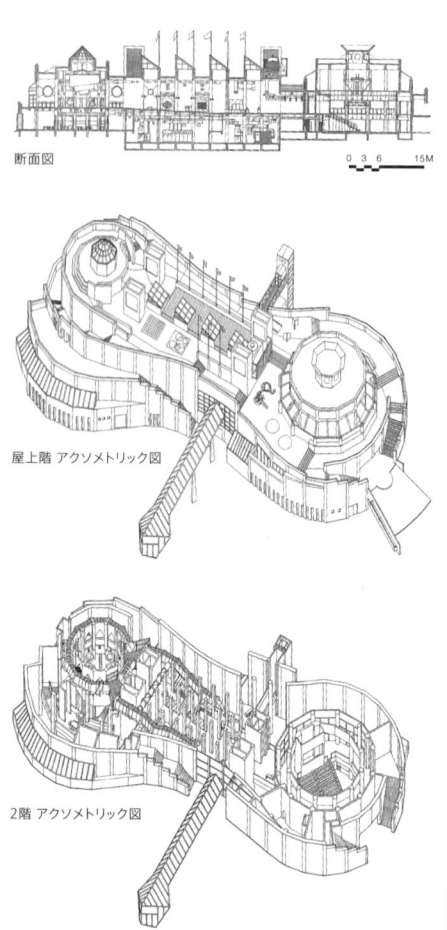

断面図

屋上階 アクソメトリック図

2階 アクソメトリック図

所在地：富山県射水市黒河太閤山ランド
主用途：児大型児童館
建築主：富山県
構造設計：構造計画研究所
設備設計：釣谷設備設計事務所
施工：熊谷組・砺波工業・山本建設JV
構造：RC造
規模：地下1階地上2階
敷地：950,000㎡　建築：2,610㎡　延床：4,014㎡

Toyama Children's Center
Kurokawa, Imizu-shi, Toyama

1991.05
中国北京科普楽園

アクソメトリック図

所在地：中国北京市
主用途：児童公園
建築主：宋慶齢基金会
構造：れんが一部S造、FRP
敷地：7,000㎡

Beijing Children's Science Park
Beijing, China

1991.11
営団地下鉄南北線

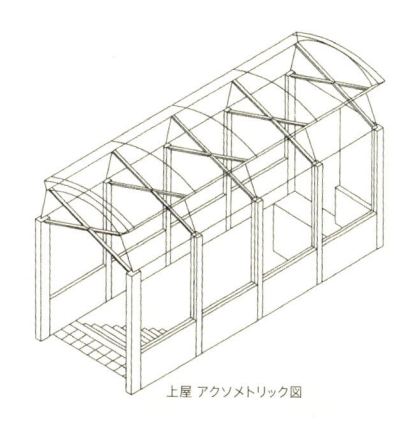

上屋 アクソメトリック図

ホーム 断面パース図

所在地：南北線駒込駅ー赤羽岩淵駅間
主用途：地下鉄
建築主：帝都高速度交通営団
プロジェクト内容：環境計画
施工：太陽工業、コトブキ、中村展設
敷地：上屋50〜100㎡、コンコース500〜1000㎡×6駅、ホーム600㎡×6駅

Eidan Subway, Nanboku Line
Nanboku Line between Komagome Station and
Akabane Iwabuchi Station

1990.06
弁天町ウォーターランド
［プールズ］

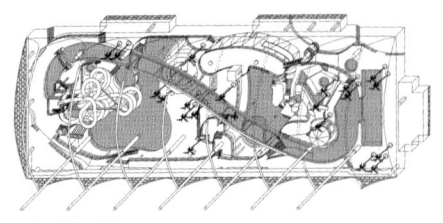

アクソメトリック図

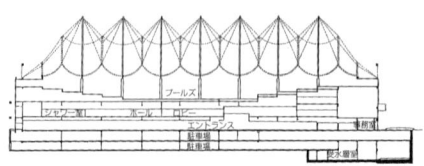

断面図

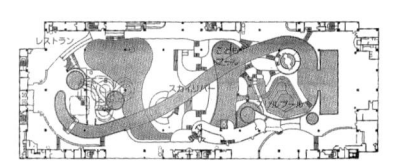

5階 平面図

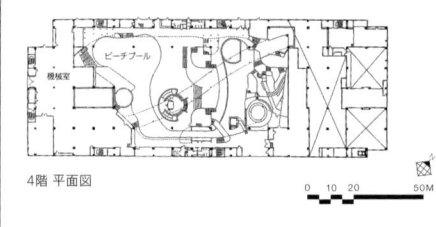

4階 平面図

所在地：大阪府大阪市港区弁天
主用途：レジャープール
プロジェクト内容：内装デザイン
共同設計：昭和設計
施工：竹中工務店・奥村組JV
構造：SRC造
規模：地下3階地上5階塔屋1階
敷地：30,123㎡　建築：8,298㎡　延床：46,677㎡

Bentencho Waterland "Pools"
Benten, Minato-ku, Osaka-shi, Osaka

1990.11
鳥の家

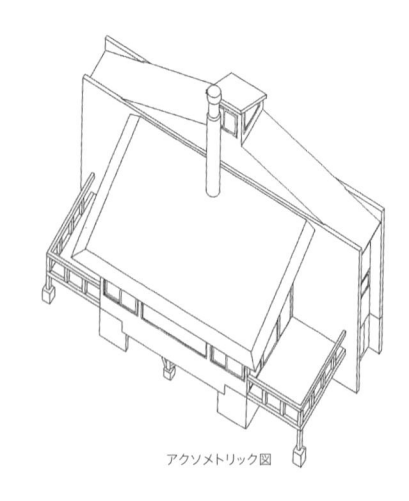

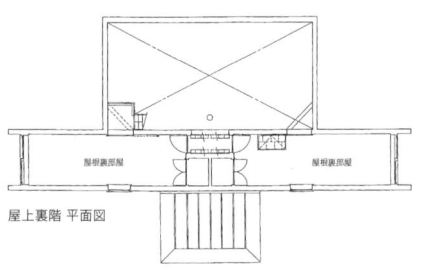

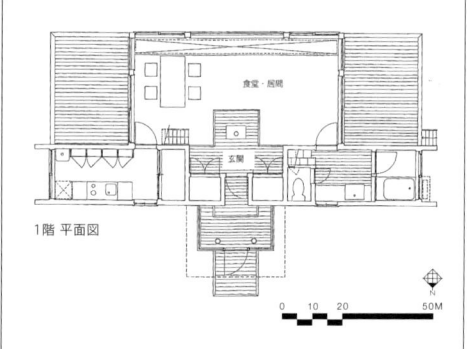

アクソメトリック図

屋上裏階 平面図

1階 平面図

所在地：長野県南佐久郡南牧村
主用途：住宅
構造：W造
規模：地上1階
敷地：2,427㎡　延床：71㎡

Bird House
Minamimakimura, Minamisaku-gun, Nagano

1990.04
鵠沼の家

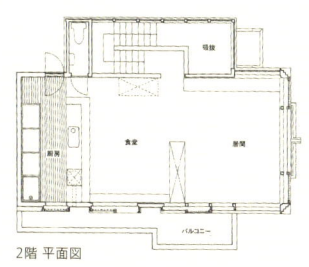

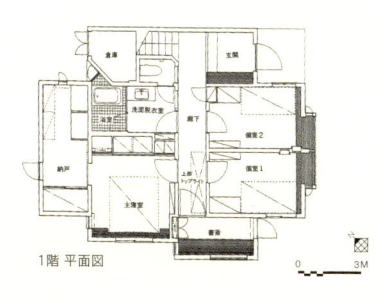

アクソメトリック図

2階 平面図

1階 平面図

所在地：神奈川県藤沢市鵠沼
主用途：住宅
設備設計：ユニ設備設計
施工：三栄ハウス
構造：W造
規模：地上2階
敷地：147㎡　建築：73㎡　延床：117㎡

Kugenuma House
Kugenuma, Fujisawa-shi, Kanagawa

1990.12
松庵の家

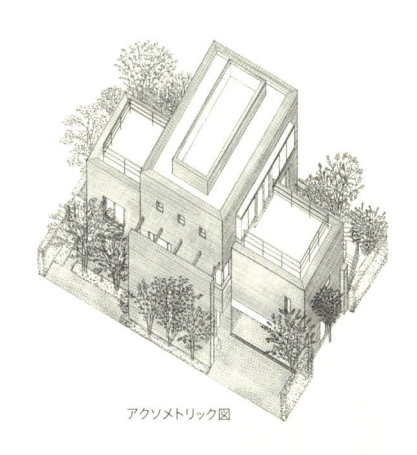

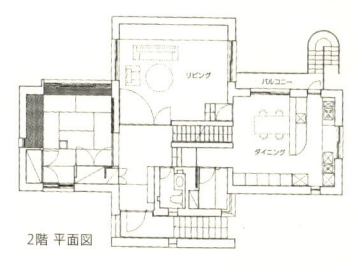

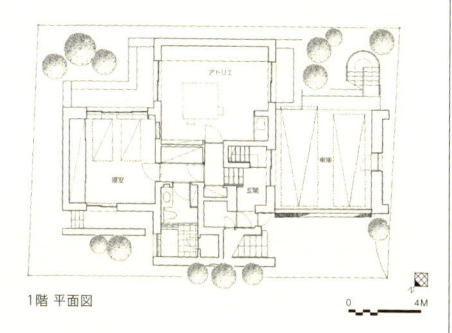

アクソメトリック図

2階 平面図

1階 平面図

所在地：東京都杉並区松庵
主用途：住宅
構造設計：構造計画研究所
設備設計：ユニ設備設計
施工：岡田建設
構造：RC造
規模：地上3階
敷地：232㎡　建築：108㎡　延床：232㎡

Shoan House
Shoan, Suginami-ku, Tokyo

1989

白金台ガーデンハウス
Shiroganedai Garden House

静かな中庭

白金台ガーデンハウス

東京都港区白金台／1989
Shiroganedai Garden House
Shirokanedai, Minato-ku, Tokyo

都心部の高級住宅地である白金台で、隣接して自然学習園がある静かな環境に位置する集合住宅である。施主個人の家を建て替え、中庭をはさんで2棟の地下1階地上3階の共同住宅としている。

This is a housing development in a tranquil neighborhood located in Shiroganedai, an upscale residential area in Tokyo, that is adjacent to a nature museum. The owner's house was replaced with a housing complex comprising two buildings with a garden in the middle. Each building has three floors and a basement.

1989

白金台ガーデンハウス

Shiroganedai Garden House

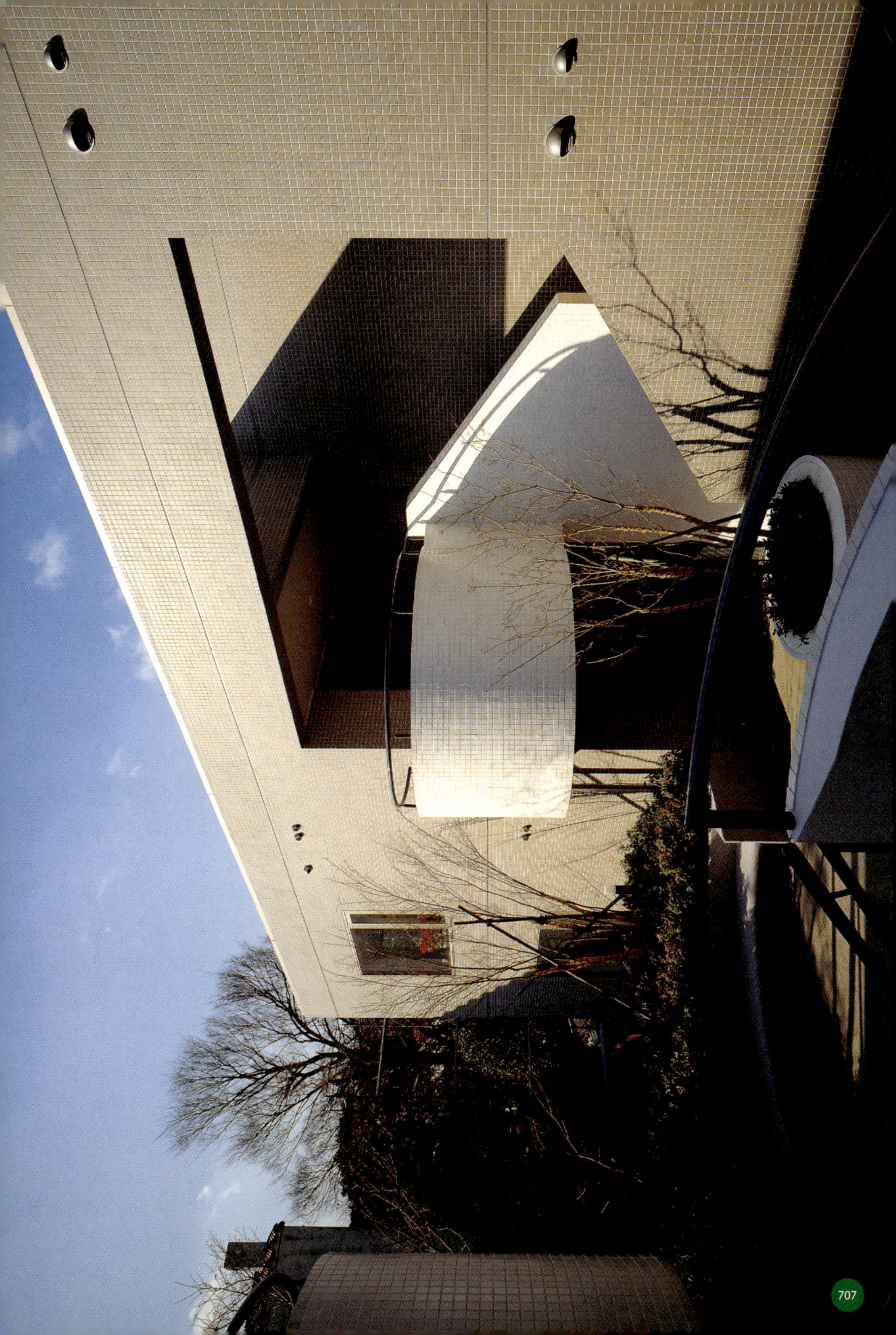

湾曲する山荘

1989

軽井沢C山荘

Mountain Villa "C", Karuizawa

軽井沢C山荘

長野県北佐久郡軽井沢町／1989
Mountain Villa "C", Karuizawa
Karuizawa-machi, Kitasaku-gun, Nagano

日本の代表的な別荘地である軽井沢に建てられた山荘である。建物の平面がC型に似た形をしているため、人々は室内を歩き回ることによってインテリアと景観の変化を楽しむことができる。

This villa stands in one of the most representative mountain resorts in Japan, Karuizawa. Being more or less like a letter "C" on plane, this makes it possible to enjoy the trees from various parts of the interior and also makes for rather interesting collection of interior spaces.

1989

軽井沢C山荘

Mountain Villa "C", Karuizawa

711

1988

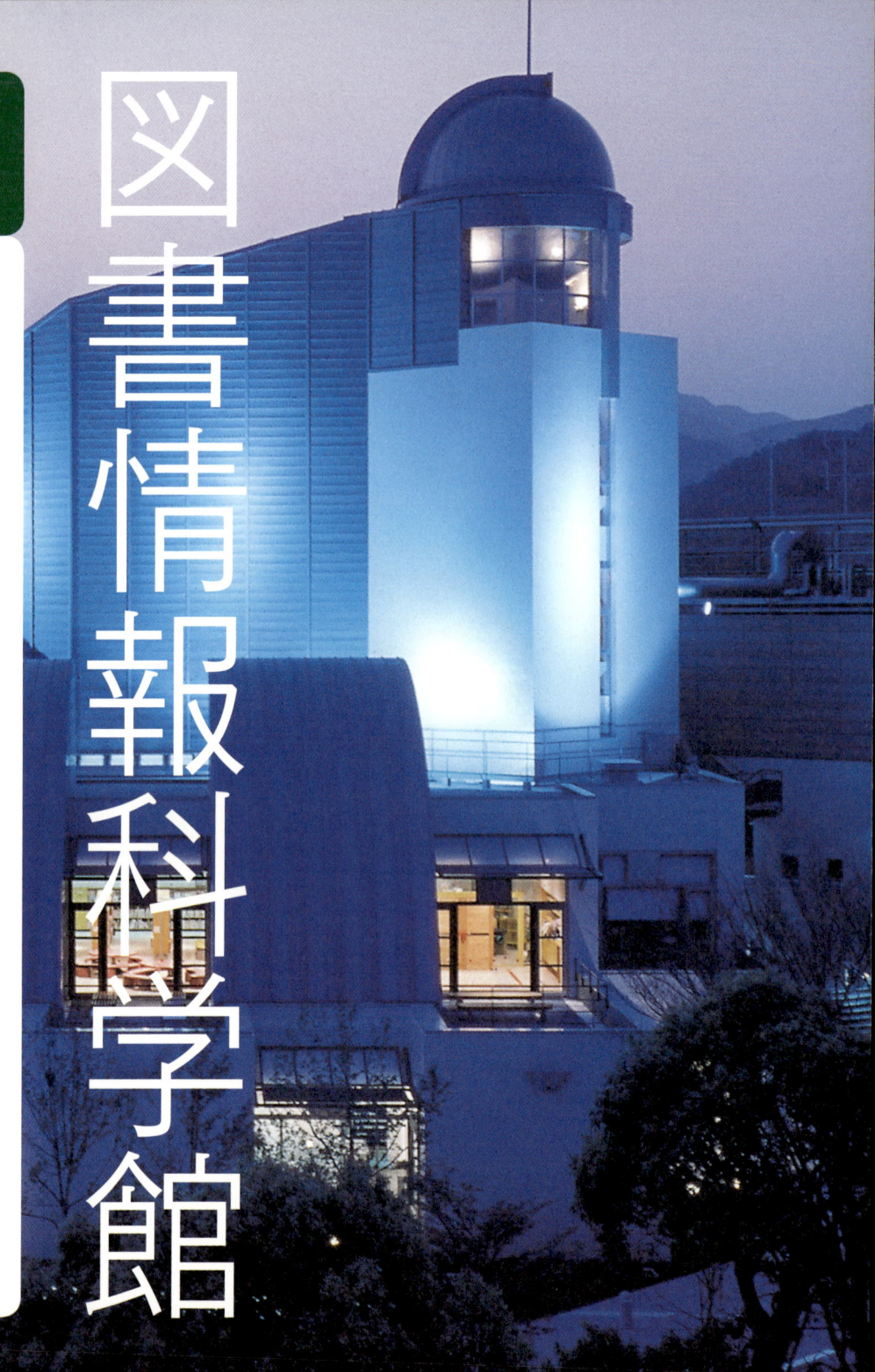

伊勢原市立図書館・こども科学館

図書情報科学館

Isehara Library and Science Museum

伊勢原市立図書館・こども科学館

神奈川県伊勢原市田中／1988
Isehara Library and Science Museum
Tanaka, Isehara-shi, Kanagawa

本施設は市役所に隣接した図書館と科学館の複合施設として計画された。私達は図書情報科学館という一体的なコンセプトを提案し、具体的には共通項である情報フロアーを2階に配し、図書館を1・2階に、科学館を2・3階とした。遊環構造建築とした構造をもち、既存の市役所・文化会館との間に市民広場を構成するような配置計画とし、図書館・こども科学館との間を抜ける通路をコミュニティ道路として広場と一体化させている。

As a combined library and science museum on an adjoining site to the city hall, we proposed a comprehensive facility comprising library and information science functions. In concrete, the information area, was provided on the second floor, and the library on the first and second floors, and science museum on the second and the third floors. The site was planned so as to have some open spaces between the existing city hall and cultural hall complex on the adjoining site and the remaining passageway between the two sites was arranged as the road for the community with circular play system.

1988

窓の外には『ヘリックス』
At the center of the window,
is "Helix," a piece of work by sculptor Aijiro Wakita

伊勢原市立図書館・こども科学館

Isehara Library and Science Museum

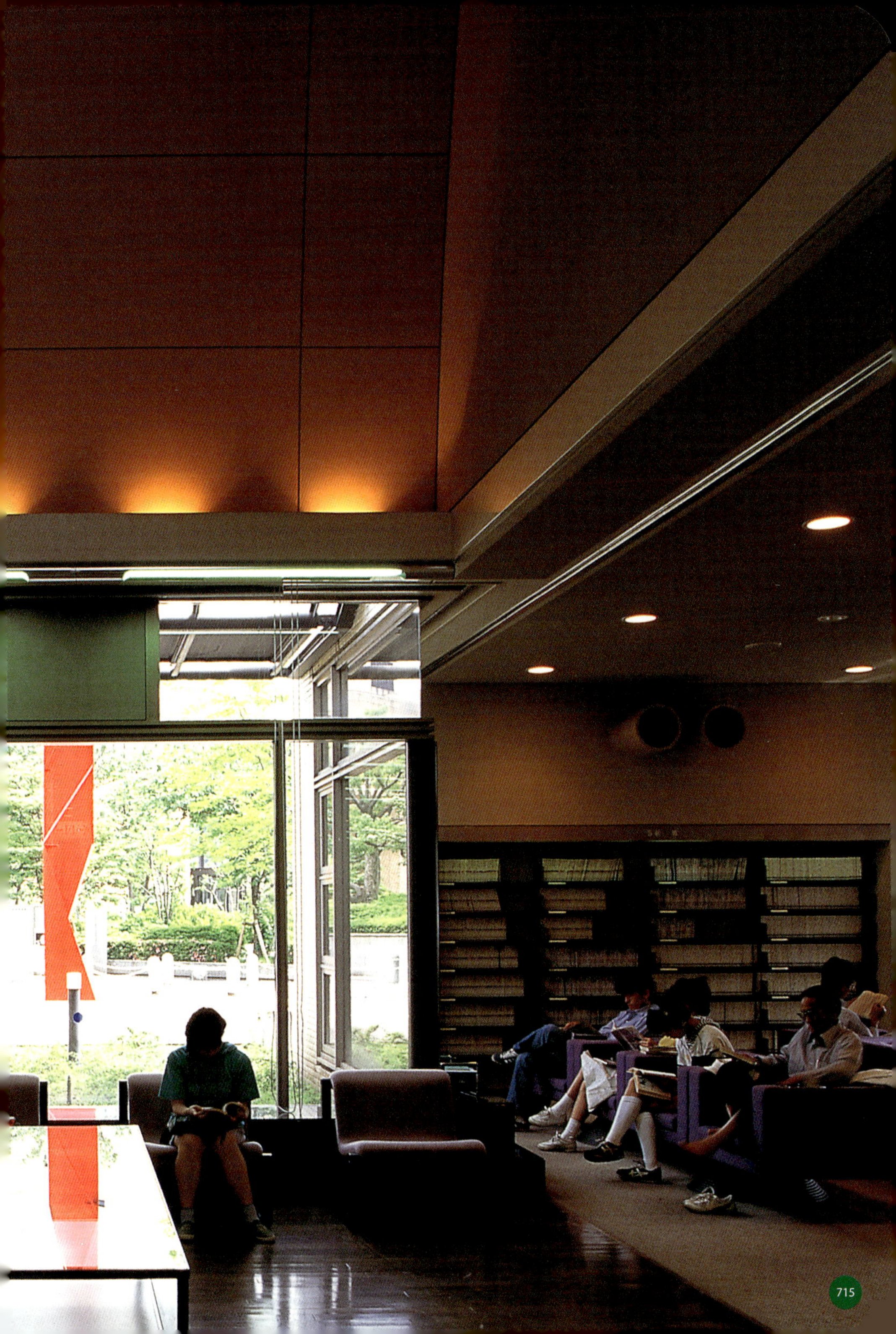

1988

伊勢原市立図書館・こども科学館

Isehara Library and Science Museum

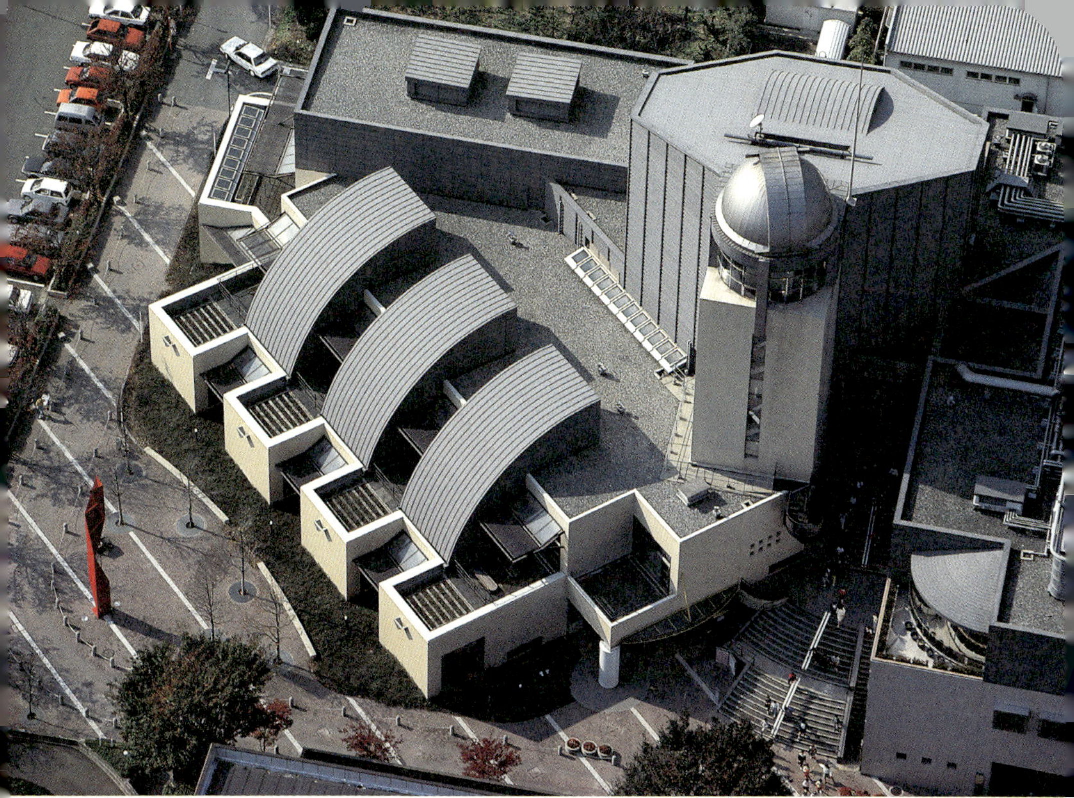

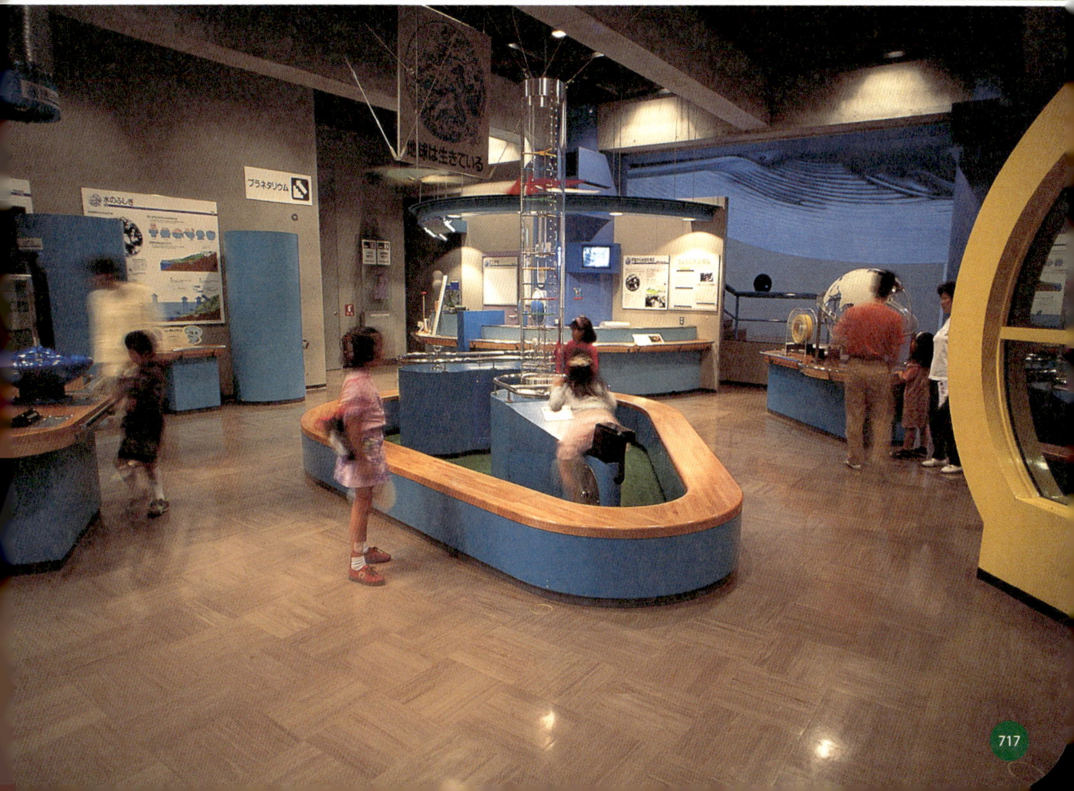
地球は生きている
プラネタリウム
水のふしぎ

彫刻のある散策路

1989

渋谷区散策路整備計画［美術館ルート］

Shibuya Promenade Design "Route to shoto Museum"

渋谷区散策路整備計画 [美術館ルート]

東京都渋谷区松濤／1989
Shibuya Promenade Design "Route to shoto Museum"
Shoto, Shibuya-ku, Tokyo

渋谷区立松濤美術館の建設にあわせ、美術館、渋谷駅、区役所という3つの核を結ぶ全長2.5kmの美術館通りという街路を提案し、デザインを担当した。特に彫刻を内蔵した方向性は新しい試みで、異なる性質の地区をつなぎながら舗装・植栽・ストリートファニチャーによって新しいイメージと快適な歩行環境を実現した。

When the Shoto Museum of Art was built, we proposed and handled the design for this 2.5-kilometer "museum street" connecting the art museum, Shibuya Station, and the ward's municipal offices. The incorporation of sculptures was a particularly novel undertaking. We were able to achieve a fresh-looking, pleasant walking environment by using decorations, plants, and street furniture while also connecting together areas of disparate characters.

1989

渋谷区散策路整備計画［美術館ルート］

Shibuya Promenade Design "Route to shoto Museum"

721

都市環境の転換

1989

渋谷区散策路整備計画［旧玉川上水ルート］

Shibuya Promenade Design "Hatsudai District"

渋谷区散策路整備計画 ［旧玉川上水ルート］

東京都渋谷区初台／1989
Shibuya Promenade Design "Hatsudai District"
Hatsudai, Shibuya-ku, Tokyo

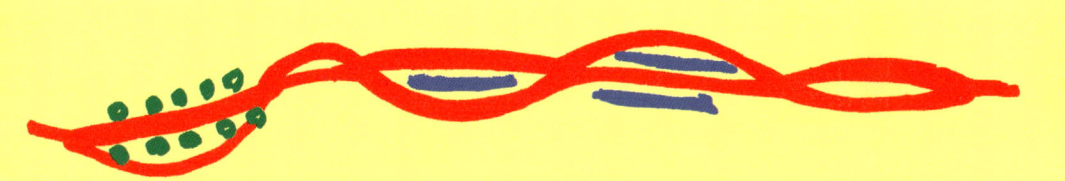

新宿駅より京王線で1.5kmのところ、初台駅より約300mの区間が、京王線の地下鉄化によって新たに緑道として整備された。この地域は住宅地ではあるが、甲州街道と高架の首都高速道路が走り、環境としてはあまりよくない。そのため、住宅地に欠けている緑と潤いのある空間の提供という2つの目標を提案し、実現した。住民は比較的若い世代が多い。水の流れ、こども達のための種々の遊具、地域のシンボルとなる彫刻等が配された。彫刻家、脇田愛二郎と共同した。

There is a park constructed about a 300 meters from Hatsudai station when the Keio Line was put underground. The area is residential but not a particularly good location due to a highway as well as an expressway spread overhead. The greenbelt was developed as a buffer between the residential area and to afford those residences some greenery and fresh air. The ward also has many young families. The greenbelt provides the sound of flowing water, various play equipment for children, and statues that have become symbols of the neighborhood. This project was taken on together with sculptor Aijiro Wakita.

1989

渋谷区散策路整備計画［旧玉川上水ルート］

Shibuya Promenade Design "Hatsudai District"

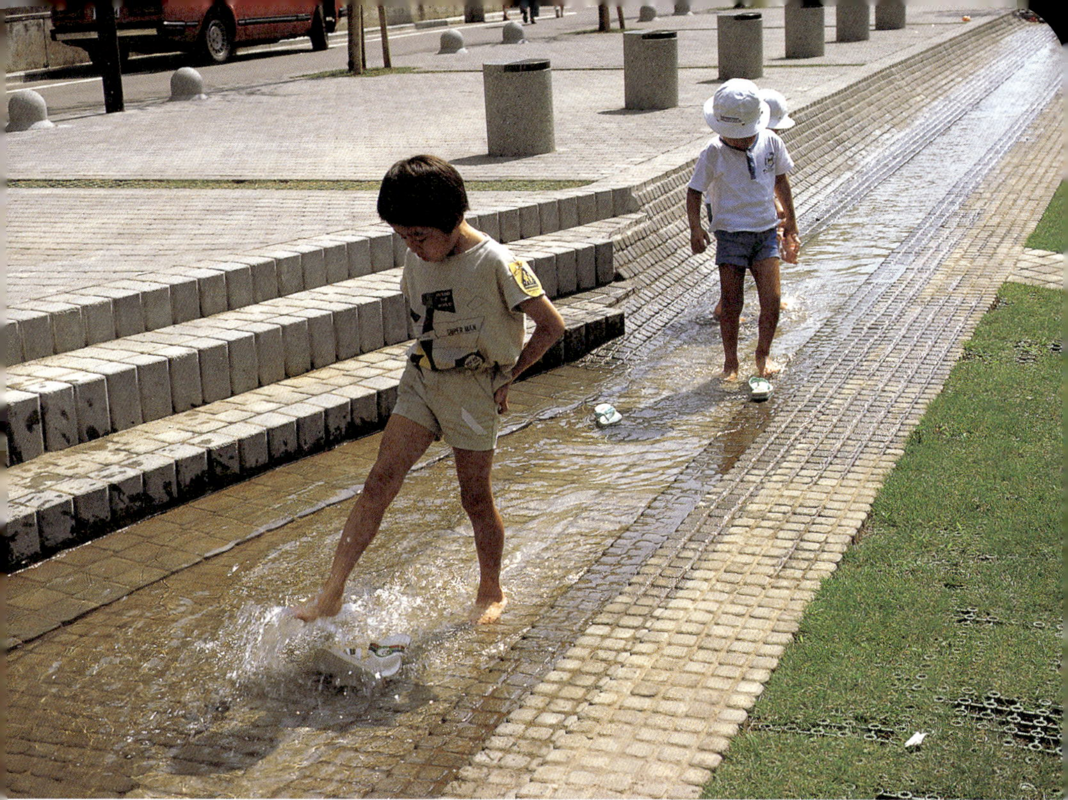

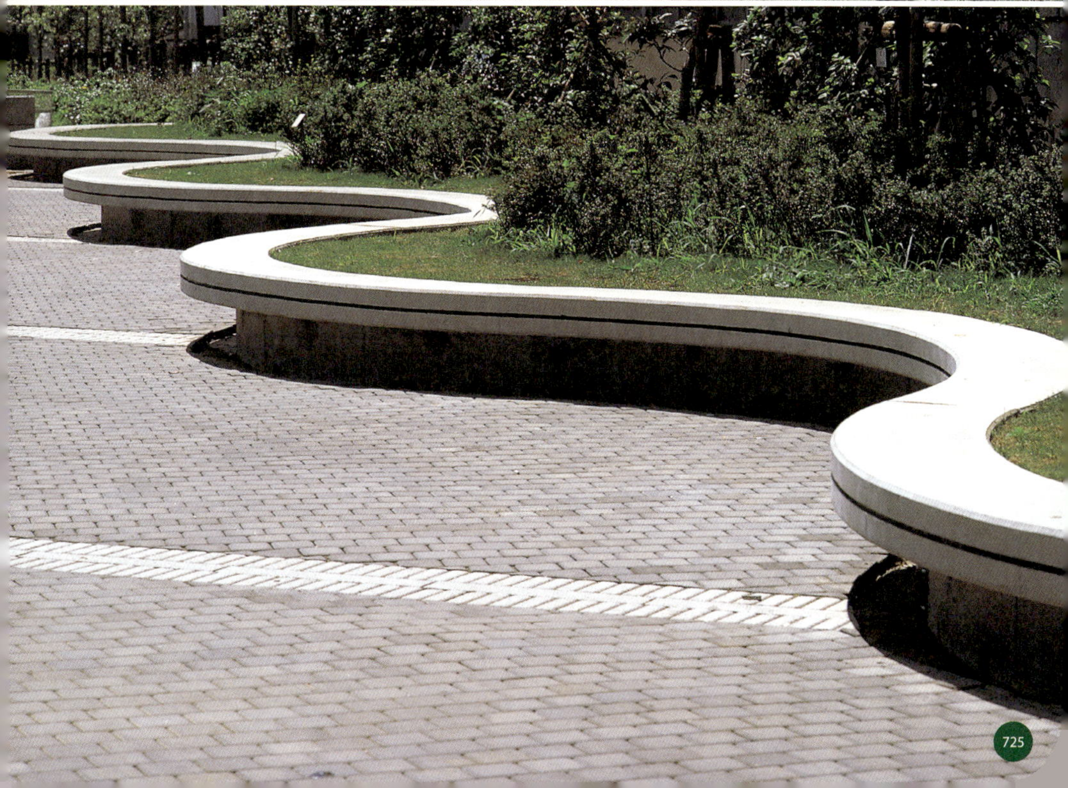

1987

戦艦三笠へ

1万Mプロムナード三笠アプローチ

Mikasa Park Approach Road in the ten thousand Meter Promenade

1万Mプロムナード 三笠アプローチ

神奈川県横須賀市小川町／1987
Mikasa Park Approach Road in the ten thousand Meter Promenade
Ogawa-cho, Yokosuka-shi, Kanagawa

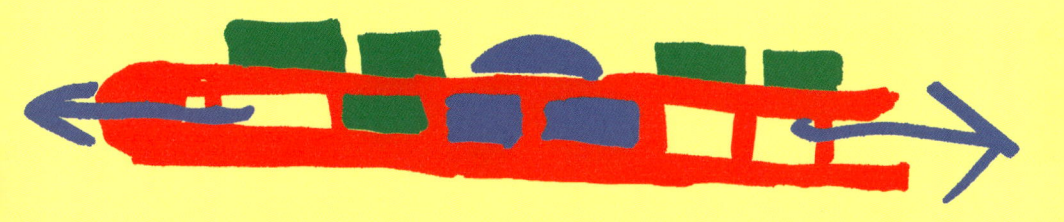

三笠アプローチと呼ばれる公園通りはJR横須賀駅から観音崎を結ぶ海沿いの長さ1万Mプロムナードのモデル区域で、米軍基地の入口から海側の三笠公園まで約300mの距離をもつ。車道を片側に寄せてつくられた、幅約26mの緑道は4つの性格の広場に分けられ、水の小さな流れによって連結されている。道そのものが横須賀の新しい文化イメージを伝えることが意図された。

Mikasa Street is a park promenade about 10,000 meters long that runs along the ocean, connecting JR Yokosuka Station and Kannonzaki. The entrance to the United States military base is about 300 meters from the sea side of Mikasa Park. Built parallel to the road on one side, Mikasa Park is nearly 26 meters wide and is separated into four different characteristically different personalities, all connected by a small flow of water. It was anticipated that this promenade heralded a new image for Yokosuka.

1987

1万Mプロムナード三笠アプローチ　Mikasa Park Approach Road in the ten thousand Meter Promenade

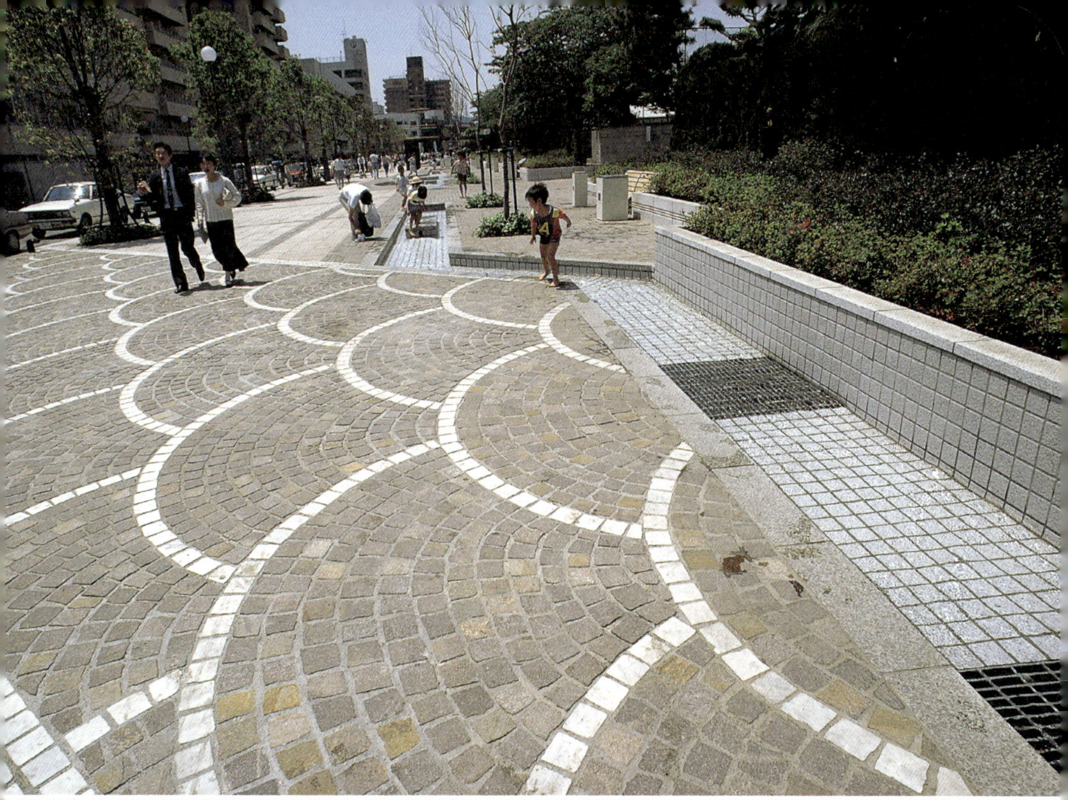

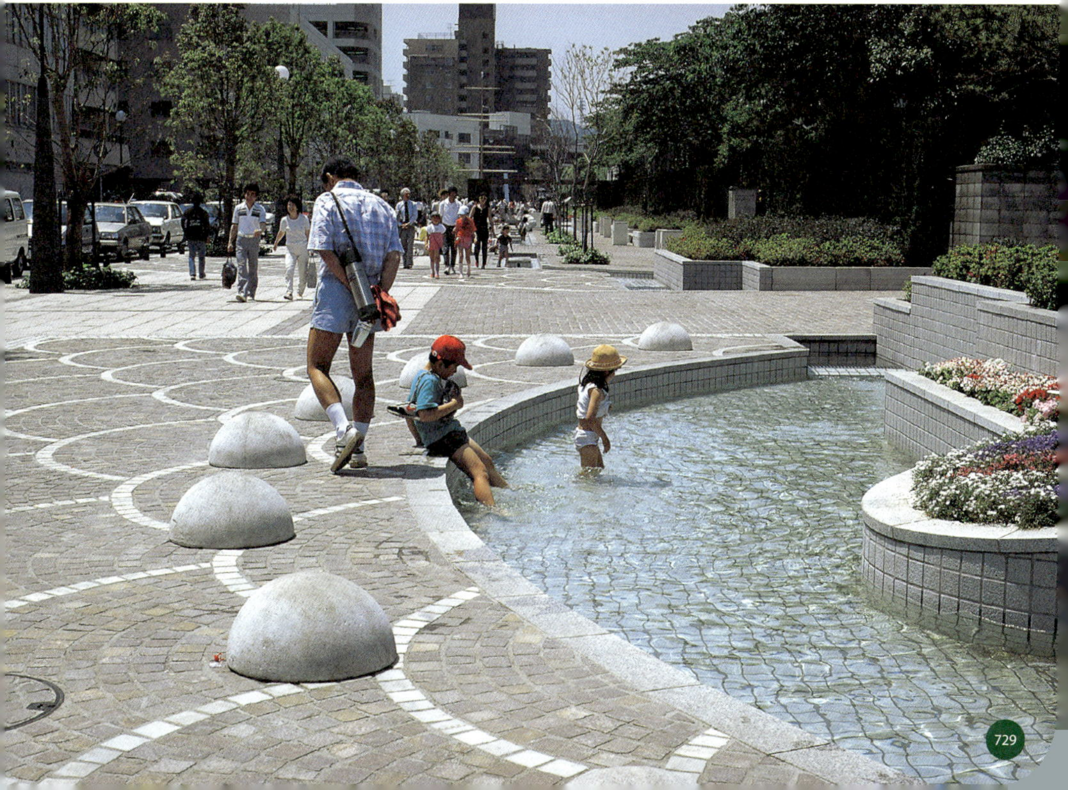

1987

名古屋市宝くじモデル児童遊園［わいわい広場］

Nagoya Children's Play Park "Wai Wai Plaza"

視・聴・触

名古屋市
宝くじモデル児童遊園
［わいわい広場］

愛知県名古屋市昭和区川名山町／1987
Nagoya Children's Play Park "Wai Wai Plaza"
Kawanayama-cho, Showa-ku, Nagoya-shi, Aichi

名古屋市の児童福祉センターの芝生広場に5つの遊具が設置された。これらの遊具は木、鉄、ゴムといった素材の特徴を生かし、視覚的な変化、聴覚的なふしぎ、触覚的な驚きをテーマとしている。

Nagoya-city installed five pieces of play structure on the lawn in front of the Children's Welfare Services location. Using wood, metal, and rubber to good effect, it is full of visual changes, various audio effects and tactile surprises.

1987

名古屋市宝くじモデル児童遊園［わいわい広場］

Nagoya Children's Play Park "Wai Wai Plaza"

733

1987

山手ヨットクラブ　Yamate Yacht Club

Pool+
Coffee+
Sandwich+
Room

山手ヨットクラブ

神奈川県横浜市中区山手町／1987
Yamate Yacht Club
Yamate-cho, Naka-ku, Yokohama-shi, Kanagawa

横浜の高級住宅地、山手につくられた小さなコーヒーショップとパーティハウスである。サンドイッチをメインとする平屋のコーヒーショップと3階建ての住居棟がL型に構成され、道路側に駐車のスペースがとられている。中心空間は中庭の美しい楕円形のプールである。

This is a small coffee shop and party house built in Yamate, a high-class residential area in Yokohama. The one-story coffee shop is known for its delicious sandwiches and has a three-story residential building running perpendicular to it in a L shape, thus creating space for a parking lot on the road side. The space's center is the gorgeous oval shaped pool located in the central garden.

1987

山手ヨットクラブ　Yamate Yacht Club

結婚式のパーティ会場として良く使われ、
花婿はプールに投げ込まれる
Often used as a venue for wedding parties,
the groom is thrown into the pool.

1987

山手ヨットクラブ　Yamate Yacht Club

建築は仙田満、
インテリアは脇田愛二郎の共同作品
A joint collaboration,
with Mitsuru Senda on the architecture
and Aijiro Wakita on the interior design.

1987

相模川ふれあい科学館

Sagamigawa River Museum

40mの連続水槽

相模川ふれあい科学館

神奈川県相模原市中央区水郷田名／1987
Sagamigawa River Museum
Suigotana, Chuo-ku, Sagamihara-shi, Kanagawa

本施設は相模川を科学の目で促えた淡水水族館である。1.2ヘクタールの敷地全体を親水公園とし、相模川の観光・レジャーとしての拠点化とそれによる地域の活性化とを目的につくられた。内部は円弧状の流れのある一体水槽で、川の上流から川の下流までを落差を設けて相模川が再現された。相模川の段丘と川と魚の関係をわかりやすく構造化されている。日本の淡水水族館のモデルとなっている。

This facility is a museum of fresh-water aquatic life that offers a scientific view of the Sagamigawa River. The museum is located on a 1.2-hectare plot of land, which includes various facilities in its role as a waterfront park. It was built with the purpose of making the area a base for sightseeing and leisure activities along the Sagamigawa River, and consequentially to vitalize the region. Inside, the museum has an arched aquarium made to look like Sagamigawa River, with water flowing downstream over steps. This is a model for other freshwater fish aquariums in Japan.

1987

相模川ふれあい科学館

Sagamigawa River Museum

長さ150kmの相模川を40mの水槽でみせる、
世界最初の環境型河川連続水槽

The world's first environmental river water tank,
the 150km long Sagami River is shown in a 40m tank

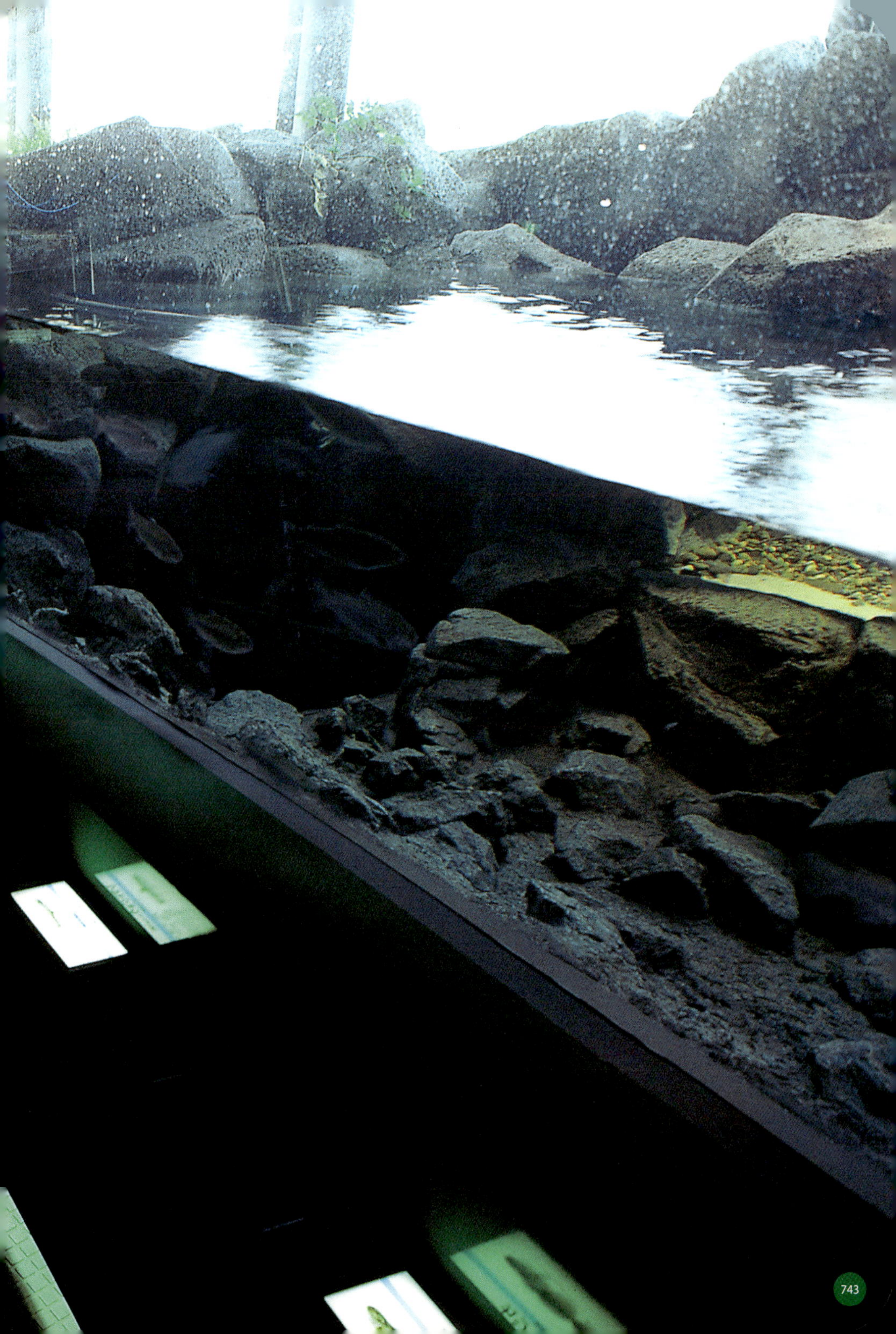

1987

相模川ふれあい科学館

Sagamigawa River Museum

745

1986

浜松科学館
Hamamatsu Science Museum

建築も
科学展示物

浜松科学館

静岡県浜松市中区北寺島町／1986
Hamamatsu Science Museum
Kitaterajima-cho, Naka-ku, Hamamatsu-shi, Shizuoka

浜松は日本を代表するものづくりの産業文化をもつ都市である。その科学的実験精神「やらまいか」を継承する科学館として計画、設計された。建築そのものをひとつの大きな科学展示物と考え、器としての建築と内容物としての科学展示装置の融合が図られた。ガラス張りの機械室、内外に露出した空調ダクト、エレベーター等の機構部、コンクリートの配筋、天井下地などの可視化が工夫され、また、太陽光の陰影によって科学者の顔が浮かび出る外壁や、太陽光追尾装置などの展示的仕掛けは建築全体に及んでいる。遊環構造建築のモデルとして設計されている。

We have advocated the treatment of architecture in these facilities as a large scientific exhibit itself. Here we have tried to fuse together the concepts of architecture as a "container" and scientific exhibitions as "content." We worked to make the glassed-in machinery room, exposed air ducts, all visible from the outside. On the exterior walls, the faces of famous scientists become visible depending on the degree of sunlight and shadows, and solar trackers and other exhibit-worthy devices are scattered all over the building. This was designed as a model for future structure with circular play system.

1986

浜松科学館

Hamamatsu Science Museum

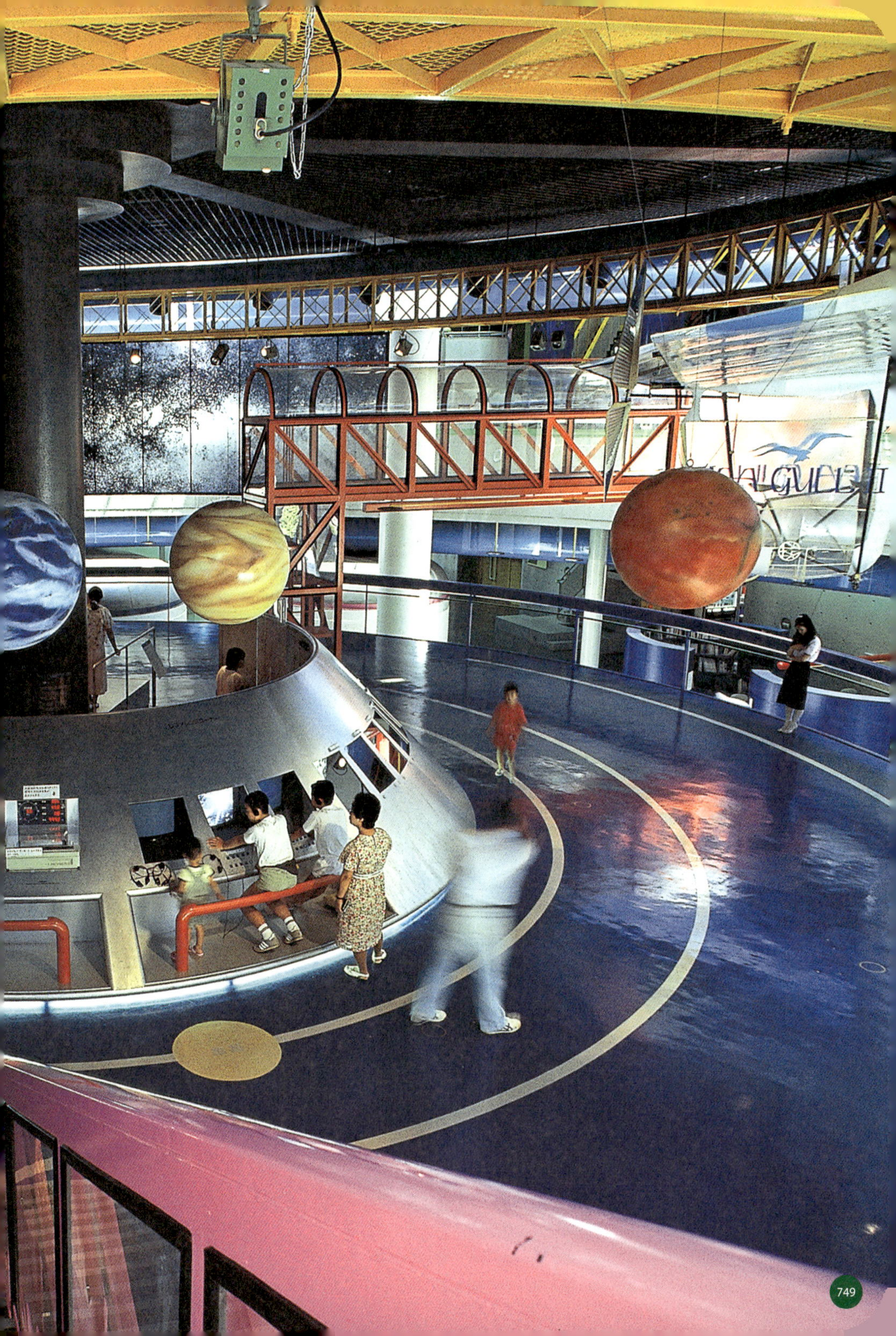

1986

浜松科学館　Hamamatsu Science Museum

751

1986

浜松科学館
Hamamatsu Science Museum

円形のドラムはプラネタリウムで、
新幹線の振動と音から守るため
コンクリート打設による外壁の上にアルミパネル、
そして内部はプラネタリウム本体のアルミパネルと
3層の壁により構成される

The spherical drum is a planetarium.
For protection from vibration and noises from the Shinkansen,
the concrete structure is made up of a three-layer wall,
with aluminum panels on the top of the outer wall,
as well as on the interior, which is the planetarium itself.

科学館

1986

浜松科学館
Hamamatsu Science Museum

淡松科学馆

1986

浜松科学館
Hamamatsu Science Museum

都市広場として街路と広場が一体的にデザインされる
Streets and squares are designed in an integral manner to form an urban square.

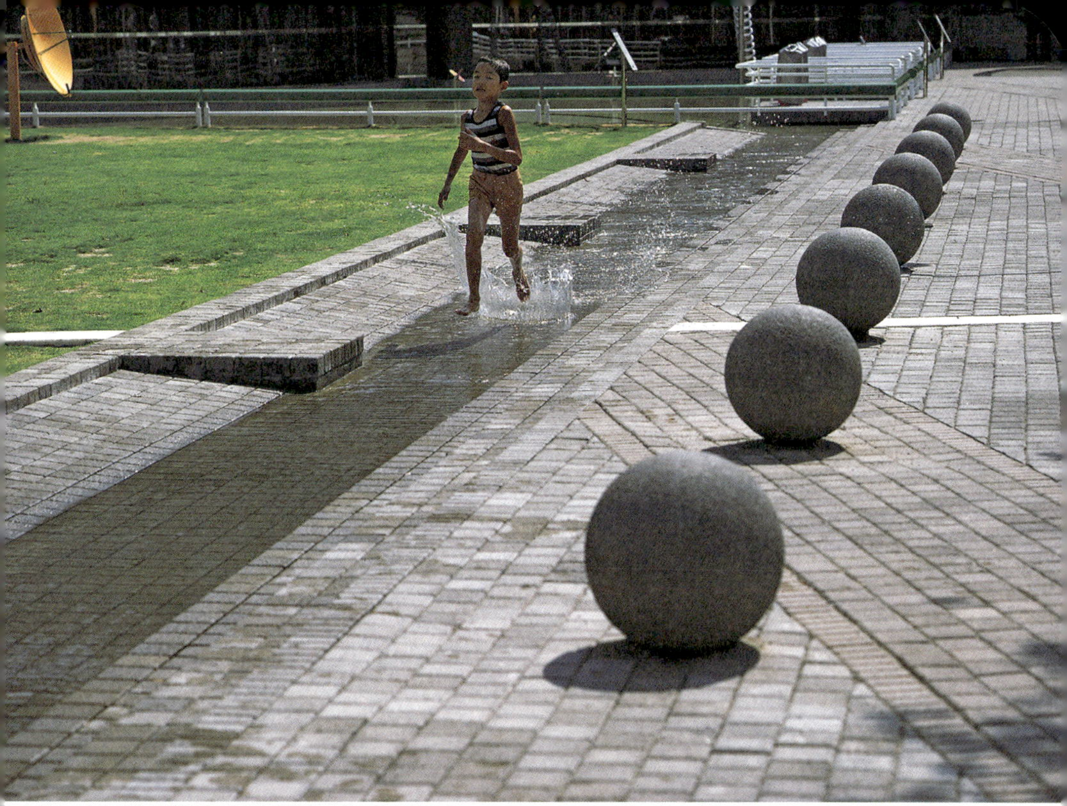

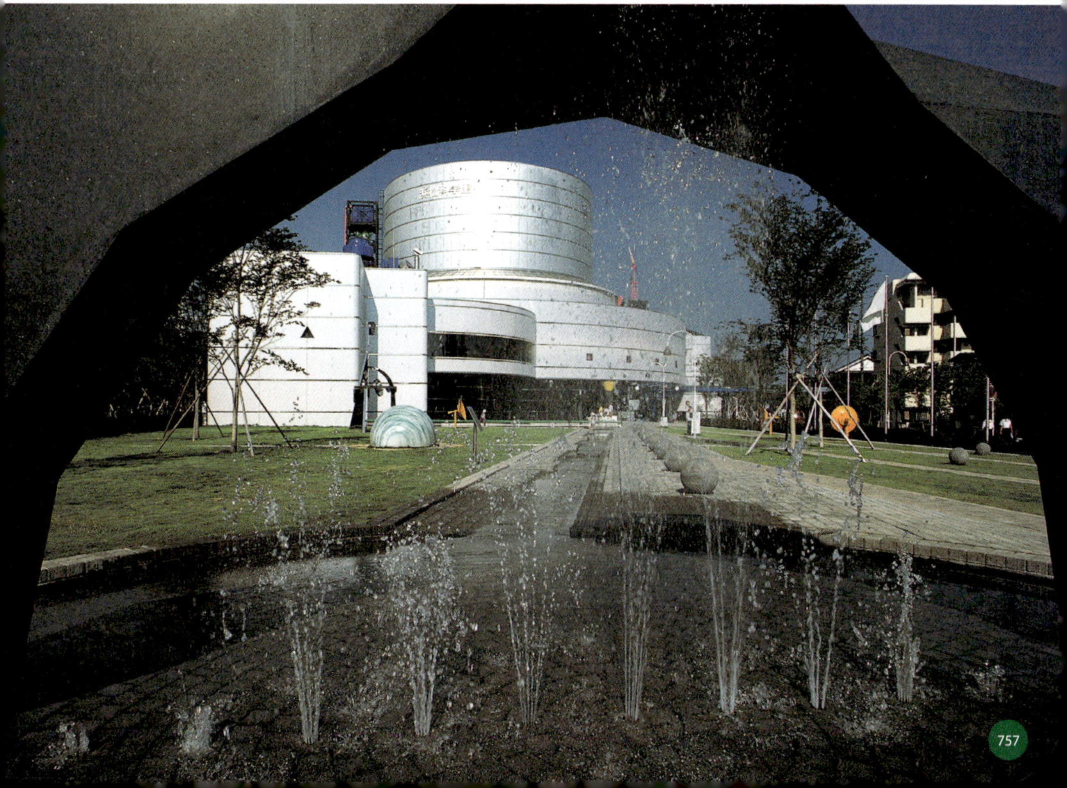

1985

多摩動物園 猛禽舎

Tama Zoo "Raptores House"

谷にかかるオーバルネット

多摩動物園 猛禽舎

東京都日野市程久保／1985
Tama Zoo "Raptores House"
Hodokubo, Hino-shi, Tokyo

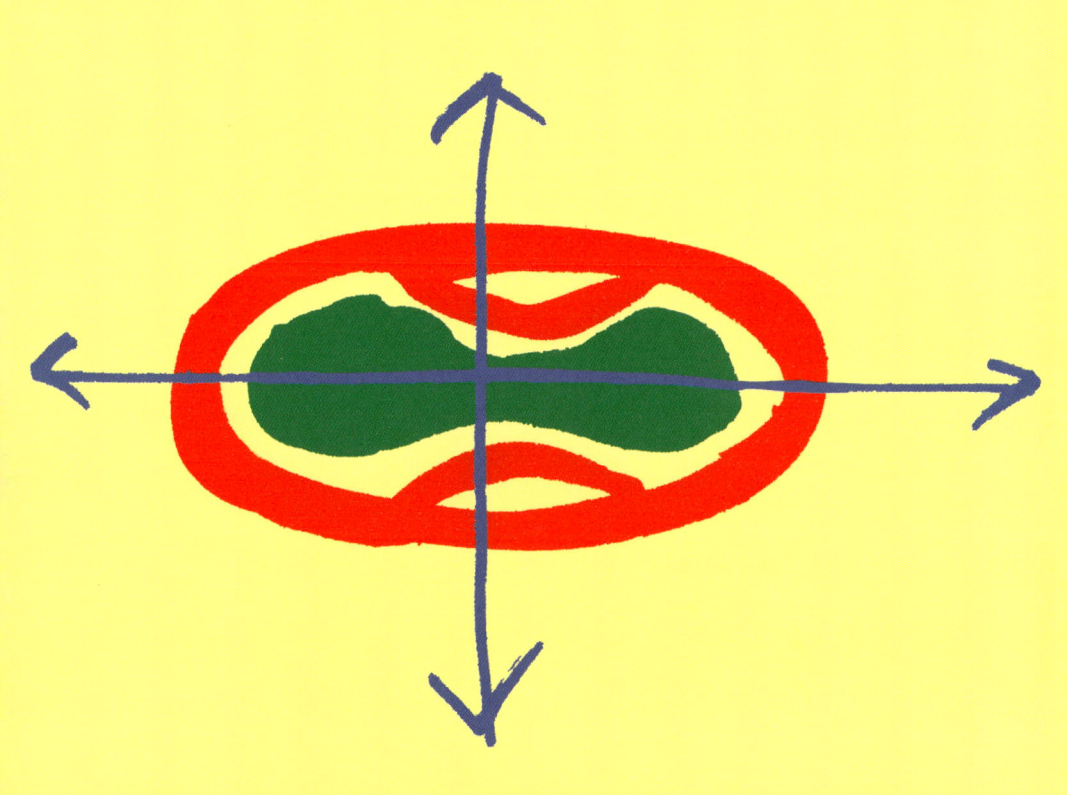

猛禽舎は多摩動物園のほぼ中央の小さな丘の間の谷間に位置している。平面は楕円形をしており直径47m、短径は31mである。2つの大きなアーチ状の鉄骨パイプと楕円形の平面梁によって、ネットはH.P.シェル面を構成する。全体的に谷部の地形を改変せず、観客の見学しやすさだけでなく、鳥たちの生活のしやすい空間が意図された。

The Cage of Rapacious Birds is located in a small dale surrounded by low hillocks in its central area. The cage measures 47m in its full diameter and 31m in its shorter dimension. Two arches of metal pipe form openings under a beam which is topped by a net of H.P. shell surface. The topography of this miniature valley was left unchanged for the benefit of the birds as well as the viewers.

1985

多摩動物園 猛禽舎

Tama Zoo "Raptores House"

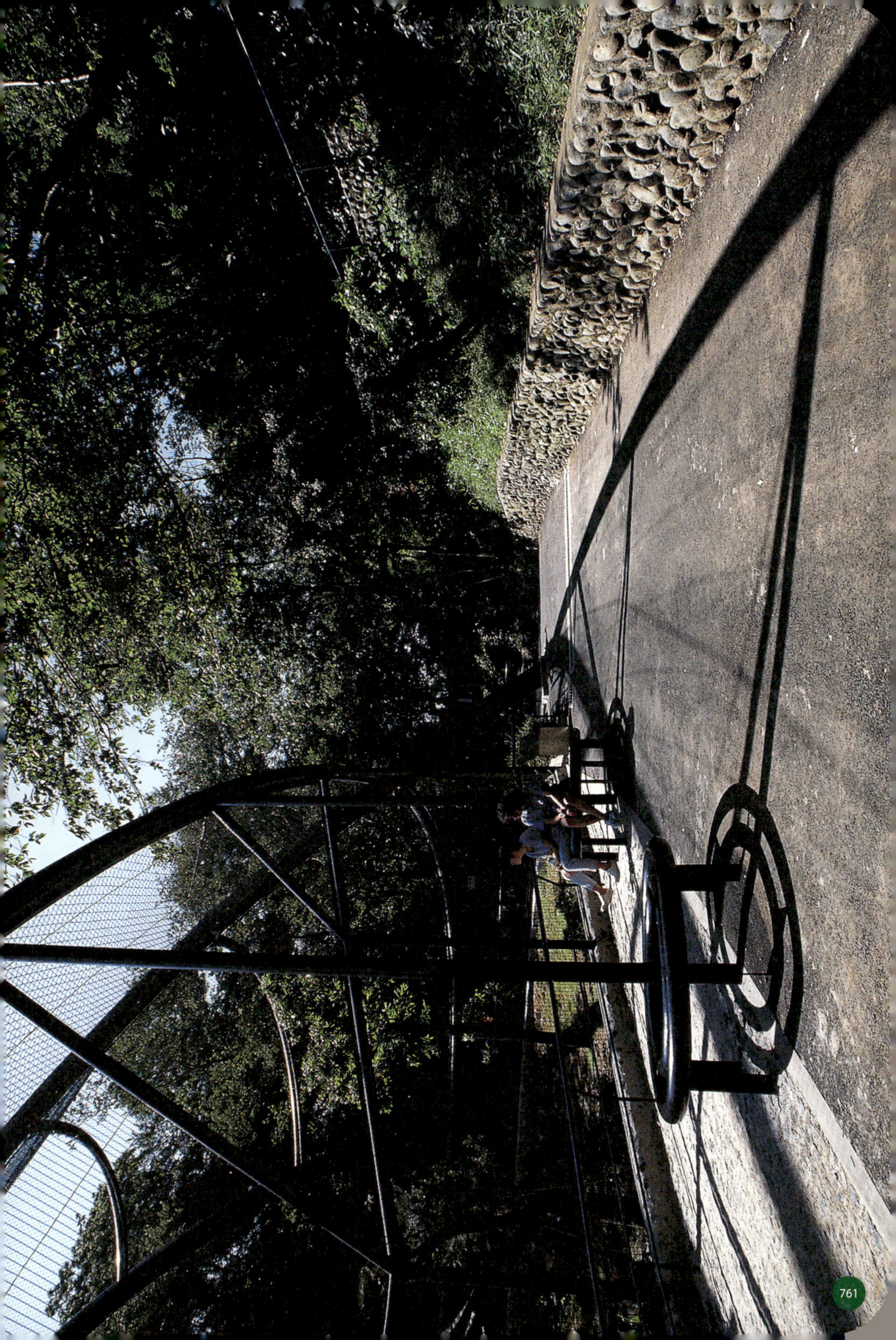

1985

筑波科学万国博覧会こども広場

Tsukuba Science Expo Children's Plaza

不思議と科学のEXPO

筑波科学万国博覧会 こども広場

茨城県つくば市吾妻／1985
Tsukuba Science Expo Children's Plaza
Azuma, Tsukuba-shi, Ibaraki

筑波科学万国博覧会政府出展施設であるこども広場は、博覧会場中央部分に位置している。4つのテーマ空間に分かれ、第1は「ふしぎの庭」と呼ぶエントランス広場である。錯視を利用した屋外版エイムズの部屋ともいうべきふしぎ回廊、ドアの迷宮など、不思議な小宇宙が体験できる広場である。第2は「おもしろチューブ」と呼ぶ、全長270mの連続科学体験遊具。第3は「地球とメカ動物園の広場」、第4は「日本列島ゾーン」で10万分の1の地図を直径36mの地球の一部として表現した。この遊具オブジェは遊環構造理論により配置された。

This children's plaza, a facility exhibited by the government at the Tsukuba Science Expo, is situated at the center of the Expo site. It is divided into four themes. The first is "Garden of Wonder," which serves as the entrance to the Expo. This area allows visitors to experience a mysterious microcosmo. The second is a "Fun Tube," which is a 270-meter long science exploratorium. The third is "Mechanimal" and the fourth is the "Japanese Archipelago Zone," which recreates a portion of the globe at a scale of 1/100,000 using 36 meters of space. These play objects were placed according to circular play system theory.

1985

筑波科学万国博覧会こども広場

Tsukuba Science Expo Children's Plaza

長さ270m、直径2.7mのサイエンスチューブ
A science tube that is 270m long and 2.7m in diameter.

1985

筑波科学万国博覧会こども広場

Tsukuba Science Expo Children's Plaza

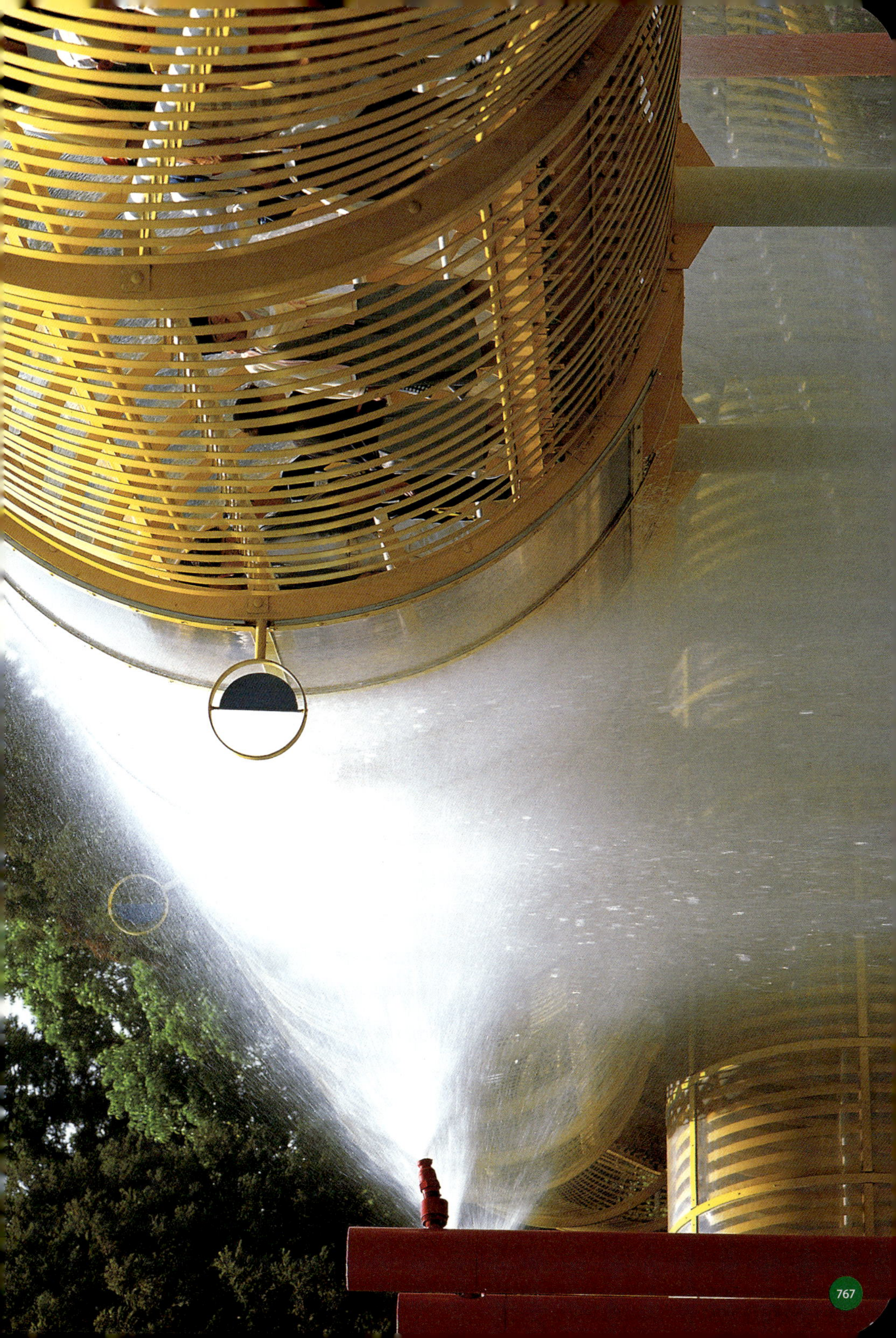

1985

筑波科学万国博覧会こども広場

Tsukuba Science Expo Children's Plaza

769

1985

筑波科学万国博覧会こども広場

Tsukuba Science Expo Children's Plaza

1/50000 の地球と日本列島
The Japanese archipelago and the earth, at 1/50000 times ratio.

錯覚と発見
Illusions and discoveries.

1985

筑波科学万国博覧会こども広場

Tsukuba Science Expo Children's Plaza

773

1985

筑波科学万国博覧会こども広場

Tsukuba Science Expo Children's Plaza

3ヘクタールのこども広場は
筑波博の政府出店中核施設

The 3-hectare children's square was a core government store facility in the Tsukuba Expo.

1984

軽井沢 640

Karuizawa 640

集合山荘

軽井沢 640

長野県北佐久郡軽井沢町／1984
Karuizawa 640
Karuizawa-machi, Kitasaku-gun, Nagano

本施設は金融企業の社員のための保養施設である。計画の条件は7つの家族もしくはグループが一年を通じ利用できることと、テニスコートを設けることであった。家族向けのメゾネットタイプの3ブロックと、1・2階に設けたグループ向けのフラットタイプの2つのブロックを敷地の奥に一列に配置し、ポーラスで大きな屋根をもつ豊かな自然の中の「大きな家」として計画された。

This is a resort facility for employees of a financial firm. The conditions for design were that it must provide for simultaneous use by seven families or groups throughout a single year period and include tennis courts. We placed three blocks of maisonette-type rooms for families and the two blocks of flats for groups on the first and second floors at the back of the site. The facility appears as a large single home with a huge, porous roof amidst a rich natural surrounding.

1984

軽井沢 640

Karuizawa 640

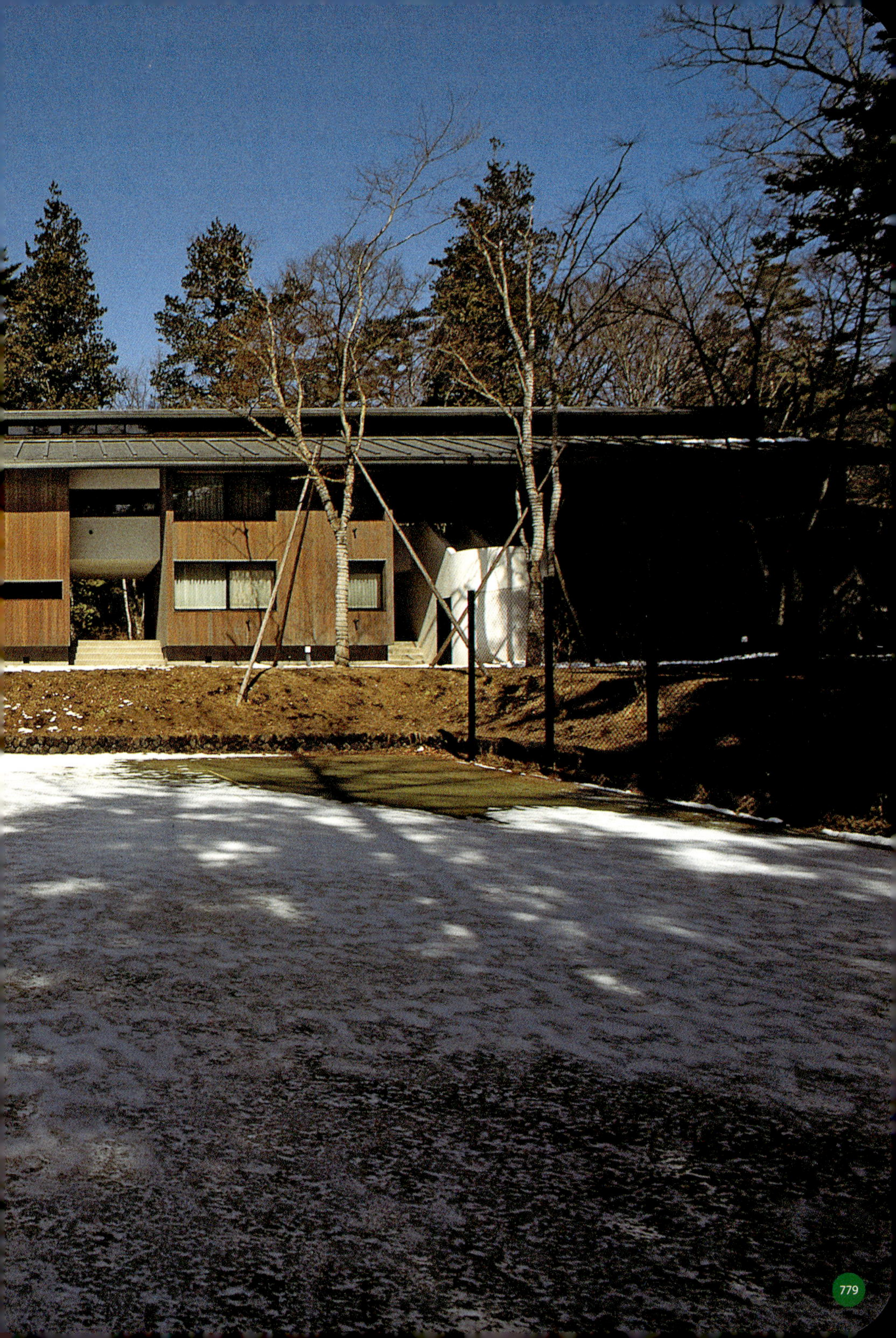

1984

軽井沢 640

Karuizawa 640

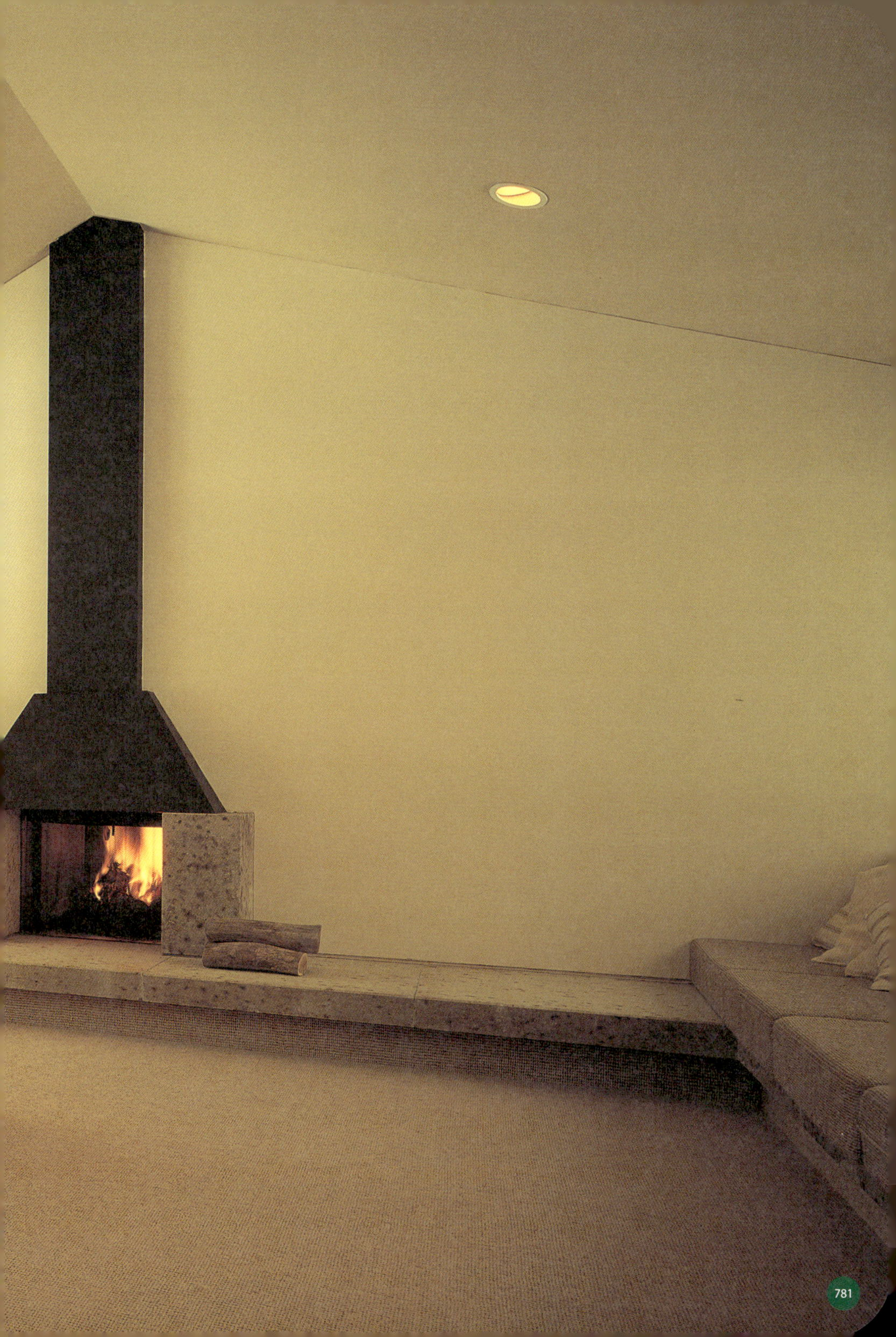

1983

静岡県吉原林間学校
Yoshiwara Camping School

心休まる
生活環境

静岡県吉原林間学校

静岡県富士市大淵／1983
Yoshiwara Camping School
Obuchi, Fuji-shi, Shizuoka

情緒障害児用短期治療施設である。周囲は松林に囲まれた丘陵地に位置する。学習棟、生活棟により構成されている。生活棟は中央に広場型のラウンジを設け、遊環構造的平面で自由に歩き回れることで、こども達の孤独感を癒すことが意図されている。

This is a short-term treatment facility for psychologically-disturbed children located in a hilly area surrounded by pine trees. The facility is composed of a building for learning and a separate building for living. The residential building has a large lounge set in its middle and a flat construction of play space so that people can walk around freely, allowing the children staying at the facility a release from their sense of loneliness.

1983

静岡県吉原林間学校 Yoshiwara Camping School

785

1983, 1982

標高1250m

鳥居平やまびこ公園[ローラースケート場・風のとりで]

Toriidaira Yamabiko Park

鳥居平やまびこ公園
［ローラースケート場・風のとりで］

長野県岡谷市内山／1983,1982
Toriidaira Yamabiko Park
Uchiyama, Okaya-shi, Nagano

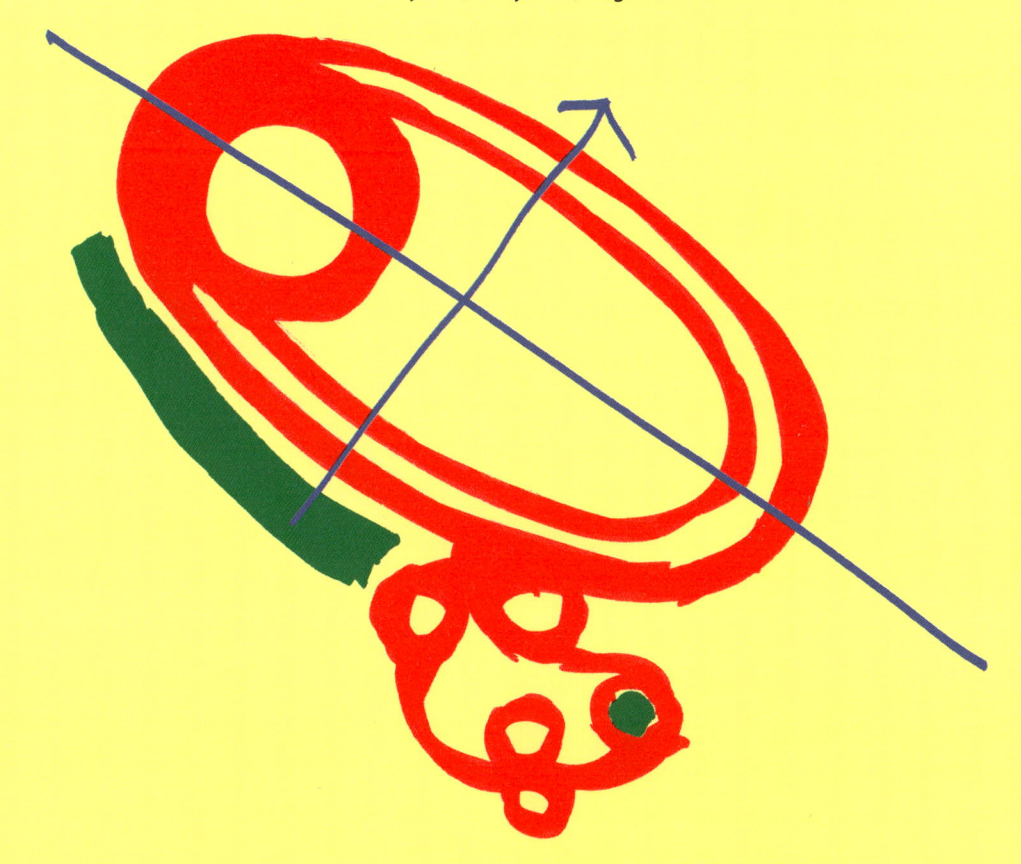

長野県岡谷市、諏訪湖と町を見下ろす標高約1,250ｍの丘の上に建設された公園。公園の広さは23ヘクタールである。レストランと展示室があるセンターハウスが中央にあり、南口広場に「ローラースケート場」と「風のとりで」と呼ぶ巨大な木製遊具がつくられている。

This 23-hectare park was built on a hill 1,250m above sea level, looking out over Lake Suwa and the city of Okaya, Nagano Prefecture. A "Center House" with restaurant, and exhibition room, stands in the center. At the south plaza is a "Roller skating area" and the "Fortress of Wind"–a large wooden play structure.

1983, 1982

鳥居平やまびこ公園［ローラースケート場・風のとりで］

Toriidaira Yamabiko Park

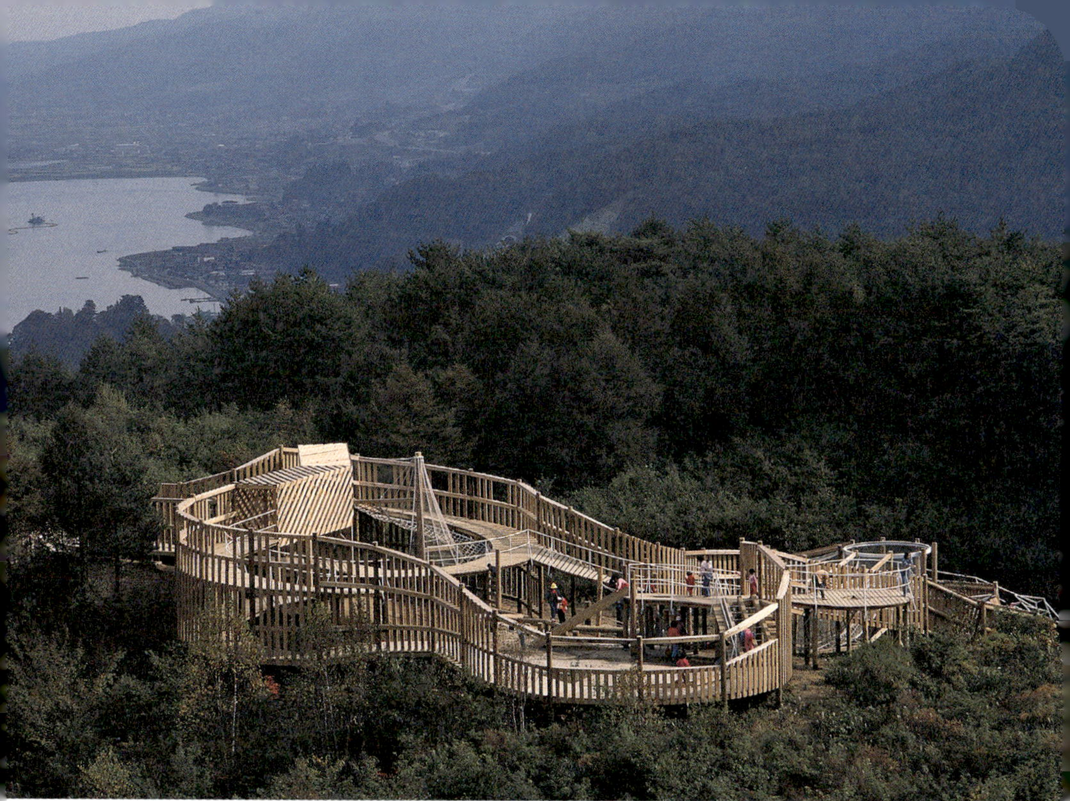

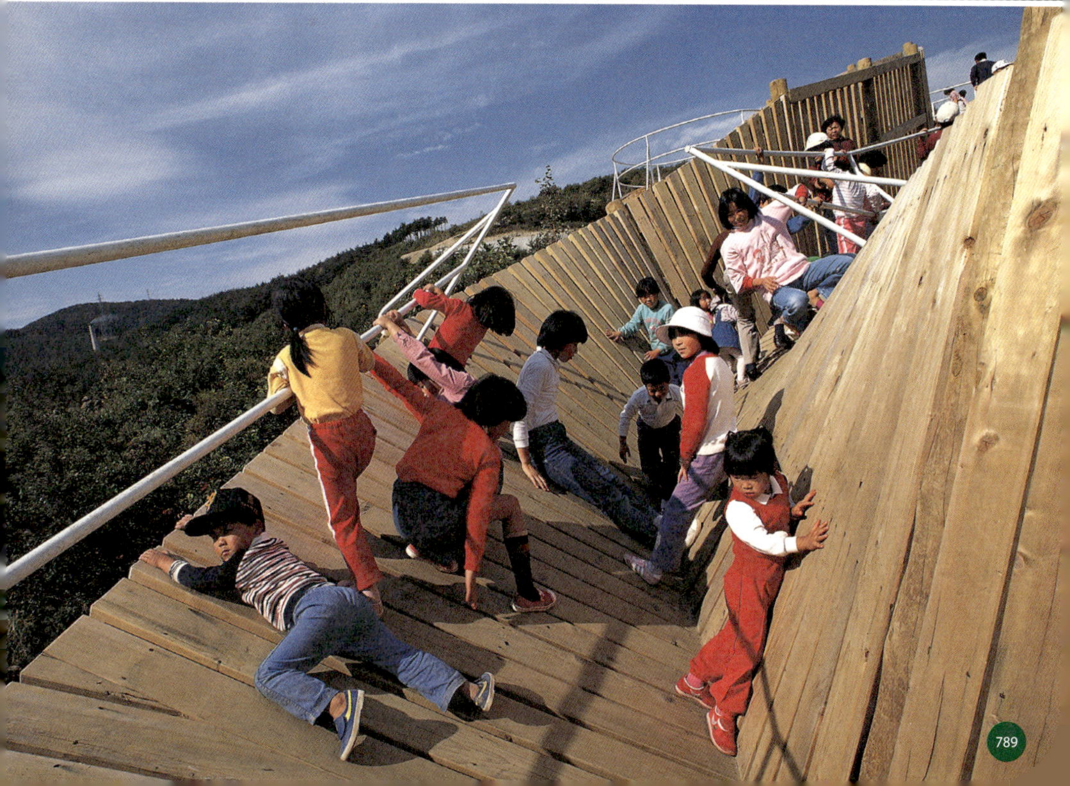

3つの役割

1982

太刀の浦緑地
Tachinoura Port Park

太刀の浦緑地

福岡県北九州市門司区太刀浦海岸／1982
Tachinoura Port Park
Tachinourakaigan, Moji-ku, Kitakyusyu-shi, Fukuoka

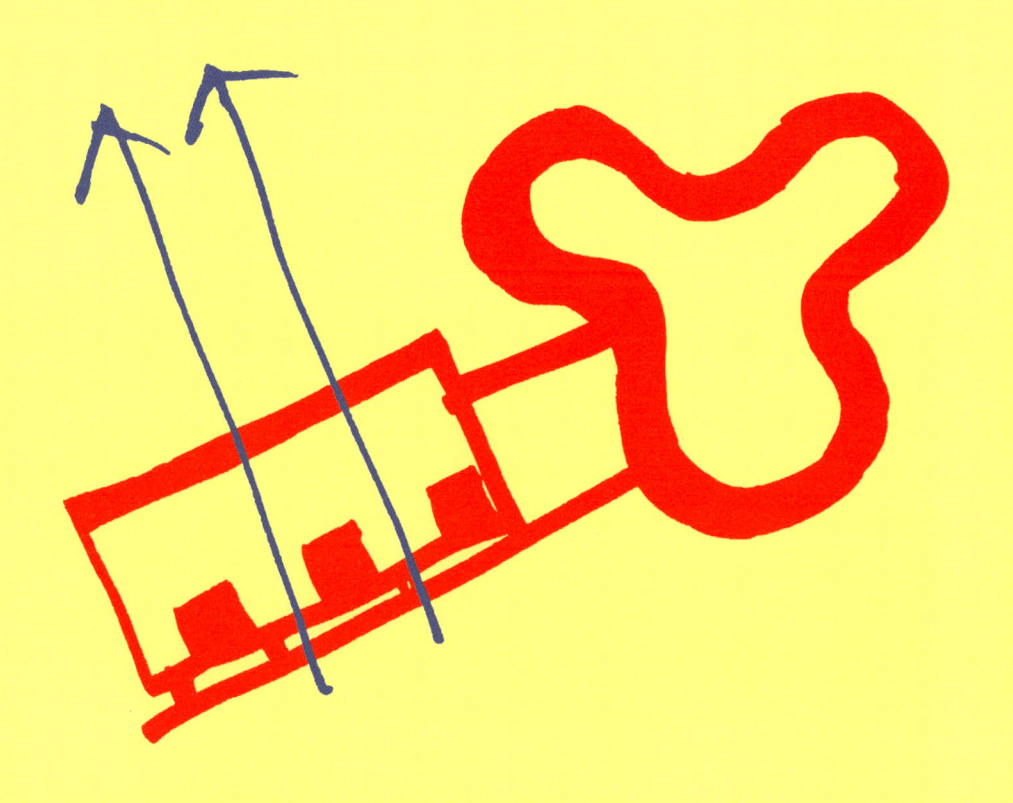

太刀の浦海浜公園は北九州門司地区に建設された港湾緑地である。この港湾緑地に3つの異なる緑地、オープンスペースが計画された。3つの地区はそれぞれ〈シンボル的、修景的スペース〉〈休憩的緑地〉、そして〈建築的・造形的なランドスケープのオープンスペース〉である。床・壁・塔というようにきわめて建築的な造形によって、遊環構造的で活動的なランドスケープをつくりだすことが意図されている。

Tachinoura port Park is a harbor-side greenbelt constructed in the Moji district of Kita-Kyushu. Three different green zones and open spaces were planned for this greenbelt. The first section is a "symbolic and landscaped space," the second a "green zone for rest," and the third an "open, landscaped space with architectural and structural characteristics." The floors, walls, and towers give the facility a very architectural construction, allowing for creating a circular play system and active landscape.

1982

太刀の浦緑地 Tachinoura Port Park

彫刻家・脇田愛二郎の作品
A work by sculptor Aijiro Wakita.

1982

脇田和邸
K. Wakita House

画家の住まい

脇田和邸

東京都世田谷区代田／1982
K. Wakita House
Daita, Setagaya-ku, Tokyo

東京近郊の住宅地に建つ。1階に吹抜けを持つリビング、2階にアトリエ、3階にバルコニーを持つ寝室という構成である。閉鎖的であるが、心落ち着く、年老いた画家の住まいである。

Located in a suburban residential area outside of Tokyo, the first floor has a living room with high ceilings, there is a studio on the second floor, and the third floor contains the balcony. Although a bit tight, this is the relaxing home of an elderly artist.

795

1982

脇田和邸　K. Wakita House

797

1982

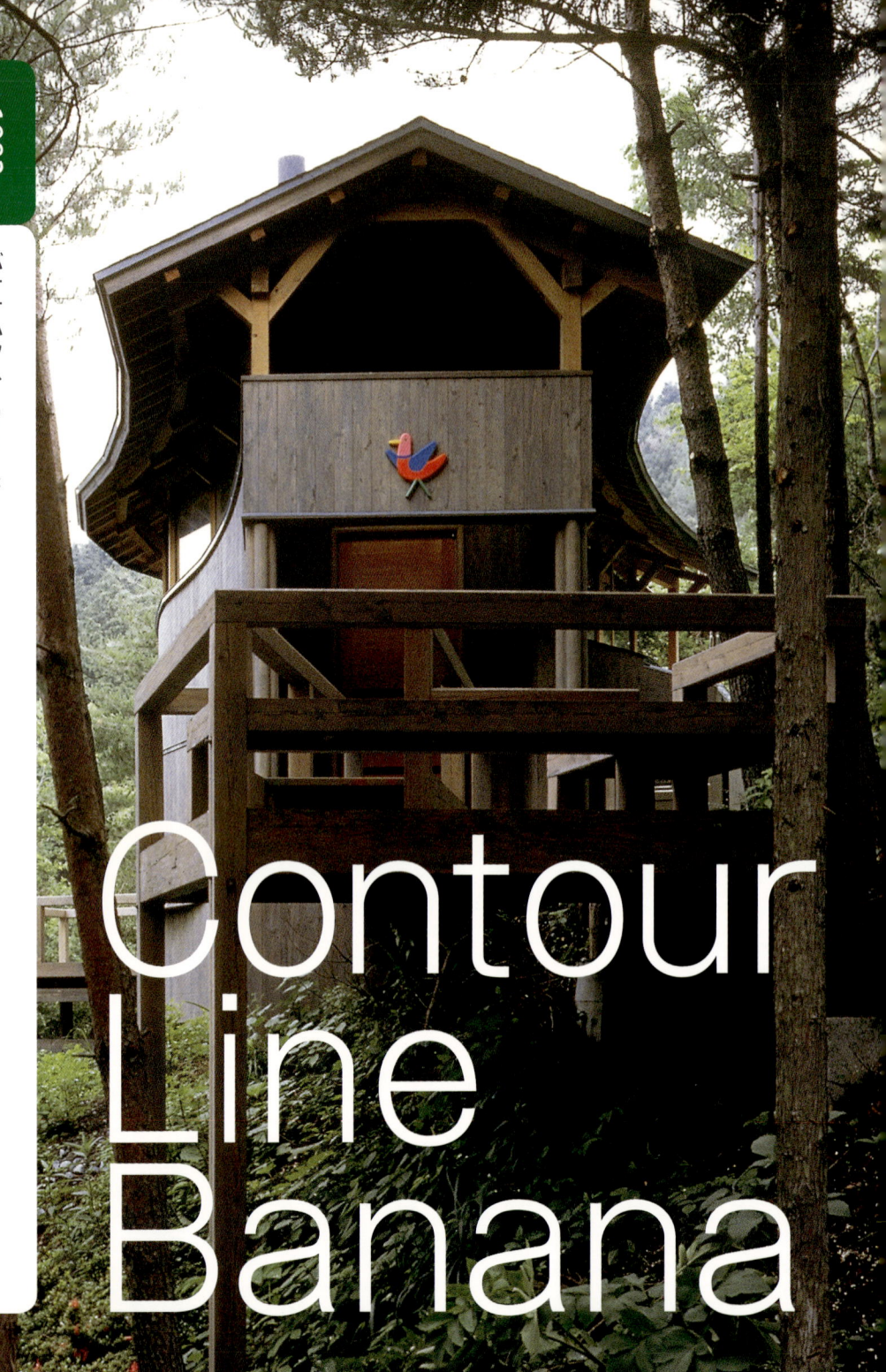

バナナハウス
Banana House

Contour Line Banana

バナナハウス

山梨県南都留郡／1982
Banana House
Minamitsuru-gun, Yamanashi

敷地は南斜面で約30度の斜度をもつ。敷地の等高線をそのままなぞり、平面形はバナナの形になった。居間からは真正面に富士山を望むことができる。

The lot faces south on a 30° slope. The outline of the house resembles a banana, hence the name of the house. Mt. Fuji can be seen directly from the living room.

799

1982

バナナハウス Banana House

801

1982

バナナハウス Banana House

803

1981

壁と丘とトンネル

八日市市城砦公園
Yokaichi Rampart Park

八日市市城砦公園

滋賀県東近江市緑町／1981
Yokaichi Rampart Park
Midori-cho, Higashiomi-shi, Shiga

木の見張り台、円形舞台、ネットの橋、白いコンクリートの滑り台、トンネル、芝生の山。これらが高く湾曲するブロック壁に、あるときは寄り添い、あるときは突き抜けて、遊具的な環境が形成されている。

A high serpentine block wall, along with a wooden viewing tower, circular stage, net bridge, white concrete slide, tunnel, and lawn-none of which are particularly functional as play structures on their own-but the area as a whole has been designed as a high-density playground providing all the necessary functions for active play.

1981

八日市市城砦公園

Yokaichi Rampart Park

807

1981

横浜市保土ヶ谷地区センター
Hodogaya Community Center, Yokohama

通り抜け
と街角

横浜市ほどがや地区センター

神奈川県横浜市保土ヶ谷区／1981
Hodogaya Community Center, Yokohama
Hodogaya-ku, Yokohama-shi, Kanagawa

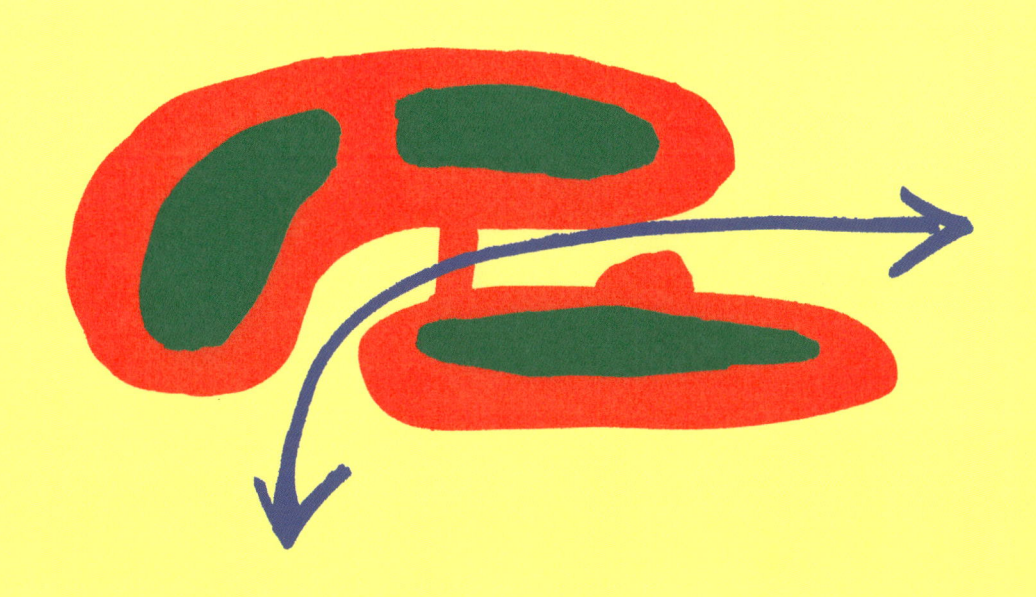

横浜市の住宅街の地域利用施設である。コミュニティセンターという性格上、まず住民に親しみやすい空間として"通り抜け"と"街角"という2つの空間コンセプトが私たちにより提案された。"通り抜け"とは住宅地の中の近道である。目的的な人びとだけでなく、通りすがりの人々にも公園のベンチのように安らぎを与え、また刺激を与えるものと考えられた。"街角"は集まりの空間であって、お祭りの空間である。この地区センターは3方の道路に面し、街の小さな広場としての機能を有している。

This is a community facility located in a residential neighborhood in Yokohama City. Due to the facility's nature as a community center, we received proposals for the two spatial concepts of having a "passing space" and "corners" to create a facility that would make residents feel welcome. The "passing space" is a shortcut located in the center of the residential space. The space offers a sense of peace, much like a park bench, to people passing through and even those just on a stroll. This community center has roads on three sides, functioning as a small common space for the city.

809

1981

横浜市保土ヶ谷地区センター　Hodogaya Community Center, Yokohama

811

白壁と切妻

1981

秋田県営御野庭団地

Akita Prefectural Onoba Housing

秋田県営御野庭団地

秋田県秋田市四ツ小屋／1981
Akita Prefectural Onoba Housing
Yotsugoya, Akita-shi, Akita

100戸の集合住宅である。秋田の伝統的な白壁の切妻町屋の妻入り連続ファサードが引用された。敷地は細長く、長辺方向が南北を向いている。そのため住戸の日照の確保を考え、中庭が設けられた。そこには緩やかな起伏と円環状にこども達のあそび場が設けられている。

This is a housing development with 100 houses. Gables including serial facades of the traditional Akita white wall gabled roof town house were employed. The site was narrow and long, with long side facing north and south, to secure illumination for living, an interior courtyard was created, and inside this space a moderately rolling terrain and a children's play space were fashioned.

1981

秋田県営御野庭団地

Akita Prefectural Onoba Housing

現代計画研究所の藤本昌也との共同作品

A joint work with Masaya Fujimoto
from the Architectural and Planning Office.

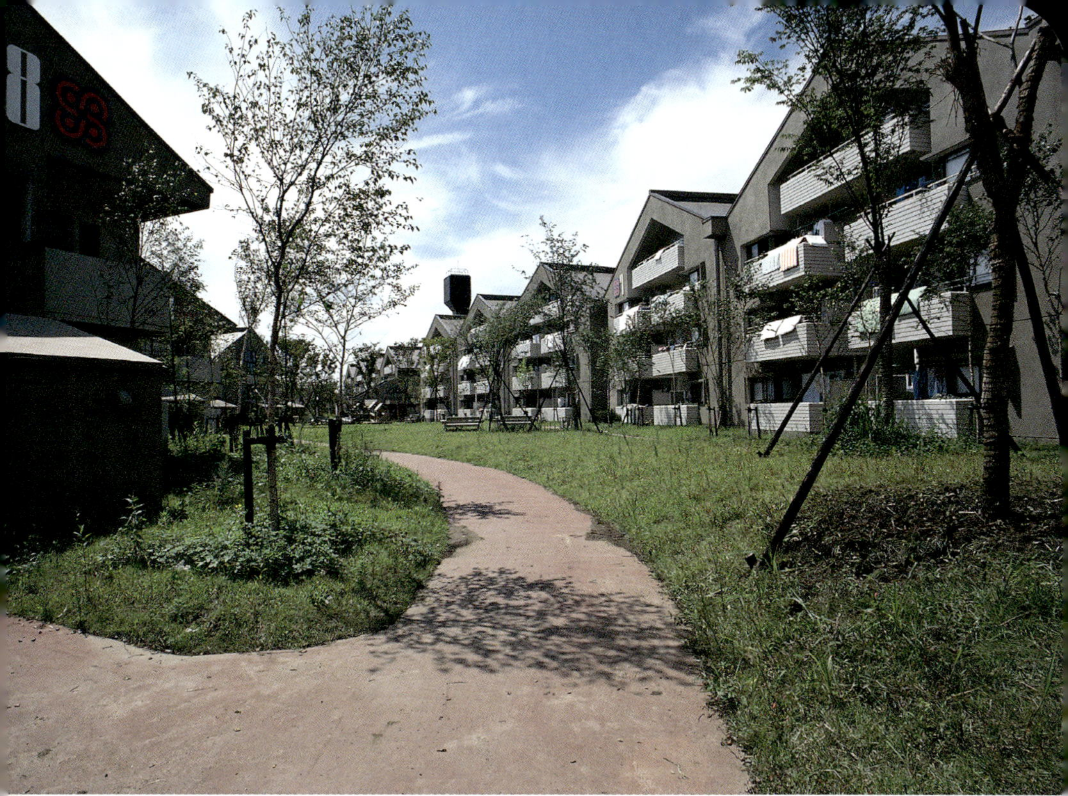

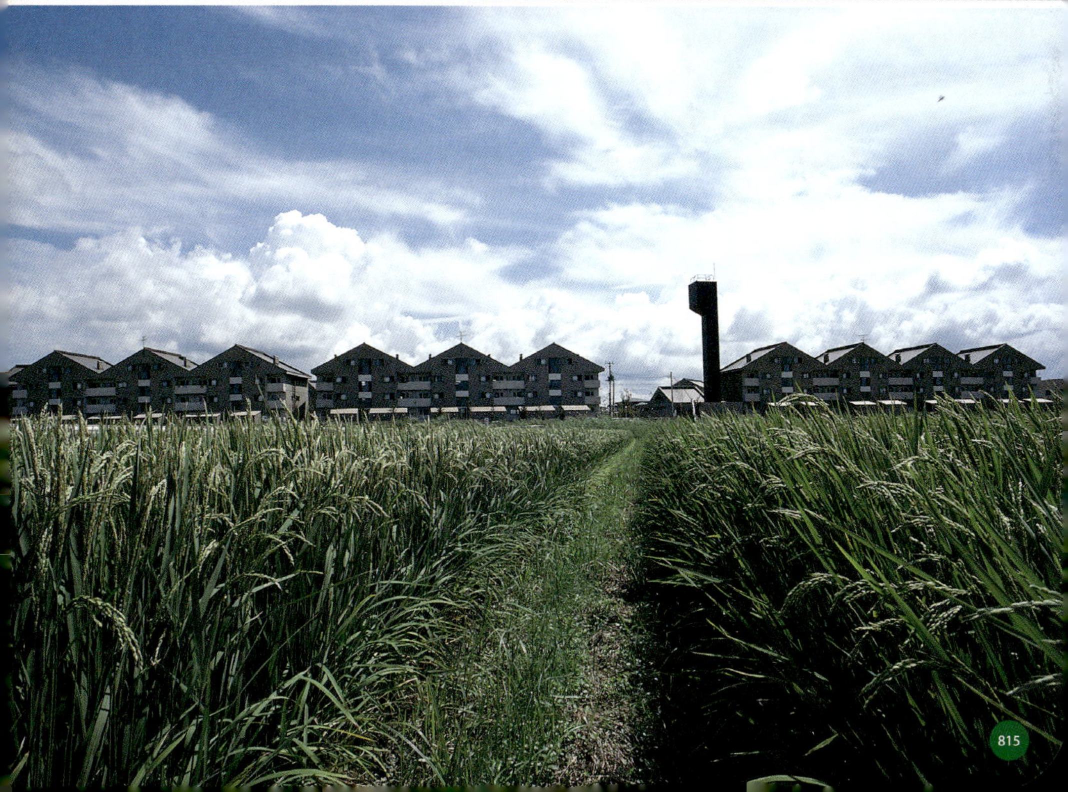

1980

片瀬山の家
Kataseyama House

光・水・森・家

片瀬山の家

神奈川県藤沢市片瀬山／1980
Kataseyama House
Kataseyama, Fujisawa-shi, Kanagawa

湘南の海に近い建築家の家である（自邸）。敷地は約600㎡で、そのうち平地が1/3、残りは斜面である。建物は平地の部分2階建てコンクリート造。屋上は10m×3mのプールと約25㎡のテラスになっており、書斎より木製の階段でつながっている。

This is the architect's own residence. The site is 600㎡, of which one-third are flat, and the rest sloping. The structure is two-story concrete construction on the level part of the site. On the roof is a small (3×10m) pool and 25㎡ terrace, connected to the study by stairs of wood.

1980

片瀬山の家　Kataseyama House

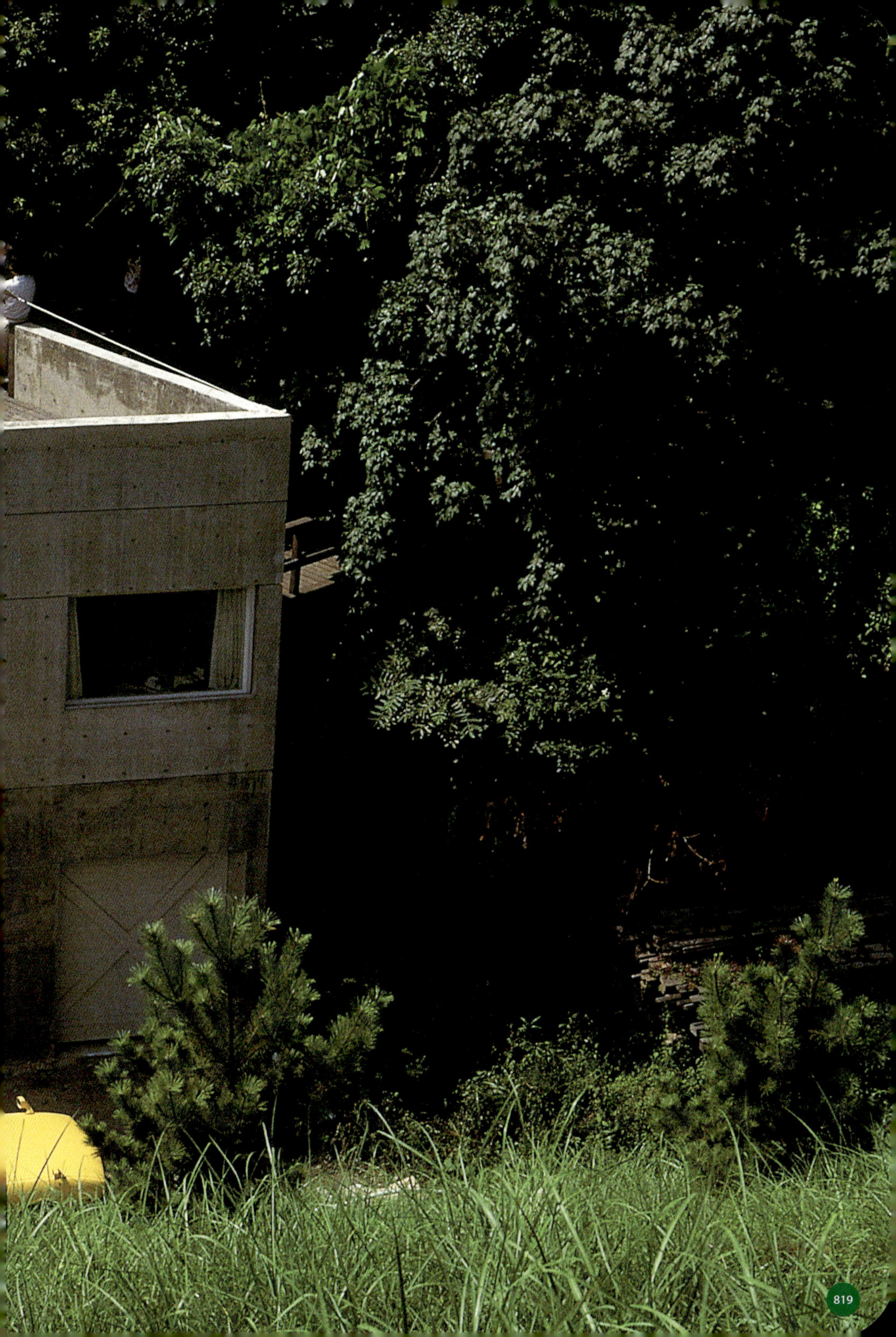

1980

片瀬山の家　Kataseyama House

築25年、緑で隠れる
25 years since its establishment,
and hidden by greenery.

こども 都市建築

1980

秋田県立児童会館・こども博物館

Akita Prefectural Children's Center, Children's Museum

秋田県立児童会館・こども博物館

秋田県秋田市山王中島町／1980
Akita Prefectural Children's Center, Children's Museum
Sannonakajima-cho, Akita-shi, Akita

秋田市の新中心市街につくられた大型児童館。こども劇場、こども博物館等が併設されている。中央にあそび広場が街角のようにつくられ、多くの機能的な空間が分節化され、こどもの都市がイメージされた。

This is a large-scale children's house built in the new city center of Akita City. The facility is set parallel to a children's theater, children's museum, and other attractions. A play area has been constructed in the center like a corner, and a wide range of different areas with different functions are offered to create a city for children.

1980

秋田県立児童会館・こども博物館
Akita Prefectural Children's Center, Children's Museum

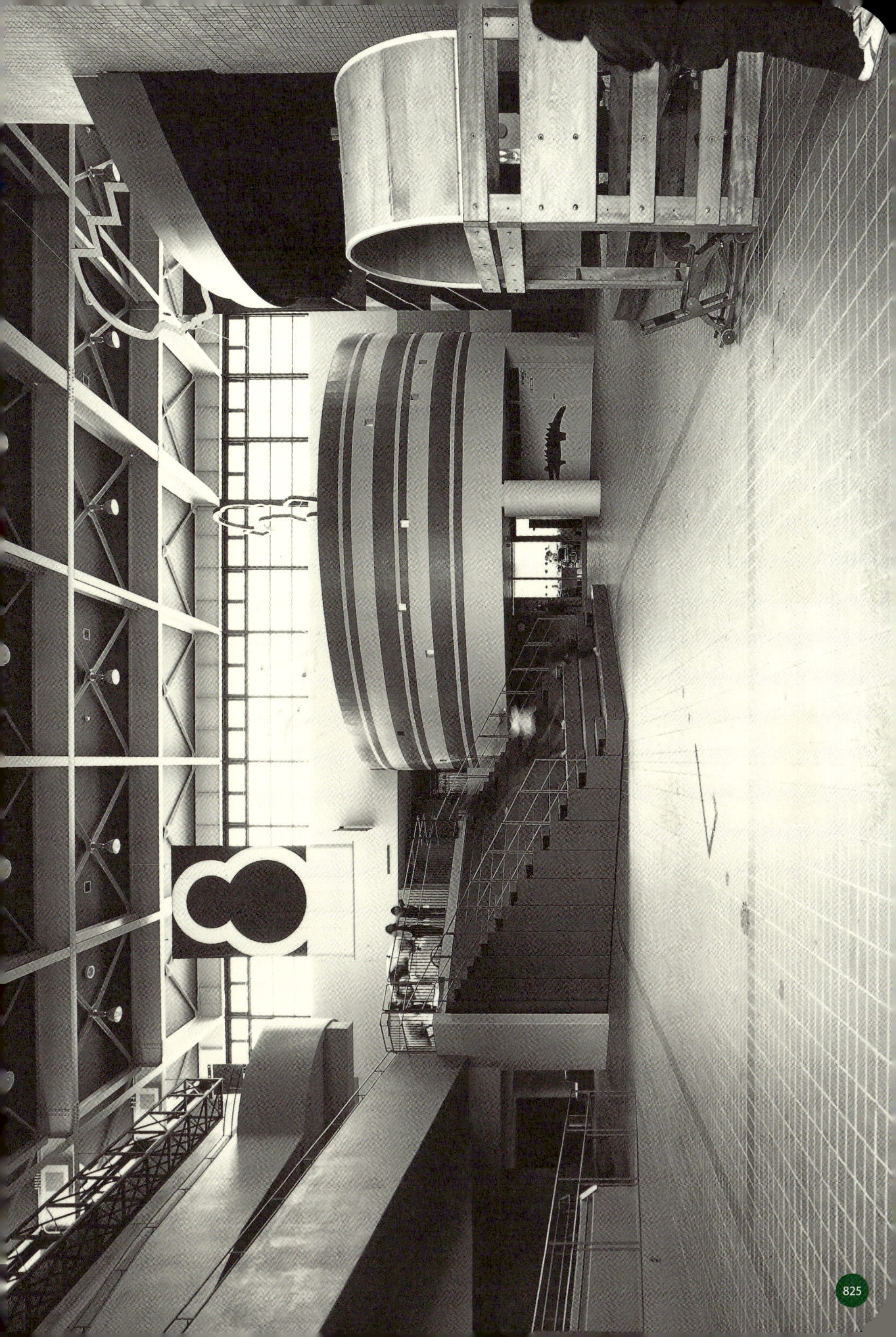

1980

秋田県立児童会館・こども博物館　Akita Prefectural Children's Center, Children's Museum

827

浜松科学館を中心に

藤塚光政×仙田 満

対談

浜松科学館を中心に
About Hamamatsu Science Museum

浜松の地域性が生んだ「やらまいか」気質

仙田 満（以下S） 浜松は実は、科学的な創造力を培った地域なんです。例えば、明治以降、山林がある木曽の岡谷や長野では養蚕が生まれて、そこでできた生糸が天竜川を経て浜松に下ってきて、繊維産業が盛んになり、それが発展して自動織機が生まれました。

藤塚光政（以下F） それがやがて、自動車メーカーとして世界にその名をとどろかせる。

S　そうそう。そして木工技術として、河合楽器やヤマハといった楽器づくりも盛んになり、その後、オートバイのホンダやヤマハ、スズキも生まれました。つまり、浜松には一つの地域としての流れがあり、地形や自然によって生まれるべくして生まれた産業があるのではないでしょうか。それと、もともと「やらまいか」という気質があったんでしょうね。

F　ヤマライカって標準語だと否定みたいに聞こえるけど、方言では「やってみよう」という意味なんだよね。「やらないで何がわかる!?」というスピリッツは、方言のほうがよく伝わる。

S　浜松には、先ほどの本田宗一郎のホンダ、ヤマハ、スズキ、河合等のワールドワイドのメーカーだけでなく、ノーベル賞を受賞した小柴昌俊東大名誉教授のカミオカンデをつくった会社（浜松ホトニクス）もあります。こうした実験精神をもっている人や会社を輩出したり、先進的なものをつくり出す気質が「やらまいか」なのでしょう。

F　最近でも、ホンダが今秋（2010年）、7〜8人乗りビジネス機「ホンダ・ジェット」の量産型認定用機体の初フライトを行うらしいです。普通、飛行機メーカーはエンジンの供給を他社から受けているけど、ホンダはエンジンから開発していると聞きました。まさに本田宗一郎の精神を受け継いでいる。「YARAMAIKA」って名前にしたらいいのに（笑）。

S　「浜松科学館」（1986年）も、こども達に科学を伝えることを「やらまいか」という精神が生んだのでしょう。この施設はもともと児童館が前身なんですよ。

F　ああ、そういう経緯なんだ。その児童館は新幹線が通る前からあったんですか。

S　今の場所より、もっと北の方にありました。昔は浜松駅の貨物ヤードがすごく大きかったんですが、新幹線を通すことで縮小し、再開発用地が確保できたので、そこに児童館を移転した。それで名前を決める時に、中学生から「僕らはこどもじゃない！」という声があがった。だから、名称に「こども」という言葉は入れずに「浜松科学館」にしたわけです。

F　「おれたちはガキじゃない」と主張するなんて、心身ともに急成長中の中学生らしいね。

S　そういう「やらまいか」精神を踏まえて、浜松科学館は僕が42,3歳の頃につくったもので、ある種、今までの自分の考え、理論とデザインをまとめたものなんです。

F　いわば、「SENDA・MANの集大成」？

S　ちょうどその頃、これまでこどものあそびを研究してきたことを博士論文にまとめたのを機に、その遊環構造理論を応用して設計

藤塚光政（ふじつか みつまさ）
1939年東京都生まれ。写真家。1961年東京写真短期大学卒業、月刊「インテリア」入社。1965年フリーになる。1987年日本インテリアデザイナー協会賞。主な著書に、『意地の都市住宅①、②』文・中原 洋。『粟津字博作品集』デザイン・田中一光。『現代の職人』文・石山修武。『建築リフル全10巻』文・隈 研吾、デザイン・秋田 寛。『PLAY STRUCTURE』文・仙田 満。

した最初の作品が浜松科学館なんです。そして「やらまいか精神を伝える」ことをコンセプトに、それまでの世界の科学博物館とは違った「新しい科学館」をつくったつもりです。

F　あそこでは、時代や科学の進歩によって展示を更新するんですか。むろん、基礎科学的な展示は別だけど。

S　そう。展示の内容は、だいたい10年ごとに変えているんですよ。

F　でも、コンピュータ関係なんか、日進月歩どころか分進日歩で、激変しているのもあるじゃない。更新していくのも大変だね。

S　お金がかかることですからね。しかし、先ほどお話ししたように、僕は浜松科学館をこれまでの集大成のつもりでつくりましたから、建築だけでなく、展示のあり方も見直したんです。科学彫刻を導入した広場も。

F　科学と環境とアートは近いものだから。

S　広場の設計は脇田愛二郎*¹さんにも手伝ってもらっていたんです。浜松科学館をつくるにあたり、海外の科学館や、国内の科学館を視察して、こども達に科学をどう伝えるかということをさまざまな角度から考えてきて、楽しい、面白い、きれいだというところから科学に興味をもってもらってもいいんじゃないのか、と。広場にアートを採り入れたのも、そうした考え方からでしたね。

こどもがあそびながら学ぶための空間の構造

F　仙田さんが提案してきた「遊環構造」には、7つの条件がありますよね。

S　そうです。「回遊性」とか。

F　「ショートサーキット遊具」とか、「シンボル性」とか。

S　そういう「遊環構造」は、それ以前につくっていたんです。先ほど話した通り、ここで初めて意識的に遊環構造理論を応用しようとしたんです。その考え方を建築やデザインに採り入れ、図式化して展示したり、壁から展示物を離したりするような見せ方をしました。

F　ここでは、建築の骨格や筋肉や内臓にあたる設備も科学として見せていますよね。水道の給排水や、水と湯を色分けしたり。

S　建物も一つの科学的展示物なんだ、というコンセプトでつくっているんですよ。これは1970年代に、倉俣史朗*²さんと仕事を一緒にやってきたことや、大阪万博*³の三井グループ館パビリオンでの経験が生かされているんです。今考えてみると、あのパビリオンの、ドラムが真ん中にあるような構成や展示のしかたは浜松科学館と似ている気がします。

F　仙田さんは昔から、建築家にしては珍しいくらい、いろんな人と積極的にコラボレーションしてましたよね。懐かしいな、三井グ

Conversation

藤塚光政 × 仙田 満

Mitsumasa Fujitsuka × Mitsuru Senda

対談

浜松科学館を中心に　About Hamamatsu Science Museum

ループ館の模型は僕も当時、撮影していたから。そういえば、浜松では、柱やコンクリートの一部分を素のまま見せてますね。エレベーターの仕組みを見せたり、自動販売機もスケスケだし。

S　設備機械室を透明にしたりね。最近、僕は遊環構造を「こどもがあそびやすい空間の構造であり、意欲を喚起する構造である」といっています。あそびたい、運動したいというような意欲を喚起するには、空間の構造が大切だと思うんですね。「あそぶ」、「運動する」、そして「学習する」ということは、つまり「考える」ということじゃないか、と。

F　じっと座っているよりも散歩しながら考えた方が、いい考えが浮かぶとは、古来いわれていることだよね。心も身体も頭脳もリンクしているから。

S　運動しながら学ぶ、あるいは、あそびながら学ぶ、とか。例えば、階段は大人の施設では「余分なもの」と見られがちですが、こどもの施設では多ければ多いほどいい。僕自身、こどもの施設を手がけることで、新しいアイデアが浮かぶことがよくある。

F　仙田さんは理論的に感じているんだろうけど、いつも僕は撮影しながら体で感じていますよ。根がこどもだから（笑）。

これまでの博物館と未来の博物館

S　浜松科学館は、最初の計画から完成まで、6年くらいかかっているんです。

F　土木や超高層並みだね。

S　そう。実は科学館というものをやりたいと思って、「秋田県立児童会館」（1980年）の中に「こども博物館」という小さな展示室を文部省の補助金でつくったのが最初です。それで博物館というものに興味が出てきた。

F　僕は何年かに一度、国立科学博物館に行くけど、行くたびに発見があって、やっぱり博物館は面白いよね。仙田さんが手がけた科学館といえば、ほかにもいろいろあるじゃないですか。

S　横浜こども科学館の基本設計は僕が担当しました。そこで実現しきれなかったアイデアや「建築も科学的展示物でなくてはならない」というコンセプトは、浜松科学館で生かされています。

F　浜松科学館のあとに、「富山県こどもみらい館」（1992年）、「愛知県児童総合センター」（1996年）ができたんですよね。やはり原理はつながっているなあ。

S　そうです。浜松科学館をつくる時に、理論とデザインのつながりのようなものをいろいろ考えたし、それが愛知県児童総合センターをつくる時の原点になっていると思うんです。

F　つくづく、こどものための空間づくりのエキスパート、「仙田小児科」ですね。看板変えたら？

S　あ・・ははは。

F　こども向けとはいえ、チューブやネットを用いた、今までに見たこともないような構造を、現実の建築で実現するのがすごい。

S　「こどもの施設だから」と言い訳しつつ、普通ならできないことをやってしまう（笑）。例えば、筑波科学万国博覧会「こども広場」（1985年）では、広さ3ヘクタールの広場に、太さ2.7m、長さ360mのチューブを回したりね。

F　あれは、明るい「恐竜の体内巡り」みた

いでしたね（笑）。ところで、科学館といえば、サンフランシスコのエクスプロラトリアム*4には、非常に敬意を感じますね。

S　アメリカでは1960年代後半から70年代にかけ、体験型の科学館が次々にできて、それが世界に影響を与えました。その後、70年代から80年代にかけて、アメリカ各地のミュージアムが体験型の展示を行うようになっていく。ヨーロッパの博物館に行くと、よく機関車など、産業革命時代の本物がありますよね。だけど、そういうものがない新大陸のアメリカでは、体験しながら科学を学ぶ展示や、盛んな映画産業と結びついた見せ方をするようになった。つまり、展示にエンターテインメント性や楽しさを求めたと思うんです。

F　そういうことやらすと、アメリカ人はうまいからね。

S　体験する展示ということ自体、ハリウッド的だし、ある意味、ディズニーランドと通じるところがありますよね。

F　実物を見せたり、エンターテインメント性を付加した博物館もいいけど、こどもの頃初めて見たプラネタリウムも、ロマンチックでわくわくしたなあ。戦前は大阪と東京にしかなくて、東京のものは戦災で消失してしまって、僕が都電に乗って見に行ったのは、戦後、渋谷の東急文化会館にできた五島プラネタリウム*5です。鉄アレイみたいに球体が2個付いていて、メカ的でよかった。

S　それはまだ水平のプラネタリウムですよね。カナダのメーカーがつくった「アイマックス」という傾斜型のプラネタリウムは、僕が横浜こども科学館で最初に導入して、浜松科学館に日本で2番目に入れたんですよ。日本でアイマックスが入った傾斜型のプラネタリウムが盛んにつくられたのは、80年代のことだと思います。

F　浜松科学館は新幹線が近いから、工事も大変だったでしょう。

S　振動と音の問題については、神経をつかいました。横浜こども科学館も浜松科学館もまだ若い頃につくったもので、ある意味で僕の原点ですね。こうして振り返ってみると、僕にとってはまさに85年からの10年間が、科学館や博物館の仕事が多い時代でした。

F　あとは何をつくりたい？新広島市民球場もやったし。あれこそ、エンターテインメント球場で、SENDA・MANしかできない建築だね。野球観戦はともかく、夜、球場で仲間とビールを飲むのが好きという人がいたよ（笑）。

S　今後はスポーツ施設がテーマですね。国内外で積極的に挑戦しています。博物館や文化会館という建築物は、戦後復興の中でつくられたものですから、もう少しあとに順番が回ってくることになるのでしょう。

F　飛行機好きの僕としては、ぜひ航空博物館をつくってほしいけどね。戦争で負け、大事な機体が壊滅してしまったのが残念。わが国の航空機の歴史を失っている気がするんですよ。

S　これからの時代、多様なミュージアムの展開が必要だと思っています。少子高齢の時代だから、地域にあるこぢんまりとした博物館を訪ね歩く楽しみも見直されていくでしょうし。こうして考えてみると、博物館というものはまだまだ奥が深い分野ですね。

*1　**脇田愛二郎**（わきた あいじろう）1942～2006　彫刻家、造形作家、父は洋画家の脇田和
*2　**倉俣史朗**（くらまた しろう）1934～1991　インテリアデザイナー
*3　**大阪万博**（EXPO'70）／三井グループ館（1970）チーフ・プロデューサー：山口勝弘、建築設計：東 孝光
*4　**エクスプロラトリアム**（The Exploratorium）／1969年、アメリカ・サンフランシスコにオープンした、こどもから大人まで楽しめる、参加・体験型科学博物館。物理学者で教育者でもあったフランク・オッペンハイマー（1912～1985）の発案と尽力でつくられ、彼が亡くなるまで館長を務めた。こどもから大人まで楽しめる、参加・体験型科学博物館
*5　**五島プラネタリウム**／正式名称は「天文博物館五島プラネタリウム」。1957年、渋谷駅前の東急文化会館8階に開館、2001年に閉館

Conversation

藤塚光政 × 仙田 満
Mitsumasa Fujitsuka × Mitsuru Senda

About Hamamatsu Science Museum
Mitsumasa Fujitsuka × Mitsuru Senda

Hamamatsu has fostered the "Yaramaika" (go the distance) spirit.

Mitsuru Senda (S): Hamamatsu was originally the area with scientific creativity. For example, Okaya and Nagano in the mountainous Kiso area started silkworm breeding, bringing produced raw silk to Hamamatsu through the Tenryu River, making the textile industry booming, and creating automatic looms through industrial developments.

Mitsumasa Fujitsuka (F): That has in turn created TOYOTA that has its name well known everywhere in the world.

S: That's right. The wood craft technology led to the flourish of musical instrument manufacturing by such companies as KAWAI and YAMAHA. After that, Honda, YAMAHA, and SUZUKI created their business as motorcycle manufacturers. What I want to say is that Hamamatsu has its history unique to the area and that the land features and nature have created certain industries fitted to this area. And we originally had the *"Yaramaika"* spirit.

F: *Yaramaika* sounds a negative expression in the Tokyo accent but it means "do everything you can" in the dialect. This dialect expression more clearly captures the essence showing nothing can be achieved without trying.

S: Hamamatsu has come up with global-level manufacturers including Honda, YAMAHA, SUZUKI, and KAWAI as well as the company (Hamamatsu Photonics) that has manufactured *Kamiokande* by Masatoshi Koshiba, a Nobel laureate and Professor Emeritus of the University of Tokyo. I believe that *Yaramaika* is the spirit that has created this sort of people or companies motivated to try new things and enabling advanced technologies.

F: More recently, Honda is planning this fall (in 2010) to give the first flight of Honda Jet, a business jet accommodating seven or eight passengers to test the aircraft to be certified for mass production. Usually aircraft manufacturers obtain engines from other companies, but Honda seems to have developed engines on their own. This is the example of the spirit fostered by Soichiro Honda. Honda should name it *"Yaramaika"* (laughter).

S: I suppose that the Hamamatsu Science Museum (1986) has been created by the *"Yaramaika"* spirit that tries to disseminate scientific information to children. This facility used to be a children's center.

F: That explains the history of the museum. Did the children's center exist before the bullet train services started?

S: It used to be located further to the north of the current location. We used to have a very large cargo yard at Hamamatsu Station, but the yard was downsized to make bullet trains pass and the land for redevelopment was made available. So, a project was started to transfer a children's center there. As we tried to name the museum, middle school students claimed that they were not kids. So we did not use the term "children" in the name and came up with "the Hamamatsu Science Museum."

F: It was very like middle school students going through a rapid change in body and mind by claiming that there were not kids.

S: Based on this *"Yaramaika"* spirit, I created the Hamamatsu Science Museum when I was

42 or 43 years old, so in a sense I created it based on the integration of my ideas, theories, and designs I had developed so far.

F: So this is the culmination of "SENDA MAN"?

S: Around that time, I had compiled what I researched on how children play in my doctoral thesis and tried to implement my circular play system theory. The first work I came up with based on this motivation was the Hamamatsu Science Museum. I targeted to create a new science museum very different from conventional science museums in the world based on the concept of disseminating the *Yaramaika* spirit.

F: How do they update exhibitions in line with the advancement of time and science? Of course, exhibitions on basic research are different matters, though.

S: Right. They are updating exhibitions around every 10 years.

F: However, things like computers are being developed every minute or second instead of in days or months. It should be tough to keep exhibitions updated.

S: Updates cost money. However, I reworked how we presented exhibitions in addition to architecture since I tried to create the Hamamatsu Science Museum as the culmination of my career as I said a while ago. I also created a square where we installed science-related sculpture.

F: Science, environment, and art are closely linked to each other.

S: I asked Mr. Aijiro Wakita[*1] to help me with the design of the square. As we tried to create the Hamamatsu Science Museum, we visited various science museums in Japan and abroad, thinking about how we should disseminate science to children from various perspectives and coming up with the idea that fun, interesting, and beautiful features could be good ways to make children interested in science. It was based on this idea that we put in place art at the square.

The structure of space where children play and learn

F: Circular Play System, the concept you have advocated, has seven conditions.

S: Yes. One condition is "migratory movements."

F: I can also name "short-circuit play structure equipment" and "symbolism."

S: I had already established Circular Play System before those days. As I told you a while ago, I specifically tried to apply my theory of circular play system on the architecture for the first time. So I tried to show it by incorporating the idea into the architecture and design, exhibiting the illustrations showing the design, and displaying objects apart from walls.

F: At this museum, you show scientific features of various facilities of the building that correspond to the bones, muscles, and intestines for the human body. For example, you color-code water supply and drainage or water and hot water.

S: My concept is creating the architecture as a piece of scientific object. This is based on what I worked on with Mr. Shiro Kuramata[*2] in the 1970s and my experiences of the Mitsui Group Pavilion of the Expo '70 in Osaka[*3]. Looking back, the way we structured and exhibited the pavilion with a drum-shaped object located in the center is somewhat similar to the way we created the Hamamatsu Science Museum.

F: You have been aggressively collaborating with various people for a long time unlike usual architects. Your story brings me back my fond memories. At that time, I took photos of the model for the Mitsui Group Pavilion. By the way, you show a part of columns and concrete structures as they are at Hamamatsu. You show how elevators function and provide transparent vending machines.

S: We also made the facility control room transparent. Recently I have been claiming

藤塚光政 × 仙田 満

Mitsumasa Fujitsuka × Mitsuru Senda

that *Circular Play System* is the structure where children can comfortably play and are motivated to do something. Motivating children to play or exercise requires the appropriate spatial structure. After all, playing, exercising, and learning all lead to thinking.

F: We have the conventional wisdom that you can hit good ideas while walking and thinking rather than while sitting still. Our mind, body, and brain are fully linked.

S: Your can learn while exercising or you can learn while playing. For example, staircases tend to be considered as something superfluous in adult facilities but we are allowed to place as many staircases as possible for children's facilities. In my case, working on children's facilities often gives me new ideas.

F: You probably feel this quality through your theory but I always feel it as I take photos. I am a child at heart (laughter).

Traditional museums and future museums

S: It took about six years to work on the Hamamatsu Science Museum from the initial planning to the completion.

F: It took as long as a civil engineering project or a super-high-rise building.

S: That's right. I wanted to create a science museum and my first project was a very small exhibition room named Children's Museum located within Akita Prefectural Children's Center (1980) made possible by the subsidy from the Ministry of Education. That experience made me more interested in museums in general.

F: I go to the National Museum of Nature and Science every few years. Every time I visit it, I come up with new discoveries. Museums are very interesting places. You have also worked on many other science museums.

S: I did the basic design for Yokohama Science Center (1984). I incorporated the ideas I could not accomplish with this project and the concept of displaying architecture as a scientific object into the Hamamatsu Science Museum.

F: The project of the Hamamatsu Science Museum led to Toyama Children's Center (1992) and Aichi Children's Center (1996). Your theory has been connected through these projects.

S: That's right. When I worked on the Hamamatsu Science Museum, I thought about ways to connect my theory and design. The experience created the basis for the project of Aichi Children's Center.

F: You are really an expert on the creation of children's space. You are such a good pediatrician. Why don't you switch jobs?

S: Hahaha.

F: The facility is targeted for children, but it is so great that you have created the structure with tubes and nets we have never seen as the real architecture.

S: I always use my excuse saying this is the facility for children and do something I usually cannot do (laughter). When I worked on the Children's Square for the Tsukuba Expo (1985), I used 2.7-meter thick, 360-meter long tubes and wrapped them around the 3-hectare square.

F: I felt like walking around inside a dinosaur fully lit (laughter). By the way, as we think about science museums, I deeply respect the Exploratorium[*4] in San Francisco.

S: The United States created participatory science museums one after another from the late 1960s to the 1970s, influencing the whole world. This trend was followed by museums across the U.S. presenting participatory exhibitions from the 1970s to the 1980s. As we go to museums in Europe, we often find real objects used during the Industrial Revolution including locomotive engines. However, the U.S. did not have such objects as the new continent, and so museums started to present participatory science exhibitions and exhibitions related to the booming movie industry.

In sum, the U.S. tried to seek for entertainment and fun in exhibitions.

F: Americans are very good at implementing something like that.

S: Participatory exhibitions are very much like Hollywood and in a sense have certain qualities linked to Disneyland.

F: Museums showing genuine objects and providing entertainment are great, but I was so excited about the planetarium that I visited for the first time as a child since it was so romantic. Planetariums were only located in Osaka and Tokyo before the war, and the one in Tokyo was burnt down during the war. So the planetarium that I went to by taking a tram after the war was Goto Planetarium[*5] established in Shibuya Tokyu Bunka Kaikan. It was so mechanical with two globes attached like an iron dumbbell.

S: What you mean is a flat planetarium. A Canadian manufacturer created a planetarium with a slanted dome named IMAX. I used it for the first time for Yokohama Science Center (1984) and for the second time for the Hamamatsu Science Museum (1986). I think it was in the 1980s that many IMAX planetariums with slanted domes were created in large numbers in Japan.

F: The Hamamatsu Science Museum is so close to bullet trains, so the construction must have been quite tough.

S: I was careful about the issues on vibrations and noises. Since I created Yokohama Science Center and the Hamamatsu Science Museum while I was still young, I can call these as the basis of my career. As I look back, I was involved in many projects related to science museums and museums during the 10 years from 1985.

F: What do you want to work on further going forward? You have done Hiroshima Municipal Baseball Stadium. That is exactly the ballpark offering entertainment and is only made possible by SENDA MAN. I know some people who want to drink beer with friends at the ballpark at night aside from watching a baseball game (laughter).

S: My future challenge is sport facilities. I am aggressively trying to work on them in Japan and abroad. Since such architectures as museums and cultural facilities were created during the recovery period after the war, it will take some more time before I can work on them.

F: Since I love airplanes, I definitely want you to create an airplane museum. It is such a pity that we lost valuable aircraft as we lost the war. It is a great loss for the history of Japanese airplanes.

S: I believe we need to implement museums in versatile ways in the coming era. With the increasingly aging population with less childbirth, we will begin to rediscover the joy of visiting small but cozy museums in local areas one by one. As we take a look at the situations we are in, museums still present very significant challenges to us.

٭1 Aijiro Wakita (1942-2006)**:** Sculptor and craft artist. His father is Kazu Wakita, oil painter.

٭2 Shiro Kuramata (1934-1991)**:** Interior designer.

٭3 The Mitsui Group Pavilion of the Expo' 70 in Osaka (1970)**:** Katsuhiro Yamaguchi (chief producer) and Takamitsu Azuma (architectural design).

٭4 The Exploratorium: A participatory science museum offering various experiences for children and adults, opened in San Francisco, the U.S.A. in 1969. Frank Oppenheimer (1912-1985), physicist and educator, created the museum based on his ideas and dedication and worked as the director of the museum until his death.

٭5 Goto Planetarium: The Gotoh Planetarium and Astronomical Museum. It was opened on the eighth floor of Shibuya Tokyu Bunka Kaikan close to Shibuya Station in 1957 and closed in 2001.

Mitsumasa Fujitsuka

A photographer, born in Tokyo in 1939. Graduated from the Tokyo Junior College of Photography in 1961 and joined monthly magazine "Interior." Became a freelance photographer in 1965. Received the Japan Interior Designers' Association Award in 1987. Publications include "Urban Housing with Presence (1), (2)," written by Hiroshi Nakahara; "Art Collection from Awazu," design by Ikko Tanaka; "Modern Craftsmen," written by Osamu Ishiyama; "Architecture Riffle" (Vols. 1-10), written by Kengo Kuma, design by Kan Akita; "PLAY STRUCTURE," written by Mitsuru Senda.

Conversation

藤塚光政 × 仙田 満

Mitsumasa Fujitsuka × Mitsuru Senda

1989.10
白金台ガーデンハウス

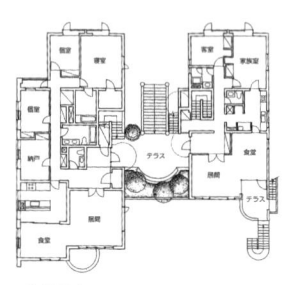

アクソメトリック図

2階 平面図

1階 平面図

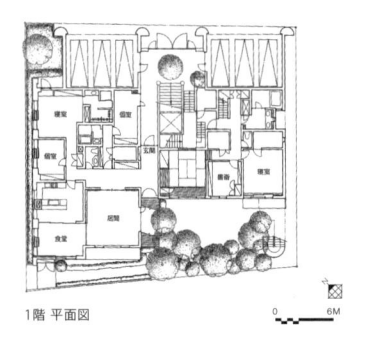

所在地：東京都港区白金台
主用途：集合住宅
構造設計：構造計画研究所
設備設計：愛住設計
施工：竹中工務店
構造：RC造
規模：地下1階地上4階
敷地：699㎡　延床：1,221㎡

Shiroganedai Garden House
Shirokanedai, Minato-ku, Tokyo

1989.04
軽井沢C山荘

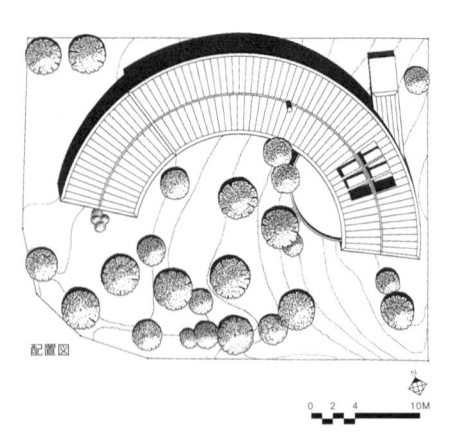

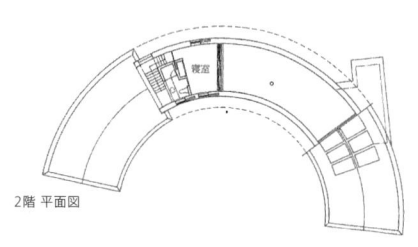

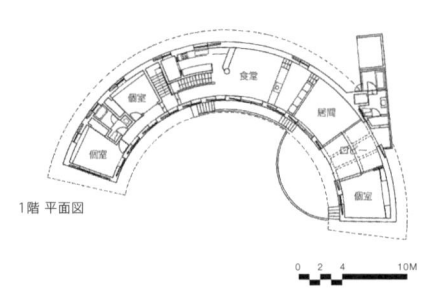

配置図

2階 平面図

1階 平面図

所在地：長野県北佐久郡軽井沢町
主用途：別荘
設備設計：知久設備計画研究所
施工：丸山工務店
構造：W造一部RC造
規模：地下1階地上2階
敷地：988㎡　建築：197㎡　延床：240㎡

Mountain Villa "C", Karuizawa
Karuizawa-machi, Kitasaku-gun, Nagano

1988.09
伊勢原市立図書館・こども科学館

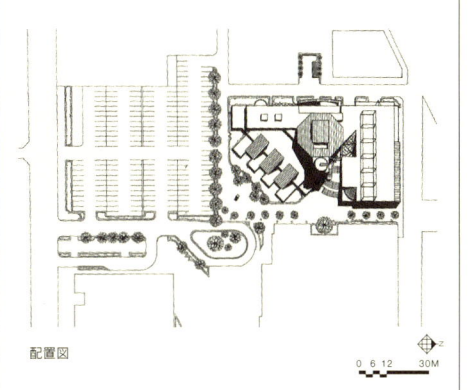

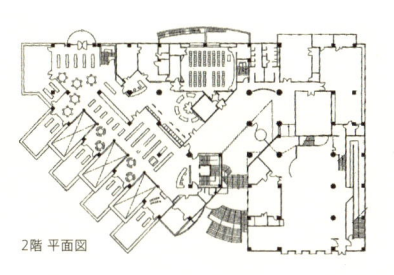

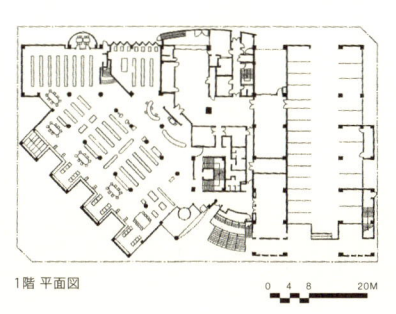

配置図

2階 平面図

1階 平面図

所在地：神奈川県伊勢原市田中
主用途：図書館、児童科学館
建築主：伊勢原市
構造設計：構造計画研究所
設備設計：共信設備設計
施工：フジタ工業・東海建設JV
構造：RC造一部SRC造
規模：地下2階地上4階
敷地：4,512㎡　建築：2,921㎡　延床：8,036㎡

Isehara Library and Science Museum
Tanaka, Isehara-shi, Kanagawa

1989.05
渋谷区散策路整備計画
［美術館ルート］

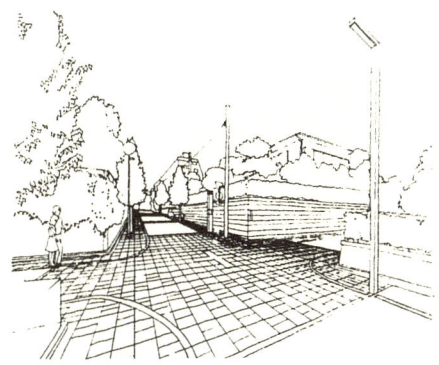

イメージパース図

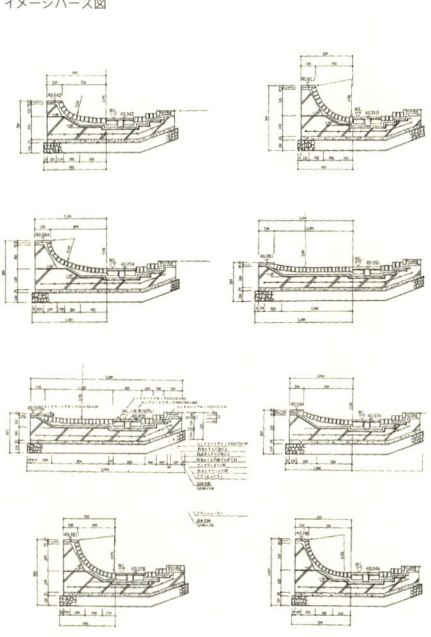

断面詳細図

所在地：東京都渋谷区松濤
主用途：散策路
建築主：渋谷区
共同設計：脇田愛二郎＋スタジオA
規模：全長約2.5km

Shibuya Promenade Design "Route to shoto Museum"
Shoto, Shibuya-ku, Tokyo

837

1989.05
渋谷区散策路整備計画
[旧玉川上水ルート]

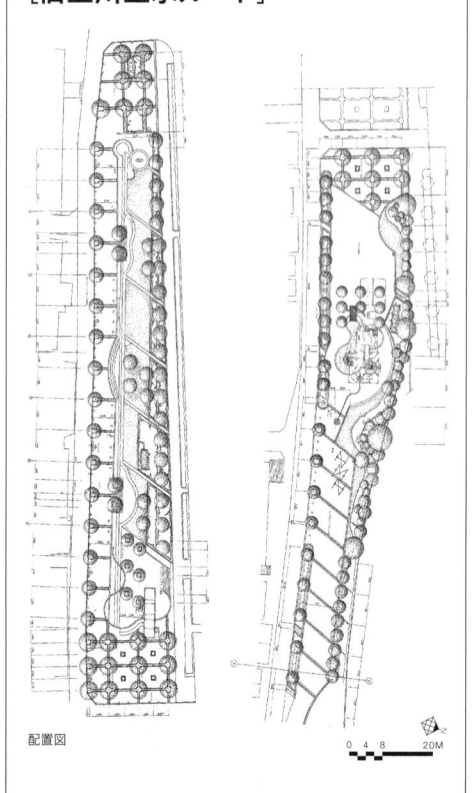

配置図

所在地：東京都渋谷区初台
主用途：散策路
建築主：渋谷区
共同設計：脇田愛二郎＋スタジオA
規模：全長3.7km

Shibuya Promenade Design "Hatsudai District"
Hatsudai, Shibuya-ku, Tokyo

1987.03
1万Mプロムナード
三笠アプローチ

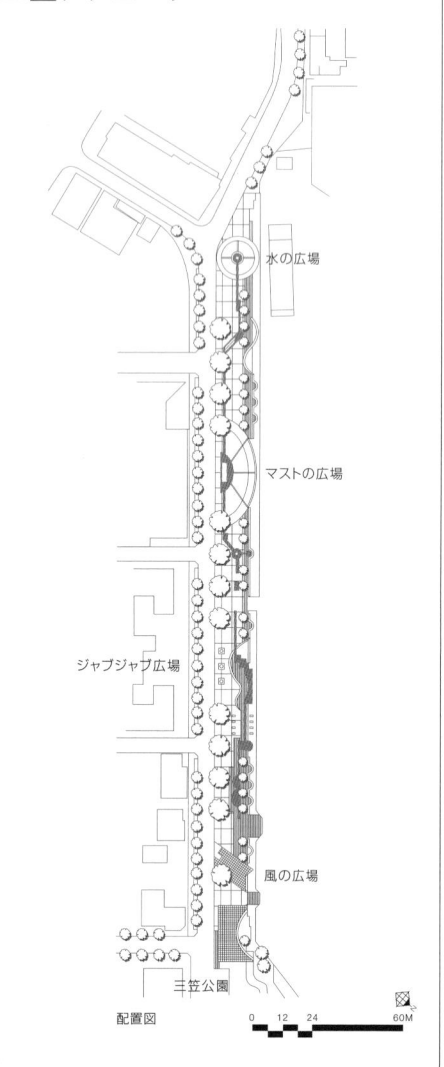

水の広場
マストの広場
ジャブジャブ広場
風の広場
三笠公園

配置図

所在地：神奈川県横須賀市小川町
主用途：散策路
建築主：横須賀市
施工：東急建設、前田道路
規模：全長約480m
敷地：10,000㎡

Mikasa Park Approach Road in the ten thousand Meter Promenade
Ogawa-cho, Yokosuka-shi, Kanagawa

1987
名古屋市宝くじモデル児童遊園
［わいわい広場］

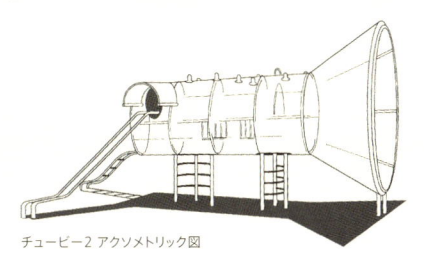

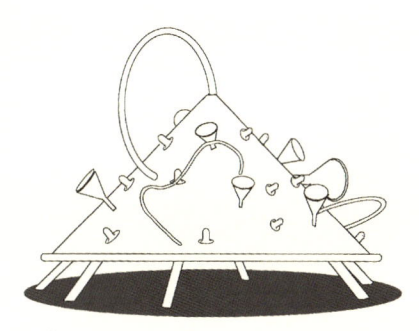

チュービー 2 アクソメトリック図

ビッグホーン アクソメトリック図

所在地：愛知県名古屋市昭和区川名山町
主用途：遊具

チュービー 2（構造：S造）
ビッグホーン（構造：S造）

Nagoya Children's Play Park "Wai Wai Plaza"
Kawanayama-cho, Showa-ku, Nagoya-shi, Aichi

1987.04
山手ヨットクラブ

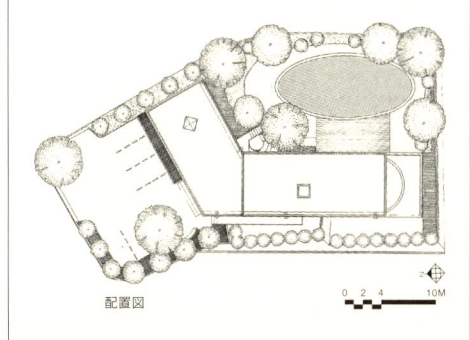

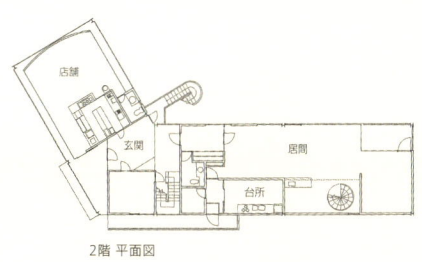

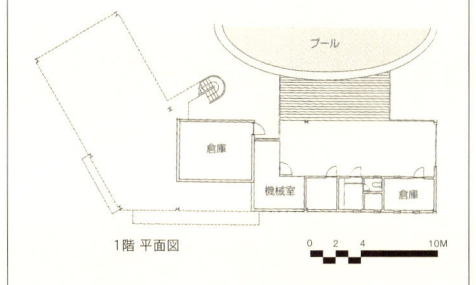

配置図

2階 平面図

1階 平面図

所在地：神奈川県横浜市中区山手町
主用途：住宅、カフェ
共同設計：脇田愛二郎＋スタジオA
構造設計：構造計画研究所
設備設計：高建築設備
施工：大林組
構造：S造
規模：地上3階
敷地：902㎡　建築：226㎡　延床：354㎡

Yamate Yacht Club
Yamate-cho, Naka-ku, Yokohama-shi, Kanagawa

839

1987.08
相模川ふれあい科学館

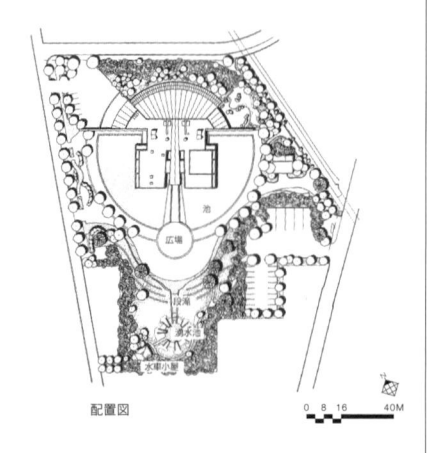

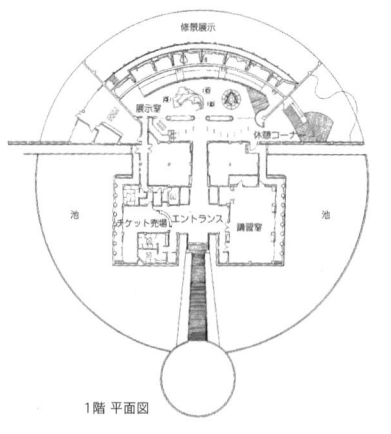

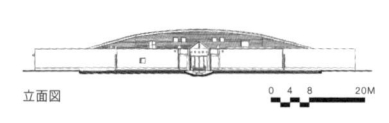

配置図

1階 平面図

立面図

所在地：神奈川県相模原市中央区水郷田名
主用途：水族科学館
建築主：相模原市
構造設計：構造計画研究所
設備設計：環境デザイン研究所
施工：相陽建設
構造：RC造
規模：地上1階
敷地：12,479㎡　建築：1,679㎡　延床：1,662㎡

Sagamigawa River Museum
Suigotana, Chuo-ku, Sagamihara-shi, Kanagawa

1985.06
多摩動物園猛禽舎

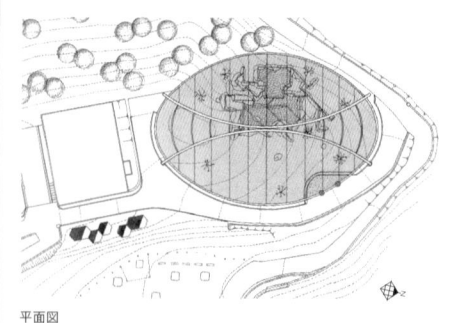

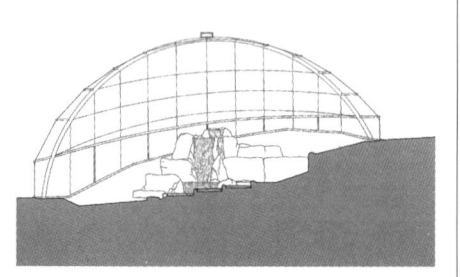

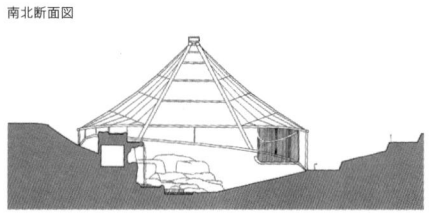

平面図

南北断面図

東西断面図

所在地：東京都日野市程久保
主用途：動物園施設
建築主：多摩動物園
構造設計：構造計画研究所
施工：山本建設
敷地：6,000㎡　建築：1,127㎡

Tama Zoo "Raptores House"
Hodokubo, Hino-shi, Tokyo

1986.04
浜松科学館

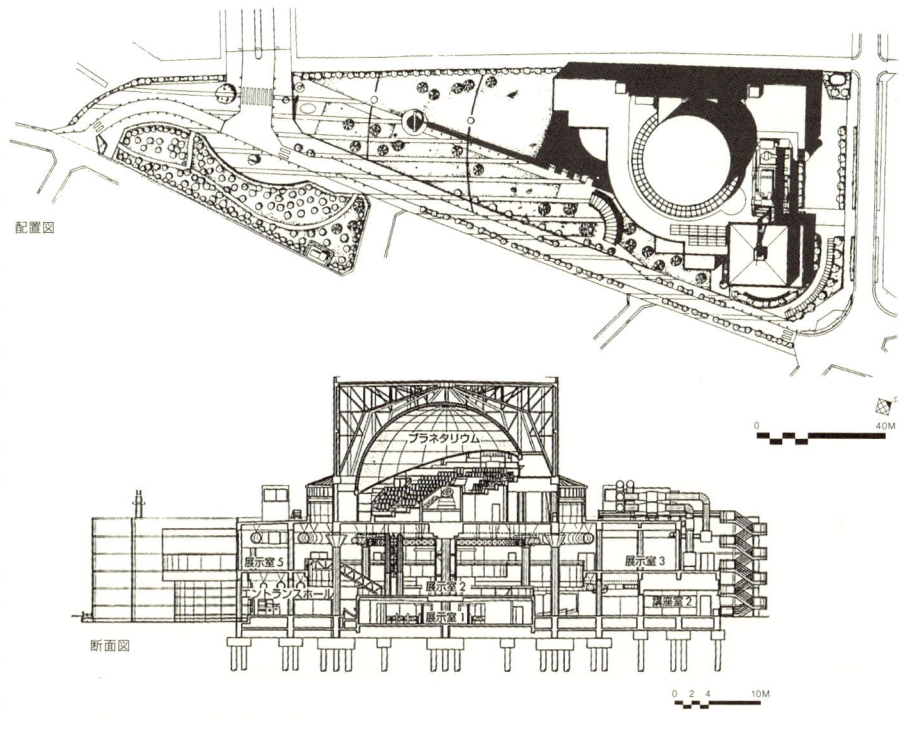

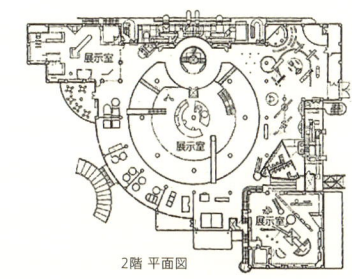

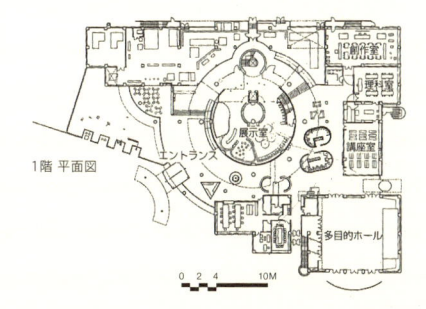

配置図

断面図

2階 平面図

1階 平面図

所在地：静岡県浜松市中区北寺島町
主用途：科学館
建築主：浜松市
構造設計：佐々木睦朗構造計画研究所
設備設計：環境デザイン研究所
施工：大成・中村JV
構造：SRC造一部S造
規模：地上4階
敷地：9,911㎡　建築：3,387㎡　延床：6,905㎡

Hamamatsu Science Museum
Kitaterajima-cho, Naka-ku, Hamamatsu-shi, Shizuoka

1985.03
筑波科学万国博覧会 こども広場

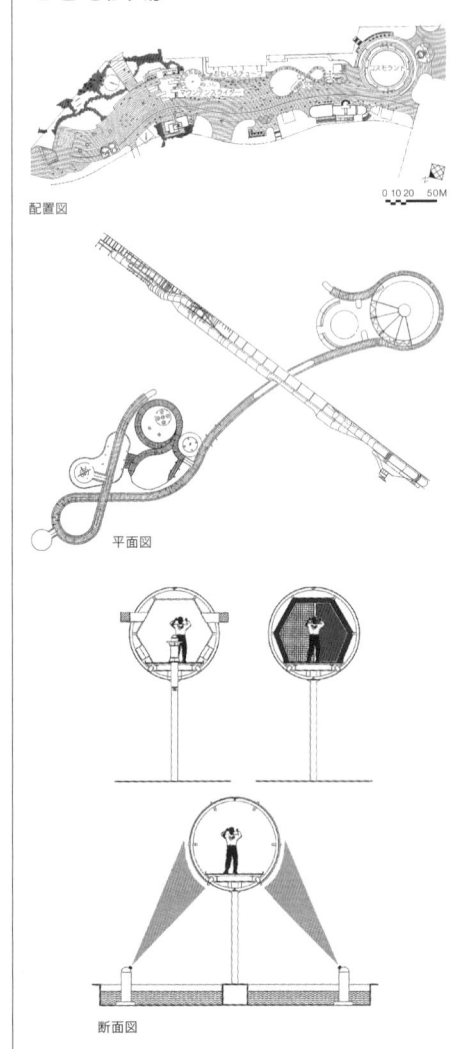

配置図

平面図

断面図

所在地：茨城県つくば市吾妻
主用途：博覧会施設
建築主：財団法人国際科学技術博覧会協会
共同設計：設計工房、博報堂
構造設計：構造計画研究所
施工：博報堂
敷地：30,000㎡

Tsukuba Science Expo Children's Plaza
Azuma, Tsukuba-shi, Ibaraki

1984.06
軽井沢 640

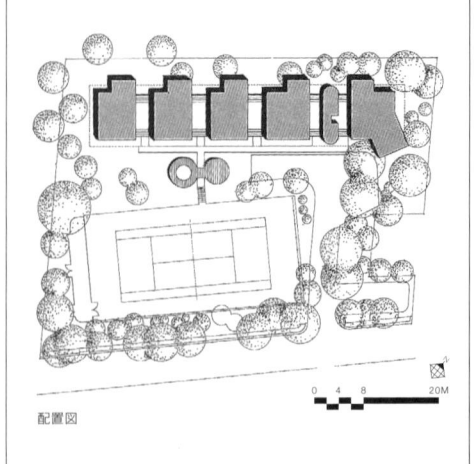

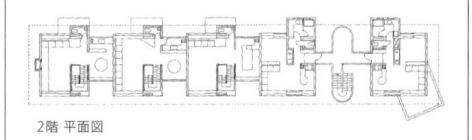

配置図

2階 平面図

1階 平面図

所在地：長野県北佐久郡軽井沢町
主用途：保養施設
建築主：ダイヤモンドリース
共同設計：脇田愛二郎＋スタジオA
設備設計：ユニ設備設計
施工：丸山工務店
構造：W造一部RC造
規模：地上2階
敷地：2,457㎡　建築：392㎡　延床：497㎡

Karuizawa 640
Karuizawa-machi, Kitasaku-gun, Nagano

1983.03
静岡県吉原林間学校

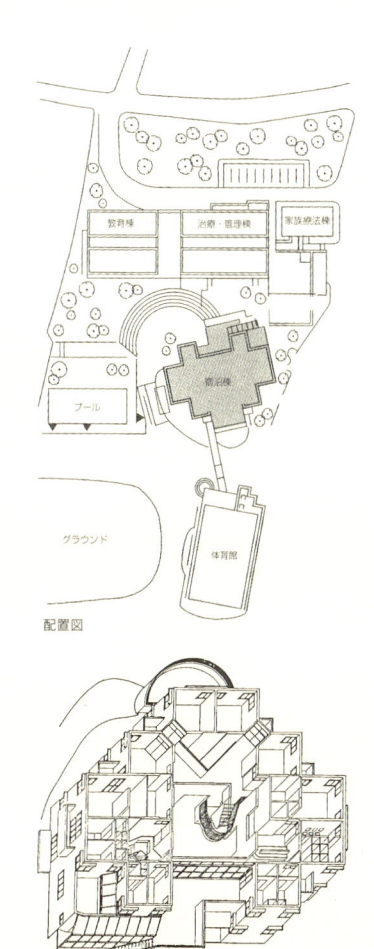

配置図

宿泊棟 アクソメトリック図

所在地：静岡県富士市大淵
主用途：情緒障害児短期治療施設
建築主：静岡県
構造設計：佐々木睦朗構造計画研究所
設備設計：森村協同設計事務所
施工：保坂組
構造：RC造
規模：地上2階
敷地：13,088㎡　建築：629㎡　延床：629㎡

Yoshiwara Camping School
Obuchi, Fuji-shi, Shizuoka

1983.05, 1982.07
鳥居平やまびこ公園
[ローラースケート場・風のとりで]

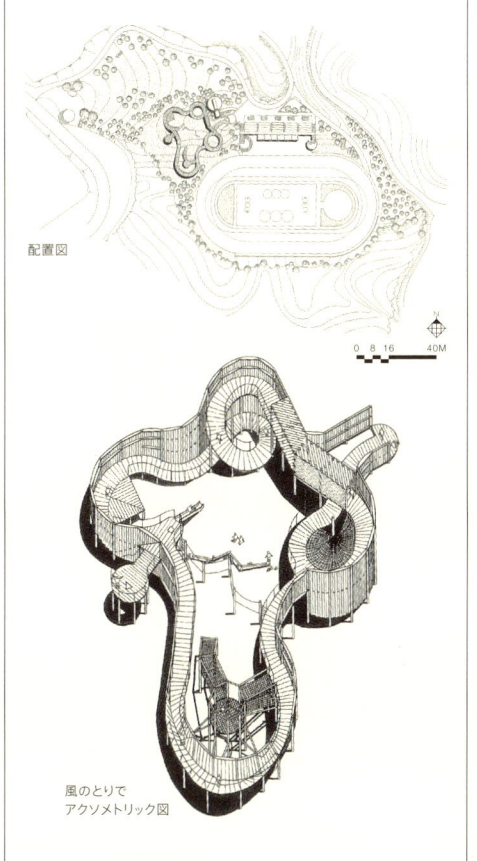

配置図

風のとりで
アクソメトリック図

所在地：長野県岡谷市内山
主用途：公園施設
建築主：岡谷市、住宅都市整備公団

ローラースケート場
構造設計：団設計同人
設備設計：ユニ設備設計事務所、やまと設備設計
施工：岡谷組
構造：RC造
敷地：300,471㎡　建築：302㎡　延床：266㎡

風のとりで
構造：W造
規模：全長外周約170m
敷地：300,471㎡

"Roller-skating Rink" in Toriidaira Yamabiko Park
"Fortress of Wind" in Toriidaira Yamabiko Park
Uchiyama, Okaya-shi, Nagano

1982.03
太刀の浦緑地

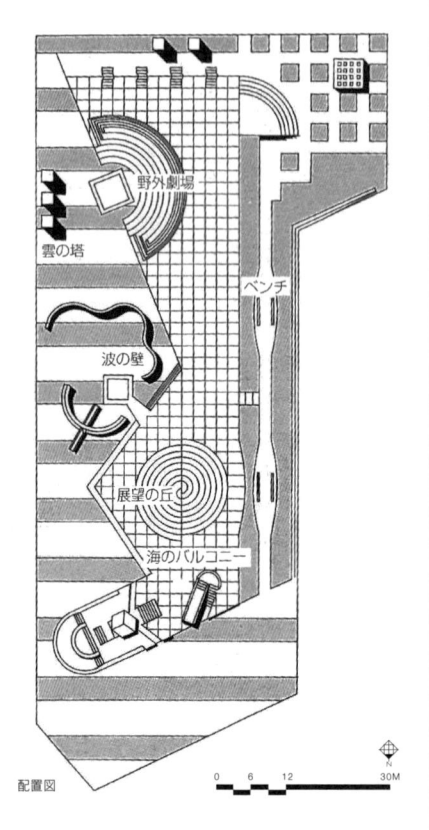

野外劇場
雲の塔
ベンチ
波の壁
展望の丘
海のバルコニー

配置図

所在地：福岡県北九州市門司区太刀浦海岸
主用途：公園施設
建築主：北九州市
構造設計：佐々木睦朗構造計画研究所
設備設計：ユニ設備設計
施工：九州緑化建設
構造：RC造、CB造
敷地：5,540㎡（A緑地）、5,875㎡（B緑地）

Tachinoura Port Park
Tachinourakaigan, Moji-ku, Kitakyusyu-shi, Fukuoka

1982.11
脇田和邸

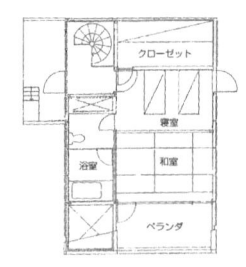

クローゼット
寝室
浴室
和室
ベランダ

3階 平面図

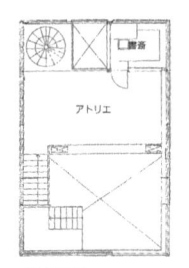

アトリエ

2階 平面図

台所
食堂
居間
玄関

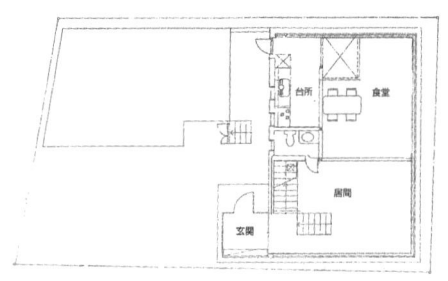

1階 平面図

所在地：東京都世田谷区代田
主用途：住宅
構造設計：佐々木睦朗構造計画研究所
設備設計：ユニ設備設計
施工：岩本組
構造：RC造、S造
規模：地上3階
敷地：211㎡　建築：85㎡　延床：174㎡

K. Wakita House
Daita, Setagaya-ku, Tokyo

1982.01
バナナハウス

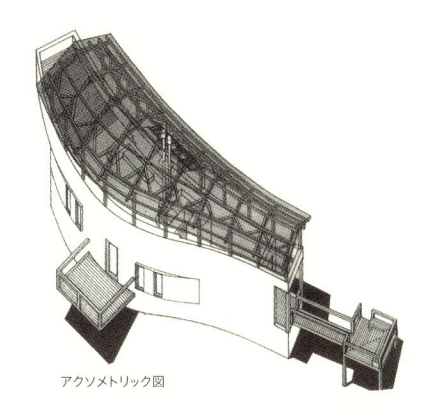

アクソメトリック図

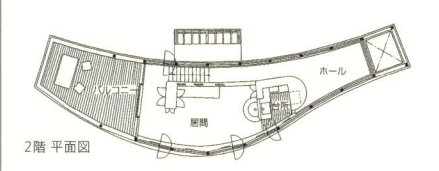

2階 平面図

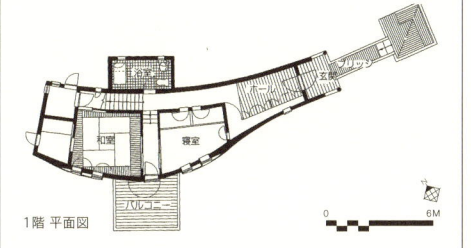

1階 平面図

所在地：山梨県南都留郡
主用途：別荘
設備設計：ユニ設備設計
施工：丸格建築
構造：W造
規模：地上2階
敷地：796㎡　建築：117㎡　延床：93㎡

Banana House
Minamitsuru-gun, Yamanashi

1981.11
八日市市城砦公園

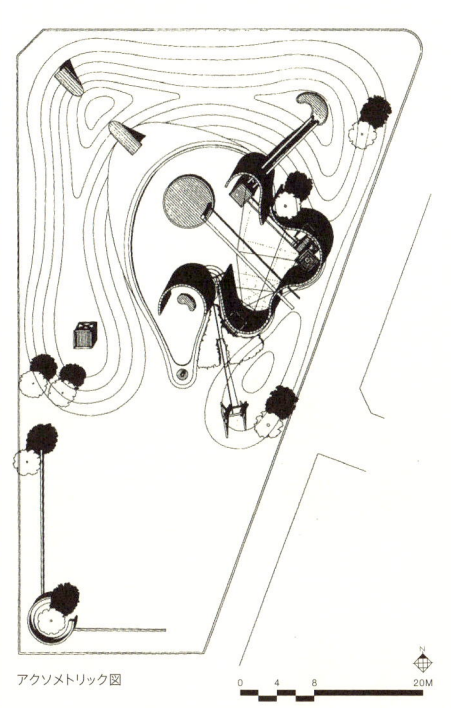

アクソメトリック図

所在地：滋賀県東近江市緑町
主用途：児童公園
建築主：八日市市、宝くじ協会
施工：奥儀建設
構造：S造、CB造
敷地：2,081㎡

Yokaichi Rampart Park
Midori-cho, Higashiomi-shi, Shiga

1981.03
横浜市ほどがや地区センター

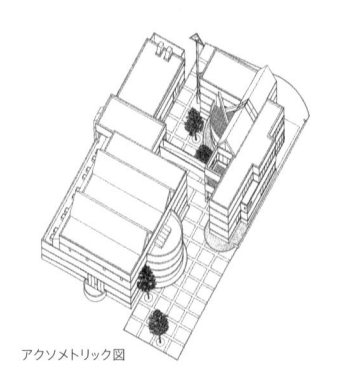

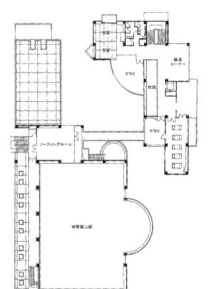

アクソメトリック図

2階 平面図

1階 平面図

所在地：神奈川県横浜市保土ヶ谷区
主用途：地区センター
建築主：横浜市
構造設計：団設計同人
設備設計：ユニ設備設計事務所、守田設備
施工：松村組
構造：RC造
規模：地下1階地上2階
敷地：3,617㎡　建築：1,454㎡　延床：2,094㎡

Hodogaya Community Center, Yokohama
Hodogaya-ku, Yokohama-shi, Kanagawa

1981.04
秋田県営御野庭団地

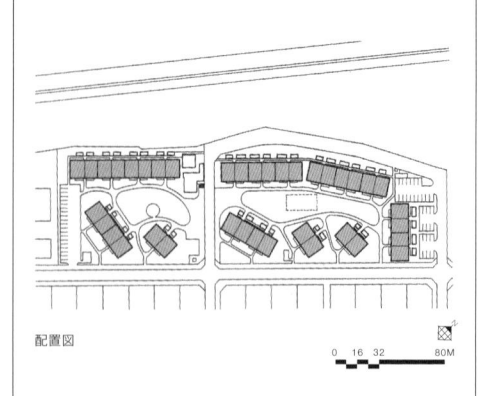

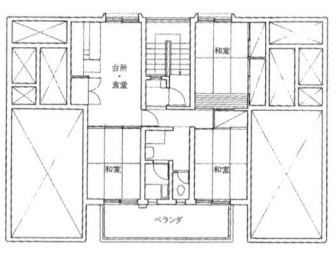

配置図

屋上階 平面図

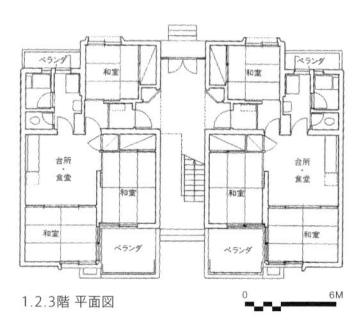

1.2.3階 平面図

所在地：秋田県秋田市四ツ小屋
主用途：共同住宅
建築主：秋田県
共同設計：現代計画研究所
構造設計：青木繁研究室
設備設計：ユニ設備設計
施工：長谷駒組、中央土建、沢木組
構造：RC造
規模：地上4階、地上3階
敷地：13,628㎡　建築：3,078㎡　延床：8,921㎡

Akita Prefectural Onoba Housing
Yotsugoya, Akita-shi, Akita

1980.03
片瀬山の家

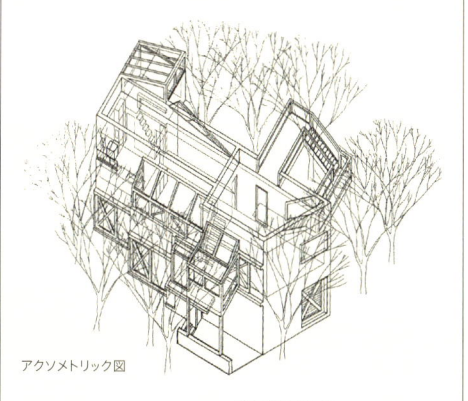

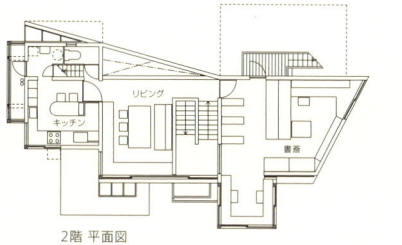

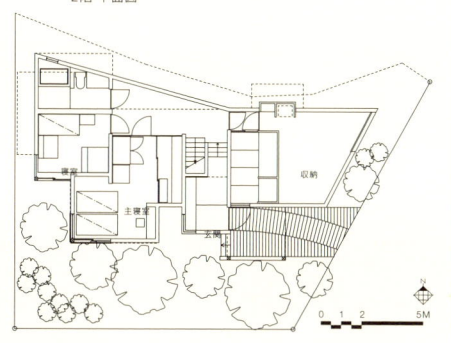

アクソメトリック図

2階 平面図

1階 平面図

所在地：神奈川県藤沢市片瀬山
主用途：住宅
構造設計：団設計同人
設備設計：ユニ設備設計
施工：友伸建設
構造：RC造
規模：地上3階
敷地：599㎡　建築：77㎡　延床：152㎡

Kataseyama House
Kataseyama, Fujisawa-shi, Kanagawa

1980.03
秋田県立児童会館・こども博物館

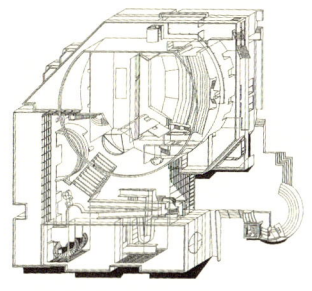

アイソメトリック図

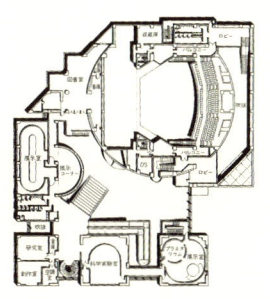

2階 平面図

1階 平面図

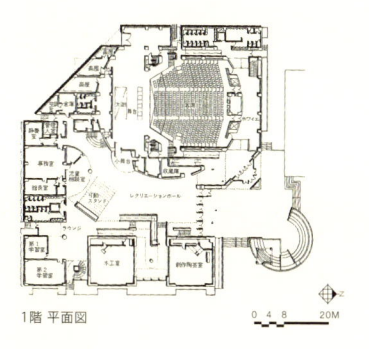

所在地：秋田県秋田市山王中島町
主用途：児童会館、劇場、博物館
建築主：秋田県
共同設計、構造設計、設備設計：日建設計
施工：戸田建設・中田建設・伊藤組 JV
構造：RC造一部S造
規模：地下1階地上4階
敷地：8,024㎡　建築：3,089㎡　延床：5,584㎡

Akita Prefectural Children's Center, Children's Museum
Sannonakajima-cho, Akita-shi, Akita

847

1978

大屋根児童館

串木野児童館
Kushikino Children's Center

串木野児童館

鹿児島県いちき串木野市下名／1978
Kushikino Children's Center
Shimonmyo, Ichikikushikino-shi, Kagoshima

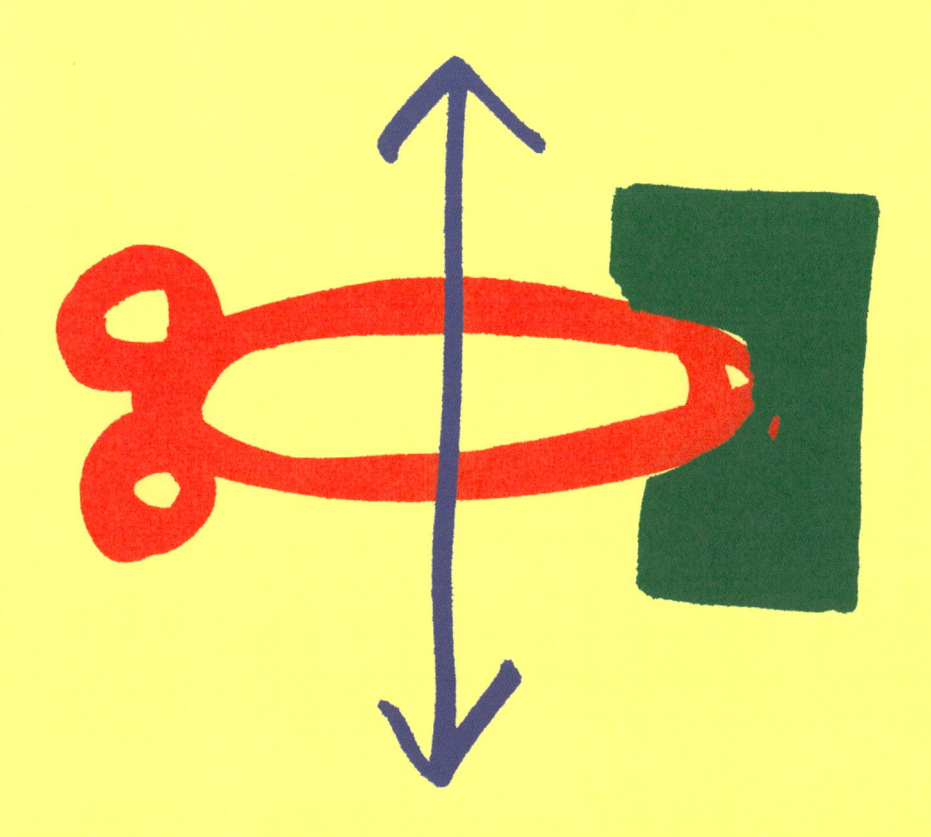

長崎鼻は串木野の海浜レクリエーションエリアとして、市民及び観光客に親しまれており、この児童館はこどもだけでなく、老人クラブ、青少年の集会というような複合的に対応できる施設となっている。機能的に明確なのは2階の児童図書室のみで、集会室、和室は、多目的に使用される。管理室、便所を除けば、あとはオープンな大屋根である。大屋根は一種の野外ホールであり、各種の催事ができる。また、海水浴シーズンには大きな日陰のシェルターになる。

As a marine recreation area in Kushikino City, this children's center is not only for children, however, as it is a multi-purpose facility that contains a club for the elderly and a club space for teenagers. The only room with a clear, distinctive functional purpose is the children's library on the second floor. The other rooms are used for multiple purposes, including the meeting room and Japanese-style room. Other than the management office and bathrooms there is also a large, open-stretching roof. The large roof is used as an outside hall and sun shade.

1978

串木野児童館
Kushikino Children's Center

851

1978

横浜市赤城林間学園

Akagi Camping School, Yokohama

民家型棟間建築

横浜市赤城林間学園

群馬県利根郡昭和村／1978
Akagi Camping School, Yokohama
Showa-mura, Tone-gun, Gunma

赤城山の麓に立つ200人のこどものための宿泊型野外活動施設である。赤城地方の民家の屋根構成が引用され、内部は中央に大きな広場をもつ。運動やあそび集会、催しのための空間となっている。宿泊室も1室8人の共同生活の場として計画され、共同体験が意図されている。初期の遊環構造建築である。

This is a stay-over outdoor activities facility that can accommodate 200 children set at the foot of Mt. Akagi. The facility has adopted a roof structure of private residents of people from the Akagi region and the inside contains a large communal space in the center. The space is used for athletics, leisure activity meetings, and events. Each guest room was designed to accommodate a community living environment for eight people, planning for joint experiences between people staying at the facility. This is one of the earliest circular play system facilities.

1978

横浜市赤城林間学園

Akagi Camping School, Yokohama

横浜市少年自然の家・赤

1975

沖縄県立石川少年自然の家
Ishikawa Children's Nature School

大屋根の
日陰と風

沖縄県立石川少年自然の家

沖縄県うるま市字石川／1975
Ishikawa Children's Nature School
Aza-Ishikawa, Uruma-shi, Okinawa

沖縄県石川岳の麓につくられた、200人収容の、こどものための自然体験宿泊施設。大屋根を中心に4つに分割された宿泊棟により構成されたポーラスな建築である。空中にブリッジが走り、中央の円形広場とともにこども達の交流の装置の役割を果たしている。宿泊棟のコンクリートの外壁の厚さは50cmあり、沖縄らしい影を生むハナブロックの建築が追求された。

This nature lodging facility for children has a capacity of 200 and is constructed at the foot of Mt. Ishikawa in Okinawa Prefecture. The lodging building is divided into four sections and centered under a massive roof to give it a porous construction. There is also a mid-air bridge that, along with the central spacious area shaped like a circle, functions as a way to promote exchanges between children. The outer concrete walls of the lodging building were made to be 50 centimeters thick in aim of a flower block construction unique to Okinawa.

1975

沖縄県立石川少年自然の家

Ishikawa Children's Nature School

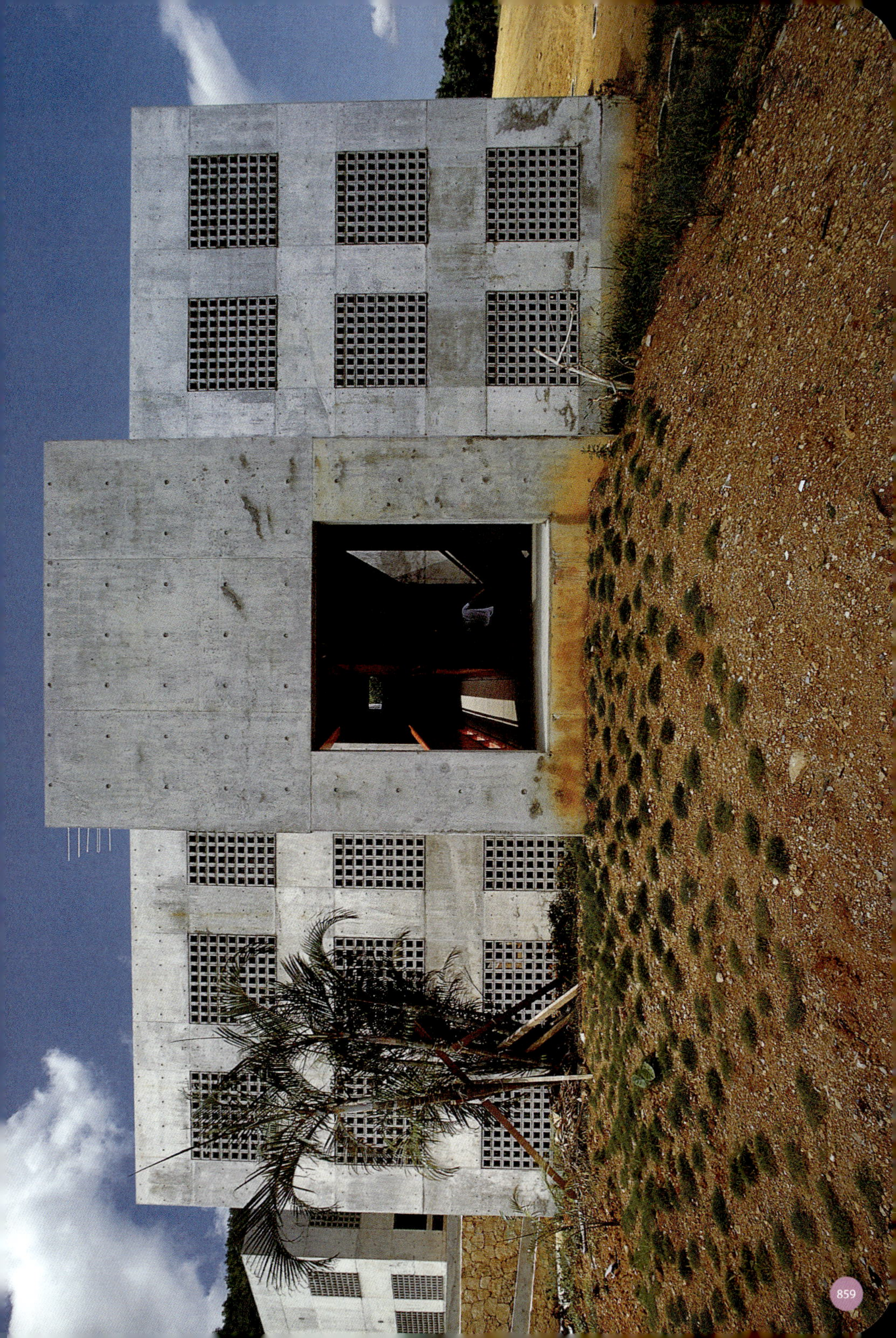

1975

沖縄県立石川少年自然の家　Ishikawa Children's Nature School

861

1975

沖縄県立石川少年自然の家　Ishikawa Children's Nature School

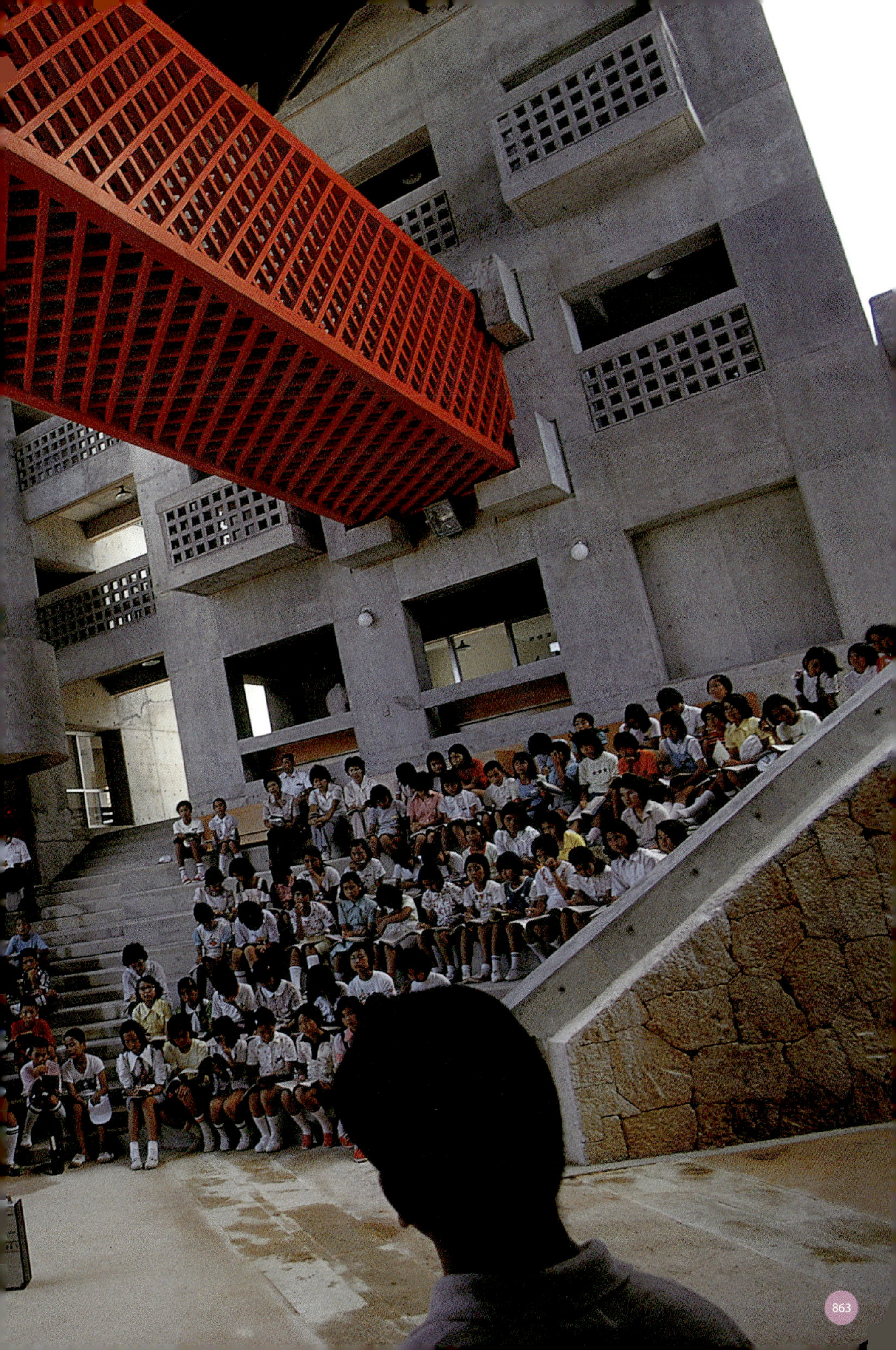

1975

沖縄県立石川少年自然の家

Ishikawa Children's Nature School

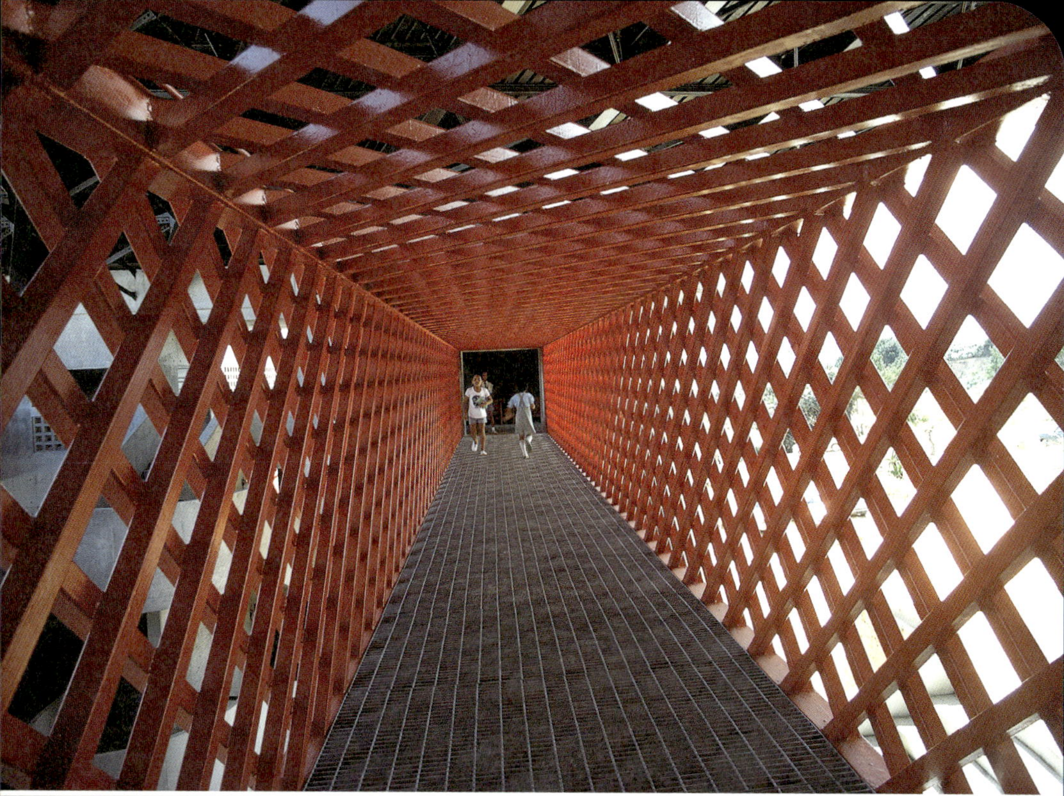

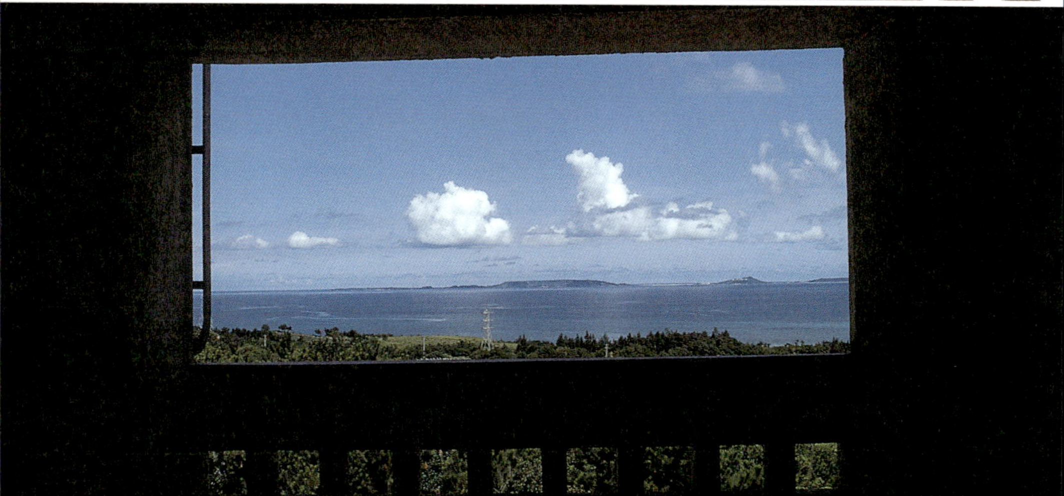

1974

愛知こどもの国 ［ドラゴン］

Giant Play Structure "Dragon" Aichi Prefectural Children's Land

僕たちのドラゴン

愛知こどもの国
［ドラゴン］

愛知県幡豆郡幡豆町／1974
Giant Play Structure "Dragon"
Aichi Prefectural Children's Land
Hazu-cho, Hazu-gun, Aichi

敷地は愛知こどもの国にある幅40m程度の長くて緩やかな芝生斜面である。このドラゴンと呼ぶ巨大遊具は直径2m、長さ200mの大きさを持っている。単にこの中でのあそび体験ばかりでなく、遊戯的な環境を形成するパブリックアートでもある。

The site is a gentle, grassy slope 40m-wide, in a park known as Aichi Children's Land. This Giant Play Structure is 200m-long and 2m in diameter. It not only offers the chance to play, but serves as public art that forms a play environment.

1974

愛知こどもの国 ［ドラゴン］

Giant Play Structure "Dragon" Aichi Prefectural Children's Land

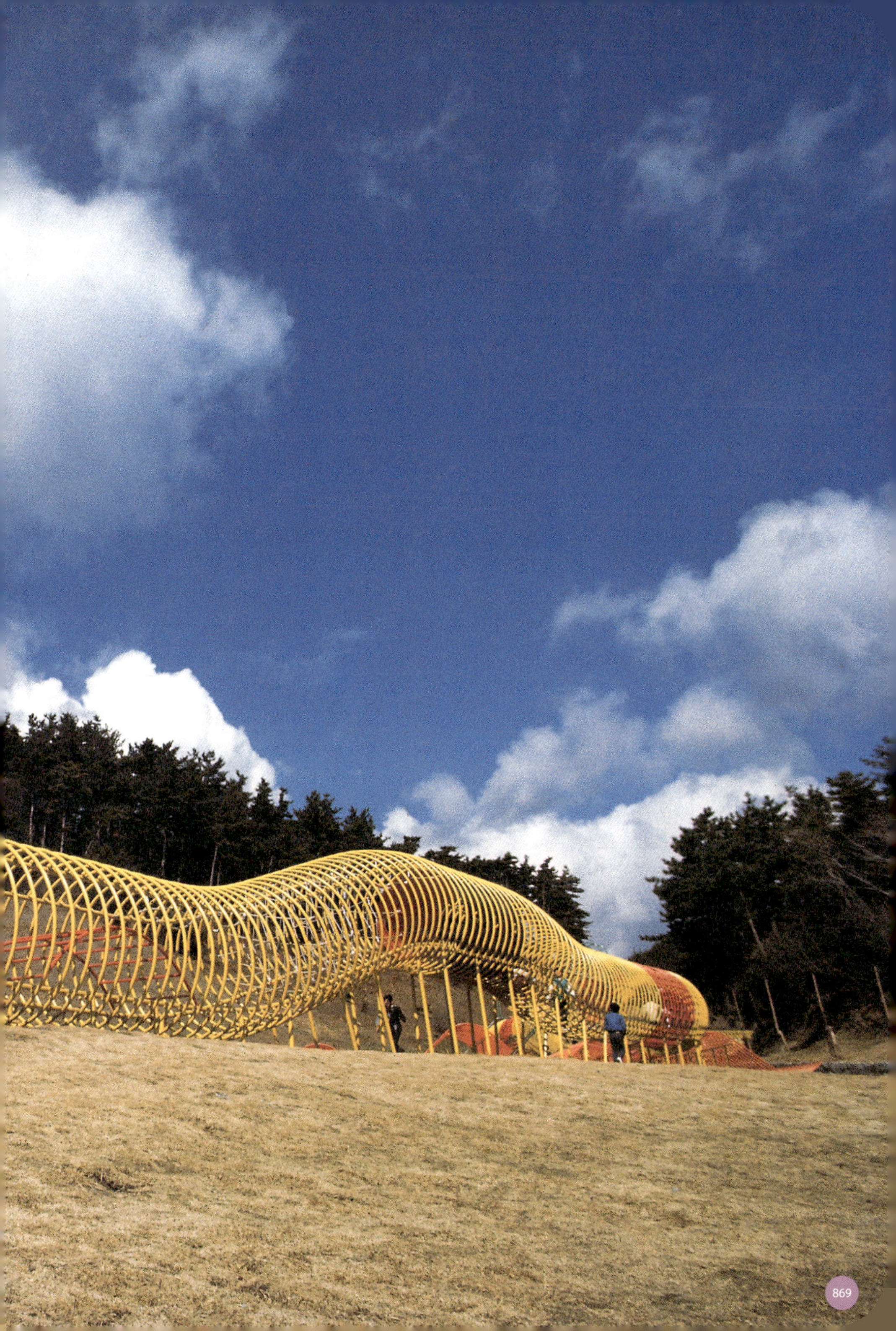

1973

山梨県愛宕山少年自然の家

Atagoyama House of Nature for Young People

山腹の
トライ
アングル

山梨県愛宕山少年自然の家

山梨県甲府市東光寺／1973
Atagoyama House of Nature for Young People
Tokoji, Kofu-shi, Yamanashi

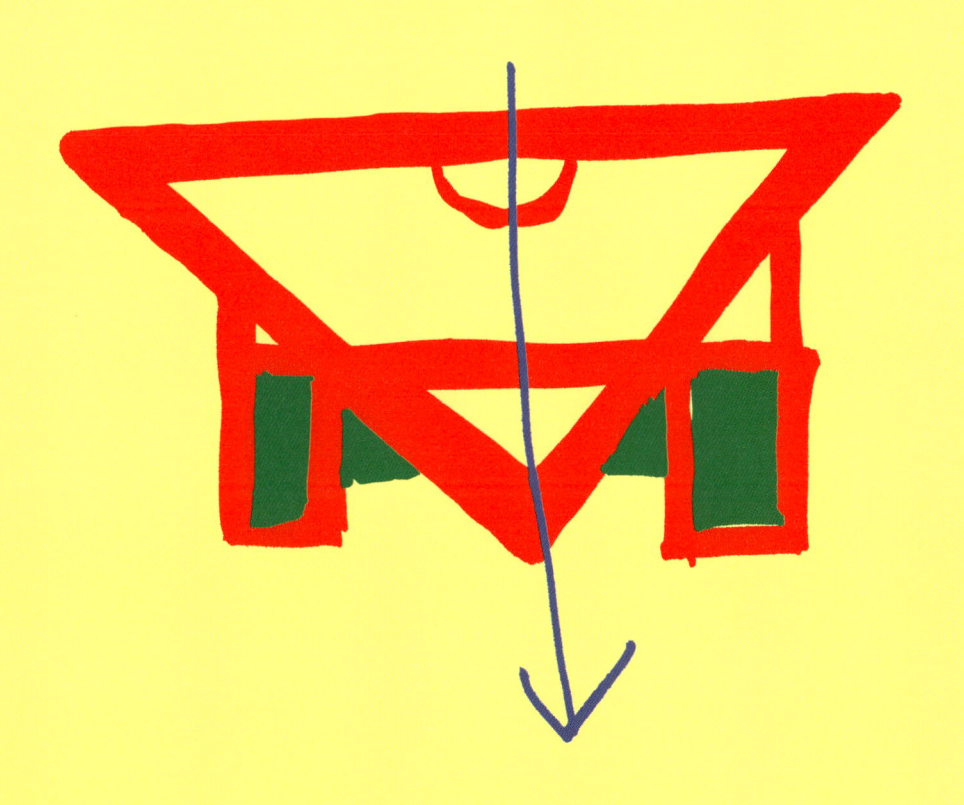

甲府を見下ろす山の斜面に沿いながら、頂点が空中に飛び出す建築構成をもつ、こどものための宿泊型の野外活動施設である。自然との一体性、演劇的な空間が目指されている。

This is a stay-over outdoor activities facility for children constructed along the slant of the mountains overlooking Kofu with the mountain's peak shooting out into midair. The facility aims to offer a construction that is almost theatrical in the way that it achieves oneness with nature.

1973

山梨県愛宕山少年自然の家

Atagoyama House of Nature for Young People

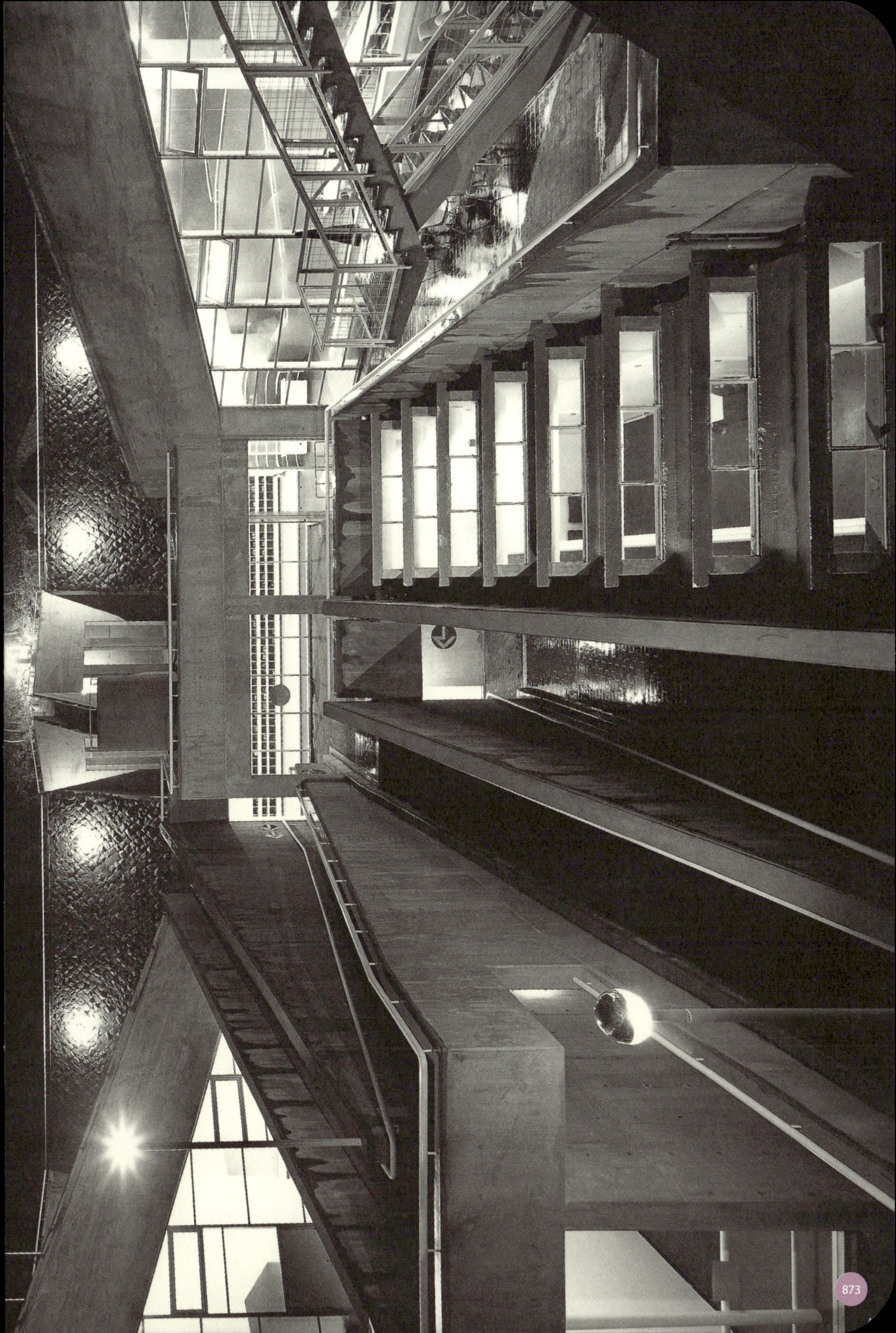

変化自在の
みんな
いっしょ

1981

野中保育園［野中丸］

Nonaka Day Nursery "Nonaka-Maru"

野中保育園
［野中丸］

静岡県富士宮市野中／1981
Nonaka Day Nursery "Nonaka-Maru"
Nonaka, Fujinomiya-shi, Shizuoka

野中保育園（野中ザウルス）の増築。保育室の隔壁が可動で、小さな体育館や劇場にも変えられる。ここでは「みんないっしょにあそべる」環境、「みんなが楽しい」環境の形成が求められた。

Expansion of Nonaka-Saurus. Partition walls in the nursery rooms are movable, so it can be transformed into a small gym or theater. We were tasked with creating an environment where everyone could play together and that would be fun for all people.

1981

野中保育園［野中丸］

Nonaka Day Nursery "Nonaka-Maru"

877

1981

野中保育園［野中丸］

Nonaka Day Nursery "Nonaka-Maru"

879

1981

野中保育園 ［野中丸］

Nonaka Day Nursery "Nonaka-Maru"

881

1981

野中保育園［野中丸］

Nonaka Day Nursery "Nonaka-Maru"

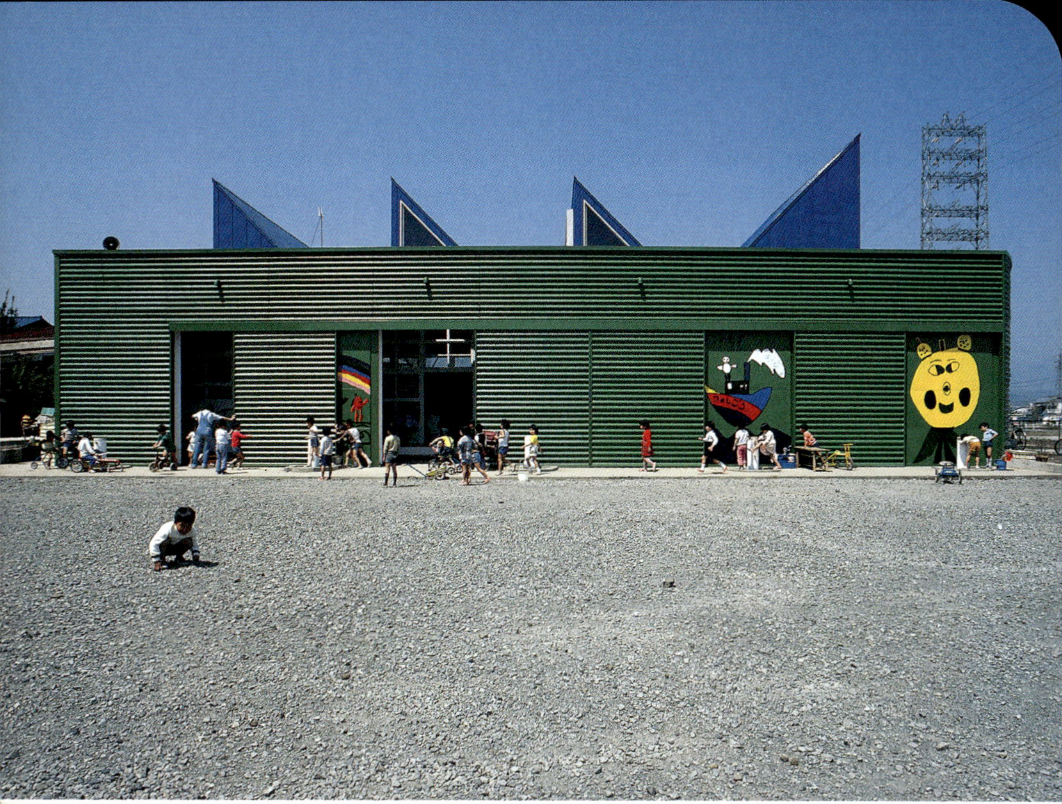

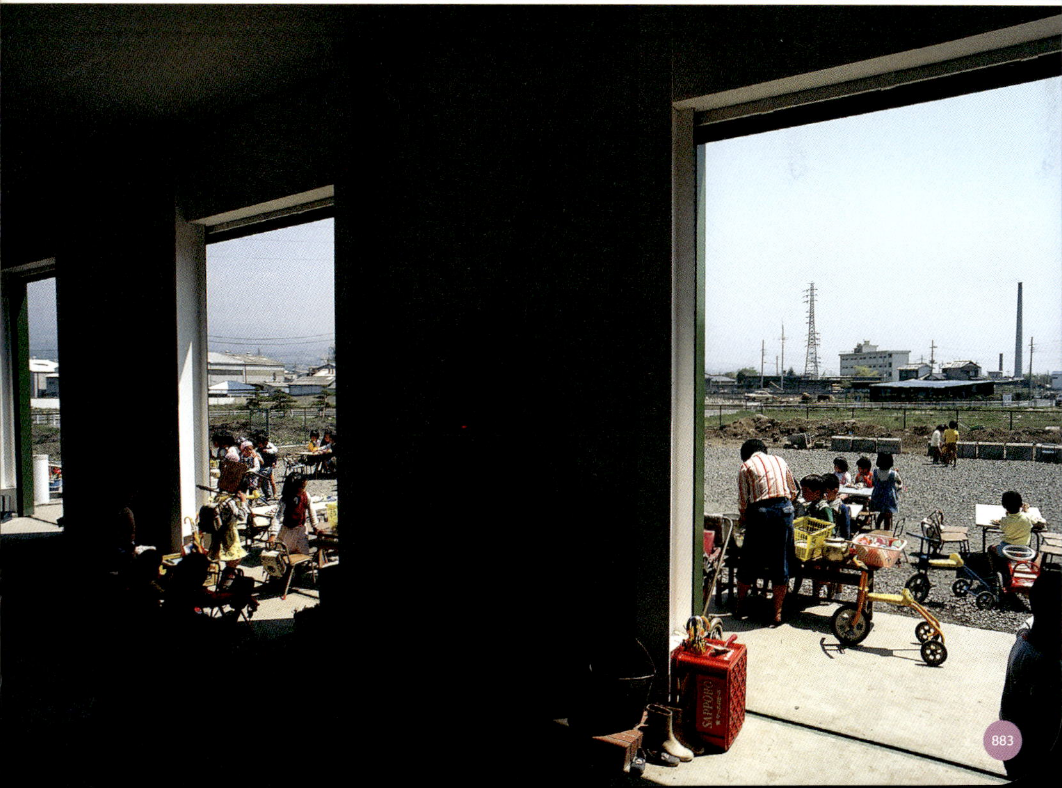
SAPPORO

1972

野中保育園［野中ザウルス］

Nonaka Day Nursery "Nonaka-Saurus"

どろんこあそび

野中保育園
［野中ザウルス］

静岡県富士宮市野中／1972
Nonaka Day Nursery "Nonaka-Saurus"
Nonaka, Fujinomiya-shi, Shizuoka

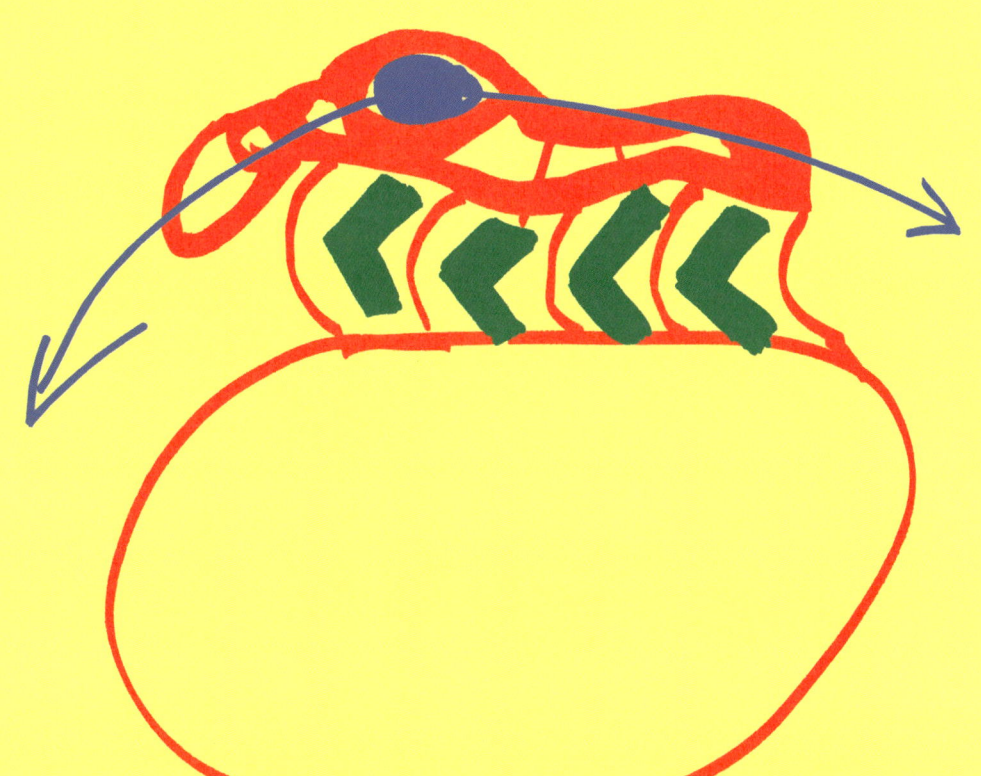

富士山を望む丘の上に立つ保育園。大地保育という保育理念の建築化が目指された。保育室は自立した空間をもち、それぞれに路地状のアプローチ空間をもってプロムナードと自然豊かな園庭に容易にアクセスできる。プロムナードは北側敷地境界線上に沿ってつくられた背の高い廊空間である。各保育室の中2階とブリッジにより連続的につながれ、プロムナードと連携し遊環構造を形成している。その動線はすべり棒、階段等によってこども達に多様な行動が引き起こされ、一体的な空間となっている。遊環構造建築の原型である。

This is a nursery school standing on hill in view of Mt. Fuji. Its design aims to manifest in a building the child-rearing ideology of raising children in close relations with nature. The nursery rooms have their own independent spaces and can be easily accessed using the promenade and nature-rich kindergarten yard, giving each room an alley-shaped approach. The circular play system is achieved by connecting each nursery room with the second floor using a bridge and then connecting that bridge to the promenade. This is the archetype of circular play system buildings.

1972

野中保育園 ［野中ザウルス］

Nonaka Day Nursery "Nonaka-Saurus"

887

1972

野中保育園［野中ザウルス］
Nonaka Day Nursery "Nonaka-Saurus"

屋根の上に富士山が見える、
風景がこどもの心に残る、いつまでも

Mt. Fuji can be seen from the top of the low roof;
Mt. Fuji is of the greatest importance in Japan.
This scenery will remain lodged
in the hearts of children forever.

889

1972

野中保育園［野中ザウルス］

Nonaka Day Nursery "Nonaka-Saurus"

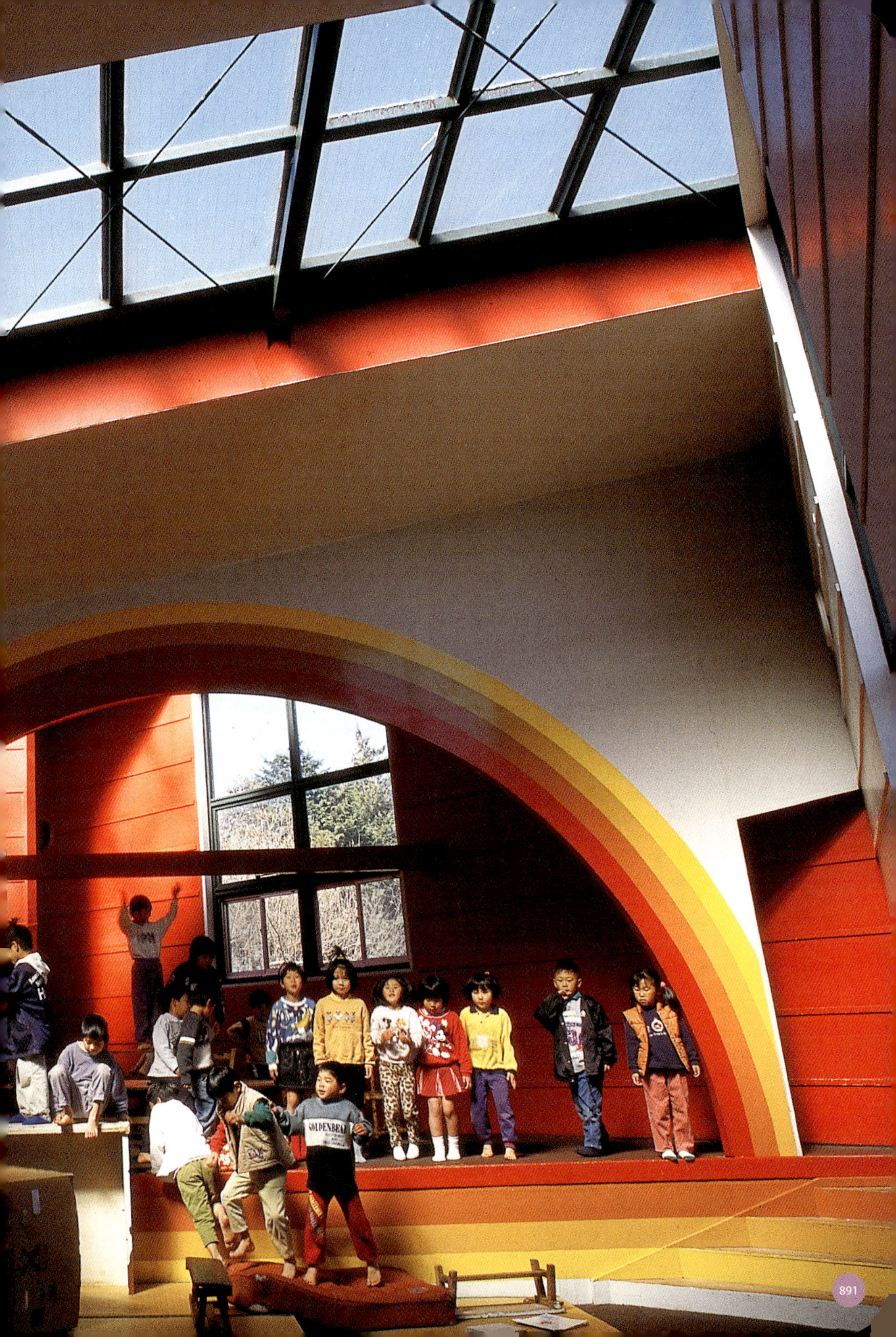
GOLDENBEAR

1972

野中保育園［野中ザウルス］

Nonaka Day Nursery "Nonaka-Saurus"

893

1972

野中保育園［野中ザウルス］

Nonaka Day Nursery "Nonaka-Saurus"

895

1972

野中保育園［野中ザウルス］

Nonaka Day Nursery "Nonaka-Saurus"

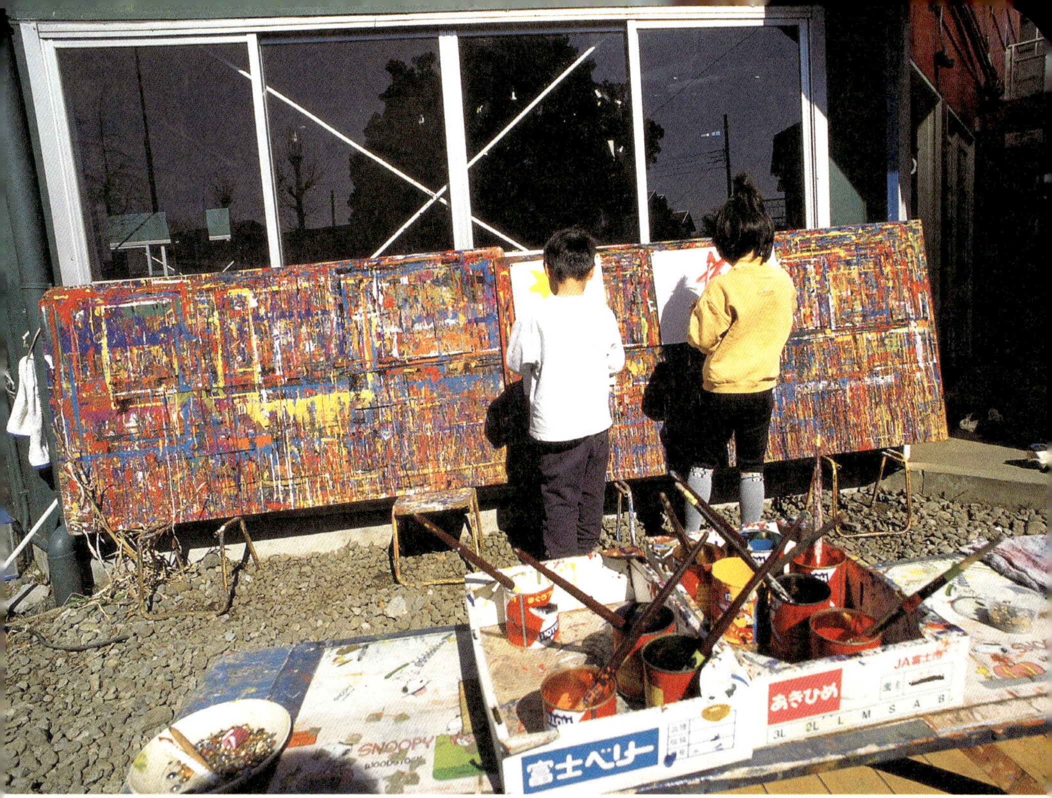
富士ベリー
あきひめ
SNOOPY

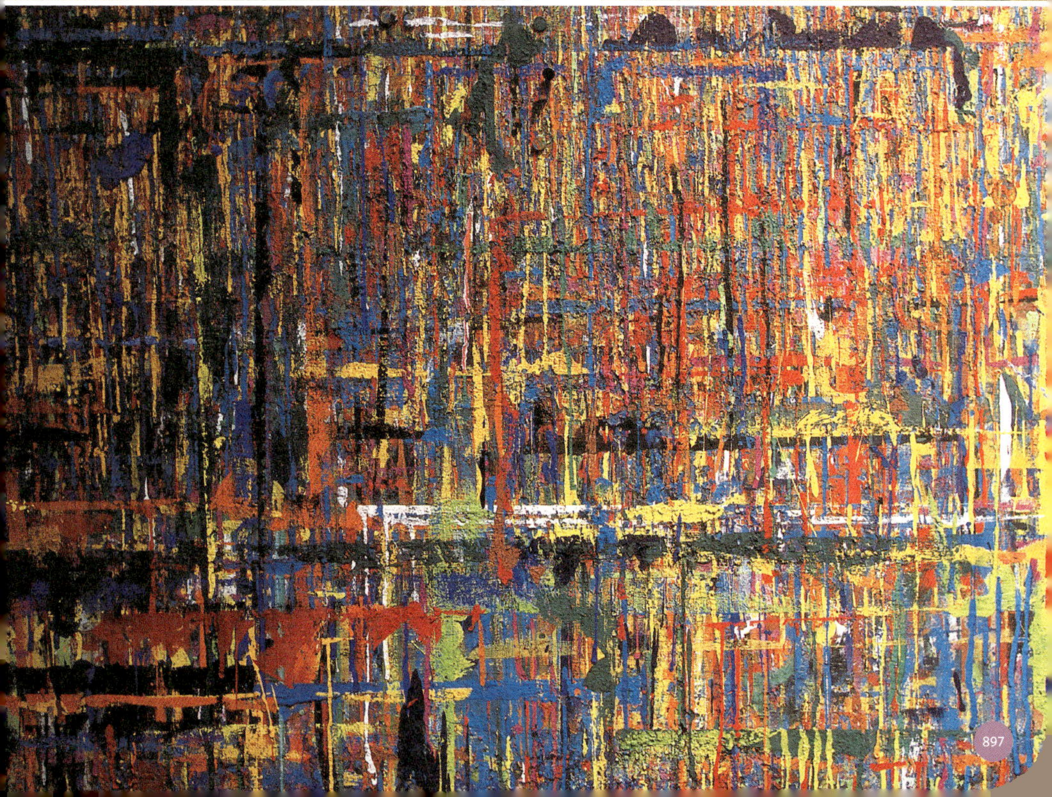

1972

野中保育園［野中ザウルス］

Nonaka Day Nursery "Nonaka-Saurus"

野中保育園はどろんこ保育、
身も心も開放する
The concept behind Nonaka Day Nursery is
that of raising children the "natural" way,
with open and liberated minds and bodies.

1972

理想のこどもの姿だ
The Nonaka children are the ideal children.

野中保育園［野中ザウルス］
Nonaka Day Nursery "Nonaka-Saurus"

901

1972

野中保育園［野中ザウルス］
Nonaka Day Nursery "Nonaka-Saurus"

903

1971

神保医院
Jinbo Clinic

回遊スロープ

神保医院

神奈川県川崎市中原区下小田中／1971
Jinbo Clinic
Shimokodanaka, Nakahara-ku,
Kawasaki-shi, Kanagawa

ベッド数18の産婦人科医院。小さな中庭をたくみに回遊するスロープによって、住居棟と診療棟を連結させ、三角形の遊環構造をなしている。

This is an obstetrician and gynecologist office with 18 beds. The residential building and treatment building are connected by a slope that cleverly crosses a small garden area, making for this triangle-shaped circular play system.

1971

神保医院
Jinbo Clinic

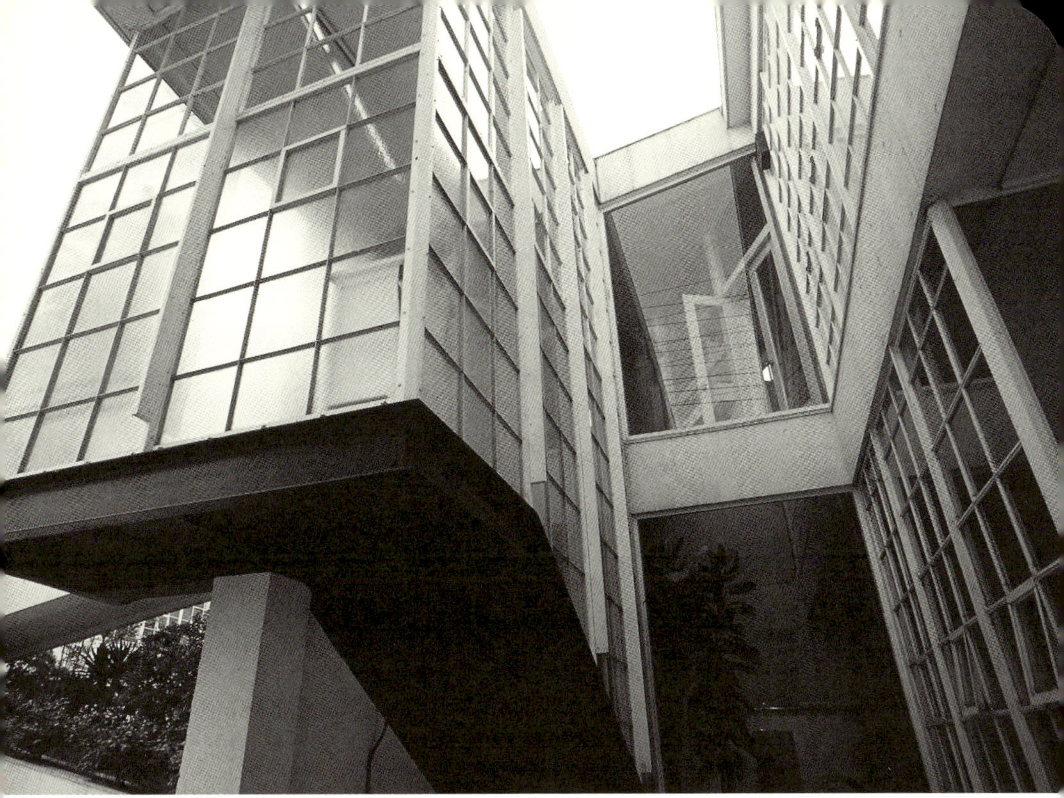

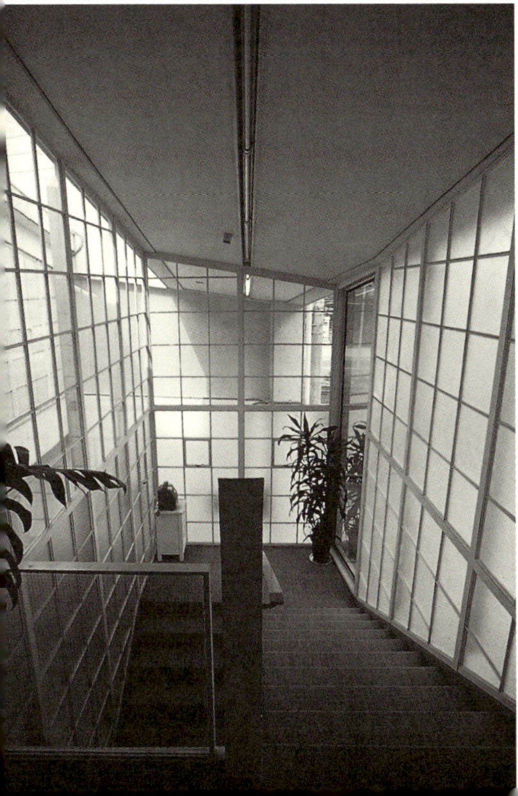

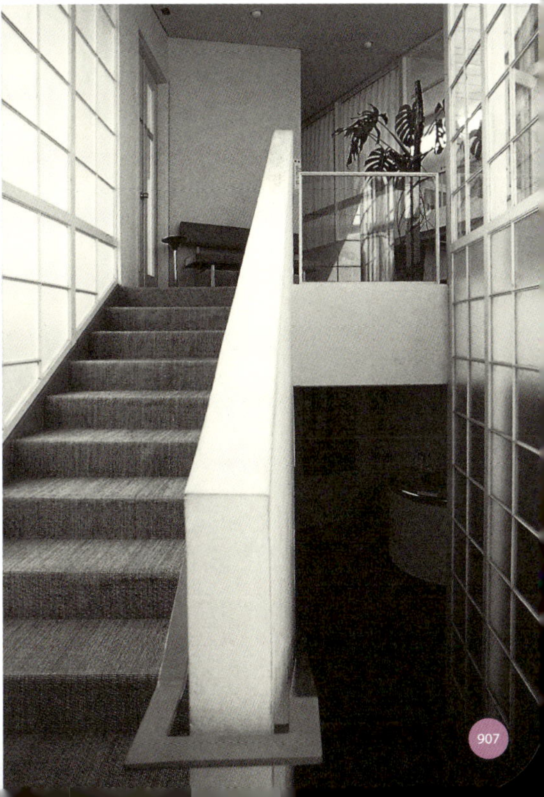

1971

テル建築

鳥取砂丘こどもの国　Children's Land at Tottori

鳥取砂丘こどもの国

鳥取県鳥取市浜坂／1971
Children's Land at Tottori
Hamasaka, Tottori-shi, Tottori

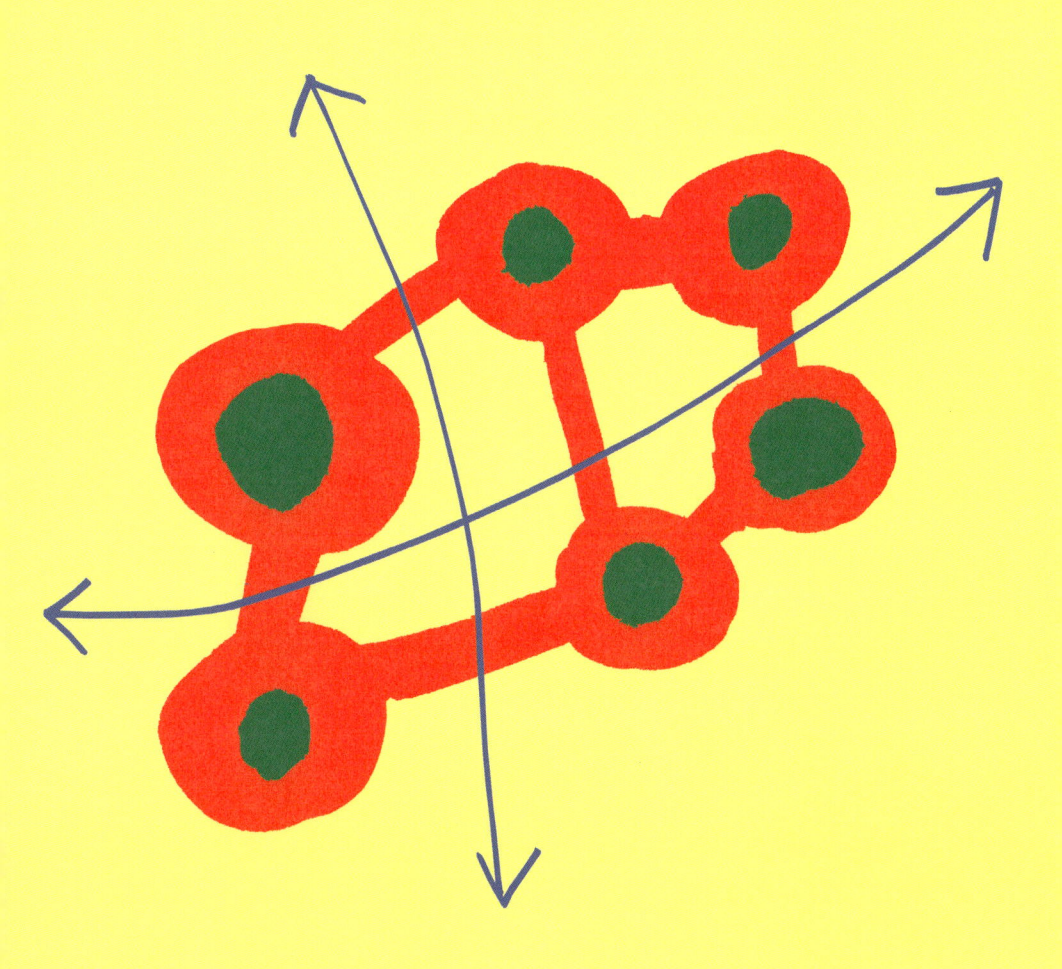

鳥取砂丘につくられた約13ヘクタールのこどものための園地。中心施設は砂漠のかつての都市の遺跡「テル」が引用され、「ビニシェル」という球状のコンクリートシェルによって遊環構造的に連携されている。

This is a 13-hectare play area for children built in the Tottori Sand Dunes. Adopting the "tell" ruins from an old desert city, the central facility it connected with a circular play system using a concrete shell called "Binishell."

1971

鳥取砂丘こどもの国　Children's Land at Tottori

911

1971

愛宕山こどもの国［展望広場］

Observation Square, Atagoyama Children's Land

標高420m

愛宕山こどもの国 ［展望広場］

山梨県甲府市東光寺／1971
Observation Square, Atagoyama Children's Land
Tokoji, Kofu-shi, Yamanashi

山梨県甲府市を見下ろす愛宕山につくられたこどものための園地。敷地面積約55ヘクタール、標高420mのレベルに主園路が幹のようにつくられ、30m×100mの展望広場が設けられている。少年自然の家、キャンプ場などが果実のように配されている。遊環構造のランドスケープとして初期の仕事である。

This is a children's play area that was constructed at Mt. Atago, overlooking Kofu City in Yamanashi Prefecture. The main path is of the nearly 55-hectare, 420-meter elevation grounds is created almost like a tree trunk and there is even a 30-meter by 100-meter observation space. The area is also rich with other facilities, including a children's nature house and camping area. The initial job was to create a landscape for play.

1971

愛宕山こどもの国［展望広場］

Observation Square, Atagoyama Children's Land

915

1971

愛宕山こどもの国［展望広場］

Observation Square, Atagoyama Children's Land

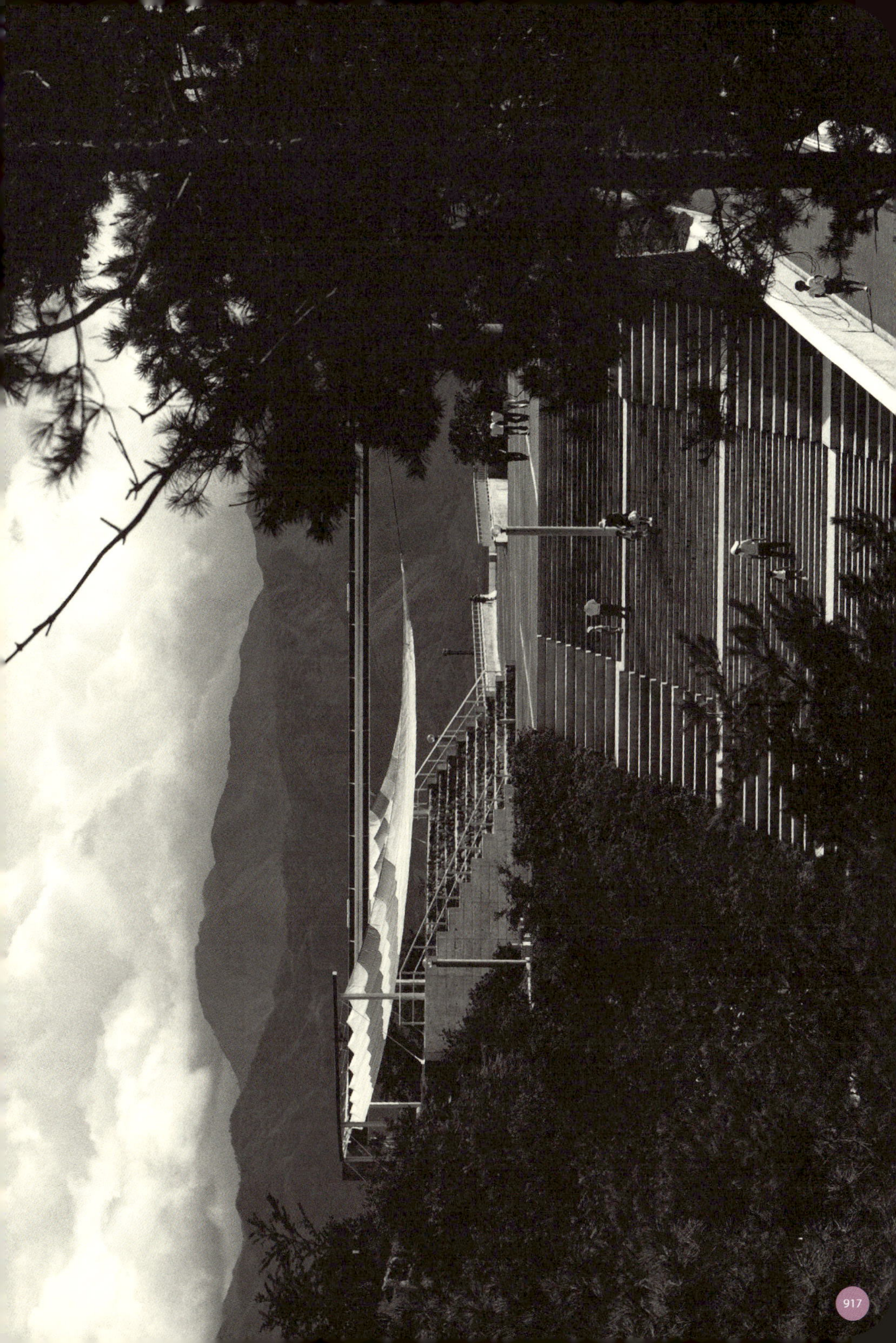

1971

コンチキ号

新川シーサイド遊園
Shinkawa Seaside Children's Park

新川シーサイド遊園

愛媛県伊予市新川／1971
Shinkawa Seaside Children's Park
Shinkawa, Iyo-shi, Ehime

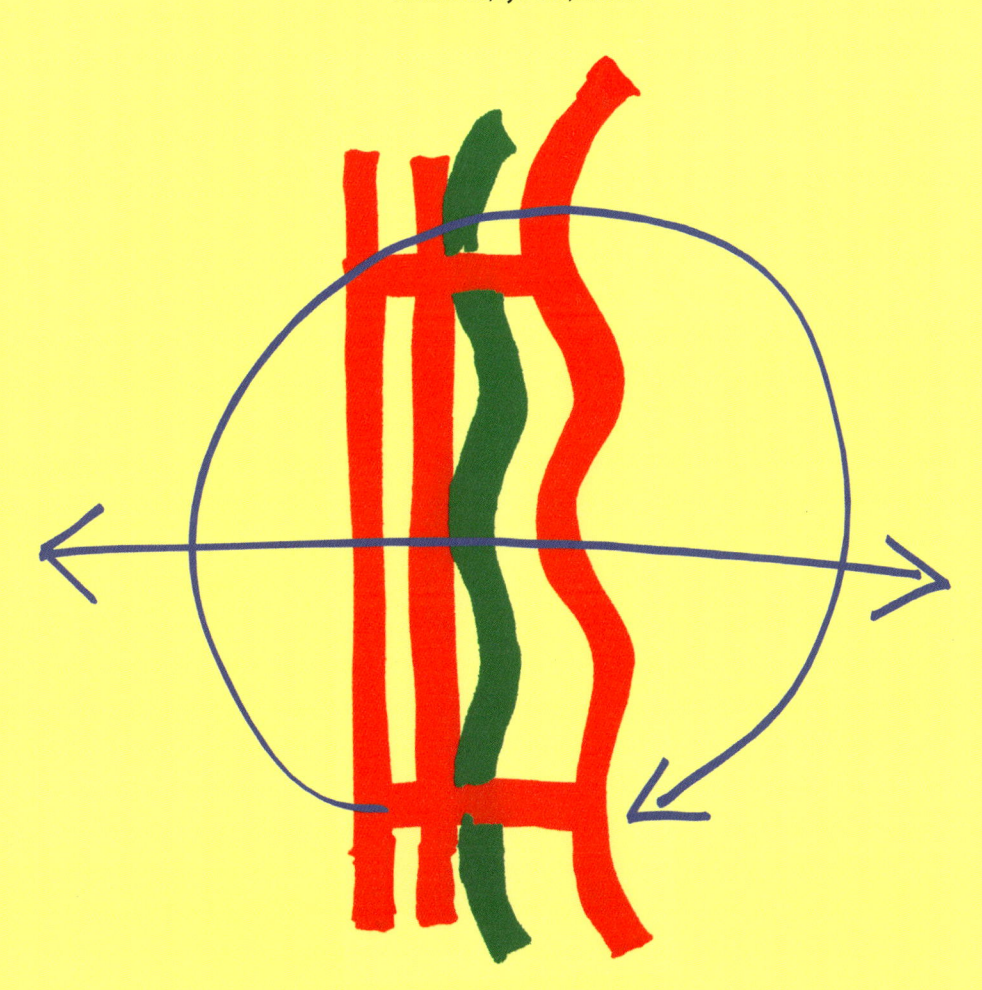

ヘイエルダールのコンティキ号をテーマとしたうねりの大地と、丸太の橋の大海に投げ出された原始的な遊環構造である。大地の彫刻としてはよかったが、こども達のスケールを超えてしまった。遊具としては大失敗作であるが、初期の遊具作品としては最も印象深い。

This primitive-like circular play system consists of a wavy piece of earth and an ocean of floating log bridges, and was created based on the theme of Thor Heyerdahl's Kon-Tiki. The carved earth surpassed the size of children, making this a failed attempt at creating play equipment. However, it is still an impressive example of early age play equipment.

1971

新川シーサイド遊園　Shinkawa Seaside Children's Park

921

1979

立体木道

ランニングサーキット

"Running Circuit"

ランニングサーキット

宮城県仙台市太白区向山／1979
"Running Circuit"
Mukaiyama, Taihaku-ku, Sendai-shi, Miyagi

木製の立体運動路。走り回りたいというこども達の運動の意欲を喚起することを目的としてつくられた遊環構造遊具である。その視覚的変化を自分の足と身体によって感じることができる。

This is a wooden three-dimensional exercise track. It was built as a circular play system that would boost the motivation of children that want to run around and play to exercise. It is possible to feel the visual changes through one's feet and body.

1979

ランニングサーキット　"Running Circuit"

こども達はただひたすら走る
The children simply keep running.

1975

キシャコゾウ
Kishakozo

キシャコゾウ

1975
Kishakozo

私の息子達が幼稚園児だった頃に彼らのためにつくった手作りの高い机である。大人達に見下ろされないように、大人の視線に近づけるために床から45cm高い位置に椅子と机が置かれた。その下はおもちゃ箱になっている。幼児には個室は不要で、彼らのものを収納できる空間があればいいと考えた。居間に置かれ、広々とした空間に向かってその存在を主張する。

This is a homemade desk that I made for my sons in nursery school. So that the child would not be looked down upon, I raised the eye level closer to that of an adult, placing the desk and chair 45cm above the floor. Under neath is a toy box. I surmise that very young children don't need their own room, just a space to store their things. Set in the living room facing an open space, this piece of furniture stands out.

1975

キシャコゾウ　Kishakozo

929

1969

元祖
巨大遊具

道の巨大遊具

"Giant Path Play Structure"

道の巨大遊具

宮城県仙台市太白区向山／1969
"Giant Path Play Structure"
Mukaiyama, Taihaku-ku, Sendai-shi, Miyagi

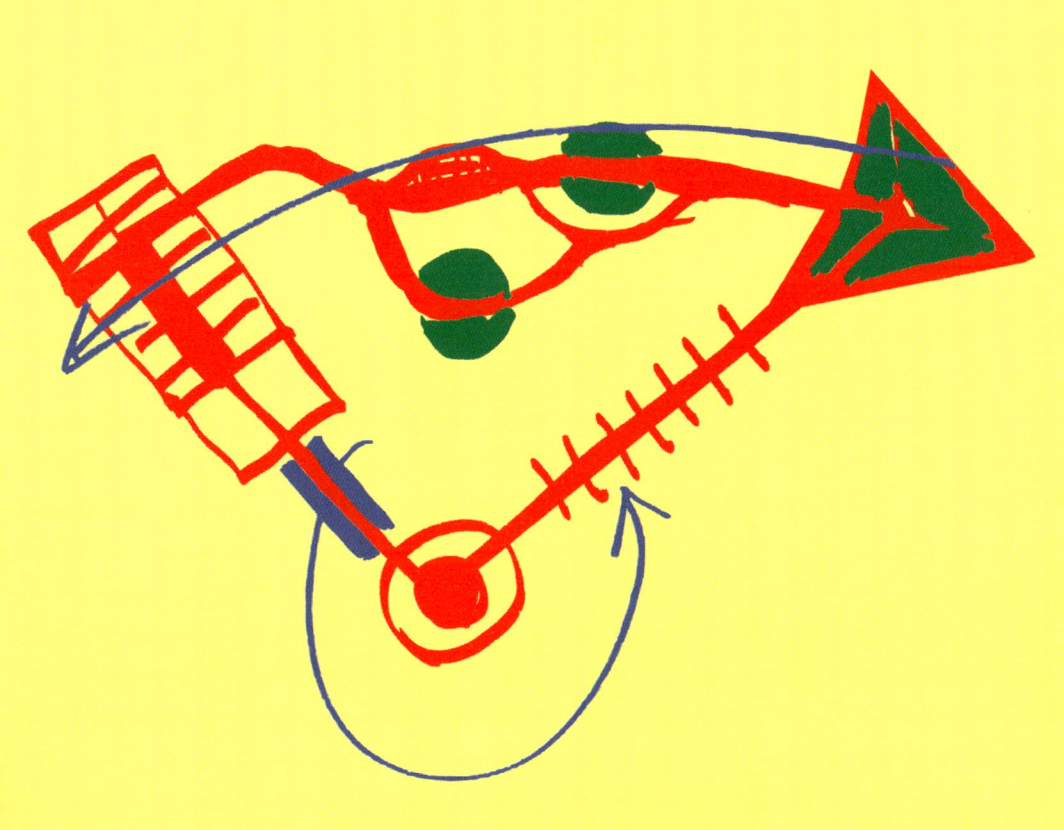

巨大遊具とは、単機能的な遊具を超え、大木のようにこども達に総合的なあそび行動を喚起する遊具として構想された。巨大遊具の考え方によって設計した最初の遊具。全長180ｍ、主構造は直径1ｍのパイプのコイル。4つのユニットで構成でき（1ユニット長さ1.8ｍ）、中でも三又型のユニットがこの遊具を特徴づけている。平面的に亀甲型プランをつくり、ルートに変化をもたせた。

This giant play structure, much like a huge tree, was conceptualized as a tool to go beyond the simplistic functions of regular play equipment and to incite comprehensive play behavior in children. This was the first play structure that I designed using the giant play structure concept. It is 180 meters in total length, and the main structure is made of steel pipe coil that is one meter in diameter. Consisting of four units each 1.8 meters in length, the structure also includes distinctive three-part units. The structure has a tortoise shell plan with variation in its routes.

1969

道の巨大遊具　"Giant Path Play Structure"

933

1968

黒い家　Black House

ロミオとジュリエットのバルコニー

黒い家

神奈川県横浜市磯子区／1968
Black House
Isogo-ku, Yokohama-shi, Kanagawa

外壁は黒色の鉄板とし、内部は小さな吹き抜けにテラスを設けた小住宅である。仙田満の処女作である。巨大遊具の家とも名づけられ、吹き抜けのギャラリーにハムレットのバルコニーがコンセプトとして埋め込まれた。生活行動の回遊性も意識された住宅である。小さな遊環構造的住宅といえる。

With black metal outer walls, this small residence has a compact area with a high ceiling and a terrace in the inside. It was the first work of Mitsuru Senda. Also named the "giant toy," the inside gallery contains a balcony that was modeled after Hamlet. The house was also designed in consideration of free movement in living in the house. It can be considered a small circular play system-like house.

1968

黒い家 Black House

バルコニーの見上げと
バルコニーからの見下げ
Looking up from the balcony,
and looking down from the balcony.

1979-1975

遊具　Play Structure

プレイストラクチャー

遊具

1979-1975
Play Structure

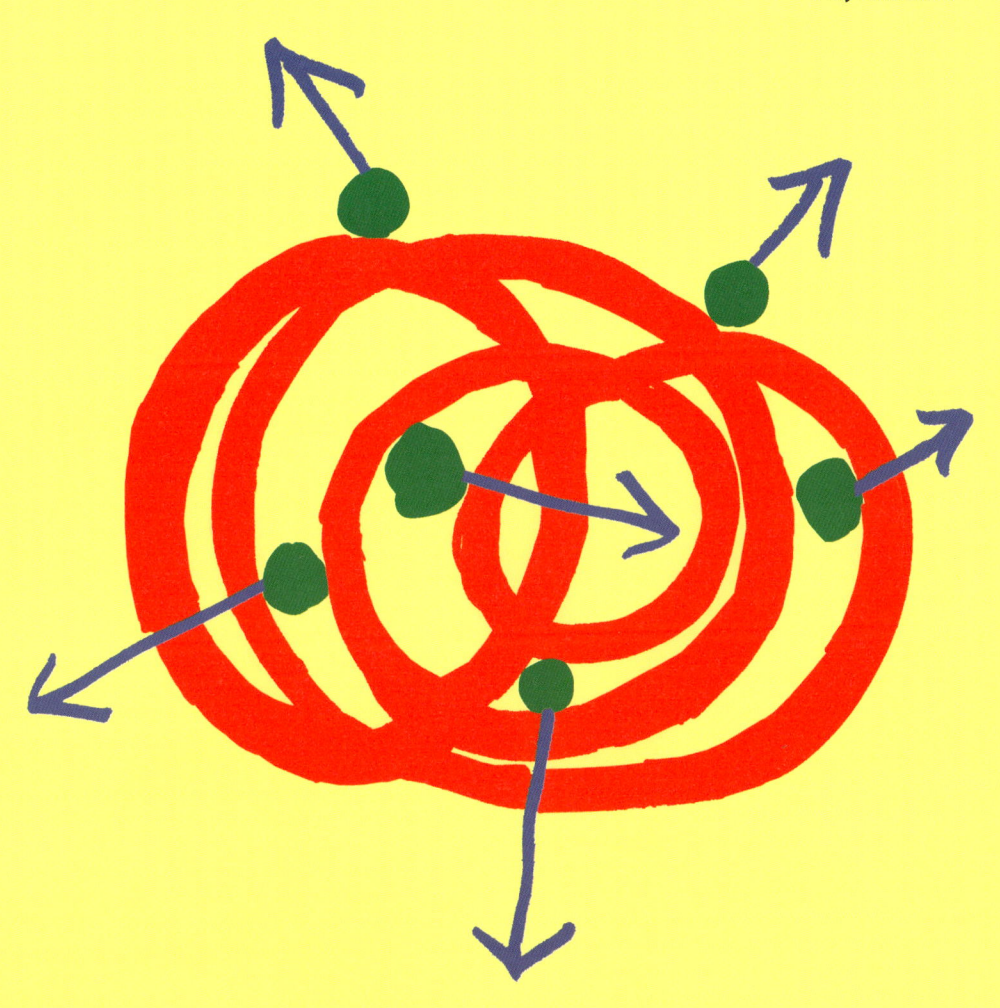

遊具はこどものあそびを引き起こし運動を誘発する装置である。あまり複雑でなく、シンプルさが必要だ。こどもの遊環行動が喚起される小さな仕掛けだ。そしてデザイナーとしては頭の体操になる。

Play structure has the purpose of invoking the urge to play in children and connecting that urge with exercise. These devices should be simple, and not too complicated. This is a small device that incites play behavior in children. This achievement was also a mental exercise for the designer.

1979-1975

遊具　Play Structure

TUBE α
1978
TUBE α

ピンポング
1979
Ping Pong

パネルトンネル
1976
Panel Tunnel

プレイロード
ステーション
1976
Play Road Station

1979-1975

遊具　Play Structure

メイズプレイス
1979
Maze Place

ポケットパーク
1981
Pocket Park

スカイネット
1979
SkyNet

赤い靴
1978
Red Shoes

野中保育園を中心に

塩川寿平×仙田 満

巨大遊具としての野中保育園

仙田 満（以下S） 野中保育園「野中ザウルス」の竣工は、1972年でしたかね。僕の事務所が43年目になるんです。だから野中保育園は39年前だと思うんですね。

塩川寿平（以下J） 仙田先生の息子さんがまだ2歳か3歳で、ちんちんの高さを測って、こども用の便器の高さを決めたんですよね。

S そういう意味ではとても長い時間使っていただいています。野中ザウルスができたあと、約10年後の81年に「野中丸」。自分でいうのもなんだけど、日本の保育史上、保育上の建築物としては、画期的なものだと思っています。当時、野中保育園は「どろんこ保育」が中心で、僕は「こどもの国」をやったあとだったこともあり、がらくた公園とか、野性的な空間のアナーキースペースといったことを主張してつくらせていただきました。

J 野中保育園の特色は、自然の中に溶け込んで、自然にたわむれることができること。もともと田んぼと柿の果樹園でしたから、何かものをつくることよりも土と会話する、たわむれるのです。そこでこども達はどろんこになったり、森にある落ち葉の山の中にもぐったり、落ち葉を飛ばしてあそぶ。心理学で言う「表出」がすごく多いんです。今の幼児教育では、形を認める、人に評価される「表現」が盛んで、汚れる、汚い、後始末が大変な「表出」はぐーっと減っているんです。

S 僕は、寿平さんのお母さんの塩川豊子[*1]先生に「こども達が来た時に、保育室におもちゃが散らばっている状態と、整理された状態とでは、朝の過ごし方が違うのよ」といわれたことをすごく覚えています。それはこどもにとって、整頓されていない中での想像力の刺激は重要だし、建物をつくってからの40年間、どんどん手あかで汚れて、べたべたとこども達の絵が貼られていったことによっても、空間としての迫力がますます出てきたなと感じます。

J 豊子先生は「片付けることから入ってはだめ」とよく言っていたんですね。自然の中に行くと、どんぐりが落ちていたり、棒切れが落ちていたり、それを目で見て感じて、そして何をしようかな、ということを考えていく。がらくたも同じで、大人から見ると散らばっているけれど、こどもにとっては整理されているんです。むしろ歩いてぶつかるようにしたり、板切れがあったり、トタンがあったり、段ボールがあったりほかのものも置いてある。三輪車も園庭に適当な間隔で置いておくことで、何かが触発されていくのです。

S こども達は刺激されますね。

J 野中保育園の建物もできてから40年近くなりますから、多くの理事から「建て替えたら」といわれていますが、理事長の塩川寿一は「これは世界遺産だから壊さないように」っていうんです。仙田さんは「こどもはごはんと寝る以外は全部あそびだ」とおっしゃって、「巨大遊具建築」という言葉をつくられた。保育園というところは、朝から夜遅くまでいる場所だから、ひとりになれる空間とか、仲良し数人でいるところとか、自分達がドキドキする空間、秘密基地がいっぱい必要なんです。

建物ができた当時の保育教育関係の学界では「危険だ」といわれましたけれど、こどもは危機になると泣いたり、大声でわめいたりして大人に知らせますからね。私は「半管理空間（相互に見え隠れする範囲のすき間）」と命名したのですが、大人から見るとすき間があって、注意をすることもできるのです。

S 基本的に平屋だけど、立体的につくっていますからね。声もよく通ります。

J 僕は見学者の方には「イースト菌でパンをふくらましたように、おもちゃをふくらませた巨大遊具」と説明しています。建物をつくってから40年近く、飽きることなく、至るところボロボロになっています。でも豊子先生や今の理事長は、ボロボロのところを嫌がるのではなく、それが自然だという。散らばっているといえばそうなのですが、こどもがあそびやすいリズムでものが整理されている。こども達は園に来てすぐ、あそび始められるところがいっぱいあるわけです。

こどもの五感を刺激し
想像力をつくる場

J 自然ほど、複雑にいろいろなものを提供してくれるものはありません。秋になれば落ち葉になるし、春になれば芽吹いてくる。園内に2カ所あるビオトープでは、こども達が朝から晩まで真剣にザリガニを釣っています。ああいう活動で、大脳へ活発に電気信号を出しているし、整理されてない空間の方が、直感が働く。汚い、汚れる、ということではないんです。木が腐って、倒れて、そのままにしておいたら皮をはいで、その木の枝でチャンバラをする。こども達自身が、自然のリズムを知って、自分にとって必要な道具をつくっていくのです。

S そういう刺激的な五感は大切です。もともと保育園を始めて何年になりますか？

J 58年です。

S 僕が野中保育園へ20年ほど前にあそびに行った時驚いたのは、成人式を迎えたこどもが挨拶に来ていたこと。やっぱりこの園はすごいなあ、と思いましたよ。野中保育園の卒業生の追跡調査をしたいですよね。ある意味、クリエイティブに、積極的に生きていると思うんです。

J 昭和28年に創立してから、卒園生は2,890名ほどいます。彼らの両親、じいちゃん、ばあちゃん、親戚も含めるとなると、だいたい1万5,000人くらい、つまり富士宮市の人口13万人の一割は園の関係者というわけです。野中保育園の「どろんこ祭り」にもたくさんの方が来てくれるし、日曜日には老人会の方が貸してほしいとやってくる。保育関係者以外の人たちも、仙田さんの園舎を見に来ます。市長も「野中保育園の貢献度は、歴史

塩川寿平（しおかわ じゅへい）
1938年満州国奉天市（現中国瀋陽市）生まれ。わが国における保育環境論の第一人者。明治学院大学大学院（修士）卒業。大中里保育園長、野中保育園理事、大地教育研究所長。淑徳大学助教授、静岡県立大学教授、東横学園女子短大特任教授。主な著書に大地保育三部作『名のない遊び』『どろんこ保育』『大地保育環境論（こども環境学会論文賞）』フレーベル館。

Conversation

塩川寿平 × 仙田満
Juhei Shiokawa × Mitsuru Senda

対談

野中保育園を中心に About Nonaka Nursery School

を超える重みがある」といってくださっています。そうなると野中保育園の理論が、いろいろな人に浸透していきます。僕も学者のはしくれなので、「こどものアニミズム論」だと思っているのですが、こどもが棒切れを刀と命名すれば刀になるし、トンネルをお城とか戦車とかいうような一人称の見方が広まっていきます。例えばどろんこを見て、大人は「黒い、汚い、汚れる、大腸菌がいる」という発想で、避けてしまいます。しかしこどもは「おしるこ、コーヒー、チョコレート工場」と表現する。あるいは、グラウンドに線を引いただけで「玄関」といって靴を脱いでいる。野中保育園のこども達は、そういうまったく創造的な世界を、自分でつくり出すことができるんです。日本保育学会でも汐見稔幸*2先生はじめ、多くの方々に野中保育園の大地保育を支持いただいているのです。

S 日本の幼稚園や保育園の幼児教育、ヨーロッパの教育論と比べても、野中保育園の環境も理論も全然負けてない。野中保育園は、世界的な幼児の環境としてもすばらしい、と思いますね。野中丸ができてから、階段でつなぎましたよね。ああいう動線をつくって、変化がありましたか。

J そうですね。改めて「体育をしましょう」と言わなくても、こども達は登ったり、降りたり、もぐったり、跳んだり、自然にからだ全部の筋肉を使っています。

S よく運動できるこどもが、脳を発達させるんですよね。

J 先日、野中保育園について講演をしてほしいと頼まれ講演したのですが、その場にいらっしゃった脳外科の先生たちから称賛を受けました。一番脳を活性化するのは、泥のつるつるや木登りなんだそうです。建物にも、こども達は慰安と休息のために来るわけではないんです。ほとんどの時間を野外であそんでい

て、雨が降った時とか、寝る時とか、食事の時くらいしか建物の中にいません。それがこどもの生活には一番合っていると思います。

S 東京の3、4歳のこども達が、自分で歩かないでバギー車に乗せられているのを見ると、こども達はどう成長するのだろうと心配しています。

J よくあそんで脳を使わない限り、あっちにぶつかる、こっちにぶつかる、というふうになりますよ。

S 今おっしゃったように、障害物があってつまずいても、手をつくこともできない、だからケガも多くなる。その点、野中保育園では、いつも中でも外でも駆け回らないといけないですからね。こども達自身が自然に危険を回避するわざが身についていますね。

J 野中保育園では、こども達を自由にさせる教育方針です。早いうちから自治の能力を身につけさせていきます。4歳で丸太にくぎを打って、5歳で小屋をつくり、卒園していきます。危険なところは先生が見ますが、ほとんどこどもに任せているんです。だから自分で転ぶとか、自分でケガをするとか、自爆が多いです（笑）。だけど自爆というのは、本人がイタイ思いをして二度とやらないように注意する。すごい教育効果がありますよ。

S みんなであそぶところと、ひとりや数人の小さな集団であそぶところ、と空間の変化や選択ができることも、こども達の心や体の成長には必要なことです。

J　そんな汚くて危なっかしいところに、卒園生が慕って成人式に来てくれたり、卒業後も自分の息子や娘を入れようと思ってくださっている、といったように、入園希望の方が来てくれるということは、支持されているということですよね。

こども達にとって自然と広さは重要

S　野中保育園は、面積も大きいじゃないですか。だからこども達は多様な体験ができますよね。

J　ちょうど3,500坪ぐらいあります。住宅部分を含めると、4,000坪、1万㎡くらいはあります。でもそれは決してぜいたくではないですね。こどもの育つエネルギーを考えると。

S　最低でも保育園には5,000㎡の広さは必要ですよ。

J　自分の仕事、あそびに打ち込んでいる時には、ケンカをする必要がまったくない。逆にいえば、過密がケンカのもとですから、広さというのは多面的に重要です。

S　広いと、みんなであそべるところと、ひとりや小さな集団であそべるところ、いろんな選択ができる。それが、こども達の心や体の成長には不可欠です。逃げ場がないところは、いじめは発生しやすいんじゃないかな。私の友人で、こども社会学者は「いじめは閉鎖空間のあそびだ」といっています。

J　あと、ブランコが混んでいれば滑り台に行くような、こっちが混んでいればあっちにと選択肢が増えれば、ケンカも減ります。幼児のケンカは、そういった利害対立ですからね。こども達のエネルギーを吸収できるくらいの広さは必要ですね。

S　もし自分の園が小さければ、園外保育で公園や自然の山を使うとかしたほうがいいと思うんです。最近保育園の環境と運動量の関係についての研究を、万歩計を使って進めているのですが、その調査の中で園庭のない保育園でも、毎日こども達を近くの公園に連れて行っている園では、こども達の運動量はそれほど変わらないことが明らかになっています。野中保育園の園児は2時間のお昼寝をしっかりとっているにもかかわらず、他の園児に比べ約1.5～3倍くらい歩いたり走ったりしています。

J　いま野中保育園ではキウイが1,000個以上なるんです。1カ月くらいねかせて、熟させて食べています。ほかにも甘柿、渋柿、びわ、みかんなど、実のなる木を植えています。

S　運動会のために広々とした運動場を用意するのではなく、本当は小学校でも木を植えるべきです。

J　木を植えるスペースなど、自然を広く取った方がいいですね。

S　これからの日本のこども達を育てる環境として、僕は40年前に塩川先生達の理念を、少なくとも建築的にお手伝いすることができて幸運だったと思います。いまはちょっとでも危ないものは排除したがる傾向が強いのですが、本質的には野中保育園のような空間がますます必要になっていると思います。

J　野菜を育てることとか、太陽や雨に感謝することとか、環境教育についていわれていますが、自然の恵みに感謝することなんです。野中保育園のこども達は、見かけのきれいさや大人の利便性ではなく、仙田さんの感性でできた戸外と直結した園舎のおかげで自然と生活することができて、本当に感謝しています。

＊1　塩川豊子（しおかわ とよこ）1915～1999　野中保育園（静岡県富士宮市）"大地保育"創立者
＊2　汐見稔幸（しおみ としゆき）1947～　教育学者

About Nonaka Day Nursery

Juhei Shiokawa × Mitsuru Senda

Nonaka Day Nursery as a huge play structure

Mitsuru Senda (S): I suppose Nonaka Day Nursery (*Nonaka-Saurus*) was completed in 1972. My office is in the 43rd year in business. So I think I worked on Nonaka Day Nursery 39 years ago.

Juhei Shiokawa (J): I remember your son was two or three years old and we decided the height of children's toilets by measuring the distance of his willie from the ground.

S: In that sense, the facility has been in place for a very long time. 10 years after I worked on *Nonaka-Saurus*, I created *Nonaka-Maru* in 1981. Looking back, it is an unprecedented achievement as the building for a nursery school in the history of children's education in Japan. In those days, Nonaka Day Nursery was famous for letting children play in mud. It was right after I completed the project of *Kodomo-no-kuni* (Children's Land) and I was involved in the design of such structures as *Garakuta-Koen* (Junk Park) by focusing on the creation of anarchical space found in wilderness.

J: At Nonaka Day Nursery, children can blend into the nature and play with it. The area used to contain rice paddies and an orchard of persimmon trees. So it is fitted for talking and playing with the soil rather than creating something. Children play there by getting covered in mud, diving into fallen leaves in the forest, and dispersing fallen leaves. You see a lot of "expressions" as defined by psychology in children here. In the current children's education, "presentations" are promoted since they lead to the recognition of shapes and are evaluated by others. We see dwindling cases of "expressions" where things get dirty, soiled, and messy.

S: Your mother, Toyoko Shiokawa[*1], once told me that children spend the morning in totally different manners in case the room is cluttered with toys or everything is tidy. I think what she meant is that children get important stimulations to their imagination in cluttered environments. 40 years after the construction, the building has become more impressive as it has got soiled with the hands of children and had its walls decorated with many paintings by children.

J: My mother used to say that we should not give precedence to keeping the space tidy. As you walk in the nature, you see acorns and sticks lying around on the ground and get inspired to do something. It is the same thing with junk. The environment is just untidy from the viewpoint of adults, but it is organized for children. So we need to create the environment where children bump into something while walking or find various objects like galvanized plates, boards, or cardboard boxes. Placing tricycles on the playground in appropriate intervals will inspire something in children.

S: Children get stimulation from those things.

J: Since the building for Nonaka Day Nursery has been in place more than 40 years, many of our board members say it is time to rebuild it but our chairperson, Juichi Shiokawa, says that we should not demolish it since this is a world heritage site. You always say that children are playing when they are not eating or sleeping and created the word of "giant play structure building." A nursery school is where children stay from early morning to late night, so children need hidden space where they can stay alone, play with several good friends, or feel excited. When the building was constructed, the academic community related to children's education used to say the environment was too dangerous. However, children give alerts to adults by crying or shrieking when they feel a danger. I name this space "the semi-managed space controlled through half-visible gaps". Adults can see how children spend their time through the gaps and take necessary precautions.

S: It is basically a building with one floor but has an effective structure where you can make your voice clearly heard from a distance.

J: I tell visitors that this is a huge toy like bread bloated with yeast. I have never got tired of the building nearly 40 years since we created it and every part of it has become tattered. My mother and our current chairperson do not hate it and say that it is just natural. You can call it untidy but it is organized in the rhythm enabling children to play. As soon as children enter the school, they find many places where they can start their fun activities.

The place stimulates the senses of children to foster their creativity.

J: Nature is the best environment providing many things in a complex manner. It provides fallen leaves in autumn and new buds in spring. At the biotope space in two locations of the school, children try hard to catch crayfish from morning to night. They actively transmit electronic signals to their brain through that sort of activities and get more instinctive in unorganized settings. This environment is not simply dirty or soiled. As trees get rotten and fall on the ground, children let them stay where they are, peel the bark, and duel with each other with branches. They get to know the rhythm of nature and create necessary tools on their own.

S: Giving stimulation to children's senses is important. How long have you been running this nursery school?

J: 58 years.

S: What surprised me when I visited Nonaka Day Nursery about 20 years ago was young people who celebrated their coming-of-age day came over to visit the school. The incident made me realize once again what a great school this was. I want to trace what kind of life people have after finishing this school. I suppose they should be leading their lives in a creative and positive manner.

J: We have come up with about 2,890 graduates since we founded this school in 1953. As I count their parents, grandparents, and relatives, approximately 15,000 people, corresponding to 10% of the total 130,000 residents of Fujinomiya City, are related to the school. Many people come to our Mud Festival and on Sundays elderly group people come to us to use our facilities. Even people not directly involved in children's education come to see the building you designed. Our mayor also says that the significance of Nonaka Day Nursery is greater than its history. This way, the principles of this school have permeated many people. I myself am a scholar and believe that this is the animism theory for children. As children call a stick a sword, it becomes a sword. They can also call a tunnel a castle or a tank based on their imagination. For example, adults try to avoid mud by associating it with such negative words as "black, dirty, soiled, and E. coli." However, children think about "*Oshiruko* (sweet red bean soup), coffee, and a chocolate factory." Or they take off their shoes as they draw a line on the playground and call it an entrance. Children of Nonaka Day Nursery can create that sort of totally creative situations on their own. Many members of the Japan Society of Research on Early Childhood Care and Education, including Professor Toshiyuki Shiomi[*2], support the educational principle rooted in natural environments offered by Nonaka Day Nursery.

S: The environment and theory offered by Nonaka Day Nursery are superb even in comparison with the children's education in Japanese nursery schools and day care centers or the European education theory. The education provided here is wonderful as the environment for global children's education. As we created *Nonaka-Maru*, the staircases connected the whole space. Did the flow bring about any changes?

J: Yes. We do not have to tell our children to exercise. They naturally use the muscles of their whole body by climbing and get down, diving and jumping.

S: Children who exercise a lot can greatly develop their brain

J: I was asked to make a lecture on Nonaka Day Nursery the other day. The brain surgeons attending the lecture praised what we do. The activities that activate our brain best are fiddling with mud and climbing up trees. Children do not come to our building to have fun or rest. They spend most of their time outside and come inside the building when it rains or when they sleep or eat. That's the most appropriate way to spend their time.

S: Watching three or four year old children placed in strollers instead of walking on their own feet makes me wonder how they will grow.

J: Unless children play and use their brain a lot, they bump into something here and there.

S: That's right. As they stumble on something, they cannot hold out their hands and get easily injured. In contrast, children here need to run around all the time inside and outside Nonaka Day Nursery. They naturally get the knack to dodge dangers.

J: Nonaka Day Nursery has the policy to let children do what they want to do. We try to allow children to control what they do at an early stage. They drive nails on tree trunks at age four, build a cabin at age 5, and finish this school. Teachers watch activities to avoid any danger, but we leave most of the activities to children. This frequently leads to stumbling or hurting themselves (laughter). Children learn quickly not to make the same mistake by hurting themselves. This is a quite effective educational process.

S: Being able to change space and select appropriate space by playing together or playing alone or in small groups is also important for the development of children's mind and body.

J: Our school involves a lot of dirty and dangers but our graduates come to visit us on their coming-of-age day and try to send their sons and daughters to this school. Many people coming to our school to place their children here means that they support what this school stands for.

Nature and spaciousness are two important requirements for children.

S: Nonaka Day Nursery is spacious. It allows children to experience many things.

J: The size of the school is around 3,500 tsubo (11,550㎡). The total space including the residential space is 4,000 tsubo, around 13,200㎡. But this size is not luxurious at all for the energy of growing children.

S: A nursery school should have at least 5,000㎡ in size.

J: When children are focused on their work or play, they should not fight each other. In other words, congestion creates fighting. So spaciousness is important in many ways.

S: When you are in a spacious place, you can make multiple choices by playing alone or in small groups. This is essential for the development of children's mind and body. I suppose bullying tend to take place where you do not find hidden places. A friend of mine who is a sociologist on children says that bullying is a play taking place in closed space.

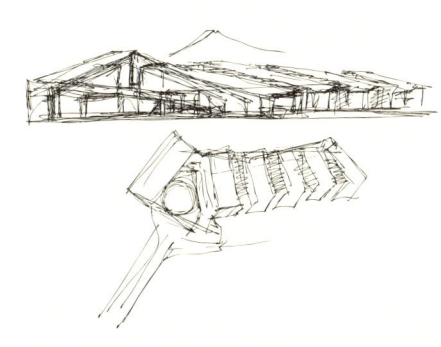

J: As children come up with many choices by avoiding congested swings and going to chutes, we see less instances of fighting. Children fight based on this sort of conflicts of interests. The space needs to be large enough to absorb the energy of children.

S: If your school is small, you need to use parks or hills by educating children off-site. I have recently been using a pedometer to study the correlation between the environment of nursery schools and the volume of exercise. The research has uncovered that exercise volume does not greatly decrease even at nursery schools without a playground as far as teachers take children to nearby parks every day. Children at Nonaka Day Nursery take a full two-hour nap, but they walk and run 1.5-3 times as much as children at other nursery schools.

J: Every year, our school grows more than 1,000 kiwis. We let them sit about one month and eat them after they get ripe. We also plant trees that bear fruits like sweet persimmons, tart persimmons, loquats, and tangerine oranges.

S: We do not need to have a spacious playing field for the sports day. We definitely need to plant more trees at elementary schools.

J: We need to have spacious natural spaces where we can plant trees.

S: I am so lucky that I was able to assist the ideals set by Mr. Shiokawa and other educators through architecture 40 years ago to create an environment to educate Japanese children shouldering the future of the country. Nowadays we have a strong trend to try to avoid danger at all costs, but we are basically seeing a growing necessity to have the space offered by Nonaka Day Nursery.

J: Many people advocate education on environment by growing vegetables and appreciating the sun or rain. We need to thank the blessings by nature at the end of the day. Children of Nonaka Day Nursery can live with nature since the building is closely linked with the outside world thanks to the sensitivity you injected into it. They do not spend their time based on superficial neatness or convenience for adults. I really appreciate what you have done for us.

✻1 Toyoko Shiokawa (1915-1999)**:** Founder of Nonaka Day Nursery (Fujinomiya-shi, Shizuoka Prefecture) and Daichi Hoiku (nature child care).
✻2 Toshiyuki Shiomi (1947-)**:** Educationist.

Juhei Shiokawa

Born in 1938 in the Chinese city of Mukden (modern day Shenyang) and one of the foremost experts in Japan on childcare environments. Graduated with a master's degree from the graduate school of Meiji Gakuin University. Serves as principal of Onakazato Nursery School, president of Nonaka Nursery School and director of the Daichi Education Institute. Serves as associate professor of Shukutoku University, professor at the University of Shizuoka, and special appointed professor at the Toyoko Gakuen Women's College. Publications include the three parts of the Daichi Education theory, "Games with No Names," "Doronko Childcare," and "Theories on the Daichi Childcare Environment" (winner of the Academic Paper Prize of the Association for Children's Environment), Froebel-kan, Co., Ltd.

塩川寿平×仙田満

Juhei Shiokawa × Mitsuru Senda

Conversation

仙田満が仙田満となるまで

藤森照信×仙田 満

卒業設計は「城」だった

仙田 満（以下S） この間、茅野市民館の展覧会で藤森さんの卒業設計を拝見してびっくりしたんですよ。大変な労作ですね。

藤森照信（以下F） ありがとうございます。仙田さんの時はどうでしたか？

S 僕の時は共同です。僕は卒論で城の研究をしました。藤岡通夫[*1]先生という城の大家がいたのですが、谷口吉郎先生の研究室で、建築論として城をやったのです。

F お城、ですか？

S そう。城はたったの50年ぐらいで、それまでの日本建築とは異なる新しい様式を完成するのですが、城をつくる人達というのは、下克上した武将も、宮大工も、田舎大工も、千利休のような時代の文化人もいると考えました。僕は結局、「城は組織である」「新しい時代をつくる様式は、多様なデザイナーのコラボレーションによる」という結論を出したのです。

F へえー。

S 結論を証明するために卒業設計を4人の共同で、計32枚の設計図で発表しました。

F すごいですね。

S そしてその延長が「環境デザイン研究所」という、僕の研究所になっているんですよ。

F そうですか。それで野中保育園のような面白いものをつくっていかれるんですね。野中保育園には、ちゃんと計画された空き地があったりと、建物に限らない建築としてうまくできていますよね。仙田さんがいつからこういうことに気づかれて、なさっているのか知りたい。

S 僕が独立したのは26歳の時ですが、大学卒業後、菊竹清訓[*2]事務所に入ったのです。

F そのあたりの話を、もう少し詳しく教えてください。

菊竹清訓事務所入所前後の仙田さん

S 大学4年の時、助教授になられたばかりの篠原一男[*3]さんが大学にいらして、僕は篠原研究室ではなかったのですが、「菊竹（清訓）事務所に入りたい」といいに行ったんです。そうしたら電話してくださって。

F 篠原先生が学生の面倒を見たり、口を利いてくれたんですか！

S そうなんです、まだその頃は（笑）。それで僕は図面を持って菊竹さんに会いに行ったのです。スカイハウスから四谷の小さなビルの3階に移った頃で、内井昭蔵[*4]さんと最初にお会いし、その後菊竹さんに図面を見てもらいました。

F 内井さんが番頭というわけですね。

S ええ。それから8月末に電報で「ニュウショキョカシマス」と連絡が来たんです。

F 電報はまだ取ってありますか？

S ないですね（笑）。僕が入所した時というのは、京都国際会館のコンペを大谷幸夫[*5]さんに取られて、事務所ががっかり感と、何くそという挑戦的な高まりの交錯する時期でしたね。長谷川逸子[*6]さんと一緒に入ったのですが、彼女は前から事務所でアルバイトをしていて、とにかく図面がうまい。僕はなぜ入れたのかよくわからなかったですね。

藤森照信（ふじもり てるのぶ）

1946年長野県生まれ。建築家。東北大学建築学科卒業。東京大学大学院に学ぶ。現在、東京大学名誉教授。工学院大学教授。専門は、日本近代建築史。45歳より設計も手がけ、神長官守矢史料館、高過庵（茶室）を設計。主な著書に『日本の近代建築』（上・下）岩波書店。

F　当時は誰がいたんですか。

S　チーフで内井昭蔵さん、遠藤勝勧*7さん、小川惇*8さんの3人。内井さんがプランとか構想を、小川さんはエレベーションを、遠藤さんはディテールを担当していました。武者英二*9さんもすごい人でしたね。今いっしょにやっている斉藤義さんも茅ケ崎パシフィックホテルを担当していました。

F　遠藤さんは、今でもディテールの人ですからね。もうその時、菊竹さんは「か・かた・かたち」*10を提唱されていたのですか？

S　はい、やっていました。僕も入って半年間は「か・かた・かたち」という理論の応用係で、プレゼンテーションを担当していました。事務所は厳しかったけど楽しかったですね。当時の菊竹事務所は、土曜日が休みだったんです。

F　土曜が休みですか、すごいですね。

S　だから毎週、菊竹事務所が手がけた作品を見に行っていました。ある工場で、菊竹さんの取り換えの理論によるサッシの現場を見たのですが、サッシを取り換えるようにアングルで留めてあったのですが、アングルがサッシより先に錆びてしまって、漏水して取り換えなければいけない状態になっていた。僕は「理論と実際は違うのだ、理論通りやってはいけないこともある」ということを学びました。

F　大事なことに気づかれましたね。

S　やがて菊竹事務所で「こどもの国」の設計をすることになり、浅田孝*11さんが仕切って、大谷幸夫さん、イサム・ノグチ*12さん、黒川紀章*13さん、大高正人*14さんなどがかかわっていました。

F　そうそうたるメンバーですね。そこに仙田さんはスタッフとして入られたのですね。

S　はい。そこで林間学校の現場に常駐していたのですが、イサムさんの仕事に感心したことがあるんです。現場で土の山をつくるのですが、ブルドーザーの職人に「5cm削れ」っていう。しかし職人は10cm削ってしまう。

F　ブルドーザーの作業誤差だけでも5cmありますよね。

S　そうなんです。でもあと5cmといいながら、たちどころに土が形を変えて、イサムワールドになっていくんですね。すごいなあ、僕も土をデザインしたいなあと思いましたよ。

こども向け施設の第一人者となる

F　こどもの国の経験が、その後の建築につながっていたのは、仙田さんだけですか？

S　そうですね。

F　結局みんな、相当違う方向の建築に行ってますよね。黒川さんも浅田さんも全然違いますね。

S　僕は「こどもの国」の仕事をした後で独立して、厚生省の方が主宰の、児童遊園研

対談

仙田満が仙田満となるまで

How Mitsuru Senda has accumulated his career

会に参加したんです。その時の議論の影響が大きいですね。それと植田実さんが編集長をしていた『都市住宅』で、こどもについての特集が組まれたことも、僕自身がこどもの環境について考えをまとめるきっかけになりました。

F 野中保育園はその頃ですか？もともとどういうご縁だったのでしょう。

S 当時の園長の息子さんの塩川寿平さんと、その研究会で知り合い、それが新園舎の設計を頼まれるきっかけになったんです。

F そこで仙田さんの人生が決まった、大事な分岐点になったのですね。当時から野中保育園はどろんこ教育をやっていたんですか？

S やっていました。園舎ができてから、いわゆる保育界、保育学会が取り上げてくださって、どろんこ保育、大地保育の野中保育園として名前が知られるようになったのです。

F 当時あった保育園はどこでも、どろんこなんて日常だったでしょう。でも仙田さんのおしゃれな園舎だから話題になったのでしょうね。行ってびっくりしたのは、仙田さんのプランと、地形と、保育園の教育方針が合っていることです。起きたい時に起きて、寝たい子は寝て、あそびたい子はあそんでいて。

S 当時の園長だった塩川豊子[*15]先生が共感してくださって。僕は前から、アナーキースペースとか、アジトスペースとか、計画されていないところについて話していたんです。

F 塩川園長は経験的にご存じだったわけでしょうが、仙田さんはどういうところで気づいたのですか？経験といっても、菊竹さんはそういう設計の進め方はしてないでしょう。

S むしろ僕はこどもの時の経験ですね、ほら僕らは防空壕世代だから。アジトをつくったり、壮大なあそびの陣地をつくったり。僕はこどもの環境形成力が必要だと思っている。

F ああ、こどもの環境づくりではなく、こども自らが環境をつくりあげることが大切だ、と。

S そうです、こども達自身が環境をつくりあげる力ですね。

F 昔はそれしかなかった、自分たちであそぶ環境をつくって、その中であそんでいた。

S だから建築家がすべてをつくりあげるのは、こどもの空間としてまずいと思うのです。

F なるほど、面白いですね。当時、そのようなことを考えている人ってほかにいましたか？

S たぶん今でも少ないんじゃないでしょうか、特に建築家は。そういう考えは、建築界ではなかなか評価されなくて。今でも日本建築家協会の25年賞には2回落ちています。

F 写真にはこの面白さは写らないですよ。僕は写真家の藤塚光政さんに「写真じゃわからないから、現物を見に行け」といわれて、見に行ったのです。現場を見て衝撃で、こどもの行為と時間がからみ合っていましたね。

S 保育界では評価されているんですよ。

F 今伺っていて、何かしら系譜がある気がしました。今和次郎[*16]さん、世界でも珍しい方向に興味をもっていた方ですが、今さんから川添登[*17]さん、吉阪隆正[*18]さん、そして僕が所属している路上観察学会[*19]、という流れがある。仙田さんもその流れにあるのですね。

S 実はこの野中保育園のことで、早稲田大学に呼ばれ講演会をしたことがあるのです。その時吉阪さんにほめられました。とてもうれしかったことを覚えています。

F そうでしょうね。仙田さんのようなプランをもっていても、吉阪さんはル・コルビュジエ[*20]

の影響が強くて理論化はできなかったのではないでしょうか。

野中保育園の設計裏話

S 最初は、塩川寿平さんが2階建てのスケッチを持ってきたんですよ。でも僕は「何よりもあの富士山を見せたいから、2階建てではだめ」と提案して、平屋の設計にしたんです。

F 取材で野中保育園には行っていますが、その話は初耳ですね。

S それは僕しか知らない話ですよ（笑）。

F 保育園としては、ほかに建築に対して強い意見はなかったんですか。

S ほとんど任せてくれましたね。北側の敷地の形をそのまま建築の外形に取り入れたり、保育室に中2階を設けてそれをつないだり、こどもの行動の連続性ということを意識していましたね。お金がないから構造は軽量鉄骨で、内装は厚さ3mmのベニヤなんです。

F ふつうは5mm以上使いたいですよね。3mmというと、ペラペラのベニヤですよね、学芸会に使うような。今でもそれですか？

S そうです。それでも残っているからすごい。しかも3mmベニヤのすごいところは、こどもがぶつかっても壁の方がへこんでくれるから、たんこぶができないんですよ。

F あれこれ聞いていると、いろいろ考え直さないといけないですね。あと、使う側の問題、ソフトの問題もありますよね。

S 建物ができたあとの問題ですね。あそこの廊下は、アスファルトなんですね。

F え・・・？

S 床がアスファルトなんで、ときどき穴が開くんですよ。

F アスファルトは中に空気があるから、弾性もある。こどもは裸足だから、その方がいいんですね、それは気づかなかったなあ。

S この建築はやはり「か・かた・かたち」をやったことが、影響していますよ。材料やディテールよりも保育園の新しい型をつくろうとしたんですね。型を優先して形としての材料やディテールは徹底したローコストです。

F 原理を考え、計画を考え、形に持っていく、という手順や理論をつくり出すということですね。

S そうです。新しい保育園の型をつくろうと懸命でしたね。とはいえ、野中保育園のこども達を見ていると、僕が建築家としてこども達の成長に何を寄与できているかわからないけれども。やはり自然やどろんこの力は大きい。

F いやいや、野中保育園はうまく生きていると思います。建築のあり方として、一つの理想形ですよ。

---

*1 藤岡通夫（ふじおか みちお）1908〜1988　建築史家
*2 菊竹清訓（きくたけ きよのり）1928〜　建築家
*3 篠原一男（しのはら かずお）1925〜2006　建築家
*4 内井昭蔵（うちい しょうぞう）1933〜2002　建築家
*5 大谷幸夫（おおたに さちお）1924〜　建築家、都市計画家
*6 長谷川逸子（はせがわ いつこ）1941〜　建築家
*7 遠藤勝勧（えんどう しょうかん）1934〜　建築家
*8 小川惇（おがわ まこと）1932〜　建築家
*9 武者英二（むしゃ えいじ）1936〜　建築家
*10 か、かた、かたち／1969年菊竹清訓が提唱した、代謝建築論
*11 浅田孝（あさだ たかし）1921〜1990　建築家
*12 イサム・ノグチ（Isamu Noguchi、日本名：野口 勇）1904〜1988　彫刻家、画家、インテリアデザイナー、造園家
*13 黒川紀章（くろかわ きしょう）1934〜2007　建築家
*14 大高正人（おおたか まさと）1923〜2010　建築家、都市計画家
*15 塩川豊子（しおかわ とよこ）1915〜1999　野中保育園（静岡県富士宮市）創立者
*16 今和次郎（こん わじろう）1888〜1973　民族学研究者
*17 川添登（かわぞえ のぼる）1926〜　建築家、建築評論家
*18 吉阪隆正（よしざか たかまさ）1917〜1980　建築家
*19 路上観察学会（ろじょうかんさつがっかい）／路上に隠れる建物（もしくはその一部）・看板・張り紙など、通常は景観とは見なされないものを観察・鑑賞する団体
*20 ル・コルビュジエ（Le Corbusier）1887〜1965　建築家

How Mitsuru Senda has accumulated his career

Terunobu Fujimori × Mitsuru Senda

My graduation project was on castles.

Mitsuru Senda (S): The other day I was amazed by your graduation project presented at an exhibition at the Chino Cultural Complex. It is a very impressive work requiring huge workload.

Terunobu Fujimori (F): Thank you. What was your graduation project like?

S: I was involved in a joint project. I researched castles in my thesis. There was a master on castles, named Michio Fujioka[*1]. I worked on the architecture theory of castles in the laboratory of Dr. Yoshiro Taniguchi.

F: You worked on castles?

S: Yes. Castles completed a totally new Japanese architectural style within a very short period of 50 years or so. I considered that people related to the construction of castles had included war lords who took their positions by killing other lords, castle builders, ordinary carpenters, and such cultural specialists of the era as Sen no Rikyu. I reached the conclusion that castle building required the organization of different elements at the end of day and that the style leading to the new era was made possible by the collaboration of multiple designers.

F: That is interesting.

S: In order to prove our theory, four students including me presented a total of 32 blue prints.

F: That is amazing.

S: This experience has led to Environment Design Institute that I am a part of.

F: I see. That has enabled you to create interesting things like Nonaka Day Nursery. Nonaka Day Nursery is very well designed as the architecture that does not fit the category of architecture by offering well-planned vacant space. I want to know when you came up with this sort of ideas.

S: I created my own business at age 26. Before that, I joined the office by Kiyonori Kikutake[*2] after finishing college.

F: Could you further elaborate on it?

Mitsuru Senda around the time he joined the office by Kiyonori Kikutake

S: In my senior year at college, Kazuo Shinohara[*3] came to my school as a new assistant professor. I was not a member of Shinohara laboratory but told him that I wanted to join the office of Dr. Kikutake. He was kind enough to call him up.

F: Professor Shinohara took care of students to help you get the job!

S: That's right. He was kind at that time (laughter). Then, I went to meet Dr. Kikutake with my blueprints. His office had just moved from Sky House to the third floor of a small building in Yotsuya, where Shozo Uchii[*4] met me first. After that, Dr. Kikutake was kind enough to take a look at my blueprints.

F: Dr. Uchii was his gate keeper.

S: Yes. Later I got a telegram allowing me to enter the office at the end of August.

F: Do you still have the telegram?

S: No, it's already gone (laughter). Around the time I joined the firm, the whole office was full of great disappointment and challenging spirit after having Sachio Otani[*5] snatch away the competition for Kyoto International Conference Center. I entered the firm with Itsuko Hasegawa[*6]. She had been working part time at the office and was very good at drawing blueprints. But I did not how I could join the office.

F: Who did you work with at that time?

S: We had three managers including Shozo Uchii, Shokan Endo[*7], and Makoto Ogawa[*8]. Dr. Uchii was in charge of planning and basic design, Mr. Ogawa took care of elevation, and Mr. Endo was into details. Another capable person was Eiji Musha[*9]. Tadashi Saito, whom I work with right now, was in charge of Chigasaki Pacific Hotel.

F: Mr. Endo is till into details. Did Dr. Kikutake advocate *"Ka-Kata-Katachi"*[*10] around that time?

S: Yes, he did. For six months after I joined the office, I was in charge of application of the theory of *"Ka-Kata-Katachi"* and working on presentations. I was run through the mill there but I had a fun time. We did not have to work on Saturdays at the Kikutake office in those days.

F: You did not have to work on Saturdays. That was rare.

S: So I visited various works done by the Kikutake office every week. When I visited a certain factory, I saw how the sashes were installed based on the replacement theory by Dr. Kikutake. I once found that the angle steel got rusty before the sashes, requiring the replacement due to the water leak. That way, I learned that theory and practice were two different things and that a theory could lead to a mistake.

F: That was educational for you.

S: Some time later, the Kikutake office was entrusted with the design for *Kodomo-no-Kuni* (Children's Land). Under the general management by Takashi Asada[*11], Sachio Otani, Isamu Noguchi[*12], Kisho Kurokawa[*13], and Masato Otaka[*14] were involved in the project.

F: You named such great people. So you worked with them on the project.

S: Yes. I was working on the site for campsite facilities and notice how Isamu Noguchi worked on the project. He was creating a mountain with soil on the site. As he told bulldozer operators to dig by 5 centimeters, they dug by 10 centimeters.

F: A 5-centimeter gap was created by the operation of a bulldozer.

S: Yes. He told the operators to dig another 5 centimeters and transformed the soil into different shapes in his own unique way. I was impressed with the work and felt like designing soil.

Becoming a specialist on facilities for children

F: Was it only you who have implemented further architecture projects based on the experience of *Kodomo-no-Kuni*?

S: That's right.

F: Other people have taken very different paths in architecture. Dr. Kikutake is not related to this area and Mr. Kurokawa and Mr. Asada are also doing completely different things.

S: I made my own business after working on the project of *Kodomo-no-Kuni* and joined the Working Group on Children's Parks hosted by the Ministry of Health and Welfare. The discussions that I had at that time gave great influence on my career. Also, Mr. Makoto Ueda featured children in his magazine *Toshi-Jutaku* (Urban Housing), which helped me sum up my ideas on the environment for children.

F: Did you work on Nonaka Day Nursery around that time? How did you get involved in the project for Nonaka Day Nursery?

S: I got acquainted with Juhei Shiokawa, a son of the then principal of the school, at the working group. That experience created the opportunity for him to ask me to design the new school building.

F: That way you encountered an important

intersection determining your career. Was Nonaka Day Nursery letting children play with mud around that time?

S: Yes. As the new school building was completed, the so-called children's education community and academic community referred to the school, which began to be known as the school educating children in mud and natural environment.

F: I suppose nursery schools everywhere used to let children play with mud in those days, but I think your stylish building made the school famous. What surprised me when I visited the school was that there was a complete match between your plan, the land features, and the school policy. Children got up, slept, or played whenever they wanted to.

S: Toyoko Shiokawa[15], then principal, had agreed with that direction. I myself had been talking with her on unplanned space, including anarchical space and secret bases.

F: Ms. Shiokawa should have known it from her experiences. How did you get the idea? You may say experiences, but Mr. Kikutake did not proceed with his design that way.

S: What I mean is my childhood experiences. As you know, we spent our childhood in air-raid shelters. I created my secret base and my grand turf to play there. I believe in the children's ability to create their own environment.

F: I see. You do not create environment for children but children create their environment on their own.

S: Right. I respect the children's ability to establish their environment.

F: That was the only way available. We created our own play environment and enjoyed out time in it.

S: So I think that it is not right if architects create everything for children's space.

F: I see. That's interesting. Were there any other people who shared your philosophy at that time?

S: I don't know. I do not think we have many people with this idea even now, especially architects. This idea has not really been evaluated in the architecture community. I have so far missed the Twenty-Five Year Award by the Japan Institute of Architects twice.

F: This charm cannot be represented on pictures. Mitsumasa Fujitsuka, a photographer, told me to see the actual site since pictures could not show the essence. Seeing the actual building shocked me. Children's actions and time were well intertwined there.

S: Children's education community highly evaluates the building.

F: As I listened to your story, I felt I saw some lineage there. Wajiro Kon[16] was interested in something very rare and very unique on a global scale. Starting with Mr. Kon, Noboru Kawazoe[17], Takamasa Yoshizaka[18], and *Rojoh-Kansatsu-Gakkai*[19] that I am a member of have created a certain movement. You are also a part of it.

S: I was actually once invited to visit Waseda University to make a speech on Nonaka Day Nursery. At that time, Mr. Yoshizaka gave me his compliment and I felt really happy.

F: I can see that. If Mr. Yoshizaka had come up with a plan like yours, he probably could not have make a theory out of it with a strong influence from Le Corbusier[20].

Anecdotes about designing Nonaka Day Nursery

S: At first, Juhei Shiokawa gave me his drawing showing a two-floor building, but I designed the structure with one floor, proposing that Mt. Fuji was the most important object we could see from there and that we should not create a two-story building to see Mt. Fuji.

F: I visited Nonaka Day Nursery for an interview, but I never heard of the story.

S: This is the secret story that only I know (laughter).

F: Did the school side have any requests for the architecture?

S: They basically let me do what I wanted to do. I focused on incorporating the northern side of the land into the exterior shape of the architecture as it was, creating the mezzanine on the nursery room and connecting it, and leveraging the consistency of children's actions. Since the budget was limited, we used light-gauge steel for the structure and 3-milimeter veneer for walls.

F: Usually we use at least 5-milimeter veneer. 3-milimeter veneer is very thin and used for props for a school play. Is it still in place?

S: I think it is wonderful that it is still there. What is great with 3-milimeter veneer is that children do not get lumps on their head since a wall absorbs the shock as children bump onto it.

F: Your story makes me rethink about many things. Furthermore, we have issues of how people use and maintain facilities.

S: You mean how we maintain the building after we complete it. The floor of the school is made of asphalt.

F: Oh…

S: Since it is made of asphalt, we get holes on it once in a while.

F: Asphalt contains air inside it and is very elastic. Children walk barefoot, so it is actually better that way. I did not notice it.

S: Working on *Ka-Kata-Katachi* influenced me in creating this architecture. I tried to create a new format of a nursery school instead of focusing on materials or details. Since I focused on the format, I applied full-scale low-cost approaches to materials and details.

F: You tried to create new procedures and theories by establishing principles, thinking about plans, and creating forms.

S: Yes. I was excited about creating a new format of nursery school. However, I do not know how I have served the growth of children as an architect as I see children play at Nonaka Nursery School. At the end of the day, nature and mud have a strong influence on them.

F: I still think Nonaka Day Nursery is very well made. It has exemplified one ideal format of what architecture should be.

✱1 **Michio Fujioka** (1908-1988): Architectural historian.
✱2 **Kiyonori Kikutake** (1928-): Architect (Ph. D. in engineering).
✱3 **Kazuo Shinohara** (1925-2006): Architect.
✱4 **Shozo Uchii** (1933-2002): Architect.
✱5 **Sachio Otani** (1924-): Architect and city planner.
✱6 **Itsuko Hasegawa** (1941-): Architect.
✱7 **Shokan Endo** (1934-): Architect.
✱8 **Makoto Ogawa** (1932-): Architect.
✱9 **Eiji Musha** (1936-):
✱10 **Ka-Kata-Katachi**: The metabolic architecture theory advocated by Kiyonori Kikutake in 1969.
✱11 **Takashi Asada** (1921-1990): Architect.
✱12 **Isamu Noguchi** (1904-1988): Sculptor, painter, interior designer, and garden designer.
✱13 **Kisho Kurokawa** (1934-2007): Architect.
✱14 **Masato Otaka** (1923-2010): Architect and city planner.
✱15 **Toyoko Shiokawa** (1915-1999): Founder of Nonaka Day Nursery (Fujinomiya-shi, Shizuoka Prefecture).
✱16 **Wajiro Kon** (1888-1973): Ethnologist.
✱17 **Noboru Kawazoe** (1926-): Architect and civilization specialist.
✱18 **Takamasa Yoshizaka** (1917-1980): Architect.
✱19 **Rojoh-Kansatsu-Gakkai**: The group established to observe and appreciate what is usually not considered as landscape, including peculiar buildings (or a part of them), signs, and posters found on the streets
✱20 **Le Corbusier** (1887-1965): Architect.

Terunobu Fujimori

An architect born in Nagano in 1946. Graduated from the Department of Architecture and Building Science of Tohoku University and studied further at a graduate school of the University of Tokyo. Currently a professor emeritus of the University of Tokyo and a professor of Kogakuin University, specializing in the history of Japan's modern architecture. Became involved in design from the age of 45 and designed the Jinchokan Moriya Historical Museum and the Taka-sugi-an tea house. Publications include "Japan's Modern Architecture" (Vols. I and II), Iwanami Shoten.

1978.04
串木野児童館

アクソメトリック図

2階 平面図

1階 平面図

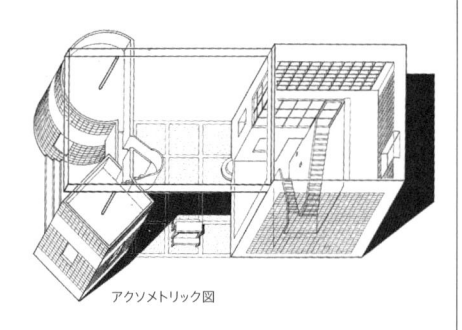

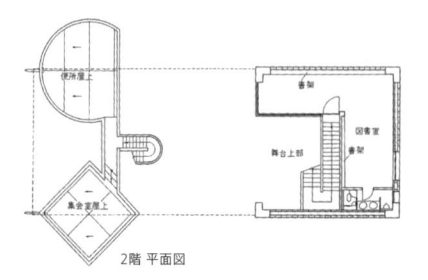

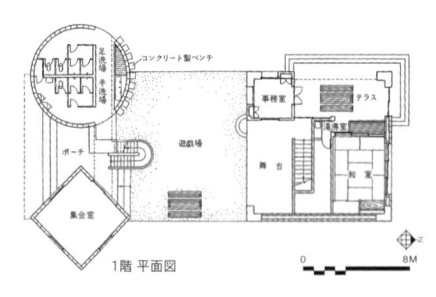

所在地：鹿児島県いちき串木野市下名
主用途：児童館
建築主：串木野市
構造設計：団設計同人
設備設計：ユニ設備設計
施工：竹下工業
構造：RC造
規模：地上2階
敷地：8,000㎡　建築：337㎡　延床：425㎡

Kushikino Children's Center
Shimonmyo, Ichikikushikino-shi, Kagoshima

1978.11
横浜市赤城林間学園

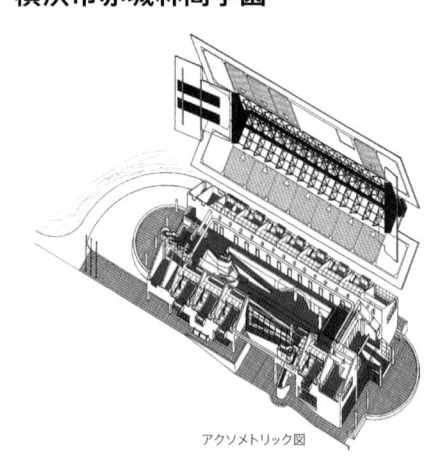

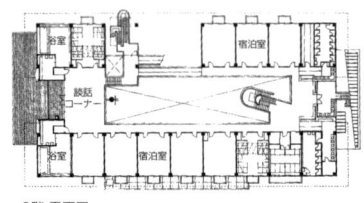

アクソメトリック図

2階 平面図

1階 平面図

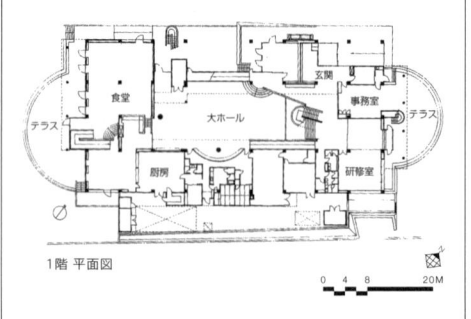

所在地：群馬県利根郡昭和村
主用途：少年自然の家、野外活動施設
建築主：横浜市
構造設計：団設計同人
設備設計：ユニ設備設計、守田設備
施工：西松・山内建設共同企業体
構造：RC造
規模：地上2階
敷地：21,160㎡　建築：1,780㎡　延床：2,450㎡

Akagi Camping School, Yokohama
Showa-mura, Tone-gun, Gunma

1975.03
沖縄県立石川少年自然の家

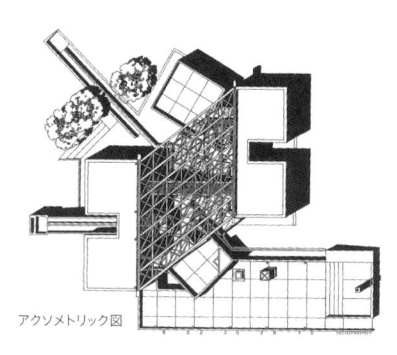

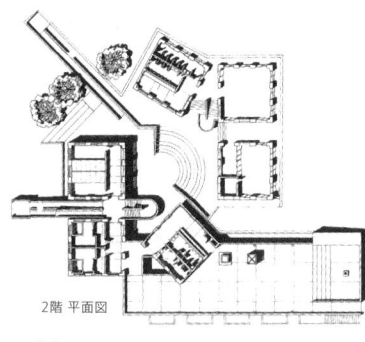

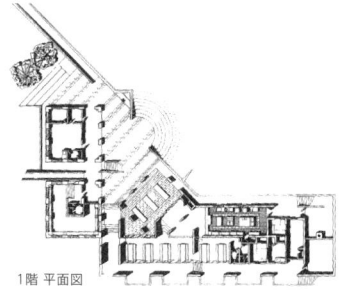

アクソメトリック図

2階 平面図

1階 平面図

所在地：沖縄県うるま市字石川
主用途：少年自然の家、野外活動施設
建築主：沖縄県
構造設計：団設計同人
設備設計：ユニ設備設計
施工：沖水建設
構造：RC造一部S造
規模：地上3階
敷地：121,361㎡　建築：1,197㎡　延床：2,172㎡

Ishikawa Children's Nature School
Aza-Ishikawa, Uruma-shi, Okinawa

1974
愛知こどもの国
［ドラゴン］

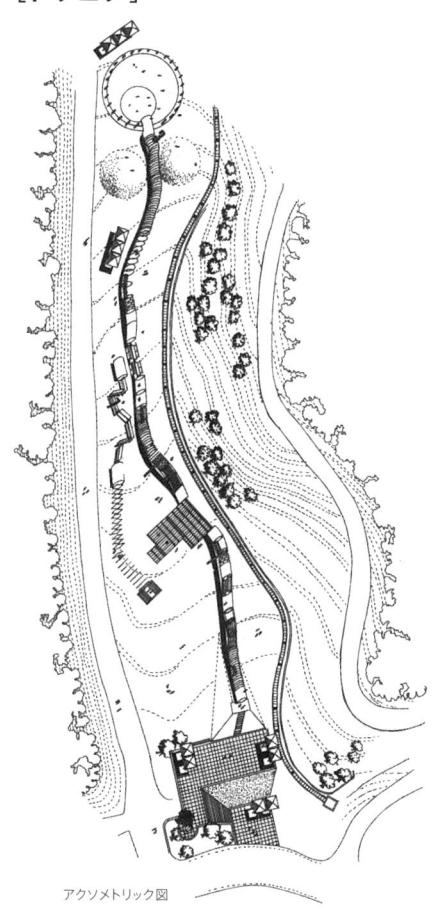

アクソメトリック図

所在地：愛知県幡豆郡幡豆町
主用途：遊具
規模：直径2m、全長200m

Giant Play Structure "Dragon" Aichi Prefectural Children's Land
Hazu-cho, Hazu-gun, Aichi

1973.08
山梨県愛宕山少年自然の家

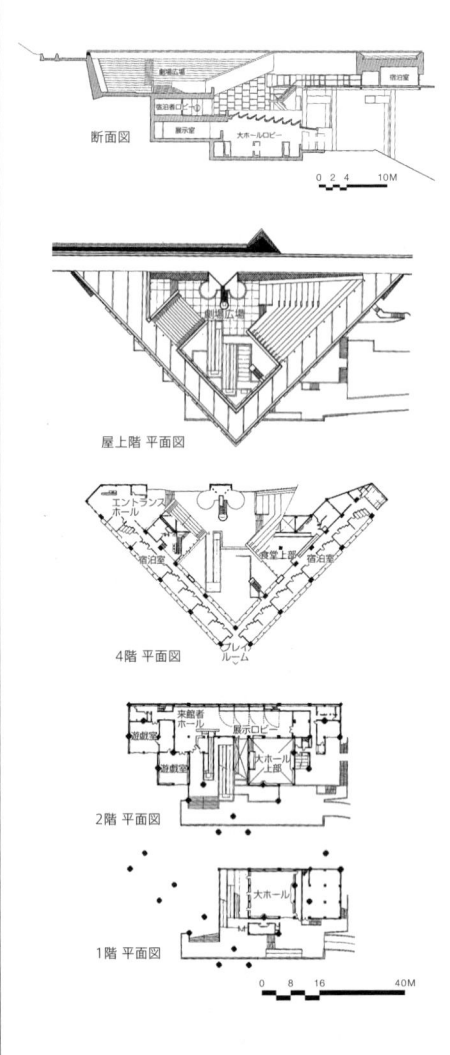

断面図

屋上階 平面図

4階 平面図

2階 平面図

1階 平面図

所在地：山梨県甲府市東光寺
主用途：少年自然の家、野外活動施設
建築主：山梨県
共同設計、構造設計、設備設計：松田平田坂本設計事務所
施工：佐藤工業
構造：RC造
規模：地上4階
敷地：550,000㎡　建築：1,693㎡　延床：2,663㎡

Atagoyama House of Nature for Young People
Tokoji, Kofu-shi, Yamanashi

1981.03
野中保育園
［野中丸］

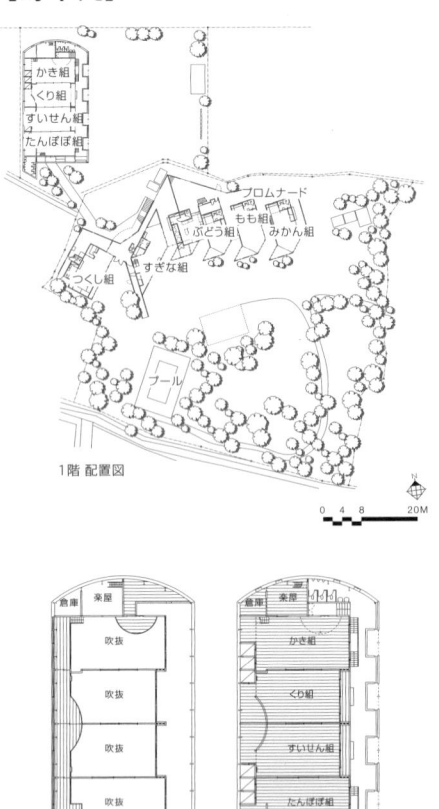

1階 配置図

2階 平面図

1階 平面図

所在地：静岡県富士宮市野中
主用途：保育園
建築主：社会福祉法人柿ノ木会
構造設計：団設計同人
設備設計：ユニ設備設計
施工：河原崎建設
構造：S造
規模：地上1階
敷地：4,485㎡　建築：328㎡　延床：325㎡

Nonaka Day Nursery "Nonaka-Maru"
Nonaka, Fujinomiya-shi, Shizuoka

1972.08
野中保育園
［野中ザウルス］

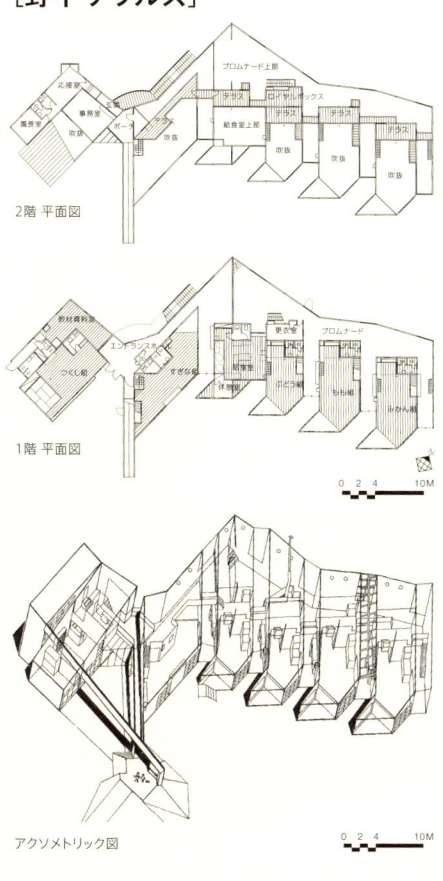

2階 平面図

1階 平面図

アクソメトリック図

所在地：静岡県富士宮市野中
主用途：保育園
建築主：社会福祉法人柿ノ木会
構造設計：団設計同人
設備設計：ユニ設備設計
施工：大和ハウス
構造：S造
規模：地上2階
敷地：6,600㎡　建築：592㎡　延床：647㎡

Nonaka Day Nursery "Nonaka-Saurus"
Nonaka, Fujinomiya-shi, Shizuoka

1971.03
神保医院

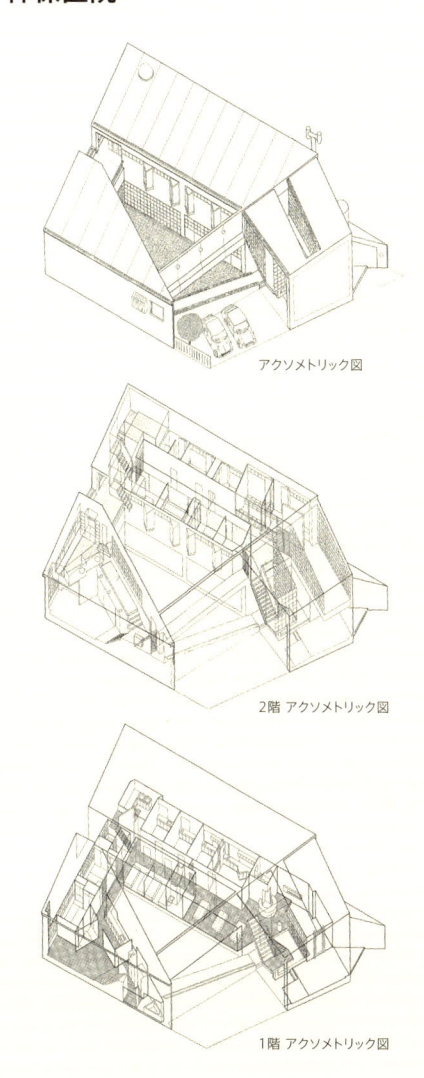

アクソメトリック図

2階 アクソメトリック図

1階 アクソメトリック図

所在地：神奈川県川崎市中原区下小田中
主用途：診療所
構造設計：平島新一
設備設計：東京建築設備研究所
施工：川崎組
構造：RC造
規模：地上2階
敷地：748㎡　建築：277㎡　延床：494㎡

Jinbo Clinic
Shimokodanaka, Nakahara-ku, Kawasaki-shi, Kanagawa

1971.03
鳥取砂丘こどもの国

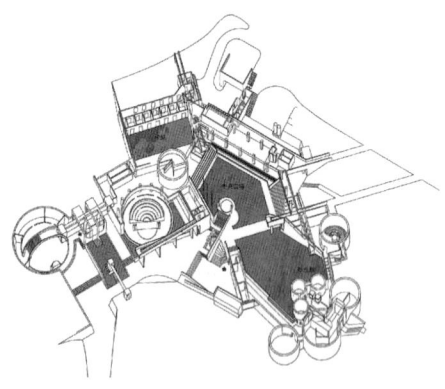

アクソメトリック図

2階 平面図

1階 平面図

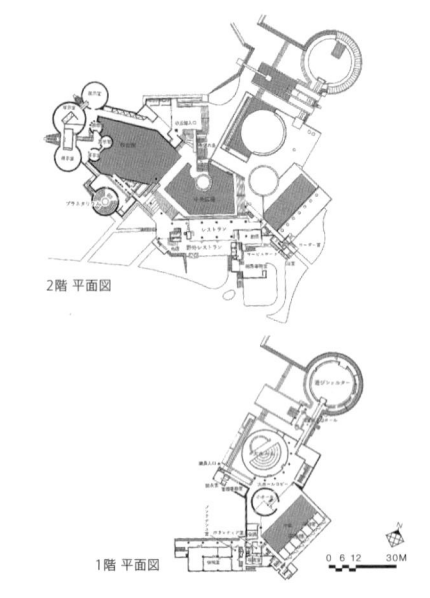

所在地：鳥取県鳥取市浜坂
主用途：野外活動施設
建築主：財団法人国立公園協会
構造設計：団設計同人
設備設計：建築設備研究所
施工：大成建設
構造：RC造
敷地：132,000㎡

Children's Land at Tottori
Hamasaka, Tottori-shi, Tottori

1971.05
愛宕山こどもの国
［展望広場］

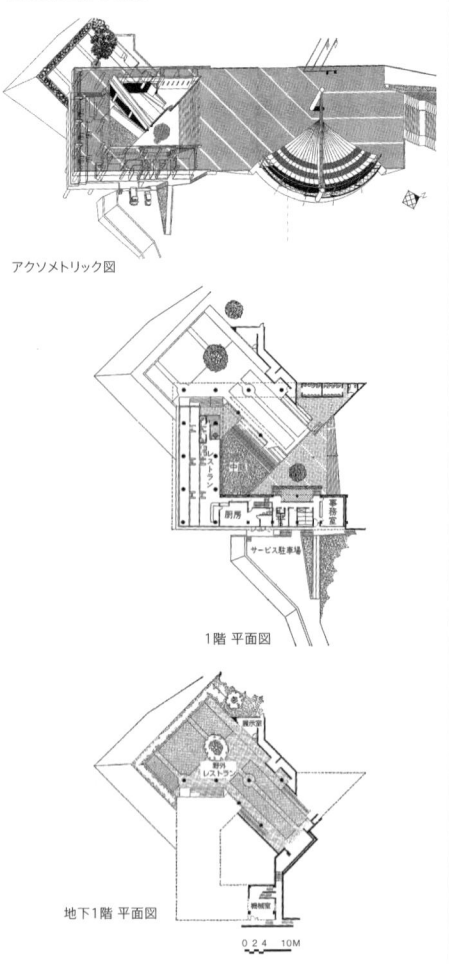

アクソメトリック図

1階 平面図

地下1階 平面図

所在地：山梨県甲府市東光寺
主用途：野外活動施設
建築主：山梨県
構造設計：団設計同人
設備設計：東京建築設備研究所
施工：早野組、小川テント
構造：RC造
敷地：550,000㎡　建築：3,053㎡（広場面積）　延床：646㎡（レストハウス部分）

Observation Square, Atagoyama Children's Land
Tokoji, Kofu-shi, Yamanashi

1971.07
新川シーサイド遊園

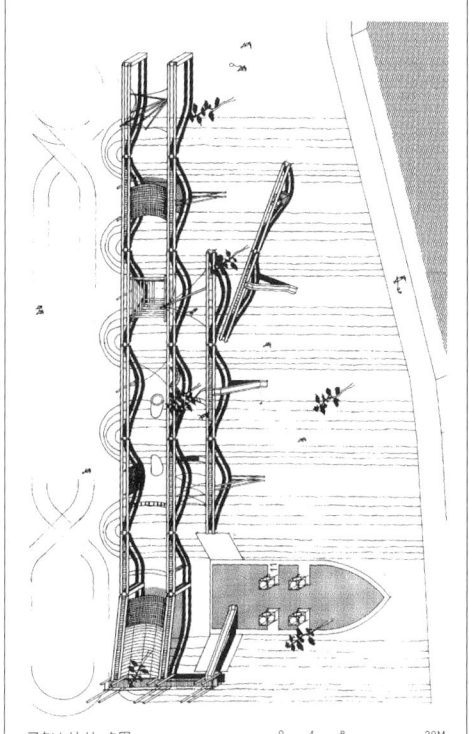

アクソメトリック図

所在地：愛媛県伊予市新川
主用途：児童遊園
施工：日本体育用具
敷地：6,000㎡

Shinkawa Seaside Children's Park
Shinkawa, Iyo-shi, Ehime

1979
ランニングサーキット

宮城中央児童館モデル児童遊園［ランニングサーキット］

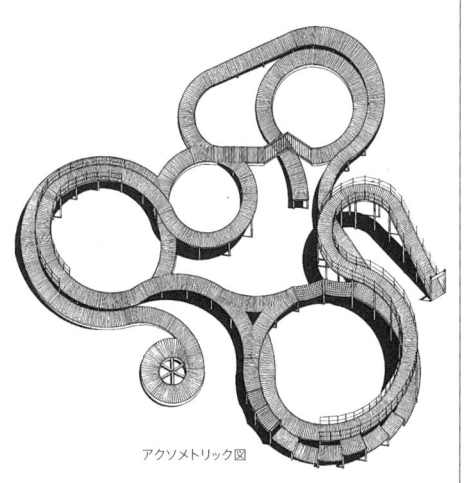

アクソメトリック図

所在地：宮城県仙台市太白区向山
主用途：児童公園遊具
建築主：宮城県
敷地：5,400㎡

"Running Circuit" in the Miyagi Prefectural Children's Center Model Playground
Mukaiyama, Taihaku-ku, Sendai-shi, Miyagi

1975
キシャコゾウ

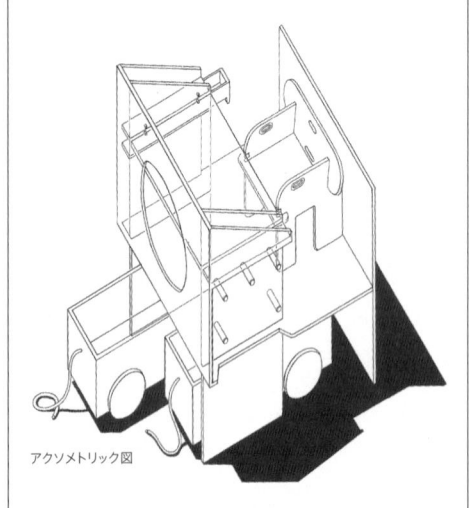

アクソメトリック図

主用途：家具
構造：W造

Kishakozo

1969.07
道の巨大遊具

宮城中央児童館モデル児童遊園［道の巨大遊具］

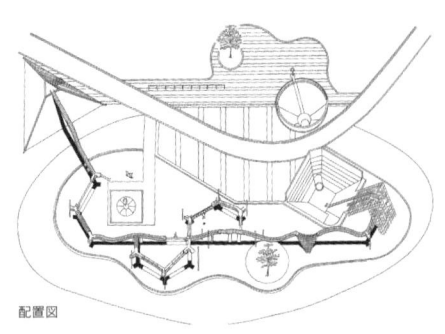

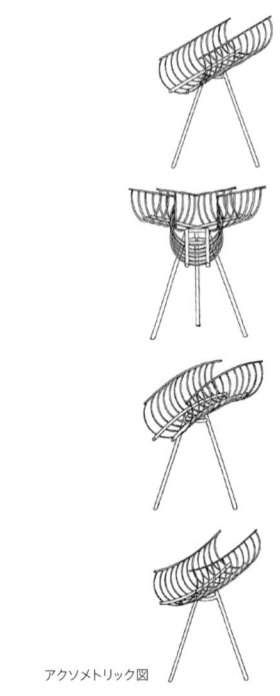

配置図

アクソメトリック図

所在地：宮城県仙台市太白区向山
主用途：児童公園遊具
建築主：宮城県
施工：日本体育用具、萩野工務店
構造：S造
規模：直径1m、全長180m
敷地：5,400㎡

"Giant Path Play Structure" in the Miyagi Prefectural Children's Center Model Playground
Mukaiyama, Taihaku-ku, Sendai-shi, Miyagi

1968
黒い家

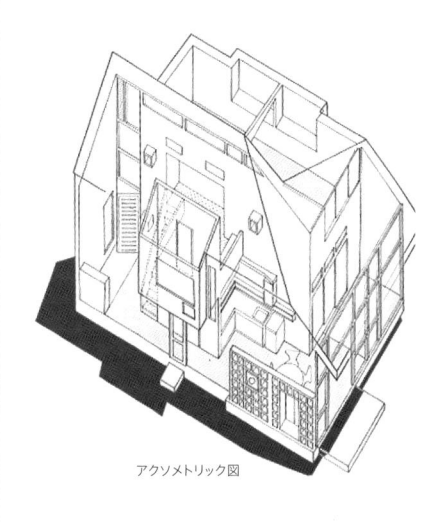

アクソメトリック図

所在地：神奈川県横浜市磯子区
主用途：住宅
施工：三共工務店
構造：W造
規模：地上2階
敷地：243.2㎡　建築：60.8㎡　延床：90.4㎡

Black House
Isogo-ku, Yokohama-shi, Kanagawa

1979-1975
遊具

ピングポング
アクソメトリック図

パネルトンネル
アクソメトリック図

プレイロードステーション
アクソメトリック図

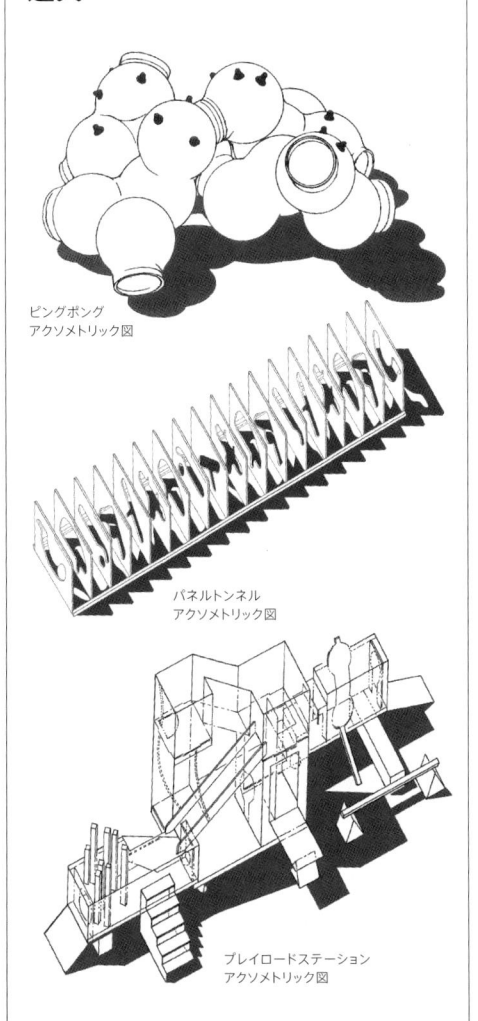

主用途：遊具

TUBEα（構造：S造）
ピングポング（構造：FRP造　規模：直径1m）
パネルトンネル（規模：1.6m×2.4m、全長16.2m）
プレイロードステーション（構造：W造　規模：幅3m、長さ6.7m（広げた時））
メイズプレイス（構造：W造）
ポケットパーク（構造：W造）
スカイネット（規模：1辺4～5m）
赤い靴（構造：W造　規模：トンネル部分 60cm角）

Play Structure

年表 Chronological table

1968〜69

1968
- 4月、環境デザイン研究所を設立、世田谷区尾山台にて業務開始
- 8月、渋谷区青山通りに移転
- 日本総合愛育研究所「モデル遊園研究会」研究員となる

- 黒い家（住宅）を新建築にて発表

- 国際コンペインター2000佳作「ロータスチェア」

- Mitsuru Senda Established the Environment Design Institute (EDI).
- In August, the office moved to Aoyama-street, Shibuya-ku.

- Honorable mention at West German Competition "Inter 2000"［Lotus Chair］

黒い家
Black House

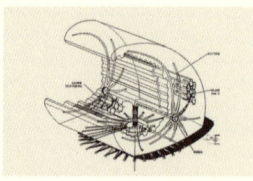

ロータスチェア
Lotus Chair

横浜市こども自然公園
Children's Nature Park, Yokohama

宮城中央児童館モデル児童遊園
［道の巨大遊具］
"Giant Path Play Structure"
in the Miyagi Prefectural Children's Center Model Playground

1970〜74

1970
- 横浜市公園利用実態調査を行なう

- 「都市の木をつくろう こども／巨大遊具」市住宅7007にて発表
- 「斜面緑地論」横浜市調査季報、都市科学研究所報にて発表

- "Making tree of cities. Children/Giant play structure", featured in City Housing 7007.

1971
- 「環築アーステクチャー」建築文化にて発表

- "KANCHIKU-Earthtecture", featured in Kenchiku Bunka.

1972
- 横浜においてこどものあそび環境の研究（自主研究）を始める
- 横浜市レクリエーション実態調査を行う
- 都市におけるフルーツパークの成立要件調査を行う

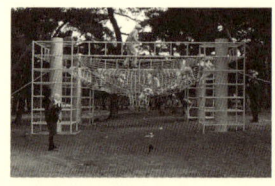

豊橋市モデル児童遊園
Toyohashi Children's Playground

愛宕山こどもの国［展望広場］
Observation Square, Atagoyama Children's Land

入来町児童センター
Iriki-cho Children's Center

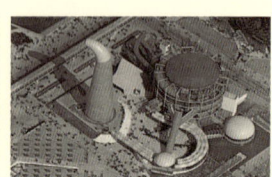

大阪万博［三井グループ館］
The Osaka Expo［The Mitsui Pavilion］

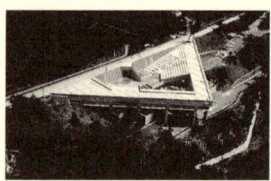

山梨県愛宕山少年自然の家
Atagoyama House of Nature for Young People

愛知こどもの国［ドラゴン］
Giant Play Structure "Dragon"
Aichi Prefectural Children's Land

- 神奈川県建築コンクール優秀賞「神保医院」
- Prize for Excellence of Kanagawa Prefecture Architectural Competition [Jinbo Clinic]

1973

- ヤマギワの照明指名コンペに[マンモス]出品
- Presented "Mammoth" in Yamagiwa Lighting Design Competition.

1974

- 日本大学芸術学部住環境デザインコースの非常勤講師となる（〜1984）
- 「新しい保育と教育の環境」家庭科学研究所「家庭医学第60集」にて発表
- 「レジャーの構造」日本経済新聞社刊分担執筆
- 「あそびの環境」療育の窓にて発表
- Mitsuru Senda appointed as lecturer at Nihon University, College of Art, Housing Environment Design Course.

鳥取砂丘こどもの国
Children's Land at Tottori

神保医院
Jinbo Clinic

新川シーサイド遊園
Shinkawa Seaside Children's Park

野中保育園［野中ザウルス］
Nonaka Day Nursery "Nonaka-Saurus"

聖徳園香里敬愛第2保育所
Shotokuen-Kori-Keiai Nursery School

照明器具［マンモス］
Lighting Fixture "Mammoth"

1975〜79

1975

- トヨタ財団より「こどものあそび環境の研究」に研究助成を得る
- 港区三の橋、皆川ビルに移転
- 思考椅展 ハート・アートギャラリーにて開催

- 「遊び環境論」ジャパンインテリアデザイン4月号にて特集
- 「＜環築＞をめざして」ジャパンインテリアデザイン9月号にて特集
- 日本建築学会にて「児童のあそび環境の研究」（1〜4）を連続して発表（1975〜76）

- Awarded TOYOTA Foundation grant for "Research and Investigation of Children's Play Environments". (The only private research institute among a total of 20 organizations)
- Moved the office to Minakawa Building, Sannohashi, Minato-ku.
- Exhibition of thinking chair at Heart Art Gallery.

- "Aiming to KANCHIKU", special featured in Japan Interior Design.
- Submitted series of research papers on children's play environment for

沖縄県立石川少年自然の家
Ishikawa Children's Nature School

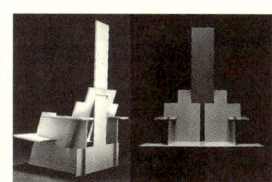

思考椅
Shikoki

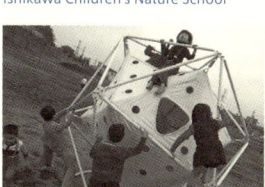

コスモス
Cosmos

キシャコゾウ
Kishakozo

井本歯科医院
Imoto Clinic

シーチェア
Sea Chair

969

Architectural Institute of Japan.

1976

- 「児童のあそび環境システムの調査開発研究」トヨタ財団報告書として提出
- 「巨大遊具論」産業デザイン振興会誌第65号にて発表
- 「道あそび論」現代文化研究所報第116号にて発表
- 「遊具に関する調査研究ノート」ジャパンインテリアデザイン5月号にて発表
- 「遊具の独創性と商業性」ジャパンインテリアデザイン5月号にて発表
- 「児童のあそび環境装置の方法」ジャパンインテリアデザイン6月号にて発表

- "Giant play structure", featured in Japan Industrial Design Promotion Organization Magazine No.65.
- "Play on street", featured in GENDAI Advanced Studies Research Organization Report No.116.
- "Research note on play structure", Japan Interior Design No.206.
- "Originality and commerciality on play structure", Japan Interior Design No.206.
- "Method of mechanism of play environment for children", Japan Interior Design No.207.

1977

- 西武春日井ショッピングセンター等商業環境計画を始める

- 「こどもの遊び環境」建築文化にて特集
- 「都市公園の再開発の方法 その1、2」日本建築学会にて発表

- Designed "Yokohama Children's Land" and Children's center. Also started commercial environment planning, Seibu Kasugai Shopping Center.

- "Children's play environment", special featured in Kenchiku Bunka.

1978

- 毎日デザイン賞展 東京デザイナーズスペースにて開催

- 「こどものあそびの原空間」伝統と現代5月号にて発表
- 「児童遊具の機能とデザイン」同文書院「現代のこども文化」にて発表
- 「コミュニティ遊具のデザイン」産業デザイン振興会誌第111号にて発表

- 毎日デザイン賞「あそび環境のデザイン」
- 商環境デザイン賞「西武春日井ショッピングセンター外構環境計画」

プレイロードステーション
Play Road Station

パネルトンネル
Panel Tunnel

森口邸
Moriguchi House

高い机
Tall Table

川西市奥池冒険公園
Okuike Adventure Park, Kawanishi

横浜市根岸森林公園
Entrance of Negishi Forest Park, Yokohama

沖縄県立聾学校幼稚部
Okinawa Prefectural Kidergarten for the Deaf

西武春日井ショッピングセンター外構環境計画
Seibu Kasugai Shopping Center

エスカルゴ
Escargot

唐津港妙見緑地
Port Karatsu, Taemi Greens

長崎鼻公園児童遊園
Nagasakibana Park Playground

田中邸
Tanaka House

- ディスプレイデザイン年鑑賞「西武春日井ショッピングセンター外構環境計画」
- "Inside world of children's play", featured in Dento-to-Gendai.
- Mainichi Design Award [Design of Children's Play Environment]
- JCD Award [Outdoor environment plan for Seibu Kasugai Shopping Center]
- Display Design Award [Outdoor environment plan for Seibu Kasugai Shopping Center]

1979

- 遊具展 西武船橋店オープンギャラリーにて開催
- 緑のマスタープラン策定調査を行う

- 「こどもの空間学」ジャパンインテリアデザイン6月号にて特集
- 「遊具プレイリーダー論」日本レクリエーション協会誌9月号にて発表
- 「住民時代」新建築社分担執筆

- Play structure exhibition at Seibu Funabashi Open Gallery.
- "Study on children's space", featured in Japan Interior Design.
- "Play leader of play structure", featured in National Recreation Association of Japan Magazine.

飛考椅
Hikoki

弥勒寺の家
Mirokuji House

横浜市赤城林間学園
Akagi Camping School, Yokohama

古市邸
Furuichi House

TUBE α
TUBE α

八王子市万葉公園モデル児童遊園
Manyo Park, Model Playground, Hachioji

串木野児童館
Kushikino Children's Center

ピングポング
Ping Pong

上山モデル児童遊園
Kaminoyama Children's Play Park

宮城県中央児童館モデル園［ランニングサーキット］
"Running Circuit" in the Miyagi Prefectural Children's Center Model Playground

横浜金沢地先埋立公園
Yokohama Kanazawachisaki Park

1980〜84

1980
- 「遊具におけるこども集団の形成の研究」日本造園学会「造園雑誌」にて発表
- 「遊具計画論」ジャパンインテリアデザイン10月号にて特集
- 「こどものあそび場を主体としたオープンスペースの設計計画」日本住宅協会「住宅」10月号にて発表
- 「イタズラのすすめ」三修社分担執筆

- "Study on formulation of children's group on play structure", Journal of the Japan Institute of Landscape Architecture.
- "Planning of play structure", featured in Japan Interior Design.

1981
- 早稲田大学理工学部建築学科非常勤講師となる（〜1984）
- 「こどものあそび環境の構造の研究」日本建築学会論文報告集にて発表
- 「子どものための建築に関する考察」ジャパンインテリアデザイン11月号にて特集
- 「ふたたび科学、技術の時代」自動車とその世界に寄稿
- 「遊び場の可能性をさぐる」REEDに寄稿

- Lecturer at the Faculty of Science and Engineering of Waseda University.
- "Study on structure of children's play environment", submitted in Architectural Institute of Japan Journal.
- "Study on architecture for children", featured in Japan Interior Design.

1982
- 横浜市公園利用実態調査を行う
- 科学技術振興財団テクノパーク委員会委員となる
- 学位論文―こどものあそび環境の構造の研究（東京工業大学）
- 「子供時代の遊び環境と原風景」ジャパンインテリアデザイン12月号にて特集
- 「子どもの遊び空間と遊具」プロセスアーキテクチュアNo.30にて特集
- 「子ども現代誌」筑摩書房分担執筆

- 秋田市都市景観賞「秋田県立児童会館・こども博物館」
- 秋田市都市景観賞「秋田県営御野庭団地」

- Mitsuru Senda received a doctorate of

文田病院
Fumita Clinic

片瀬山の家
Kataseyama House

秋田県立児童会館・こども博物館
Akita Prefectural Children's Center, Children's Museum

和歌山県モデル児童遊園
Wakayama Prefectural Model Playground

秋田県営御野庭団地
Akita Prefectural Onoba Housing

野中保育園［野中丸］
Nonaka Day Nursery "Nonaka-Maru"

大宮愛徳幼稚園
Aitoku Kindergarten, Omiya

横浜市ほどがや地区センター
Hodogaya Community Center, Yokohama

茨城県立児童センター［こどもの城］
Ibaraki Prefectural Children's Center

脇田和邸
K. Wakita House

八日市市城砦公園
Yokaichi Rampart Park

バナナハウス
Banana House

engineering from the Tokyo Institute of Technology.

- Akita City Landscape Design Award ［Akita Prefectural Children's Center, Children's Museum］
- Akita City Landscape Design Award ［Akita Prefectural Onoba Housing］

1983

・毎日デザイン賞調査委員となる（現在まで）

・「遊具の構造」現代思想2月号にて発表
・「都市化によるあそび空間の変化の研究」日本都市計画学会にて発表
・「テクノパーク基本構想報告書」を提出

- "Structure of play equipment", featured in Gendai-shiso.
- "Research on change of play spaces by urbanization", submitted in City Planning of Japan Journal.

1984

・通産省グッドデザイン商品選定委員となる（～1989）
・NIRAより「こどものあそび環境マスタープラン作成の調査研究」に対し助成を受ける
・琉球大学工学部建設工学科教授となる
・パリ・建築ビエンナーレに出品（パリ・ポンピドーセンター）

・「こどものあそび環境」筑摩書房より発行

- Awarded NIRA grant for "the Research, Investigation and Making a Master Plan of Children's Play Environments". Mitsuru Senda became professor at the department of architectural engineering of Ryukyu University in Okinawa. Then, retired from his position as president and went on as honorary chief of Environment Design Institute.

- "Children's play environment" was published in Chikuma-Shobo.

掛川市モデル児童遊園［斜面の巨大遊具］
"Giant Slope Play Structure"
Kakegawa Play Park

横浜市希望ヶ丘公園
Kibogaoka Park, Yokohama

神奈川県消防学校寮
Dormitory of School for Firemen

日田市亀山公園［メビウスバンド］
"Mobius Band" Kizan Park

太刀の浦緑地
Tachinoura Port Park

秋田県伊佐野団地
Isano Housing Development, Akita

鳥居平やまびこ公園［風のとりで］
"Fortress of Wind"
in Toriidaira Yamabiko Park

鳥居平やまびこ公園［ローラースケート場］
"Roller-skating Rink" in Toriidaira Yamabiko Park

静岡県吉原林間学校
Yoshiwara Camping School

横浜市入船公園
Irifune Park, Yokohama

軽井沢 640
Karuizawa 640

横浜市こども科学館
Yokohama Science Center

973

1985〜89

1985

- 筑波科学万博の政府出展施設こども広場を担当
- 「子どもの遊び環境を考える」まち＆すまいNo.13にて発表
- 「遊びの科学」科学博ハンドブックに寄稿
- 「町づくりとこどもの遊び環境」日本建築学会誌にて発表
- Designed Tsukuba Science Expo, "Children's Plaza".

1986

- 「現代建築 空間と方法12」同朋舎出版社より発行
- 「都市とあそび空間」INAX REPORTに寄稿
- 都市公園コンクール設計部門 公園緑地協会長賞「横浜市入船公園」
- 中部建築賞「浜松科学館」
- Award of Chairman of Parks of Open Space Association of Japan of Urban Park Design competition [Irifune Park, Yokohama]
- Chubu Architecture Award [Hamamatsu Science Museum]

1987

- 宋慶齢基金会評議員、理事となる（〜2000）
- 「あそび環境のデザイン」鹿島出版会より発行
- 国際交通安全学会賞「著書『こどものあそび環境』」
- 商環境デザイン賞「浜松科学館」
- ディスプレイデザイン 年鑑賞「浜松科学館」
- 建築業協会賞（BCS賞）「浜松科学館」
- 公共の色彩賞「浜松科学館の色彩計画」
- International Association of Traffic and Safety Sciences Award [Book "Children's Play Environment"]
- JCD Award [Display design of Hamamatsu Science Museum]
- Display Design Award [Display design of Hamamatsu Science Museum]
- Building Contractors Society Award [Hamamatsu Science Museum]

1988

- 港区一の橋、三田ソネットビルに移転
- 名古屋工業大学社会開発工学科教授となる

鳥居平やまびこ公園［中央広場・管理棟］
"Entrance Plaza, Adminstration" in Toriidaira Yamabiko Park

こどもの国［温室・自然観察センター］
National Children's Land "Green House, Nature Observation Center"

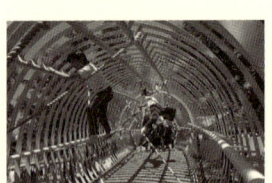

筑波科学万国博覧会こども広場
Tsukuba Science Expo Children's Plaza

名城公園無料休憩所
Meijo Park, Rest House

多摩動物園猛禽舎
Tama Zoo "Raptores House"

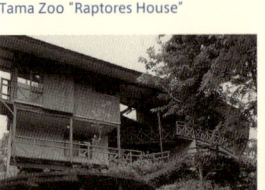

浜松科学館
Hamamatsu Science Museum

こどもの国［センターハウス］
National Children's Land "Center House"

相模川ふれあい科学館
Sagamigawa River Museum

山手ヨットクラブ
Yamate Yacht Club

宮崎科学技術館
Miyazaki Science Center

名古屋市白鳥メモリアルパーク
Shiratori Memorial Park, Nagoya

大田区石川町文化センター
Ishikawacho Culture Center

- 「環境の設計」プロセスアーキテクチュア No.79にて特集

- 商環境デザイン賞「山手ヨットクラブ」
- ディスプレイデザイン年鑑賞「相模川ふれあい科学館」
- 都市公園コンクール設計部門 建設(現国土交通)大臣賞「鳥居平やまびこ公園」
- 浜松市都市景観賞「浜松科学館」

- Moved the office to Mita, Ichinohashi Minato-ku.
- Mitsuru Senda became professor at the department of social development engineering at Nagoya Institute of Technology.

- A special featured of EDI was published in Process Architecture No.79.

- JCD Award [Yamate Yacht Club]
- Display Design Award [Sagamigawa River Museum]
- Minister of Construction (Currently, Minister of Land, Infrastructure, Transport and Tourism) Award of the Urban Park Design Competition [Toriidaira Yamabiko Park]
- Hamamatsu City Landscape Award [Hamamatsu Science Museum]

1989

- 「あそびと環境と安全性」「公園と管理」誌3月号にて発表
- 「歩行線形と都市デザイン」ESTAPにて発表
- 「私の東京改革論」朝日新聞社「東京朝日100周年記念懸賞論文集にて発表
- 「Den Kindern die Weltgestalten」 Garten + Landschaftにて発表

- 那覇市都市景観賞「末吉リバーサイドテラス」
- カナルパーク 基本デザインコンペ最優秀賞「富岩運河環水公園」
- 軽金属建築賞「浜松科学館の設計」
- 日本建築学会作品選集「渋谷区散策路整備計画［旧玉川上水ルート］」
- 日本建築学会作品選集「相模川ふれあい科学館」
- 全国公園百選入選「鳥居平やまびこ公園」
- 中部建築賞「鳥居平やまびこ公園」

- "Play, Environment and Safety", featured in Parka and Maintenance Magazine.
- "Walking line and urban design", featured in ESTAP No.12.

- Naha Landscape Award [Sueyoshi Riverside Terrace]
- Grand Prize of Toyama Canal Park Basic Design Competition. [Fugan Canal Park]
- Architectural Award of Light Metal Association [Design of Hamamatsu Science Museum]
- Winning for Architectural Design of the Architectural Institute of Japan

横浜市こども自然公園［野外活動センター］
Yokohama Children's Nature Park

末吉リバーサイドテラス
Sueyoshi Riverside Terrace

1万Mプロムナード三笠アプローチ
Mikasa Park Approach Road in the ten thousand Meter Promenade

名古屋市宝くじモデル児童遊園［わいわい広場］
Nagoya Children's Play Park "Wai Wai Plaza"

青函博スーパードーム
Super Dome for Seikan Expo

元麻布集合住宅
Motoazabu Housing

伊勢原市立図書館・こども科学館
Isehara Library and Science Museum

軽井沢C山荘
Mountain Villa "C", Karuizawa

鳥居平やまびこ公園［センターハウス］
"Center House" in Toriidaira Yamabiko Park

渋谷区散策路整備計画［美術館ルート］
Shibuya Promenade Design "Route to Shoto Museum"

白金台ガーデンハウス
Shiroganedai Garden House

国営ひたち海浜公園［おもしろチューブ］
"Fun Tube" in Hitachi Seaside Park

975

[Shibuya Promenade Design - Hatsudai District]
- Winning for Architectural Design of the Architectural Institute of Japan [Sagamigawa River Museum]
- Ministry of Construction Award of the Urban Park Design Competition [Toriidaira Yamabiko Park]
- Chubu Architecture Award [Toriidaira Yamabiko Park "Center House"]

渋谷区散策路整備計画 [旧玉川上水ルート]
Shibuya Promenade Design "Hatsudai District"

1990〜94

1990

- 朝日新聞月曜版にて「あそびの現風景」エッセイを毎週発表 (85回)
- Architect (JIA東海支部機関誌) に「こどもと環境」をテーマに1年間発表
- 1990年と1992年に「こどものあそび環境の国際比較研究」日本都市計画学会論文集にて発表
- 『こどもと住まい－50人の建築家の原風景 (上・下)』(編著) 住まいの図書館出版局より発行
- 「街路空間におけるセットバックの形態と歩行線形に関する研究」日本都市計画学会論文集にて発表
- 「感性あふれる都市」日本工業新聞に寄稿
- 「こどもの視点でみる都市デザイン」日立8月号に寄稿
- 「こどもの冒険環境論」恩賜財団母子愛育会「愛育」8月号に寄稿

- 神奈川建築百選入選「相模川ふれあい科学館」
- 神奈川県建築コンクール 奨励賞「鵠沼の家」
- 第1回読売まちづくり設計 コンペ優秀賞「レイクウッドタウン」
- 富岩運河基本デザインコンペ 最優秀賞「富山県富岩運河のデザイン」
- 日本建築学会作品選集「1万Mプロムナード三笠アプローチ」
- ディスプレイ産業大賞優秀賞「釧路フィッシャーマンズワーフディスプレイ環境計画」

- 100 Selected Architecture Prize of Kanagawa Prefecture [Sagamigawa River Museum]
- House Section Prize of Kanagawa Architectural Contest [Kugenuma House]
- Yomiuri Town Design Competition [Lakewood Town]
- Grand Prize of Toyama Fugan Canal Basic Design Competition [Design of Fugan Canal Park]
- Prize for Excellence of Display Industry Award [Kushiro Fisherman's Wharf Environment Planning]

鹿児島市立科学館
Kagoshima Municipal Science Hall

松庵の家
Shoan House

鵠沼の家
Kugenuma House

釧路フィッシャーマンズワーフ遊具
Kushiro Fisherman's Warf

弁天町ウォーターランド [プールズ]
Bentencho Waterland "Pools"

鳥の家
Bird House

川崎市青少年創作センター
Kawasaki Children's Culture Center

中国北京科普楽園
Beijing Children's Science Park

ラミアール藤沢
Lamiar Fujisawa

池田町風の丘
"Hill of Winds" in Ikeda-cho

1991

- UNDER CONSTRUCTION展（SENDA MAN個展）東京デザイナーズスペースにて開催

- 「あそびの原風景の喪失と日本の将来」富士総合研究所「φ」にて発表
- 「建築の個体距離に関する研究」日本建築学会論文報告集にて発表
- 「住宅の個体距離と十字式設計法」新建築住宅特集8月号にて発表
- 「都市化によるこどものあそび環境の変化に関する研究」日本都市計画学会学術研究論文集にて発表
- 「安全性からみた保育環境」フレーベル館「保育専科」11月号に寄稿

- 図書館建築賞優秀賞「伊勢原市立図書館・こども科学館」
- 商環境デザイン賞奨励賞「弁天町ウォーターランド［プールズ］」
- 日本建築学会作品選集「伊勢原図書館・こども科学館」
- 横浜まちなみ景観賞「市ヶ尾彫刻の森プロムナード」

- Prize for Excellence of Library Architecture Award［Isehara Library and Science Museum］
- JCD Award［Bentencho Waterland "Pools"］

1992

- 東京工業大学工学部建築学科教授となる（〜2005）
- 仙田順子が環境デザイン研究所代表取締役となる

- 「子どもとあそび〜環境建築家の眼」岩波書店
- 「都市における子どものあそび場」東京市政調査会「都市問題」に寄稿
- 「あそび環境としての学校」児童心理6月号臨時増刊に寄稿

- 商環境デザイン賞奨励賞「営団地下鉄南北線」
- ディスプレイデザイン賞「営団地下鉄南北線」

- Mitsuru Senda became professor at the department at the architecture and building engineering of Tokyo Institute of Technology
- Junko Senda, President, Environment Design Institute

- 「Design of Children's Play Environments」Mc Grow Hill

- JCD and Display Design Award［Eidan Subway, Nanboku Line］

1993

- 日本建築学会理事となる（〜1994）

営団地下鉄南北線
Eidan Subway, Nanboku Line

松ヶ丘第二公園遊具［トンネルぐるりん］
Matsugaoka Park Play Structure "Tunnel Gururin"

スターズ・アート23
Stars Art 23

富山県こどもみらい館
Toyama Children's Center

滋賀県立びわ湖こどもの国
Lake Biwa Children's Land

ジャンボード
Jamboard

稲荷公園わんぱく広場
Inari Park Wanpaku Plaza

プレイランドたけべの森
Playland "Takebe no Mori"

安浦地区沿道緑地［水の丘］
Yasuura Roadway Landscaping "Mizu no Oka"

相模原市星が丘こどもセンター
Sagamihara Municipal Hoshigaoka Children's Center

多摩六都科学館
Tama Rokuto Science Museum

常滑市体育館
Tokoname Municipal Gymnasium

977

- 「こどものあそび環境の構造的変化に関する研究」日本都市計画学会にて発表
- 「子どもと遊び環境」ジャパン・ランドスケープ No.27にて特集
- 「遊び空間と遊具の構造」住宅総合研究財団「すまいろん」春号に寄稿
- 「子どもと遊び空間」余暇開発センター「ロアジー」4月号に寄稿

- 商環境デザイン賞「富山県こどもみらい館」
- 商環境デザイン賞「スターズアート23」
- 日本建築学会霞ヶ関ビル記念賞（研究部門）「都市空間におけるこどものあそび環境開発に関する研究」
- ジャパンエキスポ大賞優秀賞「信州博アルピコ広場「円環遊具」」
- 富山県建築賞「富山県こどもみらい館」
- 中部建築賞「富山県こどもみらい館」

- JCD Award [Toyama Children's Center]
- JCD Award [Stars Art 23]
- The Kasumigaseki Building Memorial Prize of Architectural Institute of Japan [Research of Development of Children's Play Environment in Urban Area]
- Prize for Excellence of Japan Expo Award Grand Prize ["Circular Play Structure" in the Shinshu Expo Alpico Plaza]
- Toyama Architectural Award [Toyama Children's Center]
- Chubu Architecture Award [Toyama Children's Center]

1994

- 東京大学建築学科非常勤講師となる（〜1997）

- 1994年と1995年に「歩行線形の研究」日本建築学会論文集にて発表
- 「環境の設計」プロセスアーキテクチュア No.121にて特集
- 「こどもと共生」日本教育学会教育学研究第61巻第1号にて発表
- 「子どものあそび環境の変化」総合研究開発機構NIRA政策研究 VOL.7 No.3にて発表
- 「こどもにやさしいまちづくり10の提言」地域活性化センター No.56に寄稿
- 「子どもたちに『あそび基準法』を」光村図書国語教育相談室 No.1に寄稿
- 「こどもを代弁できる建築家でありたい」JIA Bulletinに寄稿

- 東京建築賞「東京辰巳国際水泳場」
- 北陸建築賞「富山県こどもみらい館」
- 照明普及賞「東京辰巳国際水泳場」
- 中部建築賞「常滑市体育館」
- ジャパンエキスポ大賞 秀作賞「94三重博覧会 ダイワハウス こども館」
- 商環境デザイン賞「多摩六都科学館」

- Tokyo Architectural Award ["Tokyo Tatsumi International Swimming Center"]
- Chubu Architecture Award [Tokoname Municipal Gymnasium]
- Japan Expo Award [Daiwa House Children's Center at Mie Expo 94]

東京辰巳国際水泳場
Tokyo Tatsumi International Swimming Center

信州博アルピコ広場［円環遊具］
"Circular Play Structure" in the Shinshu Expo Alpico Plaza

相模湖カルチャーパーク［漕艇場］
Lake Sagami Culture Park, "Rowing space"

国営ひたち海浜公園［たまごの森］
"Tamago no Mori" in Hitachi Seaside Park

姫路御立公園［たつまきロード］
Himeji Mitate Park "Tornado Road"

浦和くらしの博物館・民家園
Urawa Style of Living Museum

兵庫県南但馬自然学校
Minami Tajima Nature School, Hyogo

旭川春光台［風の子館］
Asahikawa Shunkodai Park "Kaze no Ko Kan"

川崎私立井田中学校
Ida Junior High School, Kawasaki

ミュージアムパーク茨城県自然博物館
Ibaraki Nature Museum

こどもの国［ふしぎ広場］
National Children's Land "Play Structure"

1995～99

1995

- 「SDSシリーズ第3巻美術館・博物館」新日本法規出版より発行（共著：戸尾任宏）
- 「まちづくりと子ども」児童心理Vol.49 No.12にて発表
- 「歩行線形による屋外通路空間の形状に関する研究」を日本建築学会論文集にて発表

- 商環境デザイン賞「ミュージアムパーク茨城県自然博物館」
- ディスプレイデザイン賞「ミュージアムパーク茨城県自然博物館」
- 愛知まちなみ建築賞「常滑市体育館」
- 日本造園コンサルタント協会奨励賞「姫路市御立公園たつまきロード」
- 兵庫県但馬ドーム設計コンペ最優秀賞「兵庫県立但馬ドームの設計」

- JCD and Display Design Award [Ibaraki Nature Museum]
- Aichi Architectural Award [Tokoname Municipal Gymnasium]
- Consultants of Landscape Architecture in Japan Encouragement prize [Himeji Mitate Park "Tornado Road"]
- Grand Prize of Tajima Dome Design Competition in Hyogo Prefecture [Design of Hyogo Prefectural Tajima Dome]

1996

- 港区六本木に建設移転

- 「子どものあそび」日本小児科医会会報No.12にて発表

- 日本建築学会作品選集「富山県こどもみらい館」
- 日本造園学会賞（作品）「ミュージアムパーク茨城県自然博物館」
- 神奈川県建築コンクール奨励賞「藤野芸術の家」
- 仙台ドーム設計競技佳作賞「仙台ドームの設計」
- 商環境デザイン賞 優秀賞「藤野芸術の家」

- Built a new office building in Roppongi, Minato-ku and moved there.

- Winning for Architectural Design of the Architectural Institute of Japan [Toyama Children's Center]
- The Japanese Institute of Landscape Architecture Prize [Ibaraki Nature Museum]
- Kanagawa Architectural Contest Award [Fujino Workshop for Art]
- Honorable mention of Sendai Dome Design and Application Competition [Design of Sendai Dome]
- Prize for Excellence of JCD Award [Fujino Workshop for Art]

宮崎市大淀川学習館
Oyodo River Study Center, Miyazaki

由比ヶ浜の家
Yuigahama House

さぬきこどもの国
Sanuki Children's Land

鈴廣かまぼこ博物館
Suzuhiro Kamaboko Museum

藤野芸術の家
Fujino Workshop for Art

長崎市科学館
Nagasaki Science Museum

川崎市向丘小学校
Mukaigaoka Elementary School, Kawasaki

珠洲リフレッシュ施設［二棟廊］
"Futamune-Rou"
in the Suzu Refreshment Center

愛知県児童総合センター
Aichi Children's Center

珠洲ビーチホテル
Suzu Beach Hotel

コスモアイル羽咋
Cosmo Isle Hakui

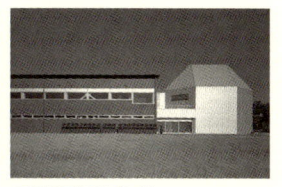

五藤光学研究所山梨工場
Goto Optical MFG. Yamanashi Factory

1997

- 日本建築学会にて谷口吉郎展を開催

- 「遊具から都市づくりまでカバーする『遊環構造』」maju(諭創社)にて発表
- 「子どもたちのための都市」国際交通安全学会誌Vol.22 No.3にて発表
- 「都市廊に関する研究」日本都市計画学会論文集にて発表
- 「野外活動施設の計画的研究(1、2)」日本建築学会にて発表
- 「こどもと都市の未来」埼玉総合研究機構「think」No.49に寄稿

- 日本建築学会賞(作品)「愛知県児童総合センター」
- 東京建築賞 優秀賞「ミュージアムパーク茨城県自然博物館」
- 日本造園コンサルタント協会 奨励賞「安浦地区沿道緑地「水の丘」」
- 石川県建築賞 知事賞「コスモアイル羽咋」
- ディスプレイデザイン賞「鈴廣かまぼこ博物館」
- 甍賞 銀賞「珠洲リフレッシュ施設「二棟廊」」
- グッドデザイン賞「五藤光学研究所山梨工場」
- IOC/IAKS賞 銀賞「東京辰巳国際水泳場」
- とやま市都市景観建築賞「富岸運河環水公園」
- SDA賞 オリジナル部門 入選「五藤光学研究所山梨工場」

- The Architectural Institute of Japan Prize [Aichi Children's Center]
- Prize for Excellence of Tokyo Architectural Award Superior Award [Ibaraki Nature Museum]
- Consultants of Landscape Architecture in Japan Encouragement prize [Yasuura Roadway Landscaping "Mizu no Oka"]
- The Governor Award of Ishikawa Prefecture Architectural Award [Cosmo Isle Hakui]
- Display Design Award [Suzuhiro Kamaboko Museum]
- Iraka Award Silver Prize ["Futamune Rou" in the Suzu Refrenshment Center]
- Good Design Award [Goto Optical MFG. Yamanashi Factory]
- IOC IAKS International Association for Sports and Leisure Facilities Silver Award ["Tokyo Tatsumi International Swimming Center"]
- Toyama Urban Landscape Architecture Award [Fugan Canal Park]
- SDA Award [Goto Optical MFG. Yamanashi Factory]

1998

- 環境デザイン研究所設立30周年を迎える

- 「こどものためのあそび空間」市ヶ谷出版社より発行
- 「環境デザインの方法」彰国社より発行
- 「プレイストラクチャー」柏書房より発行
- 「廊空間に関する研究」日本建築学会論文集にて発表

福井県児童科学館
Fukui Children's Science Center

山梨県立科学館
Yamanashi Prefectural Science Center

春日部の家
Kasukabe House

兵庫県立但馬ドーム
Hyogo Prefectural Tajima Dome

えひめこどもの城
Ehime Children's Castle

城島町総合文化センター
Jojima Cultural Center

やすらぎミラージュ
Yasuragi Mirage

藤野芸術の家 [音のプロムナード]
Fujino Workshop for Art "Promenade of sound"

世界淡水魚園オアシスパーク
Oasis Park

岐阜県先端科学技術体験センター
Gifu Advanced Science and Technology Experience Center "Science World"

富岩運河環水公園 [天門橋]
Fugan Canal Park "Tower"

アクロス荒川
Across Arakawa

- 日本建築学会作品選集「藤野芸術の家」
- 長崎市都市景観賞「長崎市科学館」
- 公共建築百選「ミュージアムパーク茨城県自然博物館」
- 都市景観大賞 景観形成事例部門(小空間レベル)「横須賀市うみかぜ公園地区」
- 京都市西京極総合運動公園プール棟他基本設計コンペ最優秀賞「京都アクアリーナ」

- The 30th Anniversary since establishment of Environment Design Institute.

- "Play Space for Children" Published by Ichigaya Publishing.
- "The Method of Environment Design" Published by SHOKOKUSHA Publishing.
- "Play Structure" Published by Kashiwa Shobo.

- Winning for Architectural Design of the Architectural Institute of Japan [Fujino Workshop for Art]
- Nagasaki City Landscape Award [Nagasaki Science Museum]
- 100 Selected Public Architectural Award [Ibaraki Nature Museum]
- City Landscape Grand Award (Minimal Space Level) [Yokosuka Umikaze Park]
- First Prize for Design Competition for Kyoto Municipal Nishikyogoku Sogo Sports Park Swimming Pool Facility [Kyoto Aquarena]

1999

- 日本建築学会副会長となる(〜2001)
- 日本建築学会司法支援建築会議発足を提案

- 「利用者の満足度より見た科学博物館の建築・展示計画に関する研究」日本建築学会論文集にて発表
- 「子どものための都市・建築12ヶ条」日本建築学会にて発表

- 日本建築学会作品選集「長崎市科学館」
- コア東京賞 優秀賞「環境建築家を目指して」
- グッドデザイン賞「山梨県立科学館」
- グッドデザイン賞「春日部の家」
- 商環境デザイン賞「山梨県立科学館」

- Mitsuru Senda assigned the Vice President of the Architectural Institute of Japan.

- Winning for Architectural Design of the Architectural Institute of Japan [Nagasaki Science Museum]
- CORE Tokyo Award, Award for Excellence ["Aiming Environmental Architect"]
- Good Design and JCD Award [Yamanashi Prefectural Science Center]
- Good Design Award [Kasukabe House]

富岩運河環水公園[泉と滝の広場]
Fugan Canal Park "Spring and falls square"

富岩運河環水公園[噴水]
Fugan Canal Park "Fountain"

谷口吉郎展
Exhibition of Yoshiro Taniguchi

大森の家
Omori House

ミュージアムパーク茨城県自然博物館[自然発見工房]
Ibraki Nature Museum "Nature Center"

兵庫県立但馬ドーム[環境発見遊具]
Tajima Dome "Environment Discovery Play Structure"

宮崎科学技術館リニューアル
Miyazaki Science Center Renewal

2000〜04

2000

- 斎藤義が環境デザイン研究所所長となる
- 東京工業大学大岡山キャンパス整備に関する会議を提案

- 「自然体験学習施設」市ヶ谷出版社より発行
- 「幼児のための環境デザイン」世界文化社より発行

- 中部建築賞「岐阜県先端科学技術体験センター サイエンスワールド」
- 日本建築学会作品選集「兵庫県立但馬ドーム」
- JIA環境建築賞「兵庫県立但馬ドーム」
- 商環境デザイン賞「福井県児童科学館」
- 商環境デザイン賞「世界淡水魚園オアシスパーク」
- グッドデザイン賞「兵庫県立但馬ドーム」
- 日本建築士会連合会賞「兵庫県立但馬ドーム」
- HIROBA賞「兵庫県立但馬ドーム」
- 都市景観大賞「富岩運河環水公園」
- いわて景観賞「きききのつりはし」
- ふるさと建築景観賞「海南市わんぱく公園」

- Tadashi Saito, Director, Environment Design Institute

- "Nature Study Facilities" Published by ICHIGAYA Publishing.
- "Environment Design for Infants" Published by Sekai Bunka-sha.

- Chubu Architecture Award [Gifu Advanced Science and Technology Experience Center "Science World"]
- JIA Award [Hyogo Prefectural Tajima Dome]
- JCD Award [Fukui Children's Science Center]
- JCD Award [Oasis Park]
- Good Design Award [Hyogo Prefectural Tajima Dome]
- Japan Federation of Architects & Building Engineers Associations Award [Hyogo Prefectural Tajima Dome]
- HIROBA Award [Hyogo Prefectural Tajima Dome]
- City Landscape Grand Award [Fugan Canal Park]
- Iwate Landscape Award [Bridge Kikiki]
- Wakayama Townscape Architectural Award [Kainan Wanpaku Park]

2001

- 「地球環境建築憲章」起草委員長として発表
- 日本建築学会会長となる（〜2003）
- 日本建築学会に建築博物館設立を提案
- まちづくり支援会議設立を提案

- 「困難な時を新しい展望の時に」日本建築学会建築雑誌にて会長就任寄稿論文

玄海エネルギーパーク
Genkai Energy Park

海南市わんぱく公園
Kainan Wanpaku Park

紙百科
Paper House

きききのつりはし
Bridge Kikiki

鳥取砂丘こどもの国
Children's Land at Tottori

アクアワールド大洗水族館
Oarai Aquarium "Aqua World"

横浜市プリンス幼稚園［三つ目コゾウ］
Play Structure "With three eyes"

君津市立坂田小学校校庭整備計画
Sakata School Grounds Improvement

和歌山県動物愛護センター
Wakayama Prefectural Animal Welfare Center

佐久市子ども未来館
Saku Children's Science Dome for the Future

桜山の家
Sakurayama House

浜松こども館
Hamamatsu Children's Center

- 「地球環境問題と21世紀の建築界」近代建築 7月号にて特集(監修)
- 「環境デザイン研究所特集」近代建築 7月号
- 「こどものふれあいの建築と環境」KJ別冊
- 「入札制度・公共施設設計は技術力で」朝日新聞(8月24日)私の視点にて発表

- 日本建築学会作品選集「山梨県立科学館」
- 日本建築学会作品選集「福井県児童科学館」
- ランドスケープコンサルタンツ協会賞 優秀賞 「海南市わんぱく公園」
- 全建賞 都市部門「富岩運河環水公園」
- IOC/IAKS賞 金賞「兵庫県立但馬ドーム」
- グッドデザイン賞「富岩運河環水公園」
- ディスプレイデザイン賞優秀賞「紙百科」
- 都市環境デザイン会議2000 JUDI賞優秀賞 「富岩運河環水公園」
- 造園作品選集「富岩運河環水公園」
- とやま市都市景観建築賞「天門橋(富岩運河環水公園)」

- Mitsuru Senda assigned the President of Architectural Institute of Japan.

- Special featured in Kindai Kenchiku Magazine (July 2001)
- "Architecture and Environment for Children's Interaction" Published as an additional volume of Kenchiku Journal.

- Winning for Architectural Design of the Architectural Institute of Japan [Yamanashi Prefectural Science Center]
- Winning for Architectural Design of the Architectural Institute of Japan [Fukui Children's Science Center]
- Consultants of Landscape Architecture Award [Kainan Wanpaku Park]
- Japan Construction Engineers' Association Award [Fugan Canal Park]
- IOC IAKS International Association for Sports and Leisure Facilities Gold Award [Hyogo Prefectural Tajima Dome]
- Good Design Award [Fugan Canal Park]
- Prize for Excellence of Display Industry Award [Paper House]
- JUDI Award [Fugan Canal Park]
- JILA Works of Landscape Architecture [Fugan Canal Park]
- Toyama Urban Landscape [Tenmonkyo (Fugan Canal Park)]

2002

- 慶應義塾大学大学院特別研究教授となる(〜2006)
- 設計者選定についての5会共同提言を提案

- 「環境デザインの展開」鹿島出版会より発行
- 「都市景観における建物のおさまり感の評価構造に関する研究」日本都市計画学会論文集にて発表
- 「地球環境建築を目指そう」新建築4月号に寄稿
- 「良い建築と社会システムのために」日本建築学会「建築雑誌」9月号に寄稿

根岸アパート
N-Patio

七尾希望の丘公園[ブリッジ遊具]
Nanao Bridge Play Structure

国立成育医療センター
National Center for Child Health and Deveropment

御所野縄文博物館
Goshono Jomon Museum

つくし保育園
Tsukushi Day Nursery

弘法湯
Bath House "Kobo-Yu"

東京工業大学[すずかけホール]設計監修
Tokyo Institute of Technology "Suzukake Hall"

東京工業大学キャンパス屋外サイン計画
Tokyo Institute of Technology, Outdoor Sign Planning

京都アクアリーナ
Kyoto Aquarena

エコールみよた
Ecole Miyota

関門海峡ミュージアム
Kaikyo Dramaship

ほうとく幼稚園
Houtoku Kindergarten

- 「劣化と創造」建築文化4月号に寄稿
- 日本建築学会作品選集「海南市わんぱく公園」
- AMERICAN WOOD DESIGN AWARD「屋根付木製遊具（世界淡水魚園オアシスパーク魚の遊具）」
- グッドデザイン賞「アクアワールド大洗水族館」
- SDA賞 入選「国立成育医療センター」
- ディスプレイデザイン賞奨励賞「国立成育医療センター」
- ディスプレイ産業賞特別賞（日本経済新聞社賞）「国立成育医療センター」

- "Development of Environment Design" Published by Kajima Institute Publishing Co., Ltd.
- "Architectural Institute of Japan American Wood Design Award" [Roofed wooden play equipment (fish play equipment at Oasis Park, an amusement park for freshwater fish from around the world)]
- Good Design Award [Oarai Aquarium "Aqua World"]
- SDA Award ["National Center for Child Health and Development"]
- Display Design Award Encouragement Prize ["National Center for Child Health and Development"]
- Nippon Display Federation Award Special Prize (Nihon Keizai Shimbun Award) ["National Center for Child Health and Development"]

2003

- 仙田満建築設計作品展 中国科学展覧センター（北京）にて開催
- 最高裁判所 裁判の迅速化に関わる検討委員会委員となる（現在まで）

- 「環境」中国建築工業出版社より発行
- 「21世紀建築の展望」丸善より発行
- 「日本の歴史的都市における景観保存と創造」日仏都市会議（京都）にて発表
- 「展望する建築学会の課題と戦略」日本建築学会「建築雑誌」5月号に寄稿
- 「子どものあそび環境の多様性と心身の活性に関する研究」日本建築学会にて発表

- 読者と選ぶ「建築と社会」賞「京都アクアリーナ」
- 日本建築学会作品選集「桜山の家」
- Interarch 2003 グランプリ受賞「兵庫県立但馬ドーム」
- 「上海旗忠森林体育城テニスセンター」国際コンペ最優秀賞
- 石川建築賞 入選「弘法湯」
- SCN&DesignShare賞「ほうとく幼稚園」
- 「佛山市岭南明珠体育館」国際コンペ最優秀賞
- グッドデザイン賞「御所野縄文博物館」
- 北九州市都市景観賞「関門海峡ミュージアム」
- 京都景観まちづくり賞優秀賞「京都アクアリーナ」

- "Environment and Architecture" Published by China Architecture and Building Press.
- "Prospects of 21st Century Architecture"

秋田市太平山自然学習センター
Akita Taiheizan Nature Learning Center

わかくさ保育園
Wakakusa Day Nursery

東京農業大学［学生サービスセンター］改修
Tokyo University of Agriculture Setagaya Campus Bldg.,10

ふじえだファミリークリニック
Fujieda Family Clinic

氷見市ふれあい健康館遊具
Fureai Kenko Kan Play Structure, Himi

やすらぎの杜
Yasuragi-no-Mori

健康パークあざい
Wellness Park Azai

福井まちなか文化施設［響のホール］
Fukui Cultural Complex "Hibiki Hall"

神楽坂の家
Kagurazaka House

上海閔行区オフィス棟コンペ案（最優秀賞）
Shanghai Minghang Shenzhuang North Community Plaza and Office Building

東京工業大学すずかけ J2棟設計指導
Suzukake Campus J2 Building

北京オリンピックテニス場コンペ案（最優秀賞）
Tennis Center Stadium for Beijing Olympic

Published by Maruzen.

- The Selection with the readers "Architecture and Society" Award [Kyoto Aquarena]
- Winning for Architectural Design of the Architectural Institute of Japan [Sakurayama House]
- IAA Award Grand Prix [Hyogo Prefectural Tajima Dome]
- First Prize for Design Competition on planning and architecture design for Shanghai Qizhong Forest Sports City Tennis Center
- Ishikawa Prefecture Architectural Award [Bath House "Kobo-Yu"]
- Designshare Awards Citation Award [Houtoku Kindergarten]
- First Prize for Design Competition on planning and architecture design for Foshan Pearl Gymnasium
- Good Design Award [Goshono Jomon Museum]

2004

- こども環境学会を創立、会長となる（～2010）
- 「国家戦略としての建築デザイン」The Japan Architect 4月号に寄稿
- 「子どものための環境デザイン」シリーズ地球環境建築・専門編にて発表（日本建築学会）
- 「新斜面緑地論－新たな都市緑化の提案－」を日本建築学会「建築雑誌」6月号にて発表
- 造園作品選集「君津市立坂田小学校校庭整備計画」
- 医療福祉建築賞「国立成育医療センター」
- 日本建築学会作品選集「京都アクアリーナ」
- 東北建築賞「御所野縄文博物館」
- 福井市都市景観賞「福井まちなか文化施設［響のホール］」
- ディスプレイ産業賞 特別賞（日本経済新聞社賞）「関門海峡ミュージアム」
- 北陸建築文化賞「福井まちなか文化施設［響のホール］」

- Mitsuru Senda assigned the President of the Association for Children's Environment.

- JILA Works of Landscape Architecture [Kimitsu Municipal Sakata Elementary School Ground Improvement Project]
- Japan Institute of Healthcare Architecture Award [National Center for Child Health and Development]
- Winning for Architectural Design of the Architectural Institute of Japan [Kyoto Aquarena]
- Tohoku Architecture Award [Goshono Jomon Museum]
- Nippon Display Federation Award Special Prize (Nihon Keizai Shimbun Award) [Kaikyo Dramaship]
- Hokuriku Architectural Culture Award [Fukui Cultural Complex "Hibiki Hall"]

北京オリンピック公園コンペ案
Beijing Olympic Green

北京オリンピック卓球会場コンペ案（次点）
Table Tennis Arena for Beijing Olympic

北京オリンピックバドミントン会場コンペ案
Badminton hall for Beijing Olympic

蘇州水族館コンペ案（最優秀賞）
Suzhou Aquarium

北京吉祥ビルコンペ案
Beijing Wangfujing building

済南サンシャイン100 CBDコンペ案
Jinan Sunshine 100 the 4th CBD Construction

武漢駅コンペ案
Wuhan Railway Station

三甲港温泉ホテルコンペ案
Sanjiagang Hot spring hotel

蘇州市世界遺産研究教育センターコンペ案
World Cultural Heritage Research Center

天津国際テニスセンターコンペ案
Tianjin Tuanbo International Tennis Center

広東科学センター コンペ案
Guandong Science Center

上海遊泳館 コンペ案
Shanghai Pool

2005～09

2005

- 日本学術会議会員となる
- 東京工業大学名誉教授となる
- 日本建築学会司法支援建築会議運営委員会委員長となる（～2008）
- 日本学術会議課題別委員会こどもを元気にする戦略的政策検討委員会を提案
- 国土交通省社会資本整備審議会建築分科会基本制度部会委員に就任し、統括建築士の提案
- 契約書の確認申請時の添付義務付を提案
- 建築司法の改正にともなう大学院のインターンシップを提案
- 愛知産業大学大学院教授となる（～2007）

- 「元気が育つ家づくり」岩波書店より発行（共著：渡辺篤史）

- 日本建築学会作品選集「御所野縄文博物館」
- 照明普及賞 優秀施設賞「福井まちなか文化施設［響のホール］」
- 環境・設備デザイン賞「京都アクアリーナ」
- 日本建築家協会優秀建築選2005「桜山の家」
- 日本建築家協会優秀建築選2005「京都アクアリーナ」
- 緑の都市賞都市緑化基金会長賞「国立成育医療センター」
- 国土交通大臣表彰「伊勢崎市iタワー花の森住宅・保育所」
- IOC/IAKS賞 銀賞「京都アクアリーナ」
- 中部建築賞入選「こばと幼稚園絵本館」

- Mitsuru Senda assigned honorary professor of Tokyo Institute of Technology and Chairman of Environment Design Institute.

- "Building houses which promote wellness"(co-authored by Atsushi Watanabe) Published by Iwanami-shoten.

- Winning for Architectural Design of the Architectural Institute of Japan ［Goshono Jomon Museum］
- Environmental and Equipment Design Award ［Kyoto Aquarena］
- Japan Institute of Architects, Selected Architecural Designs in 2005 ［Sakurayama House］
- Japan Institute of Architects, Selected Architecural Designs in 2005 ［Kyoto Aquarena］
- Green City Award - Urban Green Charity President Award ［National Center for Child Health and Development］
- The commendation of the Minister of Land, Infrastructure, Transport and Tourism ［Isesaki I tower Hana-no-mori Housing and Day Nursery］
- IOC IAKS International Association for Sports and Leisure Facilities Silver Award ［Kyoto Aquarena］

伊勢崎市iタワー花の森住宅・保育所
Hana-no-mori Housing and Day Nursery

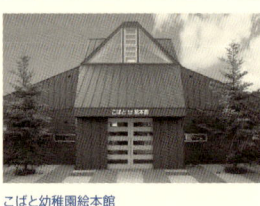

こばと幼稚園絵本館
Kobato Children's Library

高尾の森わくわくビレッジ 改修 (PFI)
Takaonomori Wakuwaku Village

たびだちの村
Tabidachi-no-Mura

こばと西幼稚園 こばと自然の森ビオトープ
Kobato Nishi Kindergarten Biotope

ハッピーローソン山下公園内装
Happy Lowson Yamashita Park

ハッピーローソン日本橋
Happy Lowson Nihonbashi

丹後海と星の見える丘公園［カフェ・管理棟］
Tango Eco-Future Park

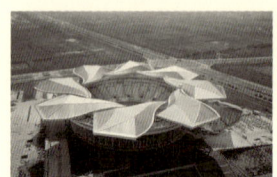

上海旗忠森林体育城テニスセンター
Shanghai Qizhong Forest Sports City Tennis Center

ゆうゆうのもり幼保園
Yuyu-no-Mori Nursery School and Day Nursery

よつば循環器科クリニック
Yotsuba Circulation Clinic

尼崎スポーツの森 (PFI)
Amagasaki Sports Forest

- Children's Library]

2006

- 日本建築家協会会長となる（〜2008）
- 国士舘大学工学部建築デザイン工学科客員教授となる（現在まで）
- 日本学術会議課題別委員会こどもを元気にする戦略的政策検討委員会委員長となる（〜2007）

- 「環境デザイン講義」彰国社より発行
- JIA仙田満週報を発信
- 「姉歯事件と設計者、技術者の独立性」学術の動向1月号に寄稿

- 岐阜市都市景観奨励賞「こばと幼稚園絵本館」
- 日本建築学会作品選集「アクアワールド大洗水族館」
- 日本建築家協会優秀建築選2006「上海旗忠森林体育城テニスセンター」
- 日本建築家協会優秀建築選2006「福井まちなか文化施設［響のホール］」
- 神奈川建築コンクール最優秀賞「ゆうゆうのもり幼保園」
- グッドデザイン賞「こばと幼稚園絵本館」
- 広島市新球場（仮称）設計提案競技最優秀賞「広島市民球場」
- 中部建築賞特別賞「福井まちなか文化施設［響のホール］」

- Mitsuru Senda assigned the President of Japan Institute of Architects.

- "Lecture of Environment Design" Published by SHOKOKUSHA Publishing.

- Gifu Urban Landscape Award Encouragement Prize [Kobato Children's Library]
- Winning for Architectural Design of the Architectural Institute of Japan [Oarai Aquarium "Aqua World"]
- Japan Institute of Architects, Selected Architecural Designs in 2006 [Shanghai Qizhong Forest Sports City Tennis Center]
- Japan Institute of Architects, Selected Architecural Designs in 2006 [Fukui Cultural Complex "Hibiki Hall"]
- Grand Prize of Kanagawa Prefecture Architectural Competition [Yuyu-no-mori Nursery School and Day Nursery]
- Good Design Award [Kobato Children's Library]
- First Prize for Design Competition for Hiroshima Municipal New Baseball Stadium [Hiroshima Municipal Baseball Stadium]
- Chubu Architecture Award Special Prize [Fukui Cultural Complex "Hibiki Hall"]

2007

- 放送大学教授となる
- 日本学術会議4委員会合同「子どもの成育環境分科会」設立を提案、委員長となる（〜2009）

川崎市宮前スポーツセンター
犬蔵中学校格技館、金工・木工室
Miyamae Sports Center, Inukura Junior High School Combative Sports Hall

浪速スポーツセンター・浪速屋内プール・アイススケート場・浪速区在宅サービスセンター
Naniwa Sports Center, Swimming Pool, Ice Skating Link, Home Service Center

佛山市嶺南明珠体育館
Foshan Pearl Gymnasium

愛和病院 ANNEX
Aiwa Hospital ANNEX

多治見市立滝呂小学校
Takiro Elmentary School, Tajimi

猿島公園
Sarushima Park

港区立飯倉保育園・学童クラブ
Iigura Day Nursery, Iigura After School Club

河口湖ステラシアター
Kawaguchiko Stellar Theatre

ふたばランド保育園
Futaba Land Day Nursery

四街道さつき幼稚園
Yotsukaido Satsuki Kindergarten

国際教養大学図書館棟
Akita International University, Library

宮前幼稚園増築
Miyamae Kindergarten

- 日本学術会議 対外報告「我が国の子どもを元気にする環境づくりのための国家的戦略の確立に向けて」を発表
- 「建築家の独立性と設計業務環境の確立に向けて」日本建築家協会「建築家」に寄稿
- 「こどもの成育環境としての都市建築」日本学術会議「学術の動向」にて発表
- 「多様化する幼稚園教育とその環境」等、幼稚園じほうに連続して1年間（12回）寄稿

- ランドスケープコンサルタンツ協会賞（CLA賞）奨励賞「猿島公園」
- 東京建築賞優秀賞「ゆうゆうのもり幼保園」
- 日本建築家協会優秀建築選2007「佛山市嶺南明珠体育館」
- 国際建築賞2007「上海旗忠森林体育城テニスセンター」
- 造園作品選集「ゆうゆうのもり幼保園」
- キッズデザイン賞入賞「ゆうゆうのもり幼保園」
- 千葉県屋外広告物コンクール理事長賞「四街道さつき幼稚園」
- DesignShare賞名誉賞「ゆうゆうのもり幼保園」
- グッドデザイン賞「ゆうゆうのもり幼保園」
- 水辺のユニバーサル・デザイン大賞大賞「富岩運河環水公園」
- 全国学校ビオトープ・コンクール2007銅賞「こばと西幼稚園 こばと自然の森のビオトープ」

- Mitsuru Senda assigned professor at the Open University of Japan.

- Consultants of Landscape Architecture Award Encouragement Prize［Sarushima Park］
- Prize for Excellence of Tokyo Architectural Award Superior Award［Yuyu-no-mori Nursery School and Day Nursery］
- Japan Institute of Architects, Selected Architecural Designs in 2007［Foshan Pearl Gymnasium］
- 2007 International Architecture Awards［Shanghai Qizhong Forest Sports City Tennis Center］
- JILA Works of Landscape Architecture［Yuyu-no-mori Nursery School and Day Nursery］
- Kids Design Award［Yuyu-no-mori Nursery School and Day Nursery］
- Chiba Prefecture Outdoor Advertisement Contest Chairperson Prize［Yotsukaido Satsuki Kindergarten］
- Designshare Awards Honor Award［Yuyu-no-mori Nursery School and Day Nursery］
- Good Design Award［Yuyu-no-mori Nursery School and Day Nursery］
- Grand Prize for The Water Front Universal Design Award［Fugan Canal Park］

2008

- 環境デザイン研究所設立40周年を迎える
- NPO JIA建築家教育推進機構設立を提案
- 日建学院と共同して一般建築士定期講習事業を実施

東大柏どんぐり保育園
Tokyo University Kashiwa Donguri Day Nursery

上海STEP
Shanghai STEP

岡崎げんき館
Okazaki Genkikan

やすらぎガーデン・石神井台
Yasuragi Garden - Shakujiidai

広島県立可部高等学校
Hiroshima Prefectural Kabe High School

あづみの公園 サテライトハウス
Alps Azumino National Government Park

埼玉県警察学校生徒寮
Saitama Prefectural Police School Domitory

峰岡幼稚園
Mineoka Kindergarten

元住吉こばと幼稚園園舎改修
Motosumiyoshi Kobato Kindergarten

六本木ヒルズスカイデッキ
Roppongi Hills Sky Deck

慶應義塾日吉キャンパス 協生館
Keio University Collaboration Complex

つつじヶ丘ふたばランド保育園
Tsutsujigaoka Futaba Land Nursery

- 日本学術会議提言「我が国の子どもの成育環境の改善に向けて－成育空間の課題と提言－」を発表
- 「環境デザイン学と教育」日本学術協力財団「学術の動向」にて発表
- 「現代日本の子どもの成育環境－課題と展望」日本教育方法学会にて発表

- 2007千葉県建築文化賞「四街道さつき幼稚園」
- 国際建築賞2008「佛山市岭南明珠体育館」
- 日本建築家協会優秀建築選2008「猿島公園」
- 日本建築家協会環境建築賞「四街道さつき幼稚園」
- 神奈川建築コンクール奨励賞「猿島公園」

- Celebrate the 40th Anniversary of Environment Design Institute.
- 2008 International Architecture Awards [Foshan Pearl Gymnasium]
- Japan Institute of Architects, Selected Architecural Designs in 2008 [Sarushima Park]
- JIA Environmental Architecture Award [Yotsukaido Satsuki Kindergarten]
- Kanagawa Prefecture Architectural Competition Encouragement Prize [Sarushima Park]

2009

- 「子どもが安全な町づくり」日本建築学会総合論文誌にて発表
- 「次世代のための都市建築環境」連続エッセイ（他4回）を新建築に寄稿
- 「子どもとあそび環境」（他5回）保育界に寄稿

- 人にやさしい街づくり賞「岡崎げんき館」
- 東京建築賞奨励賞「四街道さつき幼稚園」
- 日本免震構造協会賞「慶應義塾日吉キャンパス 協生館」
- 医療福祉建築賞「愛和病院ANNEX」
- IOC/IAKS賞銀賞「上海旗忠森林体育城テニスセンター」
- 空間デザイン・コンペティション 銅賞「慶應義塾日吉キャンパス 協生館」
- TILE DESIGN CONTEST 特別記念賞「慶應義塾日吉キャンパス 協生館」
- 神奈川建築コンクール優秀賞「慶應義塾日吉キャンパス 協生館」
- 全国学校ビオトープ・コンクール2009銀賞「四街道さつき幼稚園」
- 全国学校ビオトープ・コンクール2009銀賞「宮前幼稚園」

- IOC IAKS International Association for Sports and Leisure Facilities Silver Award [Shanghai Qizhong Forest Sports City Tennis Center]
- Prize for Excellence of Kanagawa Prefecture Architectural Competition [Keio University Collaboration Complex]
- ARCASIA Architecture Award Gold Medal [Foshan Pearl Gymnasium]

国際教養大学講義棟
Akita International University, Lecture Building

中軽井沢山荘
Villa Nakakaruizawa

こころ認定こども園増築
Kokoro Kindergarten & Nursery

さくらい保育園
Sakurai Day Nursery

広島市民球場
Hiroshima Municipal Baseball Stadium "Mazda Zoom-Zoom Stadium Hiroshima"

一の台幼稚園
Ichinodai Kindergarten

Winx
Winx

勝川幼稚園
Kachigawa Kindergarten

カナリヤ幼稚園園舎改修
Kanariya Kindergarten

Y邸
Y's House

富岩運河環水公園［野鳥観察舎］監修
Fugan Canal Park "Bird Watching Huse"

富岩運河環水公園［野外劇場］
Fugan Canal Park "Open Air Theater"

989

2010〜

2010

- こども環境学会代表理事となる
- 国際交流基金の事業としてブラジル（サンパウロ、クリチバ、ポルト・アングレ）の国際会議、大学にて連続講演

- 放送大学大学院科目「都市環境デザイン論」（佐藤滋と共著）発行、開講
- 「子どもにやさしい都市」公明新聞に20回寄稿

- 造園作品選集「四街道さつき幼稚園」
- 茨城建築文化賞茨城新聞社賞「つつじヶ丘ふたばランド保育園」
- 生物多様性保全につながる企業のみどり100選「四街道さつき幼稚園」
- 日本建築家協会賞「国際教養大学図書館棟」
- 国際建築賞「国際教養大学図書館棟」
- AACA賞優秀賞「国際教養大学図書館棟」
- 建築家フォーラムアワード優秀賞「国際教養大学図書館棟」
- アルカシア建築賞ゴールドメダル「佛山市岭南明珠体育館」

- Mitsuru Senda assinged chairperson for Association for Children's Environment

- The Open University of Japan "Theories of Urban Environmental Design"

- JILA Works of Landscape Architecture [Yotsukaido Satsuki Kindergarten]
- Ibaraki Architecture and Culture Award Ibaraki Shinbun Award [Tsutsujigaoka Futaba Land Nursery]
- 100 Select Greens in Company Relating Biodiversity [Yotsukaido Satsuki Kindergarten]
- Japan Institute of Architects Award [Akita International University, Library]
- 2010 International Architecture Awards [Akita International University, Library+Lecture Building]
- Prize for Excellence of AACA Award [Akita International University, Library]
- Architect Forum Award [Akita International University, Library]
- Arcasia Architecture Gold Medal [Foshan Pearl Gymnasium]

2011

- こども環境学会（代表理事）公益社団法人として認可される
- 放送大学新科目「産業とデザイン」を制作
- こども環境学会主催「東日本大震災復興プラン国際提案競技"知恵と夢"の支援」を提案

香港プレイスコープ内装
HSBC/Playright Playscope

早苗保育園遊具
Play Structure of Sanae Day Nursery

ひかりの子保育園
Hikari-no-Ko Day Nursery

田園江田幼稚園
Den-en Eda Kindergarten

国際教養大学多目的ホール
Akita International University, Multi Purpose Hall

東京大学（柏）第2総合研究棟
Kashiwa Research Complex 2

緑の詩保育園
Green Note Day Nursery

西砂保育園増築
Nishisuna Day Nursery

昭島すみれ幼稚園
Akishima Sumire Kindergarten

袋井市風見の丘
Kazami no Oka

富岩運河環水公園［見晴しの丘］
Fugan Canal Park "Fine View Hill"

名古屋文化学園保育専門学校・幼稚園
Nagoya Bunka Gakuen

- 日本学術会議 5委員会合同子どもの成育環境分科会提言「我が国の子どもの成育環境の改善にむけて－成育方法の課題と提言－」を発表
- 日本学術会議 土木工学・建築学委員会景観と文化分科会報告「我が国の都市・建築の景観・文化力の向上をめざして」を発表
- 「新たな街づくりのコンセプト 子どもにやさしい『成育環境』構築を」The EM 教育医事新聞に寄稿

- 文部科学大臣表彰「ゆうゆうのもり幼保園」
- OECD/CELE学校施設好事例集第4版選定「ゆうゆうのもり幼保園」
- 日本建築家協会賞「広島市民球場」
- いわて広告景観コンクール 岩手県知事賞「御所野縄文公園」
- 村野藤吾賞「国際教養大学図書館棟」
- 建築業協会賞（BCS賞）「国際教養大学新校舎群」
- IOC/IAKS賞金賞「佛山市岭南明珠体育館」

- Honor Award of the Minister of Education, Culture, Sports, Science and Technology［Yuyu-no-Mori Nursery School and Day Nursery］
- Selected by OECD/CELE in the Compendium of Exemplary Educational Facilities［Yuyu-no-Mori Nursery School and Day Nursery］
- Japan Institute of Architects Award［Hiroshima Municipal Baseball Stadium "Mazda Zoom-Zoom Stadium Hiroshima"］
- Iwate Advertising Publicity Landscape Contest Iwate Prefectural Governor Award［Goshono Jomon Site］
- Togo Murano Award［Akita International University, Library］
- Building Contractors Society Award［Akita International University］
- IOC IAKS international Association for Sports and Leisure Facilities Gold Award［Foshan Pearl Gymnasium］

日本女子体育大学スポーツセンター（2012）
Japan Women's College of Physical Education Sports Center Project

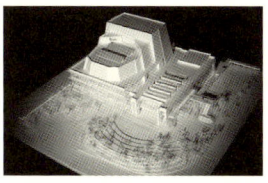

柏崎市民文化会館アルフォーレ（2012）
Kashiwazaki Civic Hall Project

町田市鶴川駅前公共施設（2012）
Public Facility around Tsurukawa Station Project

新潟市西川総合体育館（2013）
Nishikawa Gymnasium Project

横浜市瀬谷区総合庁舎及び二つ橋公園（2013）
Yokohama City Seya Ward Hall Project

三春町統合中学校（2013）
Miharu Town Middle School Integration Project

蘇州東南EV呉江地区（2013）
Suzhou Dongnan Elevator in Wujiang District Project

湘南CXアーバンライフサポートプラザ（2013）
Shonan CX Urban Life Support Plaza Project

新潟市こども創造センター（2013）
Niigata City Child Creation Center Project

東山動植物園探検温室（未定）
Higashiyama Zoo and Botanical Gardens Adventure Glasshouse Project

「SENDA・MANを撮影して40年」 藤塚光政

一人の作家の仕事を40年続けて撮影することは滅多にあることではない。たいていの場合、途中でどちらかがダメになるか、ケンカ別れするか、飽きるかがオチである。といっても、仙田とはベタベタした付き合いではなく、言うなれば君子の淡交である。

仙田満の仕事が、建築・ランドスケープ・遊具を手がけているのは周知のことである。「環境デザイン研究所」と名付けたのは1968年からと古く、「環境」という言葉は当時ごく一般的な普通名詞で、今日のように地球環境やエコロジーを意識した言葉ではなかったが、仙田はこの頃から意識していたのだ。それはたぶん、「こどものあそび空間」を研究し、自らの建築や遊具が環境と調和しなければ、構想と一致しないことを確信していたからだろう。

撮影を始めた頃、僕の頭に浮かんだのは、「こどもに遊具は必要なのか?」という疑問だった。僕らのこどもの頃にも、ブランコや滑り台やジャングルジムなど古典的なモノが公園にはあったし、別にデザインした遊具がいるのか、棒があれば鉄砲にも刀にもなるし、木に登れば世界が見えるし、水辺であそべば池は海洋に、小川は急流になる。何も、色つきのデザインをして、与えなくてもイイじゃ、という思いだった。

しかし、撮影し始めるとすぐに、なるほどなぁと分かった。もとより、僕は大人になってもガキ気分が色濃く残っているから、そのあたりはよく見える。

たとえば、風もない何もない丘には何も起こらないが、たった一本の管を置き、軽くテーパーをつけるか、中ほどで絞ってやると、風が流れる。空気力学でいう、いわゆるヴェンチュリ効果だ。こどもは一時も止まらない流体であるから、こどもにとって、丘にある一本のヒューム管は空気にとってのヴェンチュリ管なのだ。つまり、動きを誘発する装置なのである。これが仙田の遊具だ、建築もそうなんだと理解した。

普通、建築物を撮影するとき、大型カメラでアオリを使って垂直を出し、ひとを入れないで撮影するのが専門的な建築写真であり、ひとが必要な場合、雑誌ではヤラセで所員や編集者を立たせるぐらいである。なぁんかダサイ。通常のように人間を排除して撮影するのは、建築家の意志で作った表現空間を壊さないためのようだが、ま、そんな方法もあるだろ、それはそれでイイ。

しかし、仙田の建築や空間はこどもが入って動き回らないと、スケールも動線も空気も、なによりこどもと反応しあう空間が見えないのだ。しかも、ガキどもは決してこちらの言うようには動いてくれない。だから、行動を読み取るか、わざと挑発したり、追いかけるか、または、予測して待つしかないのだ。その際、建築内部では場所をとる大型カメラは使いにくい。こちらも動き回って撮影するので、小型カメラで撮影するしかない。だから、仙田の空間を撮影した写真はスタティックな建築写真ではなく、いわばデザインの報道写真である。

こども相手の現場では何が起こるか分からない。時には後ろからぶつかられ、身体もカメラもバッグもネットの中にぶちまけたこともあるが、自分はともかく、こどもの方が悪くても怪我をさせる

わけにはいかない。撮影しながら、僕のレーダーは常時警戒モードである。さらに、遊具の内部は建築よりもっと狭く、大柄ではない僕でもチューブの中にいるときは、ほとんど腸内の排泄予備群になったような気持ちになるんだよ、ウン。思い出しても悔しいけど、今まで、くぐれなかったのが一カ所だけである。

なんといっても印象深いのは、1972年に竣工し、何回か通っている「野中保育園」だ。静岡県富士市にできた園舎は、屋根が富士山の裾に沿って山頂に続くように見える。「ノナカザウルス」とこどもに呼ばれるのは、濃い緑色の連続した傾斜屋根のうねっている様子が、大好きな恐竜のように見えるからだろう。

塩川園長の「ドロンコ保育理論」と仙田の誘発装置によって、こども達はナニモノからも解放され、王国で先祖返りをしているのだ。むろん、こども達は仙田のことなど、誰かはチィーとも知りはしないし、園長すら「ジジィ」呼ばわりである。

仙田の建築は「仙田の建築はこども相手だから…」といった具合に、児童文学が純文学より低く見られるような損をしている気がする。しかし、仙田は「こどものためだからできた装置」というが、たとえば、人間が2〜3層の吹き抜けを浮遊しながら自在に移動するつくりなどは、普通の建築では想像もできないものではないか。もしかすると、こうした発想は現代建築の何かを打ち破ることにつながるのかもしれない。

撮影に行くたびに、樹木が成長し、ミニ豚、犬ネコ、ヤギがデカイ面してうろつく楽園で、ノナカザウルスは風景に馴染みながら、いっそうの迫力を見せてくれる。

建築の価値は、最先端のデザインや静謐な「美」、または自らのありようを問う精神性ばかりにあるのではない。ここでは、こども達が巨大な「ノナカザウルス」を小突き回すように使いながら、あそび、食べ、眠り、樹木・草花・動物・魚・水・泥と戯れている。ミニ豚を「ハナちゃんは頭がいいよ」と友人の如く僕に紹介してくれる園児と、動物の間には垣根が全くない。ひとと万物の活発な反応が38年間も休むことなく続き、臨界状態は現在も進行中である。こんな建築は他に見たことがないよ。

建築と遊具における仙田の調査研究と実践は、失敗が許されない分野ゆえに試行錯誤の繰り返しだっただろう。仙田は小児科医や獣医にも似て、症状や自ら欲することを伝えられない相手に、最適なことを選ぶ名医のようにみえる。

Forty Years of Shooting SENDA MAN Mitsumasa Fujitsuka

It is not common for one photographer to shoot for one artist continuously over a span of forty years. In most cases, they are defeated when one or the other gives up halfway, break up over conflicts, or become tired of each other or of the work. Yet, my relationship with Senda had not been an unpleasant one; rather, it had been honest and open.

It is generally known that the work of Senda Man involves experimentation with architecture, landscapes, and playground equipment. The "Environment Design Institute" was named quite a long time back in 1968. Then, the term "environment" had simply been a commonly used noun, and did not have the global environmental and ecological connotations that it does today. Yet, Senda had been aware of such issues and ideas even then, possibly as a result of his research into the play environments of children, and of his firm conviction that a lack of harmony between the environment and his architecture and playground equipment would lead to inconsistency in his vision.

When we first began shooting, one of the doubts that had arisen in my mind had been, "Do children need playground equipment?" During my own childhood days, our parks had been equipped with the "classics"—swings, slides, and a jungle gym. Did we need specially designed playground equipment? If we had sticks, they would serve as guns and swords; if we climbed onto the trees, we could see the world; if we played by the water, ponds became oceans, and rivers became rapids. I felt that there was no need to add special elements of color or design to any of the equipment.

However, once we started with the photography sessions, I began to understand why. Since I have retained much of my childhood sentiments even after entering adulthood, I could well understand the logic and reasoning.

For instance, nothing will happen on a hill that has neither wind nor any other elements. However, if we simply lay down a pipe and lightly place a taper on it, then squeeze it in the middle, we would be able to create wind flow. This is known as the Venturi effect in aerodynamics. As children are a "fluid" that does not stop flowing even for a single second, a single Hume pipe on a hill is to children what the Venturi pipe is to air. In other words, it is a motion-inducing device. I then understood that this was what Senda's playground equipment was about, and what architecture was about.

Typically, in professional architectural photography, we use tilt-shift photography techniques with large-format cameras to bring out the vertical planes, and leave people out of the photographs; where people are needed, magazines usually make their staff or editors stand-in as photo models. I find this somewhat unrefined and tacky. Apparently, the usual practice of leaving people out of photographs arises from the intention to preserve the space of representation and expression created intentionally by the architect; such methods are also used, and that is fine.

However, in Senda's architecture and spaces, the lack of moving children in a frame would mean that it would become difficult to see scale, flow, and atmosphere; more importantly, we would then not be able to see the space that children respond to, and which in turn, reacts to the children. Furthermore, children never move the way they are told to. Consequently, we have no choice but to read their movements, deliberately provoke them, chase them, or attempt to predict their movements and wait. During such shoots, it is difficult for us to use large-format cameras within the architectural structures as these cameras take up much space. As we also move around as we shoot, our only alternative is to use small-format cameras. As such, the photographs taken in Senda's spaces are not static architectural photographs; rather, they are journalistic pictures of designs.

We cannot anticipate what may happen in a child-centric location. At times, they knock into us from behind, wreaking havoc with our bodies, cameras, bags, and the inside of our nets; even when the children are at fault, we must never inflict injury on them. As I shoot, my radar is constantly tuned to its alert mode. In addition, the interior spaces of playground equipment tend to be more narrow and constrictive than other architectural structures. Even for someone like myself who is not of a large build, when I am inside a tube, I often feel as if I have become part of the matter in intestines, about to be discharged through the body. Although the memory leaves me frustrated and regretful, until now, there has only been one place that I failed to get through.

The work that had left the deepest impression on me was the Nonaka Day Nursery completed in 1972, which I visited several times. Situated in Fuji City, Shizuoka Prefecture, the roof of the nursery follows the edge of Mount Fuji, and to all appearances, seems to be a continuation of the mountain peak. The architecture is known as "Nonaka Zaurus" among the children; perhaps it is because the continual, dark green rolling slopes of the roof look like the dinosaurs they love.

Principal Shiokawa's "Muddy Childcare Theory" (the ideology of raising children the "natural" way) and Senda's stimulating equipment help to liberate children from whoever they are; it is a backward revolution in their kingdom. Of course, the children do not have the slightest inkling of who Senda is. They even call the Principal "*Jijii*" (old man)."

I feel that Senda's architecture is being undermined in the same way that children's literature is seen as being of a lower class as compared to pure literature—"Because Senda's architecture is for children…" Yet, even though Senda declares that his equipment is made for children, is it not inconceivable in "normal" architecture to have structures in which humans may move around freely while suspended in two to three layers of openings? Perhaps, concepts like these may lead to the creation of something groundbreaking in modern architecture.

Whenever we go on a photo-shoot, the Nonaka Zaurus emanates greater power even as it becomes a familiar sight in the landscape; it is a paradise where trees grow, where miniature pigs, dogs, cats, and goats reign supreme and roam around freely.

The value of architecture does not lie solely in its pioneering design or its tranquil "beauty," or in the spirit of questioning what the self is. Here, while children use the Nonaka Zaurus by "knocking about," they play, eat, sleep, and have fun with trees, grass and flowers, animals, fish, water, and mud. There are no barriers between the animals and the children, who introduced the miniature pig to me as they would a friend—"Hana-chan is so clever!" The active feedback and response between humans and all other living creatures have persisted for 38 years, and despite being in a critical state, continues even now. I have never seen another architectural structure quite like this.

Senda's investigative research and practice in architecture and playground equipment had been a continuous process of trial and error, perhaps because it was a field one simply could not afford to fail in. Like pediatricians and veterinarians, Senda is a renowned doctor who decides on the best treatment for patients who are unable to convey their symptoms and wants.

おわりに

この本は多くの協同者によってつくられた。写真はほとんどが藤塚光政さん、グラフィックデザインは秋田寛さんである。2人とも長い友人である。環境建築家として40余年をまとめるという企画は美術出版社の水越弘(現:広隆社代表)さんによるものである。対談には先輩、友人の手を煩わせ、一緒に遊環構造の作品について見ていただき、評価をいただいた。環境デザイン研究所の落合千春さん、そして秋田寛さんのスタッフの皆さんにも大変なご苦労をおかけした。そして長年の仕事のパートナーである環境デザイン研究所 仙田順子社長、斎藤義所長他多くの環境デザイン研究所所員(もちろんかつての所員も含めて)とともにこの本の完成を喜びたい。

「遊環構造理論」は1970年頃より環境デザイン研究所で私が始めたこどものあそび環境の研究の成果である。総事業抑制という福田内閣の政策によっておきた建設不況の中で、1974年に幸運にも「トヨタ財団」から研究助成を受けることができた。助成を受けた20機関中唯一の民間組織であった。遊具やあそび環境調査、原風景調査等を行い、1982年にその研究をまとめ、東京工業大学にて「こどものあそび環境の構造の研究」により、工学博士の学位を取得した。それを基に筑摩書房より『こどものあそび環境』と題して出版し、その結論として「遊環構造」を提案した。もともと建築家であるから実証的な研究を行う前に、さまざまな仮説をたててデザインしてきた。従って、この遊環構造理論を意識して建築の設計に応用したのは、1985年に竣工した「浜松科学館」が最初であるが、それ以前の作品もその多くは遊環構造的な環境をつくってきた。今回40余年の多くの作品を遊環構造BOOKとしてまとめられたことを大変幸せに思い、作品をつくる機会を与えていただいた多くの関係者の皆様に感謝したい。

とにかくこの本は写真家である藤塚光政さんとの共同作品でもある。すべてに渡って彼の提案によりつくられたといっても良い。カジュアルで楽しい写真集ができた。前出の彼の「SENDA・MANを撮影して40年」にも涙がでる。また、秋田寛さんにはこの本の長い制作期間にお付き合いいただき、このようにアイデア溢れる美しい本にまとめていただいたことに、素直に喜びたい。

Acknowledgements

This book as well was created along with numerous copartners. Most of the photographs are thanks to Mitsumasa Fujitsuka and the graphic design was handled by Kan Akita. Both of these individuals are longtime friends of mine. The idea to come up with a work to compile my 40 years as an environment architect was the idea of Hiroshi Mizukoshi of Bijutsu Shuppan-Sha Co., Ltd. (Currently the president of Koryusha Ltd.). I held discussions with my superiors and friends, looking at play structures with circular play system together and receiving their feedback. Mr. Fujitsuka and Mr. Akita were both extremely helpful in coming up with editing ideas in order to express the essence of an environment architect and SENDA MAN. I would like to extend my gratitude to the sincere efforts of Chiharu Ochiai of Environment Design Institute and Mr. Akita's staff. In the completion of this book I would also like to thank my longtime working partner Junko Senda, president of the Environment Design Institute, Tadashi Saito, Chairman of the institute, as well as the many staff (current and past) of the institute.

I started the circular play system theory at the Environment Design Institute in the 1970s. It was the fruit of research conducted on the play environments of children. Amidst a sluggish construction industry spawned by the policies of the Fukuda Administration that restricted operating costs, I was fortunate enough to receive a research grant from the Toyota Foundation in 1974. It was the only grant awarded to a private sector organization from among the 20 that received them. After conducting surveys on play structure and environments, landscapes, and other areas, I compiled my research in 1982 and received my doctor of engineering degree from the Tokyo Institute of Technology for submitting my dissertation entitled, "Research on the structure of children's play environments." Based on my dissertation, Chikuma Shobo Publishing published a book titled "Children's Play Environment" (Japanese: *Kodomo no Asobi Kankyo*), suggesting the concept of "circular play system" in its conclusion. As first and foremost I am an architect, I employed many hypotheses in my designs before commencing empirical research. That is why I first applied circular play system theory to my architectural designs for the Hamamatsu Science Museum, which was completed in 1985. However, I had created numerous circular play system like environments before that as well. I am tremendously happy to have compiled the vast number of works that I have completed over the past 40 years into this book of circular play system. I would like to extend my gratitude to the large number of people that have been in involved in allowing me the opportunity to create these pieces.

仙田 満 （せんだみつる）

環境建築家
環境デザイン研究所会長

Environmental Architecture,
Chairman of Environment Design Institute

略歴

1941	12月8日、神奈川県横浜市生まれ
1964	東京工業大学理工学部建築学科 卒業 株式会社菊竹清訓建築設計事務所 入所
1968	環境デザイン研究所を創設
1974	日本大学芸術学部住環境デザインコース 非常勤講師（～1984）
1982	工学博士（東京工業大学）論文題目「こどものあそび環境の構造の研究」
1984	琉球大学工学部建設工学科 教授（～1987）
1988	名古屋工業大学社会開発工学科 教授（～1992）
1992	東京工業大学工学部建築学科・大学院理工学研究科建築学専攻 教授（～2005）
2001	日本建築学会 会長（～2003）
2002	慶應義塾大学大学院 特別研究教授（～2006）
2004	こども環境学会 会長（～2010）
2005	日本学術会議会員（～2011） 東京工業大学 名誉教授 愛知産業大学大学院教授（～2007）
2006	日本建築家協会 会長（～2008）
2007	放送大学 教授（～現在）
2010	こども環境学会 代表理事（～現在）
2011	日本学術会議連携会員（～現在）

主な著書

1984	「こどものあそび環境」筑摩書房
1986	現代建築空間と方法12「巨大遊具、環築、都市の木」同朋舎出版
1987	「あそび環境のデザイン」鹿島出版会
1990	「こどもと住まい―50人の建築家の原風景（上・下）」（編著）住まいの図書館出版局（住まい学大系32・33）
1992	「Design of Children's Play Environments」NewYork McGraw-Hill社 「子どもとあそび―環境建築家の眼―」岩波書店
1998	「子どものためのあそび空間」市ヶ谷出版社 「環境デザインの方法」彰国社 「プレイストラクチャー」柏書房
2001	「幼児のための環境デザイン」世界文化社
2002	「環境デザインの展開」鹿島出版会
2003	「環築」中国建築工業出版社 「21世紀建築の展望」丸善
2006	「環境デザイン講義」彰国社
2009	「環境デザイン論」放送大学教育振興会
2010	「都市環境デザイン論」（共著）放送大学教育振興会

主な受賞

1978	毎日デザイン賞「あそび環境のデザイン」
1987	国際交通安全学会賞「著書『こどものあそび環境』」 建築業協会賞（BCS賞）「浜松科学館」
1993	日本建築学会霞ヶ関ビル記念賞（研究部門）「都市空間におけるこどものあそび環境開発に関する研究」
1996	日本造園学会賞（作品）「ミュージアムパーク茨城県自然博物館」
1997	日本建築学会賞（作品）「愛知県児童総合センター」 IOC/IAKS賞 銀賞「東京辰巳国際水泳場」
2001	IOC/IAKS賞 金賞「兵庫県立但馬ドーム」
2003	Interarch '2003 グランプリ受賞「兵庫県立但馬ドーム」
2005	IOC/IAKS賞 銀賞「京都アクアリーナ」
2009	IOC/IAKS賞 銀賞「上海旗忠森林体育城テニスセンター」
2010	アルカシア建築賞ゴールドメダル「佛山市嶺南明珠体育館」 日本建築家協会賞、AACA賞優秀賞、建築家フォーラムアワード優秀賞「国際教養大学図書館棟」
2011	日本建築家協会賞「広島市民球場」 村野藤吾賞「国際教養大学図書館棟」 建築業協会賞（BCS賞）「国際教養大学新校舎群」 IOC/IAKS賞 金賞「佛山市嶺南明珠体育館」

MITSURU MAN SENDA

Biography

1941	Born on December 8 in Yokohama, Kanagawa Pref.
1964	Graduated from the faculty of architecture of Tokyo Institute of Technology
	Worked for Kiyonori Kikutake Architects and Associates
	Established Environment Design Institute and takes position as president
1974	Lecturer at Faculty of Art of Nihon University (-1984)
1982	Took a doctorate in engineering at Tokyo Institute of Technology Dissertation title: Research on the structure of children's play environments
1984	Professor at Department of Architectural Engineering of Ryukyu University in Okinawa (-1987)
1988	Professor at the department of social development engineering of Nagoya Institute of Technology (-1992)
1992	Professor at the Department of Architecture and Building Engineering at the Engineering School and the Department of Architecture and Building Engineering at the Science and Engineering Graduate School of the Tokyo Institute of Technology (-2005)
2001	Mitsuru Senda assigned the President of Architectural Institute of Japan (-2003)
2002	Special Research Professor for Keio University, Graduate School
2004	Mitsuru Senda assigned the President of the Association for Children's Environment (-2010)
2005	Memberships of Science Council of Japan
	Professor Emeritus of Tokyo Institute of Technology
2006	Mitsuru Senda assigned the President of Japan Institute of Architects. (-2008)
2007	Professor at the Open University of Japan.
2010	Mitsuru Senda assinged chairperson of Association for Children's Environment

Books

1984	"Children's Play Environment" Chikuma Shobo
1986	Modern Architectural Space and Method 12 [Giant Play Structure, Environmental Architecture, Urban Tree] Dohosha Shuppan
1987	"Design of Children's Play Environment" Kajima Institute Publishing Co., Ltd.
1990	"Children and Their Home – 50 Architects' Solutions" Sumai no Toshokan Syuppankyoku
1992	"Design of Children's Play Environments" New York McGraw–Hill
	"Child and Their Play – Vision of Environmental Architect – " Iwanami Shoten
1998	"The Method of Environment Design" SHOKOKUSHA Publishing
	"Play Space for Children" ICHIGAYA Publishing
	"Play Structure" KASHIWASHOBO
	"Environmental Design for Small Children" Sekai Bunka–Sha
2002	"Development of Environmental Design" Kajima Institute Publishing Co., Ltd.
2003	"Environment and Architecture" China Architecture and Building Press
	"Prospects of 21st Century Architecture" Maruzen
2005	"Building houses which promote wellness" (joint authorship) Iwanami–Shoten
2006	"Lecture of Environmental Design" SHOKOKUSHA Publishing
2009	"The Theories of Environmental Design" The Society for the Promotion for The Open University of Japan
	"Children's Play Environment" (Reprinted) Kajima Institute Publishing Co., Ltd.
2010	"The Theories of Urban Environmental Design" (joint authorship) The Society for the Promotion for The Open University of Japan

Awards

1978	Mainichi Design Award [Design of Children's Play Environment]
1987	International Association of Traffic and Safety Sciences Award [Book "Children's Play Environment"]
	Building Contractors Society Award [Hamamatsu Science Museum]
1993	The Kasumigaseki Building Memorial Prize of Architectural Institute of Japan [Research of Development of Children's Play Environment in Urban Area]
1996	The Japanese Institute of Landscape Architecture Prize [Ibaraki Nature Museum]
1997	The Architectural Institute of Japan Prize [Aichi Children's Center]
2001	IOC IAKS International Association for Sports and Leisure Facilities Gold Award [Hyogo Prefectural Tajima Dome]
2003	IAA Award Grand Prix [Hyogo Prefectural Tajima Dome]
2010	Arcasia Architecture Gold Medal [Foshan Pearl Gymnasium]
	Japan Institute of Architects Award [Akita International University, Library]
	Prize for Excellence of AACA Award [Akita International University, Library]
	Architect Forum Award [Akita International University, Library]
	Japan Institute of Architects Award [Hiroshima Municipal Baseball Stadium "Mazda Zoom–Zoom Stadium Hiroshima"]
2011	Togo Murano Award [Akita International University, Library]
	Building Contractors Society Award [Akita International University]
	IOC IAKS International Association for Sports and Leisure Facilities Gold Award [Foshan Pearl Gymnasium]

写真クレジット（下記以外はすべて藤塚光政）

上田 宏：P76, P78-79
河野政人 (Nacasa & Partners)：P100, P102-107
河口湖ステラシアター：P170, P172-173
環境デザイン研究所：P188, P190-191, P226, P230-233, P330, P332-333, P342-343, P386, P388-389, P400-401, P448(下), P474(下), P480-481, P664, P666-667, P821, P911
澤田聖司：P204, P206-209, P240, P242-243, P288, P290-291
上海旗忠森林体育城有限公司：P228-229
伸和：P238, P241
新建築写真部：P316, P318-323, P626-627, P774-775, P827(上)
御所野縄文博物館：P324-325
コトブキ：P592, P596-597, P943(上)
稲村不二雄：P636-637
大橋富夫：P804, P806-807, P904, P906(上), P852, P910
古舘克明：P824-825
川辺明伸：P829
白鳥美雄：P868-869, P930, P932-933, P941(上)
鈴木 悠：P908, P918, P920-921, P934, P936-937
櫻井ロクスケ：対談写真

遊環構造BOOK
SENDA MAN 1000

2011年10月30日 初版第1刷発行

著者	仙田 満＋環境デザイン研究所
撮影	藤塚光政
アートディレクション	秋田 寛
デザイン	橋本祐治、岩松亮太（アキタ・デザイン・カン）
編集・制作	藤塚光政／水越 弘、川崎章吾（広隆社）
対談原稿	藤田千彩
発行者	大下健太郎
発行・発売	株式会社 美術出版社 〒101-8417 東京都千代田区神田神保町3-2-3 神保町プレイス9F [編集、営業] TEL：03-3234-2153 振替 00130-3-447800 http://www.bijutsu.co.jp/bss
プリンティングディレクション	熊倉桂三
印刷	株式会社 山田写真製版所
製本	株式会社 渋谷文泉閣

©2011 Man SENDA
Printed in Japan ISBN978-4-568-60040-7 C3052

著作権上の例外を除き、本誌の全部または一部を無断で複写複製（コピー）・転載をすることは禁じられています。
乱丁・落丁本はお取替え致します。